The Lubyanka Gambit

Sergei Grodzensky

The Lubyanka Gambit
Author: Sergei Grodzensky
Chess editor: Anastasia Travkina
Translated from the Russian by Ludmila Travkina
Typesetting by Andrei Elkov
Photos are taken from the author's archive and the editorial board of the magazine *64-Chess Review*
Front cover: Maria Yugina

First published in Russian in 2004. The English edition contains some updates.
Follow us on Twitter: @ilan_ruby
www.elkandruby.com
ISBN 978-5-6041770-0-6 (paperback); 978-5-6046766-1-5 (hardback)

Contents

In memory of my parents
Nina Evgenievna Karnovskaya and
Yakov Davidovich Grodzensky

We need to know how this happened
so that no one can ever steal our future again.
The study of the past is the salvation of the future,
its guarantee.
From The Manifesto of Memorial

I would like to name everyone by name,
but they took away the list and there is no way to find them out.
Anna Akhmatova. Requiem

Index of Games

Game	White	Black	Opening	Year
1	A. Kubbel	I. Rabinovich	Vienna Game	1923
2	A. Ilyin-Zhenevsky	A. Kubbel	Spanish Opening	1925
3	A. Kubbel	S. Vainstein	Four Knights Opening	1925
4	A. Kubbel	I. Rabinovich	Alekhine's Defense	1925
5	A. Kubbel	A. Rabinovich	Sicilian Defense	1925
6	F. Duz-Khotimirsky	A. Kubbel	Slav Defense	1925
7	A. Kubbel	A. Sergeev	Sicilian Defense	1926
8	A. Kubbel	A. Poliak	Sicilian Defense	1926
9	A. Kubbel	G. Levenfish	Sicilian Defense	1928
10	G. Ravinsky	A. Kubbel	Fragment	1928
11	A. Kubbel	V. Ragozin	Sicilian Defense	1929
12	A. Kubbel	L. Kubbel	Four Knights Opening	1929
13	M. Botvinnik	S. Kaminer	Fragment	1924
14	M. Barulin	Krestovsky	Dutch Defense	1924
15	B. Munster	M. Barulin	Fragment	1924
16	V. Petrovs	Gailis	Fragment	1924
17	S. Tartakower	V. Petrovs	Queen's Pawn Game	1930
18	V. Mikenas	V. Petrovs	Tarrasch Defense	1933
19	L. Rellstab	V. Petrovs	Colle System	1937
20	S. Reshevsky	V. Petrovs	Queen's Gambit	1937
21	V. Petrovs	E. Eliskases	Fragment	1937
22	V. Petrovs	A. Alekhine	Catalan Opening	1938
23	G. Thomas	V. Petrovs	Sicilian Defense	1938
24	V. Petrovs	S. Tartakower	Dutch Defense	1939
25	V. Petrovs	R. Grau	Queen's Gambit	1939
26	V. Petrovs	A. Kotov	Catalan Opening	1940
27	E. Gerstenfeld	V. Petrovs	Fragment	1940
28	V. Petrovs	G. Levenfish	King's Indian Defense	1940
29	V. Petrovs	V. Makogonov	Catalan Opening	1940
30	V. Petrovs	M. Stolberg	Grunfeld Defense	1940
31	V. Petrovs	G. Bastrikov	Fragment	1942
32	P. Izmailov	L. Staroverov	Queen's Gambit	1928
33	P. Izmailov	M. Shebarshin	Slav Defense	1928
34	P. Izmailov	I. Kan	Bogo-Indian Defense	1928
35	P. Izmailov	M. Botvinnik	Queen's Gambit	1929
36	P. Izmailov	M. Botvinnik	Queen's Indian Defense	1931

37	I. Kan	G. Schneideman	French Defense	1931
38	Dmitrievsky	G. Schneideman	King's Indian Defense	1937
39	G. Schneideman	V. Makogonov	Fragment	1936
40	E. Zagoryansky	G. Schneideman	Queen's Gambit	1936
41	G. Schneideman	M. Gergenreder	Queen's Gambit	1936
42	V. Baturinsky	G. Schneideman	Spanish Opening	1938
43	A. Konstantinov	G. Schneideman	Catalan Opening	1938
44	A. Tolush	G. Schneideman	Caro-Kann Defense	1939
45	G. Lisitsyn	G. Schneideman	Reti Opening	1939
46	G. Schneideman	Geyer	Queen's Gambit	1940
47	A. Tolush	G. Schneideman	Spanish Opening	1940
48	I. Tyurn	G. Schneideman	Queen's Gambit	1941
49	M. Shebarshin	N. Katalymov	Catalan Opening	1915
50	B. Koyalovich	M. Shebarshin	Bird's Opening	1923
51	M. Shebarshin	A. Poliak	Grunfeld Defense	1926
52	M. Shebarshin	A. Sokolsky	Queen's Gambit	1928
53	M. Shebarshin	S. Kosolapov	Nimzo-Indian Defense	1928
54	M. Shebarshin	M. Shalaev	Queen's Gambit	1930
55	V. Skotorenko	M. Shebarshin	English Opening	1952
56	A. Sokolsky	N. Salmin	Fragment	1929
57	N. Krylenko	V. Likum	Evans Gambit	1925
58	A. Rassadnev	N. Krylenko	Reti Opening	1927-1928
59	A. Gerbstman	N. Krylenko	Reti Opening	1927
60	V. Likum	N. Krylenko	Alekhine's Defense	1928
61	V. Zbandutto	N. Krylenko	Vienna Game	1935-1936
62	N. Krylenko	A. Serebryakov	Queen's Gambit	1935
63	Y. Karakhan	N. Krylenko	Sicilian Defense	1937
64	N. Krylenko	V. Fridberg	Queen's Gambit	1931
65	E. Bogoljubov and D. Gaukhberg	R. Shukevich-Tretyakov and A. Kaspersky	French Defense	1924
66	R. Shukevich-Tretyakov	A. Alexeev	Sicilian Defense	1930-1931
67	V. Kushnir	A. Kriger	Fragment	1953
68	N. Miroshnichenko	V. Levitsky	King's Gambit	1951
69	V. Levitsky	N. Miroshnichenko	Spanish Opening	1951
70	N. Sharansky	N.N.	Queen's Pawn Game	1971
71	G. Kasparov	N. Sharansky	Queen's Gambit	1994
72	G. Kasparov	N. Sharansky	French Defense	1996

Foreword by Alexander Yakovlev

Vita memoriae

The cancer of Bolshevism mercilessly destroyed generation after generation all around the world and, above all, in Russia. Therefore, in my introduction to the Russian edition of *The Black Book of Communism*, I noted with regret that the first book about the crimes of Bolshevism – this social disease of the 20th century – was not written by Russian historians.

The book you are now holding is based on the materials of Russian archives and is devoted to the life and work of famous chess artists who became victims of unjustified repressions.

The most terrible thing that exists in the world is the distortion of everything beautiful. The Bolshevik regime appeared out of revolutionary determination, inspired in words by humanistic ideals. The Leninists were convinced that violence was the universal and sole means of achieving these ideals. In the end, the ultimate means of creation was the struggle of all people with all others and with everything.

An ideological monopoly ensured universal control over everyone. Minds and souls were assigned to the same category as objects. Dissenters were destroyed or isolated. Free labor, free thought, and free speech were abolished. The search for truth was forbidden. Science and art were bolshevized. Moreover, agronomy, medicine, electronics – all and everything – were transferred to the ranks of ideological subjects. The book *The Lubyanka Gambit*, named after the KGB's headquarters on Lubyanskaya Square in Moscow known as the Lubyanka building, provides examples of how the USSR fought against "bourgeois ideology" and imposed a class-based approach in chess.

Everything that happens to us is our punishment for Bolshevism. Only after being cured of this social disease can Russia count on health and wellbeing today and in the future. A new wave of Bolshevism must be prevented, so that the Communist occupiers will forever remain in the dustbin of history, as the West managed to achieve with Nazism.

This is a serious book, tightly packed with facts, many of which are new discoveries. I think that the reader will find it interesting from various points of view. It is truthful and instructive.

Alexander Yakovlev, 2004
Academician of the Russian Academy of Sciences, Chairman of the Commission under the President of the Russian Federation for the Rehabilitation of Victims of Political Repression

Introduction by the Author

The idea of writing this book came to me at the time of the birth of Memorial – at its founding conference, which was held on January 28, 1989, in the Palace of Culture of the Moscow Aviation Institute. This meeting was unusual. People who had been deprived of the opportunity to speak freely for many years rose to the stage. Because, as Mandelstam wrote in the 1930s:

We live without feeling the country under us,
Our speech cannot be heard ten steps away,
But when we are able to say half a word,
The Kremlin mountain-dweller will inevitably be mentioned.

But under the vaults of the Palace of Culture, people wanted to speak out, or even shout out, or even cry their eyes out.

Millions of people were lost to our country during these times of trouble, which lasted for almost three quarters of the twentieth century. After the delegates and guests of the conference observed a minute of silence in memory of the victims, someone remarked that if we gave one minute to the memory of each deceased person, we would be there for another half century.

Thousands of victims of Stalinism (I use this generally accepted term to characterize the single era of Leninism-Stalinism-Khrushchevism-Brezhnevism – from the Bolshevik coup in October 1917 to the collapse of the Putsch in August 1991) have been named, but millions more remain a faceless, human mass.

It is our duty to pull back from oblivion as many names as possible of people whose destinies were broken during the era of totalitarianism. Among the victims of terror there are many cultural figures. And chess players could not avoid the repressions, many of them falling down a steep path. It is now known that the lives of dozens of chess masters, composers and organizers were tragically cut short during the years of Stalinism, and their mournful list continues to grow.

This book is the result of many years of research in the following areas: identifying chess figures who were repressed, analyzing the cult of personality with respect to chess (specifically, the impact of lawlessness and arbitrariness on chess life in the country), collecting the best works of chess players and composers who fell victim to such arbitrariness, and collecting memories of how chess helped people to survive the labor camps.

But how should I write about this subject? Varlam Shalamov noted: "It should be recounted exactly, without sounding bombastic. With brevity, simplicity, cutting off everything that might be called 'literature.'"

This book was also difficult to write because it was necessary to name those who – for the sake of their career, due to cowardice or simply out of indifference – signed the incriminating documents. Alas, there were always "do-gooders" who, in an act of self-affirmation, or sometimes in the hope of taking someone else's place, tarnished the attempts of courageous individuals to resist what was prescribed by the "script".

The time has come to carry out what was foreseen by Alexander Galich in his poem *In Memory of B.L. Pasternak*:

We won't forget that laughter
Or that boredom!
We will remember by name all those
Who raised their hand!

This book names for the first time those, including popular figures, who were guilty in the tragic fate of colleagues, and the reader will be repeatedly convinced that the 20th century refuted the formula of Pushkin's Mozart: that "genius and villainy are two incompatible things."

There's been a lot said about "repentance" lately. But do we interpret this word correctly? It is typical that this word was not included in any of the Soviet encyclopedias (either the Big or Small editions). Only in the last edition of the *Big Soviet Encyclopedia* (1975) do we find the term "church repentance", classified as a Christian rite. In the *Dictionary of the Russian Language* (1987) we find: "Repentance is the recognition of a committed offense, a mistake."

Well, in my opinion, the closest definition is the one from the 19th century *Explanatory Dictionary of the Living Great Russian Language* compiled by Vladimir Dal: "To repent something, to bring repentance, to confess a misdemeanor, to confess your sins and repent; to renounce the old, bad, sinful life, to consciously proceed to a better one."

If this book helps someone to intentionally embark on a better life, the author will consider his goal accomplished.

Chess and Soviet Totalitarianism

You would have thought that Stalinism did not hinder the progress of the art of chess. After all, even during the reign of the "father of nations", Soviet grandmasters occupied leading positions in the world, and the flow of victories at tournaments continued unchecked. Moreover, for decades the regime exploited the fact that the Soviets possessed the chess crown and their other successes on the 64 squares as proof of the advantages of the socialist system.

And yet... It all began with the fact that on August 20, 1924, at the Third Congress of Chess Players of the USSR, the then head of the prosecutors supervisory body of the country, Nikolai Vasilyevich Krylenko, was elected chairman of the All-Union Chess Section. So chess players had now got their own "curator" – much earlier than "curators" and "commissars" appeared in scientific institutions.

In 1925, in a resolution on Krylenko's report, the Fourth All-Union Chess Congress proclaimed the class character of chess: "The art of chess must become a proletarian art, chess must become a proletarian game – these are the slogans under which the chess movement of the working masses everywhere has to develop and to be developed... The Congress considers it absolutely inadmissible for members of proletarian organizations to join international chess organizations of a non-proletarian nature, to participate organically and permanently in international tournaments at their own discretion and without the approval of the Central Committee of the organization of which they are members."

That year, the chess organization of the USSR joined the Workers Chess International, but four years later, for political reasons, it broke with that organization, instead deciding to "start preparing for the World Congress of Red Organizations".

Having forbidden communication with "non-Proletarian" chess players, Krylenko in 1928 declared the world champion Alexander Alekhine, who was in exile, an enemy. In his article introducing *Shakhmatny listok* ("Chess List") magazine issue No. 6 that year, the following words were highlighted: "**We have now finished with the citizen Alekhine – he is our enemy, and we can now treat him only as an enemy.**" The article ends with a tirade: "However, we must draw one conclusion from Alekhine's behavior: all those who still cherished the hope in our Soviet chess circles that Alekhine would return one day must now abandon these hopes."

The Supreme Commander Krylenko subjected all those who continued to cooperate with the "king of chess" to a fierce attack: especially the magazine

Shakhmaty ("Chess") published by Nikolai Grekov, as well as the state publishing house Gosizdat.

"This kind of 'Manilovism' *(impractical dreaming – from a character in Gogol's Dead Souls)* and this kind of political attempt at 'keeping silence' must be ended," Krylenko wrote, and he highlighted: **"Alekhine is our political enemy, and no one should forget this fact. Whoever is with him now, even to a small extent, is against us.** We must state this clearly and it should be understood and realized by everyone. Talent is talent, and politics is politics, but it is prohibited to maintain relations with renegades, be they Alekhine, Bogoljubov or whoever."

Krylenko's "prohibition", highlighted separately in the original text, separated the brilliant Russian chess player from his homeland for many years. Wasn't this a precedent for the expulsions and bans of the best representatives of Russian culture (not only the culture of chess, of course) in the following decades, including in the years of stagnation under Brezhnev?

In 1929, *Shakhmaty*, despite being perhaps the best chess publication in the 1920s, one which aimed to establish a connection between Russian chess players scattered around the world, was closed for its "apolitical stance". Soon *Shakhmatny listok*, which was named after the first Russian chess periodical published in 1859-1863, was renamed *Shakhmaty v SSSR* ("Chess in the USSR"), an event which essentially symbolized the construction of an "iron curtain" in chess.

That idea didn't seem enough to one of the "raging zealots" of that time, Yakov Rokhlin. In an article dedicated to the 10th anniversary of *Shakhmatny listok*, he proposed renaming it *Shakhmatny front* ("Chess Front"): "...We believe that the idea of changing the name of *Shakhmatny listok*, which has a narrowly professional and primitive name (why just "List"?) to a name that is more in tune with our revolutionary era, more international and militant, is quite ripe. In our opinion, the most sensible decision is to rename our organ *Shakhmatny front*. And Rokhlin ended his note with the following appeal: "Let's move forward, for the revolutionary *Shakhmatny front*!"

That same Rokhlin, in another article "Against bourgeois cooking", being quite unhappy with Grekov's article "Chess" for the *Small Soviet Encyclopedia*, made an appeal: "...We need a good broom that will clean out all the cracks and hiding places of bourgeois smugglers, overt and secret 'saboteurs', that will rid us of amateurism and reactionary philistinism".

In the early 1930s, Krylenko was often called the "leader of chess players". And – like the "leader of all nations" – he suppressed all dissent. Through article upon article, he espoused the idea of the political content of chess and called for a decisive struggle against apolitical chess work, for the need to "further sharpen the political line in our chess movement".

Here are excerpts from the keynote speech of the "leader" of Soviet chess players in 1929: "...Chess is played by real people, people with blood and nerves, people of certain political sympathies and antipathies. And if they cannot reveal their political sympathies and antipathies directly in the chess game, then they are far from being indifferent to everything that happens around our chess movement, and they are far from being indifferent to the slogans under which this movement develops and grows... In the pre-revolutionary period, when the imperial regime restrained all expression of thought and political activity, chess was a place where the layman could relax away from the painful problems of everyday reality, from the horrors of the old regime. Such a situation disappeared immediately after the revolution, which required everyone above all to have a clear idea, even if only in his own mind, of whose side he was on, and about how he felt about the gigantic historical change.

"Since the moment when the Soviet government took the chess movement into its own hands and made efforts to turn it into a powerful tool of the cultural revolution, and set itself the task of drawing millions of workers and peasants into it, it has lost its apolitical character. But those groups of old chess players and groups of philistine-minded people still remain... And that is why a negative attitude to political issues, in particular to political matters at chess management level (of course, not to politics as such in the game of chess itself), is now an objective slogan under which all those who in their hearts do not agree with or do not sympathize with the Soviet government, but who do not risk, do not dare to openly declare their disagreement, cannot but unite and form a group. They are, let us repeat, a reservoir from which counter-revolutionary groups can draw their adherents. That is why we cannot treat the presence of these voices with absolute indifference, we cannot ignore the slogan 'Down with politics in chess', which has recently begun to be heard with a certain determination among a certain category of our chess players.

"On the contrary, precisely because this is the case, precisely because the promotion of such a slogan is only the first stage in the further development of anti-Soviet sentiments, it is so far the first form and the first slogan under which the stratification of chess players according to their political sympathies and antipathies takes place, often even objectively independently of the will of individuals – and with a greater force, in order to deepen this stratification more sharply, we must highlight the political content of the slogan 'Chess for politics', the significance of the chess movement as a tool of cultural revolution, and the **political unity of our chess movement**

leadership with the overall leadership, which is being demonstrated by the working class in its planned socialist construction in respect of all other strata and classes of the population..."

Krylenko's article ends with a simple threat: "The Executive Bureau will highlight political points in its leadership with even greater relentlessness, and even more sharply implement the slogan 'Chess is an instrument of politics'. From this point on, supporters of the slogan 'Chess is beyond politics' are our enemies." (N. Krylenko. "More about politics and chess". – *Shakhmatny listok*, 1929, No. 24).

And here is a fragment of the editorial article "Our reply to the interventionists" (*Shakhmatny listok*, 1930, No. 23): "The lessons of the 'industrial party' cannot pass without trace for our chess organization. The swamp of apoliticism and neutrality, still partially preserved as rusty spots among Soviet chess players, must be drained to the end and in the shortest possible time... The healing process of self-purification has only slightly affected the chess organizations of the USSR."

So much nonsense was written then by orthodox believers in a class struggle in chess. And the doctrinal fanaticism of many of Krylenko's ideas gave them a farcical character: "We must organize shock brigades of chess players and begin the immediate implementation of a five-year plan for chess." (From a speech by Krylenko in 1932.)

In one of the reactions to Krylenko's line, we can read: "All work must be imbued with politics. We have to increase the number of instructive political articles in chess journals... Remember that tournaments develop individualistic traits of character: the desire to profit at the expense of another, to be a point higher, to take advantage of your opponent's nervousness, etc. Eventually, the chess player ceases to take account not only of his comrades, but also of his chess organization... But educational work should also be carried out among problemists, who have little regard for the chess organization and its goals. Let's take for example the following apparently insignificant matter: all sorts of 'dreams' appear every time at chess competitions, 'Lucies', 'Lyalis', 'Neptunes' and 'Jupiters', while problems with political mottos are rare exceptions." (*Shakhmatny listok*, 1930).

The "struggle" escalated, and at the beginning of 1932 the magazine *Shakhmaty v SSSR* wrote: "Our Soviet chess and checkers organization sets two requirements (inseparable from each other) at the forefront of all its work: rallying the proletarian masses of the chess players of the capital countries to Lenin's banner, and providing all possible assistance to the fulfillment and over-fulfillment of the plans for socialist development in the USSR.

Forgetting these tasks inevitably leads the chess and checkers movement into a swamp of bourgeois sportsmanship".

The resolution of the First Plenum of the All-Union Chess and Checkers Sector, adopted upon a report by I. Zholdak, states: "...In modern class society, chess, like every form of art, sport, science, etc., is one of the many tools used by the bourgeoisie and the proletariat in the interests of their class. The main forms of the use of chess by the classes include unifying solid masses of chess and checkers amateurs around chess culture, including workers, under the ideological leadership of bourgeois circles. When gathering dispersed groups in circles, and then organizing an association (club, union, federation) of chess and checkers amateurs, various bourgeois organizations mainly pursue at the same time a goal through these associations, under the guise of talking about the apolitical nature of chess ('chess for chess', 'in chess there is only art and no ounce of politics', etc.), to raise the masses in the Fascist spirit".

In his pamphlet "International Tasks of Soviet Chess Organizations" (1931), Zholdak holds forth on the same topic: "Not only in petit bourgeois, but even in working-class circles, there are always people who do not understand that there is a class struggle going on around chess." Then, Zholdak criticizes FIDE, which he calls "the chess international of the bourgeoisie", and its slogan *Gens una sumus* ("We are one family").

The press is not forgotten either. A lead article on this topic by Samuil Vainstein (*Shakhmaty v SSSR*, 1932, No. 2) occupies about two pages. The tone of the article is strikingly monotonous: we can quote any paragraph of it: "We do not need some standard chess column consisting of problems, games and international news, which should disappear from the pages of our press as soon as possible. The main emphasis should be on creating a solid entity around the chess columns and establishing through it a connection with all enterprises and collective farms where chess work can be organized or is already organized. Its rules will ensue from this, which, in a nutshell, should be highlighting and developing the main directives of the central chess organizations based on particular examples, linking chess work with the tasks of socialist construction, fighting sabotage and the class enemy in certain sections of our chess front, while drawing general lessons from local experience, etc. Chess material can and should be published, but inseparably connected with the socio-political material published in the column..."

In 1935, on the occasion of Krylenko's 50th birthday, the magazine *Shakhmaty v SSSR* called the hero of the day "a deep expert of the chess movement, its true leader, an ardent conductor of the ideas of Lenin and Stalin in the chess arena of the cultural front," and continued: "with such extraordinary insight he is able to identify our mistakes in certain areas of our work and expose both ultra-left deviations and right inclinations in the chess movement... Always and everywhere he has been merciless to all manifestations of apoliticism, laxity and irresponsibility, and has bitterly reproached us for our inability to cope with 'objective reasons'. He has taught us not only to be chess organizers, but also to be true Bolsheviks, who have managed to overcome obstacles in the way and to recognize the machinations of the class enemy in time... He has a great memory, and he is able, if necessary, to recall the long-forgotten performances of particular comrades or some of their mistakes, which had earlier been confined to the past."

That much was true – Krylenko had students who tried to keep up with the leader (and almost all of them shared his fate).

From the report of the later repressed Vladimir Fridberg "Priority tasks of chess and checkers work in the Moscow Region" (1930): "There is no doubt that chess and checkers work, as well as other areas of our political life, requires an acute formulation of the question of fighting both manifestations of all kinds of opportunism and the erasure of the class line under any pretext in the chess and checkers movement."

Vadim Vorchenko, at the time editor of *Shakhmatny listok*, strongly criticized the non-partisan nature of chess, attempting to convince readers that the spread of theoretical achievements is only possible in the conditions of dictatorship of the proletariat: "Like all ideological superstructures, chess, despite all its 'etherealness', is inevitably painted in those social tones that prevail in a particular society and in a particular environment. The chess historian of the future, who will be able to move from the mechanical gathering of facts to their understanding, will undoubtedly provide many interesting illustrations of how the development of chess is determined by 'social demand' and, ultimately, by the economic structure of society."

Vorchenko's main idea was as follows: "...The mass distribution of theoretical chess improvements is only possible in conditions of the dictatorship of the proletariat, and this will guarantee unprecedented growth of chess work with similar inevitability." And he concludes: "From here we are obliged to draw a conclusion about the goals of our chess organizations in the historical era we are living in. Generally speaking, this conclusion is known and obvious: to enhance the revolutionary-proletarian, effective-international work among our ranks, mercilessly driving out the spies of capitalist restoration, potential spies of intervention from every dark corner, lasciviously covering their ideological nakedness with rags of apoliticism." (Vorchenko, "Chess and the class struggle", *Shakhmatny listok,* 1930, No. 24).

In Vorchenko's book *Chess in Our Days* (OGIZ-FIS, 1932) we find: "Chess 'in general' is that same fiction, that same lifeless fiction, as, for example, human society 'in general' or the national economy 'in general'."

Well, Vorchenko was repressed in the first half of the 1930s. Leonty Spokoiny, his replacement as editor of the magazine, by then known as *Shakhmaty v SSSR* (he, too, later turned out to be an "enemy of the people") held the same line. Discussing the different styles of chess players, he wrote: "The Soviet chess style, as is already generally recognized, is characterized by aggressiveness... *Stalin demands victories!* said the poet Comrade Lahouti. Stakhanovites do fight and win. They win by mastering technique. Technique is their weapon. In chess, the theory of the game, all knowledge and principles, also comprise a means of struggle. Chess theory, chess analysis and commentary, chess composition – all this plays an auxiliary and subordinate role in relation to the main part of chess – the game, which is nothing but a struggle. And it is characteristic that usually the styles were always divided into combinational and positional ones, and the Soviet chess playing style was given a definition that was not related to this traditional classification." (*Shakhmaty v SSSR*, 1936, No. 1). *(Editor's note – the text really does combine the words 'usually' and 'always' – such was the level of Shakhmaty v SSSR writers in those times.)*

Real chess masters were also willing to declare their support for the party line. In *64* (1930, No. 2) there is a letter from Abram Rabinovich:

"Letter to the editor.

Fully supporting the points put forward by the Chairman of the Chess and Checkers Sections of the All-Union Committee for Physical Education and Sports *(the "VSFK")* N. V. Krylenko in his article 'More about Politics and Chess', published in issue No. 24 of the magazine *Shakhmatny listok*, I consider it necessary to finally raise the matter of our enemies and in a more concrete fashion – I mean a thorough purging of our ranks. Cases involving some chess players – cases that have come to the surface of our chess life by chance – show that the matter of a purge is long overdue.

With chess greetings

A. Rabinovich"

However, not everyone silently endured the dictates of Krylenko and his adherents. After the "Commander-in-Chief" once again excoriated leading players, a laconic appeal by Peter Romanovsky was published in the 21st issue of *Shakhmatny listok* in 1929: "Considering the publication of Krylenko's article in the 20th issue of *Shakhmatny listok* technically and factually incorrect, I am hereby declaring my withdrawal from the editorial board and from the magazine staff."

And on June 29, 1932, the newspaper *Vechernaya Moskva* published a satirical article by Evgeny Vermont "Bobka Lapis and Capablanca", which ridiculed the statement taken from *Shakhmaty v SSSR* that "politically educating each chess player and checkers player, we help them to rise up through chess and checkers to the level of those goals which our great era is attaining."

Vermont did not try to hide his irony on this occasion: "But the editorial board doesn't tell us how to rise up to the level of the great era through chess and checkers. How many games do you have to win? Or perhaps, it's enough to queen."

Krylenko's answer was immediately published in *Shakhmaty v SSSR* (1932, No. 15). Considering Vermont's article as politically harmful, Krylenko concludes: "Vermont does not realize that to preach apoliticism inside the chess movement, to preach that, sitting at the chessboard, chess players should only think about the struggle of black versus white and forget about the political struggle, is to preach a typical kind of incorrigible opportunism, which is equally harmful wherever it manifests itself, including the chess aspect of the cultural front."

The editorial board reacted even more harshly: "No falsification will be achieved enabling Vermont to cover up his attack against the line of the Soviet chess organization. Vermont likes to pretend not to understand how it is possible to educate players through chess and checkers *politically*, raising them up to the level of the goals of our era. Vermont likes to pretend to be a simpleton and, with a clownish attitude, to provoke the Soviet chess community, trying to present the matter as though the proletarian policy inside the chess movement were an 'excess' and a 'private initiative' of individual chess players allocated by the organization to work in the press. Vermont likes to think that such a double-dealing incursion will go unpunished and – you never know – will drive a wedge into the ranks of the Soviet chess movement, causing a crack through which – if he lucks out – anonymous 'cultural workers' lurking in dark corners, still dreaming, together with Vermont, of getting rid of 'Krylenko's era', will rise to the surface. Vermont hopes with vulgar giggling to cut away the Bolshevik Party's formulation of the struggle against the class enemy and the penetration of class-hostile influences in the Soviet and international workers' chess movement... As for the ideological image of Vermont that emerges from the article in question, this ugly appearance is alien and hostile to us. The enemy does not need to be persuaded or engaged in conversation: he must be **exposed** – in order to then be **neutralized**." (*Shakhmaty v SSSR*, 1932, No. 13.)

And all that was written some years before 1937...

An active dislike for the social-democratic movement was also found on the pages of chess publications. "...We consider the leading center of the Social-Democratic Party to be the worst servants of the capitalists, their main hope and support. That is why our task is to expose in every possible way and everywhere the hypocrisy and treachery of the Social-Democratic leaders, to expose them wherever possible, even at the chessboard and during a game with the Social-Democratic minded workers... for us, the chess movement under all conditions has never been and will never mean an end in itself, but has been and will be a means not only of cultural, but also of revolutionary class struggle..." Thus Krylenko set the tone in his article "A classic example of confusion", which aimed to "expose the machinations of the chess bourgeoisie." (*Shakhmatny listok*, 1929, No. 3.)

In 1932, *Shakhmaty v SSSR* marked the 20th anniversary of the founding of the German Workers Chess Union: "The history of the German Workers Chess Union is basically... an instructive page on the activities of German social democracy... Chess was publicly turned into a means of distracting workers from politics and was reduced to a cultural activity. This hypocritical act, typical social-fascist policy, was deeply exposed in our press at that time." (S. Vainstein. "An inglorious anniversary" – *Shakhmaty v SSSR*, 1932, No. 9.)

Poor Grekov continued to bear the brunt of attacks. Spokoiny, who had not yet been labeled an "unmasked enemy of the people" at the time, selected the sharpest words from Grekov's book *A History of Chess Competitions* in his article "How not to write the history of chess" (*Shakhmaty v SSSR*, 1935, No. 7): "Instead of giving the reader a comprehensive picture of the international chess movement, the simultaneous victorious growth of the Soviet chess movement and attempts to develop the workers chess movement abroad, Grekov, hiding behind the sign of formalism, limited himself to a description of international competitions, which he understood in a strange way... Grekov is not a newcomer on the chess front. He used to publish his own magazine *Shakhmaty*. His magazine was closed for its apoliticism, since apoliticism at a time when we were striving to raise chess as a mass working-class movement and as a means of cultural revolution was nothing more than a demonstration of hostility towards the Soviet chess movement and its slogans."

In 1937, the All-Union Chess Section adopted a resolution "On measures to rejuvenate chess and checkers organizations and purge them of class-hostile, random and decayed elements, and raise the level of political literacy, cultural development and active participation in the public and political life of highly qualified chess players (checkers players)".

Half of the presidium of the All-Union Chess Section elected in 1936 was repressed in 1937. In the press, they were mostly attacked for underestimating the class struggle and ignoring political and educational work.

By that time, portraits of the "father of nations" were being placed in chess publications more often than portraits of all the chess kings taken together. The general hysteria with Stalin's deification did not spare competitions for young chess players: "In their greetings to Stalin, the participants of the All-Union junior competitions write: 'Comrade Stalin, we promise you to succeed in mastering the basics of science, we promise to be the trail-blazers and organizers for all children, we promise to fight to catch up and overtake the capitalist countries in the field of chess technique'" (*Shakhmaty v SSSR*, 1934, No. 2).

Issue dated December 21, 1939, of the newspaper *64* was entirely dedicated to the 60th birthday of the "best friend of chess players".

In addition to the collective greeting "To the Leader of the peoples, the best friend of physical education students, wise Stalin", signed by all the leading chess players, grandmaster Alexander Kotov personally congratulated the leader with words coming right from the heart: "Stalin has got rid of need. He opened the doors of university for me. He gave me the leisure time I needed for creative improvement in chess. Millions of workers owe everything they have achieved primarily to Stalin. He is the people's happiness. The only true democratic Constitution in the world has been created by the wise Stalin... Soviet chess players should celebrate the sixtieth birthday of our father and best friend, Comrade Stalin, by joining sports teams en masse..."

The grandmasters also reported on their achievements to their "true father". In 1936, Mikhail Botvinnik won the tournament in Nottingham. Soon, the newspaper *64* (1936, No. 48), published his letter to Stalin:

"Our dear and beloved teacher and leader!

With a sense of the greatest responsibility, I traveled to the international chess tournament in Nottingham to defend the honor of Soviet chess art in the most critical of chess competitions that the chess world has known in recent years. A burning desire to support the honor of Soviet chess mastery made me invest all my strength, all my knowledge and all my energy in the game. It is an absolute pleasure to be able to report that a representative of the Soviet chess art shared first place in the tournament with former world champion Capablanca.

This could only have happened because I felt the support of my entire country, the care of our government and our party, and above all, the daily care that you, our great leader, have shown and are showing in order to raise our great motherland to an unbelievable height and turn us – the representatives of Soviet youth – into a healthy and joyful next generation for all areas of our socialist construction. Inspired by the great slogan 'catch up and overtake' set by you, I am glad that I was able to implement it at least in the small area that our country entrusted me to fight in.

Mikhail Botvinnik.

London, August 29, 1936"

Decades later (in 1978), Anatoly Karpov achieved a hard-fought victory in the World Championship match over the defector Viktor Korchnoi. Later, a telegram from distant Baguio, addressed to the new leader, arrived in Moscow:

"To Comrade LEONID ILYICH BREZHNEV

Dear Leonid Ilyich!

I am glad to report that the match for the title of World Chess champion has finished with our victory. Please accept, dear Leonid Ilyich, my heartfelt thanks for the fatherly care and attention shown to me and our delegation during the preparation and course of the match. I assure the Central Committee of the CPSU *(the Communist Part of the Soviet Union)*, the Presidium of the Supreme Soviet of the USSR, the Soviet Government and you personally, Leonid Ilyich, that in the future I will make every effort to increase the glory of the Soviet chess school.

World Champion Anatoly Karpov

October 18, 1978, Baguio, Philippines".

The difference was that "the father" did not respond to Botvinnik's letter, whereas "dear Leonid Ilyich" sent a telegram to Baguio in reply. There is no need to give its text.

At the tournament in Nottingham, Mikhail Botvinnik defeated Efim Bogoljubov. This game was included in *Shakhmaty v SSSR* not only with chess analysis. Here is what Rokhlin wrote about the clash: "This meeting has not only chess, but also political significance. The former Soviet champion of 1924 and 1925, later a renegade and groveling pathetic 'racist', 11 years after that meets a young chess player of the socialist country at a major international tournament. Numerous correspondents of fascist and pro-fascist newspapers are anticipating a victory for Bogoljubov, who plays white, and are already preparing laudatory, lyrical articles in praise of the 'knights' of the capitalist world. But these hopes were never meant to come true. The Komsomol grandmaster gave the 'German' fascist Bogoljubov a proper lesson in chess strategy. Playing the game with precision and boldly, he gained an advantage in the opening and, with a direct attack on the kingside, scored a brilliant victory with his Soviet chess weapon."

The editorial article of *Shakhmaty v SSSR* No. 8 for 1937 was called "To raise the political and educational work of the chess and checkers organizations":

"It is fair to say that, in the field of political education, the situation in our chess and checkers organizations was extremely bad. The leading organizations, both central and regional, did not pay enough attention to this issue. Instructors in the grassroots circles were often politically illiterate. They could probably explain the moves of particular pieces well, but they could not say anything sensible about the question of, for example, the social role of chess in our country and in capitalist countries... A direct consequence of political illiteracy and low literacy is political myopia and a lack of vigilance... The fact that in some parts of our organization there have been morally decayed embezzlers and even direct enemies of the people who found a quiet refuge here speaks for itself. In order to be able to detect and expose our enemies in a timely manner, we must first of all be politically armed people".

And here are excerpts from the editorial of the newspaper *64* (No. 3 for 1939), entitled "To master Bolshevism": "Raising the ideological and political level of Soviet masters will contribute to the further growth of their skills... The political and educational work of chess organizations in the field among the highly-qualified chess elite will be the main means of accomplishing our tasks and implementing the slogan: 'Soviet masters must be the strongest players in the world'. It is time to put an end to the harmful practice that the enemies of the people tried to instill in chess work in the past, who have made their way into our ranks with the practice of ignoring political and educational work in the system of the Soviet chess movement. Political and educational work among chess professionals and, above all, among the highly-qualified elite, raising the ideological and political level of chess workers, mastering Bolshevism through deep study of *A Short Course of the History of the CPSU(b) ("b" = Bolshevik – S.G.)* – these are the main tasks facing each chess section, each master and chess worker."

The huge number of citations of "enemies of the people" in our book highlights that the attacks against them for underestimating the class struggle and political and educational work among chess players were unfounded. On June 15, 1937, the newspaper *64* published a report on the verdict in the case of the military guard led by Marshal Tukhachevsky. The very next issue of the newspaper contained a selection of materials naming enemies of the people on behalf of chess players:

"With the greatest satisfaction, we have learned of the execution of a brutal band of fascist spies, traitors to our socialist homeland – Tukhachevsky, Yakir, Uborevich and others. The fascist horde will fail to undermine the power of our great country no matter what tricks they use. The Soviet people are united as never before and our valiant Red Army is strong. We support the proposal of the railway workers to issue a loan for the defense of the USSR.

"Soviet masters and chess figures of Leningrad: Botvinnik, Vainstein, Volkovysky, Ilyin-Zhenevsky, Levenfish, Lisitsyn, Rabinovich, Ragozin, Ramm, Rauzer, Romanovsky, Stirius, Tyunev, Fedorov, Feldman, Chekhover".

And in 1938, Konstantinopolsky, Blinder, Kogan and Poliak hastened to report their "great satisfaction" with the judgement in the case of Bukharin and Rykov by telephone from Kiev. A letter from Leningrad approving the verdict on the "band of traitors, murderers and spies" was signed by Botvinnik, Levenfish, Romanovsky, Lisitsyn, Ilyin-Zhenevsky, Rabinovich, Ragozin, Sokov, Chekhover, Shapiro, Chernikov, Ber, Fedorov, Sokolsky, Timchenko, Nazarova, Martynova, Ritov, Korshunov, and Rozenstein.

"Participants of the chess match between the Moscow women's team and the October sports society heard with great satisfaction the verdict of the Military Collegium of the Supreme Court of the Soviet Union in the case of bandits and murderers from the Bloc of Rightists and Trotskyites." There are 66 signatures here, including from the following people: Chudova, Bykova, Rabinovich, Golubeva, Gringauz, Tomson, Mar, Mirolyubskaya, Drabkin, Rusakov, Shimbireva, and Bukhman.

It was not long for some of the "signatories" to experience a tragic fate themselves. One of them was the then chairman of the Leningrad Chess Section, the director of the Leningrad Radio Studio Zhan Stirius. At a meeting of the Leningrad chess community in the summer of 1937, the chairman of the chess section was criticized for his separation from the masses, from the grassroots collectives, mismanagement and bureaucracy. But those weren't the main accusation...

Under the headline "What carelessness leads to", the newspaper *64* (1937, No. 31) reveals the essence of the main accusation against Zhan Zhanovich Stirius: "For a long time, one of the former leaders of the sports organization of Leningrad, the enemy of the people Saikin, instilled in the chess organization a focus on the champion's title, arrogance, disregard for the masses, and ignoring the requests of the community. Like the Moscow organization, where strange and hostile people (Golts, Shebedev) worked for a long time, the Leningrad chess section overlooked the corrupting work of the enemy of the people Spokoiny – the former editor of the magazine *Shakhmaty v SSSR*. During the debate, it was repeatedly pointed out that there was a complete lack of political and educational work among chess workers. This was discussed by comrades Zelichenko, Meyer and Nogienko – and this was also admitted by comrade Stirius in his report."

One of the eyewitnesses of that society meeting told the author that when the delegate Nogienko declared that ideological work in the federation was suffering, the chairman of the federation Stirius (it was visible from the hall) turned as white as chalk. The "reproach" made could not be left without consequences. And, indeed, just a few weeks later, Stirius was arrested and disappeared without trace.

Soon, a group of leading chess players in Leningrad was called up by the then chairman of the City Committee for Physical Education and Sports Bokstein for political training. He angrily denounced the enemy of the people Stirius. But suddenly master Ilya Rabinovich, who had a firm reputation as a man of little common sense, allowed himself a remark from the floor: "Although Stirius is an enemy of the people, he is on the whole a good person." The room turned as silent as a cemetery. You could not even hear flies flying or the beating of hearts, because even the flies froze dumbstruck, and everyone's hearts stopped. Recalling this episode, a usually brave man Alexander Kazimirovich Tolush said that he wanted to disappear into thin air, or at least hide under the table. Alexander Kazimirovich later recalled that if someone had told him he would be in that psychological state, he would not have believed it...

From the editorial article of the newspaper *64* of March 30, 1939:

"The enemies of the people, exposed in physical education organizations, including chess, promoted among qualified talents participation in competitions for payment, poaching people, distracting them from productive work, separating them from social and political life. Taking into account the opinion of the general physical education community, the All-Union Committee for Physical Education and Sports under the Council of People's Commissars of the USSR on March 14, 1939 decided to cancel the issuance of all kinds of scholarships, grants and special payments for participation in competitions."

The struggle against formalism in art, which takes its inglorious beginning from the letter of the Central Committee of the Russian Communist Party "On Proletarian Culture" (1920) and was further shaped in the resolutions on ideological issues of the Party Central Committee of 1946-1948, did not pass by the art of chess composition.

"Our conclusions are as follows. Soviet problem composition, contrary to the claims of bourgeois ideologists and their followers in the USSR, should make a sharp turn towards practical chess... In any case, the time has come when a merciless war must be declared against **formalism in problem composition**, as has already been done on the art front" (Botvinnik and Spokoiny, "Confusion in chess composition" – *Shakhmaty v SSSR*, 1936, No. 3).

This strongly resembles the infamous article "Confusion instead of music", that shot down the best musicians of the country... Chess composers were not only given recommendations on what problems to compose, but also where to publish their works. A finite list of foreign publications to which domestic composers were allowed to send their studies and problems was drawn up and published.

As early as 1930, at a meeting of the Executive Bureau of the Chess and Checkers Sector of the VSFK, a resolution on entries by Soviet problemists in the foreign press was adopted, which stated the following:

"1. To recognize that in the environment of today's intensified class struggle and the increased hostile activity on the part of the bourgeoisie in relation to the Soviet Union, no entries by Soviet problemists in the foreign press that are not regulated by the Soviet political chess organizations can be made, since every case of an entry by a Soviet problemist in the foreign press brings a certain political connotation.

2. To note that until now, entries by Soviet problemists in the foreign press have been unsystematic and beyond the control of state organizations, as a result of which completely unacceptable political blunders and mistakes have been made by individual problemists. Wholly approving of the decision of the most recent plenary session of the chess sector of VSFK on the need to immediately eradicate this situation, the Commission, in developing the resolution of the chess sector about the problemists movement, considers it necessary to direct the further development of the problemists movement along a path that would completely match the fundamental political principles of the international workers chess movement, and therefore considers it necessary to propose the following to all Soviet problemists:

a) when sending their works to the foreign press, to send them first and foremost to organs of the workers press of revolutionary workers chess organizations;

b) in addition, the placement of works of Soviet problemists can take place only with organs that are loyal to the Soviet government – and which are included on a list compiled by the leading chess organizations."

Some of the "raging zealots" tried to keep up with the times. See, for example, an article by Evgeny Umnov (who later earned a reputation as a historian of chess problems) with a characteristic headline "Let's create our own Soviet three-movers!" (*64*, 1933, No. 1). Meanwhile, the publication of compositions by Alexandrov and Rotinyan in the mid-1930s in German publications led to a noisy scandal:

"Following the decision of the Chess Section of the All-Union Committee for Physical Education and Sports, chess composers R. Alexandrov and A. Rotinyan have been excluded from the ranks of the USSR Chess Organization for publishing their compositions in fascist magazines" (*Shakhmaty v SSSR*, 1937, No. 7). The same issue contained an article by the master Alexander Ilyin-Zhenevsky on this matter. This article, by the revolutionary Fyodor Raskolnikov's own brother, ends as follows: "The case of R. Alexandrov and A. Rotinyan should serve as an instructive example for our entire chess organization. Today, when the fascist aggressors are feverishly preparing for war against our great socialist motherland, when they are sending countless spies and saboteurs of all kinds to us, extensively exploiting the enemies of the people – Trotskyites, Zinovievites, right-wingers and other evil people – we must be especially careful and vigilant, and perform the work entrusted to us with special attention and care, no matter in what part of our diverse construction it is located. Let's make the flame of healthy criticism and self-criticism even stronger and more effective, so that we can identify and fix our shortcomings on the go. We will hold high the honorable title of a citizen of the great Soviet country, not allowing and fundamentally suppressing any shameful event when the name of a Soviet citizen is used to 'decorate' the pages of a fascist organ of the press."

However, it is curious that in 1939 Alexandrov's studies could again be found in the magazine *Shakhmaty v SSSR*, and that he, previously "excluded from the ranks", was appointed a judge of the annual contest – the country's most prestigious competition. Perhaps the Soviet-German (communist-fascist) rapprochement affected chess composition in this way?!

"The fateful forties", said a front-line poet referring to the first half of that decade. In fact, the second half of that decade also proved fateful for the moral atmosphere of Soviet society. In 1948, the infamous session of VASKhNIL (the Lenin All-Union Academy of Agricultural Sciences) was held which caused huge damage to the progress of biology in the Soviet Union, and a year later the government declared war on "cosmopolitanism" in science, which spread to the arts and sports, and especially to chess, where there were many prominent people with non-Russian surnames.

Sometimes, the struggle against the worship of the West took on comic forms. The rejection of the generally accepted chess notation that uses the Latin alphabet is only worth mentioning here. And today, in the library, you will definitely come across publications with the ridiculous designation of chess squares using the Cyrillic alphabet.

The "fighters" against cosmopolitans in the chess ranks usually used the name of the great Russian chess player Mikhail Chigorin as a shield. Articles from the pen of the international master and prominent chess theorist Vasily Panov were typical of that time. In them, the selection of surnames and type of argumentation resembled the journalism of the Slavophile, anti-western "Young Guard" and "Our Contemporary" of the 1990s: "Russian prerevolutionary chess literature was influenced by foreign theorists of the so-called 'new school' of Steinitz and Tarrasch, who deliberately concealed the huge contribution of Russian chess players to the world's chess art and actively fought against the advanced, creative views of Chigorin. These cosmopolitan tendencies and subservience to foreigners were especially intensified after Chigorin's death, in the period of 1908-1917, when the general ideological disintegration of Russian bourgeois culture created an extremely unfavorable situation in the chess and sports world. Among the top ten masters who represented prerevolutionary Russia in the international chess arena, there were people who were poorly connected with their native land, who spent their entire lives traveling from country to country, from one tournament to another, who were apolitical professional players who considered theoretical issues from a narrow-minded, 'variation-based' point of view. Such cosmopolitan masters include Nimzowitsch, Bernstein, Alapin, Znosko-Borovsky, and, in part, even the pre-revolutionary champion of Russia Rubinstein... The situation with chess literature also changed little in the first post-revolutionary years. In the beginning, the Soviet book market was also filled with translations of the theoretical works of representatives of the decadent, formalistic school of hypermodernists and its particularly flamboyant and prolific theorist, Tartakower" (*Shakhmaty v SSSR*, 1952, No. 2).

In another article, Panov says of Chigorin: "His creative image until 1944, under the influence of translated cosmopolitan foreign chess literature, was completely misunderstood by many Soviet chess writers... The historical decisions of the Central Committee of the CPSU, which mobilized the Soviet people to fight for the priority of Russian culture against cosmopolitanism and subservience to foreigners, played a decisive role in ensuring the correct understanding of the history of the world's chess art and the leading, progressive significance of our national school" (*Sovietsky sport* ("Soviet Sport"), January 23, 1954).

A person who fell even lower was Dmitry Petrov, a biology professor with an interest in composing studies. He penned a denouncement to the Central Committee of the CPSU(b) in February 1952 informing the supreme body "of the dominance of cosmopolitanism and formalism and the conscious disregard for the guidance of V. I. Lenin prevalent in the all-Union Commission for Chess Composition and in the magazine *Shakhmaty v SSSR*." (Russian Center for the Storage and Study of Documents of Contemporary History, f. 17, op. 132, ed. khr. 570, pp. 292-307.)

"Members of the Commission for Chess Composition have repeatedly opposed the recognition of the guiding significance of Lenin's instructions for chess composition, both in spoken form and in the press. They did so in a particularly shocking way on January 21, 1952, the anniversary of Lenin's death, during a conference on composition. The main 'activists' of the commission are the following persons: Liburkin, Gerbstman, Umnov, Kofman, Schiff, Kasparyan and Kazantsev" (p. 300). By the way, when referring to "Lenin's instructions" the informer meant a flattering review by V. I. Ulyanov (Lenin) of a study by the Platov brothers (ibid, p. 295).

Petrov's accusation was not ignored. Various bodies asked the Committee for Physical Education and Sports under the USSR Council of Ministers to investigate. Everything ended with the replacement of the main members of the Central Commission for Chess Composition, approved by the order of the All-Union Council of February 28, 1952.

The author must admit that, working in the late 1960s and early 1970s in the Central Commission for Chess Composition, before learning this story, he could not understand why his colleagues could not stand the study composer Petrov. He even included a nice essay on him in his book *Chess in the Lives of Scientists*.

The fight against "cosmopolitans" in chess encompassed over-the-board chess as well.

In August 1952, Soviet chess players made their debut at the World Chess Olympiad. On the eve of the "national tournament", it was decided not to include world champion Mikhail Botvinnik in the team. It is difficult to escape the thought that the date of that decision was close to the beginning of the anti-Semitic "poisoner doctors" case. "Some of the country's leading chess players do not work hard enough to improve their skills..." – this is what was written in the editorial of the magazine *Shakhmaty v SSSR* (1953, No. 2). "At the same time, the strongest chess players do not pass on their experience to young people, do not teach students, and do not prepare a worthy new generation to take their places." Who were these wrongdoers? The article contains several surnames – Botvinnik, Boleslavsky, and Konstantinopolsky – all Jewish, the selection of which seems symptomatic.

There was also a case with the famous coach from Leningrad, Vladimir Zak, in early 1953, at just the same time as the "doctors plot". From 1946 to 1952, he trained the future world champion Boris Spassky. However, as

Nikolai Krogius recalled, at the beginning of 1953 a number of commentators and sports figures entirely attributed the rise of Spassky to his change of coach: they praised his new mentor, Tolush, and attacked Zak.

It all started when Igor Bondarevsky told the party city council that Zak was only working with children of Jewish origin. A commission was created, but no compromising evidence was found in Zak's work, which was no surprise as the claim was false. Nevertheless, clouds gathered over the respected coach and it seemed that nothing would save him from reprisals. A joint letter by Krogius, Korchnoi, and Spassky to the party city council attempting to rehabilitate Zak didn't help either. By the way, regardless of the later lives of these grandmasters, we should admit that at that time this action took courage. After all, its initiators were also quite likely to end up alongside the accused.

The meeting of the Presidium of the Chess Federation, which was supposed to consider Zak's case, was scheduled for March 6, 1953, but it was postponed due to the national mourning for the "greatest genius of all mankind", who had died the day before. And when it did take place, it followed quite a different script. Bondarevsky left the meeting early, and Zak and his supporters emerged victorious. The first signs of the "Khrushchev thaw", which briefly weakened the oppression of totalitarianism, were felt here.

We have given only a few examples to highlight that the moral decline of society under Bolshevik rule did not ignore such a specific sphere of human activity as chess.

Chess Composers

Lazar Zalkind – A Debt of Conscience

In the middle of 1931, in one of the issues of the magazine *64*, a demand was published that would pain the eye of today's reader: "The traitor Zalkind must be expelled from the ranks of Soviet problemists!" Two resolutions were published there as well: one, anonymous, "on behalf of all the composers of chess problems of the USSR", branded "the adventurous, corrupt activities of this renegade and traitor to the cause of the working class" an "embarrassment"; the other deserves to be cited in full.

"On behalf of the chess composers of the North Caucasus, strictly condemning the subversive and interventionist activities of the 'Union Bureau' of the Menshevik Central Committee, and welcoming the fairer verdict of the proletarian court, which has completely exposed the treacherous role of the Second International, we pledge to unite even more closely around the CPSU(b) and its Leninist Central Committee, steadily implementing the general line of the Party. The composition team of the region, emphasizing the treasonous participation in the work of the Mensheviks of one of the former leaders of Soviet composers L. B. Zalkind, makes a promise to carry out chess and checkers cultural work widely among the workers and collective farmers in order for this work to become one of the elements of the cultural revolution, to saturate this work with political and class content. We undertake to establish international relations with proletarian groups of composers in the imperialist countries, providing these groups with assistance both in words and deeds. We commit ourselves to fighting for the purity of the class line in chess and to put an end to all and every attempt to cast a mask of apoliticism and classlessness on chess.

A. O. Gerbstman, N. V. Proskurnin, E. I. Umnov".

There we go! Note that the murder of Kirov and the beginning of mass terror would occur more than two and a half years later. And yet people continued to imagine 1937 as the beginning of the approaching era of socialism.

Eventually, Lazar Zalkind got eight years in prison, which turned into the termination of his active creativity.

But who was he, Lazar Borisovich Zalkind, one of the biggest Russian chess composers for two decades but now forgotten by everyone?

The fate of many victims of Stalinist tyranny is such that even after posthumous rehabilitation, it is a very difficult task, if not a completely hopeless one, to establish their biography. And there are encyclopedias where instead of the date of death of the now famous luminary, a question-mark stands, and the biography occupies just a few lines. Hence all the more satisfied you feel every time you manage to find new material that allows you to finish drawing a portrait of one of the people featured in this book.

The author's publication earlier about L. B. Zalkind, which appeared in issue No. 11 of the magazine *64. Chess Review* for 1989, gained the attention of his granddaughter – Moscow engineer Tatiana Alexeevna Cherenkova. Tatiana Alexeevna had carefully preserved documents and letters of her grandfather, whom she never met. She heard a lot about him from her mother. From the facts reported by Tatiana, I managed to identify the key milestones of Zalkind's life.

He was born on January 2 (14 New Style), in 1886 in Kharkov in the family of a tradesman. When Lazar was still a child, his family moved to Kostroma. Since childhood, the boy had been addicted to science. He graduated from Kostroma grammar school with a gold medal, which allowed him to overcome the notorious "percentage quota" established for persons of the Jewish faith when competing for a place at Moscow University.

In 1909, in order to marry N. V. Andreeva, he agreed to be baptized, since the bride's parents would not agree to their daughter's marriage to a Jew. However, activist of the Social Democratic Party Lazar Zalkind was indifferent to all religion. Back in 1903, he joined the RSDLP (the future Communist Party), and took the Bolshevik side. After the February Revolution of 1905, he took a Menshevik position on certain issues, and from April 1917, as the manager of the Moscow City Election Council, he led work on elections to the Constituent Assembly.

Upon graduation from the Faculty of Law (Economics Department) of Moscow University, he taught a course Economics and Trade Turnover at the university, employed as an associate professor. In the first years of Soviet power, his career as an economist progressed well. By the end of the 1920s, he was working as the head of the accounting and statistical sector of the People's Commissariat of Trade.

After the October Revolution, he withdrew from all party work, and engaged in public activities only in the field of chess. From 1926, he headed the Society of Chess Problems and Studies Fans of the All-Union Chess Section.

Lazar Zalkind discovered chess relatively late, at the age of fifteen, and did not strive for top sporting results. Rather, he immediately became interested in composing problems. His first composition appeared in 1903 in the chess column of literary appendices to *Niva*. Rapidly progressing in composition, Zalkind found himself at the forefront of Russian problemists. For many years, he edited the study columns in the magazines *Shakhmatny bulleten* ("Chess Bulletin") and *Shakhmaty*. He created more than 500 compositions. And even though he competed in composing tournaments infrequently, he won more than 60 commendations in international and Russian competitions.

In his work, Zalkind not only preserved the best traditions of Russian classical composition of the late 19th century, but also gave them an enlivening touch – a combinational element.

The following two-mover by Zalkind was one of the first successful attempts by a Russian problemist to implement the modernist ideas of the so-called "new school".

Composition No. 1
Western Daily Mercury
1913, 3rd prize

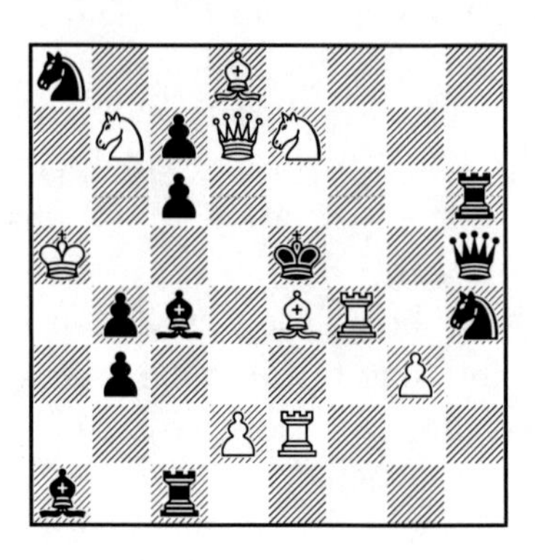

White to mate in 2 moves

An excellent first move **1.♕e8!** with the threat of 2.♘xc6#, leaving the black king two empty squares. If he moves to them, black checks white: 1...♔d4+ 2.♗f5#; 1...♔e6+ 2.♗d5#. And here are two more beautiful symmetrical variations that were possible: 1...♗e6 2.♗f3#; 1...♕xe8 2.♗d3#. The four variations highlight the wholeness of the problem.

Composition No. 2
Deutsche Schachzeitung
1907

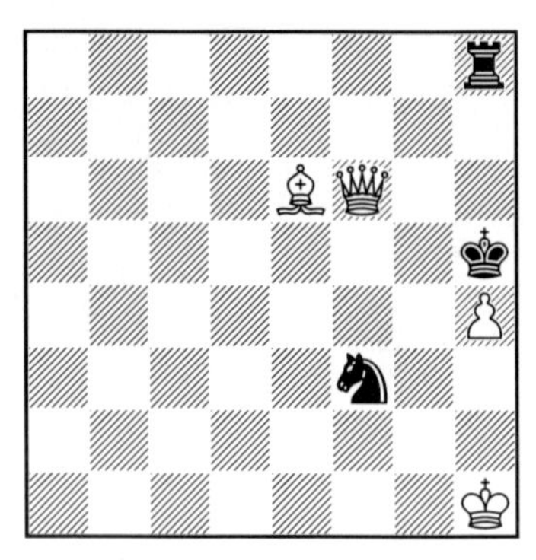

White to mate in 2 moves

1.♕g7! Zugzwang. 1...♔xh4 2.♕g4#, 1...♖h6 2.♕g4#, 1...♖~ 2.♕h7#, 1...♘xh4 2.♗g4#, 1...♘~ 2.♕g5#. A great first move. Checkmates accompanied by blocking squares next to the black king.

Most of all, Zalkind enjoyed composing three-movers. The following one is typical of the early period of his work.

Composition No. 3
Novoye Vremya
1909, Honorable mention

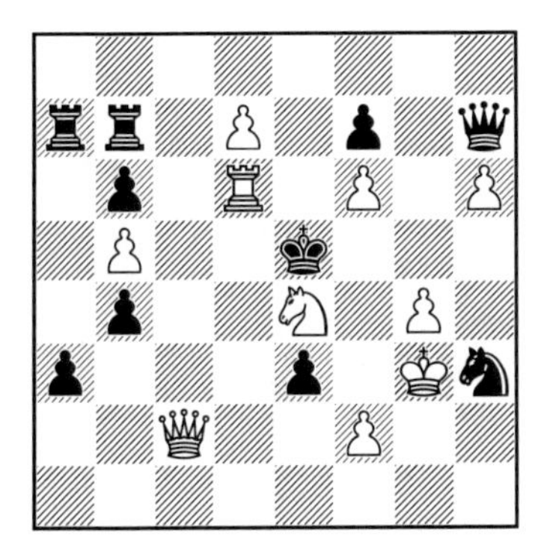

White to mate in 3 moves

1.♘g5! With the first move, white puts all his pieces (the queen, the rook and the knight) en prise, but creates a threat via 2.♘f3+ ♔xd6 3.♕c6#. 1...♕xc2. Black takes the queen, but removes the protection from the f7 square, and therefore white continues 2.♘xf7+ ♔e4 3.f3#. Black can eliminate the aggressive knight by playing 1...♘xg5, then the deflection from the f4 square via 2.f4+ ♔xd6 3.♕c6# is used. Finally, removing the white rook from the board with 1...♔xd6, the black king takes a step towards death: 2.♕c6+ ♔e5 3.♘f3#. If black tries to avoid the threat by playing 1...♖c7 he loses after 2.♕e4+ ♔xd6 3.♕d4# or 2...♕xe4 3.♘xf7#.

In 1913, the editorial office of the newspaper *Odessky List* held a competition for composing chess problems on an innovational basis: each participant had to assess the work of all their competitors. As a result, the highest amount of points was scored by Zalkind's three-mover.

Composition No. 4
Odessky List
1913, 1st prize

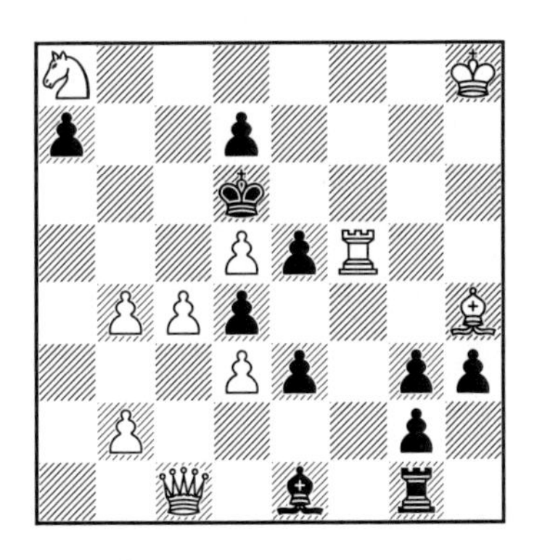

White to mate in 3 moves

1.♕c3! If black does not accept the queen sacrifice, then white threatens 2.♕b3 and 3.c5#. If the bishop captures 1...♗xc3, it will be met by 2.♖f7 and 3.♗e7# (2...e4 3.♗xg3#). If 1...dxc3, then 2.d4 and 3.c5#. Here is another variation for this combination: 1...a5 2.♕xd4 exd4 3.c5#.

Composition No. 5
Deutsches Wochenschach
1913

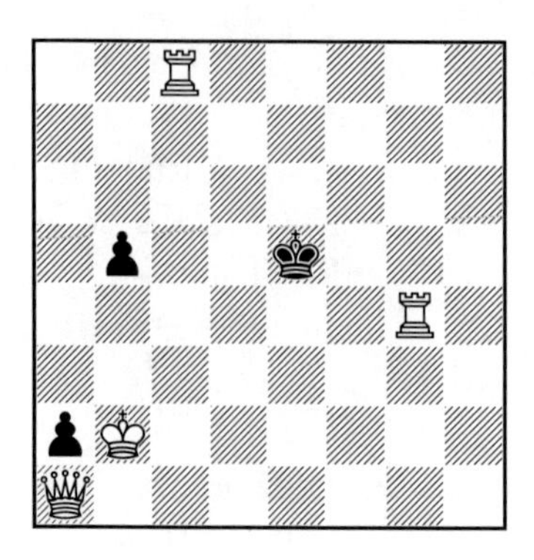

White to mate in 3 moves

1.♖gg8!, threatening 2.♕e1+ ♔d5 3.♖gd8#, 2...♔f5 3.♖cf8#, 1... ♔d6 2.♖ge8, 1...♔f6 2.♖ce8. The black king has eight free squares and a number of model mates from files in the center of the board.

Composition No. 6
Deutsche Schachzeitung
1908

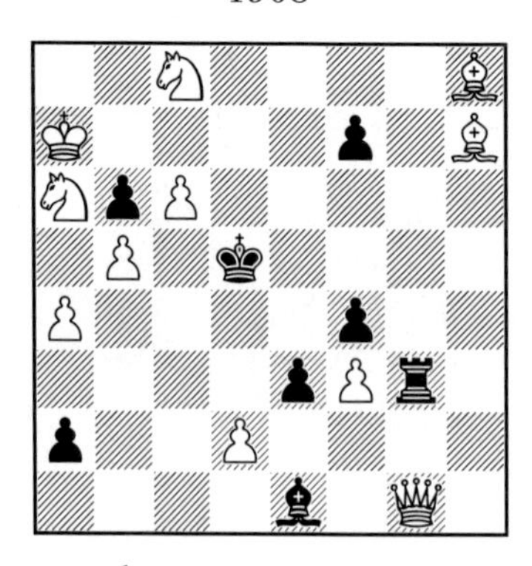

White to mate in 3 moves

1.♗a1! ♖xg1 2.♗c2, 1...♗xd2 2.♕d1, 1...♖xf3 2.♕g8, 1...♖h3 2.♕g6. Magnificent play built on zugzwang and ending with six model mates.

The term "model mate", which is common in chess composition, describes the principle of economy in the combination. A checkmate is called "model" if it is at the same time "pure" (the squares of the mating zone are either occupied by black pieces or attacked no more than once by white pieces) and "economical" (all pieces except the king and pawns take part). Model mates were a characteristic feature of the Czech school's problems.

Composition No. 7
Ceskoslovensky Sach
1923

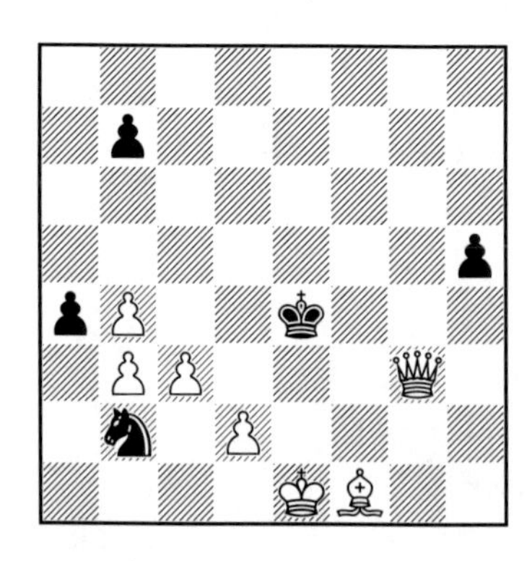

White to mate in 3 moves

1.♗h3!, threatening 2.♕e3+, 1... ♔d5 2.♕g5+, 1...♘d3+ 2.♕xd3+, 1...♘d1 2.♗e6. A Meredith problem (a chess composition with at least 8 but no more than 12 pieces) with nine (!) model mates.

The fate of the next three-mover, which received honors at two international competitions at once, is unusual. It so happened that *Arbeiter Schachzeitung* announced a competition on the eve of the First World War. Zalkind sent his problem, but, not waiting for the results and apparently believing that the competition was canceled because of the war, submitted the same composition to a competition held by *Westminster Gazette*. The jury of the English competition awarded Zalkind a prize, but *Arbeiter Schachzeitung* unexpectedly published its results eight years later (!), and the same three-mover received a prize there as well.

I suppose the double prize-winning problem should still be "assigned" to the German competition.

Composition No. 8
Arbeiter Schachzeitung
1914-1922, 3rd prize

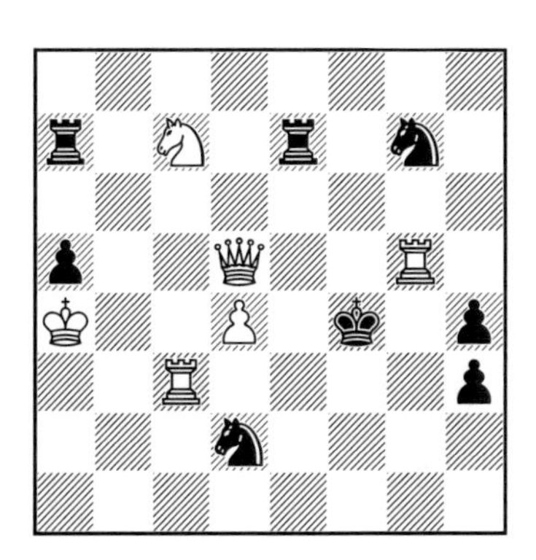

White to mate in 3 moves

1.♖g1!, threatening 2.♕g5+, 1...♘e4 2.♕f5+!, 1...♘f5 2.♕e4+, 1...♘h5 2.♕xh5.

Composition No. 9
FIDE Competition
1926, 3rd-4th prize

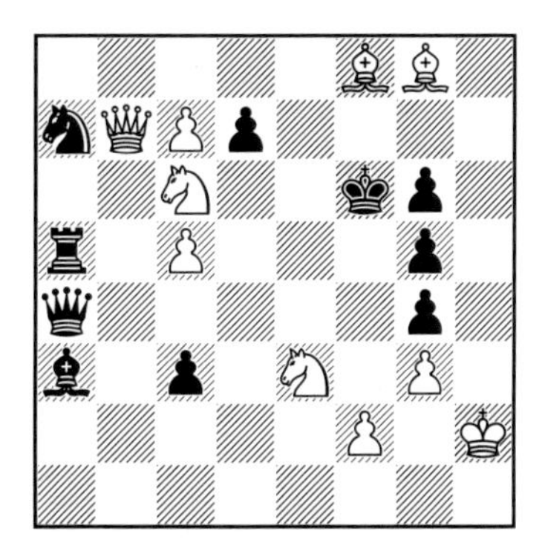

White to mate in 3 moves

1.♘e5!, threatening 2.♕c6+, 1...♕d1 2.♕f3+, 1...d5 2.♕b4, 1...♕d4 2.♕d5. Two diagonal and two frontal queen sacrifices.

Composition No. 10
Prager Mustermesse
1926, 3rd prize

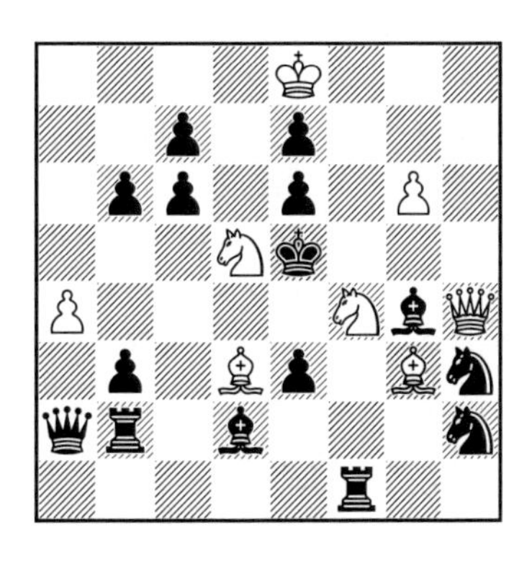

White to mate in 3 moves

1.♘b4!, threatening 2.♕h8+, 1...♗c3 2.♔d7!, 1...c5 2.♔xe7, 1...♘f3 2.♘e2+, 1...♔d6 2.♕xe7+, 1...♔d4 2.♘e2+, 1...♗h5 2.♘xh3+. In this problem, the first two variations, blocking the c3 and c5 squares, involving maneuvers of the white king and model mates with the pinned black bishop, are particularly interesting.

Composition No. 11
Shakhmaty
1923

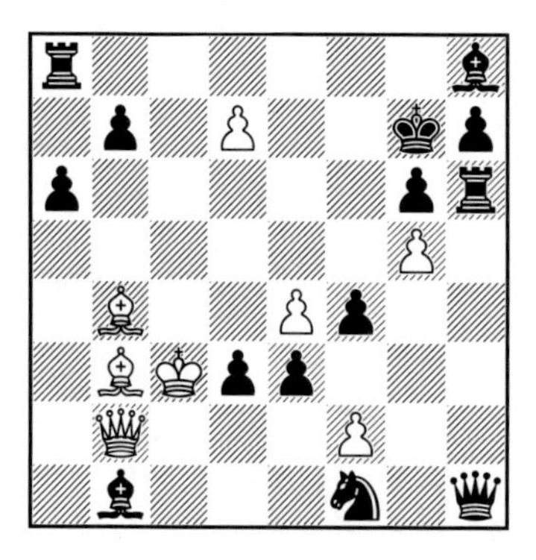

White to mate in 3 moves

1.♔d4! It is not often that a chess problem is solved by a king move. But it is extremely rare to find a three-mover in which all three moves including the checkmate move are made by the main white piece!.. No one seems to have implemented this idea before Zalkind. In the two main variations, black's attempt to defend will be followed by a white king march: 1...a5 2.♔c4+ and 3.♔b5#, 1...b6 2.♔d5+ and 3.♔c6#, 1...♖c8 2.dxc8=♕, 1...♖e8 2.dxe8=♘#, 1...♕xe4+ 2.♔xe4#.

The following problem, which shared first and second places in a competition held by the main newspaper of the country, was a milestone in Zalkind's work.

Composition No. 12
Pravda
1928, 1st-2nd prize

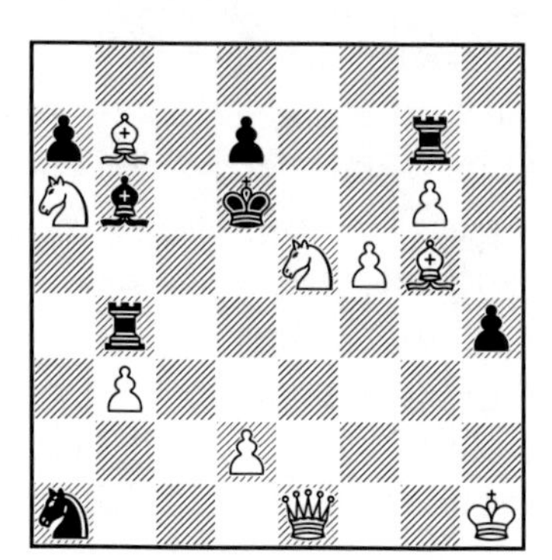

White to mate in 3 moves

The variations of this problem demonstrate how the d4 square – the interference of the lines of action of black's pieces (♖b4 and ♗b6) – becomes a critical square for both of them during the game.

This problem can be solved by playing **1.♕e2!**, which creates a threat 2.♕h2 and 3.♘c4#. It is possible to defend by playing any of the three bishop moves: 1...♗e3, 1...♗f2, 1...♗g1. This will be met by 2.♕b5 with a new threat 3.♕d5#. In the case of 2...♖d4 white has 3.♕c5# (the rook occupied the d4 square, which was critical for the bishop) or 2...♖xb5 3.♘c4#.

In another variation, the roles of

the black pieces are different: first, the rook, parrying the threat, crosses the d4 square: 1...♖e4, 1...♖f4; 1...♖g4, which is met by 2.♕d3+ ♗d4 (the bishop moves to the square that was critical for the rook) and 3.♘c4#. In this combination, the following attempts also look great: 1...♗c5 2.♕c4 and 1...♗d4 2.♕e4. In the latter case, there is a dual (besides 2.♕e4, 2.♕g2 is a solution, too), which can be eliminated by adding a black pawn on h3.

In chess composition, it is common to name themes that have become popular after the discoverer. Perhaps, the theme "turning the interference square of two black pieces into a critical square for both of these pieces" could have been called "Zalkind's Theme": after this problem was published, many compositions were created based on it and even special thematic competitions were held.

Composition No. 13
British Chess Magazine
1924, 2nd prize

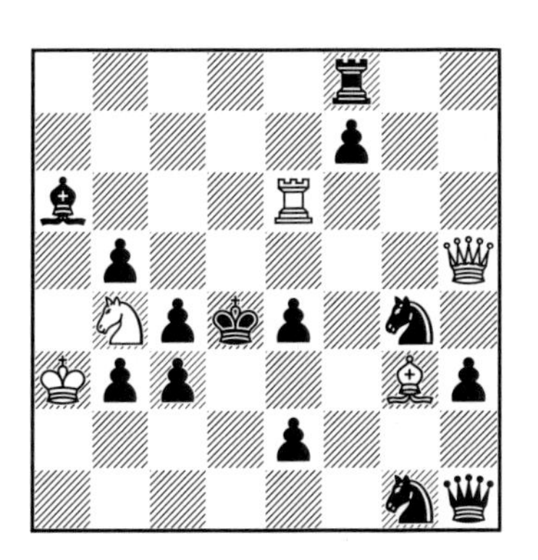

White to mate in 3 moves

1.♕h6!, threatening 2.♖xe4+ ♔xe4 3.♕f4#, 1...fxe6 2.♕g7+! ♖f6 3.♕a7#, 2...♔e3 3.♕xc3#; 1...♘xh6 2.♗f2+ e3 3.♗xe3#; 1...f6 2.♖d6+ ♔c5 3.♘xa6#; 1...♔c5 2.♘xa6+ ♔d4 3.♖d6#. The queen cleverly covers the key b6 and a7 squares.

Composition No. 14
Narodni Osvobozen
1930

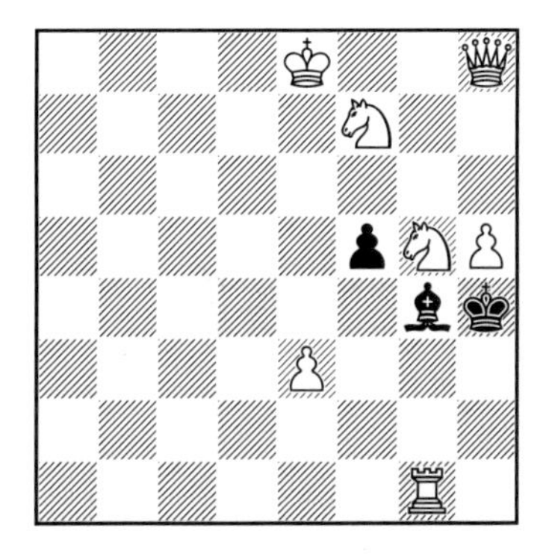

White to mate in 2 moves

1.♘e5! ♗xh5+ 2.♘g6#, 1...♔xg5 2.♘f3#, 1...f4 2.♖xg4#. "An excellent example of the near-extinct artistic two-mover" – this is what Leonid Kubbel wrote about this problem (*Shakhmatny listok*, 1930, No. 4).

Composition No. 15
Shakhmatny vestnik
1915

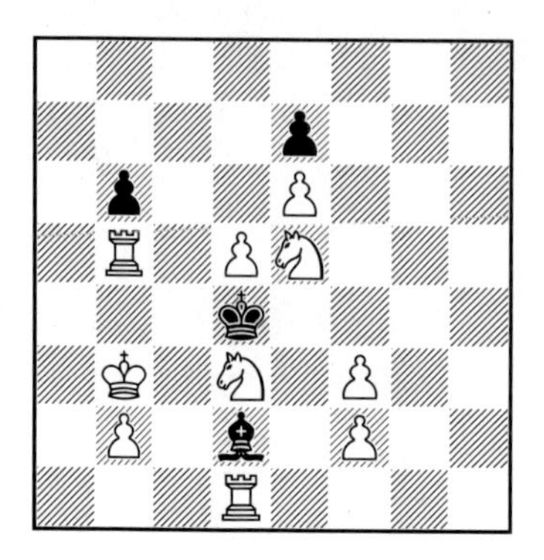

White to mate in 2 moves

This is a blockading problem: in the initial position, any move of the bishop will be met by 2.♘c6#. **1.♘c4!** is the solution.

Composition No. 16
Shakhmatny vestnik
1913

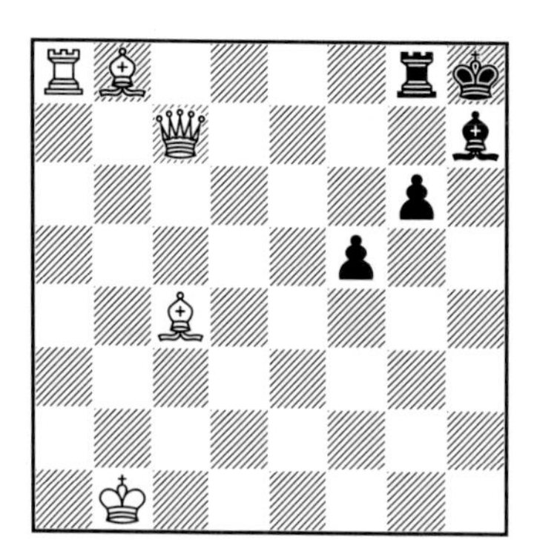

White to mate in 2 moves

1.♕h2!, threatening 2.♗e5#. The variation 1...♖xb8+ 2.♕b2# is neat, too.

The following problem by Zalkind was submitted before publication to be used for a problem solving competition of the Moscow Chess Circle on November 18, 1913.

Composition No. 17
Shakhmatny vestnik
1913

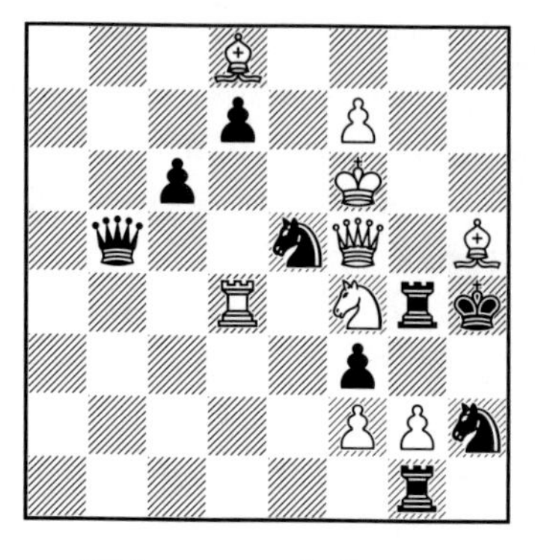

White to mate in 2 moves

1.♕h7!, threatening 2.♗g6#, 1...♖xf4+ 2.♔g7#, 1...♖g7 2.♔xg7#, 1...♘e~ 2.♘g6#.

At the first international competition for two-movers of the magazine *64* in 1925, three of Zalkind's problems won recognition. Note that the contest was held anonymously (the authors of the problems were unknown to the judges).

Composition No. 18
64
1925, 3rd prize

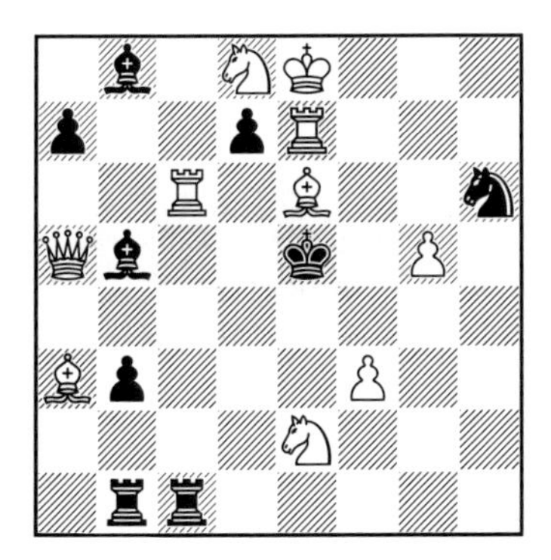

White to mate in 2 moves

1.♖c3!, threatening 2.♖e3#, 1...dxe6+ 2.♕xb5#, 1...d6+ 2.♘c6#, 1...d5+ 2.♗d7#. The nice first move leads to unusual pawn play, accompanied by checks to the white king in three variations.

Composition No. 19
64
1925, 4th prize

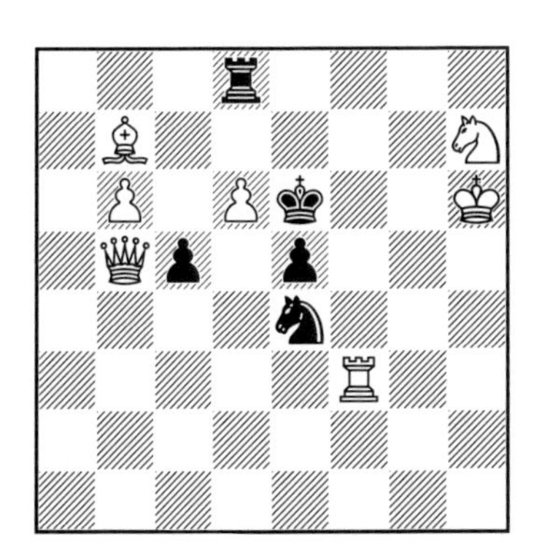

White to mate in 2 moves

1.♖f7! "A spectacular first move sets zugzwang in this graceful yet simply constructed problem. Six elegant variations, one of which is a model mate," the judge's report noted. We will let the reader evaluate the "elegance" of the following variations: 1...♔xf7 2.♗d5#, 1...♔xd6 2.♕c6#, 1...♖xd6 2.♕e8#, 1...♖~ 2.♕d7#, 1...♘xd6 2.♘g5#, 1...♘~ 2.♖f6#, 1...c4 2.♕d5#.

Composition No. 20
64
1925, 4th honorable mention

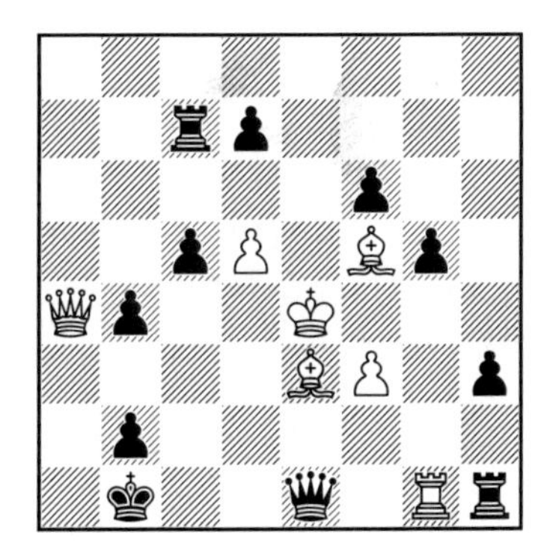

White to mate in 2 moves

In this two-mover, the most active piece is the white king. **1.♔d3!**, threatening 2.♔c4#, 1...♕c1 2.♔e2#, 1...♕f1+ (xg1) 2.♔d2#, 1...c4+ 2.♔d4#, 1.d6? ♕d1!

Composition No. 21
64
1927, 1st honorable mention of the contest of the second semester

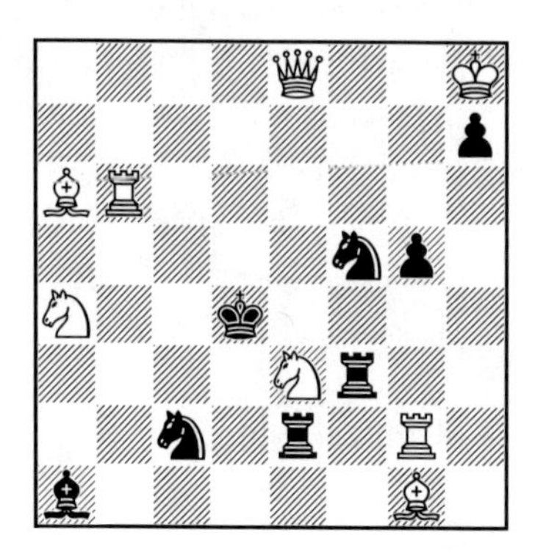

White to mate in 2 moves

1.♕e6!, threatening 2.♘xc2#. This problem contains six symmetrical pins of black's pieces and is simply constructed. The main variations are as follows: 1...♖exe3 (♖d2) 2.♖d2#, 1...♖ff2 (1...♘a3, 1...♘e1) 2.♘xf5#, 1...♘b4 (♘cxe3) 2.♖b4#, 1...♘fxe3 2.♖d6#.

Composition No. 22
Shakhmaty
1925

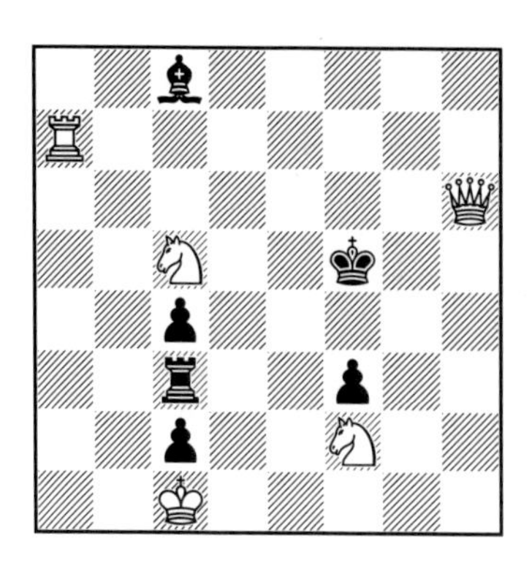

White to mate in 2 moves

1.♖a5!, threatening 2.♘b3#, 1...♖a3 2.♘a4#, 1...♖d3 2.♘cxd3#, 1...♖e3 2.♘ce4#, 1...♗a6 2.♘xa6#. In total, there are eight mating moves made by the white knight. The author managed to do without white pawns.

Composition No. 23
Shakhmaty
1925

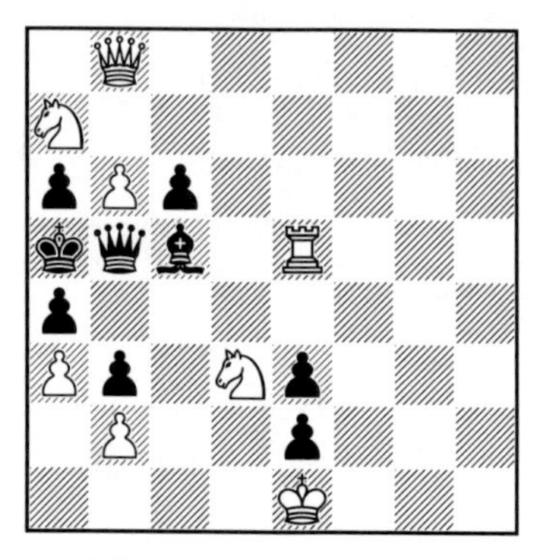

White to mate in 2 moves

1.♕c7! Zugzwang. 1...♗b4+ 2.axb4#, 1...♗~ 2.♘xc6#, 1...♕xb6 2.♖xc5#, 1...♕c4 2.b7#; 1...♕b4+ 2.axb4#. Five semi-pins of black's pieces.

Composition No. 24
Shakhmatny listok
1926

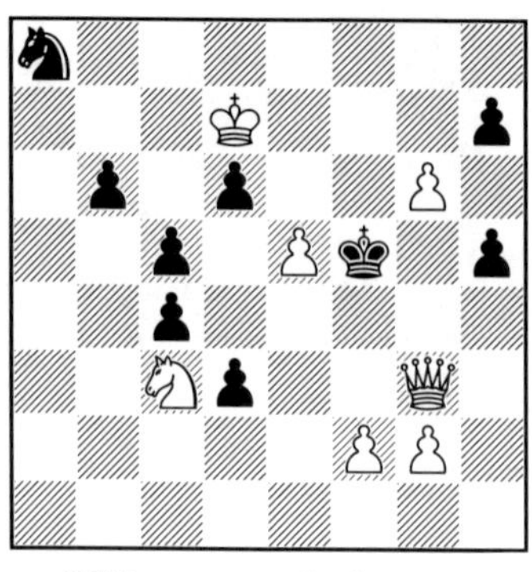

White to mate in 3 moves

1.♕h4!, threatening 2.♕xh5+, 1...dxe5 2.♘d5!, 1...♔xe5 2.♕g5+, 1...hxg6 2.f4.

Composition No. 25
Shakhmatny listok
1927, 3rd honorable mention of the contest of the first semester

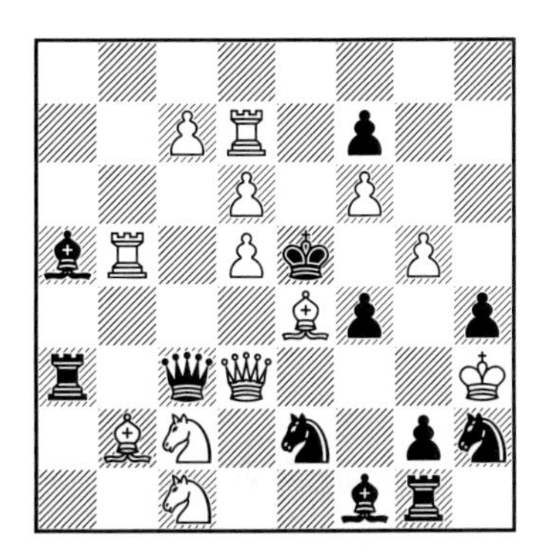

White to mate in 3 moves

1.♗h7!, threatening 2.♕e3+, 1...♘xc1 2.♘d4!, 1...♕xb2 2.♖e7+. "This is an interesting problem, which combines several ideas. Both main variations lead to model mates. A less cumbersome form would have been more desirable" (L. Kubbel).

This combination turned out to be a hard nut to crack for many solvers. Not only the solvers, but also the editors went for a false try: 1.♖e7+ ♔xd6 2.c8=♘+, which they hastened to declare a side solution. In the next issue of the magazine, the editors reported that after 2...♕xc8+ there is no solution – the combination is correct.

Composition No. 26
Nova Praha
1908, 4th prize

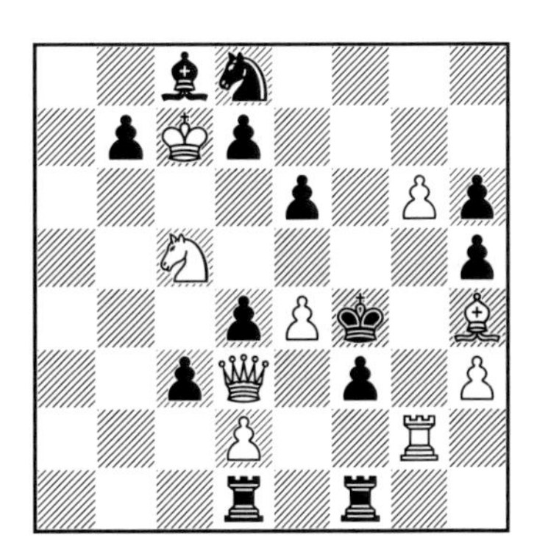

White to mate in 3 moves

1.♖e2! threatening 2.♕xd4. 1...♔e5 2.♕a6 bxa6 3.♘d3#, 1...cxd2 2.♕c3!, 1...e5 2.♕e3+! dxe3 3.dxe3#, 1...♖h1 2.♕xf3+! ♔xf3 3.♖f2#, 1...♖xd2 2.♕xd2+ cxd2 3.♘d3# with six sacrifices of the white queen!

Composition No. 27
Dzintanes Vehnesis
1914

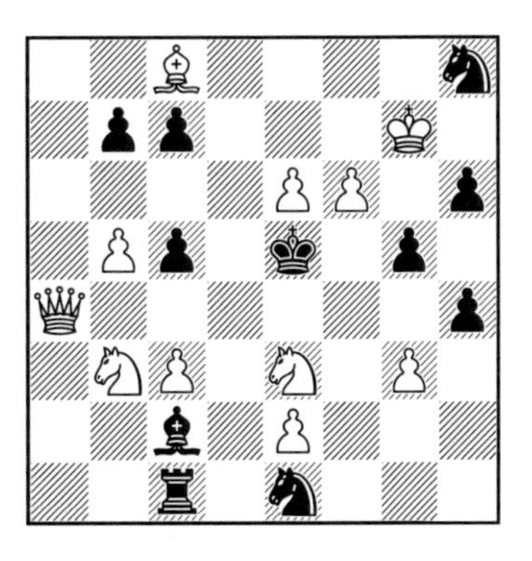

White to mate in 3 moves

1.♘d2! threatening 2.♕e4+, 1...♗xa4 2.♘ec4+, 1...hxg3 2.♕g4; 1...c6 2.♕a7.

Composition No. 28
Niva
1913

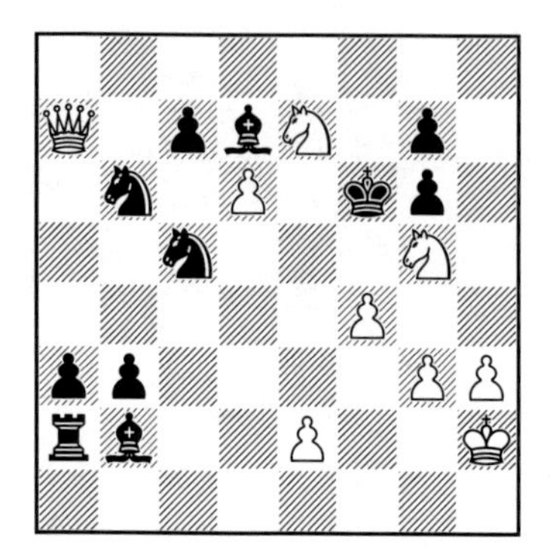

White to mate in 3 moves

1.♕a4! threatening 2.♘g8+ and 3.g4#. With his first move, white leaves his queen under attack from three pieces at once. 1...♘bxa4 2.♘d5+, 1...♘cxa4 2.♘g8+, 1...♗xa4 2.g4!

Composition No. 29
Shakhmaty
1922

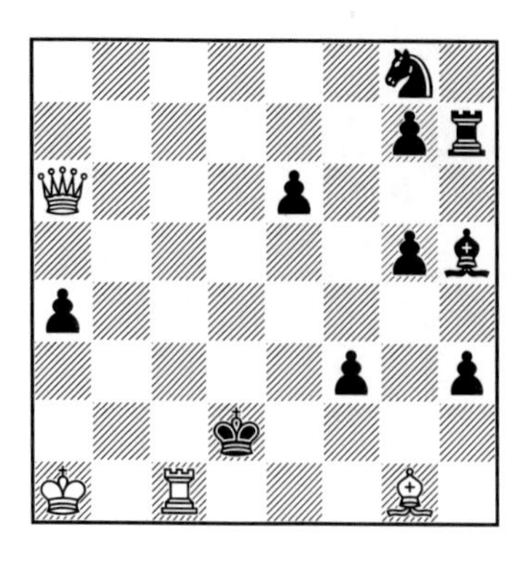

White to mate in 3 moves

1.♗c5! threatening 2.♕xa4, 1...g6 2.♕c4, 1...♗e8 2.♕f1, 1...♔xc1 2.♕d3. The continuation 1.♗b6(a7)? g6! 2.♕xa4 ♖a7 turns out to be a false try, with the white queen pinned. Four quiet queen moves when white's forces are limited and he has no pawns on the board.

Composition No. 30
Shakhmaty
1924

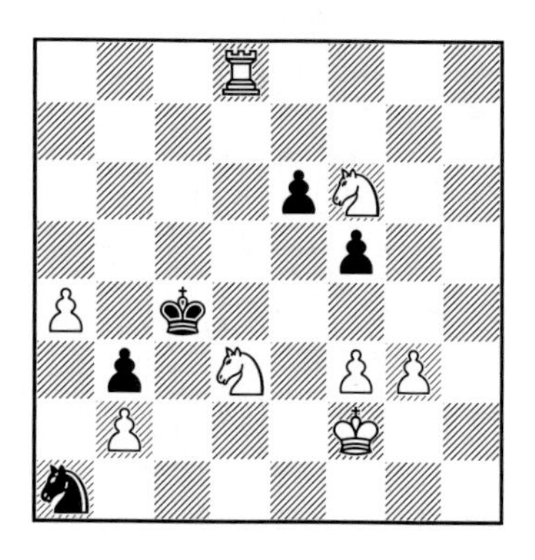

White to mate in 3 moves

1.g4! ♘c2 2.♘d7, 1...e5 2.♘d5, 1...f4 2.♘e4, 1...fxg4 2.♘xg4. The white knight makes four quiet moves. It leads to pretty knight checkmates around the king 3.♘e5# and 3.♘e3#.

Composition No. 31
Ceske Slovo
1923, Honorable mention

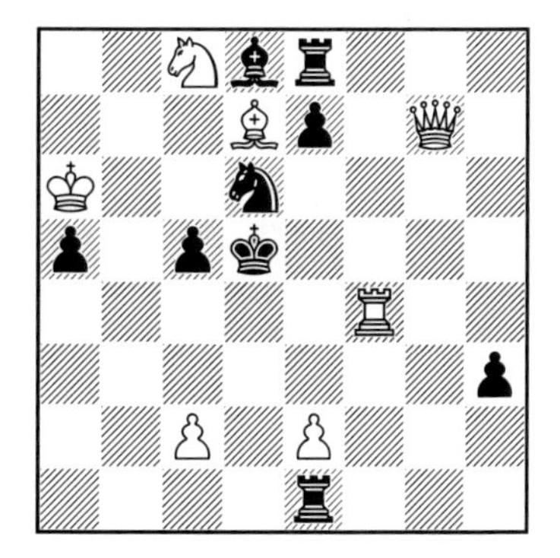

White to mate in 3 moves

1.c3! threatening 2.♖d4+. 1...♖d1 2.c4+, 1...e5 2.♕f7+, 1...♘e4 2.♕e5+. The central piece of the composition is the black ♘d6. His moves, which are the result either of black's own initiative (to e4 or c8) or of white's maneuvers (2.♕f7+ and 2.c4+), create four magnificent variations. An authentic example of the Czech school.

Composition No. 32
Narodni Osvobozeni
1926, Honorable mention

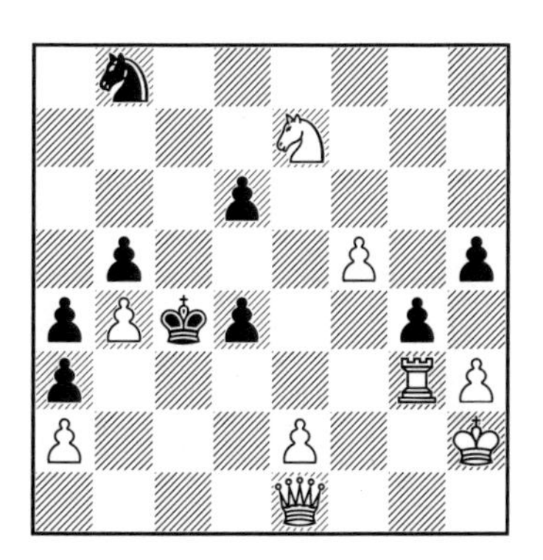

White to mate in 3 moves

1.f6! gxh3 2.♖c3+, 1...h4 2.♕c3+; 1...d5 2.♘f5; 1...d3 2.exd3+, 1...♘~ 2.♕c1+. In zugzwang, black can play four variations. Two of them involve the black g- and h-pawn moves, leading to queen and rook sacrifices, and end in frontal checkmates.

Composition No. 33
British Chess Society
1923, 1st honorable mention

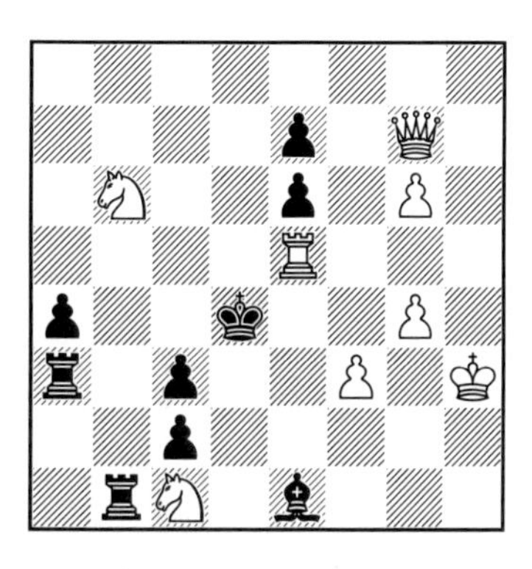

White to mate in 3 moves

1.♕h8! threatening 2.♘e2+, 1...♖xc1 2.f4!, 1...♖xb6 2.♕h5!, 1...♖b5 2.♖xe6+, 1...♗f2 2.♖f5+. This problem was very difficult to create.

Composition No. 34
Zadachi i etyudy
1928

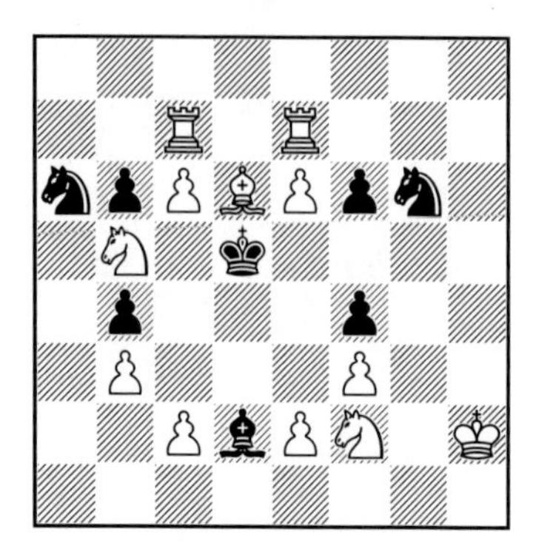

White to mate in 3 moves

1.♘d3! threatening 2.♘xb4+, 1...♘xc7 2.c4+, 1...♘xe7 2.e4+, 1...♗c3 2.♘xf4+. An unusual interpretation of the position with capture en passant. The symmetry in this game is based on the change of functions of the white knight and pawns. Four model mates.

Composition No. 35
Zadachi i etyudy
1928, 3rd honorable mention

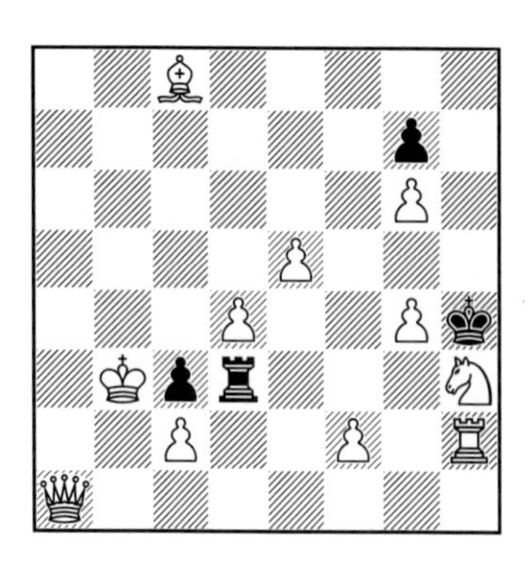

White to mate in 3 moves

The line 1.♕g1? ♖e3! 2.g5 ♖g3! or 2.♕c1 ♖xh3! is a false try. **1.♗f5** threatening 2.♕a8, 1...♖f3 2.♕e1! with a zugzwang. 1...♖xh3 2.♖xh3+, 1...♖~ 2.♘f4+.

This two-mover contains a so-called "albino" theme – a white pawn standing on its original square which moves four times in different ways in the solution with 1...♖f3 2.♕e1!, each time mating black, i.e. f3, f4 or a capture on either side depending on where the black rook moves.

Four-movers in the work of Zalkind are rare, but he managed to create several memorable works in this genre, among which you can find the following problem with three variations.

Composition No. 36
Shakhmatny vestnik
1913

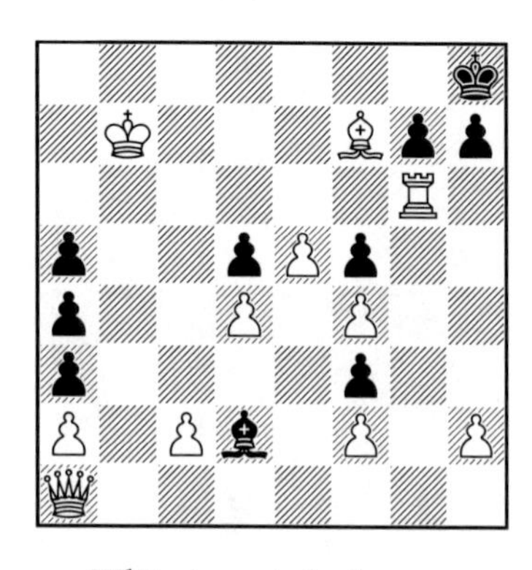

White to mate in 4 moves

1.♕f1! ♗b4 2.♕a6 threatening 3.♕a8+, **2...♗f8 3.♕f6**, 2...h5 3.♖h6+, 2...hxg6 3.♕xg6, **1...♗xf4**

2.♕b5 with the threat of 3.♕e8#, 2...hxg6 3.♗xg6, **1...h5 2.♖h6+ gxh6 3.♕g1.**

Having made his name as an author of wonderful problems, Zalkind also composed endgame studies. He focused on specific themes in his studies. This was no easy expansion, as unlike with problems, where the initial position is artificial and must only meet the requirement of being legal, i.e. theoretically possible, the initial position of a study is usually a natural one and resembles a real chess game position (usually starting in the endgame, or less often in the middlegame).

Zalkind's first foray into studies dates back to 1908, and even then in his works you could trace features of a problem composer. Problem techniques occupy a central place in his studies: zugzwang and underpromotions. In the last period of Zalkind's work, which was tragically ended prematurely, the idea of converting problem themes into study form took hold.

The following study, which won first prize, is on the so-called "Indian theme" – one of the oldest in problem composition. The idea of the Indian theme is that in order to avoid stalemating black, white performs a maneuver consisting of logically connected elements: a critical move, temporarily locking a critical piece out of the game by occupying a critical square with the locking piece, and then unlocking the critical piece with the locking piece.

Composition No. 37
64
1928, 1st prize

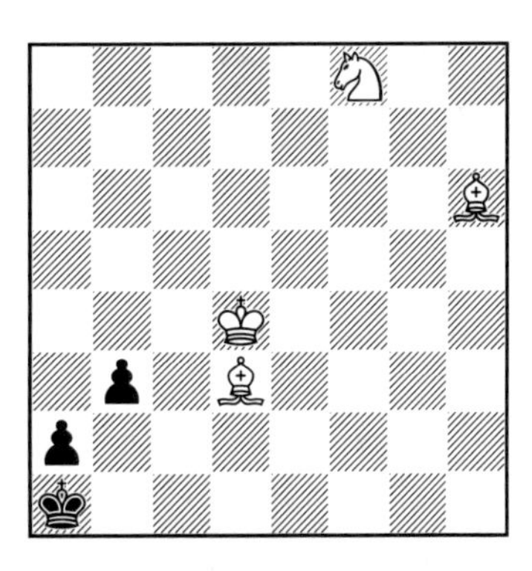

White to move and win

1.♗d2! b2 2.♗h7! (the critical move) **2...b1=♕** (2...b1=♘ 3.♗c1! wins). **3.♗c3+ ♕b2 4.♘g6!** – a locking move.

4...♔b1 5.♘e5+! unlocks the critical piece. If now 5...♕c2 6.♗xc2+ ♔xc2 7.♘c4 ♔b1 8.♘a3+, winning. Or 5...♔a1 6.♘d3! ♕xc3+ 7.♔xc3 ♔b1 8.♘c5+ with a win.

In another variation, play is more prosaic: 1...♔b2 2.♗c3+ ♔a3 (2... ♔c1 3.♗c4) 3.♔c4 b2 4.♗b4+ ♔a4 5.♗c2#.

Zalkind also composed studies that incorporated rook endgame theory:

Composition No. 38
Shakhmaty
1927, 2nd prize of the contest of the second semester

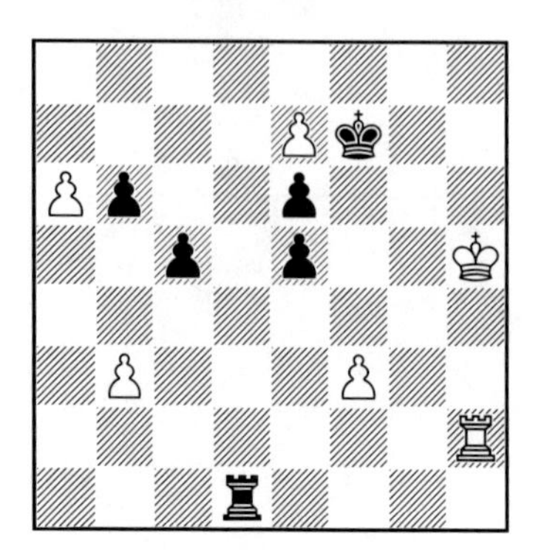

White to move and win

1.a7! ♖a1 2.e8=♕+ ♔xe8 3.♔g4! The continuations 3.♔g5? or 3.♔g6? ♔e7 4.♖h1 ♖a2! 5.♖h8 ♖g2+ 6.♔h6! ♖h2+ 7.♔g7 ♖g2+! are false tries and lead to draws. **3...♔d7** (3...♔f7) **4.♖h1!** Not 4.♖h8? due to 4...♖g1+, and black wins. **4...♖a2 5.♖h8 ♖xa7 6.♖h7**+ with a win.

Composition No. 39
La Strategie
1916

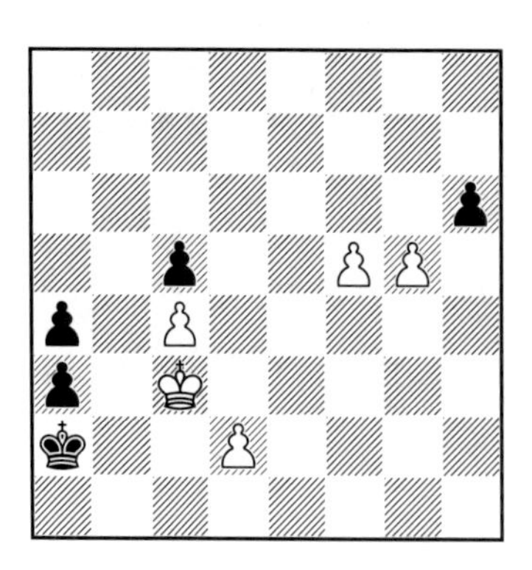

White to move and win

1.♔c2 Otherwise, black will play 1...♔b1 and win easily. **1...h5 2.g6!** This move is the only one that wins, its importance will become clear later. **2...h4 3.g7 h3 4.g8=♗!! h2 5.♗d5** with a win.

We admire the subtlety of white's second move, which interferes with black's fifth move. Only the bishop, to which white promotes his g-pawn, is able do this. If 4.g8=♕, then after 4...h2 5.♕d5 black would respond with 5...h1=♕, and white cannot take the black queen due to stalemate.

The following alternative is similar: 1...hxg5 2.f6 g4 3.f7 g3 4.f8=♗ g2 5.♗xc5 with a win. To prevent black from playing 5...g1=♕, white should promote to a bishop instead of a queen or rook, this time on f8, in order to avoid stalemate.

"This study, the only one of its kind, is remarkable because with its simple construction, the idea of promoting a pawn to a minor piece is implemented here logically in two variations on different squares. The importance of this promotion is hidden and becomes clear only when carefully examining the position after black's fifth move. This study should undoubtedly be counted among the classics, because the theme has been technically implemented in a totally new way. Working on this theme, the author competes with such a virtuoso in this field as Troitsky," the Platov brothers enthusiastically commented.

Composition No. 40
Barcelona Chess Club Competition
1914, 4th prize

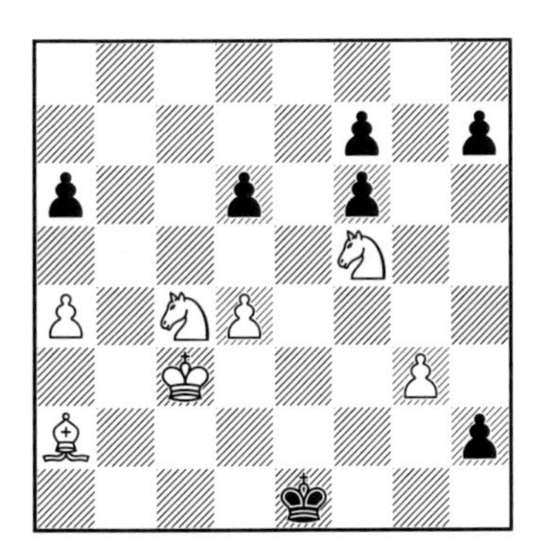

White to move and win

1.♘e5! This is quite a paradoxical move, but let's see what happens next. **1....h1=♕ 2.♗d5 ♕h5.** 2...♕xd5 3.♘d3+, 2...♕f1 3.♘e3, 2...♕h3 3.♘d3+ ♔f1 4.♗g2+. **3.♘d3+ ♔f1 4.♘e3+ ♔g1 5.♘f4 ♕h2.** 5...♕h6 6.♘e2+ and 7.♘g4+. **6.♗g2**, with a win.

Composition No. 41
Tidskrift for Schack
1910, 3rd prize

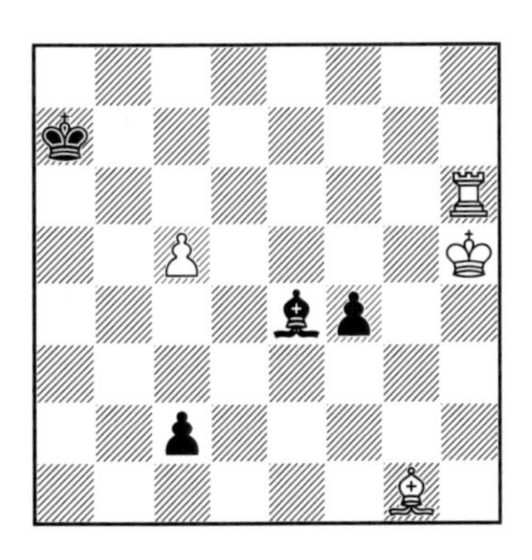

White to move and draw

1.c6+! ♔b8!? If 1...♔a6, then 2.c7+ ♔b7 3.♖b6+ ♔c8 4.♖b8+ ♔xc7 5.♖b5 c1=♕ 6.♖c5+ with a draw. **2.♖h8+!** 2.c7+? (but here is a dual – the continuation 2.♗b6! leads to a draw, too) 2...♔xc7 3.♖h7+ ♔d6 4.♖c7 ♗c6! with a win for black. **2...♔c7 3.♖h7+! ♔xc6**

3...♗xh7 4.♗h2, and so on, if 3...♔d6, then 4.♗c5+! ♔xc5 5.c7 ♗f5 6.c8=♕+ ♗xc8 with a draw. **4.♖c7+! ♔xc7 5.♗h2 c1=♕.** 5...c1=♗ 6.♔g4 with a draw.

6.♗xf4+ ♕xf4. Stalemate.

Composition No. 42
Tidskrift for Schack
1916

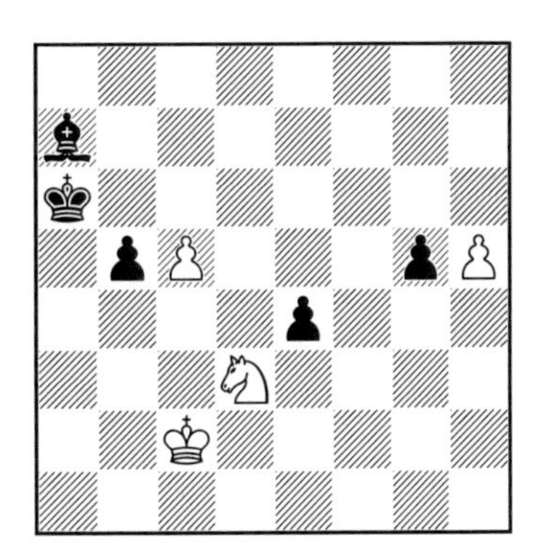

White to move and win

1.h6! ♗b8. 1...exd3+ 2.♔xd3 ♗b8 3.♔e4, winning. **2.♘b4+ ♔b7 3.c6+ ♔c8! 4.c7! ♗xc7 5.♘c6**, winning.

Composition No. 43
64
1925, 1st honorable mention

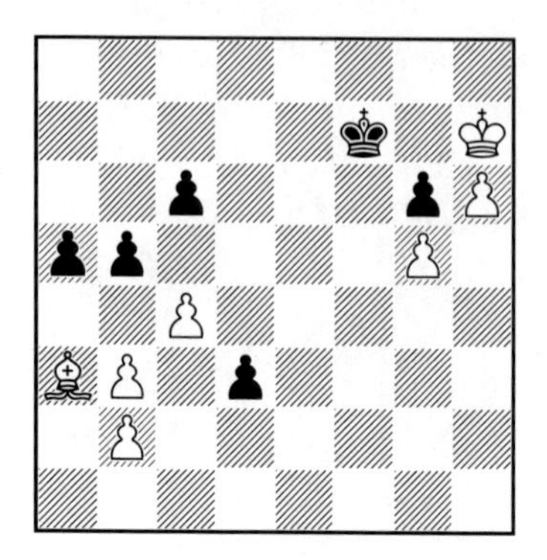

White to move and draw

1.♗b4! axb4 2.cxb5 d2 3.b6 d1=♕ 4.b7 ♕d8 5.b8=♕ ♕xb8, stalemate. **2...cxb5 3.♔h8 d2 4.h7 ♔e6.** 4...d1=♕, stalemate. **5.♔g7 d1=♕ 6.h8=♕ ♕d4+ 7.♔xg6 ♕xh8**, stalemate.

"An elegant study with an interesting position. Though play is not complicated, it leads to three stalemate positions" – competition judge Nikolai Grigoriev.

Composition No. 44
La Strategie
1916

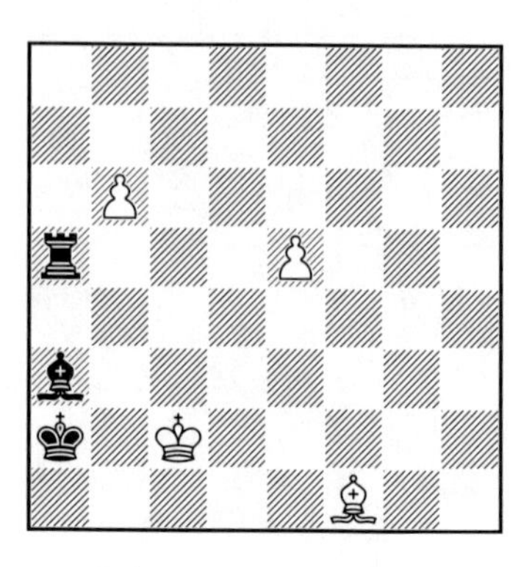

White to move and win

1.♗c4+! ♔a1 2.b7 ♖a8! 3.bxa8=♘! ♗d6 4.e6! with a win. The study is all the more interesting because white here turns a pawn into a knight without a check, which usually accompanies the promotion of a pawn to a knight. It is impossible to swap the first two moves.

Composition No. 45
Shakhmaty
1924

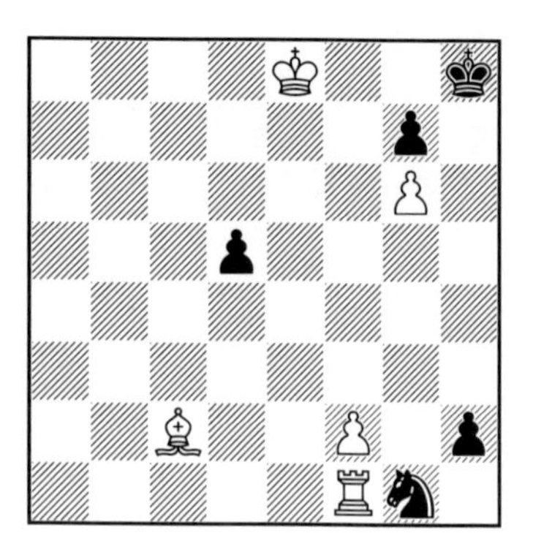

White to move and win

1.♗e4! The lines: 1.♖a1? h1=♕ 2.♖a8 d4 and 1.♖b1? h1=♕ 2.♖b8 ♕h2! 3.♖c8! ♕h3! are false tries. **1...dxe4 2.♖d1 h1=♕ 3.♖d8 ♕h4 4.♖a8!** with inevitable checkmate in two moves.

Composition No. 46
Shakhmaty
1925, 2nd prize

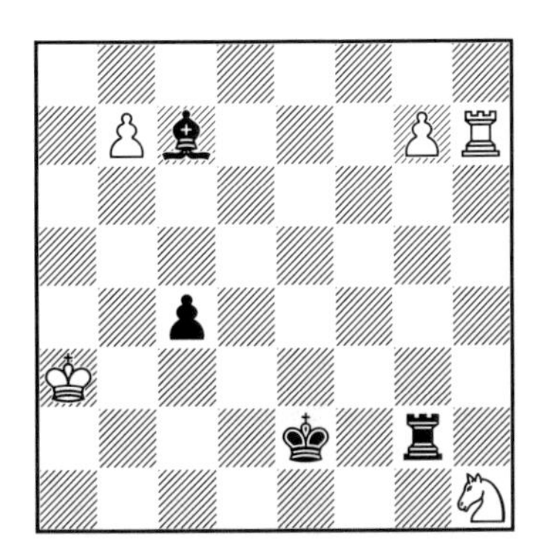

White to move and win

1.♔a4! threatening 2.g8=♕ ♖xg8 3.♖xc7, **1...♗e5 2.♖h2! ♗xh2 3.♘g3+ ♖xg3 4.b8=♕**, 3...♗xg3 4.g8=♕.

A wonderful example of the use of interference. Unfortunately, a dual somewhat spoils the overall impression, since after 1...♗e5, apart from the author's move 2.♖h2!, other continuations also win for white, such as 2.g8=♕.

Composition No. 47
Shakhmaty
1927, 4th prize of the competition of the first semester

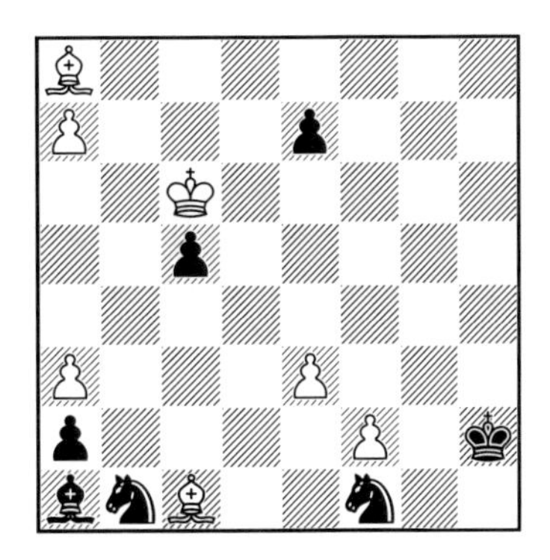

White to move and win

1.♔d7! ♗e5 2.♗b2!! ♗xb2 3.♗h1! ♔xh1. 3...a1=♕ 4.a8=♕! ♔h3 5.♕f3+, winning. **4.a8=♕+ ♔g1.** 4...♔h2 5.♕b8+ and 6.♕xb2. **5.♕g8+** and **6.♕a2.** A combination of two ideas in a study, with a nice first white move.

Composition No. 48
Shakhmaty
1929, 1st prize of the competition of the first semester

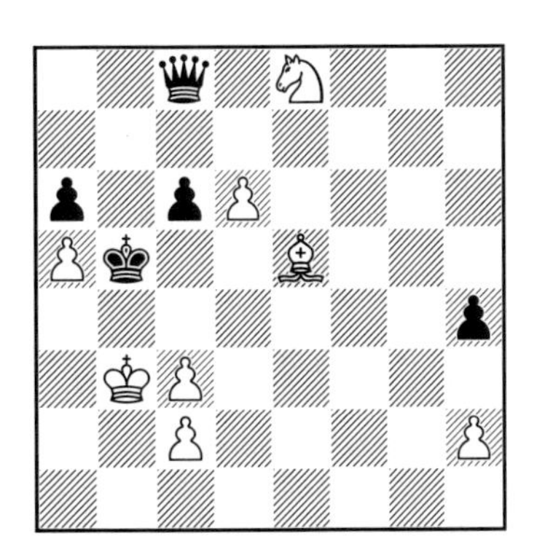

White to move and win

1.d7! ♕xd7 2.c4+ ♔c5 3.♘d6! ♕h7 4.♔c3 h3 5.♘e8!, winning. 5.♘c8? ♕h8! is a draw. "Here, the old theme of the struggle of two minor pieces against a queen is expressed in a completely new interpretation, which brought an enthusiastic reaction from our readers" (V. Platov).

Composition No. 49
La Strategie
1916

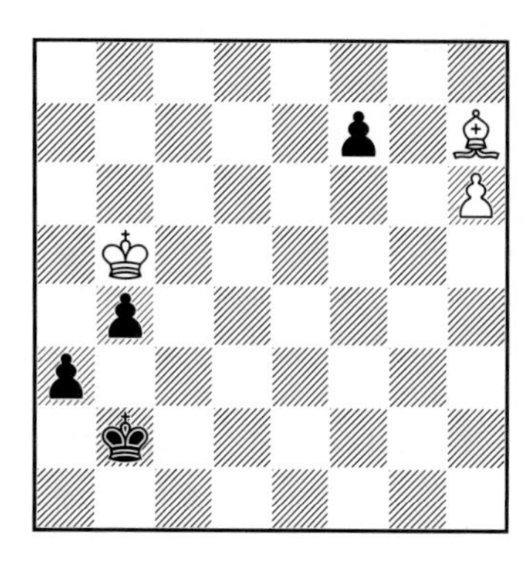

White to move and win

1.♗c2! This move was the last thing that have been expected. **1...a2** Black has to hurry to play this move. If 1...♔xc2, then 2.h7 and after 2...a2 or 2...b3, the continuation 3.h8=♕ leads to a win. If 1...b3, then 2.♗xb3 ♔xb3 3.h7 and so on.

2.h7 a1=♕ 3.h8=♕+ ♔a2 4.♗b3+! Nice! And yet the importance of white's first move is not yet clear. For example, after 1.♗d3, white could now play 4.♗c4+ without putting his bishop at risk. **4...♔b1 5.♕h7+ ♔b2.** Now all the unpleasant consequences of white's first move for black are felt: because of the queen checkmate on c2, the black king cannot move to c1.

6.♕c2+ ♔a3 7.♗d5! Defending against check from the queen on e5 and threatening checkmate himself. **7...♕f1+ 8.♔a5** with inevitable checkmate.

Composition No. 50
La Strategie
1915

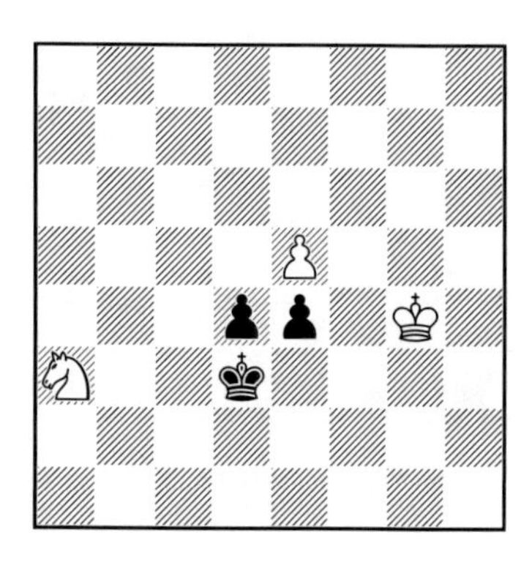

White to move and win

1.e6 e3 2.e7 e2 3.e8=♖! If 3.e8=♕, then 3...e1=♕! 4.♕xe1, with an elegant stalemate. The idea of this study is to promote a pawn to a rook, however, the game does not end there, but enters the second stage, full of interesting events. **3...♔d2 4.♘c2! d3 5.♘d4 ♔d1 6.♖a8! e1=♕.** The move 6...d2 is followed by 7.♖a1#, or 6...♔c1 7.♖a1+ ♔b2 8.♖h1.

7.♖a1+ ♔d2 8.♘f3+, winning. 100+ years after publication, we have the Nalimov tables which show that white mates in 18 moves after both 1.e6 and 1.♔g3.

In the middle of 1926, the Society of Chess Problems and Studies Fans was organized at the All-Union Chess Section. Zalkind was unanimously elected Chairman.

Shakhmatny listok No. 7, 1928 published a resolution of the plenum of the All-Union Chess Section on Zalkind's report on the activities of the Central Bureau of the Association of Problemists of the USSR. That report approved its work and noted the achievements of Soviet chess composers.

Meanwhile, Zalkind's achievements in competitions had also built up spectacularly. 1930, his last year of freedom, turned out to be especially fruitful. Lazar Borisovich won second prizes in competitions of *Vechernaya Moskva* and *Pravda*. One of his last studies shared 1st-2nd place in a competition for the *Zadachi i etyudy* book of studies, whose judge was none other than Troitsky.

Composition No. 51
Zadachi i etyudy, 1929-1930
A. A. Troitsky International Competition, 1st-2nd prize

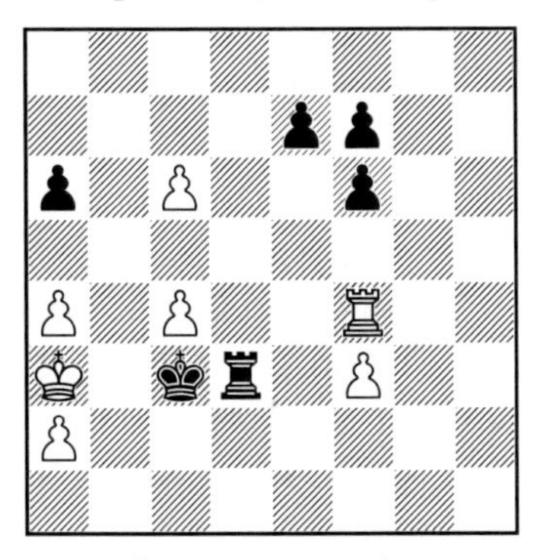

White to move and win

1.c7! a5!? 2.♖d4! ♖xf3. 2...♖e3 3.♖e4 ♖xf3 4.♖e2, winning. **3.♖f4!**. 3.♖d2? ♔xd2+ 4.♔b2 ♖c3 5.c8=♕ ♖c2+ and a draw, **3...♖g3.** 3...♖d3 4.♖f2 or 3...♖xf4 4.c8=♕, winning.

4.♖g4! 4.♖f2? ♖g8! and a draw. **4...♖h3 5.♖h4! ♖g3 6.♖h3! ♖xh3 7.c8=♕ ♖d3**. If 7...♖e3 with the idea of playing 8...♖e5, then the continuation 8.♕c5 ♖e5 9.♕b5 decides the outcome. **8.♕f5 ♔c2+ 9.♕xd3+ ♔xd3 10.c5**, winning.

"What is interesting is the maneuver of the white rook. This maneuver occurs in one of my studies in a shortened form, but in the work of Zalkind this maneuver has a different purpose and looks new to me... The construction looks impeccable." (From the report by the judge Troitsky.)

It seemed that Lazar Zalkind had every chance of winning the first All-Union Composition Championship, scheduled for 1930. Alas, he was unable to take part in this composers' forum...

In 1931, the "Union Bureau of the Mensheviks" case was investigated. Solzhenitsyn wrote about it in *The Gulag Archipelago*: "The GPU *(the secret police)* set the following structure: there were two people from the Supreme Economic Council, two from the People's Commissariat of Trade, two from the State Bank, one person from the Central Union and one from Gosplan. (So depressingly unoriginal!) Therefore, they selected suitable candidates for these posts. Actually, it was only according to rumors that they were Mensheviks. Some of them were not Mensheviks at all, but the order was to consider them Mensheviks. The true political views of the accused did not interest the GPU at all. Not all the convicted persons even knew each other. The GPU scraped for information from witnesses to unmask the Mensheviks. (All the witnesses were themselves then given prison sentences.)" (Alexander Solzhenitsyn *The Gulag Archipelago, Vol. 1*, Moscow: Sov. pisatel, 1989, p. 391).

The trial was fabricated with the participation of Nikolai Krylenko, and the accusation formulated by him referred among other matters to the defendants' attempts to restore the capitalist system, collaboration with counter-revolutionary fascist organizations, sabotage, preparation of intervention, betrayal of the world revolution and treachery towards the world proletariat. The prosecutor repeatedly mentioned the "Kulak-SR group of Chayanov–Kondratiev", and made the following claim about Zalkind: "He carried out wrecking work quite specifically, the only question that should be raised is about his long-term isolation...".

Perhaps the decisive role in Zalkind's fate was played by the fact that he, an economist by profession, adhered to the views of Chayanov and Kondratiev – outstanding academics who were illegally repressed in the late 1920s, and have since been rehabilitated.

The magazine *Shakhmaty v SSSR* No. 2 for 1932, reporting on the results of the international three-mover competition of the *Zvyazda* newspaper (Minsk), noted that "the problem by the convicted Menshevik traitor Zalkind was disqualified." Not only were authors repressed, but also their works of art.

Efim Rossels, who replaced Zalkind as chairman of the composers' commission, wrote in the preface to the book *300 Chess Problems* published in 1933: "The All-Union Association, headed by Zalkind and Levman, made no attempt to correct the ideological line of the composer's movement, but tried to deepen the separation of composition from the general chess movement. At present, there are hardly any of our readers who do not know what a counter-revolutionary, wrecker and Menshevik Zalkind was, whose 'artistic creativity' spilled far beyond the boundaries of chess composition..."

Lazar Borisovich Zalkind was sentenced to eight years in prison. He spent the entire term, from start to finish, in the Upper Urals political isolation ward. In prison, Lazar Borisovich read a lot, and he was able to work on chess theory and composition. Prisoners of that time still had the hope of being released one day.

In August 1938, the sentence imposed by the court expired. But instead of his expected freedom, Zalkind was given a new sentence. This time, there weren't even any new accusations: a Special Council of the NKVD (the precursor to the KGB) gave him 5 years of correctional labor camps (CLC). The CLC in which Lazar Borisovich found himself was located in Komsomolsk-on-Amur. Prison was a holiday compared with the regime here. The former economist was saved from an early death by a lucky chance to get a job as an accountant at a clothes factory.

1943 brought terrible grief – news of the death of his son Boris. The 18-year-old son of an "enemy of the people" died a hero's death on the 1st Belorussian front. In the same year, the 5-year sentence of the Special Council expired. But his release turned out to be restricted – the right to consider himself "free" in the settlement in Komsomolsk-on-Amur without the right to leave his place of internal exile. Further, Lazar Borisovich's health was seriously compromised by that time.

His life during that period was somewhat brightened up by his acquaintance with Emilia Davydovna Plinka, a teacher from Latvia who was also living in internal exile, and had once studied with Lazar Borisovich's younger brother, Aron Zalkind, a teacher and psychologist. Here are lines from a letter from Plinka addressed to Zalkind's daughter: "34 notebooks of his scientific work on the theory of the game of chess remain in the archive of the Upper Urals prison, where he spent eight years. Evidently, he worked a lot on this area and I think that this work should be interesting, especially since (as he told me) no one has worked on this area before."

The letter is dated June 24, 1945, and from another letter we learn that at 4 o'clock in the morning of June 25, Lazar Borisovich died of a heart attack. Maybe Zalkind's notebooks will still be found. He suffered an extremely tough life, yet was devoted to chess until his very last breath.

Lazar Borisovich Zalkind died while at the peak of his chess talent. An issue of collected problems by *Zadachi i etyudy* in 1929 reported that the next issue would be entirely devoted to Zalkind's work. However, this issue was never published...

In 1929-1930, the Society of Chess Problems and Studies Fans under the All-Union Chess Section began an international four-mover competition to honor the 25th anniversary of Zalkind's career. However, that contest was later scrapped...

In 1928, the magazine *Shakhmaty* published an article about Zalkind's work which concluded with the following words: "A collection of Zalkind's compositions has not yet been published, which is impossible not to regret". No collection has yet been published...

Zalkind's works have returned to the library shelves from the restricted access archives, and the publication of his best problems and studies in this book you are holding is an attempt to repay a debt of conscience to a person who did so much for the development of chess composition in our country.

Arvid Kubbel – Kubbel's Brother

The career of Arvid Kubbel, the eldest of three famous chess composer brothers, was quite diverse. He was an over-the-board master and at the same time a versatile composer who left a noticeable mark in the history of both problem and study composition. However, in Evgeny Umnov's Russian-language book *Chess Problem of the XX Century* (1966), he was mentioned only in passing, as Leonid Kubbel's brother, while Filipp Bondarenko's Russian-language monograph *Gallery of Chess Study Composers* (1968) does not say a word about Arvid Ivanovich...

I learned a lot about him and his family from conversations and correspondence with his daughter Renata Arvidovna Volovikova. Arvid Kubbel was born on November 12, 1889, in St. Petersburg in the family of factory workman Ivan Ivanovich Kubbel. In early childhood, Arvid discovered chess watching his father play, and by 1900, together with his younger brothers Leonid and Evgeny, he was already battling enthusiastically at the board. Soon, the Kubbel brothers became interested in solving problems and studies, and then tried their hands at composing them. Arvid Kubbel's debut came in 1903, when two of his problems appeared in the newspaper *St. Petersburger Zeitung.*

Composition No. 52
St. Petersburger Zeitung
1903

White to mate in 2 moves

1.♕d3!, threatening **2.♕c2#**, 1...cxd3 2.♘b3#, 1...b3 2.♕c3#, 1...♗e4 2.♕d1#.

Composition No. 53
St. Petersburger Zeitung
1903

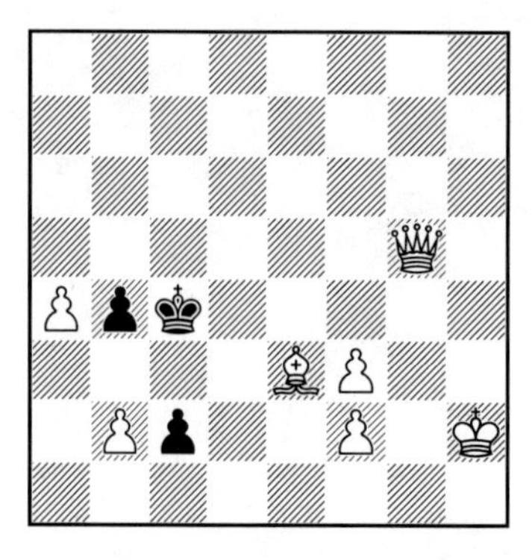

White to mate in 3 moves

1.♗c1! ♔b3 2.♕d5+ ♔xa4 3.b3#, 1...♔d3 2.♕b5+ ♔d4 3.♗e3#.

The problems were sent by Leonid Kubbel and published under his name, but the Kubbel brothers' archive materials show that the author of these problems was actually Arvid. This marked his debut in composition.

By the end of 1904, Arvid Kubbel had already produced 13 works, five more than Leonid, though the latter would become more famous. In February 1906, the Kubbel brothers experienced a painful loss – their father died. This meant that Arvid did not manage to finish his grammar school, as he had to go out to work to raise his younger brothers. Until the end of his life, Arvid Ivanovich worked as a ledger clerk and then as a proper accountant.

Although Arvid Kubbel had already shown his ability as a mature composer in his first works, he was attracted by over-the-board play, in which he surpassed his brothers since his youth.

The first time that Arvid achieved major tournament success was at the Congress of the Baltic Chess Union in 1913, in which he took first place. In 1916, Arvid won a small tournament in Petrograd ahead of Peter Romanovsky.

In the first Soviet Championship in 1920, Arvid shared 5th place with Nikolai Grigoriev and Abram Rabinovich, ahead of Blumenfeld, Ilyin-Zhenevsky, Zubarev and other masters. He was also ahead of a whole cohort of famous players in the Soviet 1923 championship, beating Bogatyrchuk and Nenarokov, though they finished above him in the table. The following game was played on July 8, 1923, in the first round of the Soviet Championship.

Game No. 1
A. Kubbel – I. Rabinovich
2nd Soviet Championship,
Petrograd, 1923
Vienna Game C29
Commentary by A. Kubbel

1.e4 e5 2.♘c3 ♘f6 3.f4 d5 4.fxe5 ♘xe4 5.♘f3. It was also possible to play 5.♕f3, which also has its own nasty threats.

5...♗e7. Recently, this old move has been used more often than 5...♗g4, since it leads to a quiet and equal game.

6.d4. In the case of 6.d3 black would have played 6...♘xc3 7.bxc3 0-0, followed by 8...f6, and his pieces would have stood well.

6...0-0 7.♗d3 f5 8.exf6

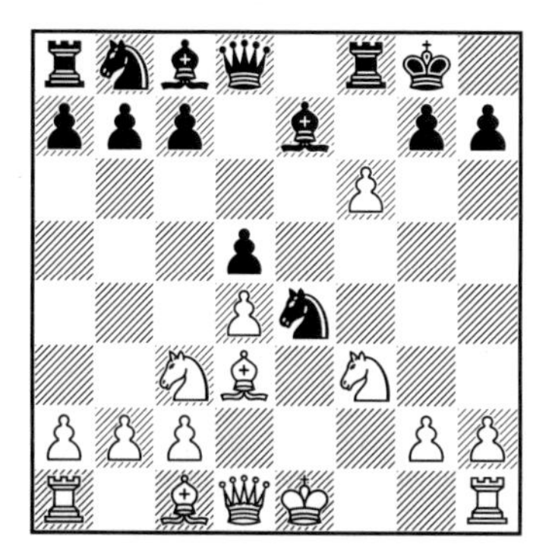

8...♗xf6. A novelty first tried by Reti against Spielmann in the Vienna tournament of 1922, thanks to which black manages to avoid all difficulties.

With the previous continuation 8...♘xf6, white would get great prospects after 9.0-0 ♘c6 (or 9...♗g4? 10.♕e1 c5 11.♘e5 c4 12.♘xg4 [12.♗xh7+ was also strong – S.G.] 12...cxd3 13.♕e6+ ♔h8 14.♘e5!, with an advantage for white) 10.♗g5 ♗g4 11.♕e1 h6 12.♗e3! ♗xf3 13.♖xf3 ♘g4 14.♖xf8+ ♗xf8 15.♕g3 ♘xe3 16.♕xe3 ♕d7 17.♖f1!.

9.0-0 ♘c6 10.♘xe4 dxe4 11.♗xe4 ♘xd4 12.c3. In the above game, Reti played 12.♘g5 ♗f5!, and the opponents agreed to a draw after another 10 moves, but the move played is sufficient for complete equality.

12...♘xf3+ 13.♗xf3 c6. At this point, I offered a draw, because the position was completely symmetrical and it would have been impossible to win with correct play.

14.♕xd8 ♗xd8 15.♗e3 ♗e6 16.a3 ♗b3 17.♗c5 ♗b6 18.♗xb6 axb6 19.♖fe1 ♖f7. Obviously, the invasion of the rook on e7 must be prevented.

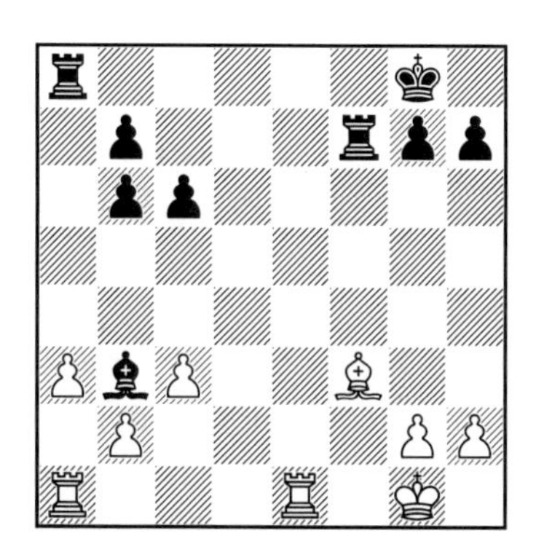

20.♖e2 ♖d8 21.♖ae1 ♔f8 22.♗g4. Forcing black's next move (threatening 23.♗e6).

22...♗d1. As I mentioned in the note to the 13th move, I was playing for a draw and therefore tried to force exchanges to achieve it soon. In this case, black has no other choice, for example, in the case of 22...♖f4 white would play 23.♖f2.

23.♖e4 ♗xg4 24.♖xg4 ♖d2. Finally, black has achieved his goal and confidently occupied the d2 square, but at the same time, the white rook on b4 will occupy an equally magnificent square.

25.♖b4 b5 26.♖f1. This continuation ruins all of black's attempts, since it brings the game to an endgame (rook and pawns against rook and pawns), in which black is held back by the weakness of the b7 square.

26...♖dd7. In the case of 26...♖c2 27.a4 bxa4 28.♖xb7 ♖xf1+ 29.♔xf1 c5 30.♖a7 ♖xb2 31.♖xa4 it would be a draw.

27.♖e4 ♖d2 28.♖b4 ♖xf1+ 29.♔xf1 ♖d1+ 30.♔e2 ♖g1 31.♔f2 ♖b1. Trying to win, black takes advantage of all the available opportunities and moves his rook to b1, thus neutralizing the move 32.c4, which is to a certain extent unpleasant for him.

32.♔e3 ♔e8.

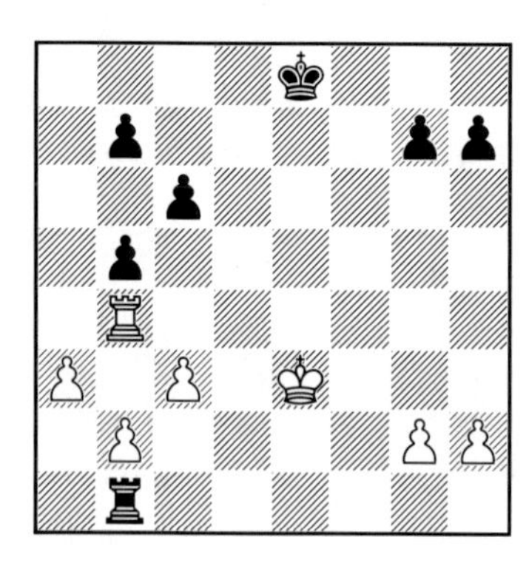

33.c4! My sealed move. White temporarily sacrifices a pawn, but gets better chances due to the passed a3 pawn.

33...bxc4 34.♖xb7 c3 35.♔d3

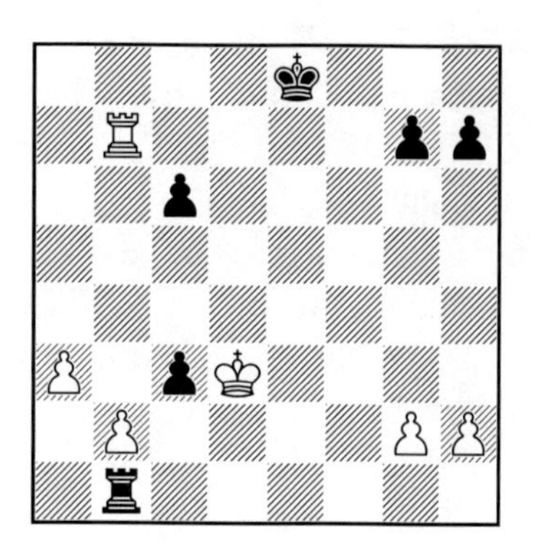

35...cxb2. The continuation 35... ♖xb2 led to a draw, too, for example, 36.♖xb2 cxb2 37.♔c2 b1=♕+ 38.♔xb1 ♔d7 39.♔c2 ♔d6 40.♔c3 ♔c5 (however, not 40...♔d5 since after that 41.a4 ♔c5 42.♔b3 ♔d4 43.a5 ♔c5 44.♔a4, and black would find himself caught in zugzwang) 41.a4 ♔d5 42.♔b4 ♔d4! 43.a5 c5+ (This continuation loses because of 44.♔a3! – S.G.). 44.♔b5 c4 45.a6 c3 46.a7 c2 47.a8=♕ c1=♕ 48.♕a7+ and 49.♕xg7. This variation for black can be improved through first playing g5 and then h6 on the 41st move, so as not to give white the opportunity to capture the pawn on g7.

36.♔c3 ♖g1. If 36...♖h1, then 37.♔xb2 ♖xh2 (the line 37...♔f8 38.a4 ♖xh2 39.a5 ♖xg2+ 40.♔b3 ♖g3+ 41.♔b4 ♖g4+ 42.♔c5 ♖a4 43.♔b6 h5 44.a6 h4 45.a7 h3 46.♖b8+ ♔f7 47.♖h8 looks dangerous) 38.♖xg7 h5 39.♔b3 h4 40.a4 h3 41.gxh3 ♖xh3+ 42.♔b4 ♖h4+ 43.♔a5 ♔d8 and a draw.

37.♖xb2 ♔e7 38.♖d2. Now it has definitely become clear that if anyone has a chance of winning, it is white.

38...♔e6 39.a4 c5

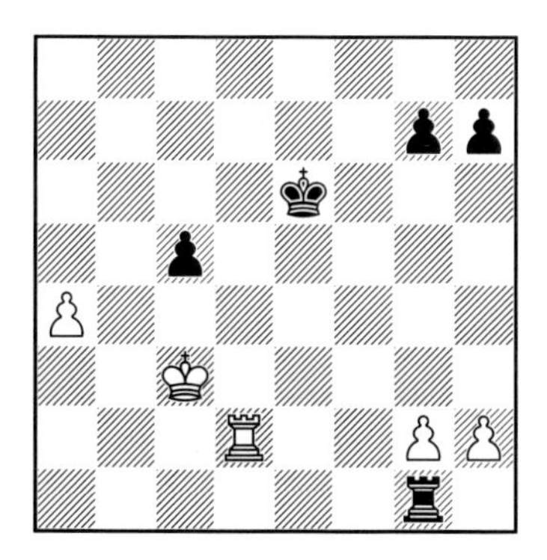

40.♖a2? This move has the disadvantage that the black king, who had been cut off from the action, can now get back into it. However, due to a lack of time, I could not calculate the benefits of the move 40.♔b2, although it seemed better to me. In fact, with the move of the king white controls the a1 square that the black rook wants to occupy, and the a-pawn threatens to go forward unhindered; black, it seems, is unable to prevent this maneuver, for example 40...c4 41.a5 ♖f1 42.♔c3 ♖a1 43.♔b4 c3 44.♖c2 ♔d6 45.♖xc3. Or 40...♖f1 41.a5 ♔e5 42.♔b3 ♖f6 43.♖a2 ♖a6 44.♔c4.

40...♔d5? An instructive mistake, after which there is no way for black to escape. Not the rook, but the king should stand in front of the pawn, therefore the correct continuation was 40...♔d6 41.a5 ♔c7 42.a6 ♔b8 43.a7+ ♔a8 44.♔c4 ♖c1+ 45.♔d5 c4 46.h3 h5. There is no forced win in sight, and it is doubtful whether it even exists in this position.

41.a5 ♖e1 42.a6 ♖e3+. After the game ended I found out that black had placed his hopes in this check.

43.♔d2 ♖e8 44.a7 ♖a8 45.♔c3 (the rest is a matter of technique) **45...♔c6 46.♔c4 ♔b6 47.g4 ♔b7.** It is obvious that the continuation 48.♔xc5 ♖c8+ and 49...♔a8 is a trap.

48.♖a5 g6 49.g5 ♔b6 50.♖b5+ ♔c6. Not 50...♔a6 due to 51.♖b1 ♔a5 52.♔xc5 ♖c8+ 53.♔d6, winning.

51.♖xc5+ ♔b6 52.♖b5+ ♔a6 53.♔b4. Black resigned.

In 1924, Arvid Kubbel, together with his brother Leonid, edited the problems and studies column in the magazine *Shakhmatny listok*. Arvid was content with fifth place in the Leningrad Championship of 1924, in which the six strongest chess players faced each other twice. *Shakhmatny listok* (1924, No. 7, p. 51) commented on his performance with the following words: "Two antipodes – the prudent Ilyin-Zhenevsky and the headstrong Arvid Kubbel – fitted well together." Arvid Kubbel was "headstrong" only at the board, but in real life he was always gentle and sensitive. As for his sporting results, though, his impulsiveness sometimes prevented him from greater achievements.

Thus, his relative failure in the Leningrad Championship of 1924 happened to some extent because in the first round he blundered and lost from a good position against Ilya

Rabinovich and could not recover from that defeat until the end of the tournament.

The right to be called the champion of Leningrad in 1925 depended on the outcome of the last round game between Alexander Ilyin-Zhenevsky and Arvid Kubbel. Victory would have delivered clear first place for Ilyin-Zhenevsky, but...

Game No. 2
A. Ilyin-Zhenevsky – A. Kubbel
Leningrad Championship, 1925
Spanish Opening C64
Commentary by A. Kubbel

1.e4 e5 2.♘f3 ♘c6 3.♗b5 ♗c5 4.c3. According to Tartakower, this continuation is the correct one; the moves 4.0-0 or 4.♘xe5 would have been much weaker.

4...♕f6. The start of extravagant play by black.

5.0-0 ♘ge7

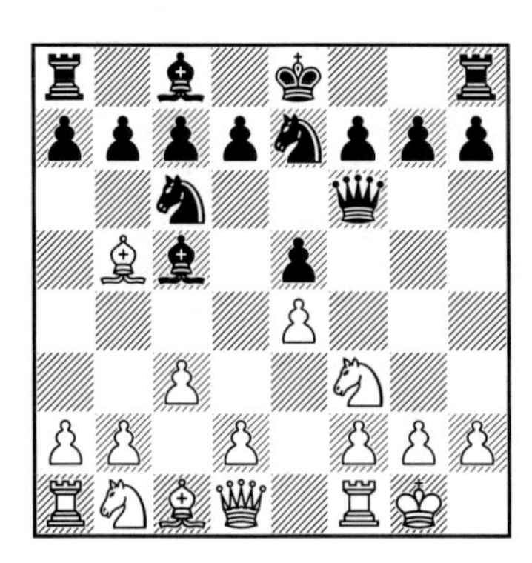

6.d3. In the case of 6.d4 exd4 7.♗g5 ♕d6 8.♗xe7 ♔xe7 9.♗xc6 dxc6 10.cxd4 ♗b6 black is left with two bishops against two knights. The move in the game is better. Because black still cannot prevent the advance of the d-pawn, it will follow anyway with greater force.

6...h6 (otherwise the move 7.♗g5 would have been most unpleasant).

7.♗e3 ♗b6. It is definitely impractical to exchange the bishops, since the open file would promise white good prospects.

8.d4 0-0 9.♗xc6 ♘xc6 10.d5 ♘e7 11.♗xb6 axb6 12.d6! A correct pawn sacrifice, which gives white much freer space due to the disarray of black's pawns on the queenside and the difficulty of developing the c8 bishop.

12...cxd6 13.♘a3 d5. The best thing about this move is that black voluntarily returns the pawn, but at the same time frees up his bishop. In other continuations, black would lose his pawn under worse conditions.

14.exd5 d6 15.♘d2. Avoiding a pin after ♗g4 and at the same time threatening 16.♘dc4 and 16.♘e4.

15...♕g6 16.♘dc4 ♗h3. A tempting and, at the same time, poor move, refuted by white. The correct continuation was 16...♖a6 and 17...♗d7.

17.♘e3 ♖fc8? This move was completely incomprehensible. The exchange sacrifice is not a sufficiently serious threat. Black needs to admit his mistake and either move the bishop back to d7 or play 17...♘f5 18.♕f3 ♘xe3 19.fxe3 ♗g4 20.♕g3 ♕e4.

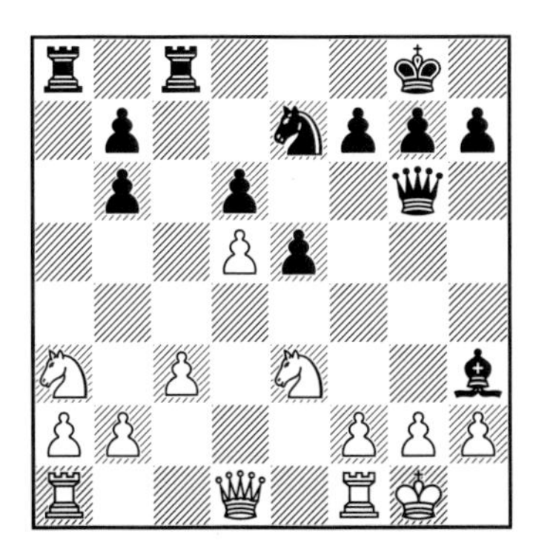

18.♕b1! With the aim of exchanging queens, after which white has an advantage in the endgame.

18...e4. Probably not the best continuation. 18...f5 19.♔h1 ♗g4 was preferable.

19.♔h1 ♗f5? Another poor move that takes away the e7 knight's best square. Here too, the move 19...♗d7 was quite suitable.

20.♘ac4 ♖e8? An unjustified pawn sacrifice, since black does not get anything in return. Obviously, he should've played 20...♖a6. Black's last 4-5 moves were very weak.

21.♘xb6 ♖a5 22.♘bc4 ♖c5 23.b4 ♖c7 24.♕b3 b5 25.♘a5 ♗d7 26.c4. In order to convert his advantage on the queenside as soon as possible.

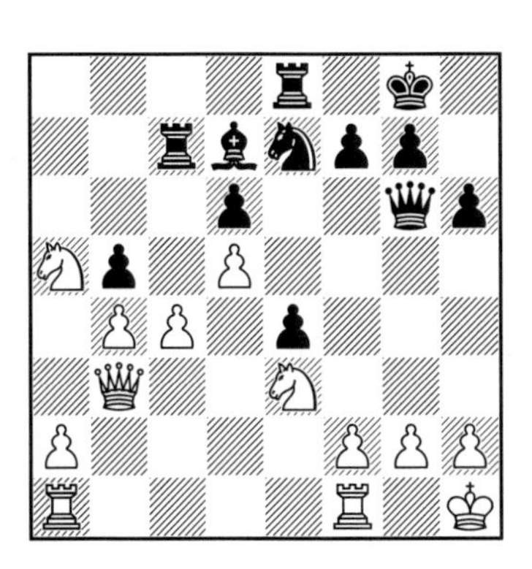

26...f5. A last throw of the dice, that leads to a favorable result beyond all expectations. Anyway, black has no other option, since he will be slowly but surely crushed with a waiting game.

27.cxb5? In his understandable intoxication of the coming victory (winning this game would have placed Ilyin above his competitors, since by this time it had already become clear that Romanovsky would lose to Levenfish), white makes a huge mistake, giving him, it's true, two strong pawns, but still ceding all his chances. Black's bishop now becomes active, and the black pawns on the kingside start to advance ominously. The fact that white did not continue by playing 27.c5 (27.c5? loses to 27...f4 – S.G.) can only be explained by an optical illusion, because after 27...dxc5 28.d6+ ♗e6 black could not save his pieces, as after a queen move, the knight on e7 would die. If black does not take on c5, then white has c6 and so on.

27...♗xb5 28.♖fc1 ♖xc1+ 29.♖xc1 f4 30.♘c2. The critical moment of the game. White thought over his move for a long time, and as a result, he had very little time left for the next 15 moves. The knight's retreat to c2 in order to occupy the e1 square to protect g2 is probably better than 30.♘ec4, for example, 30...♘f5 31.a4? ♗xc4 32.♘xc4 e3 33.fxe3 fxe3 34.♖e1 ♘h4 35.♕b2 e2, with a win. Or 35.♖e2 ♕g4 36.♕c2

♖c8, with a win. The variation given here does not exhaust all the possibilities, but it clearly shows what risks white got exposed to due to his 27th move.

30...♘f5 31.♘c6. This move cannot be considered bad, on the contrary, it fits both for the attack (♘e7+) and for the defense (♘d4).

31...♗d3! An extremely important move, since it prevents the transfer of the white queen to h3.

32.♘e1. Here's the logical continuation of white's defensive idea (move 30!), whereas the move 32.♘6d4, which seemed to be much stronger, led to extremely tense play, for example: 32...♗xc2 33.♘xc2 ♖c8! 34.♕b2! (not 34.♖f1 due to 34...e3 35.fxe3 ♖xc2) 34...♕f6 35.♕xf6 gxf6 36.b5 ♘d4 37.b6 ♘xc2 38.b7 ♖b8 39.♖xc2 ♖xb7, with a possible draw. If black preferred to continue his attack, then he could have continued 32...♘h4 33.♘e1 (not 33.♖g1 e3 34.fxe3 ♗f1! 35.♘e1 ♖xe3, with a win), and given the opportunity, white would have had the move ♘e6 in reserve.

32...♘h4 33.b5? This was the decisive mistake. White's hopes, placed on his 35th move, were too high. And here, with 33.♘d4, it was still possible to put up stubborn resistance.

33...e3! A pretty move, although quite obvious. It would be a mistake to capture the bishop in view of exf2, but now there's no strong means of protection against exf2.

34.fxe3. In the case of 34.f3 black achieves victory in an elegant way: 34...♗f1 35.♕c2 ♕g5 36.♘d4 e2 37.♘e6 ♗xg2+ 38.♔g1 ♘xf3+! 39.♘xf3 (or 39.♔f2 ♕h4+! 40.♔xg2 ♘xe1+, with a win) 39...♕g4! 40.♘e1 ♗e4+ and so on.

34...♖xe3 35.♕b2. Now it would seem that the worst is over for white, but...

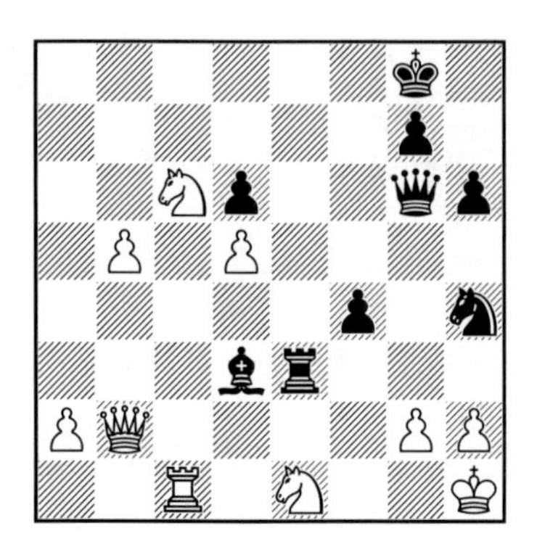

35...♗c2!! A spectacular, purely problem-like move (reminiscent of the finale of the Reti – Bogoljubov game, New York, 1924) that forces white to capitulate immediately, since the only possible continuation 36.♕xc2 ♖xe1+ 37.♖xe1 ♕xc2 38.♖g1 f3 leads to checkmate. White resigned.

Game No. 3

A. Kubbel – S. Vainstein

Leningrad, June 8, 1925

Four Knights Opening C49

Commentary by A. Kubbel

1.e4 e5 2.♘c3 ♘f6 3.♘f3 ♘c6 4.♗b5 ♗b4 5.0-0 0-0 6.d3 d6 7.♘e2

♗g4 8.♗xc6 bxc6 9.♘g3 ♔h8 10.h3 ♗xf3 11.♕xf3 ♘g8.

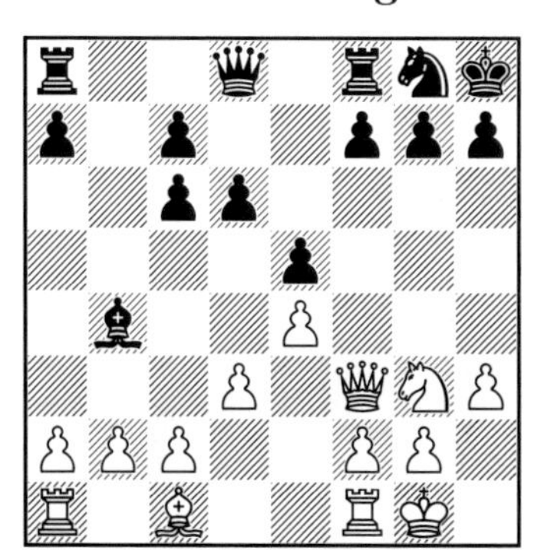

This explains the king's enigmatic move: black takes up a strong defensive position.

12.a4. Threatening with 13.c3, etc. to take the bishop. At the same time, this move provides white with good prospects in the future.

12...d5 13.♕g4 ♕c8 14.♘f5 g6 15.exd5 gxf5. In keeping with his plan, black intends to use the file to attack.

16.♕xb4 cxd5 17.f4. The strongest continuation, which requires an accurate response from black.

17...f6. The only correct move, others are not suitable here, for example, 17...c5 18.♕b3! ♕e6 19.fxe5 ♕xe5 20.♗d2 and so on. Or 17...e4 18.♕d4+ and 19.♕xd5. (17...f6 loses after 18.fxe5 and 17...c5 is still the best option, though white is easily better – S.G.).

18.♕c5 ♕e6 19.a5. Avoiding the exchange of queens after black's ♕b6 and at the same time creating an outpost on the queenside.

19...e4. This move has a pro and a con. The former is that the pawn becomes a passed pawn, but the latter is that it opens the b2-f6 diagonal for the bishop. However, black had a certain reason to play it, since he was afraid of 20.b3, 21.♗b2 and 22.♖ae1, or even the exchange on e5.

20.b4 ♘e7 21.♗a3. There is nothing for the bishop to do here, so 21.♗b2 was of course better.

21...♖g8 22.b5 ♘g6. Now white's position has become unenviable, because a concentrated attack by all of black's pieces on the kingside will follow.

23.c4. 23.♖fe1 was probably more solid, but the move in the game was made to sharpen play.

23...♘h4 24.♖a2.

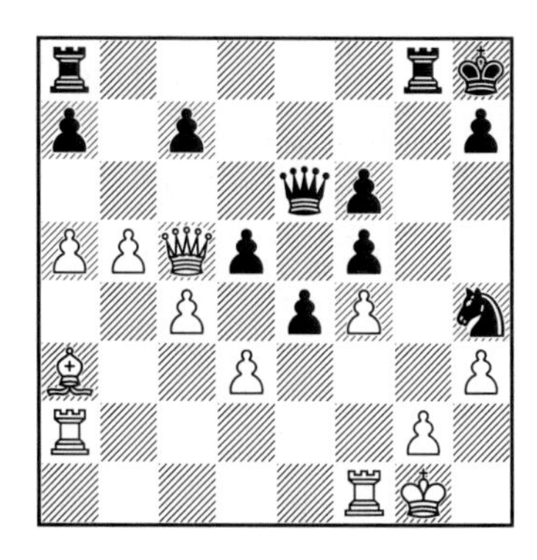

24...dxc4. Black misses the chance to win via 24...exd3, for example, 25.♕xd5 (not 25.cxd5 ♕e4 26.♖ff2 ♖xg2+ 27.♖xg2 ♕e1+ and checkmate next move) 25... ♕e3+ 26.♔h2 (the continuation 26.♔h1 is a mistake [the only correct continuation – S.G.] 26... ♘xg2! 27.♖xg2 [white should play 27.♕xf5, protecting the h3 pawn and threatening 28.♗c5 – S.G.] 27...♕xh3+ 28.♔g1 ♖xg2+ 29.♕xg2 ♖g8, with a win) 26...♖ae8 27.♗c5 ♕g3+ 28.♔h1 ♖e2 and so on.

25.dxc4 ♕f7. A complex maneuver to transfer the queen to g6, but one which allows white to concentrate his forces on defense. However, in the case of 25...♖g6, white could respond by playing an unpleasant move 26.♕d5!, forcing the exchange of queens (26...♕e8 is clearly bad), and therefore the attack would be neutralized.

26.♖c2 ♕g6 27.♔h1! A subtle response, moving the king away from the dangerous g-file without losing a tempo.

27...♖ad8. 27...♘xg2 was pointless, for example, 28.♖g1 ♕g3 29.♖gxg2 ♕xh3+ 30.♔g1, and white is no longer in danger (actually, it was only pointless if white plays 28.♗b2, any other white move loses – S.G.). If 27...♕g3 28.♗b2 ♖g6 29.♕e7 ♘f3! 30.♗xf6+ ♔g8 31.♕e6+ ♔f8, white has to make-do with perpetual check. White, however, does not need to choose this option, he can simply play 29.♕f2 instead of 29.♕e7.

28.♗b2 ♕f7. In order to prevent the move ♕e7. Unfortunately, the move 28...♖d3 could not help here in view of 29.♕e7 ♖d6 30.c5 ♖e8 31.cxd6 ♖xe7 32.dxe7 ♔g8 33.♗xf6, with a win.

29.♕xa7. This move looks too risky, because the queen moves far from the action, but in fact it is precisely calculated. White has enough resources to defend, and the passed a-pawn soon turns out to be disastrous for black.

29...♖d3 (29...♖a8 would have had no effect after 30.♕d4).

30.♕c5 ♖dg3. The capture of the g2 pawn could be refuted as follows: 30...♘xg2 31.♖xg2 (the capture of the pawn is actually refuted by the move 31.♕xf5+– – S.G.) 31...♖xg2 32.♔xg2 ♕g6+ 33.♔f2 ♕g3+ (?+–, 33...e3 – S.G.) 34.♔e2, and everything would be fine. Or 31...♖xh3+ 32.♔g1 ♖xg2+ 33.♔xg2 ♕g6+ 34.♔xh3 ♕g4+ 35.♔h2 ♕h4+ 36.♔g2 ♕g4+ 37.♔f2 and the king escapes.

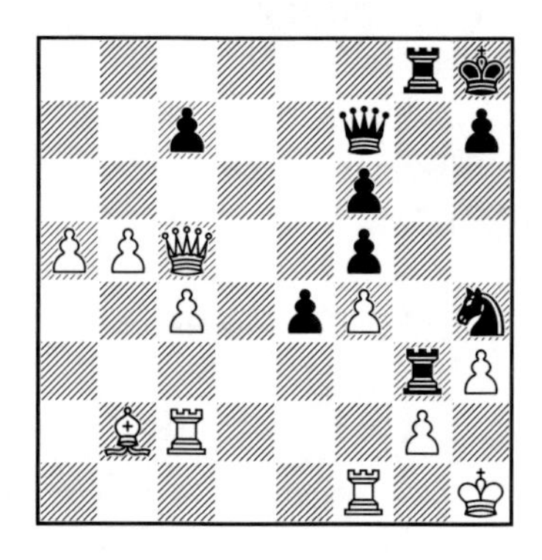

31.♕d4 (now playing is easy) **31...♖8g6 32.♕d8**+ **♔g7 33.♖d1 ♘f3.** This is the last trap in case white plays the reckless move 34.♖d7 – which is met by a pretty checkmate in two moves. 33...♘xg2 would not help here, for example, 34.♗xf6+ ♕xf6 35.♖d7+ ♔h6 36.♕xf6 ♖xh3+ 37.♔g1 ♘xf4+ (the continuation 37...♖xf6 38.♖xg2 e3 39.♖h2 ♖xh2 40.♔xh2 ♖e6 41.♖d1 is no good either) 38.♕xg6+ ♔xg6 39.♖xc7, with a win.

34.♕d7. This move completely eliminates all black's attempts to resist, although it was possible to continue by playing 34.gxf3 ♖xh3+ 35.♖h2 ♖xh2+ 36.♔xh2 ♖h6+ 37.♔g1 ♕g6+ 38.♔f2 ♖h2+ 39.♔e3 ♖xb2 40.♕xc7+, and black loses his queen.

34...♘h4 (in the case of 34...♖h6, the simplest continuation was 35.♕xf5) **35.c5!** (an inconspicuous, but totally adequate move) **35...♘xg2 36.♗xf6+.** The finale of the combination started on the 29th move.

36...♖xf6. A sad necessity. In the case of 36...♔xf6 white mates in four moves: 37.♕d4+ ♔e7 38.♕d8+ ♔e6 39.♖d6+ cxd6 40.♕xd6#.

37.♖xg2 (the mass exchanges immediately decide the game) **37...♖xg2 38.♔xg2 ♔g6 39.♕xf7+ ♖xf7 40.a6 ♖f8 41.a7.** Black resigned.

Perhaps the biggest event in Arvid Kubbel's over-the-board career was the Soviet championship of 1925. This time, the start looked promising. In the first round, he defeated Ilya Rabinovich.

Game No. 4
A. Kubbel – I. Rabinovich
4th Soviet Championship,
Leningrad, 1925
Alekhine's Defense B05
Commentary by A. Kubbel

1.e4 ♘f6 2.e5 ♘d5 3.♘f3. This is how Bogoljubov played against Tarrasch in Breslau in 1925. This move is all the better because it has not been studied sufficiently yet.

3...d6 4.d4 ♗g4. In the above-mentioned game, Tarrasch played 4...♗f5 and, after making a few more weak moves later in this game, quickly lost. The move in the game is much better, because it is important for black to exchange the f3 knight and thereby force a recapture by the d-pawn after dxe5.

5.h3 ♗xf3 6.♕xf3 dxe5 7.dxe5 e6 8.♘c3 ♗b4 9.♗d2 0-0 10.♖d1 ♘c6 11.♕g3 f6. After the opening, black seems to have got a freer game and now combines defense with attack, parrying the threat of ♗h6 and at the same time being willing to open the f-file for action. However, white has a smart answer that not only equalizes, but gives him a small positional advantage.

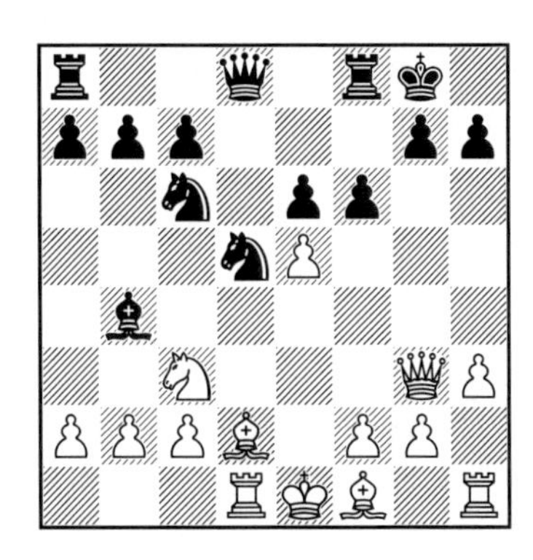

12.♘e4! I precisely calculated the combinations after this move. The knight's move was a surprise for my opponent, since after it he spent about 40 minutes thinking.

12...♗xd2+. Evidently, the only possible continuation. Not 12...♘xe5 due to 13.♗xb4 or 12...♗e7 13.♗h6 ♖f7 14.c4 and so on.

13.♖xd2 ♘xe5 (again, forced) **14.c4 ♕e7 15.cxd5 exd5 16.♖xd5.** If 16.♕b3, then 16...♘f7! 17.♕xd5 c6, which is less advantageous for white than in the game.

16...♘c6 (in the case of 16...♕b4+ white would play 17.♘c3, preserving the piece) **17.♗d3 f5.** Now, the move 17...♕b4+ would have been followed by 18.♔f1, and the king would have moved through g1 to the safe square h2.

18.0-0 fxe4 19.♖e1 ♕f6 20.♖xe4 ♖ad8 (obviously, not 20...♕xb2 21.♖h4 h6 22.♕g6 and so on) **21.♖xd8.** The continuation 21.♖h4 h6 22.♖f5 (22.♖f5? misses a chance to win, it would be necessary to play 22.♖d7 with the idea of ♖xg7-♕xg7-♖g4 – S.G.) 22...♕d6 is useless, and black has nothing to be afraid of.

21...♘xd8 22.♖e2? This continuation looks weak. The rook should stay on e4, from where it could be active. The correct continuation was 22.b3, and white's game is preferable.

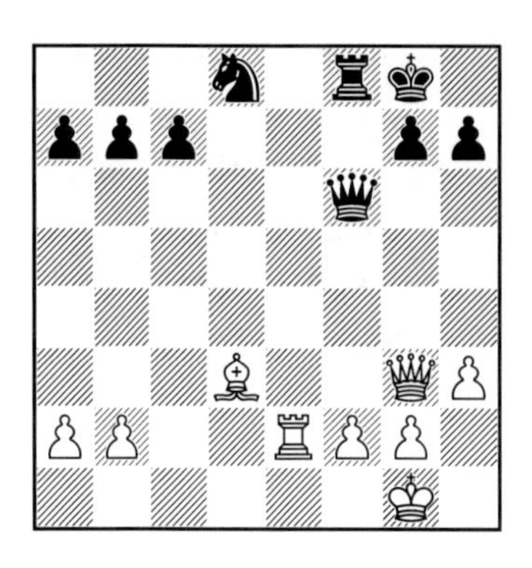

22...♘c6! 23.♖e4 (23.♕xc7 led to the loss of the exchange and hence the game after 23...♘d4 24.♖d2 ♘f3+ and 25...♕g5+. [Actually white has 24.♖e7! with the idea of 24...♕xf2+? 25.♔h1 – black has run out of checks, but white continues to threaten – S.G.]) **23...♘d4 24.f3 ♘f5?** In time pressure, black makes several poor moves now and later in this game. However, white suffered from the same problem. It was necessary to cement the position of the knight on d4 by means of c5.

25.♕xc7 ♕xb2 26.g4? This continuation weakens the f3 square unnecessarily and generally exposes the white king. There is, however, an explanation for this – the time control. Instead, he could have played 26.♕c5, which was stronger.

26...♘h4 27.♗c4+ ♔h8 28.♗e2 ♕f6. At this point, black could create an escape route for his king by playing 28...h6.

29.f4 g5?? A terrible move, which black would no doubt not have chosen under normal conditions, since its disadvantages are too obvious. The knight's retreat to g6 was correct.

30.f5 ♖d8? Black fails to see the last opportunity to save the knight by playing 30...♘g6, since white cannot play 31.fxg6 because of 31...♕f2+ with mate in a few moves. In tournament games, the 30th move often turns out to be fatal!

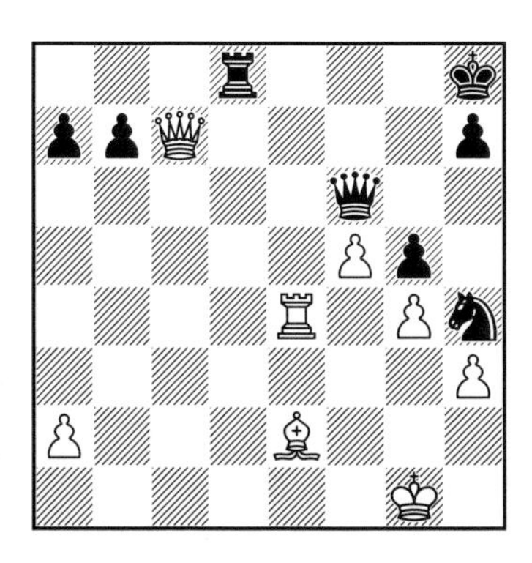

31.♕e5! The exchange of queens leads to a winning endgame for white due to the passed f5 pawn, the free rook and the black king, which is cut off from the other pieces. Other continuations leave black better chances, for example, after 31.♖e7 ♕d4+ 32.♔f1 ♕a1+ black already has a chance to draw.

31...♕xe5 32.♖xe5 ♔g7 (if 32...♖d7, then 33.f6 h6 34.♖e7, with a win) **33.♖e7+ ♔f6 34.♖xb7 ♖d2 35.♔f1 ♖xa2 36.♖xh7 ♖a3.** 36...♘g2 leads to a losing rook ending, for example, 37.♔xg2 ♖xe2+ 38.♔f3 ♖a2 39.♖h6+ ♔f7 40.♖g6 ♖a3+ 41.♔e4 ♖xh3 42.♖xg5 and so on.

37.♖h6+ ♔g7 38.♖d6! (it is here that the rook must stand to control the square) **38...♖xh3?** (38...♖a1 – S.G.) **39.f6+ ♔f8.** If 39...♔h6, then 40.♗d3 ♖f3+ 41.♔e2 ♖f4 42.f7+ ♘g6 (42...♔g7= – S.G.) 43.♗f5, with a win, and if 39...♔g6, then 40.♗d3+ ♖xd3 41.♖xd3 ♔xf6 42.♖d5!, with a win.

40.♗c4 ♖f3+ 41.♔e2 ♔e8 42.f7+ ♖xf7 (42...♔e7 would have been met by 43.♖e6+ ♔xf7 44.♖e3+, with a win) **43.♗xf7+.** Black resigned.

In the third round, Arvid Kubbel vigorously attacked Abram Rabinovich's position. In response to black's counterplay on the queenside, white developed a decisive attack on the enemy king.

Game No. 5
A. Kubbel – A. Rabinovich
4th Soviet Championship,
Leningrad, 1925
Sicilian Defense B24
Commentary by A. Kubbel

1.e4 c5 2.g3. The closed variation of the Sicilian Defense is the one that Tarrasch prefers; however, I chose it simply because I wanted to avoid well-trodden paths.

2...♘c6 3.♗g2 g6 4.♘c3 ♗g7 5.♘ge2 d6 6.b3. Another idea is the setup with 6.d3, 7.♗e7, and so on.

6...♗d7. If 6...♗g4, forcing 7.f3 to close the diagonal for the g2 bishop, this factor would play a secondary role in a closed game and, moreover, costs black a tempo.

7.♗b2 ♖c8 8.0-0 b5. Taking advantage of the vulnerability of the b2 bishop, black blocks the queenside. The standard development via 8...e6 and so on would have been too passive for a person of Rabinovich's playing style.

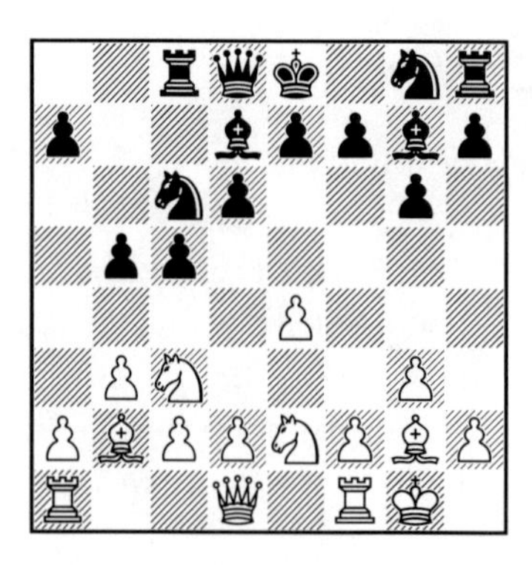

9.♖b1 (otherwise, after 9...b4 white would have had to move his knight to a4) **9...b4 10.♘d5 e5 11.♘e3 ♘ge7 12.f4** (white attacks immediately) **12...0-0 13.f5 f6.** It was better to play 13...gxf5, and then 14.exf5 f6, since then black still has the opportunity for counterplay in the center (d5).

14.g4 gxf5. Now this is hardly a good variation, because white attacks with the g-pawn and prevents d5. Besides, white opens up a path to attack the exposed black king.

15.gxf5 ♗e8 16.♖f3 ♘d4. Not 16...d5 due to 17.exd5 (17.♖h3! – S.G.) 17...♘xd5 (17...♘d4! – S.G.) 18.♘xd5 ♕xd5 19.♖d3! ♕f7 20.♗d5, winning the queen; if 16... ♗h6, then 17.♘g4 ♗g5 18.♕e1.

17.♖h3 ♖c7 18.♘g3 ♔h8

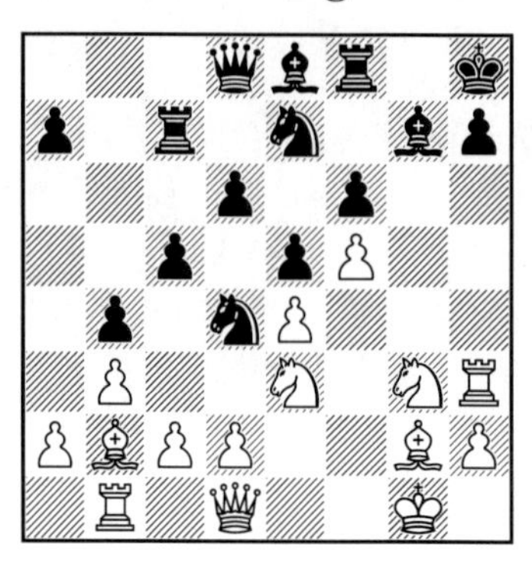

19.d3. Under time pressure, white chooses a slow plan to mobilize the b2 bishop on the c1-h6 diagonal, which gives black time to advance the a-pawn and at the same time open this file for a counter maneuver. The correct continuation was 19.♔h1, then c3, moving the queen away and ♖g1.

19...a5. Black skillfully uses his only chance.

20.♗c1 a4 21.♔h1 ♖a7 22.♗d2. The points expressed in the note to white's 19th move are proven here, since it is now obvious that white has not made a single step forward, but is just marking time.

22...axb3 23.axb3 ♕a8 24.♘c4 ♘c8 (not 24...d5 due to 25.♘b6 [25.exd5+– – S.G.] and 26.♘xd5) **25.♕g4 ♗f7?** Having prepared a break along the a-file with his last moves, black wrongly abandons his idea to play ♖al, which was required for the exchange of the white rook and the invasion of the black queen into the enemy camp. Indeed, after 25...♖a1 26.♖xa1 ♕xa1+ 27.♗f1 ♗f7 28.♘e3 the position remains tense; all variations are highly complex and do not lend themselves to perfect calculation. However, it is clear that black had some opportunities with the suggested continuation, whereas the move in the game leads to a quick defeat.

26.♖g1. A decisive move – the rook is transferred in order to accumulate forces on the kingside. It is interesting that the denouement will take place not on the h-file, but on the g-file.

26...♗g8 27.♘h5 ♖d7. If 27... d5 then 28.♘e3. Black is completely helpless.

28.♗f1 d5 29.♖hg3! Black's vulnerable points are the g7 and g8 squares, where the fatal blow is directed.

29...dxc4.

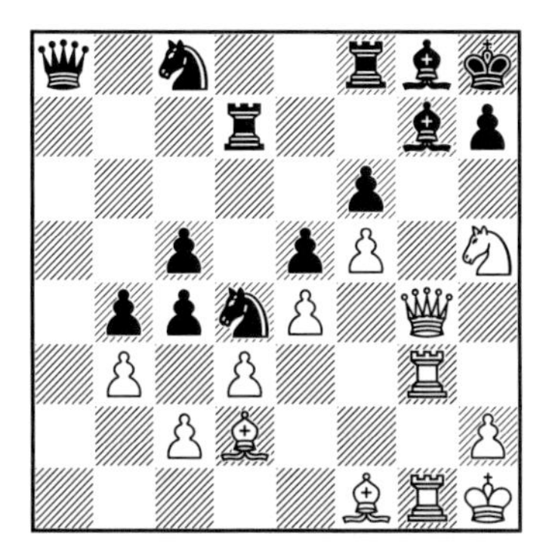

30.♗h6!! A spectacular move that totally destroys black's position. By the way, I made the last 4-5 moves under time pressure.

30...♕b7 (30...♘xf5 would have been followed by 31.♕xf5 ♗xh6 and a pretty sacrifice 32.♕xf6+! ♗g7 33.♖xg7, with a win) **31.♘xg7 ♗f7 32.♘h5 ♗xh5 33.♕g8+.** Black resigned.

In the fifth round, Arvid Kubbel faced the 1924 Soviet Champion and future winner of the 1925 championship Efim Bogoljubov. Bogoljubov was definitely the favorite in that game, especially since he played with white. However, Arvid managed to score a draw with a skillful defense, and after defeating Zubarev, he became one of the leaders.

The best creative achievement of A. Kubbel in the Soviet Championship of 1925 was his game with Duz-Khotimirsky, for which he was awarded a beauty prize.

Game No. 6

F. Duz-Khotimirsky – A. Kubbel

4th Soviet Championship

Leningrad, 1925

Slav Defense D13

Commentary by A. Kubbel

1.d4 d5 2.♘f3 ♘f6 3.c4 c6 4.cxd5. This continuation is very rare, the move 4.e3 is more common.

4...cxd5 5.♘c3 ♘c6 6.♘e5 e6 7.e3 ♘xe5. Black follows his plan, which leads to a lively game.

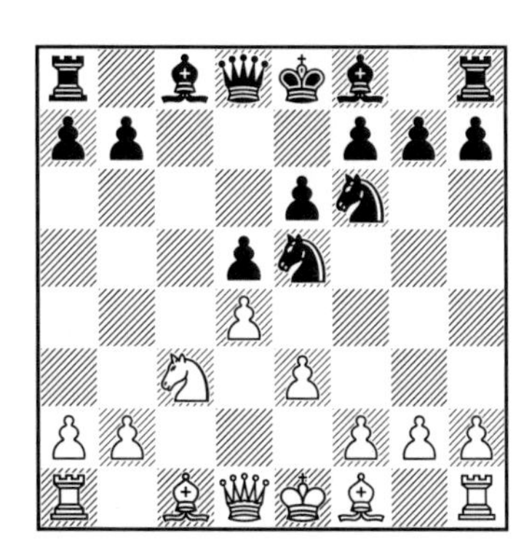

8.dxe5 ♘d7 9.f4 f6. This move seems risky, but in reality it forces white to commit, since it threatens to isolate the e-pawn.

10.♕h5+. This check and the pressure on e6 looks tempting, but it only creates difficulties for white, which he eventually proves unable to cope with. It was necessary to take on f6 and continue piece development.

10...g6 11.♕h3 ♕b6 12.♗d3 (threatening ♗xg6+) **12...♗g7 13.exf6.** Forced, and black gets better play, because the white queen is out of position on h3, while black's occupies an excellent position on b6. Another advantage is the possession of the a1-h8 diagonal.

13...♘xf6 14.♗b5+ ♔f7 15.0-0 ♖f8 16.♕h4 ♔g8 (black castles by hand) **17.a4 a6 18.a5** (in order to drive the queen away from the a7-g1 diagonal) **18...♕d6 19.♗a4 ♗d7 20.b3.** Black's response shows that this is not a good move. However, the situation white finds himself in is already difficult.

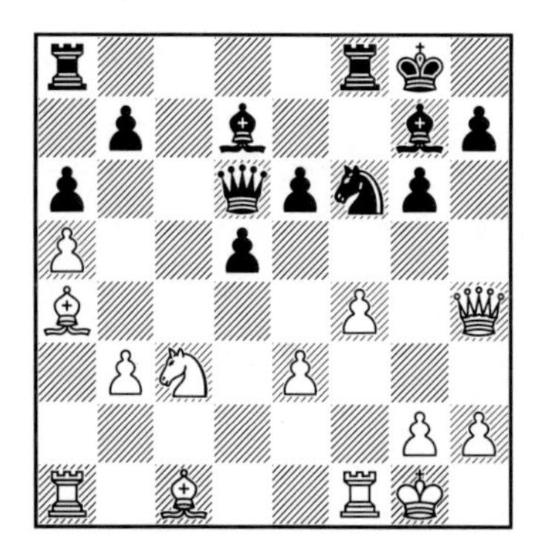

20...♕b4! (fixes the weakness of the b3 and a5 pawns) **21.♗d2 ♖ac8 22.♗xd7 ♘xd7 23.♖a4.** If 23.♘xd5, then 23...♕xd2 24.♖ad1 (or 24.♘e7+ ♔f7 25.♘xc8 ♕xe3+ and 26...♖xc8, getting two pieces for a rook) 24...♕xd5! 25.♖xd5 exd5 with equivalent material for the sacrificed queen.

23...♕xb3. An obvious move that required precise calculation. Black conducts the rest of the game decisively.

24.♖b1 ♕c2 25.♖a2 ♕d3 26.♖xb7 ♖f7. Quietly and firmly; at the same time avoiding complications that could have followed after 26...♗xc3, for example, 27.♖xd7 ♖f7 (27...♗g7 is met with 28.♕e7 with checkmate in a few moves) 28.♖xf7 ♔xf7 29.♗xc3.

27.♘a4 (for the purpose of defense, it was more correct to continue 27.♘d1) **27...d4 28.♕e1 dxe3 29.♗xe3 ♗d4! 30.♖e2?** This continuation loses quickly. White could have held on for longer with 30.♗xd4 ♕xd4+ 31.♔h1 ♕xf4 32.♖a1 ♘e5 and so on, but being under time pressure he failed to notice black's problem-like move.

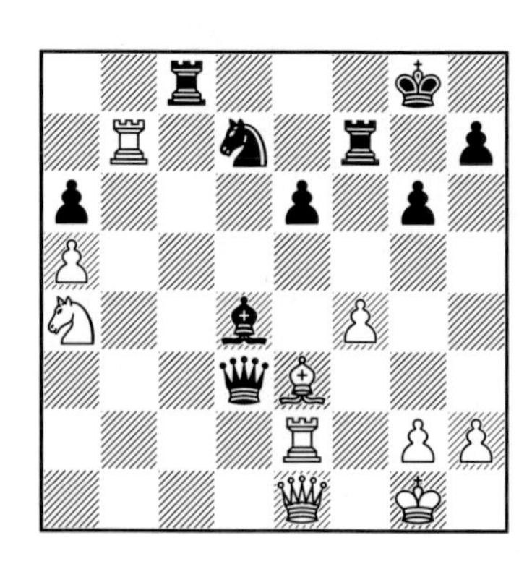

30...♖xf4 31.♖xd7. The allows black to finish the game spectacularly, however, there is no salvation at all. If, for example, 31.♘b2, then 31...

♗xe3+ 32.♖xe3 ♖f1+ 33.♕xf1 ♕xe3+ 34.♔h1 ♖c1 35.♘d1 ♕d2, with a win.

31...♕xe2!! A murderous attack that was possible due to the mating position of the white king. The continuation 31...♗xe3+ is weak in view of 32.♖xe3 ♕xd7 33.♘b6 and so on. The rest is agony for white.

32.♖d8+ ♔f7 33.♖f8+ ♔xf8 34.♕b4+ ♔g8. White resigned.

Despite a poor run-in, Arvid fulfilled his masters norm at the 1925 national championship. For the next few years, master Arvid Kubbel was one of the strongest Leningrad chess players. He usually played on one of the top boards in the traditional Leningrad – Moscow match.

On May 22 and 23, 1926, in the Leningrad – Moscow match, Arvid Kubbel scored one-and-a half points out of two against Alexander Sergeev. He won a brilliant game on the first day of the match.

Game No. 7
A. Kubbel – A. Sergeev
Moscow, 1926
Sicilian Defense B23
Commentary by A. Kubbel

1.e4 c5 2.♘c3. This leads to a closed, relatively unexplored game. 2.♘f3 and 3.d4 are still considered stronger.

2...d6 3.g3 ♘c6 4.♗g2 ♘f6. Another development system, often used by Saemisch, is also worth considering, namely 4...g6, then ♗g7, ♗d7 and ♕c8.

5.♘ge2 e6 6.0-0 a6 7.d3 ♗e7 8.h3 ♕c7 9.a4 (preventing b5, which, prior to the move ♕c7, could be refuted by a simple e5) **9...0-0 10.g4.** Simultaneously freeing up the g3 square for the knight and preparing an attack on the kingside.

10...b6 11.f4 ♗b7 12.♘g3 ♖fd8.

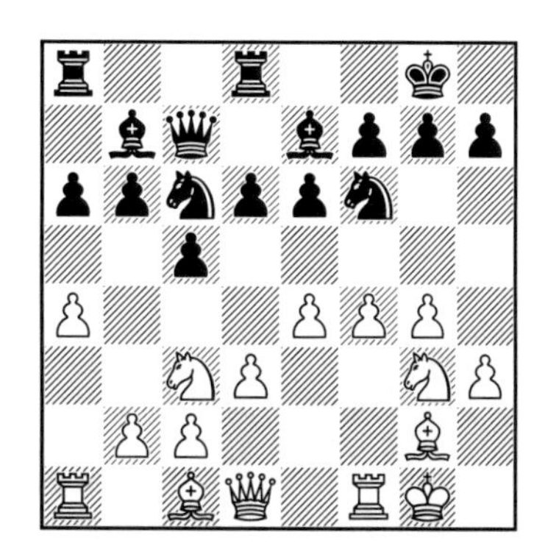

A typical situation for the Sicilian Defense: black possesses an advantage on the queenside, and white on the opposite flank. However, white has better chances in this position, since the white pawn chain advances and creates real threats to black.

13.g5 ♘e8. The best continuation here was 13...♘d7, since the knight is cramped on e8, but in that case it would be necessary to postpone the d6–d5 advance.

14.h4 ♘b4 15.♗d2 d5 16.e5 ♔h8? An incomprehensible move. The most logical continuation was 16...d4, in order to give the knight an outpost on d5 after 17.♘ce4.

17.♖c1 (to release the queen from the protection of the c2 pawn) **17...♗c6 18.b3 b5 19.axb5 axb5 20.♕e2 ♘a2?** Black fails to spot white's threat and therefore wants to occupy the a-file unchallenged. It was necessary to play 20...g6, and if 21.h5 then 21...♘g7.

21.♘xa2 ♖xa2 22.f5! (this move was overlooked by black) **22...♗d7?** This move loses very quickly. Like it or not, it was necessary to take the pawn via 22...exf5, although after 23.♖xf5, black's weak f7 square will tell.

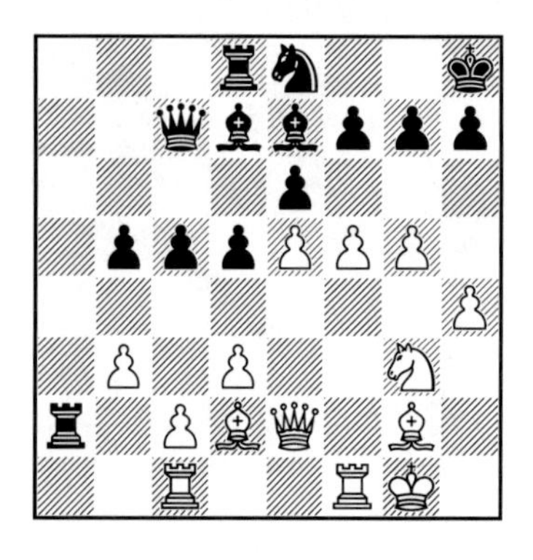

23.g6!! A fatal blow! There is no antidote to the double threat of gxf7 and ♕h5.

23...f6. Other moves don't help, for example, 23...fxg6 24.fxg6 hxg6 25.♖f7 ♗c6 (25...♗f6 26.exf6 ♕xg3 27.♖f8+ ♔h7 28.f7 with a win, or 25...♗xh4 26.♖f8+ ♔h7 27.♕g4 with inevitable checkmate) 26.h5 g5 27.♗xg5 ♖d7 28.♗xe7 ♖xe7 29.♖f8+ ♔h7 30.♕g4 g5 31.hxg6+ ♔g7 32.♖cf1, with a win.

24.♕h5. Black resigned.

In December 1926 in Leningrad, during a match between the teams of the Moscow and Leningrad Departments of the Union of Soviet Trade Workers, Arvid Kubbel beat one of the strongest chess players in Moscow at that time, Abram Poliak, on third board (in the 1925 championship of the capital, Poliak shared 5th-6th place).

Game No. 8
A. Kubbel – A. Poliak
Leningrad, 1926
Sicilian Defense B24
Commentary by A. Kubbel

1.e4 c5 2.♘c3 ♘c6 3.g3 g6. In our opinion, this continuation looks better than the 3...e6 and ...d6 system, although that is how Emanuel Lasker played against Ilyin-Zhenevsky at the Moscow International Tournament in 1925.

4.♗g2 ♗g7 5.♘ge2 d6 6.0-0 ♗d7

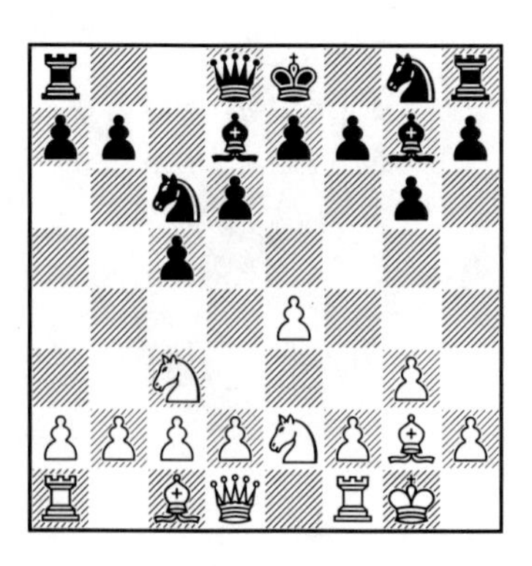

7.d3 (the continuation 7.h3 deserved consideration, so that in response to ♕c8 white could play 8.♔h2) **7...♕c8 8.♘f4 ♘f6 9.♗d2 0-0 10.♖b1 ♖b8 11.a4 ♘b4.** In order to prevent the occupation of d5 by one of the white knights.

12.b3 a6 13.f3. A kind of waiting move, which, at the same time, prepares g4.

13...e5 14.♘fe2 ♘c6. The knight has completed its task and is returning back, which could have been postponed until a more appropriate time. It would be more energetic to continue by playing 14... h5, in order to interfere with white's plan; in this case, there would be no good prospects for white.

15.g4 ♘d4 16.♘g3 h6 17.h3 ♘e6 18.♘ce2. White wants to play f4 in order to open the f-file and get a freer game.

18...g5. Completely preventing the f4 advance, but allowing the white knight to invade on f5. As a result, the next part of the game is replete with tense moments.

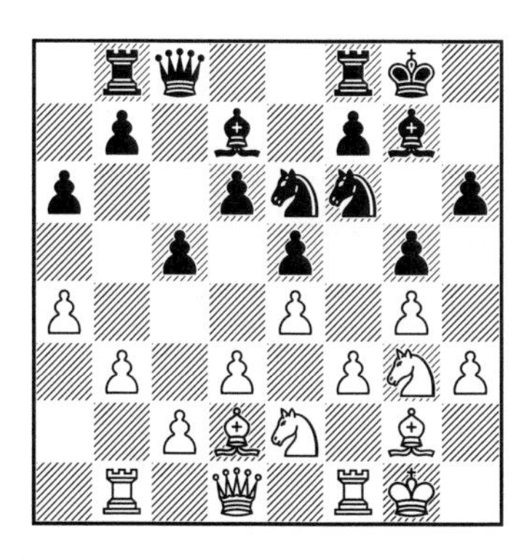

19.♘f5 ♕c7 20.h4 ♘f4 21.hxg5 hxg5 22.♘e7+. This intermediate check leads to complications, but is almost forced, because exchanging the f5 knight would destroy any chance for white to attack.

22...♔h7 (the king on h8 would have looked much worse) **23.♘xf4 exf4 24.♔f2 ♗xg4.** Instead, black could safely play 24...♗e6, after which white had no choice but to play 25.♘f5; then 25...♗xf5 26.gxf5 ♘g8 with a strong position. The move in the game plays into white's hands, and is all the worse because he retains the initiative.

25.♖h1+ ♗h6 (after 25...♗h5 white continues 26.♘f5 ♖h8 27.♗c3 [27.♗c3? ♔g6!; 27.♕g1+!= – S.G.]) **26.♘d5 ♘xd5 27.fxg4 ♘e7.** After 27...♘e3 28.♗xe3 fxe3+ 29.♔xe3 white's position, despite the opposite-colored bishops, is clearly preferable.

28.♗xf4 f6 29.♗g3 ♔g6 (if 29... ♘g6 then 30.♕f3 ♕d7 31.♖h5 ♘e5 32.♖bh1 and so on) **30.♕g1 ♖h8 31.♖h5** (this move was made after the adjournment) **31...♘c6.**

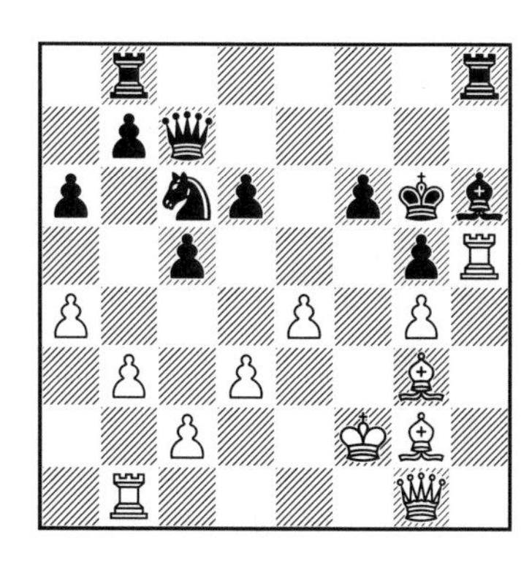

32.e5! A positional pawn sacrifice, forced due to the threat of

32...♘e5, after which the g2 bishop finds himself locked in. Now this bishop provides active and important support during the attack.

32...dxe5. Evidently, the best continuation. If, for example, 32...♘xe5, then 33.♗e4+ ♔f7 34.♗xe5 dxe5 35.♕h2 ♗g7 36.♖h1 with an excellent position for white.

33.♗e4+ ♔g7? A crucial mistake, since black will not have time to move the bishop from h6. The correct continuation was 33...♔f7 34.♗d5+ ♔e7! 35.♕h2 ♗g7 36.♖h7 ♔d6!

34.♕h2 ♕d6. Obviously, the only defense against the threats of 35.♖h1 and 35.♖xh6 ♖xh6 36.♕xh6+. If 34...♕a5, then 35.♔e3, or else 34...♘e7 35.♖h1 ♘g8 36.♗d5.

35.♖h1 f5 36.gxf5 ♖be8 37.♖e1? (37.♗xc6 ♕d4+ 38.♔g2 bxc6 39.♖e1 e4 40.dxe4 would win easily) **37...♘d8 38.♔g2 ♖hf8?** This continuation is equivalent to surrendering, since white wins two pawns by playing the ensuing combination. Black could have resisted longer by continuing 38...b5.

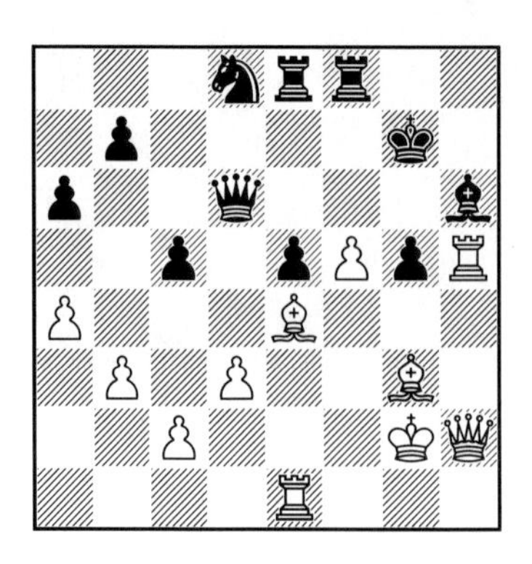

39.♖xh6! ♕xh6 40.♗xe5+ ♖xe5 41.♕xe5+ ♕f6 42.♕xc5 g4 (42...b6 was relatively better) **43.♕c7+ ♖f7 44.♕g3 ♘c6 45.♗d5!** White puts a knife to his opponent's throat. The rook can't run away because of 46.♕xg4+.

45...♘d4 46.♗xf7 ♕c6+ 47.♖e4 ♔xf7 48.c4 ♘xf5 49.♕f4. Black resigned. 49...♔f6 could have been met by 50.d4 and 51.d5.

The 1928 Leningrad championship brought together a very strong group of competitors. A. Kubbel put in an uneven performance, scoring 7.5 points out of 15 and sharing 8th-9th place. Analyzing this result in more detail, we note that he scored 2 points against the top three in the table (I. Rabinovich, Levenfish and Ravinsky). So his final standing would have been much higher had he not so generously given away points to tail-enders. Commenting on the results, the magazine *Shakhmatny listok* named the master A. Kubbel "a wizard of ingenuity". He demonstrated this feature of his play in the next game.

Game No. 9
A. Kubbel – G. Levenfish
Leningrad, 1928
Sicilian Defense B23
Commentary by A. Kubbel

1.e4 c5 2.♘c3 e6 3.g3 ♘c6 4.♗g2 ♘f6 5.♘ge2 ♗e7 6.0-0 0-0

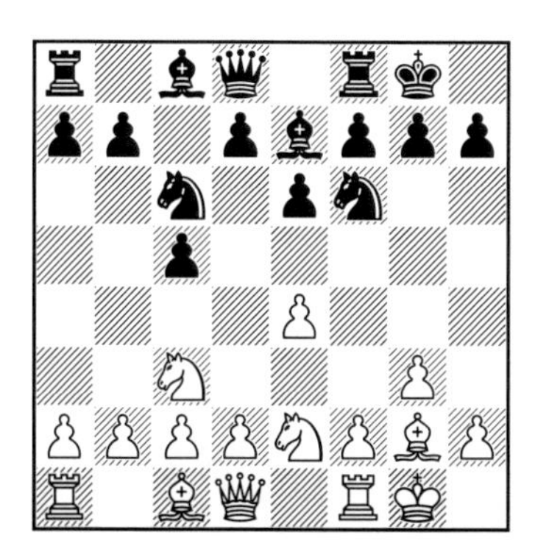

7.d3? Somewhat formulaic and cautious play. Given the following d5, white should have prevented ♗g4 via 7.h3.

7...d5. Black's whole system of development was aimed at playing this move; in our opinion, it is better than advancing through 7...d6, 8...♗d7 and 9...g6.

8.exd5 exd5 9.d4. White gives up a tempo to isolate the black pawn on d5. This is done, however, not as a principled decision, but out of necessity, since after 9.♗g5 d4 10.♗xf6 ♗xf6, black has a completely satisfactory game.

9...cxd4 10.♘xd4 ♗g4 11.f3. It is of course unpleasant for white to close the diagonal for the bishop, but, unfortunately, this is forced, since 11.♗f3 ♗xf3 12.♘xf3 d4 13.♘e2 ♗c5 brings an advantage for black.

11...♗d7 12.♔h1 ♕c8. 12...♖c8 seems more logical.

13.♗g5 h6 14.♗e3 ♘e5 15.♗g1 ♘c4 16.♕c1. As a result of bad opening play by white, black has seized the initiative, and white has to fight back with great care. For example, 16.b3 led to an immediate loss: 16...♘b2 (16...♘b2? 17.♕d2!±, it was better to play 16...♘e3! – S.G.) 17.♕d2 ♗b4 18.♘de2 ♗b5 and so on.

16...♗b4 17.♘ce2 ♗d2 18.♕d1 ♗e3 19.b3 ♗xg1 20.♖xg1 ♘e3 21.♕d3 ♖e8.

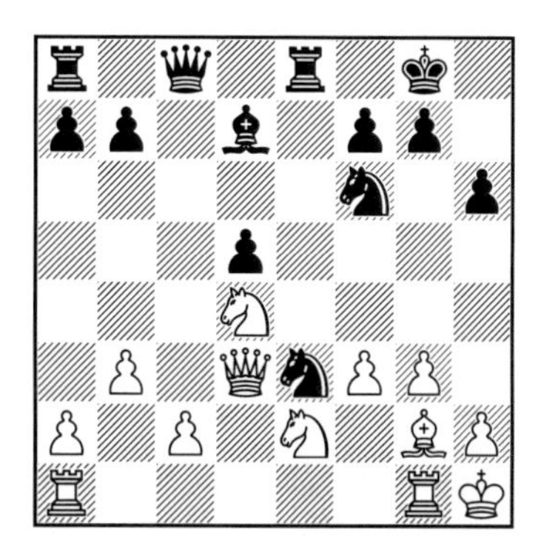

Now we can review the outcome of the entire operation initiated by black's 14th move: the occupation of the e3 square, and even then not for long.

22.♖ae1 ♖e7 23.♘c3 ♕e8 24.♖e2 ♘xg2 25.♖gxg2 ♖c8 26.a4 ♕f8 27.g4! With their last moves, both sides have fought for the c-file, the possession of which black failed to keep. Instead of developing an offensive in this part of the board, white changes his plan and aims for an attack on the kingside, while simultaneously limiting the scope of black's minor pieces.

27...♖xe2 28.♘cxe2 ♕e7 29.♕d2 ♘h7. This simple move, which prevents the g4–

g5 advance, nullifies all white's calculations.

30.♘c3? The beginning of a slow and unfortunate maneuver that worsens white's position. 30.♘f4 ♕c5 31.♖e2 was much more energetic, maintaining a positional advantage.

30...♕c5 31.♘d1 ♘g5 32.♘e3 ♖e8. Threatening 33...♘f3.

33.♖e2 ♘h3. An extremely strong outpost for the knight, which restricts white's play to a large extent.

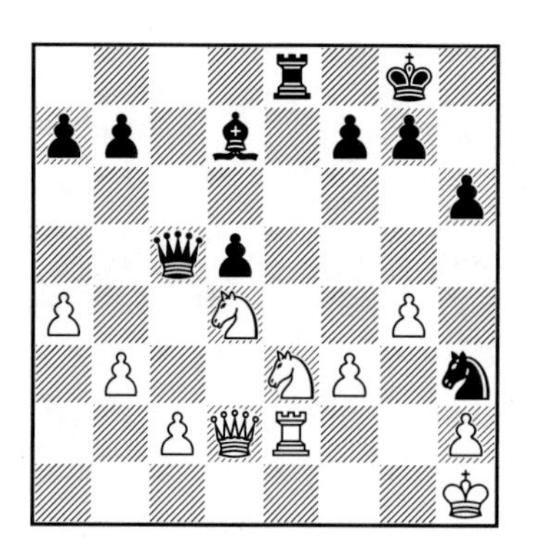

34.♖e1 ♖e5 35.♘g2 f6 36.♖d1 h5. This continuation significantly disrupts white's kingside. That said, 36...g5, preventing ♘f4 was also very strong.

37.gxh5 ♖xh5 38.♘f4. Forces the exchange of the h3 knight and thus makes it easier for white to defend.

38...♘xf4 39.♕xf4 ♕e7 40.♖g1 ♕e5 41.♕xe5? After the exchange of queens, white gets a hopeless endgame. It was necessary to play 41.♕d2, and it would have still been unclear whether black could have won due to the strong position of the d4 knight.

41...fxe5 42.♘b5 ♗f5? It was simpler and stronger to play 42...a6 immediately. The move in the game will give white a chance to draw again.

43.♖g2 ♖h6 44.♖e2. Not 44.♘xa7 due to 44...e4 45.♖g5 e3 46.♖xf5 ♖e6, with a win.

44...e4 45.♘d4 ♗h3 46.♔g1? A mistake that again hands black a winning chance. Despite the apparent danger, it was necessary to play 46.fxe4, for example 46...♖f6 47.♘f5 dxe4 48.♘g3 ♗g4 49.♖e1 ♖f2 50.♔g1 ♖xc2 51.♘xe4.

46...♖f6 47.♔f2 ♗g4 48.♖e3

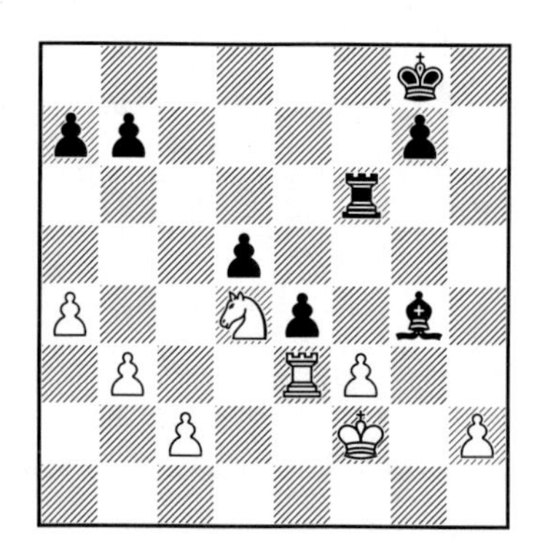

48...exf3? Under time pressure, black commits an inaccuracy that costs him an important half-point. The correct continuation was 48... ♗xf3 49.♘xf3 ♔f7 50.♔g3 ♖xf3+ 51.♖xf3+ exf3 52.♔xf3 ♔f6 53.♔f4 g5+ and the pawn ending is won for black (actually this pawn ending is a draw so black's move is not a mistake – S.G.).

49.♖e5 ♖h6 50.♔g3 ♖f6 51.♔f2 ♖h6 52.♔g3 ♖g6. In response to this move, white forces a draw in an elegant way. In any event, it would be hard for black to win this.

53.♘xf3 ♗f5+.

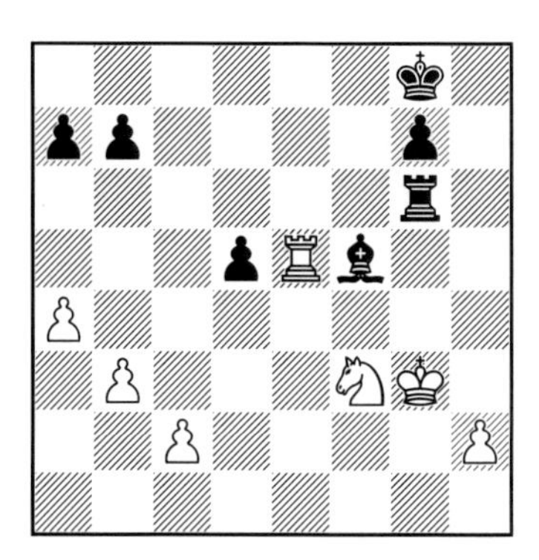

54.♘g5! An unexpected but pretty knight sacrifice due to the large number of threats: 55.♖e8#, ♖xf5 and ♖xd5. Black has to submit to his opponent's will and move to a rook endgame, and although he has an extra pawn, it's an easily achievable theoretical draw for white.

54...♖xg5+ 55.♔f4 ♖g2 56.♔xf5 ♖xh2 57.♖e7 ♖f2+ 58.♔g6 ♖f6+ 59.♔g5 ♖f7 60.♖e8+ ♔h7 61.♖d8 ♖c7 62.♖xd5 ♖xc2 63.♖d7 b6 64.♖xa7 ♖c5+ 65.♔g4 ♖c3 66.a5. Draw agreed.

Arvid Kubbel finished his game against Grigory Ravinsky with an elegant combination.

Game No. 10
G. Ravinsky – A. Kubbel
Leningrad Championship, 1928
Commentary by S. Grodzensky

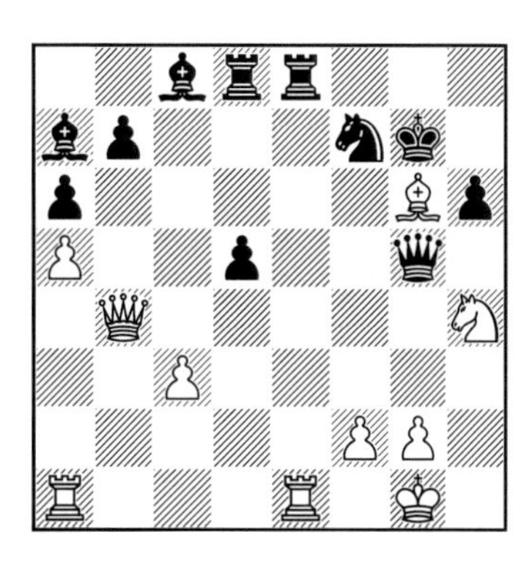

Black to move

There followed **33...♘e5! 34.♗xe8 ♗xf2+!** This sacrifice, possible due to the withdrawal of the bishop from the b1-h7 diagonal, ensures white's defeat. Not 35.♔xf2 due to 35...♘d3+.

35.♔f1 ♗xe1 (35...♗xh4 also won) **36.♖xe1 ♖xe8 37.♕d4.** The obvious move 37.♘f3? would not help due to 37...♕f6 38.♕d4 ♗h3! 39.♖xe5 ♕xf3+ 40.♔e1 ♕g3+.

37...♗g4 38.♔g1 ♔h7 39.g3 (if 39.♕f2, then 39...♗f3 with a win) **39...♗f3.** White resigned.

Kubbel chose not to participate in the final of the 1929 city championship, but he played several interesting games at the preliminary stage; in the next one, he played against the future grandmaster and world correspondence champion.

Game No. 11
A. Kubbel – V. Ragozin
Leningrad, 1929
Sicilian Defense B24
Commentary by A. Kubbel

1.e4 c5 2.♘c3 ♘c6 3.g3 d6 4.♗g2 f5?

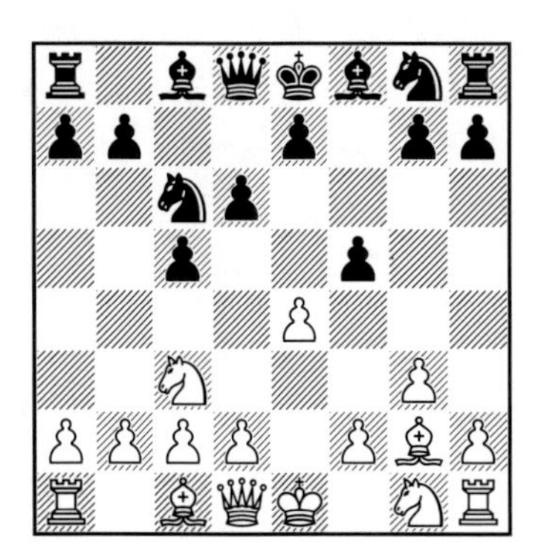

A novelty of dubious merit. Its disadvantage is mainly that the g2 bishop, which usually remains locked out of action in whatever variation is chosen by white, here owns the h1-a8 diagonal with good prospects.

5.♘ge2 ♘f6. It is clear that 5...fxe4 or 5...e5 also have their own disadvantages. In the first case, after 6.♘xe4 e5 7.d3 d5 8.♘4c3 ♗e6 black gets a "hanging center", while the second option prevents d4, but gives white the d5 square. Still, the last continuation was probably the lesser evil.

6.d4. White turns play into an open game, which in these conditions is advantageous for him due to the rapid development of his pieces.

6...cxd4 7.♘xd4 ♘xd4 8.♕xd4 e5 9.♕d3! 9.♕c4, which would prevent black from castling, seemed more obvious. However, the move in the text creates combinational complications, which, thanks to accurate play, give white a well-deserved victory.

9...♗e7. In order to castle, black is willing to sacrifice a pawn. Besides, the white pawn on f5 looks weak and it seems possible to win it back in the near future. This calculation, however, is incorrect, as the further course of the game will show.

10.exf5 0-0

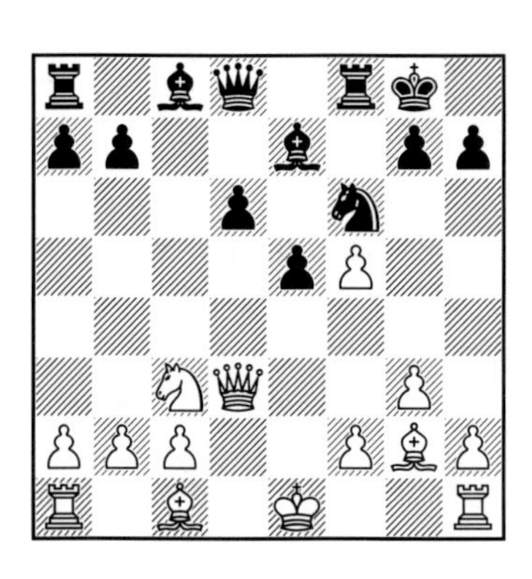

11.g4! The first subtlety! The pawn cannot be captured because of 12.♕c4+.

11...e4! Still the best chance, although it is insufficient to equalize. 11...h5 can be repelled by the simple 12.h3.

12.♗xe4 ♘xg4 13.♖g1 ♘e5 (if 13...h5, then 14.h3 ♘e5 15.♕g3 g6 16.♗f4 ♗h4 17.♕g2! ♗xf5 18.♗xe5, with a win) **14.♕g3 g6.** The continuation 14...♗f6 15.♗h6 ♕d7

16.♘d5! and so on was absolutely hopeless.

15.fxg6 hxg6.

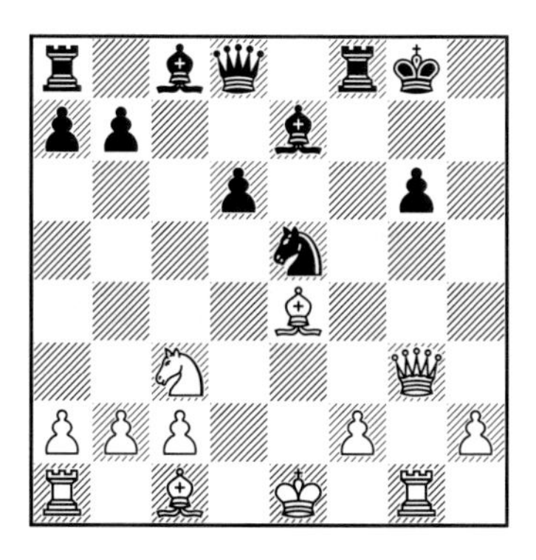

16.♗d5+! The continuation 16.♗xg6 would have been a mistake. In this case black would have chosen not 16...♗h4? in view of 17.♗h7+! ♔f7 18.♕g7+ ♔e6 19.♗g8+!, but 16...♗g4! with unpleasant threats of ♗h4 or ♘f3+.

16...♔h7? More stubborn resistance could be provided by black via 16...♔g7, for example, 17.♗f4 ♗f5 18.0-0-0 (not 18.♗xe5+ dxe5 19.♕xe5+ ♗f6 and the capture of the f5 bishop is impossible due to 20...♗xc3+) 18...♗h4 19.♗xe5+ dxe5 20.♕xe5+ ♕f6! 21.♕c7+ ♔h8. Therefore, white should play 19.♕g2!, after which black's situation is still difficult, but 19...♕f6 fends off the direct threats 20.♗xe5+ and ♗e6.

17.♕e3! Again, the strongest move. In response to 17.h4, black could play 17...♘g4.

17...g5. Black is forced to close the diagonal for his e7 bishop, and this is the beginning of the end, since he has no chances of counterplay left.

18.♗d2! Before proceeding to decisive operations against black's broken kingside, it is necessary to get the king to a safe place by long castling. Black cannot prevent such an intention; if, for example, 18...♘g4 (18...♗g4? 19.♖xg4!), then 19.♕h3+ ♘h6 20.♗e4+ ♗f5 (20...♔g7 21.♕h5) 21.0-0-0 and so on.

18...♗f5 19.0-0-0 ♖c8. 19...♕d7 and then ♖ae8 was somewhat better. Black does not have time to create pressure along the c-file.

20.f4! White finishes off his opponent energetically and without unnecessary hiccups.

20...♘g4. A magnificent finale could have been played after 20...♘c4, namely 21.♕e2 ♘xd2 22.♕h5+ ♔g7 23.fxg5! – and only big material losses would save black from early checkmate.

21.♕e2 ♕d7 22.h3 ♘f6 23.♖xg5. Definitely not 23.fxg5? in view of 23...♘xd5.

23...♔h6 (♖h5+ was threatened) **24.♖dg1 b5 25.♖xf5.** The simplest variation. The continuation 25.♕e1 ♘h5 and then 26.♖xf5 ♕xf5 (26...♖xf5 27.♗e6) 27.♗e4 also won.

25...♕xf5 26.♕xe7. Black resigned.

The brothers Arvid and Leonid Kubbel met in the preliminary group of the Leningrad Championship in

1929. In over-the-board play, Arvid appeared to be much stronger

Game No. 12
A. Kubbel – L. Kubbel
Leningrad, 1929
Four Knights Opening C49
Commentary by S. Grodzensky

1.e4 e5 2.♘f3 ♘c6 3.♘c3 ♘f6 4.♗b5 ♗b4 5.0-0 0-0 6.d3 ♗xc3 7.bxc3

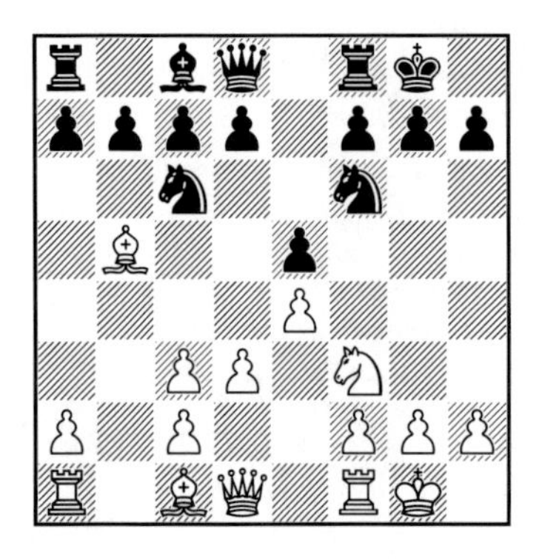

7...d5. The continuation 7...d6 8.♗xc6 bxc6 9.♖b1 c5 10.c4 h6 leads to an equal position. With the move 7...d5, black begins the so-called Svenonius Attack, which leads to a double-edged struggle with slightly better chances for white.

8.♗xc6. The variation 8.exd5 ♕xd5 9.c4 (9.♗c4 ♕a5 10.♖b1 a6 11.♖e1 b6 12.♕e2 ♗g4 13.♗g5 e4! is weaker) 9...♕d6 10.♗xc6 bxc6 11.♗b2 ♖e8 12.♕e1! is considered the strongest.

8...bxc6 9.♘xe5 ♕d6 10.♗f4 ♖e8 11.exd5 ♖xe5 12.d4 ♖e1 13.♗xd6 ♖xd1 14.♖fxd1 cxd6 15.dxc6

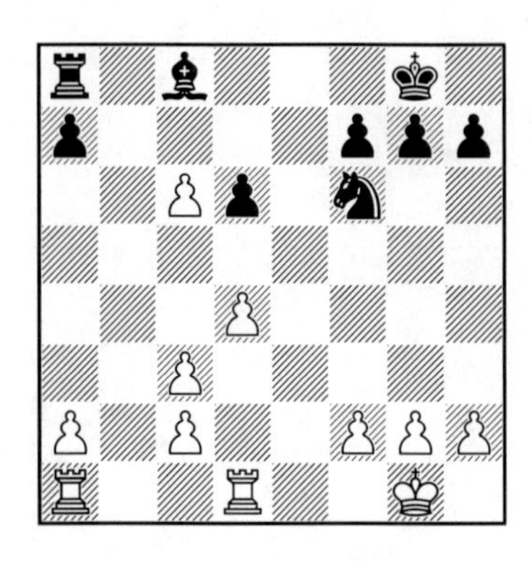

15...♔f8? It was necessary to continue by playing 15...♗e6, although in this case, according to analysis by Paul Keres, after 16.♖ab1 ♖c8 17.♖b7! white keeps the best chances in the endgame.

16.d5, and white achieved a strategically won position.

In the same year, master Arvid Kubbel received an invitation to the Soviet Championship, but declined to play in it. Perhaps the reason for his refusal was the realization that it would be difficult to count on a high score. Arvid's sharp, risk-taking playing style brought him some pretty victories, but sometimes led to disappointments. On occasions, Arvid Ivanovich tried to squeeze more out of the position than was possible, with unfortunate consequences.

His performance in the Leningrad masters tournament of 1933 was characteristic – 5 wins out of 13 games and no draws, Starting with three defeats, he then won four fairly ordinary victories, then another five losses, and only after did he achieve a victory in the final round. At the same time, the list of those he defeated was impressive: Ilyin-Zhenevsky, Grigoriev, Sozin, Nenarokov and Model.

In 1934, Arvid became one of the finalists of the championship of the RSFSR (Soviet Russia). Twenty players were divided into two preliminary groups, and the three winners of each progressed to the final stage. Arvid Kubbel finished fourth in his group.

At the board, he sometimes demonstrated a composer's fine technique. And, by contrast, the best of his compositions – especially studies – showed not only the genius of a composer, but also the experience of a chess master.

Arvid Kubbel's work as a composer is no less interesting than his over-the-board games. In total, he created over 700 problems of different genres and several dozen studies. In pre-revolutionary years, Kubbel published many works on the pages of various periodicals, and played a significant role in popularizing study composition in Russia. After 1917, he continued composing, at the same time working at the magazine *Shakhmatny listok*, and later at *Shakhmaty v SSSR*.

Responding to the request of the editors of the *Zadachi i etyudy* books to give them his best works, Arvid Ivanovich chose several, including two-movers.

In his early period he tried to emulate the Czech School, and model mates in particular. Later, he took more of a liking for the combinational school, but more focusing on overall harmony than creating records in expressing that idea. The following two-mover is characteristic of that focus.

Composition No. 54
64
1925, 1st honorable mention

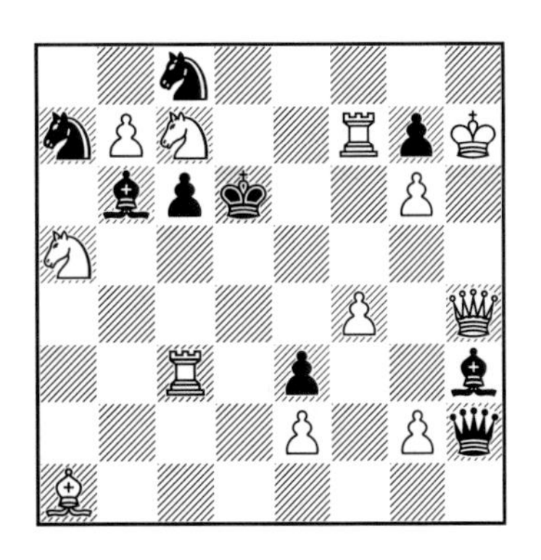

White to mate in 2 moves

1.f5! Zugzwang. 1...♗c5 2.♘c4#, 1...c5 2.♖d3#, 1...♕e5 2.♕d8#, 1...♗~ 2.♕xh2#.

Arvid Kubbel's single biggest theme was nevertheless the three-mover. Here his style was most clearly manifested. From the very beginning, he joined the artistic school and remained faithful to its principles until the end. Usually, there are a number of model mates in his problems. The final net is skillfully spread all across the board, most often with the participation of white pawns, but at the same time material is limited.

Arvid Ivanovich, creating his works, would imagine the future solver in front of him. The artistic content of his problems included not only model mate pictures, but also other elements characteristic of difficult problems. It is all about a magnificent first move that is hard to find, white's quiet moves as part of the solution along the way, piece sacrifices and false tries. It is difficult to select the best among the hundreds of three-movers created by Arvid. But here we focus on those that, in our opinion, are most characteristic of his style.

Composition No. 55
Shakhmaty
1924, 2nd prize

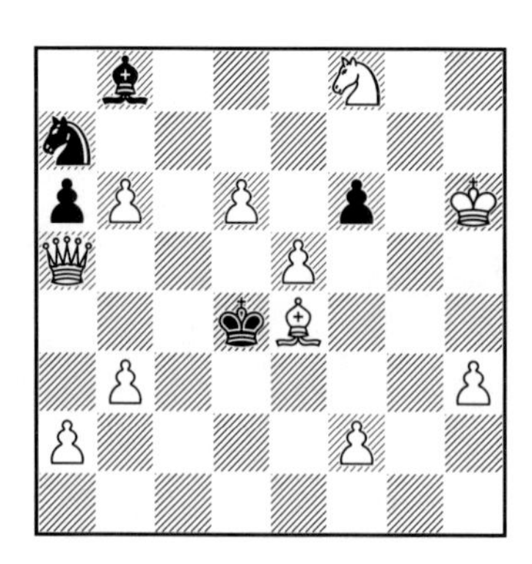

White to mate in 3 moves

1.♕e1! Threatening 2.♘d7, 1...♔xe5 2.f4+ ♔xf4 3.♘g6# 2...♔xd6 3.♕b4#, 2...♔d4 3.♘e6#, 1...♔c5 2.♘d7+ ♔b5 3.a4#, 1...♗xd6 2.♕e3+ ♔xe5 3.f4#

Composition No. 56
Shakhmaty v SSSR
1934, 1st prize

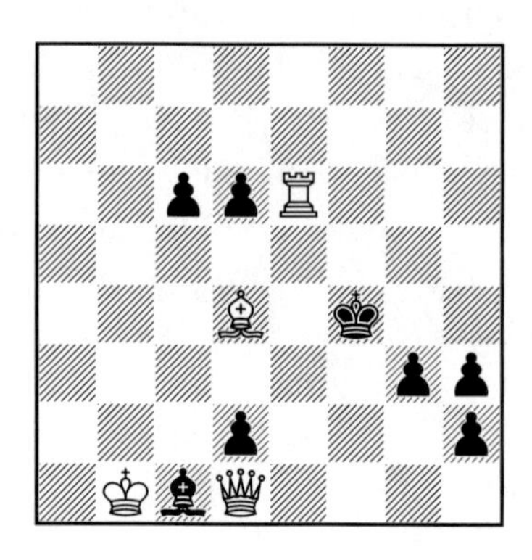

White to mate in 3 moves

1.♖h6! threatening 2.♖h4+. The main variation here is 1...♔f5 2.♕f3+ ♔g5 3.♗e3#

Composition No. 57
Neue Leipziger Zeitung
1933

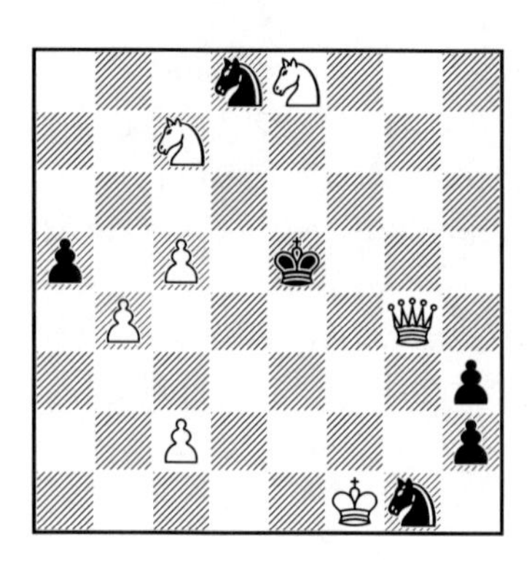

White to mate in 3 moves

1.♘d6! Threatening 2.♕g5+, 1...♔f6 2.♘d5+ ♔e5 3.♕e4#, 1...♘e6 2.♕g3+ ♔d4 3.c3#, 1...♘f7 2.♘c4+ ♔f6 3.♘d5#, 1...♘f3 2.♕g7+ ♔f4 3.♘d5#.

The most interesting variations are those that end with model mates, blocking squares next to the black king.

Composition No. 58
Neue Leipziger Zeitung
1929, 2nd prize

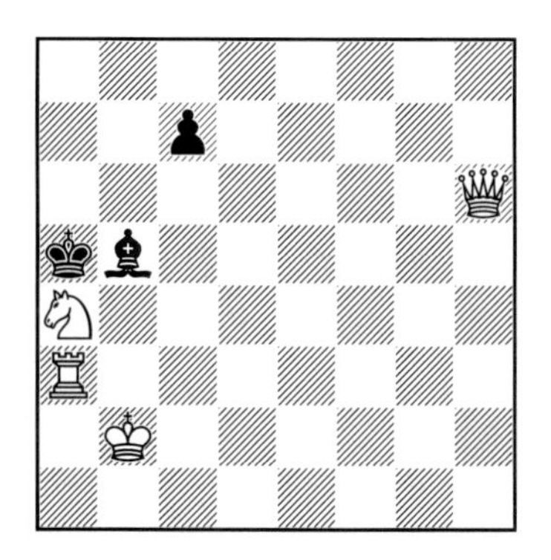

White to mate in 3 moves

1.♕e3! With the threat of 2.♘c3+ ♗a4 3.♖xa4#, 1...♔a6 2.♕b6+ cxb6 3.♘c5#, 1...♗xa4 2.♕b3 ♔a6 3.♖xa4#, 1...c5 2.♕xc5 ♔a6 3.♕b6#.

In this miniature, the main combinational variation with the sacrifice of the white queen, ending with the model mate, is especially beautiful.

Composition No. 59
Shakhmaty
1923, 2nd prize

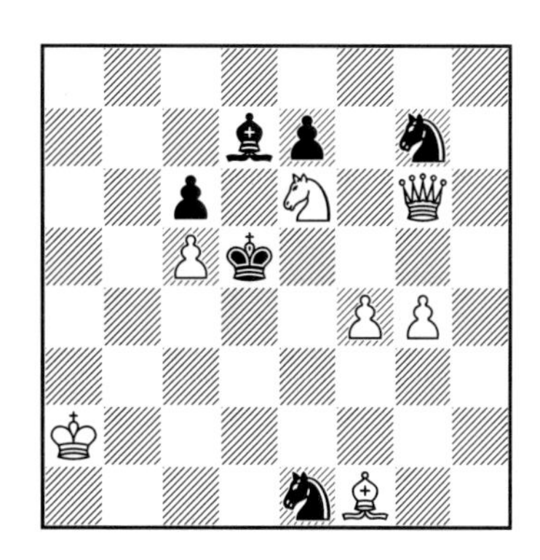

White to mate in 3 moves

1.♕b1! Threatening 2.♗c4+! ♔xc4 3.♕b3#, 1...♗xe6 2.♕b4 and 3.♕c4#, 1...♘xe6 2.♕f5+ ♔d4 3.♕e5#, 1...♔xe6 2.♗c4+ ♔f6 3.g5#.

Composition No. 60
Shakhmaty
1923, 3rd prize

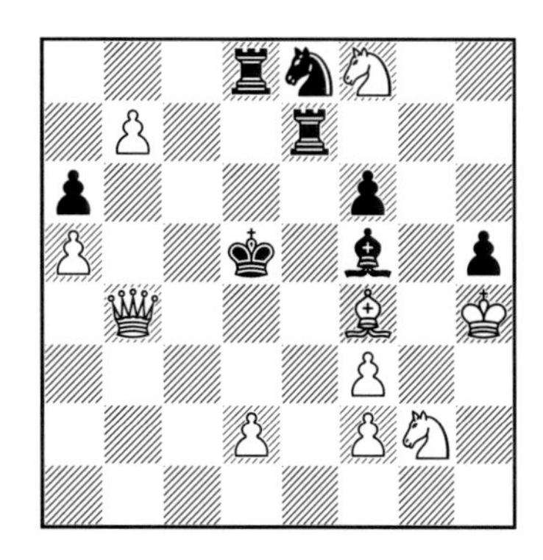

White to mate in 3 moves

1.♗e5! ♔xe5 2.♕c5+, 1...♔c6 2.♘f4, 1...fxe5 2.♘e3+, 1...♗e4 2.fxe4+

Composition No. 61
Shakhmaty
1925, 2nd honorable mention

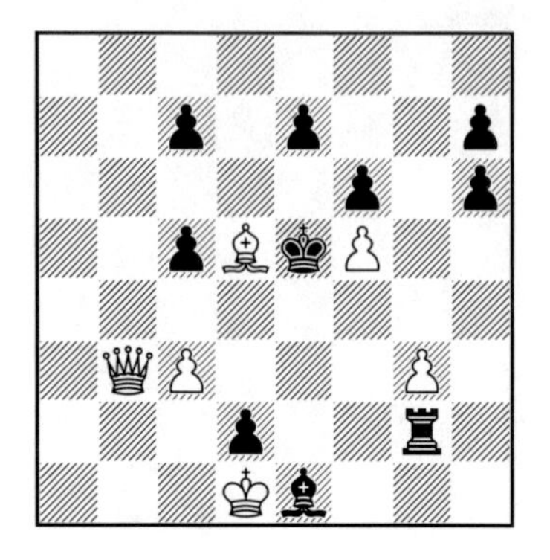

White to mate in 3 moves

1.♕c4! With the threat of 2.♕e4+, 1...♖e2 2.♕xe2+, 1...♔d6 2.♗e6, 1...♔xf5 2.♕f4+, 1...c6 2.♕f4+.

Composition No. 62
La Strategie
1909-1910, 3rd prize

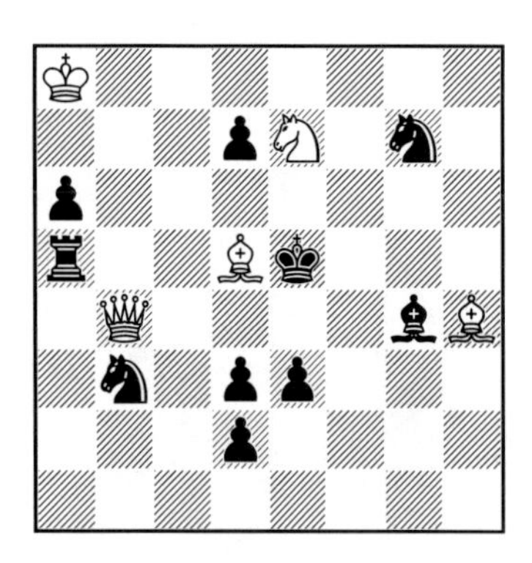

White to mate in 3 moves

This three-mover brought Arvid Kubbel his first great success.

1.♕c4! ♖a4 2.♘g6+ (with a threat) 2...♔f5 3.♗e4#, 1...♘c5 2.♕d4+! ♔xd4 3.♗f6#, 1...♘f5 2.♕f4+! ♔xf4 3.♘g6#.

The threat and both queen sacrifices after blocking the squares end in model mates. Another such finale takes place after the barely noticeable involvement of the queen: 1...♗~ 2.♗g3+ ♔f6 3.♕h4#

Composition No. 63
Shakhmaty
1923

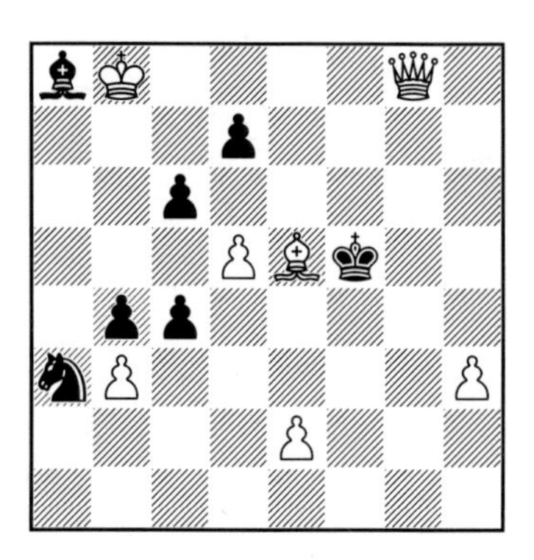

White to mate in 4 moves

1.♗d6! ♔f6 2.e4 cxd5 3.e5+, 1...cxb3 2.♕f7+ ♔e4 3.♕f3+, 2... ♔g5 3.♗f4+, 1...c5 2.h4! ♔f6 3.h5!, 2...♗xd5 3.♕g5+. The idea of this combination is to achieve a model mate. The continuation 1.♗g7? ♔f4! 2.♗d4 ♔e4! is a false try.

The following composition was his first published study.

Composition No. 64
Rigaer Tageblatt
1905

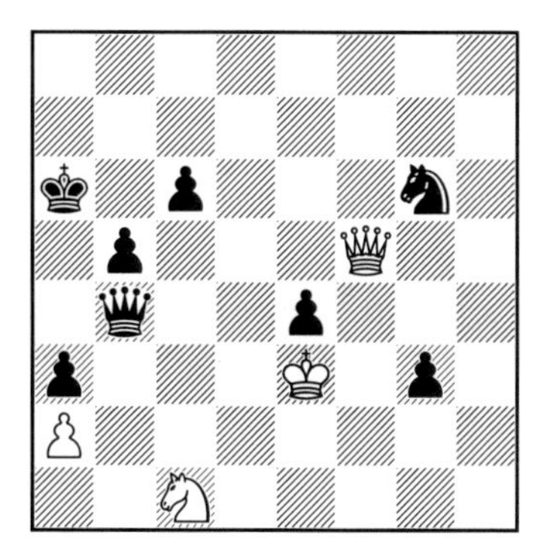

White to move and draw

1.♕c8+! ♔b6 2.♕b8+ ♔c5 3.♘d3+! exd3 4.♕e5+!! ♘xe5. A stalemate.

In total, Arvid Kubbel created around thirty studies, mainly on the theme of catching the black queen with white pieces. In his best works, you can sense not only the intelligence of the composer, but also the experience of a skillful player.

Composition No. 65
Zadachi i etyudy
1927

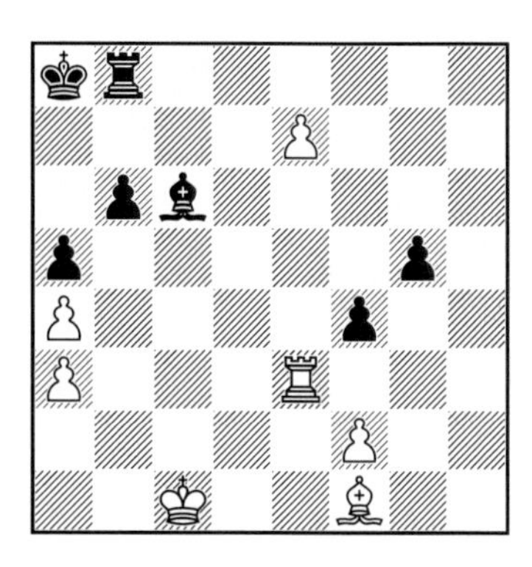

White to move and win

The variation 1.♗g2? ♗xg2 2.e8=♕ fxe3 3.♕xe3 g4 doesn't help, and there is no obvious way to win. The continuations **1.e8=♕! ♖xe8 2.♗g2! ♖c8** (2...fxe3 3.♗xc6+ ♔b8 4.♗xe8 exf2 5.♗b5 ♔c7 6.♔d2) **3.♖e8!** or 1...♗xe8 2.♗g2+ ♔a7 3.♖e7+ ♔a6 4.♗f1+ b5 5.♖xe8 ♖xe8 6.♗xb5+ decide the outcome of the game.

And yet, perhaps his best study was the following one.

Composition No. 66
Shakhmatny listok
1925, 1st-2nd prize

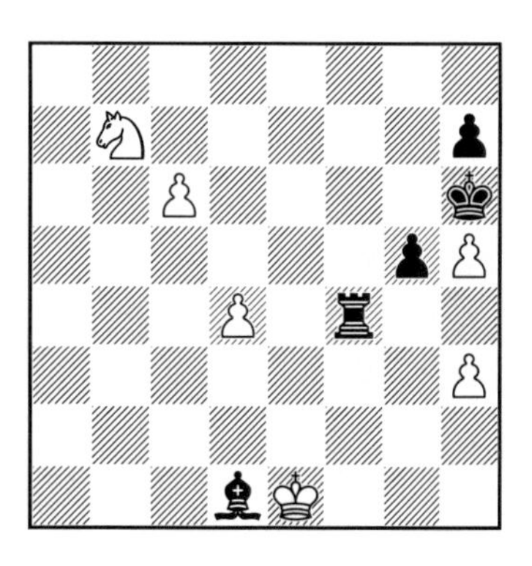

White to move and win

1.c7! ♖e4+ 2.♔d2! This is the only possible continuation! 2.♔f2?! ♖e8 3.♘d8 (or 3.♘d6 ♖f8+ 4.♔g3 ♔xh5 5.c8=♕ ♖xc8 6.♘xc8 and a draw) 3...♖e2+ 4.♔g3 ♖c2 5.♘e6 ♖c3+! 6.♔f2 ♗c2, and black should win. 2.♔f1?! ♖e8 3.♘d8 ♗e2+ 4.♔g2 ♗a6, and black wins.

2...♖xd4+ 3.♔c3 ♗g4!? (the most resilient) **4.hxg4** (4.♔xd4 ♗xh3, and it's time for white to think about a draw) **4...♖d7**

5.♘d6! 5.c8=♕? ♖c7+ 6.♕xc7 and stalemate. **5...♖xc7+ 6.♔b4** and **7.♘f5#**, or 6...♔g7 7.♘e8+, winning.

The judges of the contest were Leonid Kubbel and grandmaster Grigory Levenfish, who provided the following assessment: "This is one of those rare studies where the center of gravity is located in black's play, which makes it very difficult to solve. An unexpected and deeply conceived combination by black meets an equally subtle response from white. The final position with the active participation of the white king is most pretty."

In the 1930s, Arvid Kubbel ran a chess circle at the First Five-Year Plan Central City Club in Leningrad. His pupils recalled his highly cultured manners and fanatical devotion to chess. There is not much information about his last tournament performances. In May 1935, he took fourth place in an exhibition tournament of the Volodarsky district of Leningrad. In April 1936, he participated in an All-Union qualifier for the Soviet Championship. As always, his play was uncompromising, however, he scored only 6 points out of 14.

In summer 1937, he didn't participate in the match against

The Black Raven was the nickname of the GAZ M-1 automobile, supplied to the NKVD as well as other government ministries in the 1930s.

Moscow, and a few months later they came for him... Late in the evening of November 21, 1937, the car known as the "Black Raven" stopped at his house. Suddenly, the doorbell rang, and three people entered the building. Kubbel's home was searched, but this did not uncover any results, and Arvid Ivanovich was taken away. No one in his family ever saw him again...

Why was a modest functionary incriminated, one who at the time of his arrest was working as an accountant at the Spartak Voluntary Sports Society, a person far removed from politics? According to the late Professor Lev Evgenievich Kubbel (Arvid's nephew), his uncle's misdemeanor was publishing several problems in the German magazine *Die Schwalbe*, when such actions were already punishable. Lev Evgenievich told the author that the more prudent Leonid Kubbel had managed to withdraw his compositions from *Die Schwalbe* in good time.

Indeed, in one of the vicious articles in the magazine *Shakhmaty v SSSR* of those years, Arvid Kubbel was listed among composers who sent their works to foreign publications without the permission of the leadership of the chess federation.

However, was it really necessary to commit a real offense in order to be arrested under Article 58? Perhaps the local authorities failed to fulfill their "quota" of eliminated counter-revolutionaries, or maybe a false denunciation by a chess opponent whose mood Master Arvid Kubbel had spoiled played a role?

Arvid Ivanovich's wife learned just a few words about her husband's fate from the judicial authorities in January 1938: "He has been sentenced under Article 58 to ten years in prison in the Russian Far East, without right of correspondence".

The certificate of Kubbel's posthumous rehabilitation, dated June 11, 1958, reads as follows: "The resolution of 03.01.38 in respect of Arvid Ivanovich Kubbel is annulled and the case is terminated due to an absence of crime. Kubbel A. I. is posthumously rehabilitated".

The date of Arvid Ivanovich's death was only confirmed in later years. The Soviet-era *Chess Dictionary* indicated the year 1941, and his relatives received a message in response to their request that he died on December 12, 1943 from acute nephritis. However, it was clear that both dates were false. It was logical for Arvid Ivanovich's life to be cut short at the very beginning of 1938, immediately after sentencing. Now we know the ominous meaning of the words "sentenced to ten years without the right of correspondence" – the standard response of the authorities to queries instead of confirming a person's execution, which has now become a euphemism.

The truth was uncovered once the prosecutor's archive was made available to the public and they

Форма № 30

Военная Коллегия
Верховного Суда
Союза ССР

„11“ июня 1958 г.

№ 4н-02987/57

Москва, ул. Воровского, д. 15.

С П Р А В К А

Дело по обвинению КУББЕЛЬ Арвида Ивановича работавшего до ареста бухгалтером Спортивного общества "Спартак" ~~Кингисеппского района~~ Ленинградской ~~области~~, пересмотрено Военной коллегией Верховного Суда СССР 22 августа 1957 года.

Постановление от 3 января 1938 года в отношении КУББЕЛЬ А.И. отменено и дело за отсутствием состава преступления прекращено.

КУББЕЛЬ А.И. реабилитирован посмертно.

НАЧАЛЬНИК СЕКРЕТАРИАТА ВОЕННОЙ КОЛЛЕГИИ
ВЕРХОВНОГО СУДА СОЮЗА ССР
ПОДПОЛКОВНИК ЮСТИЦИИ

(И.ПОЛЮЦКИЙ)

аб

could read Arvid Kubbel's file. The information in it stated that he was incriminated in the Miller (Muller) group case – Miller was the deputy prosecutor in the town of Kingisepp of the Leningrad Region. The group included 45 people with German-sounding surnames. They were all charged with treason (Article 58-1a) and sabotage (Article 58-9). They were all sentenced to death on January 3 and the sentence was carried out on January 11. Twenty years later, all the accused were rehabilitated posthumously...

The fate of Arvid Ivanovich's family was sad, too. In January 1938, his wife Elizaveta Adamovna, who did not yet know that she had become a widow, was exiled to the Chkalovsky region together with her young daughter Renata. From November 1942, she worked hard on the labor front, digging trenches as best she could, sparing no effort to bring Victory closer. But soon after the end of the war, in 1946, she was sent even further – to the town of Kazalinsk (now Kazaly) in the Kyzyl-Orda region of Kazakhstan. And only in 1969, shortly before her death (Elizaveta Adamovna died in 1971), was the widow of Arvid Kubbel able to return to Leningrad.

In 1989, the Leningrad Composition Commission organized an international competition for composers of three-movers, dedicated to the 100th anniversary of the birth of A. I. Kubbel. At the same time, an All-Union correspondence tournament, the Arvid Kubbel Memorial, was organized by the author of this book.

Mikhail Platov – Co-Author of "A Beautiful Thing"

During the Soviet era, the following study was published in the press just about more often than any other chess composition (and not only in the chess press, but for example, in tear-off calendars as well).

Composition No. 67
V. and M. Platov
Rigaer Tageblatt
1909, 1st prize

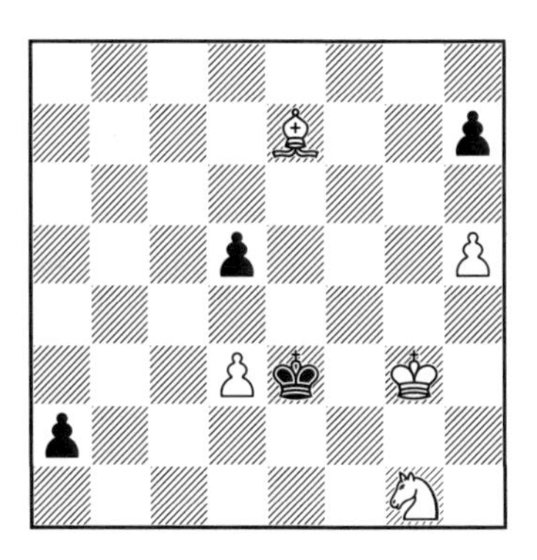

White to move and win

1.♗f6 d4 2.♘e2!! 2.♘f3 leads to a draw after 2...a1=♕ 3.♗xd4+ ♕xd4 4.♘xd4 ♔xd4. **2...a1=♕ 3.♘c1!! ♕a5.** 3...♕xc1 4.♗g5+, with a win. **4.♗xd4+! ♔xd4 5.♘b3+**, winning.

The reason for the huge popularity of the work, which was awarded first prize at a competition held by a Riga newspaper, was not only its undoubted artistic merits. It happened that on February 1, 1910, this study was reprinted by the St. Petersburg newspaper *Rech*, and here it caught the eye of Vladimir Lenin himself. In his letter to his brother Dmitry Ulyanov, dated February 17, 1910, he notes that he gained aesthetic pleasure from the solution. "A beautiful thing!" – this is how Lenin reacted to the composition by the Platov brothers, which became a part of chess "Leniniana" – the study of Lenin in popular culture.

The career of one of the brothers,

Vasily Nikolaevich Platov (1881-1952), was relatively successful. After retiring from creativity in the late 1920s, he worked as an editor of chess columns and judged composition competitions. His work in healthcare was marked by government awards, the honorable title "Distinguished Doctor of the RSFSR" and an academic degree of Candidate of Medical Sciences.

For some reason, the name of Mikhail Nikolaevich Platov got to be mentioned in muted form, only in relation to the "beautiful thing" and when a general assessment of the joint creative work of the Platov brothers was raised. Chess composition veterans with whom the author had a chance to talk recalled that in 1937 there was a rumor that Mikhail Platov had been arrested. However, that was a time when asking questions had become very dangerous. It was only clear that since then no one had seen or heard anything about M. N. Platov.

In books on compositions published up to the mid 1970s, the dates of his life were not included. Only in the monograph by composition grandmaster Genrikh Kasparyan *555 Miniature Studies*, published in 1975, was the year of his death eventually reported – 1937.

In response to the author's request, Genrikh Moiseevich Kasparyan wrote: "I learned about the year of Mikhail Platov's death, as far as I remember, from some article where 1937 was indicated as the year of arrest and presumably the year of his death."

Platov was born in Riga in 1883 in the family of a trader, Nikolai Mikhailovich Platov. After graduating from the local grammar school, he started at the Riga Polytechnic Institute and qualified as a production engineer. Mikhail Platov began composing studies at the same time as his older brother Vasily, probably in 1899. And the first works of the Platov brothers appeared in the Riga newspaper *Rigaer Tageblatt* four years later. Here is one of the first studies by Mikhail Platov.

Composition No. 68
Rigaer Tageblatt
1903

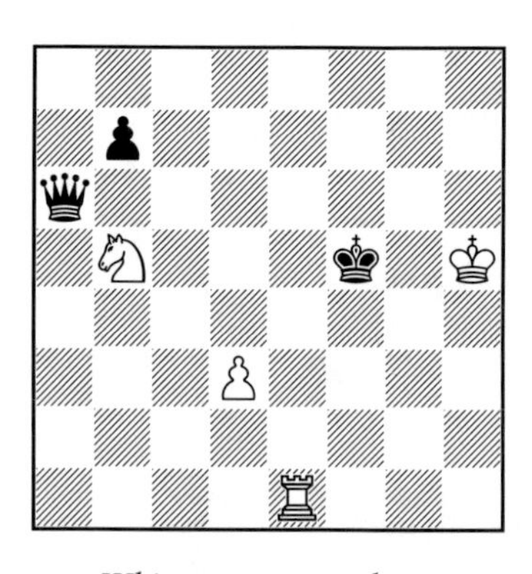

White to move and win

1.♖f1+ ♔e5 2.♔g5. The black queen has several moves at her disposal that parry the threatening 3.♖f5+ ♔e6 4.♖f6+ winning. 2... ♕a2 (or 2...♕a4) 3.♖e1+ ♔d5 4.♘c3+, winning; 2...♕a5 (or 2... ♕c6) 3.♖f5+ ♔e6 4.♘d4+, winning.

Composition No. 69
Rigaer Tageblatt
1903

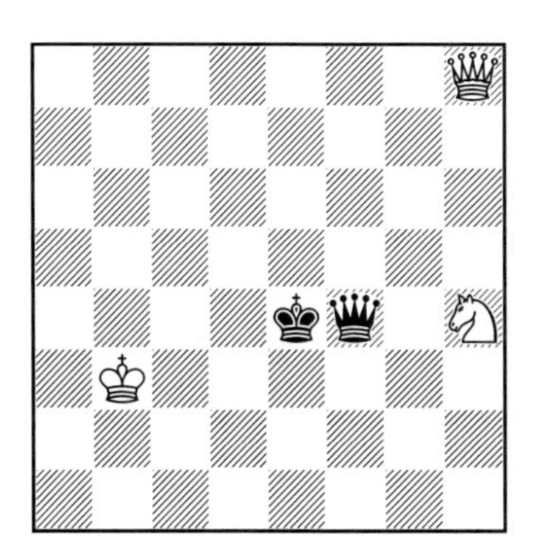

White to move and win

1.♕a8+! ♔d3. 1...♔d4 2.♕a4+, and the black king moves to one of the squares that is ruinous for him: 2...♔e5 3.♘g6+ or 2...♔e3 ♘g2+.

2.♕a6+ ♔d2 (2...♔e4 3.♕c4+) **3.♕a2+ ♔d3** (3...♔d1 4.♕c2+ ♔e1 5.♘g2+) **4.♕c2+ ♔d4 5.♕c4+ ♔e5.** 5...♔e3 6.♘g2+, winning.

1.♗d7! There are several main variations in this study. **1...♕b6 2.♘f6+ ♔xe5 3.♘g4+ ♔d5 4.♘e3+!** The continuation 4.♔f4?, threatening 5.♘f6# would be a mistake due to 4...g5+!, and not 5.♔f5?? since after 5...♕f2+! black wins. **4...♕xe3+** 4...♔e5 5.♘xc4+, winning.

5.♔xe3 f5 6.♗c8 ♔c6 7.♔f3 d5 8.♗b7+ ♔d6 9.b5 ♔c5 10.♗xd5 g2 11.♔xg2 ♔xd5 12.b6, with a win.

1...♕xd7 2.♘f6+ ♔e6 3.♘xd7 ♔xd7 4.b5 ♔c7 5.exd6+ ♔xd6 6.b6, winning. **1...g2 2.♗xc6+ ♔xc6 3.♔xg2 dxe5 4.♘f6 ♔b6 5.♔f3,** winning. **1...♕xa6 2.♘c7+ ♔xe5 3.♘xa6 d5 4.♘b8 ♔d6 5.♗a4 d4 6.cxd4 ♔d5 7.♘c6 c3 8.♘xa7 ♔xd4 9.♗b3,** winning.

The same Riga newspaper published Mikhail Platov's first study, which was awarded a prize in the competition.

Composition No. 70
Rigaer Tageblatt
1903

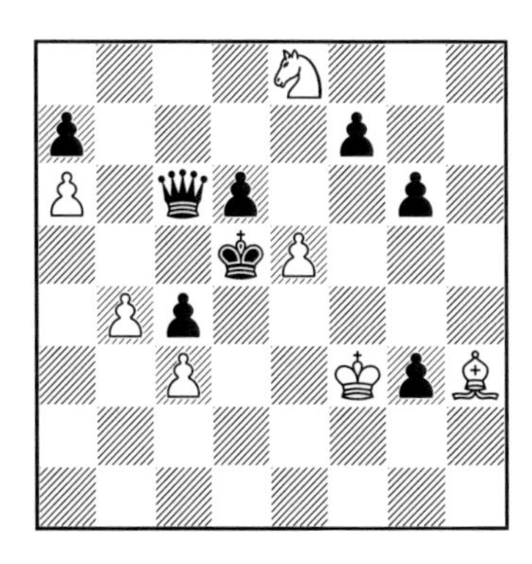

White to move and win

Composition No. 71
Rigaer Tageblatt
1905, Honorable mention

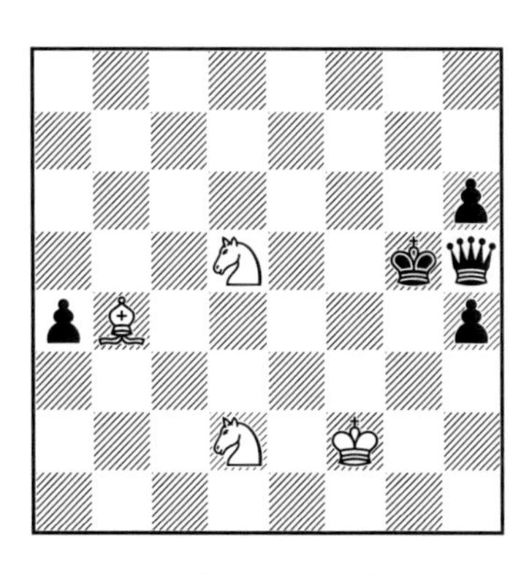

White to move and win

1.♘e4+! ♔f5!? 2.♗a3 ♔e5. Any other move made by black leads to the immediate loss of the queen. **3.♗b2+ ♔f5.** Taking any of the knights is impossible due to the following continuation: 3...♔xe4 (3...♔xd5) 4.♘f6+ ♔d3 5.♘xh5 ♔c2 6.♗g7 a3 7.♘f6 a2 8.♘d5 ♔b1 9.♘c3+ ♔b2 10.♘b5+, winning.

4.♘d6+ ♔g5 5.♗c1+ ♔g6 (♔g4) 6.♘f4 (♘f6)+, winning.

In 1914, the Platov brothers published a collection of 153 of their studies, in the preface to which they wrote that they tried "to present the struggle of varied forces as fully as possible in order to show certain combinations and features inherent to a particular piece, as well as methods of attack and defense possible in the struggle between different pieces." In 1928, a second collection of studies by the brothers was published, containing 200 works, about 140 of which were joint ones.

In the preface to the second edition of their collection, the Platov brothers formulated their creative credo in more detail: "The content of the study is a particular idea, which finds its expression in a combination or positional play; the completeness of the form lies in the simplicity of construction, combined with the greatest economic use of pieces: the simpler the initial position is, the stronger the effect caused when the idea hidden in the position is revealed."

The works of V. and M. Platov are characterized by the naturalness of the initial position and economy in the use of material. The German composer Franz Zackmann described the place of the Platov brothers in the history of composition in the following way. "Rinck is especially distinguished by his technique, accuracy and elegance of play, and unsurpassed knowledge of the board, while Troitsky, with no less successful works, impresses with the extraordinary power of ingenuity. The Platov brothers probably occupy a place between them."

Although these evaluations relate to the joint work of the Platov brothers, they objectively characterize the work of Mikhail. Here are some studies, the authorship of which belongs to Mikhail alone.

Composition No. 72
Rigaer Tageblatt
1905

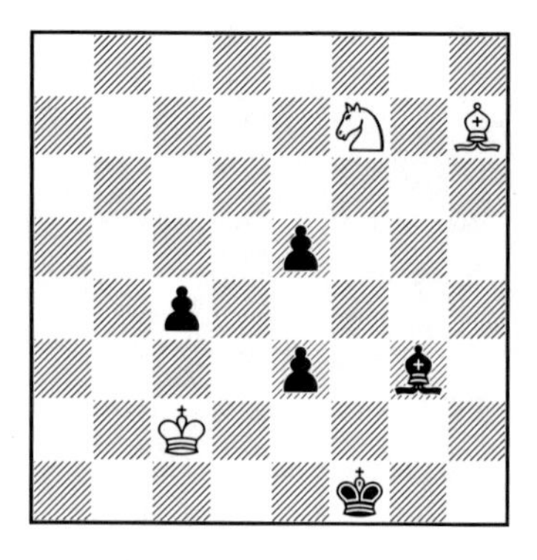

White to move and draw

1.♗g8 e2. The path to a drawn ending for white can be found in another variation, too: 1...e4 2.♘g5 e2 3.♗xc4 e3 4.♘e4 ♗e5 5.♘d2+! with a draw. **2.♘xe5 e1=♕ 3.♗xc4+ ♔g2 4.♗d5+ ♔h3 5.♗e6+.** Draw.

One of Mikhail Platov's favorite themes, later wonderfully embodied in the "beautiful thing", was when the black pawn promotes to a queen, which is then outplayed by white's minor pieces.

Composition No. 73
Niva
1905

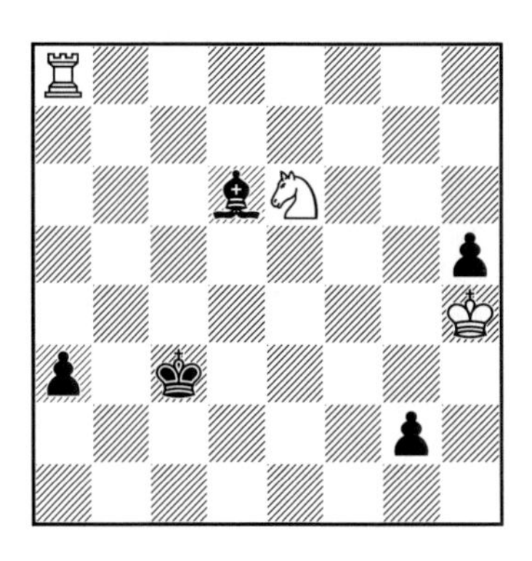

White to move and draw

1.♘f4! ♗xf4 1...g1=♕ 2.♘e2+ **2.♖xa3+ ♔b2 3.♖g3! ♗xg3+ 4.♔h3 g1=♕(♖).** Stalemate. If 4... g1=♘+ or 4...g1=♗, then 5.♔xg3, with a positional draw.

Composition No. 74
Deutsche Schachzeitung
1906

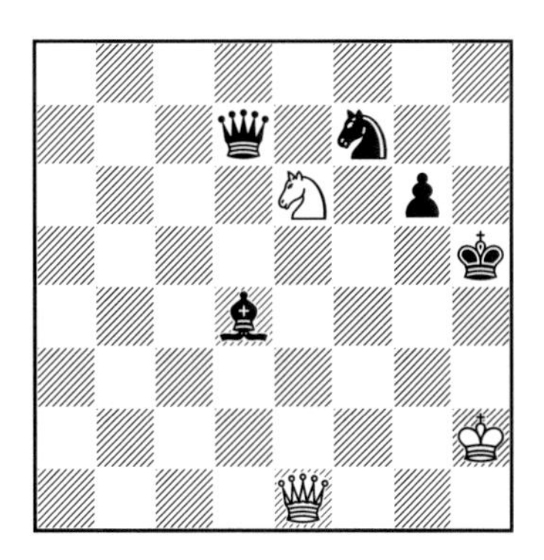

White to move and win

1.♕h1! ♕xe6 2.♔g3+ ♔g5 3.♕h4+ ♔f5 4.♕f4#, 1...♕d6+ 2.♔g2+ ♔g4 3.♕h3#, 1...♗f2 2.♕f3+ ♔h6 3.♕h3+, 1...♔g4 2.♕e4+ ♔h5 3.♕f3+, 1...g5 2.♔g3+ (or 2.♔g2+) 2...♔g6 3.♘f8+, winning.

In 1914, due to the outbreak of war, the Platov brothers were mobilized and their creative activity was interrupted. It was renewed only eight years later. It was reported in an issue of the magazine *Shakhmaty* in 1922 that "the famous study composer M. N. Platov is staying at Srednaya Syzrano-Vyazemskaya village". Soon, new studies by M. N. Platov appeared with diverse and original ideas.

Composition No. 75
Shakhmaty
1922

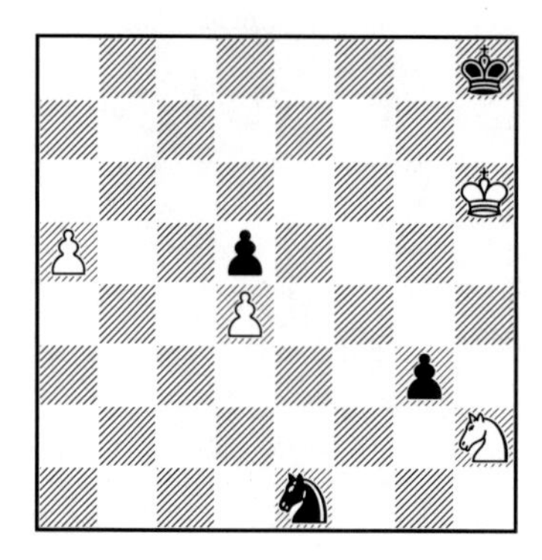

White to move and draw

1.♘f3! ♘xf3 2.a6 g2 3.a7 g1=♕ 4.a8=♕+ ♕g8 5.♕e8! ♕xe8, stalemate.

Composition No. 76
Shakhmaty
1924

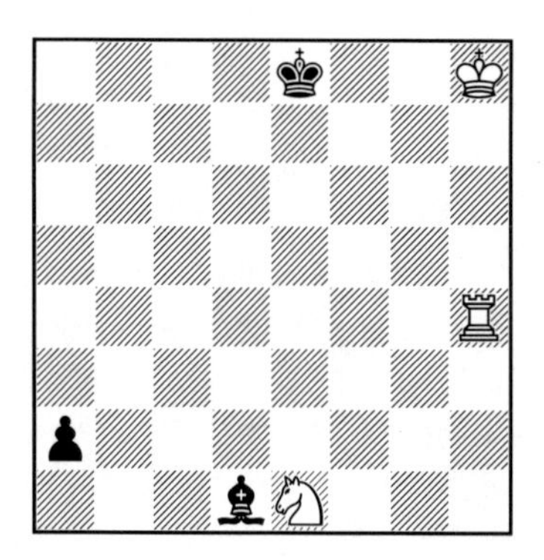

White to move and draw

1.♖e4+ ♔f7! 2.♘c2 ♗xc2 3.♖e1! However, not 3.♖e5?? a1=♖ and black wins. **3...♗b1 4.♖e5 a1=♖**. 4...a1=♕ is stalemate. **5.♖a5! ♗a2 6.♖a7+**. Draw.

Composition No. 77
Shakhmaty
1925, 1st honorable mention of the competition of the second semester

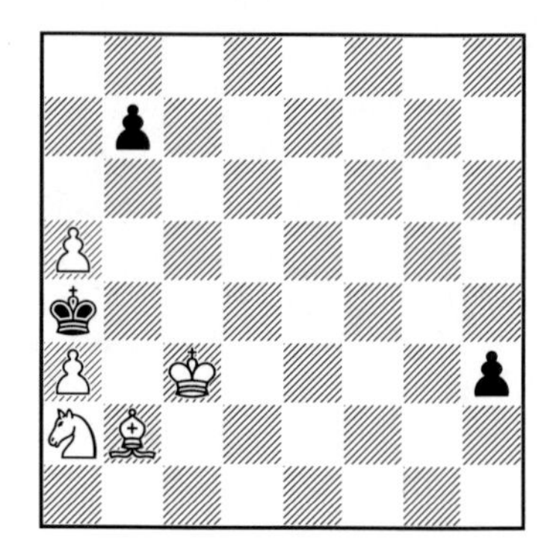

White to move and win

1.a6! bxa6 2.♔c2! h2 3.♗e5 h1=♕ 4.♘c3+, and checkmate on the next move. An elegant study with an inconspicuous second move and two model mates.

Composition No. 78
Shakhmatny listok
1925

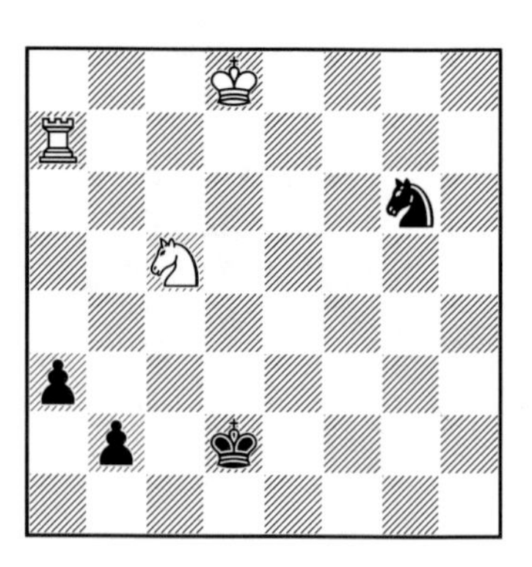

White to move and draw

When looking at the initial position, it is difficult to imagine that the final position will be a stalemate. **1.♘e4+!** The move 1.♘b3+? won't help in view of 1...♔c3!

1...♔c2 2.♘c3! And here it was easy to go the wrong way via 2.♖c7+? ♔d3! and white loses.

2...♔xc3 3.♖xa3+ ♔c4. Obviously, both 3...♔b4 4.♖a7 and 3...♔c2 4.♖a2 lead to a draw.

4.♖a4+ ♔c5 5.♖a5+ ♔c6. 5...♔b6 6.♖a8 ♔b7 7.♖a5 and so on.

6.♖a6+ ♔b7 7.♖a5 b1=♕. 7...b1=♖!? 8.♖f5, and there is no way for black to win.

8.♖b5+ ♕xb5 stalemate.

Composition No. 79
64
1925

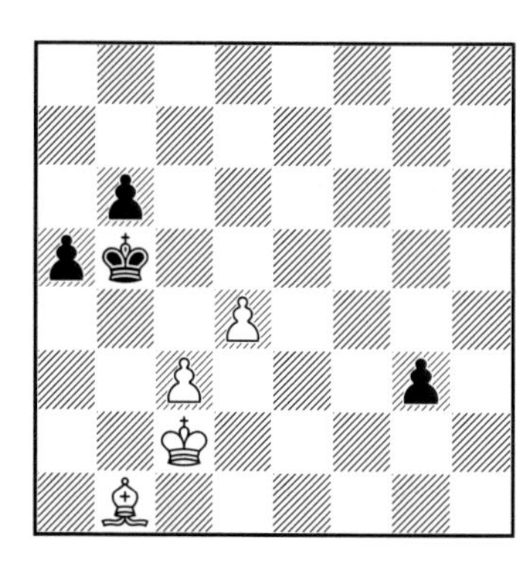

White to move and win

1.♔b2! It was wrong to play 1.♔b3? due to 1...a4+!, and black wins.

1...g2 2.♗d3+! An important intermediate check due to which the black king is pulled into a mating position.

2...♔a4. If 2...♔c6, then 3.♗e4+, and the g2 pawn is lost.

3.♗e4 g1=♕ 4.♗c6+ b5 5.♗e4 ♕f2+ (5...b4 6.♗c6#) **6.♗c2+ ♕xc2+ 7.♔xc2 b4 8.c4.** If 8.d5?, then 8...♔b5, and black achieves a draw.

8...b3+ 9.♔b2! It wasn't too late to lose – 9.♔c3?? ♔a3!, while 9.♔b1? led to a draw.

9...♔b4 10.c5! 10.d5?? a4 11.d6 a3+ 12.♔b1 ♔c3, and black wins.

10...a4 11.c6, winning.

The influence of Troitsky is felt throughout Mikhail Platov's work. In the following study, you can see how one of Troitsky's ideas is developed.

Composition No. 80
Shakhmaty
1925
Dedicated to A. A. Troitsky

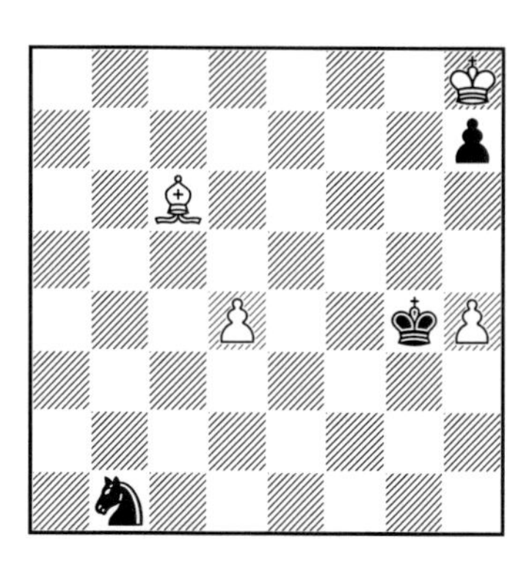

White to move and win

1.d5! ♘d2! 2.h5! Switching the first two moves is impossible, since 1.h5? is refuted through the following subtle play: 1...♔xh5 2.d5 ♔g6 3.♔g8 ♔f5! 4.♔f8! (4.♔f7 ♘d2 5.d6 ♘c4 6.d7 ♘e5+) 4...♘c3 5.d6 ♘e4! 6.♗xe4+ ♔e6! (or 6.d7 ♘c5). Draw.

2...♔xh5. Nearly forced. If 2...♘e4, then 3.h6 ♔g5 4.♔xh7 ♘d6 5.♗d7 ♘f7 6.♗e6 ♘xh6 7.d6 ♔f6 8.d7, winning; if 2...♔g5, then 3.d6 ♘c4 4.d7, winning, since the d-pawn promotes with a check.

3.d6 ♘c4 4.♗e8+! ♔h6! Stalemate play.

5.d7 ♘e5 6.d8=♖! winning.

Composition No. 81
Cheskoslovensky Sach
1927

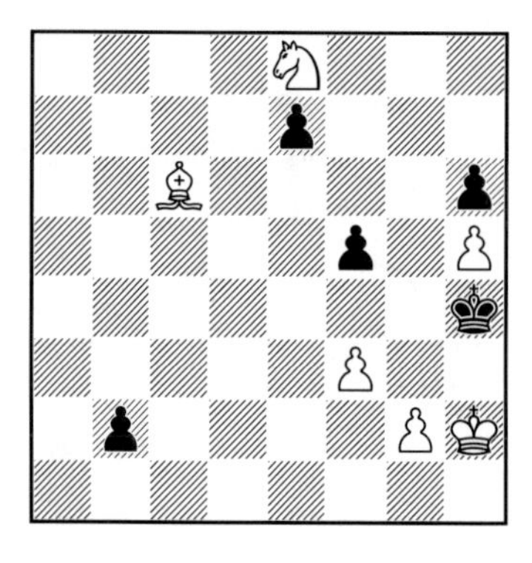

White to move and win

1.♘f6! exf6. In the case of 1...b1=♕, the newborn queen is unable to parry the blatant threat of checkmate in three moves: 2.g3+ ♔g5 3.♘h7+ ♔xh5 4.♗e8#.

2.g3+ ♔xh5 3.♗e8+ ♔g5 4.f4+ ♔g4 5.♗b5! ♔f3 (5...b1=♕ 6.♗e2#) **6.♗d3,** winning. There was one extra variation possible: 1...♔g5 2.♘e4+ (2.♗e4? ♔xf6! 3.♗c2 ♔g5 with a draw) 2...fxe4 3.♗xe4, winning.

Two variations with model mates and a third one with a knight sacrifice.

Composition No. 82
Shakhmaty
1927, 1st honorable mention of the competition of the second semester

White to move and win

1.♖a4+! A thematically false try was 1.♖c4+? ♔g5 2.♖a5+ ♔f6 3.♖c6+ ♔e7 4.♖a7+ ♔d8, and black is saved.

1...♔g5! 2.♖c5+ ♔f6 3.♖a6+ ♔e7 4.♖c7+ ♔d8 5.♖h7! ♕g2! 6.♖a8+ ♕xa8 7.♖h8+, winning.

Composition No. 83
Vechernaya Moskva
1927

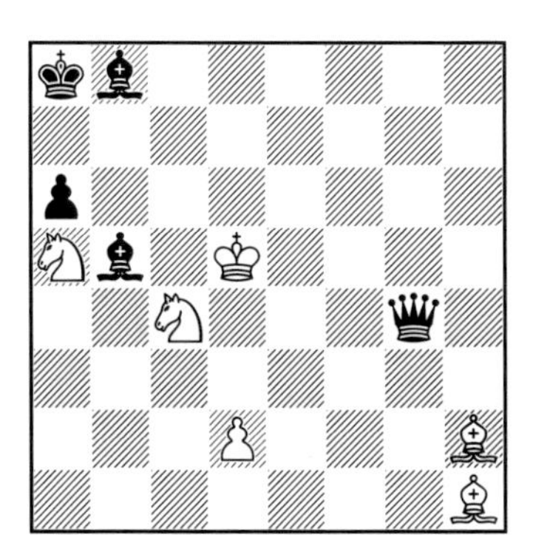

White to move and win

1.♘b6+ ♔a7 2.♘c8+ ♕xc8 3.♗g1+ ♔a8. Now the white king starts "climbing the ladder", declaring discovered checks with one bishop and blocking the other. A kind of "white valve".

4.♔d4+ ♔a7 5.♔e4+ ♔a8 6.♔e3+ ♔a7 7.♔f3+ ♔a8 8.♔f2+ ♔a7 9.♔e1+, with checkmate on the next move.

In the late 1920s, the Platov brothers retired from active composing (simultaneously!). They did not publish any studies after 1929. Why? The argument that they failed to find a way to develop further their creative work is hardly convincing. The sudden departure from the ranks of composers of two talented experts remains a mystery.

In the early 1930s, Mikhail Platov worked as a lead engineer at a defense enterprise in Serpukhov. At the time, the future science fiction writer and master of studies composition Alexander Kazantsev worked at the same factory. Many years later, in the novel *A Fateful Mine*, Kazantsev wrote about his first steps as an author of studies under the mentorship of Mikhail Platov.

The writer and study composer recalls that Mikhail Nikolaevich played chess a lot and did so with pleasure. He played for Zenit in team competitions. Platov avoided the question of why he stopped composing studies. The last time Kazantsev saw him was in 1935.

The last, dramatic period of Mikhail Platov's life was told by the grandson of Vasily Nikolaevich Platov, i.e. Mikhail's great-nephew – Alexander Andreevich (*64. Shakhmatnoye obozreniye*, 1990, No. 13, pp. 12-14).

In the first days of October 1937, the engineer M. N. Platov held a planning meeting, at which he did not speak sufficiently respectfully about the "Father of all nations" – Joseph Stalin. Reckoning was not long in coming. On the night of October 4, Mikhail Nikolaevich was arrested. The court, quick and unfair, handed down a sentence – 10 years of correctional labor camp.

Mikhail Nikolaevich was transported to the Arkhangelsk region and placed in the Kargopol camp. At the beginning of 1938, he wrote to his brother Vasily from the camp: "I did not attach much importance to my arrest and kept hoping that I would be released, believing that this was a misunderstanding, since throughout my whole life I have been far from politics and never belonged to any group or party."

Despite the conditions of camp life, Mikhail Platov managed to maintain his interest in chess. He asked his brother to send him new chess magazines. In a letter dated May 9, 1938, Mikhail Nikolaevich reported the onset of illnesses: "My health, which, of course, is not to my advantage, has declined a lot. I now suffer from shortness of breath, swelling of the legs and wounds that have appeared on my legs, which are the result of a weakening of cardiac activity. On February 20, I was taken to hospital and am still there. Now the swelling on my legs has subsided, the wounds and the incision made in them are healing. I'll probably be out of hospital in a few days. I don't know for how long and whether this can happen again."

But even in the camp, Platov thought about creating studies. Here's touching evidence – his letter to his brother Vasily dated June 11, 1938:

"Dear Vasya!

On May 27, I sent a letter addressed to you and dated May 8. I see now that you received it late, because on June 7 I got your first parcel, a suitcase, and on June 9 a small parcel. But it doesn't matter: the cap fitted perfectly. I rush to thank you and Ekaterina Alexeevna warmly for such great help for me, since any news from Moscow greatly raises my mood, which is being spoiled by the illness. Thank you very much, again. Meanwhile, I spend the days as I wrote to you in my letter of May 27, I often lie down, because when walking and sitting I get tired quickly: my health today is beyond comparison with last year, when I roamed for days in the mountains of the Caucasus; now, after walking a few dozen steps, I am already exhausted. I've lost a lot of weight: I don't want to go to hospital again. It's terribly depressing; anyway, chess now saves me from that: I played several games with local amateurs; they are less skilled than me, but now, being in this state, I make bad mistakes.

I looked through the chess literature you sent me – I read 2 issues of *Shakhmaty v SSSR* with pleasure. I hope that you will not refuse to send me more issues in the future. I just don't know if it's possible to send them as a small parcel. If you are going to send something, then inform me in advance: when they hand out parcels, they ask from where and from whom you are expecting a parcel. I need some other things sent to me, for example, shoes, but wait for now; the old ones, of course, suffered the same fate as the rest of my clothes.

One of the games played here gave me the idea of composing a study on the theme of discovered attack. Here's the position:

Composition No. 84
1938

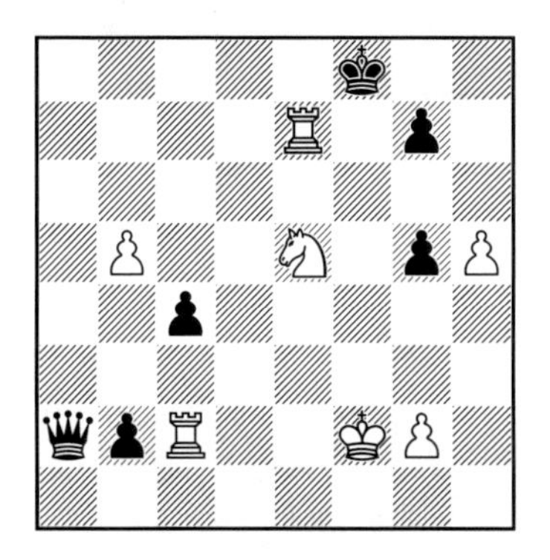

White to move and win

1.♘g6+ ♔g8 2.♖ce2, threatening a mate in 2 moves. **2...♕a3! 3.♖e8+ ♔f7 4.♘e5+ ♔f6** with the sacrifice of the rook. **5.♖e6+ ♔f5** and another rook sacrifice. **6.g4+ ♔f4 7.♖e4+ ♔xe4** with the sacrifice of the second rook. **8.♘xc4+**, winning.

Anyway, I wish you all the best. Greetings to Ekaterina Alexeevna, Pasha, Alyosha.

Your M.

P.S. I'll let you know in case I need anything. Looking forward to your reply to my letters. As for the 25 rubles, I've been coping thus far, but not very well. I don't know yet if they have arrived."

In his last letter, dated August 22, 1938, Mikhail Nikolaevich writes about the general deterioration of his health. Parcels addressed to him to the Kargopol camp were sent back at the end of 1938. Mikhail Nikolaevich was probably no longer alive by the autumn of that year.

...When in 1951 the chess community widely celebrated the 70th birthday of the outstanding study composer V. N. Platov, his brother and co-author was mentioned only in passing, and the hero of the day was not disturbed with questions about Mikhail. The time when it became possible to speak freely about Mikhail Nikolaevich Platov had not yet come.

Sergei Kaminer – The Interrupted Song

Recalling the beginning of his epoch-defining chess career, Mikhail Botvinnik writes in his memoirs: "After I was accepted as a member of the Petrograd Chess Union on June 1, 1924, I got an opportunity to cross swords with stronger opponents. I played a training match with Sergei Kaminer and... I lost all three games – I had no positional experience."

Sergei Kaminer was three years older than Mikhail Botvinnik. He was born on August 26, 1908 and lived just thirty years. It took many years, until 2000, to finally establish when and where he died.

Little is known about the biography of Sergei Mikhailovich. At the age of twelve, he started work at a factory called "Engine of the Revolution" in Nizhny Novgorod as an apprentice operator. He spent his school years in Leningrad. In 1926, he moved to Moscow and started at the Chemical Faculty of Moscow State Technical University (now the Bauman Moscow State Technical University). After graduating from the institute, Kaminer worked as an engineer at the Kauchuk (rubber) factory, led design work at the ebonite workshop at Rezinproject, and in 1936 became the head of the technical department at Glavrezin.

He became interested in chess during his school years. In 1924, he met and immediately became friends with the 13-year-old Botvinnik. It was then that the small match took place which remained etched in the future world champion's memory. The ending of one of their games was later published.

Game No. 13
M. Botvinnik – S. Kaminer
1924

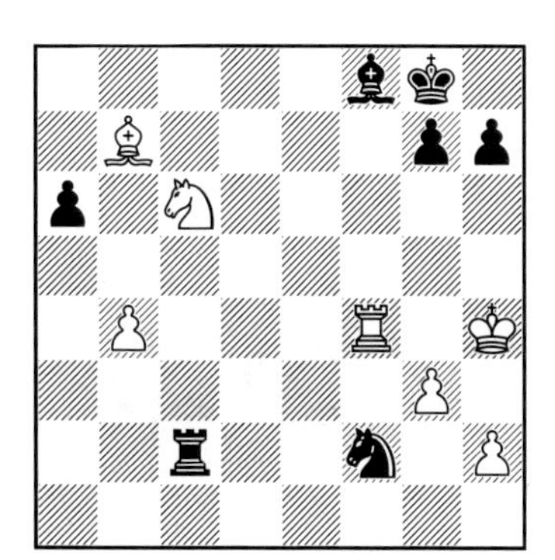

White carelessly played **1.♖d4?** and had to pay for it: **1...♖xc6! 2.♗xc6 ♗e7+ 3.♔h5 g6+ 4.♔h6 ♘h3,** with inevitable checkmate. An ending worthy of a future study composer.

Soon, Botvinnik's tournament successes would vastly outweigh Kaminer's, who, however, played for some time in competitions at the level of first category. In the photo reproduced here, Sergei Kaminer is playing a tournament game. Shortly before leaving for Moscow, he took part in a provincial chess Olympiad, and gained fifth place in his preliminary group. By that time, he was already known as a study composer. His first study was published in 1924.

Composition No. 85
Shakhmaty
1924, Commendation

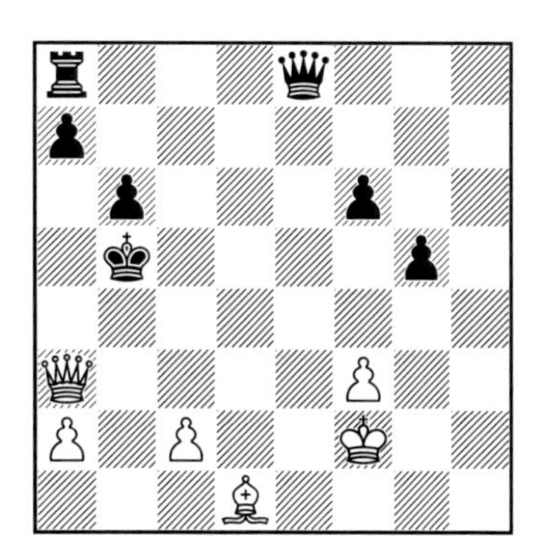

White to move and win

1.c4+! ♔xc4. Forced, otherwise black loses his queen.

2.♗b3+ ♔d4! The only possible move. If the black king withdraws to the third rank, then white will win the queen with discovered check. **3.♗f7!** Taking the bishop leads to the loss of the queen on the a2-g8 diagonal: 3...♕xf7 4.♕e3+ ♔c4(d5) 5.♕b3+. At the same time, after 3.♗f7 white threatens 4.♕e3#, and therefore the black queen cannot leave the e-file.

3...♕e5. Now, the square that is important for the king is blocked, and the queen gets lost along the b1-h7 diagonal. **4.♕b4+ ♔d3 5.♗g6+ f5 6.♗xf5+ ♕xf5 7.♕b1+,** winning.

"Not bad at all for his first effort," wrote Vasily Platov, the studies column editor of *Shakhmaty* magazine.

The following study by the newborn composer received a flattering assessment from Vasily Platov: "This study can take its place alongside the best studies by Henri Rinck on similar themes".

Composition No. 86
Shakhmatny listok
1925

White to move and draw

1.♗h4! The white bishop has almost no choice. The variation 1.♗c7(e7)? loses after 1...♖b7, while 1.♗g5? would be met by 1...♖b7 2.♗h3 (2.♗f5 ♖b5) 2...♖h7 3.♔h2 ♗e5+ 4.♔g2 ♖g7 and 5...♖xg5, winning.

1...♖b7 2.♗f5! ♖b5 3.♗g4! It is necessary to prevent 3...♖h5. If 3.♗g6?, then 3...♔g7! 4.♗e8 ♖b8, winning, but not 3...♖b6? 4.♗g3!, in which case white is saved.

3...♖b4. White seems to have achieved nothing and one of his bishops is lost anyway. But the idea of his maneuvers is to lure the rook to the g-file, which will create conditions for a stalemate combination.

4.♗g3! ♖xg4 5.♗e5+ **♗xe5** and stalemate.

The most characteristic aspect of Kaminer's early work is the principle of equality of the contending sides, which brings the study closer to the real game.

Composition No. 87
Shakhmaty
1925, 2nd honorable mention of the competition of the second semester

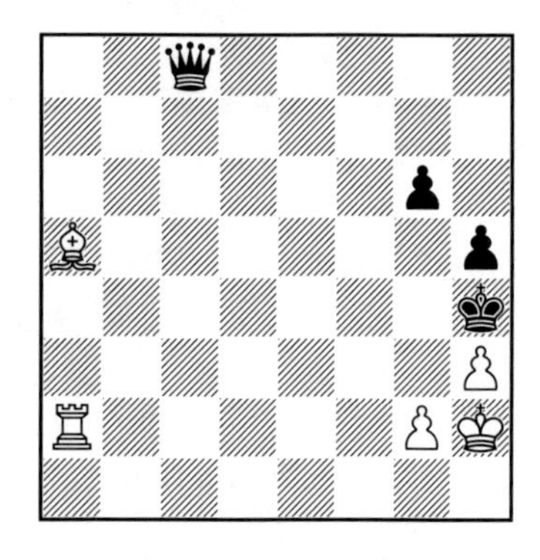

White to move and win

There is approximately equal material on the board. But the position of the black king looks bad. **1.♖c2!** White distracts the queen from defending the d8-h4 diagonal.

1...♕xc2. If 1...♕d7, 2.♖d2 and 3.♗d8+ or 1...♕e8 2.♖c5 threatening checkmate, while in the case of 1...♕f8, after 2.♖c4+ ♔g5 3.♗d2+ and ♖f4+, the black queen is lost.

2.♗d8+ **g5 3.♗a5.** Having returned to the initial point with the bishop, white threatens 4.♗e1+, continuing to keep the d8 square under attack (3...g4 4.♗d8#). **3...♛e2.** The g2 pawn must remain pinned. **4.♗c7,** creating a checkmate threat and forcing black's response. **4...♛f2.**

5.♗d6! Black falls into zugzwang. He is forced to either unpin the pawn, or stop attacking the g3 square. **5...♛f4+ 6.g3+ ♛xg3+ 7.♗xg3#.**

Composition No. 88
Shakhmatny listok
1925

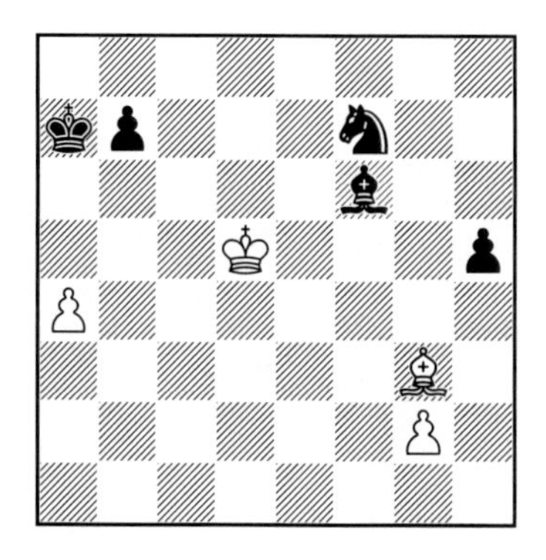

White to move and draw

1.♔e6 ♘g5+ 2.♔f5. Not 2.♔xf6? due to the fork 2...♘e4+ and 3...♘xg3. **2...♗d8 3.♗f4 ♘h7.** Or 3...♘f7 4.♔g6 ♘h8+ 5.♔g7 and a draw. **4.♔g6 ♘f8+.** After 4...♘f6 5.♗g5, the drawn ending becomes obvious.

5.♔f7 ♘d7 6.♔e8 ♘c5. Hoping for a fork again: 7.♔xd8? ♘e6+ and 8...♘xf4. However, now the knight gets pinned.

7.♗e3 ♗b6 8.a5. Draw.

"An interesting study with lively play, characteristic of our young and promising composer" (Leonid Kubbel).

Composition No. 89
Shakhmaty
1925, 1st honorable mention of the competition of the first semester

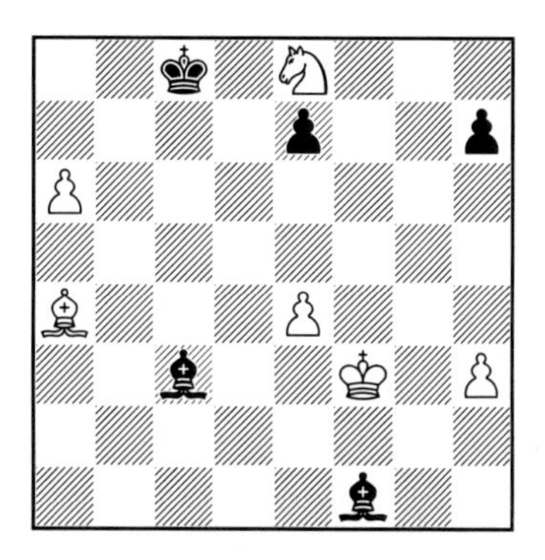

White to move and win

1.a7! ♔b7 2.♗b5! A wonderful maneuver that wins black's light-squared bishop.

2...♗xh3. The move 2...♗xb5 would be met by 3.♘c7, and if 3...♔xa7, then 4.♘xb5+ capturing both bishops, while if 3...♔xc7, then 4.a8=♕ winning, for example: 4...♗f6 5.♕a7+ ♔c6 (5...♔d6 6.e5! and so on) 6.e5 ♗xe5 7.♕xe7 and so on.

3.♔g3 ♗e6. 3...♗c8 4.♗a6+, winning.

4.a8=♕+ ♔xa8 5.♘c7+, winning.

"Here, the author presents the normally dry and insipid theme of catching an enemy piece in a sharp combinational spirit" (V. Platov).

Composition No. 90
Shakhmaty
1925, 3rd prize of the competition of the first semester

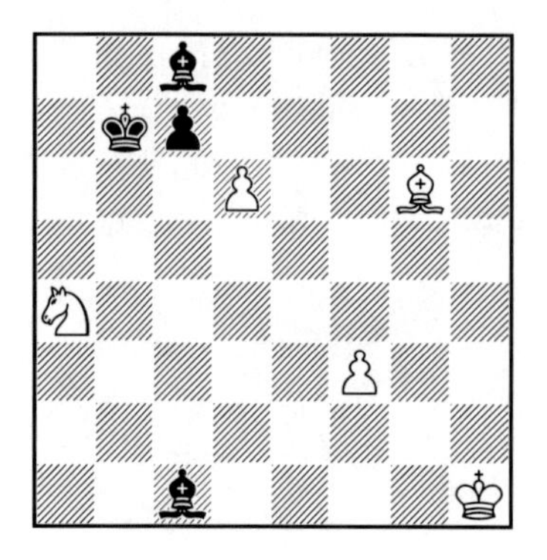

White to move and win

1.♘c5+! ♔c6 2.d7! Luring the bishop to a square that is fatal for it.

2...♗xd7 3.♘d3 ♗g5. In response to a random bishop move white plays 4.♘e5+ and wins the bishop without compensation.

4.♘e5+ ♔d5 5.♘xd7 ♔e6 6.♘c5+.

It should be noted that while developing the theme of the struggle of minor pieces Kaminer found a number of new combinational variations and created a number of memorable works. In the above study, the unusually playful white knight turns out to be stronger than two black bishops.

From the commentary of the judge V. Platov to the two studies above: "These are two great works on the now popular theme of catching an enemy piece. Here this idea is not carried out mechanically, but is wrapped in the flesh and blood of a lively combination; the knight shows especially amazing mobility in the second study... Kaminer is a very young composer, and it is all the more pleasant for us to emphasize his success because he shows amazing sensitivity to the modern study composing art, occupying the very channel of its flow."

Composition No. 91
Shakhmaty
1926, 2nd prize of the competition of the second semester

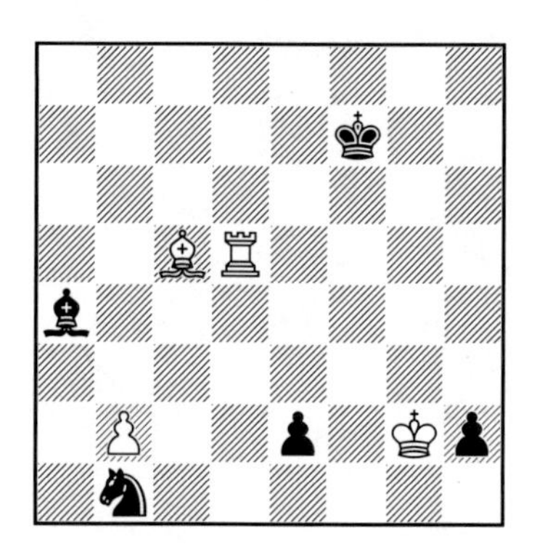

White to move and win

Although white has an exchange for a pawn, black's counter-threats make white's path to victory very tricky. **1.♖e5! ♘d2!** An unobvious defensive resource. **2.♖xe2.** Forced, since black threatened 2...♘e4 3.♗b4 ♔f6 and so on.

2...h1=♕+ 3.♔xh1 ♘e4. Now the bishop is under attack, a fork on g3 is threatened, and the knight is under the indirect protection of the black bishop.

4.♗f2 ♗d1. Exploiting the restricted position of the white rook. Again, it is impossible to continue via 5.♖xe4? because of 5...♗f3+ with a draw.

5.♖e1! What a far-sighted move! Black temporarily wins the bishop, but then will be forced to return one of the pieces.

5...♘xf2+ 6.♔g2 ♘d3. In an attempt to achieve a drawing balance of forces.

7.♖xd1 ♘xb2 8.♖d4, winning. In the case of 8...♔e6, the white king comes just in time to protect the rook.

"This is an extremely complicated study with subtle play. Beautiful counterplay from the black pieces" (V. Platov).

Composition No. 92
Shakhmaty
1926, 3rd prize of the competition of the second semester
Dedicated to A. A. Troitsky

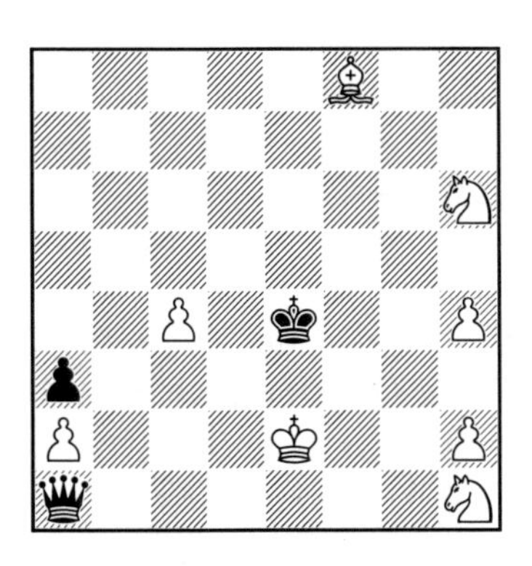

White to move and win

1.♘g3+! In the case of 1.♘f2+? ♔e5 2.♗g7+ ♔f4! 3.♘h3+ ♔e4 4.♘g5+ ♔f4 5.♘e6+ ♔e4 6.♘c5+ ♔f4 7.♘d3+ ♔e4 8.♘f2+ white has to make do with perpetual check.

1...♔e5 2.♗g7+ ♔f4 3.♘h5+. Obviously not 3.♗xa1? due to stalemate.

3...♔e4 4.♘f6+ ♔f4. Due to the threat of losing the queen, the king cannot gain his freedom.

5.♘d5+ ♔e4 6.♘c3+ ♔f4 7.♔f2! Black is in zugzwang.

7...♕h1. If 7...♕b2+, then 8.♘e2+ and 9.♗xb2.

8.♘e2+ ♔e4 9.♘g3+, white wins.

"Here is a perfectly developed theme. The circular journey of the knight is very attractive" (V. Platov).

Composition No. 93
Shakhmaty
1927, 5th prize of the competition of the second semester

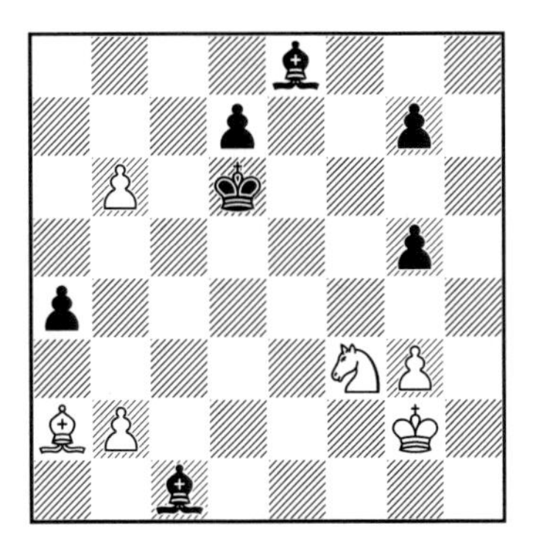

White to move and win

1.♘e5 ♗h5. Black must take countermeasures against the hidden threat of 2.♗g8, then 3.♘c4+ ♔c6 4.♗d5+, and it is no longer possible to hold back the pawn.

2.♔f1. Preventing the attempt at defense via 2...♗e2 and forcing the bishop to occupy a less advantageous position on d1.

2...♗d1 3.♗d5! If 3.♗g8?, then obviously 3...♗b3! Now white threatens not only 4.♘f7(c4)+, but also 4.b7 ♔c7 5.♘xd7.

3...♗e3. The second bishop is heading for death. If the white king were now on f2, black would escape: 3...♗xb2 4.b7 ♗d4+ or 4.♘c4+ ♔xd5 5.b7 (5.♘xb2 a3) 5...♔xc4 (but not 5...♗d4+ 6.♘e3+ with a win) 6.b8=♕ a3, and there is no win.

4.♘c4+ ♔xd5 5.♘xe3+ ♔c6 6.♘xd1, with a win. For example, 6...♔xb6 7.♔e2 ♔c5 8.♔d3 ♔b4 9.♔c2, then 10.♘c3 and so on.

The dual on the second move somewhat spoils the impression: 2.♔f2 ♗d1 3.♘d3 ♗d2 4.♘c5 ♗b4 5.♘a6 ♗a5 6.b7, winning.

This was Kaminer's best study on the theme of a bishop and knight taking on two bishops. Here, the black bishops without much firepower voluntarily occupy squares where they become victims of successive knight forks.

Kaminer's studies remind one of over-the-board play. Botvinnik annotated several of his works, as we will now see.

Composition No. 94
Shakhmaty
1927, 1st prize of the competition of the first semester

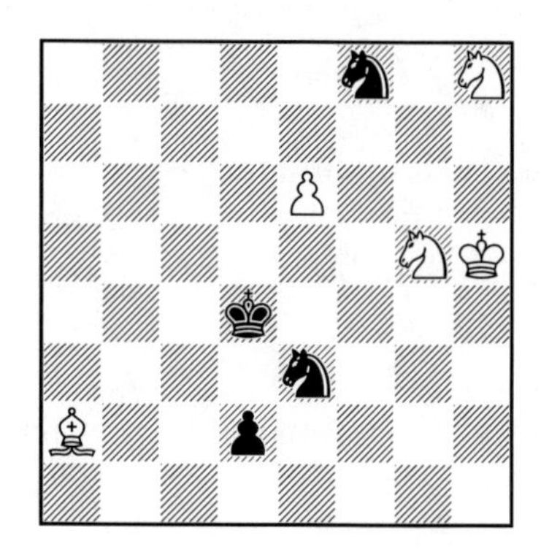

White to move and win

Commentary by Mikhail Botvinnik:

"White possesses a material advantage, but it is well known that two knights on their own without pawns cannot bring victory, and this complicates white's task. Moreover, two knights and a bishop against two knights when there are no pawns on the board don't ensure victory either.

1.♘f3+. This move is useful. White covers the d1-h5 diagonal and, if necessary, can give up the knight for the d2 pawn.

1...♔c3. As will be seen later, the king's retreat to d3 simplifies white's task.

2.e7 ♘d7. If 2...d1=♕, then 3.exf8=♕, and two extra pieces with queens guarantee success.

3.♘xd2 ♘f5. In the case of 3...♔xd2 4.♔g5 the white pawn easily queens. Now we can see that if the black king were on d3 (1...♔d3), then the move 4.♗b1+ would lead to an immediate win.

4.♘e4+ ♔d4 5.e8=♘! What a fantastic position! Three knights and a bishop guarantee victory against two knights. It would be a mistake to make the pawn a queen because of 5...♘g7+ with a draw. Instead of creating a queen on e8, protecting the e4 knight, white creates a knight there, sacrificing a piece.

5...♔xe4 6.♗b1+. This hunt for the f5 knight unexpectedly brings success. **6...♔e5.** Or 6...♔f4 7.♘g6+, and white wins the knight.

7.♘g6+ ♔e6 8.♗a2#. From an ordinary initial position, the game reached a mating ending. Almost in the center of the board, the black king got check mate, and a pure mate at that!"

Sergei Kaminer was the author of the first cooperative checkmate problem in the USSR.

Composition No. 95
Zadachi i etyudy
1927
Dedicated to M. B. Neiman and E. I. Kubbel

Cooperative mate in 3 moves

In cooperative checkmate problems, black makes the first move and helps white to checkmate the black king.

1.♕h3 ♘e4 2.♗f4 ♘g3 3.♔e5 ♗c3#!

Here is what Moisei Neiman, the founder and one of the most prominent proponents of this genre of composition in the USSR, wrote about this study: "...What is curious here is the exile of the black queen. This graceful problem of our talented study composer contains a subtle strategic maneuver and is built remarkably economically."

Anyway, a couple of problems on the theme of cooperative checkmate could not distract Kaminer from composing studies. Kaminer was a key representative of the practical tendency in studies composition, and one of his best works won a prize from the *Trud* newspaper in 1935.

Composition No. 96
Trud
1935, 2nd prize

White to move and win

1.h7! Needless to say, the first move was obvious. But here is what the outstanding study composer Alexander Gerbstman wrote about it: "The obviousness of the first move in this study is not a disadvantage, since it leads to false obviousness, to a position apparently winning for white, in which it is quite difficult to find black's counterplay".

1...♗h5. At first glance, black has nothing to oppose the appearance of his opponent's queen. But he has already conceived clever counterplay: 2.h8=♕? ♗xg6+ 3.♔a1 ♗e7!, and white will have to give up his queen for the bishop, after which a draw becomes obvious.

2.♘f4! In turn, white responds with a sparkling and deep counter-combination. Surely it doesn't matter where the knight perishes? After all, after taking it black's counterplay still works...

2...gxf4. Obviously, 2...♔g7 would be met by 3.♘xh5+, with an easy win.

3.h8=♕ ♗g6+ 4.♔a1 ♗e7. Or 4...♗f8 5.♘f3 ♗g7+ 6.♘e5+ ♔f6 7.♕g8, with a win.

5.♘f3 ♗f6+ 6.♘e5+ ♔e7. Black was counting on this variation. The exchange of the bishop for the queen seems inevitable (the queen cannot leave because of checkmate). But here follows the sacrifice of the doomed queen, after which black's bishops perish because of the fork.

7.♕h4! That's why white forced his opponent to open the d8-h4 diagonal on the second move! Now it is necessary to take the queen, otherwise white plays 8.♕xf4.

7...♗xh4 8.♘xg6+ ♔f6 9.♘xh4, winning.

The acute and tense situation is resolved by a spectacular and fresh combination. Note that during the battle all the black pieces are gradually lured to squares that are fatal for them.

Kaminer presented a substantial analysis of this dynamic period in the development of Soviet studies and his creative views in two works were published in the "Chess Yearbook" (1936) and in the collection "Soviet Chess Composition" (1937).

He begins with a reference to the book written by V. Platov (1925), which "perfectly reflects the general state of study creativity of the time... The material arranged thematically in this book, depending on the forces acting in a study, is very characteristic of that period... However, already in this book of Platov, two chapters occupy a special place: 'Studies with the promotion of a pawn into a minor piece' and 'Studies on different themes' with content other than battle between particular forces."

He highlights that "Soviet composers have given a friendly rebuff to Rinck's mechanical tendencies. *(The outstanding French studies composer of the first half of the 20th century, Henri Rinck, saw the expansion of the framework of studies creativity in the choice of a new balance of forces, for example, in the struggle of pieces without pawns – S.G.)* In our search for a new balance of forces, we have got interested not so much in the novelty of the material, but in the expansion of the combinational possibilities arising from the use of this material. We have categorically rejected the restrictions of Rinck, which were expressed in the refusal to use pawns."

Kaminer sees the main ways of developing studies as being in expanding their framework, by repeating the same idea several times, by transferring some ideas from problems to the basis of studies and, finally, by proclaiming the principle of equal play by white and black. Here, Kaminer identifies seven groups of themes that were at the time "the leitmotif of the creativity of composers: 1) the conversion of pawns into minor pieces; 2) studies with lively piece battles, mostly ending with mate; 3) the expression of a number of ideas from problems in study format; 4) versatile development of the theme of immuring; 5) studies where maneuvering follows clear geometric rules; 6) studies with several repetitions of the same idea or maneuver, or with the synthesis of different ideas; 7) studies on the theme of a positional draw".

The articles written at the end of such a short life highlight the composer's growing creativity and extensive plans, which were not destined to be achieved. One of Kaminer's last works was the following interesting position:

Composition No. 97
64
1937

Can white win?

Play will be as follows: white starts, and black tries to draw.

1.♘f3 ♗f1. 1...b1=♘+ 2.♔c1 and black loses the knight, since he is also threatened with checkmate.

2.♘c3 ♗h3 3.♗h5 ♗f5 4.♗f7 b1=♕ 5.♘xb1 ♗xb1 6.♗d5 ♔g2! Draw, since the discovered check (7.♘d2) is impossible due to the occupation of the square, and if 7.♔c1 then 7...♗a2 with a draw. Here the black bishop already successfully fights off two knights.

Kaminer composed a little over sixty works. At competitions, he won 27 prizes, including three first prizes. A dozen of his studies were included in the FIDE Album (a collection of the best works of chess composers of the world for a particular period), covering the period from 1914 to 1944, and released decades after the author's death.

Mikhail Botvinnik wrote about his last encounter with Sergei Kaminer: "It was the autumn of 1937. I was playing the match for the Soviet Championship with Levenfish in Moscow. I got an unexpected phone call, and Sergei Kaminer showed up at my room in the National Hotel. 'Here in the notebook,' he said, 'you can find all my studies, some of which are still work in progress. Take them. I'm afraid that they will be lost otherwise.' His premonition came true..."

I asked the author of a book on Kaminer, the late chess composition international master Rafael Kofman, about Kaminer's fate. Rafael Moiseevich assumed that Sergei Mikhailovich, who held a respectable job in the management of Glavrezin in 1937, fell victim to the unjustified repressions inflicted on business managers after the death of Ordzhonikidze.

According to Botvinnik's memoirs, some Penza address was written on Kaminer's notebook, and one of his relatives lived there. Eventually, it transpired that Kaminer was arrested on August 17, 1938, and tried for belonging to a counter-revolutionary and terrorist organization on September 27, 1938 in Moscow. He was found guilty, sentenced to death and executed that same day. The information is contained on the Memorial website in the section Victims of Political Terror in the USSR, citing the book *Shooting Lists: Moscow 1937-1941: "Kommunarka", Butovo*, published in the year 2000. He was buried at the Kommunarka execution site near Moscow (today on the city's outskirts) and rehabilitated on July 11, 1956.

Pavel Neunyvako – "To the Madness of the Brave..."

Veteran of the Civil and Second World wars, Army General Mikhail Kazakov, recalling his youth in the Civil War, wrote:

The personnel of the 408th Rifle Regiment, which had been recently replenished with Siberians, fought very hard. This regiment was commanded by Pavel Neunyvako, whose bravery was legendary in the division. Whenever a difficult situation occurred, he appeared among the battle troops on horseback.

But one day the situation had become extremely complicated, and the commander of the regiment was wounded and could not ride properly. What was going to happen? Would the regiment survive without him? The regiment survived. However, at a critical moment, Neunyvako nevertheless appeared among his fighters. He drove up in a horse-drawn machine-gun cart. Subsequently, I encountered this remarkable man many times during my military service. In 1922, I served in Pavel Efimovich's regiment as an assistant commissar. And in 1928, we met at the Frunze Military Academy. He was already finishing his studies, while I was just starting mine at the time.

Nature generously endowed Neunyvako with many talents. We knew him not only as a brave soldier and as a brilliant commander. Pavel Efimovich was also an excellent chess player, and he masterfully composed diverse chess problems. Over a hundred of them were published. (Kazakov M. I. *On the Map of Past Battles*. Moscow, 1971.)

Pavel Efimovich Neunyvako was a famous chess composer in the pre-war years. His name is mentioned on the pages of the novel *Twelve Chairs* by Ilf and Petrov. Neunyvako met Ilf and Petrov in the editorial office of Pravda. Soon he became friends with the writers. Their sharp, witty feuilletons did not leave

Neunyvako indifferent – he loved and understood their humor. They also met in the editorial office of the newspaper *Gudok*, where Pavel's problems were sometimes published. One can guess that the "Machine" in the novel of the great satirists is *Gudok*, a railway workers newspaper in which the chess column was edited at one time by the master Duz-Khotimirsky. It was he who became the prototype of maestro Sudeikin in the novel *Twelve Chairs*. Let us recall the text of the novel: "The editor of the chess column, Maestro Sudeikin, was the first to run to the secretary of the editors' office. He asked a polite question, but one full of bitterness: 'What, there won't be any chess today?' 'There isn't room,' the secretary replied, 'the bottom article is large. Three hundred lines.' 'But today is Saturday. The reader is waiting for the Sunday column. I have the solution to the problems, I have a charming study by Neunyvako...'"

That "charming study" was never found. Neunyvako only left chess problems for posterity.

Pavel Efimovich was born in 1897 in the Crimea. At the age of twenty, he joined the ranks of the Red Army. During the Civil War, he was the commander of the famous 408th Rifle Regiment. He crushed the Basmachi movement in Central Asia, fought in the battles for Perekop and Chongar, and finished off Wrangel's army.

He became interested in chess at the age of 18, when he studied at the school of ensigns. Once Pavel saw a page from the magazine *Niva* in the hands of a platoon leader: there were some strange-looking shapes on black and white squares. So the platoon leader turned out to be Pavel Neunyvako's first chess teacher. Pavel played a lot during the "chess fever" of 1925, when the USSR hosted its first international tournament, and he even managed to defeat Capablanca in a simultaneous game. However, solving and composing chess problems turned out to be more interesting for him than fighting at the board.

Pavel published his first problems in the chess column of the *Izvestia* newspaper. A problem by the novice composer gained the first honorable mention in the *Izvestia* contest of 1924. A year later, he won a major competition organized by the magazine *64*.

Composition No. 98
64
1925, 1st prize

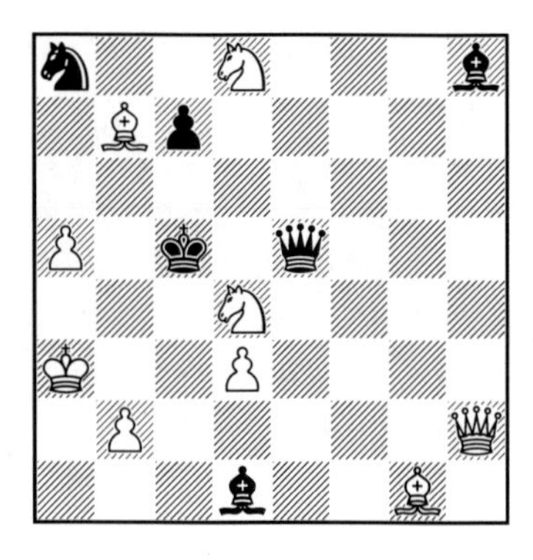

White to mate in 2 moves

1.♗c6! threatening 2.♘b7#; 1...♕xd4 2.b4#; 1...♕e3 2.♘4e6#; 1...♔d6 2.♘f5#. Three model checkmates with the pinning of the black queen.

Initially, Neunyvako tended towards the ideas of the Czech school. He created problems with model mates and pinning (or self-pinning) of the black pieces.

He could only work on creating problems in rare moments of rest. Pavel Neunyvako, the commander of the Third Turkestan Regiment, was constantly moved from one hot spot to another. The latest location of the regiment could be found by the addresses from which his problems were sent. The following two compositions, which were prize winners, were sent from Bukhara.

Composition No. 99
Shakhmaty
1925, 1st-2nd prize of the contest of the first semester

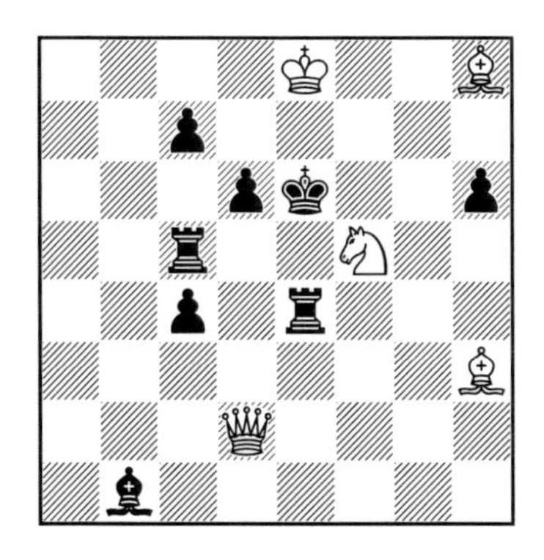

White to mate in 2 moves

1.♕g2!, threatening 2.♕g8#, 1...♖g4 2.♘d4# , 1...♔d5+ 2.♘e7#. Here are two self-pinnings of the black rook, leading to model mates.

The most active period of Neunyvako's chess career was when he studied at the Frunze Military Academy of the Red Army, from which he graduated with top marks in 1928. In addition to two-movers, Pavel Efimovich also composed three-movers.

Composition No. 100
Shakhmaty
1926

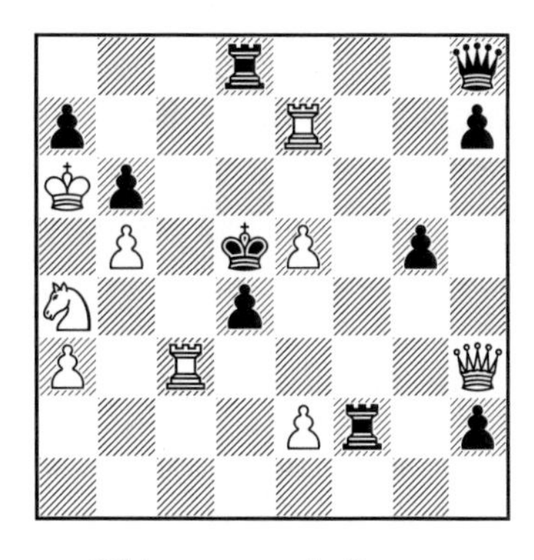

White to mate in 3 moves

1.♖c4!, threatening 2.♖xd4+ ♔xd4 3.♕d3#, 1...♔xc4 2.♕d3+ ♔d5 3.e4#, 1...♔e4 2.♘c3+ ♔f4 3.e3#, 1...♖f4 2.e4+ ♔xe4 3.♘c3#, 2...♔xc4 3.♖c7#, 1...♖xe2 2.♕f3+ ♖e4 3.♕f7#, 2...♔xc4 3.♖c7#.

The three main variations of this problem form a spectacular chain of model mates with the pinning of the same black pawn in each of them, while the black king stands on different squares (d5, e4, f4).

Composition No. 101
Zadachi i etyudy
1927

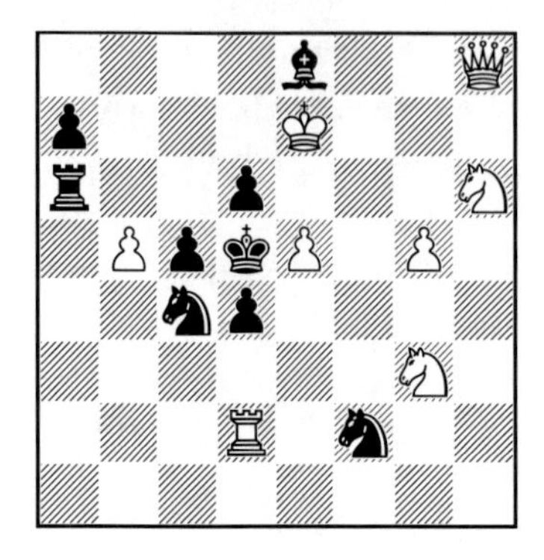

White to mate in 3 moves

1.♘g4!, threatening 2.♕g8+, 1...dxe5 2.♕xe5+, 1...d3 2.♕h1+, 1...♘xg4 2.♕h1+, 1...♗xb5(♗f7) 2.♕a8+.

Composition No. 102
Shakhmaty
1926

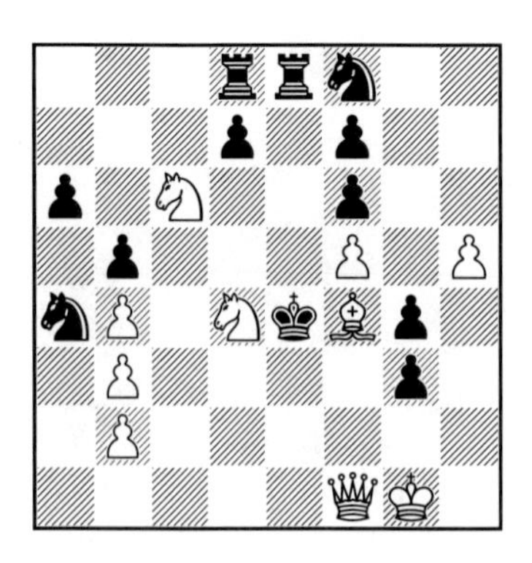

White to mate in 3 moves

1.♘e2!, threatening 2.♕g2+, 1...♔xf5 2.♕b1+, 1...♘xb2 2.♘c3+, 1...dxc6 2.♘xg3+.

Pavel Neunyvako also tried to make the opening move in his problems as spectacular as possible.

Composition No. 103
Shakhmatny listok
1926

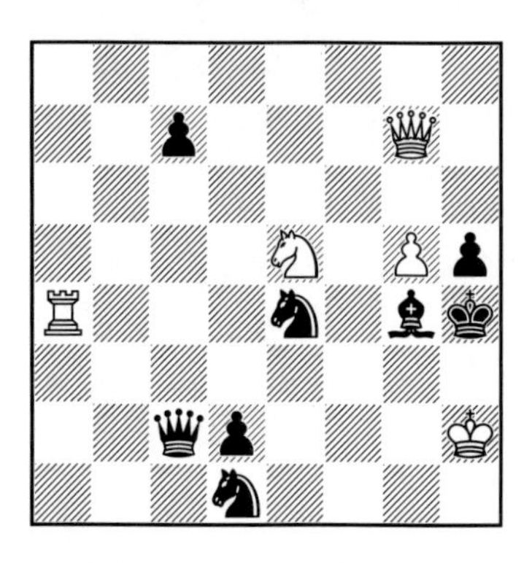

White to mate in 2 moves

1.♕f6!, threatening 2.♘g6#, 1...♗~ 2.g6#, 1...♘xf6 2.♘f3#.

"A study on the theme of semi-pinning in an artistic implementation (three model mates with a beautiful first move). How well this elegant problem differs from the sometimes cumbersome and downright anti-artistic works on this theme that are published in large numbers by followers of the New American school and are even awarded at competitions" (Leonid Kubbel's comments in the magazine *Shakhmatny listok*).

Composition No. 104
Shakhmaty
1926

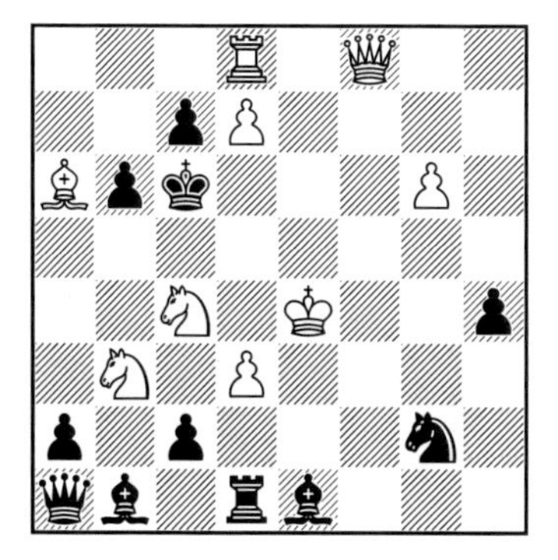

White to mate in 2 moves

In the initial position, there are several ready responses to checks to the white king: 1...♕d4+ 2.♘xd4#, 1...♕e5+ 2.♘xe5#. In the solution to this problem, after **1.♕f3!,** threatening ♔f4# the checkmate responses to the same checks change: 1...♕d4+ 2.♔xd4#, 1...♕e5+ 2.♔xe5#. And the king's discovered mate is played three more times: 1...♘e3 2.♔xe3#, 1...♘f4 2.♔xf4#, 1...♖xd3 2.♔xd3#.

Composition No. 105
Shakhmatny listok
1926

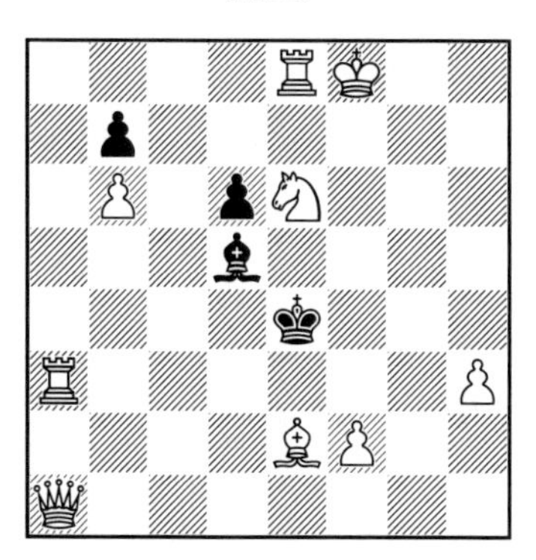

White to mate in 2 moves

1.♖a5! and zugzwang. There are two pins of the black bishop with model mates: 1...♔f5 2.♗d3#, 1...♗xe6 2.♕a4#. 1...♗~ 2.♕h1#.

Composition No. 106
Shakhmatny listok
1926

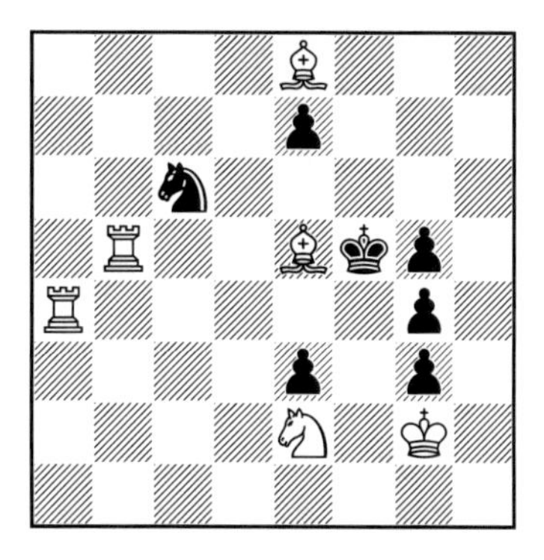

White to mate in 2 moves

1.♖a6! and zugzwang. 1...♔e6 2.♘d4#, 1...♔e4 (♘xe5) 2.♗g6#, 1...e6 2.♘xg3#.

"A simple, but elegant problem with two pinnings of the black knight in an artistic style, which, unfortunately, has recently been completely replaced in two-move problems by the New American school" (L. Kubbel's commentary in *Shakhmatny listok*).

Composition No. 107
Shakhmaty
1927, 4th prize of the competition of the second semester

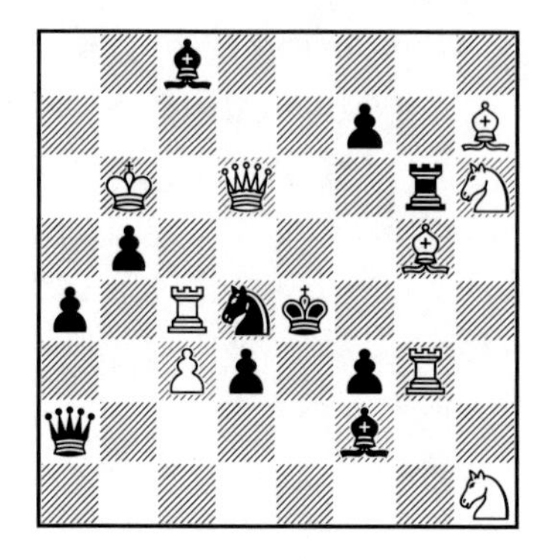

White to mate in 2 moves

1.♖c5! The black piece (♘d4), pinning white's ♖c5 that was threatening mate, also unpins another white piece (♕d6). Thematic variations: 1...♘c6 2.♕f4#, 1...♘e6 2.♕e5#. Additional variations: 1...♘b3 2.♕c6#, 1...♘f5 2.♖g4#, 1...♘c2 2.♘xf2#.

Composition No. 108
64
1927, 1st-2nd prize of the contest of the first semester

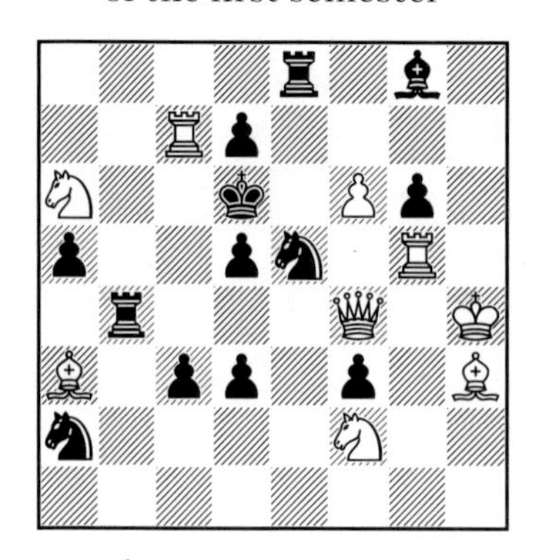

White to mate in 2 moves

1.♕d4!, threatening 2.♘e4#, 1...♘c4 2.♕c5#, 1...♘g4 2.♕b6#. This problem contains the theme of mutual unpinning of white's and black's pieces (Howard's Theme): moving along the line of her own pin, the white queen unpins the black knight, who then, defending from checkmate, is forced to unpin the queen.

Composition No. 109
Shakhmatny listok
1927, 1st honorable mention of the competition of the second semester

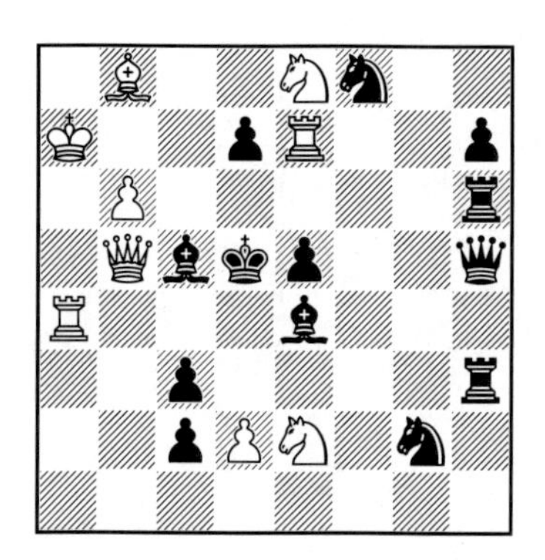

White to mate in 2 moves

1.d4!, threatening 2.♕xc5#, 1...♖c6 2.♕c4#, 1...♗d3(♗f3) 2.♘xc3#, 1...♗f5 2.♖xe5#, 1...♗g6 2.♘f6#, 1...♘e6 2.♖xd7#, 1...d6 2.♘c7#. "A technically nicely created problem with a number of interferences and blockings" (L. Kubbel).

Composition No. 110
Shakhmatny listok
1927, 3rd honorable mention of the competition of the second semester

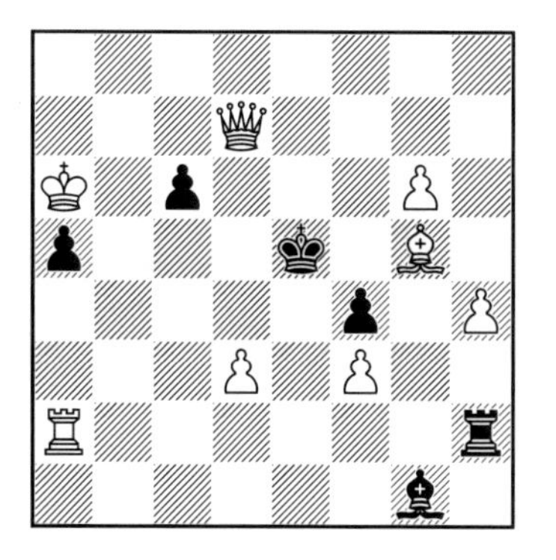

White to mate in 3 moves

1.♗d8!, threatening 1...♖xa2 2.♗c7+, 1...♗b6 2.♖xa5+, 1...♖xh4 2.♖e2+.

Composition No. 111
Vechernaya Moskva
1927, 4th prize

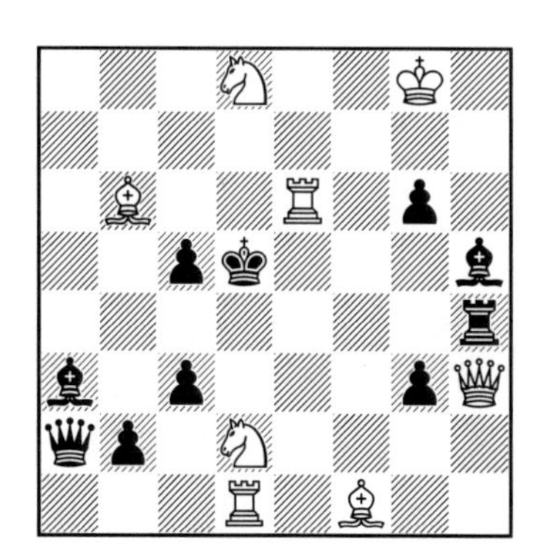

White to mate in 2 moves

1.♖e8!, threatening 2.♕d7#. A combination of two ideas. In the variations 1...♔d6+ 2.♘c4# and 1...♔d4+ 2.♘b3# we see discovered mates in response to the checks, while in the variations 1...♖g4 2.♘e4# and 1...♗g4 2.♘f3# we see a Grimshaw interference.

Pavel Neunyvako sometimes also created "tasks" – problems in which a particular theme was covered in as many variations as possible.

Composition No. 112
Shakhmaty
1923, 3rd honorable mention

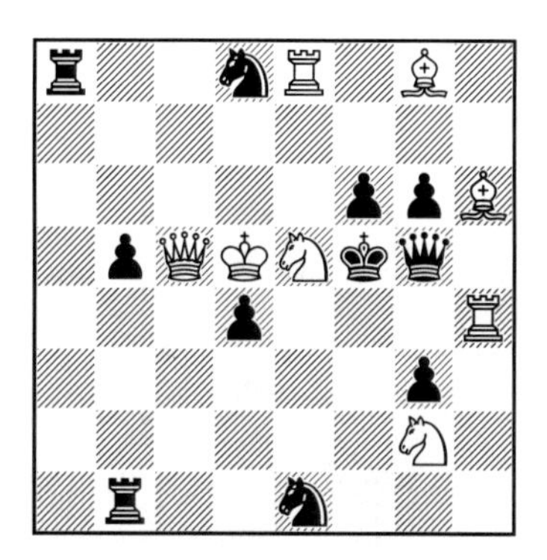

White to mate in 2 moves

Many years later, this problem was included in the FIDE Album. The white king is encircled by enemy pieces, and therefore the first move is quite spectacular **1.♔xd4!** Almost any jump by the ♘e5 leads to mate. Now, black has many ways to defend with a check to the white king, but none of them works! 1...♖b4+ 2.♘c4#, 1...♖d1+ 2.♘d3#, 1...♘c2+ 2.♕xc2#, 1...♘f3+ 2.♘xf3#, 1...♖c8 (♘c6) 2.♘c6#, 1...♘e6+ 2.♗xe6#, 1...♕d2+ 2.♘d3#, 1...♕e3+ 2.♘xe3#, 1...♕f4+ 2.♖xf4#,

1...♕g4+ 2.♘xg4#, 1...♕xh4+ 2.♘xh4#, or 1...fxe5+ 2.♕xe5#.

"A brilliant problem that sets a record number of checks (13) to the white king, which delivers eleven different mates," the magazine *Shakhmaty* noted.

Soon, Neunyvako adopted the ideas of the New American School and gained even more success.

Composition No. 113
De Problemist
1928, 2nd prize

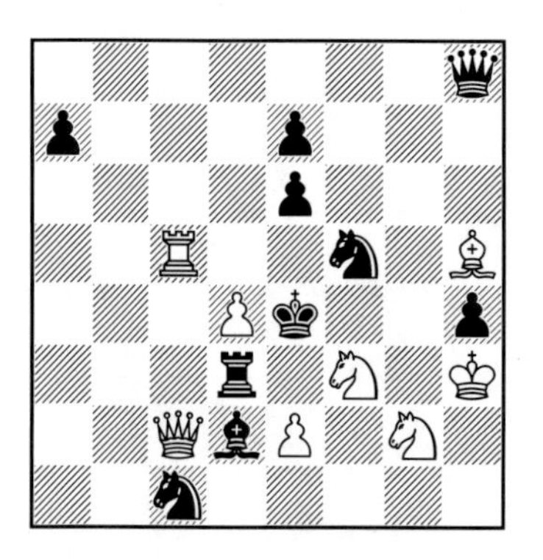

White to mate in 2 moves

1.♕a4!, threatening 2.♕c6#.

With his first move white unpins the black rook, and now there are three possible variations in which black's pieces, defending themselves from the mating threat, perform self-pinning (a Nitvelt Defense): 1...♖xd4 2.♘xd2#, 1...♘xd4 2.♗g6#, 1...♕xd4 2.♖e5#. There were also two extra variations: 1...♘e3 2.♘g5# and 1...♖xf3+ 2.♗xf3#.

A more intricate representation of these combinations was achieved in the following problem by Neunyvako.

Composition No. 114
Shakhmaty
1928, 2nd commendation of the competition of the second semester

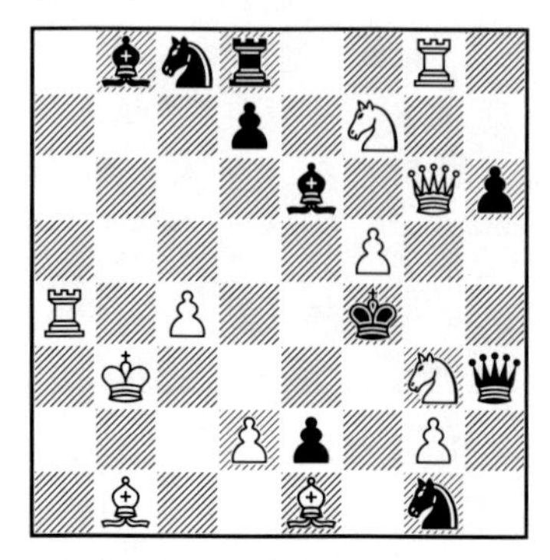

White to mate in 2 moves

1.♕f6! threatening 2.♕d4#, 1...♗xf5 2.c5#, 1...♕xf5 2.♘h5#.

This problem was composed in Vinnitsa, to where Pavel Efimovich was sent after graduating from the Academy.

Composition No. 115
Zadachi i etyudy
1928

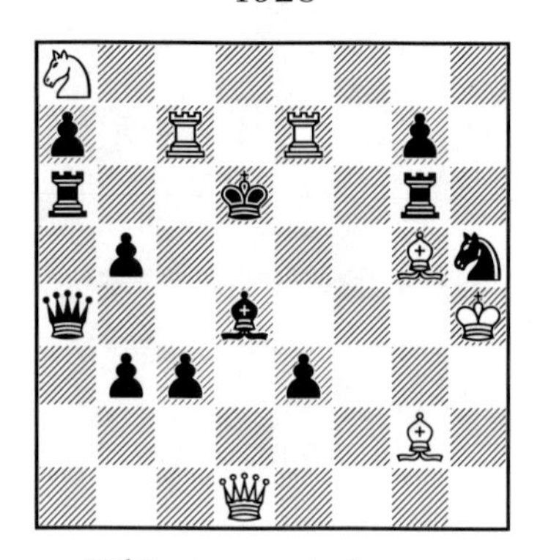

White to mate in 2 moves

1.♕g4! threatening 2.♕d7#, 1...♗e5 2.♖ed7#, 1...♗f6 2.♖e6#, 1...♗c5 2.♖cd7#, 1...♗b6 2.♖c6#. There were also extra variations: 1... b4 2.♕xd4# and 1...♘f6 2.♕e6#. Here we see the pinning of the white queen in four symmetrical variations with a thematic first move.

Composition No. 116
64
1928, 1st-2nd prize of the competition of the second semester. Dedicated to V. Schiff

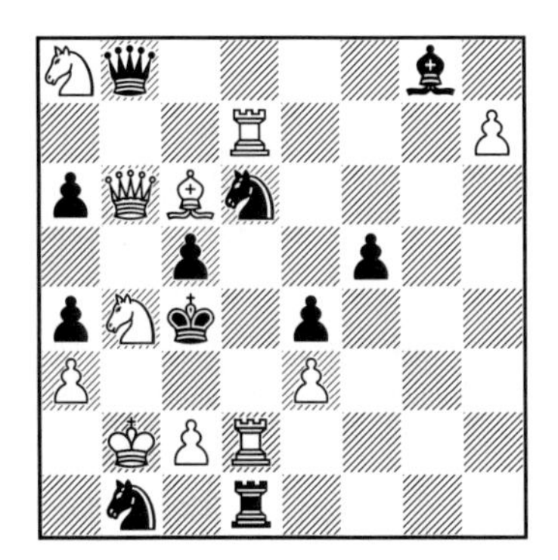

White to mate in 2 moves

1.♘d3! threatening 2.♘e5#. The theme of a valve, which consists of the simultaneous opening and closing of one of black's pieces along different lines, complicated by the unpinning of the white piece. The main variations are 1...♘b5 2.♕xc5# and 1...♘b7 2.♕xa6#.

Composition No. 117
Zadachi i etyudy
1928, Special prize of the 4th competition for two-movers

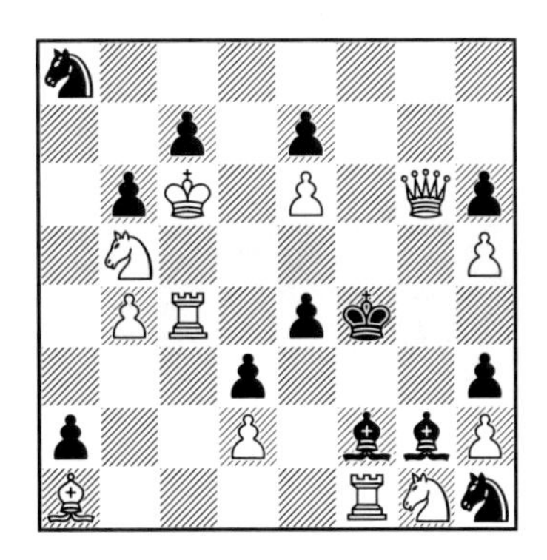

White to mate in 2 moves

1.♘d4! threatening 2.♕f5#: 1... e3+ 2.♘df3#, 1...♘g3 2.♕xg3#. The judge I. D. Katsenelenbogen awarded this problem a special prize for the best blocking: "A difficult Getgart combination with a check has been composed very nicely here. The bulkiness of the construction is justified by the type of blocking."

At the end of 1929, Neunyvako moved with his family to Kharkov, where he worked in the defense sector of the State Planning Committee of Ukraine. Several compositions created by him in Kharkov won awards at competitions.

Composition No. 118
64
1929, 4th commendation of the competition of the first semester

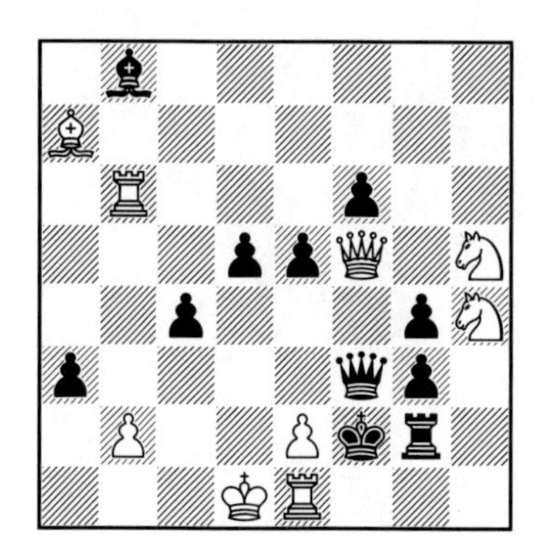

White to mate in 2 moves

1.♕c2! threatening 2.exf3#. The so-called "albino" theme – when the maximum activity of the white pawn comes on the mating move – is found in the threat and the three main variations: 1...♕d3+ 2.exd3#, 1...♕f4 2.e3# and 1...♕f5 2.e4#. There are extra variations as well: 1...♕b3(♕c3) 2.♖xf6# and 1...♕xe2+ 2.♕xe2#.

In 1930, Neunyvako was elected chairman of the All-Ukrainian Chess and Checkers Section. He headed the Union of Chess Players of Ukraine until 1933. In the same year, Pavel Efimovich left Kharkov.

The dramatic period of Pavel Neunyvako's life came as Stalinism turned rampant. On July 7, 1933, a member of the Government of Ukraine, Nikolai Skripnik, who was later declared an "enemy of the people", committed suicide. Skrypnik's supporters (and Neunyvako was one of his direct reports) were quickly disposed of: the "exposure" of the so-called "Ukrainian military organization" soon followed.

Obviously, the "competent authorities" were also aware of Pavel Neunyvako's personal friendship with Mate Zalka and Vasily Blukher...

In 1938, Pavel Efimovich was arrested and exiled to Alma-Ata. However, he managed to publish an excellent miniature, jointly composed with Lev Loshinsky, later a grandmaster and multiple Soviet champion at chess composition.

Composition No. 119
Shakhmaty v SSSR
1938 (with Lev Loshinsky)

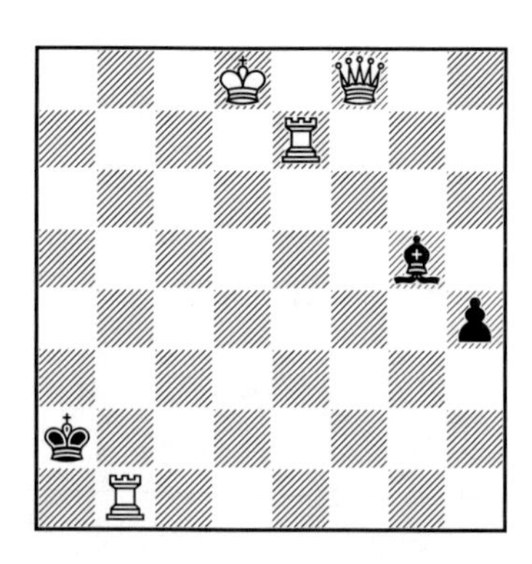

White to mate in 3 moves

1.♖b8! h3 2.♕f2+ ♗d2 3.♖a7#, 1...♔a1 2.♕f1+ ♗c1 3.♖a7#, 1...♔a3 2.♕f3+ ♗e3 3.♖a7#. Three echo-chameleon model mates (mating positions in which the arrangement of the pieces is repeated in different variations when the opponent's king is found on both light and dark squares) with the unpinning of the white rook, accompanied by the pinning of the black bishop who has just unpinned it. Other moves by the rook don't help: 1.♖b5? ♔a1! or 1.♖b6? h3!

This three-mover, characteristic of the composer's style, was later included in a collection of miniature problems and in a monograph on Loshinsky. However, it was not mentioned either among the prize winners of the 1938 contest, or among those excluded. Evidently, there were special circumstances, and the composition was "repressed".

When the final results of the 1938 contest were revealed, Neunyvako's situation had turned tragic. In Alma-Ata, where he worked as an accountant at a concrete asphalt factory, he was arrested again. He was executed by shooting on March 14, 1940.

He was remarkable not only for his risk-taking courage in cavalry attacks, but also for his courage in judgment. In the 1990s, chess composition veteran Alexander Pavlovich Gulyaev (1908-1998, pseudonym Grin/Green), who in the 1920s composed several problems together with Neunyvako, told the author that in private conversations Pavel Efimovich did not hide his sympathy for Leon Trotsky, whom he considered the main hero of the civil war. If already in the mid-1920s making such pronouncements was unsafe, then in the late 1930s it could cost you your life. It was Gulyaev who provided the key elements of Neunyvako's story.

Vladimir Neishtadt in his book *No Matter the Fate, It's a Tragedy* cites a fragment from the recollections of Ilya Dubinsky, who in the early 1930s was the Secretary of the Defense Soviet of the Ukrainian Council of People's Commissars: "One day Pavel Neunyvako – that 'enemy of the people' for whom I got into trouble – said to me, 'look, my reputation has been sullied. Why? In 1927, one-fifth of the students at the Frunze Academy belonged to the opposition. I was one of the sinners. But was I really against the party, against Soviet power? I faithfully carried out and continue to carry out everything I was told to do. I'm not criticizing anything. During the Civil War I commanded a platoon in the Fedko division. I have a piece of shrapnel fired by Denikin's forces wedged in my liver. We voted at the time because we were guided by Lenin's testament. We thought that the party would gain from a change of First Secretary.'"

In 1963, Pavel Efimovich Neunyvako was posthumously rehabilitated.

...He was a brave man, a talented leader. His abilities would have been so useful in the Second World War. And what heights could he have reached in composition?

However, there is no answer to this sad question.

Mikhail Barulin – He didn't Sign Anything

Often, the "personal" side of the biography of scientists and artists contains just a few words: born... studied... got married... died. This happens because their life achievements entirely consist of scientific discoveries or works of art.

This can also be applied to the outstanding problemist Mikhail Mikhailovich Barulin, whose life up to his own doom did not contain any noticeable excesses. He was born in 1897 in the family of a factory owner. The head of the family, Mikhail Nikitich Barulin, was said to be a brilliant scientist who made several inventions in the field of applied chemistry. And it seemed that his only son Mikhail would follow in his father's footsteps. After graduating from a commercial college, Barulin gained a specialism as a chemist, then worked as the technical director of the factory. Perhaps he would have made a notable career in the field of engineering inventions, if not for chess composition, where his ingenuity was truly boundless.

In the view of chess fans, Barulin was a "pure" problemist. It was all the more interesting to find in an old *64* magazine from 1924 a fragment of his biography as a chess player. That year, Mikhail Barulin participated in a tournament of workers circles, held simultaneously with what become known as the Third Soviet Championship. In the preliminary group, he confidently took first place with a score of 8 out of 9 and reached the final, where he shared 1st-3rd place. At the same time, neither at the preliminary nor at the final stage, did the future major problemist lose a single game. The power of his victories can be seen from the two games that made it to print.

Game No. 14
M. Barulin (Moscow) – Krestovsky (Kiev)
Tournament of workers circles, Moscow, 1924
Dutch Defense A04
Commentary by S. Grodzensky

1.♘f3 f5 2.b3 d6 3.d4 g6 4.c4 ♗g7 5.♗b2 ♘d7 6.♘bd2 ♘gf6 7.♕c2 b6. The plan to continue by playing 7...e6 and 8...♕e7 looks more logical.

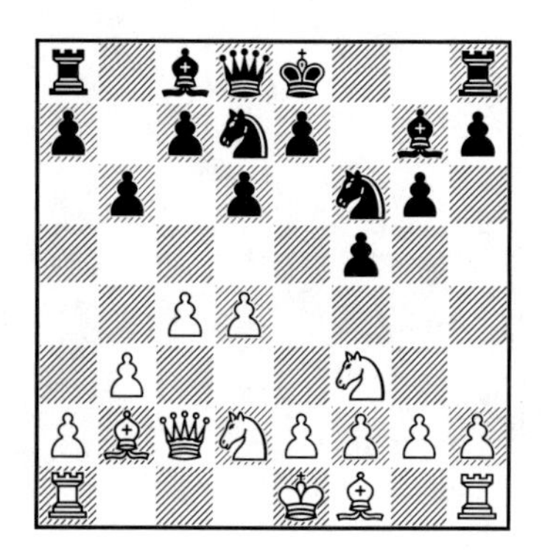

8.e3. The move 8.e4, with the obvious continuation 8...fxe4 9.♘xe4 ♗b7 10.♘eg5 ♘f8 11.d5, was more energetic. Then, by sending the knight along the ♘f3-d4-e6 route, white gets a clear advantage.

8...h6 9.♗d3 ♗b7 10.♘h4 ♘f8 11.d5 ♔f7 12.g4? And here, after 12.e4, white's position is definitely better.

12...♘xg4 13.♗xg7 ♔xg7 14.♘xg6 ♘xg6 15.♗xf5 ♘4e5 16.f4 e6 17.0-0-0 exf5 18.fxe5 ♘xe5 19.♕xf5 ♕f6? This was a crucial mistake. Meanwhile, after 19...♘g6 20.♖hg1 ♕e8! black had chances to repel white's attack, maintaining a material advantage. Now, white storms to victory almost unhindered.

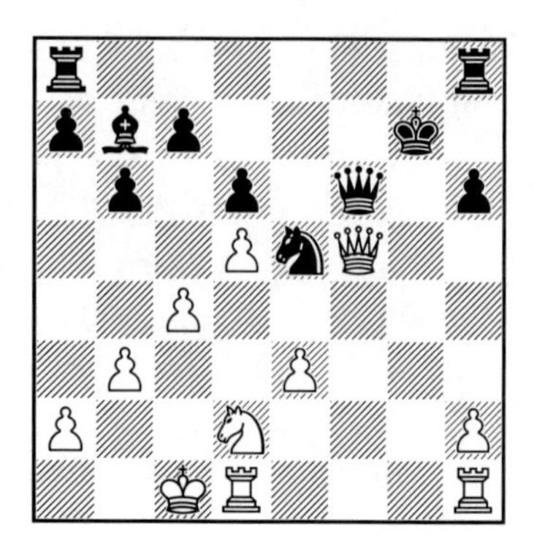

20.♖hg1+ ♘g6 21.♕d7+ ♔g8 22.♖df1 ♕c3+ 23.♔d1 ♖h7 24.♖xg6+ ♔h8 25.♕f5 ♖e7 26.♖xh6+ ♔g8 27.♖g1+ ♖g7 28.♕e6+. Black resigned.

In the final stage of the tournament of workers' communities Barulin's game against Munster representing Orel turned out to be decisive, after white's 35th move reaching the following position:

Game No. 15
B. Munster (Orel) –
M. Barulin (Moscow)
Tournament of workers circles,
Moscow, 1924
Commentary by S. Grodzensky

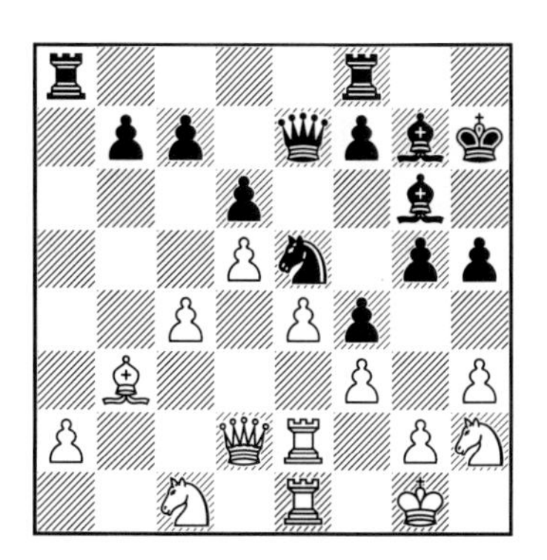

Sluggish positional maneuvering has led to an advantage for black, who is ready to take decisive action.

35...f5! 36.exf5 ♗xf5 37.♔h1?! The move 37.♗c2!? with the idea of exchanging the bad bishop deserved consideration.

37...♕f6 38.♖f1 ♗h6 39.♖ef2 ♖g8 40.♖g1 g4! Black makes a decisive breakthrough.

41.fxg4 hxg4 42.hxg4 ♖xg4! 43.♘xg4 ♕h4+. White resigned in view of inevitable checkmate.

By the time these games were played, Barulin's first problems had already appeared in print. And soon he found himself drawn increasingly into composition. His "apprenticeship" in composing passed by quite unnoticed, and so his first two-move composition was already a mature work.

Composition No. 120
Izvestia VTsIK
1923

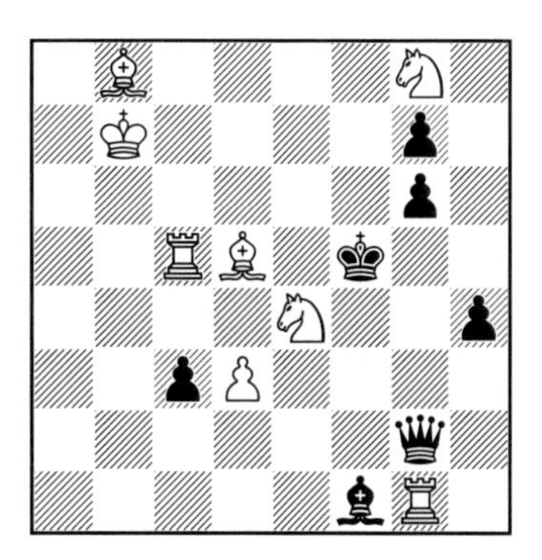

White to mate in 2 moves

1.♘g5! threatening 2.♗f3#. The threat is maintained in the variation 1...♔g4, since the black queen is pinned due to the king's retreat. The blunt reply 1...♕xd5+ is met by 2.♖xd5# (as white's ♖g1 is now involved). The variation 1...♕b2+ unpins the white bishop, allowing 2.♗b3#.

Mikhail Mikhailovich himself wrote about his first work: "In general, in the first period of my composing activity, I was totally influenced by the ideas of the New American School, and only occasionally composed works in a different style. Later, as will be seen, the 'standardized' ideas of the New Americans ceased to interest me and all my attention was directed at finding and exploring new ways to develop two-movers."

Barulin specialized in two-movers. If composition is "chess

poetry", then he was a true poet of two-move compositions, going down in the history of chess composition as the discoverer of several new themes, and in many ways anticipating the development of two-move compositions years in advance. Among his 250 or so problems, many received awards at competitions. The following one was his first to be awarded a prize:

Composition No. 121
Izvestia VTsIK
1924, 4th prize

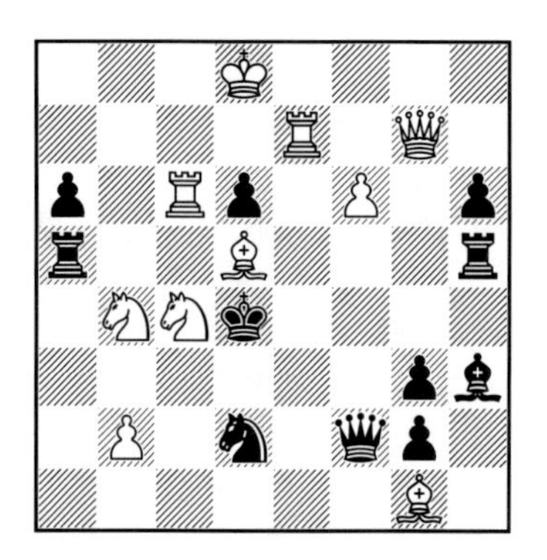

White to mate in 2 moves

1.♖e3! threatening 2.♖d3#. The variation **1...♕xf6+ 2.♖e7#** was quite spectacular. Here are several extra variations: 1...♗f5 2.f7#, 1...♖xd5 2.♘c2#, 1...♖a3 2.♕a7#.

Barulin created three-move compositions rarely and mainly in the early period of his work. Nevertheless, even in this genre, he produced works of great interest.

Composition No. 122
Pravda
1926

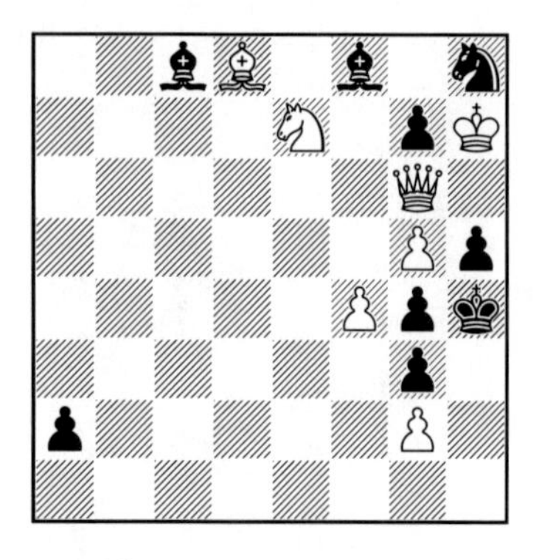

White to mate in 3 moves

1.♕b1! threatening 2.♕h1#. **1...axb1=♕+ 2.g6.** "In the starting position, the queen is an excess piece for white, and if it were not there, then checkmate would be achieved in two moves. The queen has to leave the g6 square, and, moreover, move precisely to b1, threatening to checkmate on h1 and thus gaining the necessary time for the pawn to move to g6. It is interesting that the newborn black queen can in no way prevent white from executing his plan, and in a certain sense even helps him by causing the pawn to move to g6. In general, however, this problem is just an amusing trifle, and it should be attributed to the 'sins of my composing youth'. Anyway, after creating this problem, I presented it in one of the Moscow chess clubs. A group of chess players who attempted to solve the problem could not understand for a long time why there was a black pawn on a2. Finally, one of them thoughtfully remarked: 'It is clear to me that the black pawn on a2 is placed only to prevent the white queen from moving to b1 (with the threat 2.♕h1#).' Everyone quickly agreed with him. Here I pointed out to those present that this queen move was the one that solves the problem" (notes by M. M. Barulin).

Composition No. 123
Pravda
1927, 3rd prize

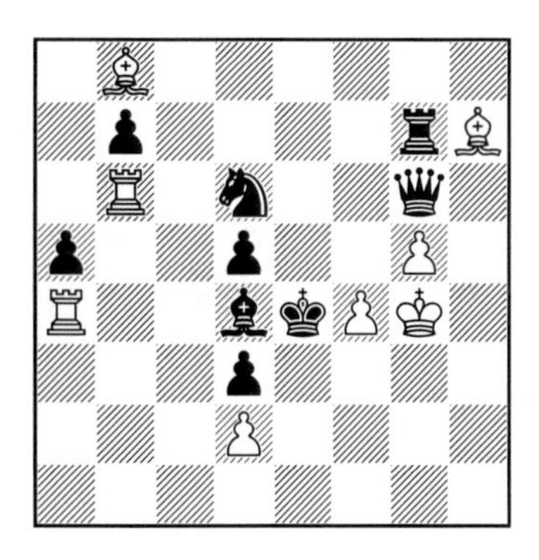

White to mate in 3 moves

1.♗a7! threatening 2.♖xd4+; 1...♘f5 2.♖e6+, 1...♘c4 2.♖e6+ (2...♗e5 3.♖xe5#).

"Lively play here from the knight who, while defending his king, creates two semi-pinning mechanisms, remaining pinned in both cases on the mating move. Not being that interested in creating three-move mates, I was content in this case with a simple demonstration of my idea and did not particularly make any effort in respect of its artistic construction, which, as is clear to me, was inadequate" (notes by M. M. Barulin).

Composition No. 124
Shakhmaty
1925, 2nd-3rd prize

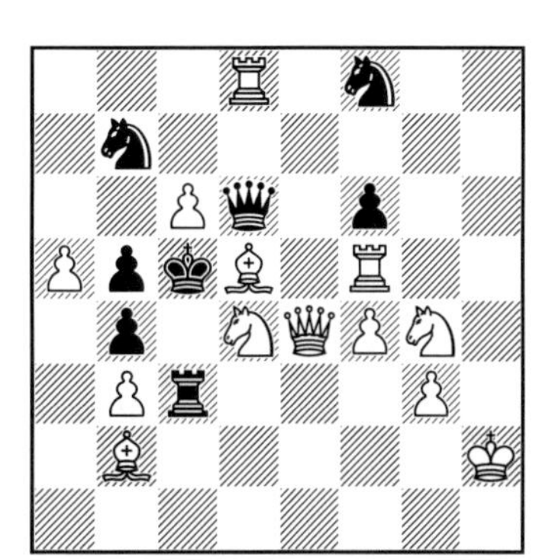

White to mate in 2 moves

This is one of the first problems on the theme of changing responses to check against the white king. In the initial position, 1...♖c2+ is met by the prosaic 2.♕xc2#. The decisive continuation was **1.♕e7!** zugzwang. Then, after 1...♖c2+ the bishop checkmates via 2.♗g2#. Here are other variations: 1...♘f~ 2.♘e6#; 1...♖e3 2.♗e4#; 1...♘b~ 2.♕a7#; 1...♕xe7 2.♗e6#.

Composition No. 125
64
1926,1st prize

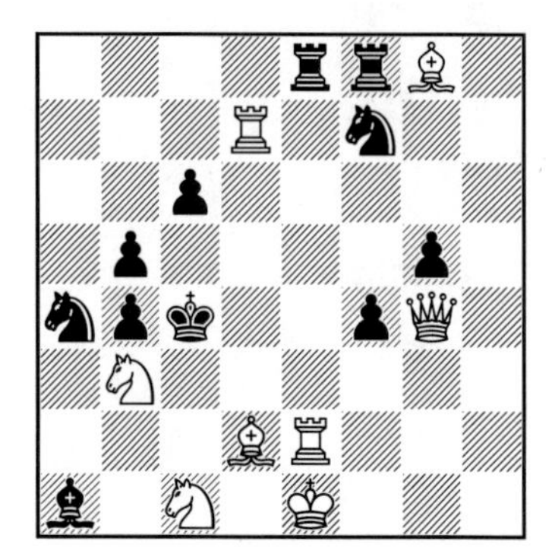

White to mate in 2 moves

Here is a problem on Howard's theme. The essence of the theme is that the first move of the pinned white piece unpins a black piece, which gets the opportunity to parry the threat, but at the same time unpins the white piece, and that piece gives checkmate. White begins with **1.♖e6!** threatening 2.♕e2#. The pinned white rook unpins the black knight; it parries the threat of **1...♘e5**, but at the same time unpins the white rook, which solves the problem with **2.♖xc6#**.

In 1927, Barulin made one of his key discoveries in composition, suggesting an original theme, which he called "white combinations". The essence of the author's idea is as follows: combinations usually carried out by black are now performed in false tries by white. The first problem on the theme of white combinations was published in a Dutch magazine.

Composition No. 126
Tijdschrift v.d. NSB
1927

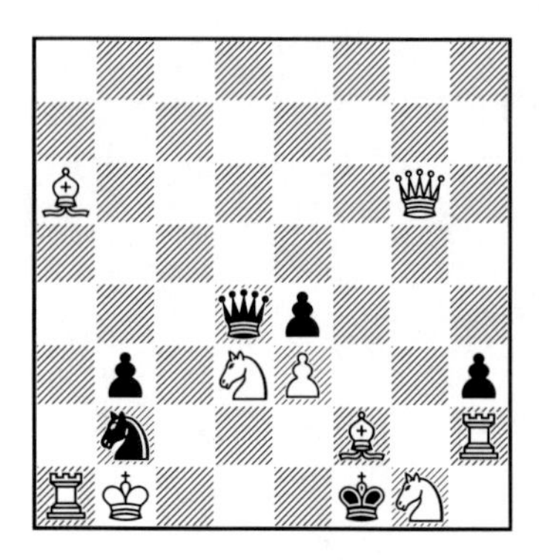

White to mate in 2 moves

1.♕f5! Barulin wrote: "With this problem, I started developing the idea of so-called 'white combinations'. Without going into any historical or theoretical excursions about this idea, I will try to explain to the reader its essence using examples that are arranged here in the order of the development of the idea itself. I approached white combinations based on Getgart combinations. Trying to invent some new combination, I came up with the following idea: Getgart combinations are particularly characterized by the fact that an attempt to solve the problem by giving a check does not work due to the fact that a black piece is unpinned, i.e. an unpinning combination takes place. But if so, why not replace the unpinning combination with some other combination, for example, a blocking one? I implemented this idea in this problem. If the immediate 1.♘xb2+?, giving a check, then 1...♛d3+ (the only possible defense), and there is no checkmate with 2.♔xb2?!, since the b2 square is blocked by the white knight. Obviously, a **white block** – a term used here for the first time – has happened. The variation 1...♛xd3+ 2.♔xb2# then works in the actual solution. However, due to the fact that by the nature of such a blocking combination, it can only happen on the second move, the whole essence and character of this attempt have diverged so much from the essence and character of the Getgart combination that it immediately became obvious to me that I had found a new idea: the possibility of expressing in 'illusory' solutions the most diverse combinations that have only ever been carried out up to now in play by black's pieces (including the most complex combinations)."

Mikhail Mikhailovich compiled several problems on the theme of "white combinations" almost at the same time. The most impressive of these won a prize at a competition organized by the magazine *Shakhmatny listok*.

Composition No. 127
Shakhmatny listok
1927, 2nd prize

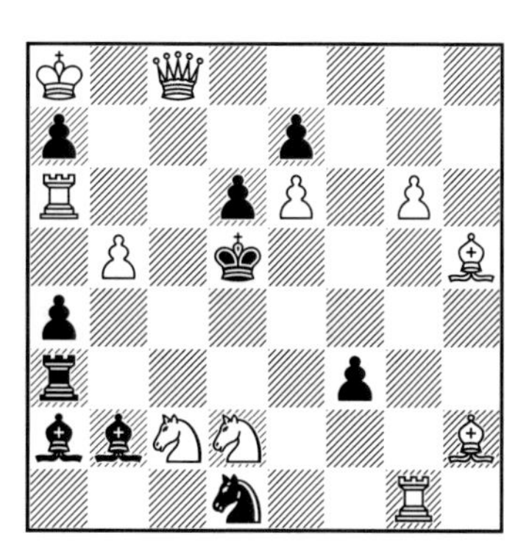

White to mate in 2 moves

1.♖a5! threatening 2.b6#. 1...♖c3 2.♖g5#; 1...♗c3 2.♗xf3#.

The false tries were as follows: 1.♗g4? ♖c3! (2.♖g5?) and 1.♖g4? ♗c3! (2.♗xf3?), and they form a "white Grimshaw", while the moves that refute these false tries are a "black Grimshaw".

Barulin wrote that he "was looking for the opportunity of artistically complicating a two-move problem in white combinations by adding illusory solutions to real play". One of his best problems on the theme of "white combinations" was published in 1930 in the same Dutch chess magazine.

Composition No. 128
Tijdschrift v.d. NSB
1930

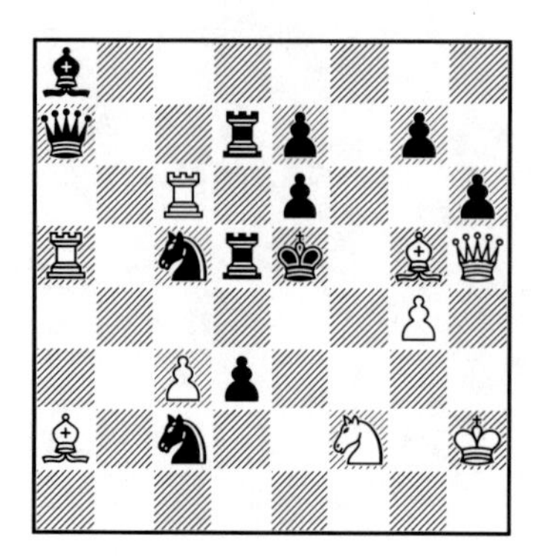

White to mate in 2 moves

To create a threat with his queen along the b8-h2 diagonal, white would like to clear the h2 square. However, in response to 1.♔h1? black plays 1...♖d4!, and 2.♖xe6# is an illegal move, since the white c6 rook unexpectedly turns out to be pinned. In the case of 1.♔g1? ♘e4!, the white knight falls under the pin and 2.♘xd3# is also impossible. The move **1.♕h4!** is the solution, after which the pinning of black's pieces via the semi-pinning mechanism is at white's disposal: **1...♖d4 2.♖xe6#; 1...♘e4 2.♘xd3#.**

"Barulin Defense" – this name was established in composition on another theme: when making a threat, white prevents any action by one of his long-range pieces on the square next to the black king; black parries the threat by preventing any action on that square by another long-range white piece. The "Barulin Defense" was first encountered in the following problem:

Composition No. 129
Shakhmaty
1928, 2nd prize

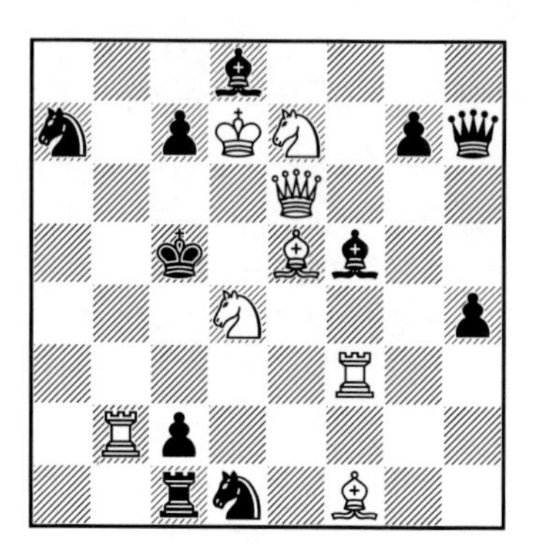

White to mate in 2 moves

After **1.♖f4!** white threatens 2.♘b3# with the white rook being simultaneously prevented from attacking the b4, b5 and b6 squares, which is enabled by the fact that these squares are attacked by other white pieces. Black's defense is based on disconnecting the white pieces from the thematic squares. **1...♗e4** (so that the ♖f4 no longer attacks b4) **2.♕c4#**; **1...♗d3** (stopping the ♗f1 from attacking b5) **2.♕d5#**; **1...c6** (so that the ♕e6 no longer attacks b6) **2.♗d6#**.

In 1929, the first All-Union composition championship took place. In the two-move problem section, first prize went to Barulin for his problem on the "Barulin Defense" theme.

Composition No. 130
Shakhmatny listok
1929, 1st prize

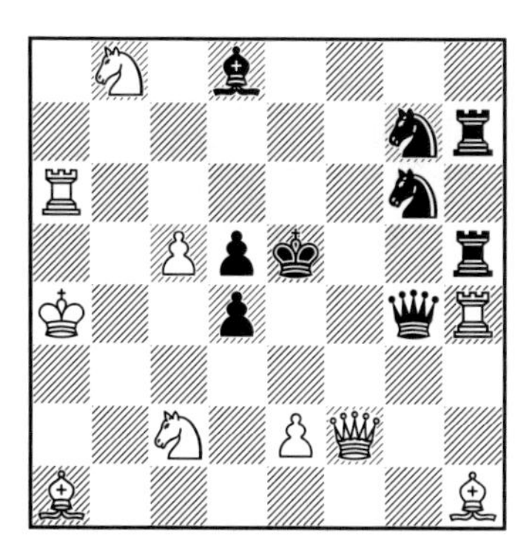

White to mate in 2 moves

Here, the Barulin Defense is presented in conjunction with other tactical ideas. The first move **1.♘xd4!** creates a thematic threat 2.♘bc6#, disconnecting the white a6 rook from the f6 square as it is controlled by the white queen. Black's thematic defenses are based on disconnecting the white queen from this square: **1...♖f5 2.♘d7#; 1...♘f5 2.♖e6#; 1...♕f5 2.♘f3#; 1...♘f4 2.♕e3#.** Additionally: 1...♕e6 2.♘dc6#; 1...♘e7 2.♕f6#.

In 1930, Barulin introduced the theme of "combinations in attempts": on the mating move, only one of several seemingly equivalent continuations leads to the goal.

Composition No. 131
Bristol Times
1930

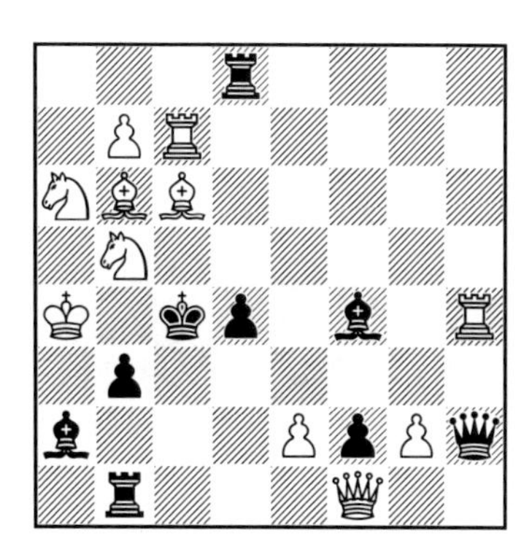

White to mate in 2 moves

1.♗a5! threatening 2.♘a3#. **1...d3.** The black f4 bishop is pinned and the frontal discovered attack is checkmate. The bishop has two ways of opening up the rook, however, the move 2.♗e4 fails due to the unpinning of the black bishop, so the only solution is **2.♗f3#**. Similarly, after **1...♗c1**, the only mating move is **2.e3#**, but not 2.e4? because of the unpinning of the black d4 pawn.

It is characteristic of the "combination in attempts" that the tactical technique (in the given problem – the unpinning of a black piece), which parries all white's attempts, is the same in all thematic variations. In the work of Barulin we find problems in which the choice of right move is determined by additional defensive points contained in black's move.

Composition No. 132
Tridtsat dnei
1930

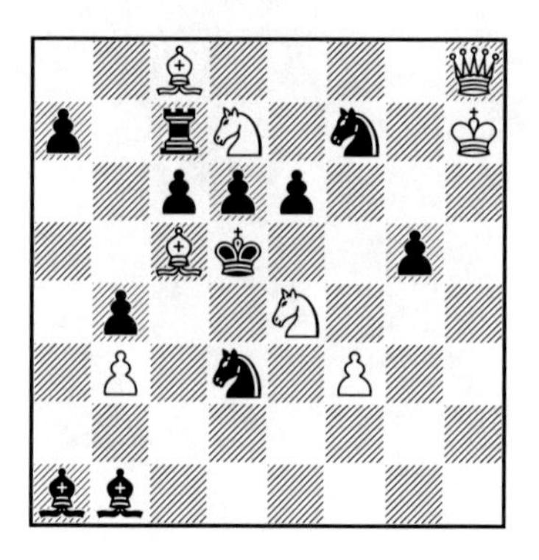

White to mate in 2 moves

1.♗a6! threatening 2.♗c4#. **1...♘de5 2.♘df6#** (2.♘ef6?) and **1...♘fe5 2.♘ef6#** (2.♘df6?). The choice of white's mating knight in the thematic variations is determined by alternating pins.

Composition No. 133
Ukrainian SFK Competition
1930, 1st prize

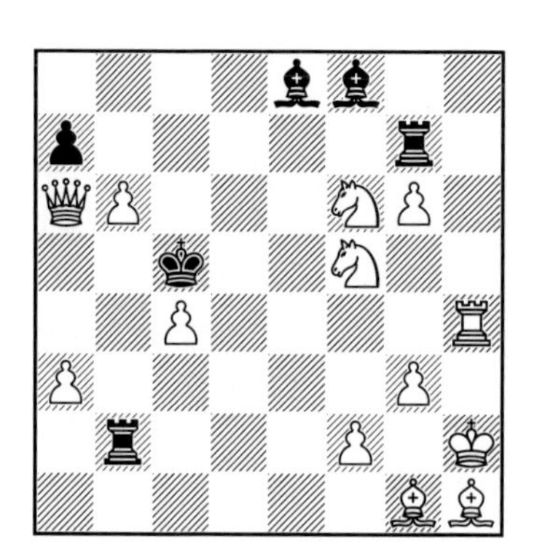

White to mate in 2 moves

1.b7! threatening 2.♘e4#, disconnecting the rook and bishop, since the c4 and c6 squares are attacked by the queen. Black uses the Barulin Defense mechanism – **1...♖b5** or **1...♖b6**, unpinning the white f-pawn. White must play accurately: in the first case, only **2.f3#** is possible, in the second – **2.f4#.** Barulin called this type of combination "neutralizing activations".

An excellent problem on the theme of "neutralizing activations" won the competition of the magazine *Problem.*

Composition No. 134
Problem
1932, 1st prize

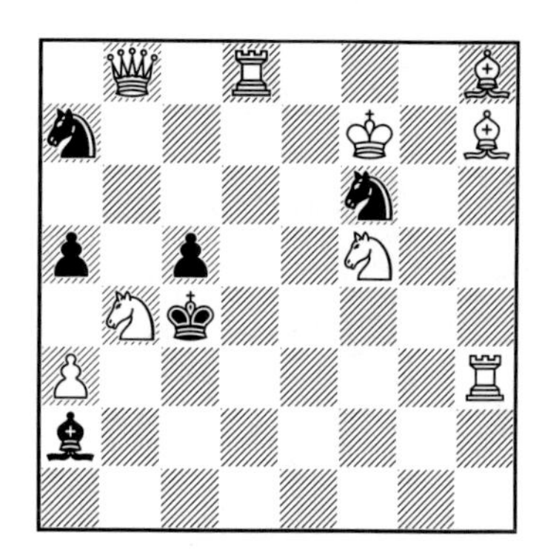

White to mate in 2 moves

1.♘d5! threatening 2.♖c3#. **1...♘d7 2.♘fe3#** (2.♘e3?) and **1...♘e4 2.♘de3#** (♘fe3?). Here are two extra variations: 1...♘xd5 2.♘d6# and 1...♘b5 2.♘b6#.

Here's another problem with "neutralizing activations".

Composition No. 135
Shakhmaty v SSSR
1931, 1st prize

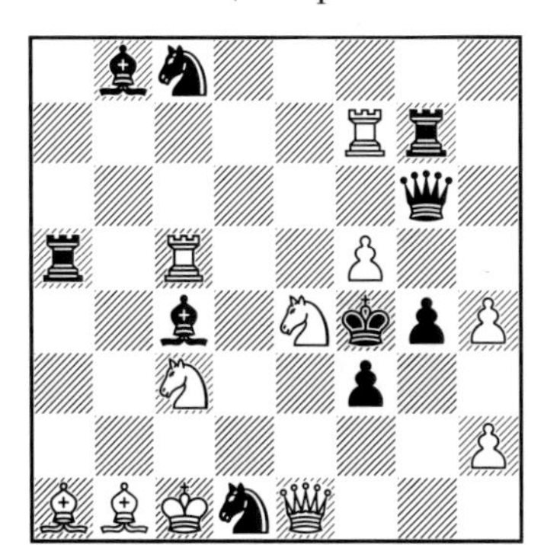

White to mate in 2 moves

1.♘f6 ♗d3 2.♘fd5#; 1...♗e2 2.♘cd5#. There were also additional variations: 1...♕xf5 2.♘h5# (in the initial position checkmate with 2.♖fxf5# would have been available); 1...♘d6 2.♕e5# and 1...♘e3 2.♕g3#.

In the composition match between Moscow and Rostov problemists, the theme "Blocking with a very recent theme in the solution" was set for one of the boards.

Composition No. 136
Moscow – Rostov Match
1930, 4th prize

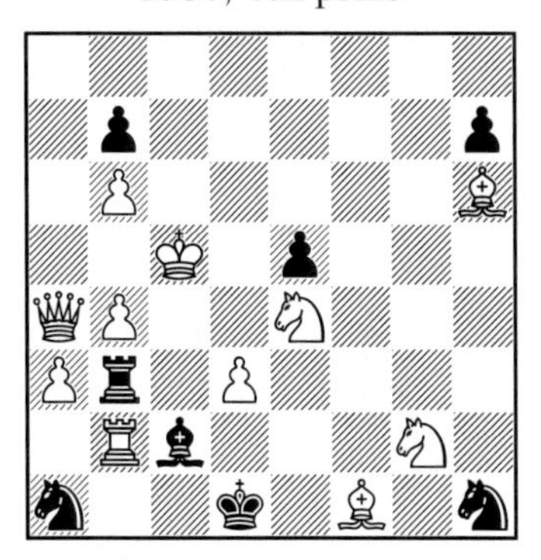

White to mate in 2 moves

In the initial position there is a complete half-pin: 1...♖xd3 2.♖b1#; 1...♗xd3 2.♘c3#. The move **1.♕d7!** is decisive. The first move breaks the virtual play and the "Nitvelt Defense" mechanism kicks in: **1...♖xd3 2.♘c3#; 1... ♗xd3 2.♗e2#.**

When the title of Master of Sport in Chess Composition was established in 1934, Mikhail Mikhailovich was one of the first recipients. Starting in 1935, he edited the problems column in *64*, and later in *Shakhmaty v SSSR*. In 1939, he got a full-time job with *64* – heading the letters department. His daughter, Lyubov Mikhailovna, told the author that her father used to come home from the editorial office with folders full of letters.

In the early 1930s, shortly after Lazar Zalkind's arrest, the Society of Chess Problems and Studies Fans that he headed was liquidated and the Central Commission for Composition was formed instead. Barulin was appointed its executive secretary, a position he held until his arrest in 1941. At the same time, he continued to compose problems that won the highest honors in major competitions.

Composition No. 137
Barcelona Radio Competition
1935, 1st prize

White to mate in 2 moves

1.♕e8! ♘e5 2.♘5e4# (2.♘3e4+ is illegal) and **1...♘xf5 2.♘3e4#** (2.♘5e4+ is illegal). The black knights in the main variations block different squares, simultaneously bringing white's pieces into the game. The variety of mates is due to the pins of white pieces.

Composition No. 138
Competition of the Park of Culture and Recreation
1939, 1st prize

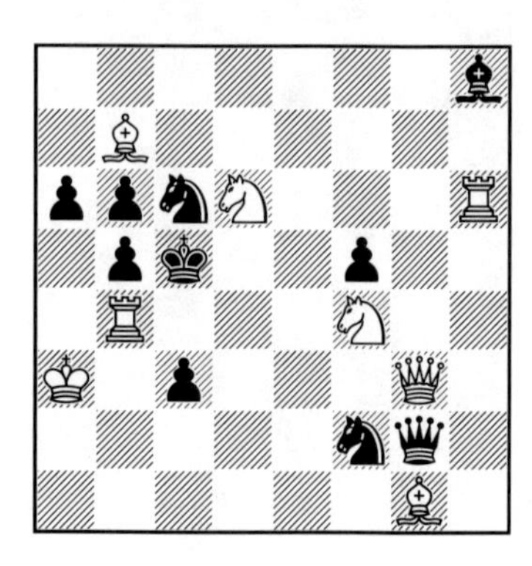

White to mate in 2 moves

1.♗a8! threatening 2.♘b7#. The c6 knight defends against the threats: 1...♘xb4 2.♘e6#; 1...♘d8 2.♘d3#; or 1...♘d4 2.♕xc3#; 1...♘e5 2.♕e3#. An original interpretation of the theme of continuous defense.

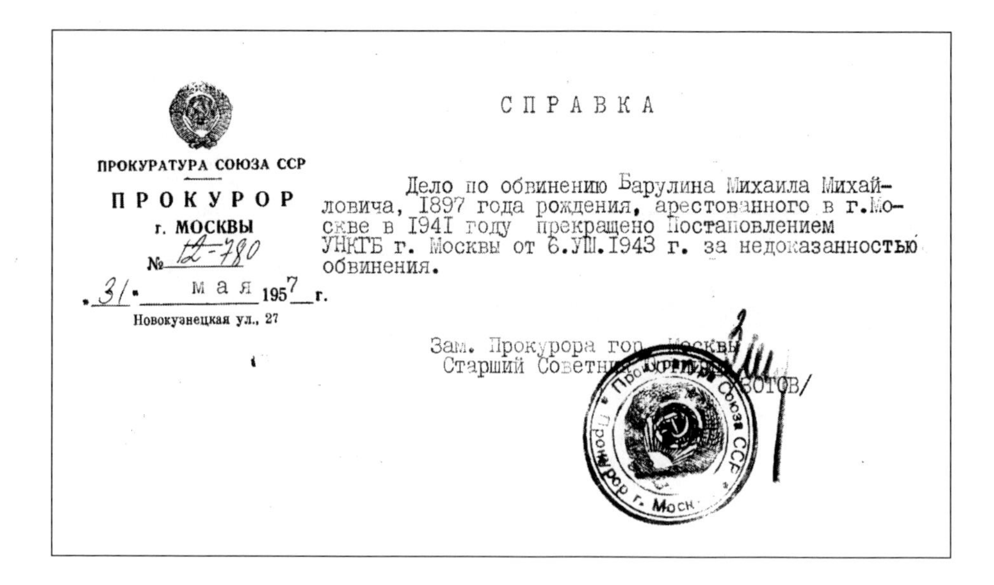

ПРОКУРАТУРА СОЮЗА ССР
ПРОКУРОР
г. МОСКВЫ
№ 12-780
„31“ мая 1957 г.
Новокузнецкая ул., 27

СПРАВКА

Дело по обвинению Барулина Михаила Михайловича, 1897 года рождения, арестованного в г.Москве в 1941 году прекращено Постановлением УНКГБ г. Москвы от 6.УШ.1943 г. за недоказанностью обвинения.

Зам. Прокурора гор. Москвы
Старший Советн[illegible] /[illegible]ОТОВ/

"Chess gatherings" were often held in M. M. Barulin's flat. Among the regulars, there were checkers master D. G. Ginzburg, artist Y. V. Yuzepchuk, who drew cartoons of almost all famous chess players, and M. M. Yudovich, already a veteran master and journalist. The "chess gatherings" ended quite abruptly after Barulin's arrest on the night of November 13, 1941. There was a rumor circulating that the host was arrested after someone filed a denunciation alleging that he was telling anti-Soviet jokes to his guests... Then it looked like Barulin was going to be released, but it was too late – Mikhail Mikhailovich died in prison. The *Chess Dictionary* (1964) indicates the year of his death – 1942.

Barulin's daughter told me, "Several days before the arrest, Yuzepchuk's wife ran to our flat, very agitated, and said that her husband had been 'taken away'. Soon after my father's arrest, I was summoned before the investigator. I got to realize that many others were being investigated in the same case, including Yuzepchuk and Ginzburg... We only received one letter (a 'triangle' – *a letter folded into a triangle and sent like that, as there was a shortage of envelopes*) from my father, telling us that he was in a remand prison in Kazan. Shortly after the war, a man in shabby clothes, with the appearance of a former camp inmate, came to our apartment one day. He said that he had been sitting in the same cell with Barulin for some time. My father was creating chess problems in prison, and taught his cellmates to play chess. During the interrogations, Mikhail

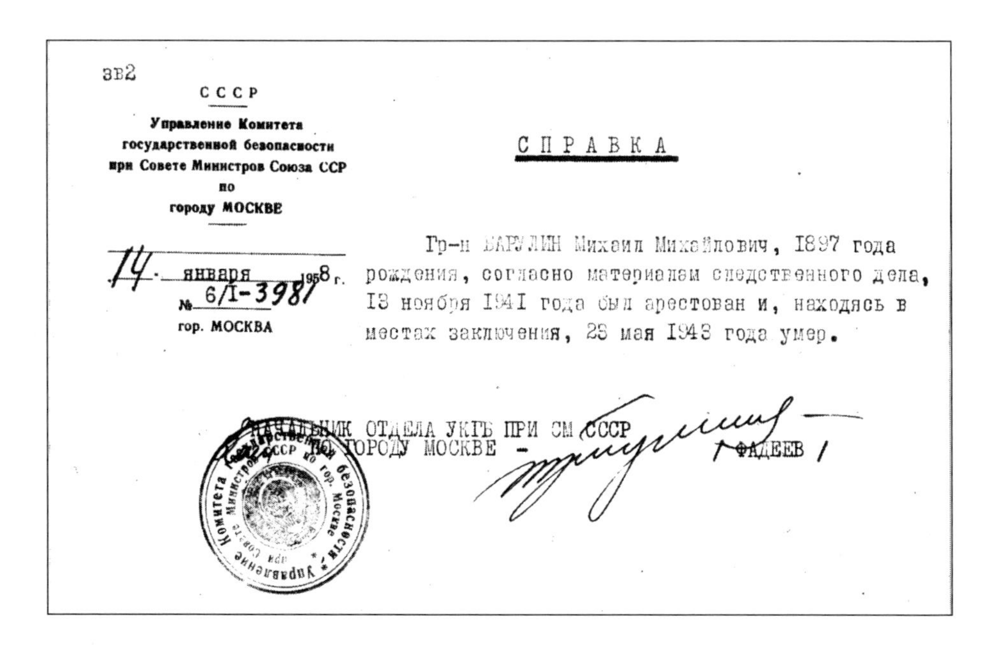

зв2

СССР

Управление Комитета
государственной безопасности
при Совете Министров Союза ССР
по
городу МОСКВЕ

14. января 1958 г.
№ 6/I-3981
гор. МОСКВА

С П Р А В К А

Гр-н БАРУЛИН Михаил Михайлович, 1897 года рождения, согласно материалам следственного дела, 13 ноября 1941 года был арестован и, находясь в местах заключения, 23 мая 1943 года умер.

НАЧАЛЬНИК ОТДЕЛА УКГБ ПРИ СМ СССР
ПО ГОРОДУ МОСКВЕ – /ФАДЕЕВ/

Mikhailovich held firm, despite the physical torture applied to him, and did not sign any confession to having committed any 'crime'. Our unusual visitor was going to come back and tell me more, but he didn't show up again. Maybe he was just afraid to visit the apartment of an 'enemy of the people' one more time."

"Lyubov Mikhailovna, did you see Yudovich since your father's arrest?" I asked her.

She replied: "I never saw Yudovich since my father's arrest. Except for one episode. I once went into a cafe on the first floor of the Central Chess Club, and suddenly heard, 'Here's Yudovich.' I reflexively looked at the door, and my eyes meet with Yudovich's. I thought that he recognized me, even though so many years had passed. Yudovich soon left the cafe. And about two weeks later, I learned that he had died." *(Yudovich died in 1987.)*

Lyubov Barulina saved two certificates received back in 1957-1958: one from the Prosecutor's Office of the USSR, and the other from the Moscow Department of the KGB. From these certificates it appears that Barulin died in prison on May 23, 1943, and two and a half months after his death, his case was dismissed "for lack of proof of charges". And it is not that difficult to understand today what is hidden behind the dry language of the certificates. Most likely, Mikhail Mikhailovich failed to survive the prison regime. He remained brave to the very end, refusing to sign fake "confessions" that were handed to him.

Over the Board Chess Players

Vladimirs Petrovs – "A Star Prematurely Extinguished"

Once, looking through the sad list of masters who fell victim to repression, the author began to wonder: which of them was the strongest over the board player?

The answer to this question is almost indisputable – this person is Vladimirs Petrovs from Riga, who was considered a grandmaster in the late 1930s (the title was not an official status at the time), but in the early 1940s he quietly disappeared without trace. "A Star Prematurely Extinguished" – this was the name of one of the first articles about him, which was published in the era of glasnost (*Shakhmaty v SSSR*, 1989, No. 3). It was written by Andris Fride and the grandmaster's widow Galina Mikhailovna Petrova-Matisa. Information in this chapter is largely drawn from it. More on this article, and on Petrovs, can be found on page 263 of the second volume of Sergei Voronkov's *Masterpieces and Dramas of the Soviet Championships: Volume II (1938-1947)* published by Elk and Ruby in 2021. Moreover, an English translation of the book by Petrova-Matisa and Dmitry Kryakvin *Hero of the Pre-War Olympiads: Grandmaster Vladimirs Mikhailovich Petrovs* (Riga 2013) by Elk and Ruby is being published simultaneously with the book you are now holding.

Vladimirs Petrovs was born in Riga on September 27, 1908, in the family of a cobbler. His parents were natives of Riga. His father owned a small workshop in the working-class district of the city, while his mother was a homemaker.

Vladimirs began studying chess at the Riga Russian Secondary School (semi-officially called the Lomonosov Grammar school), which he attended since 1919. Chess had always been held in high esteem there. Schoolmates of Petrovs – V. Rosenberg, V. Berzins, V. Hermeyer-

Knoch and N. Kampar – were strong chess players in pre-war Latvia. In the first school championship (1921-1922), Vladimirs took second place, but in all subsequent ones he was first.

In January 1923, Petrovs joined the Riga Chess Society, and in February he won second prize in the blitz handicap. When he joined the society, the student Petrovs was provisionally assigned third category. Therefore, in the handicap tournament against the strongest (first category) players, he got a head start – a pawn and two moves.

After graduating from school in 1925, Petrovs got a place at the Faculty of Law of Latvian University. However, he did not make a career as a lawyer (it was limited to serving in the Riga marriage registration bureau) – the main business of his short life was chess.

In April 1924, Vladimirs was admitted to the side tournament of the first Latvian Chess Congress. This was the first time that the name of this schoolboy, who turned out to be the winner in his preliminary group and received the right to play in the main tournament of the Second Latvian Chess Congress, appeared in the press.

Game No. 16
V. Petrovs – Gailis
Riga, 1924

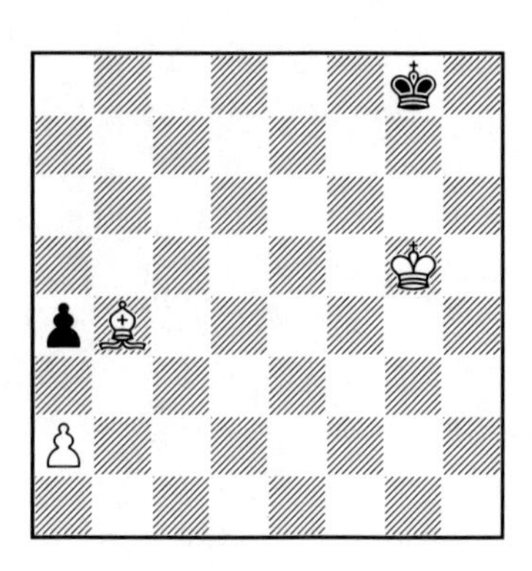

To achieve victory, white needs to take the black pawn without allowing the black king to reach a8.

48.♔g6 ♚h8 49.♗f8 ♚g8 50.♗g7! (zugzwang) **50...a3 51.♗h6 ♚h8 52.♗f8 ♚g8 53.♗xa3 ♚h8 54.♗e7**, and white won.

In 1926, Petrovs exercised his right to participate in the Second Latvian Chess Congress and obtained an excellent score: 11 points out of 14, sharing 2nd-3rd place. And even earlier, in January 1925, this first-year student won the first Riga championship, two points ahead of the second prize-winner F. Apsenieks. Petrovs also won the Riga championship in 1932 and 1936.

In the club competitions of 1926, Vladimirs had the opportunity to play a tournament game with the strongest chess player of Latvia at that time, Hermanis Matisons, for the only time in his life. However, during the game Petrovs did not know that he was playing with the maestro: it was a team tournament played "incognito", in which the opponents were chosen by the drawing of lots and were in different rooms. The game ended in a draw.

In 1928, at The Hague, Petrovs played for the Latvian team at the World Olympiad for the first time. His score – 8.5 out of 16 on third board – was not bad at all for a debutant. And the subsequent "tournaments of nations" (this is how the chess Olympiads were called at that time) cemented his reputation as a master of international class.

Game No. 17
S. Tartakower – V. Petrovs
Poland vs Latvia, III Olympiad, Hamburg, 1930
Queen's Pawn Game A45
Commentary by S. Grodzensky

1.d4 ♘f6 2.g3 d5 3.♗g2 e6 4.♘f3 c5 5.0-0 ♘c6 6.b3 cxd4 7.♘xd4 ♗c5 8.♗b2 ♕b6 (the continuation 8...♗d7!? was preferable) **9.e3 0-0 10.♘c3?** It was better to continue by playing 10.♘xc6 bxc6 11.♗xf6 gxf6 12.♕g4+ ♔h8 13.♕h4, and white gets an advantage in the middlegame.

10...♗xd4! 11.♘a4? It was better to play 11.exd4 ♕xd4 12.♖e1 with slight compensation for the pawn.

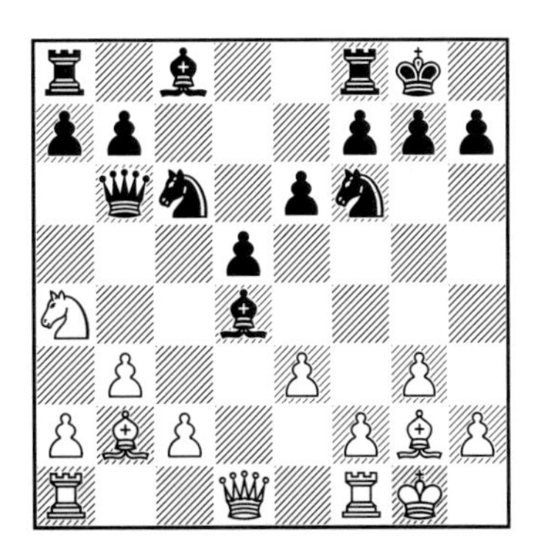

11...♗xb2! 12.♘xb6 axb6 13.♖b1 ♖xa2. The further course of the game confirms that three active minor pieces and a pawn are more than sufficient compensation for the sacrificed queen.

14.c4? (14.♕d2! was stronger) **14...♗e5 15.♕c1 ♘e4 16.♗xe4 dxe4 17.b4 ♗f6 18.♕d1 ♘e5 19.♕b3 ♖e2 20.♖bd1 ♘f3+ 21.♔g2 ♖b2 22.♕a4 ♘d2 23.♕b5 ♘xf1 24.♔xf1 e5 25.♕xb6 ♗g4 26.♖a1 ♗f3 27.♔g1 ♖d8 28.h4 h5 29.♕xb7 ♖bd2 30.♔h2 ♖d1 31.♕a6 ♖xa1?!** The easiest way to win was via 31...♖8d2! with inevitable checkmate.

32.♕xa1 ♖d1 33.♕xd1 ♗xd1 34.b5 ♗d8 35.c5 ♗a4 36.b6 ♗c6 37.♔h3 ♗e7 38.g4 ♗xc5 39.gxh5 ♗xb6 40.♔g4 ♗d7+. White resigned.

At the very beginning of the 1930s, Petrovs entered the international arena. In 1931, in Kaunas, he beat the master Aleksander Macht with a score of 2:0, and then shared 2nd-5th place at the first Baltics Chess Congress in Klaipeda, while representing Latvia. A Latvia –

Lithuania match was held in Riga on December 31, 1932 – January 1, 1933, and Vladimirs Petrovs scored one-and-a half points on second board in two games against Vladas Mikenas. The final game demonstrated the improved skill of the young chess player from Riga.

Game No. 18
V. Mikenas – V. Petrovs
Riga, 1933
Tarrasch Defense D34
Commentary by S. Grodzensky

1.d4 d5 2.c4 e6 3.♘c3 c5 4.cxd5 exd5 5.♘f3 ♘c6 6.g3 ♘f6 7.♗g2 ♗e7 8.0-0 0-0 9.h3. In the early 1930s, just like today, theory suggested a choice between Reti's move 9.dxc5, aiming at pressuring the isolated d5 pawn, and 9.♗g5, which also promised somewhat better prospects.

9...♗e6 10.♗e3 b6 11.♘e5. White wants to exploit the weakening of the a8-b1 diagonal. However, black is causing him difficulties.

11...♘xe5 12.dxe5.

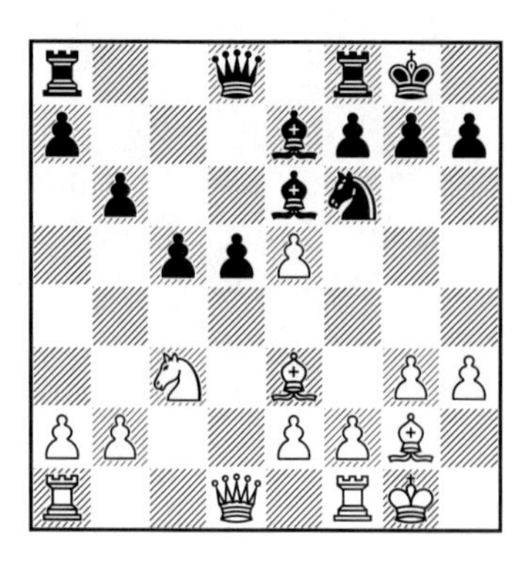

12...d4! A spectacular exchange sacrifice, which gives black a chance to execute a strong attack.

13.exf6 ♗xf6 14.♗xa8. In the case of 14.♘e4 dxe3 15.♘xf6+ ♕xf6 16.♗xa8 ♖xa8 17.fxe3 ♕xb2 18.♔h2 ♗xa2 black gets three passed pawns.

14...♕xa8 15.♔h2 dxe3 16.fxe3. Very soon it will become clear that in this position black's two bishops and a rook are stronger than white's two rooks and a knight.

16...♗e5! 17.♕e1 h5! 18.h4 b5! It would have been a mistake to continue by playing 18...g5 19.hxg5 h4 because of a possible reciprocal exchange sacrifice by white: 20.♖f4 hxg3+ 21.♕xg3. The move in the game creates an unpleasant and, it seems, irresistible threat of 19..b4.

19.a3. The move 19.♘xb5 would have been met by 19...♕e4 20.♖f4 ♕xe3 with a crushing attack.

19...b4 20.axb4 cxb4 21.♘d1 ♕e4 22.♖f4 ♗xf4 23.exf4 ♗d5 24.♕f1 ♖e8 25.e3 (or 25.♖xa7 ♕xe2+ 26.♕xe2 ♖xe2+ 27.♔h3 ♖e1! 28.♘f2 ♖f1 29.♖a5 ♗f3 with an easy win) **25...♖c8! 26.♘f2 ♖c2.** White resigned.

Vladimirs Petrovs also won the Third Chess Congress of Latvia (1930-1931) and it brought him the title of master. In the preliminary tournament, he had come first with a 100% result – 13 points out of 13. And then in the decisive match with the winner of the second tournament,

M. Feigin, he won by the score of 5.5:2.5. By that time, V. Petrovs' chess philosophy had already taken shape.

In 1933, answering a question: "What is chess?" he replied: "Some people think that chess is a waste of time, many will say that it is just a board game, but in my opinion, chess is an art. Perhaps, it is not such a kind of art that stands out for its endless number of ideas, unlike the widely accepted types of art, but it is richly saturated with elements of struggle. Chess is a battle! A battle that gives aesthetic pleasure... Chess fans who spend hours sitting at the board are mistaken believing that they are already playing chess. This illusion must be dispelled, because chess is a special art that has its own laws and foundations, which must be constantly studied. If we consider chess as an aesthetic struggle, then it can be characterized by its unusual intuitive logic. Chess intuition is something inexplicable, peculiar, but at the same time it can serve everyone, provided that the studying of chess art is managed by a highly qualified coach."

In the Fifth Chess Congress of Latvia (1934), which was also called the first championship, Petrovs shared 1st-2nd place with F. Apsenieks, and in the second national championship he convincingly won with a score of 12 points out of 13. Vladimirs Petrovs also finished first in the third championship (1937), in which the three strongest chess players of Latvia played in a quadruple round robin. Meanwhile, in 1934 Petrovs narrowly lost to Spielmann in a match with a score of 3.5:4.5, while in 1936 he won a competition in Helsinki representing Latvia.

Petrovs recorded an outstanding grandmaster result at the international tournament in Kemeri (1937). With 12 points out of 17, he shared 1st-3rd place with Flohr and Reshevsky, half a point ahead of Alekhine and Keres. Moreover, Fine, Tartakower, Stahlberg, Mikenas, Steiner and other famous maestros also played in that tourney.

Game No. 19
L. Rellstab – V. Petrovs
Kemeri, 1937
Colle System D02
Commentary by V. Sozin

1.d4 d5 2.♘f3 c5 3.e3 ♘f6 4.♗d3 g6. This defense against the Colle System at the very least deserves more attention than has been paid to it so far.

5.♘bd2 ♘bd7 6.b3. Black satisfactorily develops even after 6.c3, as was seen, for example, in the Colle – Widmar game (Karlsbad, 1929), and the Prins – Landau game (Zandvoort, 1936).

6...♗g7 7.♗b2 0-0 8.h3? In order to prevent e7–e5 followed by ♘g4; however, this move leads to a serious weakening of the kingside, so it was better to play 8.0-0 and then 9.e4 or 9.c4.

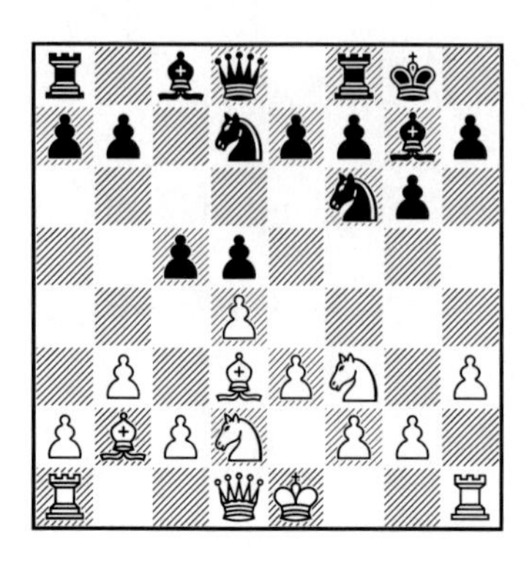

8...cxd4 9.exd4 ♘h5 10.g3 (otherwise, an unpleasant 10...♘f4 was threatened) **10...♕c7 11.♕e2 ♘c5 12.♘e5 ♘xd3+ 13.♘xd3 ♗f5 14.♖c1 ♖ac8 15.♕e3 ♕d6 16.c3 ♖fe8 17.f4** (17...e5 was threatened) **17...g5! 18.0-0 gxf4.** (The continuation 18...♗xh3 gives a clear advantage – S.G.)

19.♘xf4 ♗h6 20.♕f3 ♘xf4 21.gxf4 ♔h8 22.♖f2 ♖g8+. The invasion of the rooks along the g-file, supported by the strong position of the bishops, ends the fight very quickly.

23.♔h2 ♖g6 24.c4 ♖cg8 25.cxd5.

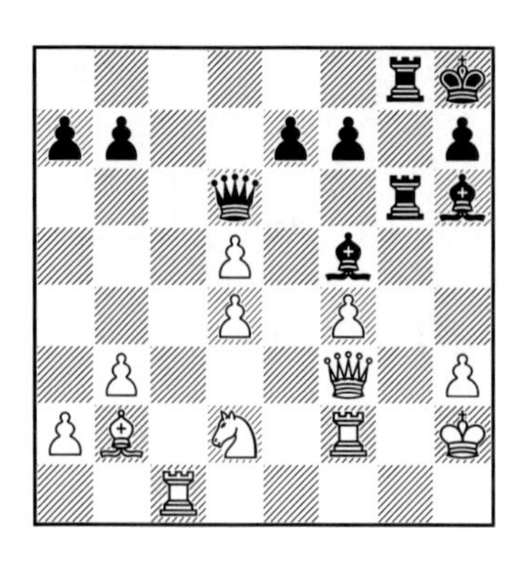

25...♗xf4+! 26.♕xf4 ♖g3. White resigned as he cannot avoid checkmate.

The result of the tournament in Kemeri would have been even better had Petrovs not blundered at a critical moment in a key game with Reshevsky, which he had played brilliantly until then.

Game No. 20
S. Reshevsky – V. Petrovs
Kemeri, 1937
Queen's Gambit D49
Commentary by M. Euwe

1.d4 ♘f6 2.c4 e6 3.♘f3 d5 4.♘c3 ♘bd7 5.e3 c6 6.♗d3 dxc4 7.♗xc4 b5 8.♗d3 a6 9.e4 c5 10.e5 cxd4 11.♘xb5 ♘xe5 12.♘xe5 axb5

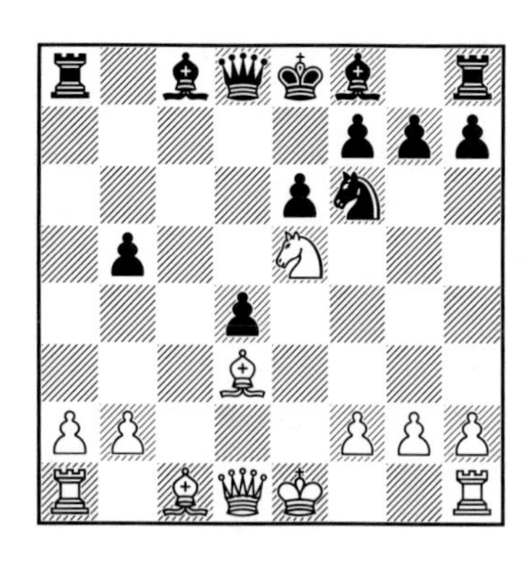

13.♕f3. The continuation devised by Stahlberg, which is currently considered the strongest. It seems that the opinion that this variation provides the best course of the game for white is correct.

13...♗b4+ 14.♔e2 ♖b8 15.♕g3.

This strong move was Reshevsky's own. However, it is strange that, on his next move, the author of the line failed to find the strongest continuation.

15...♕d5. The relatively best way of defense is the move 15...♕d6, followed by 16.♘f3, threatening ♗f4 and 17.♕xg7. After 16...♕xg3 17.hxg3 black obtains an unfavorable endgame. After 16.♘c6 (instead of 16.♘f3), white gets into difficulties even though he wins the exchange, for example: 16...♕xc6 17.♕xb8 0-0 with excellent chances to attack.

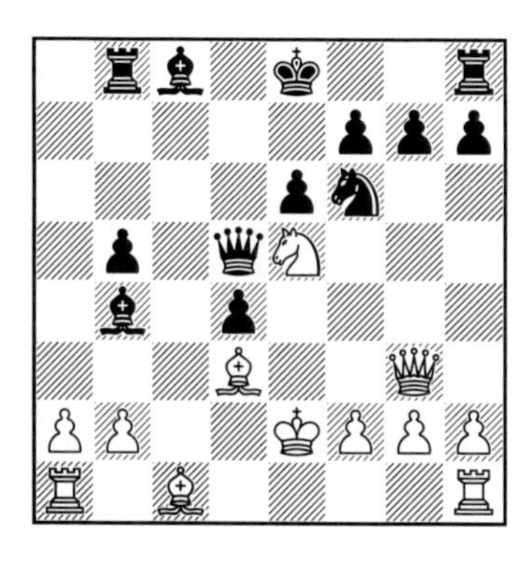

16.♘c6. This continuation leads to the above-mentioned position after winning the exchange (after 15...♕d6 16.♘c6). The correct continuation was 16.♘f3. Here, this move is even stronger than on 15...♕d6, since the ♖b8 is under attack and, moreover, white threatens 17.♕xg7 winning a piece. Black will have to continue by playing 16...♘d7 (the variation 16...e5! 17.♕xg7 ♖g8 18.♕xf6 e4 is stronger, and white's advantage is minimal – S.G.), but after 17.♕xg7, white gets a decisive advantage.

16...♕xc6 17.♕xb8 0-0 18.f3 ♗b7 19.♕e5 ♘d5. A really strong move. White is unable to capture the d4 pawn due to black's response 20...e5 followed by 21...♘f4+ or 21...f5. After elimination of the d4 pawn, the white king is even more exposed to black's attack.

20.♗d2 (after 20.♕xd4! e5 21.♕h4 f5 22.♖f1!! white has great prospects – S.G.) **20...♕c5.** Threatening 21...♘c3+, winning the queen.

21.♗f4 ♘xf4+ 22.♕xf4 e5 23.♕f5 g6 24.♕f6. Just about forced, since otherwise this will be followed by 24...f5 and 25...e4.

24...e4!

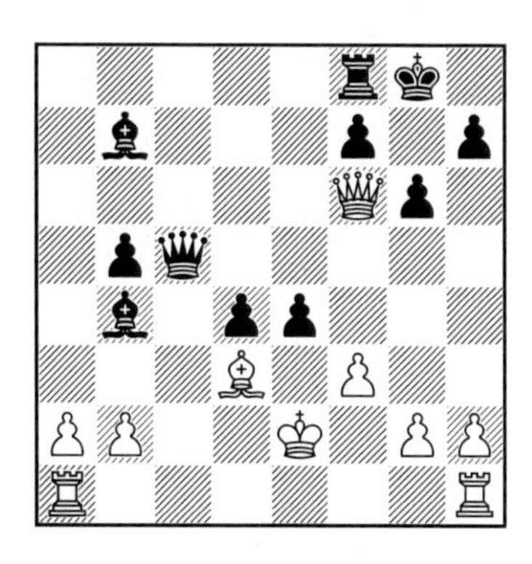

A beautiful combination, due to which black gets new resources for his attack.

25.fxe4 ♗xe4! 26.♗xe4 ♖e8. This is the idea of the e5-e4 advance. Now, 27.♕f3 will be met by 27...♕c2+ or 27...f5, while if 27.♔d3??, then 27...♕c4#, or 27.♔f3 ♕h5+

28.g4 (28.♔g3 ♖xe4) 28...♕h3+ 29.♔f4? ♗d2#.

27.♖hc1 ♖xe4+ 28.♔f2 ♕f8. The only move, which, however, is quite satisfactory.

29.♕f3 ♕e7 30.♖c7 ♕e6 31.♖c2 ♖e3 (the simplest way to win was 31...d3! – S.G.) **32.♕f4 ♖e5 33.♔g1.** Black threatened to capture the white queen, the best defense against which was retreating the king. At first glance, it seems that white has avoided all the dangers, but after a few moves it turns out that black has achieved a decisive advantage.

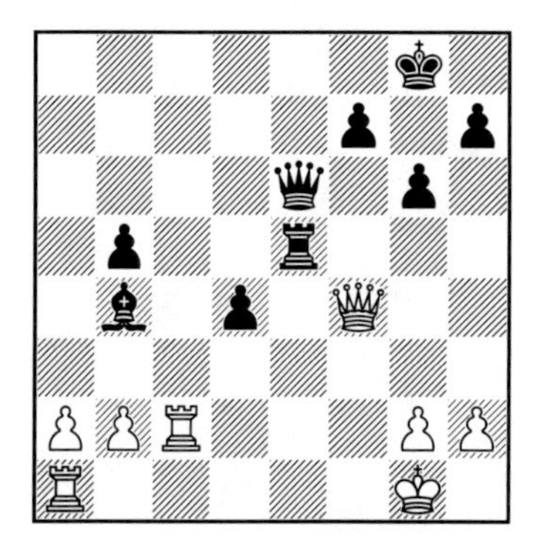

33...d3 34.♖c8+ ♔g7 35.♕d4 ♔h6?? A blunder leading to an immediate loss. The correct continuation was 35...♗d2! when white's position is critical due to the threats of 36...♗e3+, 36...♗g5 followed by 37...d2 and 38...♖e1+, and 36...♕xc8. The relatively best continuation would be 36.♖c6, for example, 36...♗e3+ 37.♕xe3 ♖xe3 38.♖xe6 fxe6! 39.♖d1, and white must counter black's planned ♔f6-e5-d4, for example, 39...♔f6 40.♔f2 ♖e2+ 41.♔f3 ♖xb2 42.♖xd3 ♖xa2 43.♖b3 ♖a5 with two passed pawns.

Thus, 35...♗d2! led to a win, while the unfortunate move in the game leads to the loss of the rook.

36.♕xb4 ♕xc8 37.♕f4+ ♖g5 38.h4 ♕c5+ 39.♔h1. Black lost on time.

Vladimirs Mikhailovich was very friendly. Knowledge of several European languages, a kind attitude and his joy of life brought Petrovs closer to very different people, including Alekhine, Flohr, Euwe, Najdorf, Bogoljubov and Keres.

After the tournament in Kemeri, Petrovs' reputation as a grandmaster grew so high that even his solid performances were sometimes treated almost as failures. At the tournament in Semmering-Baden, held shortly after the competition in Kemeri, Petrovs performed poorly overall, yet here he played several good games.

Game No. 21
V. Petrovs – E. Eliskases
Semmering-Baden, 1937
Commentary by S. Grodzensky

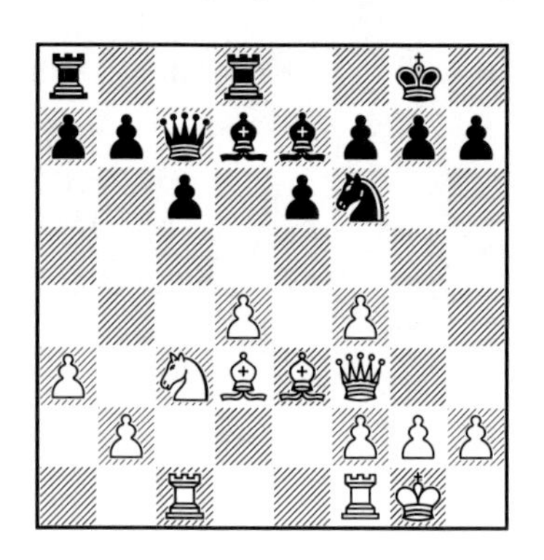

15.g4! ♗e8 16.g5 ♘d5 17.♘xd5 exd5 18.f5. The continuation 18.♕h3 g6 19.f5 looks better.

18...g6 (18...f6!) **19.h4! ♗d7?! 20.fxg6 hxg6 21.h5 ♔g7 22.♔g2.** 22.h6+! ♔f8 23.♗xg6 with a decisive advantage.

22...gxh5 23.♗f4! ♗d6 24.♗g3 ♗g4 25.♕f6+ ♔g8 26.♕h6 f5 27.gxf6 ♕f7 28.♗e5, threatening 29.♗h7+ ♕xh7 30.f7+ with a win, but it was simpler to continue 28.f3 ♗e6 29.♗xd6 ♖xd6 30.♔h2! ♕c7 31.f7+.

28...♗xe5 29.dxe5 ♖d7 30.f3 ♕e6 31.♕g5+. Black resigned.

In 1938, at a tournament in Margate, England, Petrovs finished third after Alekhine (whom he defeated in their game) and Spielmann, but ahead of Golombek, Milner-Barry and Thomas.

Game No. 22
V. Petrovs – A. Alekhine
Margate, 1938
Catalan Opening E02
Commentary by S. Grodzensky

1.d4 ♘f6 2.c4 e6 3.g3 d5 4.♗g2 dxc4 5.♕a4+ ♘bd7 6.♘f3 a6 7.♘c3 ♖b8 8.♕xc4 b5 9.♕d3 ♗b7 10.0-0 c5 11.dxc5 ♘xc5 12.♕xd8+ ♖xd8 13.♗f4 b4 14.♘d1 ♘d5 15.♖c1 ♘xf4 16.gxf4 ♗d6 17.♘e5 ♗xg2 18.♔xg2 b3 19.axb3 f6 20.♘c6

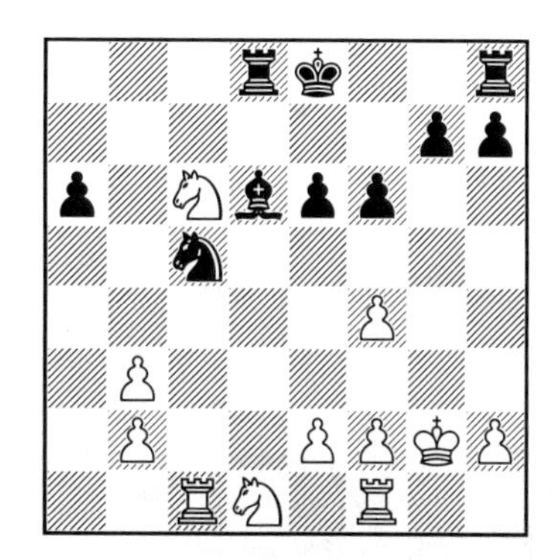

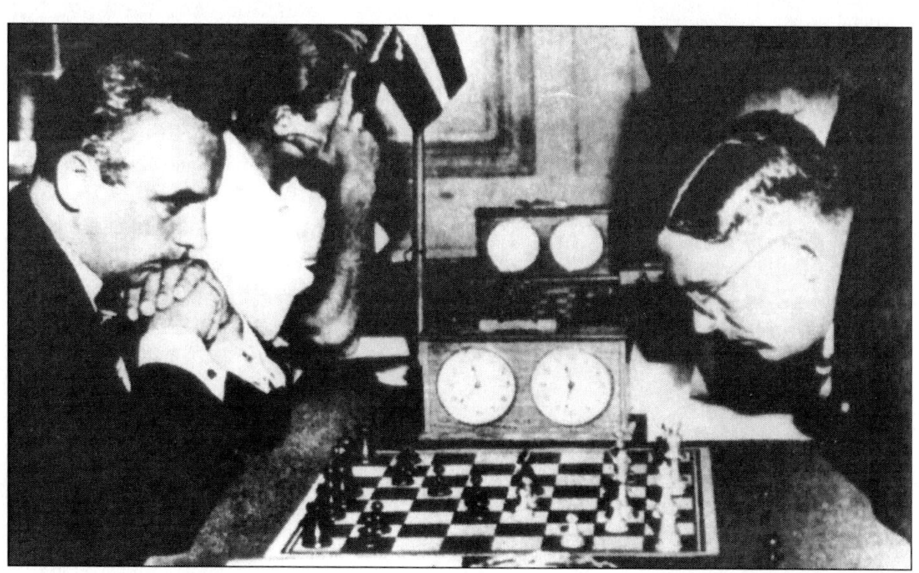

Stockholm Chess Olympiad, 1937. Euwe versus Petrovs on board 1

20...♖c8. It was also possible to play 20...♘xb3 21.♘xd8 ♘xc1 22.♘xe6 ♔f7 23.♘d4 ♗xf4 with a slight advantage for black.

21.♘d4 ♔d7 22.♘e3 ♗xf4 23.♖fd1 ♔e7 24.b4 ♗xe3 25.fxe3 ♘d7 26.♖a1! ♘b8 27.b5! axb5 (white has a better position) **28.♖a7+ ♔d6 29.♘xb5+ ♔c5 30.♘d6 ♖c6?** A blunder in an already worse position. He could have prolonged the resistance by playing 30...♖cd8 31.b4+ ♔c6 32.b5+ ♔c5 33.♖c7+ ♔b6.

31.b4+! ♔xb4. 31...♔b6 is met by 32.♖b7+ with checkmate.

32.♖b7+ ♔c3 33.♘e4+ ♔c2 (33...♔c4 34.♖d4#) **34.♖bb1!**

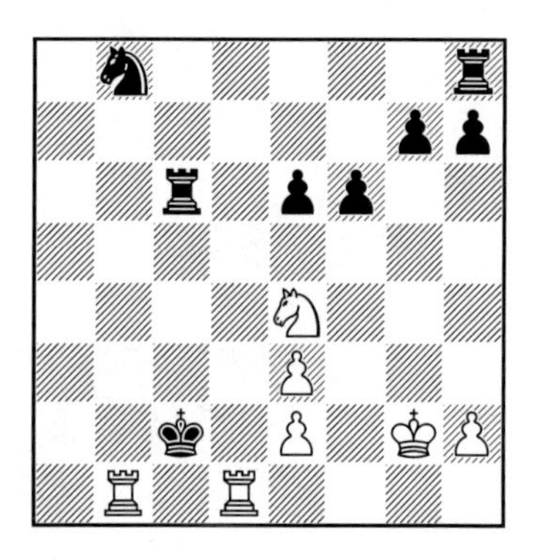

Black resigned: there is no defense to the threat of 35.♖dc1#.

Game No. 23
G. Thomas – V. Petrovs
Margate, 1938
Sicilian Defense B80
Commentary by S. Grodzensky

1.e4 c5 2.♘f3 d6 3.d4 cxd4 4.♘xd4 ♘f6 5.♘c3 e6 6.♗e3 a6 7.a4 b6 8.♗e2 ♗b7 9.f3 ♗e7 10.0-0 0-0 11.♕d2 ♘bd7 12.♗f2 ♕c7 13.♘a2 ♘c5 14.b4 ♘cd7 15.c4 ♖fd8 16.♖fc1 ♘e8 17.♖ab1 ♘e5 18.♘b3 ♘f6 19.♕e3 ♘fd7 20.f4 ♘c6 21.♗f3 a5! 22.b5 ♘b4 23.♘xb4 axb4 24.♖a1 ♘c5 25.♘xc5 dxc5 26.e5 ♖d4 27.♗xb7 ♕xb7 28.♕g3.

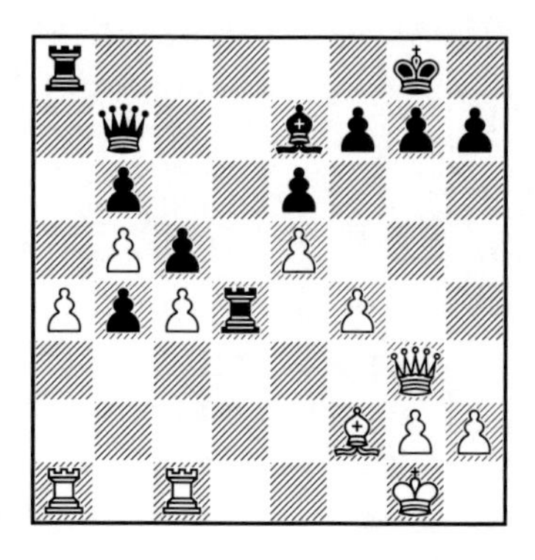

28...♖d2! 29.♗e1 ♗h4! 30.♕g4 h5 31.♕f3 (31.♕h3!?) **31...♕xf3 32.gxf3 ♗xe1 33.♖xe1 ♖c2 34.♖e4 b3.** White resigned.

In that same 1938, Petrovs shared 3rd-5th place in Lodz with Stahlberg and Eliskases (ahead of Pirc and Tartakower), leaving behind Frydman and Najdorf. In 1939 in Rosario (Argentina), the man from Riga came first, dropping only half a point to his rivals.

From 1928, Petrovs regularly participated in the tournaments of nations. In 1931, he achieved the best performance on third board. He also played very well at the Olympiad in 1936 (13.5 out of 20 on first board) and 1939 (9.5 out of 13 on first board). Note that players could not take rests at several of those Olympiads. The following games were played at what turned out to be the last Olympiad for Grandmaster Petrovs.

Game No. 24
V. Petrovs – S. Tartakower
Buenos-Aires, 1939
Dutch Defense A81
Commentary by N. Riumin

1.d4 f5 2.g3 ♘f6 3.♗g2 e6

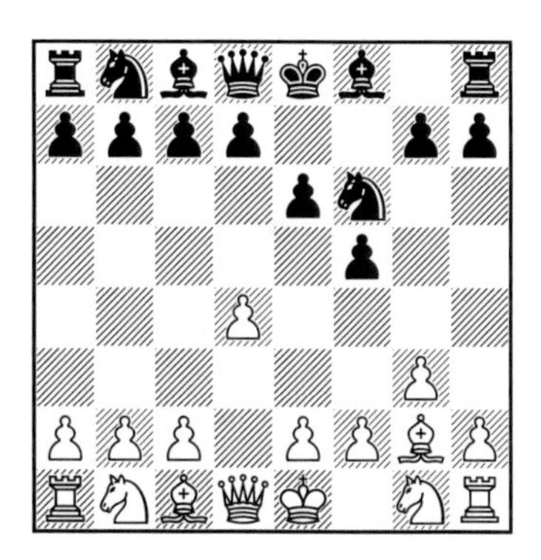

4.♘h3. Here, most masters play 4.♘f3. To be fair, it should be noted that the move in the game has a number of advantages: it retains the possibility of preparing the explosive e4 break and the white bishop creates dangerous pressure on the b7 square. The main point is that white significantly complicates black's play by preventing the possibility of any counterplay on the kingside.

4...♗e7 5.c4 0-0 6.♘c3. It was more accurate to play 6.0–0, and if 6...d6 then 7.♕b3 c6 8.♘d2 ♔h8 9.♕c3, preventing the e6-e5 advance as far as possible.

6...d6. This is the most natural way to develop. Black tries to restrict the scope of action of the b3 knight. The solid 6...d5 would have sentenced black to a long defense.

7.0-0. Evidently, the move 7.♕b3 was dubious in view of 7...♘c6 8.d5 ♘a5! 9.♕a4 c6 with great counterplay for black.

7...♕e8. Black could get a satisfactory game after 7...e5. For example, 8.dxe5 dxe5 9.♕xd8 ♖xd8 10.e4 ♘xe4 11.♘xe4 fxe4 and so on. However, black evidently wanted to avoid simplifications.

8.♕b3 ♘c6. Here black nevertheless had to play c6, accepting a cramped position. Now white seizes the initiative and achieves some advantage.

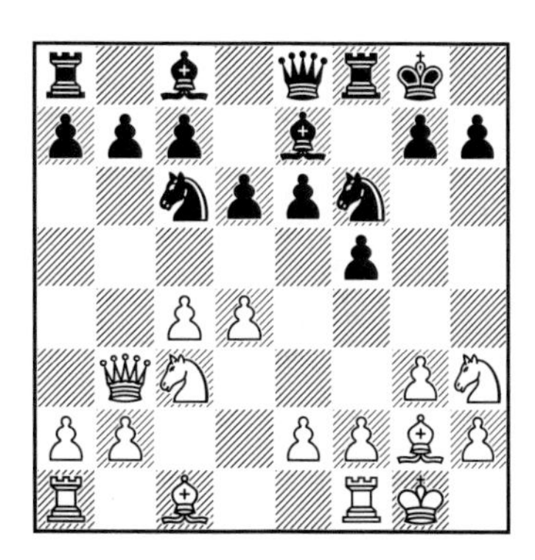

9.d5! exd5 (9...♘a5!? 10.♕b4 b6! deserved consideration – S.G.) **10.cxd5 ♘e5 11.♘b5 ♗d8 12.♘d4 ♔h8 13.♘f4.** The e6 square becomes a powerful outpost for white. All this is a consequence of the move 8...♘c6.

13...c5 14.♘de6 ♖g8 15.♘xd8. 15.♕c2 was much stronger, since each exchange makes it easier for black to defend. There was no reason to be afraid of black's counterattack via g5, since this led to an even greater weakening of black's kingside.

15...♕xd8 16.♘e6 ♕e7. Tartakower probably rejected exchanging the knight on general considerations: white's bishop pair and the weakness of his own pawns, etc. In fact, after 16...♗xe6 17.dxe6, black's position looks unattractive, although defense is still feasible. Therefore, the move in the game should be considered objectively the best, although black will have to withstand a dangerous attack.

17.f4 ♘f7 18.e4! Sacrificing a pawn in order to strengthen the position of the e6 knight.

18...♘xe4 19.♗xe4 fxe4 20.f5 ♘e5! Obviously, the continuation 20...♗xe6 21.fxe6 ♘e5 22.♗f4 ♘f3+ 23.♔g2 was much worse, when the strong e6 pawn ensures white's victory. Instead, black skillfully uses his counter-chances. Now white, in order to save the initiative, has to make new material sacrifices.

21.♗g5 ♕f7 22.f6 ♘f3+ 23.♖xf3 exf3 24.♖f1! It would not have been enough to play 24.fxg7+ ♖xg7 25.♘xg7 (but not 25.♗d2 f2+ 26.♔g2 ♗xe6 27.dxe6 ♕f5!) 25...♕xg7, and black has nothing to be afraid of.

24...gxf6. Not 24...♗xe6 25.dxe6 ♕g6 26.♗h4!, and white keeps his advantage.

25.♖xf3 ♖g6? After 25...♖xg5 26.♘xg5 ♕g6, black should not lose the game. Black's attempt to retain a material advantage is refuted by Petrovs' simple but effective combination.

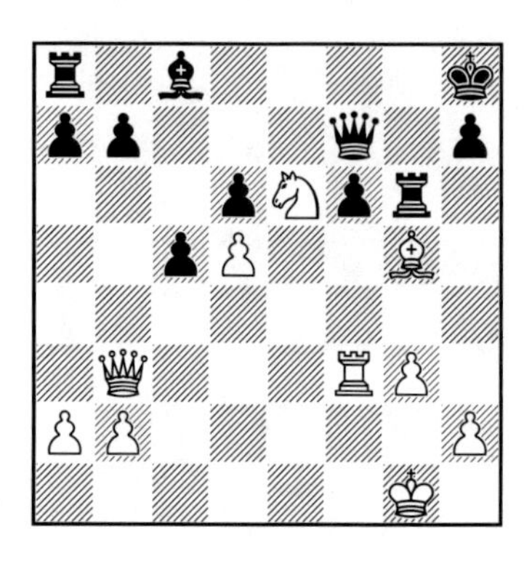

26.♗xf6+ ♔g8. Not 26...♖xf6 due to 27.♕c3!

27.♗e5 ♕e7 (the continuation 27...♗xe6! 28.♖xf7 ♗xf7 29.♕xb7 ♖e8 with counterplay was stronger – S.G.)

28.♖f8+ ♕xf8 29.♘xf8 ♔xf8 30.♗f4. The resulting endgame is lost for black due to the underdevelopment of his queenside. In any event, he could have dragged out the resistance for a long time, but, preferring to maintain the material balance, he perishes in a few moves.

30...b6 31.♕b5 ♗h3 32.♕c6 ♖d8 33.♕c7 ♖d7 34.♕c8+! ♔g7 35.♗d2.

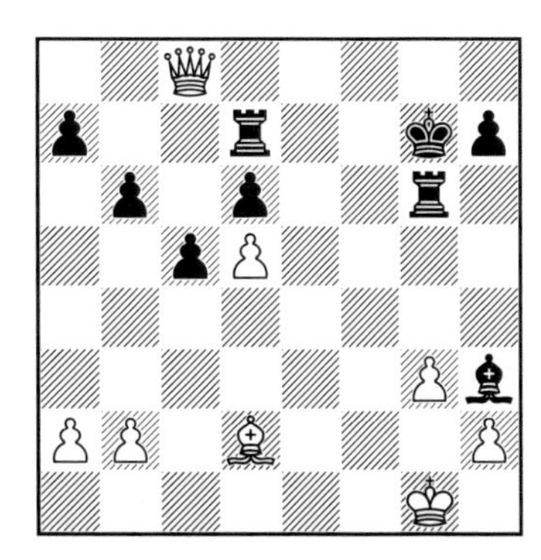

It is puzzling how black has got into such a helpless state. All his pieces are in zugzwang. If now 35...♗g4, then 36.♗c3+ ♔h6 (or 36...♔f7 37.♕h8!) 37.♕f8+ ♔h5 38.♔g2 and then h3. Therefore, black decides to give up the exchange, but it is already impossible for him to save the game.

35...♖f6 36.♗c3 ♔f7 37.♗xf6 ♔xf6 38.♕h8+ ♔f5 39.♔f2 ♔e4. This move leads to the loss of another piece, but black's position is already hopeless. White continues:

40.♕e8+ ♔xd5 41.♕h5+ ♔c6 42.♕xh3 d5 43.♕e6+ ♔c7 44.♔e3 a5 45.a4 d4+ 46.♔d2 ♖d6 47.♕f7+ ♖d7 48.♕f4+ ♔c6 49.h4 ♖d6 50.♕e4+. Black resigned.

Game No. 25

V. Petrovs – R. Grau

(Latvia vs. Argentina, Buenos Aires, 1939)

Queen's Gambit D02

Commentary by Y. Averbakh

1.d4 d5 2.♘f3 ♗f5 3.c4 e6 4.♕b3 ♘c6

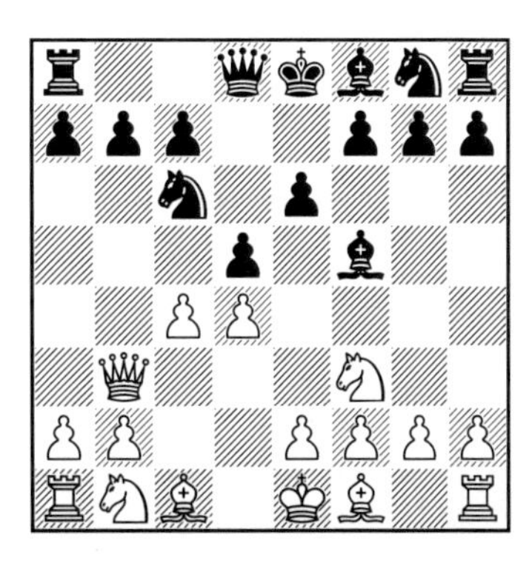

5.♗d2. Not 5.♕xb7? because of 5...♘b4 with complications that are advantageous for black.

5...♖b8 6.e3 a6. After the exchange on d5, white threatened an unpleasant ♗f1-b5 pin.

7.♗d3. Exchanges simplify black's task. 7.c5, played in order to create pressure on the queenside, would have led to a complicated game.

7...♗xd3 8.♕xd3 ♘b4 9.♗xb4. 9.♕b3 dxc4 10.♕xc4 ♕d5 promised white little.

9...♗xb4+ 10.♘bd2 ♘f6 11.0-0. If 11.c5, then 11...♘e4 with some simplifications.

11...0-0. This move leaves white the opportunity to attack on the queenside. Approximate equality could have been achieved via 11...♗xd2 12.♘xd2 dxc4.

12.c5! ♗xd2 13.♘xd2 c6 14.f4 ♘d7 15.b4 f5. Now the chances of either side getting anything on the kingside are zero. Does white have enough forces to break through on the queenside? The fate of the game will depend on this question.

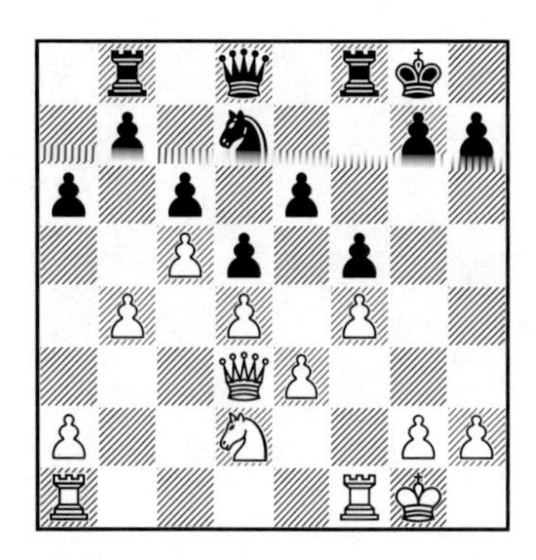

16.a4 ♕c7 17.♖fc1 ♖a8 18.b5 ♖fb8 19.♘f3 axb5. The continuation 19...♕d8 deserved consideration, since 20.bxc6 bxc6 left black an opportunity for counterplay in view of ♕d8-a5.

20.axb5 ♕d8 21.b6 ♖xa1 22.♖xa1 h6. 22...♖a8 23.♕c3, followed by 24.♖a7 or 24.♖a5, wouldn't change anything.

23.♖a7 ♔f7 24.♕e2 g6 25.♘d2 ♘f6 26.♘b3 ♔e8 27.♘a5 ♕c8 28.♕a2 ♘d7.

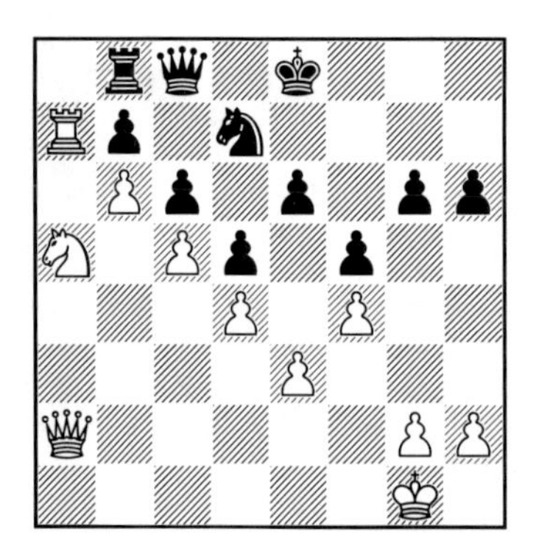

White has strengthened his position as much as possible, but black has managed to defend against the only opportunity to break through – 29.♘xb7 ♖xb7 30.♖xb7 ♕xb7 31.♕a7, which can be repelled via 31...♕b8. Therefore, white starts preparing a new manouver, the purpose of which is to deprive black of this defense.

29.♕f2! ♘f6 30.♕h4 ♘g8 31.g4 ♔f7.

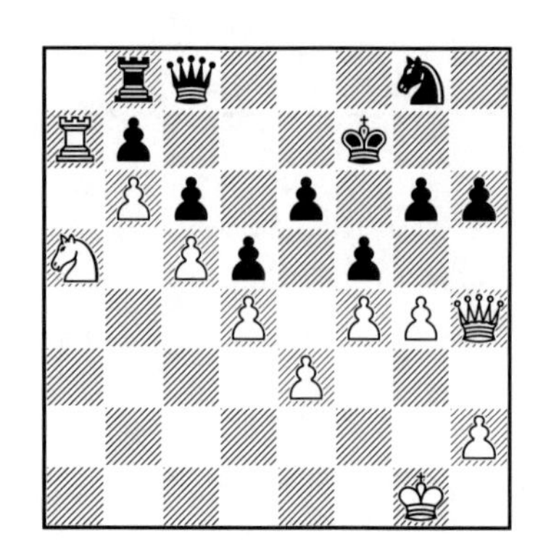

Black has defended himself against the threat of a breakthrough on the kingside, but white has completely different intentions.

32.g5 h5. Not 32...hxg5 33.♕h7+. Now, though, the black knight cannot occupy d7. In the case of 32...♔g7 white wins by playing 33.♕e1! or 33.gxh6+.

33.♕f2! ♔e8 34.♕a2 ♘e7. The continuation 34...♔d8 35.♘xb7+! ♖xb7 36.♖a8 ♖b8 37.♖xb8 ♕xb8 38.♕a7 ♔c8 39.♕f7! wouldn't help either.

35.♘xb7! ♖xb7 36.♖xb7 ♕xb7 37.♕a7. Black resigned.

In 1940, the strongest chess player of Latvia, Vladimirs Petrovs, became a Soviet citizen. Being recognized as an international grandmaster, he was awarded the title of Master of Sport of the USSR.

In the first round of the Soviet championship, Petrovs convincingly beat Kotov, who already had the title of grandmaster of the USSR.

Game No. 26
V. Petrovs – A. Kotov
12th Soviet Championship,
Moscow, 1940
Catalan Opening E02
Commentary by V. Petrovs

1.d4 ♘f6 2.c4 e6 3.g3 d5 4.♗g2 dxc4 5.♕a4+

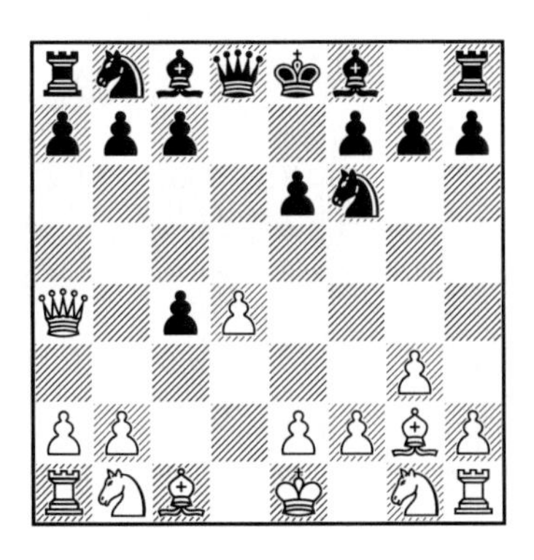

5...♗d7. Recently, this variation has been chosen the most frequently. It seems to me that 5...♘bd7 ultimately gives black the same chances of equality, regardless of whether white plays 6.♘d2 c5 7.♘xc4 or 6.♘f3 a6 7.♘c3.

6.♕xc4 ♗c6 7.♘f3 ♗d5 8.♕d3 (8.♕a4+ ♗c6 9.♕d1! also deserved consideration) **8...♗e4 9.♕d1 c5 10.♘c3 ♗c6 11.0-0 ♘bd7 12.♕d3.** With the obvious threat of e4, which forces black's next response.

12...cxd4 13.♘xd4 ♗xg2 14.♔xg2 ♗e7 15.♖d1 0-0.

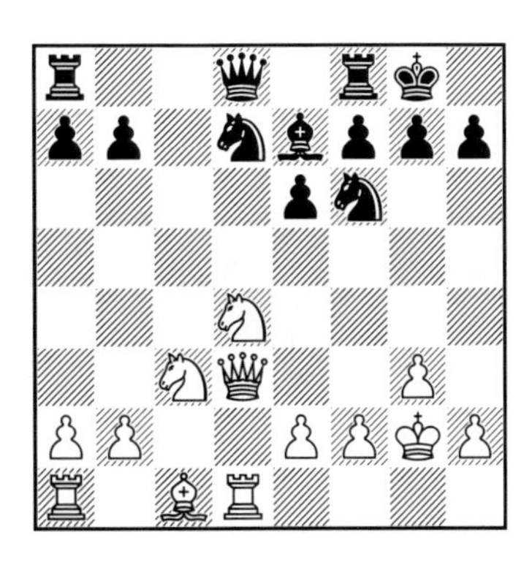

After the opening, white retains a minimal advantage, which consists of the active arrangement of his pieces. The fact that he can bring a rook into the game faster is also of importance. Therefore, black must play very accurately.

16.♕b5 ♕c8. Condemning himself to passive defense. It was necessary to play 16...♕b6 with good chances for equality. After black's erroneous move, white begins a vigorous attack in the center.

17.♗f4! a6 18.♕d3 ♘b6. Black now notices that 18...b5? does not help because of 19.♕f3! followed by ♖ac1 and ♘c6.

19.♖ac1 ♕d7. The move 19...♕c4 was wrong due to 20.♕f3 ♘bd5 21.♘xd5 ♕xd5 22.♖c7, and not 19...♘c4? 20.♘a4! b5 21.♘b6 and so on.

20.♕f3 ♘bd5 21.♘f5. Increasing the pressure in the center; however, it was more accurate to play 21.♘xd5 ♘xd5 first, and only then 22.♘f5.

Then 22...♖ac8 could have been met by 23.♖xd5! exd5 24.♕g4, winning the queen. After the move in the text, black could have put up stubborn resistance.

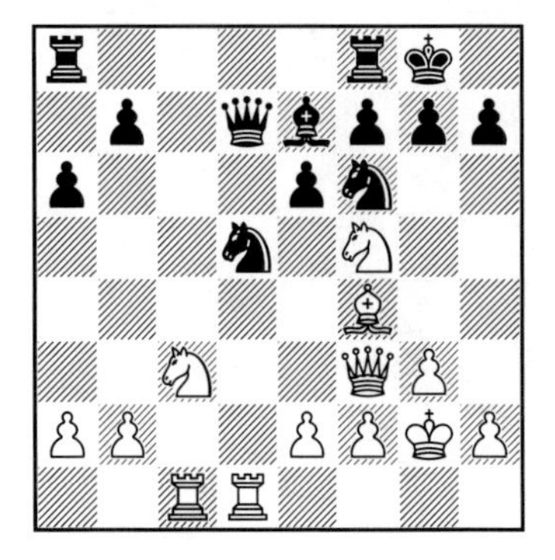

21...♖fc8? This is a crucial mistake. Black could have taken advantage of white's inaccuracy by exchanging on f4, maintaining a reinforced position.

22.♗e5! exf5 23.♗xf6 ♗xf6 24.♘xd5 ♕b5 25.♖xc8+ ♖xc8 26.♕xf5 ♖e8 27.♘xf6+ gxf6 28.♕xb5 axb5 29.♔f3 ♖e6 30.♖d7 ♖b6 31.b4 ♔g7 32.e4 ♔g6 33.♔e3 ♔g7 34.h4 h5 35.♔d4 ♔g6 36.f4 ♔g7 37.e5 fxe5+ 38.fxe5 ♔f8 39.♖d6 ♖c6 40.♖xc6 bxc6 41.♔c5 ♔e7 42.♔xc6. Black resigned.

Petrovs played unevenly during this championship. For example, he agreed to a draw with Lilienthal in the fifth round in a position where he had winning chances. In the twelfth round, having an advantage against Dubinin, he made a losing blunder in a time scramble. However, the grandmaster from Riga posted several good results, too. The fourth round game Gerstenfeld – Petrovs

Moscow, 1940, during the 12th Soviet Championship. From left to right: Petrovs, Smyslov, Keres, Rokhlin, Mikenas

was adjourned with a small advantage for black in a rook endgame.

Game No. 27
E. Gerstenfeld – V. Petrovs
12th Soviet Championship,
Moscow, 1940
Commentary by S. Grodzensky

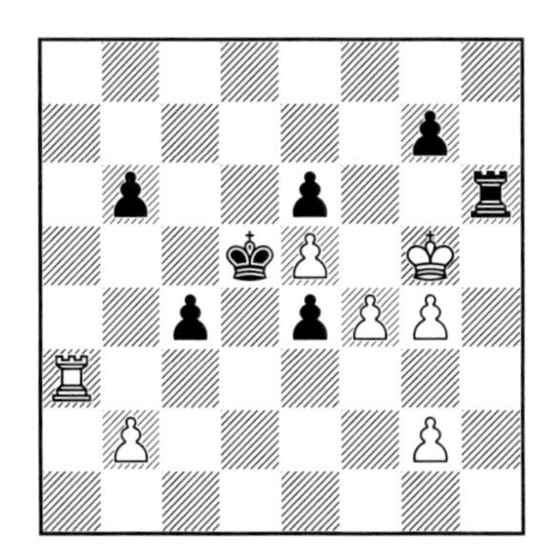

Vladimirs finished the game demonstrating excellent technique to achieve victory: **41.♖e3 ♖h1 42.♖e2 ♖d1 43.♔g6 ♔d4 44.f5 ♔xe5 45.fxe6 ♖d6 46.♔xg7 ♖xe6 47.g5 ♖c6 48.g6 ♔f5 49.g4+ ♔xg4**

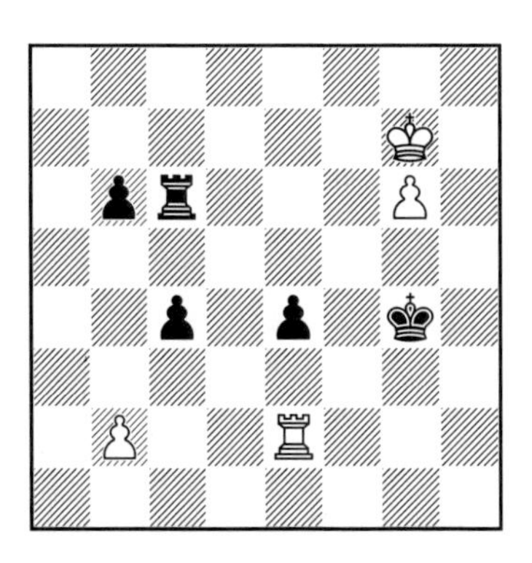

50.♖xe4+? White had to continue 50.♔h7 ♔f3 51.♖e1 or 51.g7 with an opportunity to get a draw.

50...♔f5 51.♖d4 ♖xg6+ 52.♔f7 ♖c6 53.♖d5+ ♔e4 54.♖b5 ♖d6 55.♔e7 ♖d3 56.♖xb6 ♖b3 57.♖c6 ♔d3 58.♖d6+ ♔c2 59.♖d4 ♖b4 60.♔d6 ♔xb2 61.♔c5 ♔b3 62.♖d1 ♖a4. White resigned.

Game No. 28
V. Petrovs – G. Levenfish
12th Soviet Championship,
Moscow, 1940
King's Indian Defense A53
Commentary by V. Petrovs

1.d4 ♘f6 2.c4 d6 3.♘f3 ♘bd7 4.g3 e5 5.♗g2 g6 6.b3!

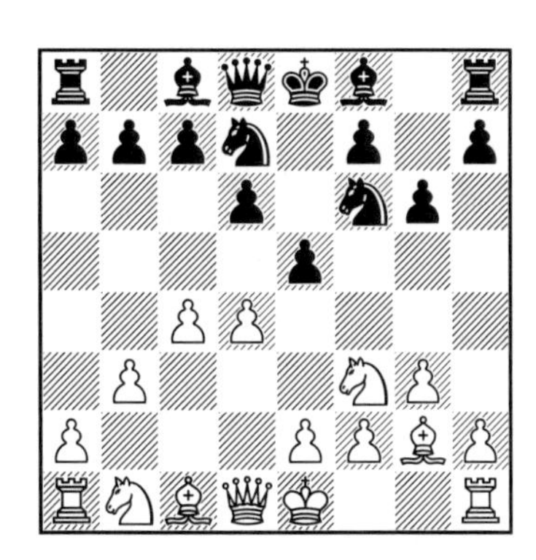

This is the best continuation, since white forces black to exchange on d4, giving up the pawn center. It is impossible to play 6...♗g7 because of 7.dxe5 dxe5 8.♗a3 e4 9.♘d4, and black must eventually play c7-c5, thereby weakening the most important strategic points d5 and d6.

6...exd4 7.♘xd4 ♗g7 8.♗b2 0-0

9.♘c3 ♘c5 10.0-0 a5 11.a3 ♖e8 12.♕c2.

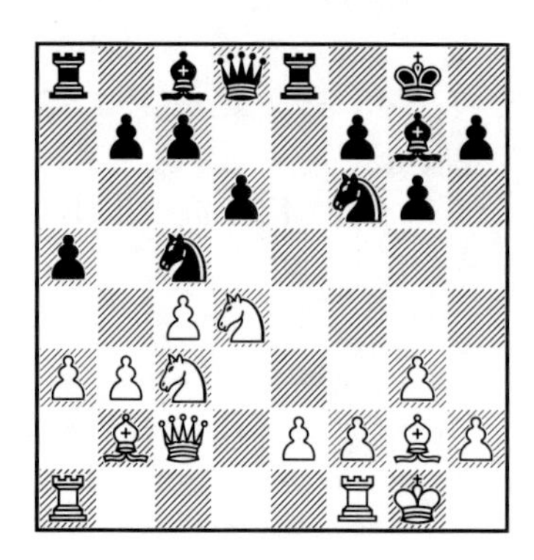

White's plan has now become clear: after placing the rooks on d1 and e1, he wants to start a general occupation of the center via e4, f4, ♘d5, etc.

12...c6. Black has to find a way for counterplay, even at the cost of weakening the d6 pawn. White has only one weakness – b3, and of course, this is the foundation black builds his game on.

13.♖ab1. White is temporarily forced to abandon the straightforward implementation of his plan. Now, in the case of 13...♕b6, white would have continued 14.♗a1!, threatening b3-b4-b5, and if then 14...♘g4 he just continues 15.e3 ♘e5 16.h3 followed by ♔h2, ♖fd1 and ♘e4, with a better position in all variations.

13...♘g4 14.♖bd1. Obviously not 14.♘e4? due to 14...♗xd4 15.♗xd4 ♗f5 and so on.

14...♕g5? Black is looking for complications in vain. He should have continued 14...♕b6. For example, 15.h3 ♘e5 16.♔h2 f5! with the following ♘f7, and black has a completely defensible position. Now, white prepares a strong attack on the queenside.

15.b4! axb4 16.axb4 ♘a6 17.b5 ♘b4 18.♕b3 c5 19.♘f3

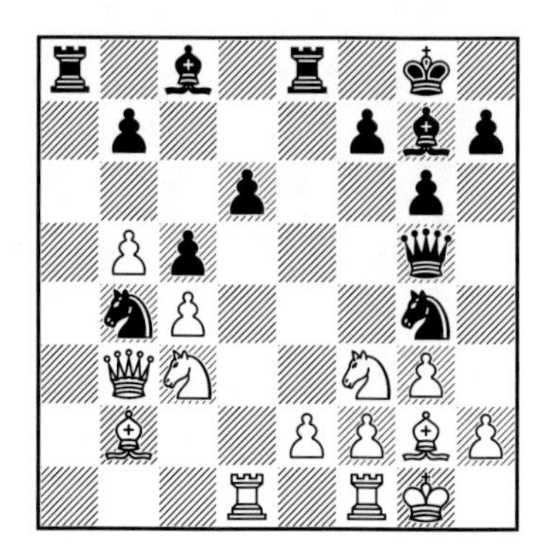

19...♕h5? This continuation loses quickly. Black could have put up stubborn resistance defending the d6 pawn via 19...♕e7.

20.♖xd6 ♗f5! What a clever move! Black threatens 21...♗c2, catching the white queen. Interestingly, white is forced to give up a pawn for freedom, but the black queen will have to pay more for her freedom!

21.e4 ♗xe4 22.♘xe4 ♖xe4 23.♗xg7 ♔xg7 24.♕c3+ ♔g8. If 24...f6, then 25.h3 ♘e5 26.♘xe5 ♖xe5 27.♖d7+, winning the b7 pawn.

25.h3 ♘h6 26.g4! Winning the knight, since the black queen has no squares to retreat to.

26...♘xg4 27.hxg4 ♖xg4

28.♘e5! This is the shortest path to victory. White uses the weakened dark squares of the kingside.

28...♖f4 29.♘d7 ♕h4 30.♘f6+ ♔f8 31.♘d5 ♖d4 32.♘xb4 ♖xd6 33.♕h8+ ♔e7 34.♕xa8. Black resigned.

Vladimirs Petrovs scored 9 points out of 19 in the Soviet Championship and was placed in the middle of the table. The magazine *Shakhmaty v SSSR* compared his playing style to Vladimir Makogonov's. The individual meeting between Petrovs and Makogonov went the Latvian's way.

Game No. 29
V. Petrovs – V. Makogonov
12th Soviet Championship,
Moscow, 1940
Catalan Opening E02
Commentary by S. Flohr

1.d4 ♘f6 2.c4 e6 3.g3. Petrovs successfully deployed this opening in the 12th Soviet Championship. Other participants of the championship started their games with the Catalan quite rarely, since it is considered rather harmless. Nevertheless, neither Kotov nor Makogonov managed to achieve an equal position against Petrovs in a real game.

3...d5 4.♗g2 dxc4 Thanks to this premature exchange, black never managed to completely equalize in the game. It was therefore preferable to continue development via 4...♗e7.

5.♕a4+ ♘bd7. This move has long been considered the best here. However, after white played 6.♘d2 in the Flohr – Euwe game during the Amsterdam tournament (1938), it was necessary to give preference to the move 5...♗d7.

6.♘d2

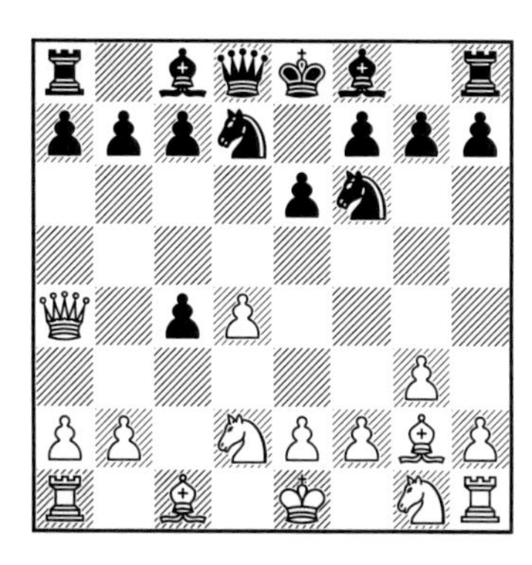

6...c6. In that Flohr – Euwe game, the continuation was 6...c5 7.♘xc4 ♗e7 8.dxc5 ♗xc5 9.♘f3 0-0 10.0-0 ♘b6 11.♕b3? ♗d7, and black achieved a good game. But after the correct 11.♕c2 or 11.♘xb6, white would have retained a positional advantage. The move chosen by Mikenas against Petrovs in the third round game 7...cxd4 was not good, since after 8.♗f4 black lost the right to castle. That game continued 8...♗e7 9.♘d6+ ♔f8 10.♘f3 ♕b6 11.♘c4 ♕b4+ 12.♕xb4 ♗xb4+, and then instead of 13.♔f1, white could have continued 13.♗d2 with a slightly better game. For example: 13...♗xd2+ 14.♔xd2 ♘e4+ 15.♔e1, and white would have won the pawn back, with the g2 bishop being stronger than the c8 bishop.

7.♕xc4 ♘b6. This move only chases the white queen to a better square. The only possible way to achieve equality for black here is by playing 7...e5. This continuation was seen in the Flohr – Petrovs game (Kemeri, 1937). After 8.♘gf3 ♘b6, white has only a minimal advantage. Now black gets a cramped position.

8.♕d3 c5 9.♘gf3 a6 10.0-0 ♗e7. If black plays 10...cxd4 at this moment, white doesn't have to capture on d4 immediately, but can achieve a better game by playing 11.♘b3 followed by ♘bxd4 and ♘e5. Black would have been constrained and the development of his queenside would have been complicated.

11.♖d1 0-0 12.b3 cxd4. Black does not have any good developing moves at his disposal and therefore must defuse the tension in the center.

13.♕xd4. White retains a significant advantage even after the exchange of queens. It was possible, of course, to capture with the knight.

13...♘fd5. As a rule, the exchange of queens is beneficial for the side under pressure. Therefore, Makogonov should have exchanged queens without much thought. Black's position would have remained cramped, but with careful defense it could be held. The knight maneuver initiated by the move in the text facilitates white's development.

14.♘e4 ♘b4. 14...f5 would have been met by the intermediate 15.♗b2 with the threat of checkmate.

15.♗b2 ♕xd4. Black is still forced to exchange queens, but on less favorable terms than on the 13th move. The knight looks bad on b4.

16.♗xd4 ♘6d5 17.♘c3 ♖d8. It was better to exchange on c3 and then play ♘bd5. The rook cannot stay on the d8 square and after a few moves is forced to leave it with a loss of tempo.

18.♘xd5 exd5. Black must allow the pawn to be isolated. In the case of 18...♘xd5, white would have played 19.e4 with tempo and then ♘e5 with strong pressure.

19.♗b6 ♖e8 20.♘d4 ♗e6 21.a3 ♘c6 22.♘xe6 fxe6

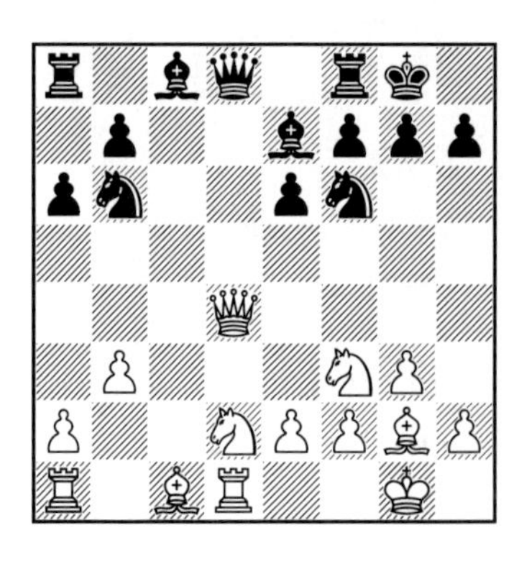

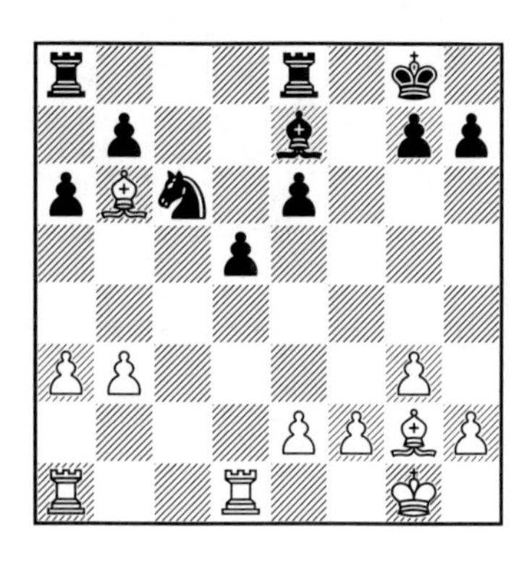

23.e4! By opening the diagonal, white significantly enhances the action of the two bishops.

23...d4. Black hopes to continue e6-e5 to limit the mobility of the g2 bishop. However, Petrovs' next move ruins Makogonov's hopes.

24.e5! This move is the decisive one. White's bishops become very active. Of course, it would have been wrong to play 24.♗xd4?? Here, due to the swap with the subsequent ♗f6, black wins the exchange.

24...♘xe5. It was necessary to try to "appease" his opponent with the sacrifice of a pawn and play 24...♖ac8.

25.♗xd4 ♘c6 26.♗b6 ♗d8 27.♗c5 ♖c8 28.♖ac1 ♘a5 29.♗e3! ♖xc1 30.♖xc1 b5. In the case of 30...♘xb3, the continuation 31.♖c8 decides the game. Now, black loses an exchange, but his position, given the inevitable loss of a pawn, was already hopeless.

31.♖c8 ♔f8 32.b4 ♘c4 33.♗c6. Black resigned.

One of Petrovs' greatest creative achievements in the Soviet Championship of 1940 was the game from the 14th round with Stolberg.

Game No. 30
V. Petrovs – M. Stolberg
12th Soviet Championship,
Moscow, 1940
Grunfeld Defense D71
Commentary by V. Petrovs

1.d4 ♘f6 2.c4 g6 3.g3. In this system, the order of moves is very important. White must prevent the c7-c5 break.

3...d5 4.♗g2 ♗g7 5.♘c3! The d5 pawn has already been attacked three times, and black must defend it or give up the center. In the case of 5...e6, the bishop's diagonal gets closed. While after 5...c6 black has to give up the more energetic c7-c5. Thus, the early development of the bishop on g2 is completely justified.

5...e6 (black is still trying to perform c7-c5) **6.♘f3 0-0 7.0-0 b6 8.♘e5 ♗b7 9.♕a4**

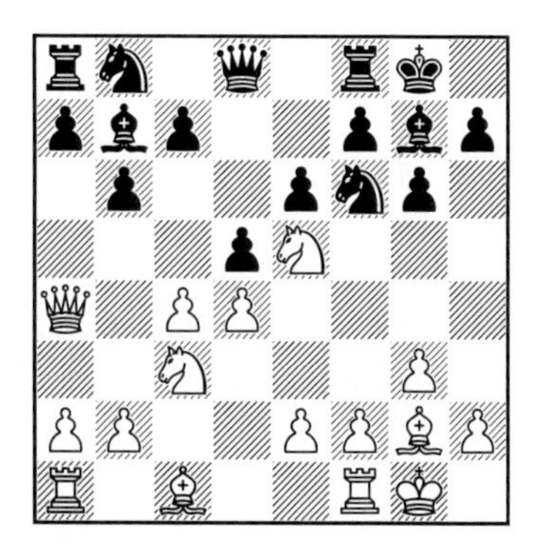

9...c6. A bitter necessity, since 9...c5 leads to the loss of a pawn after 10.dxc5 bxc5 11.♖d1.

10.♖d1 ♘e8! The best move in this difficult situation. Black is willing to move his knight to d6 and end the pawn tension in the center. White is faced with a dilemma: either to retreat his knight, giving black the opportunity of easy equality, or to choose a sharper continuation, which is somewhat risky, but proactive. White chooses the latter.

11.b4. Blocking black's queenside, but weakening the c4 square. White's plan is to create play on the dark squares after the forced exchange of his opponent's black bishop.

11...♘d6 12.c5 ♗xe5 13.dxe5 ♘c4 14.♗h6 ♘b2 15.♕b3 ♘xd1

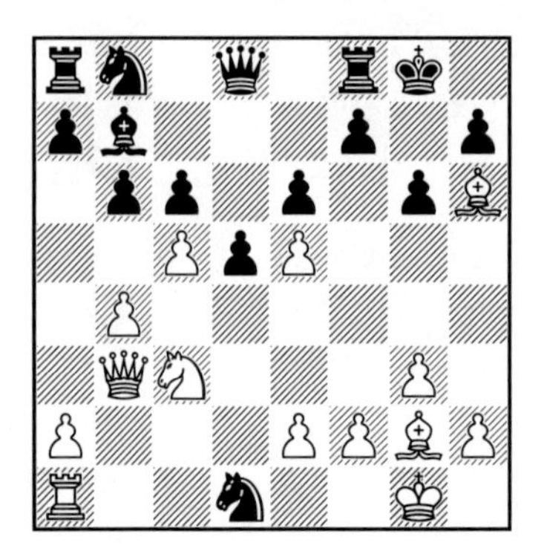

16.♘xd1! In the case of 16.♖xd1 black can continue 16...♘d7, and the white c3 knight will be unable to get to the kingside. After 17.♗xf8 ♕xf8 18.cxb6 axb6 19.f4 c5 black achieves the better game.

16...♖e8 17.♘e3 f5. The only possible continuation, otherwise black will quickly lose, falling under a mating attack. For example: 17...♘d7 18.♘g4 followed by ♕e3, ♗g5, etc.

18.exf6 ♕xf6 19.♖d1! ♘d7 20.♘g4 ♕e7 21.h4 ♗a6. Black's position is extremely tough, since he does not have any chance of counterplay. It was impossible, for example, to play 21...bxc5 22.bxc5 ♘xc5? because of 23.♕b2 or 21...e5 22.♗g5 ♕e6 23.♗h3. With the move in the text, black tries to bring his bishop back into the game.

22.♕b2! Defending the e2 pawn and occupying the important al-h8 diagonal.

22...♗c4. 22...e5 would have quickly led to a catastrophe, in response to which white would have effectively played the following rook sacrifice and decided the outcome of the game: 23.♖xd5 cxd5 24.♗xd5+ ♔h8 25.♗g5 ♕g7 26.c6, with a win.

23.♗g5 ♕g7 24.♘h6+ ♔h8 25.♘f7+ ♔g8 26.♘h6+. In order to gain time, white repeats moves.

26...♔f8? Leads to a quick loss. It is strange that black is not satisfied with a draw in this position. However, white, of course, would not have been satisfied with perpetual check, and after 26...♔h8 would have continued 27.♘f7+ ♔g8 28.♕xg7+ ♔xg7 29.♘d6, winning the exchange back. If now 29...♗xe2 30.♖e1 ♗g4, then 31.cxb6 axb6 32.b5! with the better game for white. Nevertheless, here black had chances for a draw in the endgame, whereas after the move in the text he falls under a mating attack.

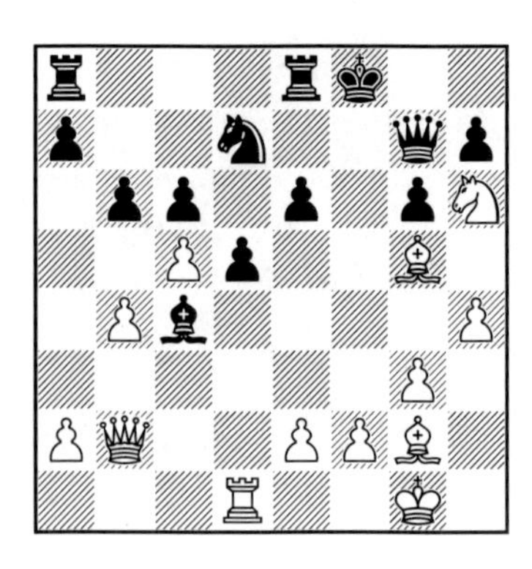

27.♖d4!! Black did not see this killer move. In the case of a queen retreat – ♕a3, ♕c1 or ♕d2 – he had sufficient defense from the check along the f-file via ♘e5 or ♕e5.

27...e5 (the only possible defense) **28.♕d2!!** The punches just keep coming! White threatens ♖f4+. In the case of 28...exd4, the continuation 29.♕f4+ ♘f6 30.♗xf6 ♕d7 31.♗xd4+ ♔e7 32.♕f6# wins.

28...♖ed8. If 28...♖e6, then 29.♖xc4 dxc4 30.♕c3 b5 31.♗xc6, and black's position, despite the two extra exchanges, is hopeless.

29.♖xc4 dxc4 30.♕d6+ ♔e8 31.♗xc6 ♖ac8 32.♕e6+ ♔f8 33.♗e7+. Black resigned in view of inevitable checkmate.

In June 1941, Petrovs played in the semi-final of the Soviet Championship at Rostov-on-Don. In the first six rounds, he achieved two victories and four draws, keeping a chance of reaching the final of the All-Union championship. But then came June 22...

Once the semi-final of the Soviet Championship was abandoned, Petrovs tried to get to Riga, where his wife and two-year-old daughter were living. But he was not allowed to go further than the Abrene border station – by that time the Germans had already reached Latvia. At first, Petrovs served in the headquarters of the 201st Latvian Rifle Division, and then, as he could speak several languages, he was recalled to Moscow to work at TASS. His name was found among the participants of the 1941 Moscow championship. In that legendary tournament held in a capital under siege, Vladimirs Petrovs finished second with the score of 9.5 points out of 14, behind Mazel but ahead of Panov, Alatortsev, Zagoryansky, Zubarev and others.

In 1942, a Masters Tournament held in Moscow was won by Bondarevsky. Petrovs scored half a point less, but 2.5 points more than Alatortsev, Mikenas, Panov and Yudovich, who shared 3rd-6th place. Just like other chess players, Grandmaster Petrovs gave simultaneous displays in hospitals.

Sports photojournalist Zigurds Mezavilks recalled that, in March 1942, at the Udelnaya station near

Moscow, where the Latvian division was preparing for battle, he took part in a simultaneous display by the Riga grandmaster and was among the four players who achieved a draw.

In the same year of 1942, Vladimirs Mikhailovich was evacuated to Sverdlovsk. In a strong tournament held there, he scored 7.5 points out of 10, which was enough for second place (grandmaster Ragozin won the event). One of Vladimirs Petrovs' last ever games was against Sverdlovsk local Bastrikov:

Game No. 31
V. Petrovs – G. Bastrikov
Sverdlovsk, 1942
Commentary by S. Grodzensky

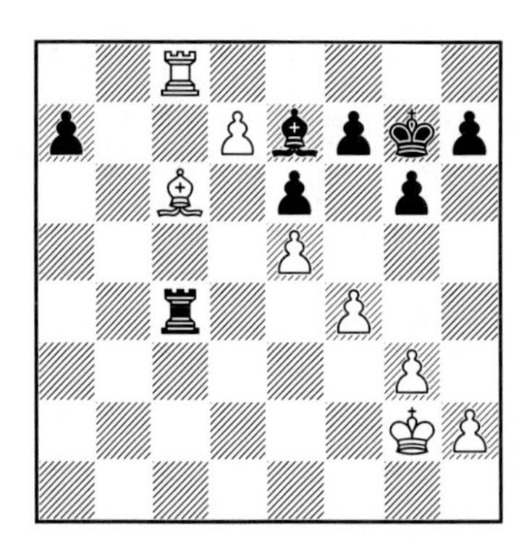

Despite the opposite-colored bishops, white gradually steers the game to victory: **41.♔f3** (the sealed move) **41...f5 42.♔e3 ♗c5+ 43.♔d3 ♖d4+ 44.♔c3 ♗b6 45.♖b8 ♖d1 46.♔c4 ♔f7 47.♔b5 h6 48.h4 ♖d2 49.♔a6 ♖d1 50.♖e8 ♖d2 51.♔b7 ♖d1 52.♔c8 ♖c1 53.d8=♘+! ♗xd8 54.♔xd8 ♖xc6 55.♖e7+ ♔f8 56.♖xa7**

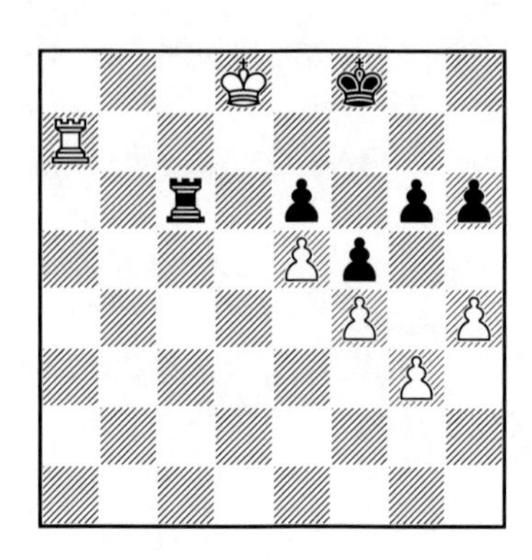

56...g5?! Black should have held his defensive lines via 56...♖b6 or 56...h5.

57.♖c7 (57.♖h7 looks more natural) **57...♖a6 58.♔d7 gxf4 59.gxf4 ♔f7 60.h5! ♖b6 61.♖c6 ♖b4 62.♖xe6 ♖xf4 63.♖f6+ ♔g8 64.♖g6+ ♔f8 65.♔e6 ♖h4 66.♔f6 ♖xh5 67.e6 ♖g5 68.♖xh6 ♖g8 69.♖h7 ♔e8 70.♖a7.** Black resigned.

After the Sverdlovsk tournament in 1942, all trace of Vladimirs Mikhailovich was lost. Sverdlovsk master G. Ilivitsky, who played with Petrovs in the 1942 tournament, recalled that after the tournament Vladimirs travelled to Kazan for another competition: there he was arrested.

Vladimirs Mikhailovich's trip to Rostov-on-Don in June 1941 destroyed his family's life. During the war, Galina Mikhailovna and her daughter Marina lived with friends in Tukums, near Riga. When she returned to Riga in the spring of 1945, she discovered that her husband had been arrested, and that their apartment was occupied by strangers. She approached the government authorities in order to get at least some official news about her spouse, and received a spoken response to a request to the Ministry of Internal Affairs: V. M. Petrovs was sentenced to 10 years imprisonment, and sent to Vorkuta. After multiple requests, the head of the Vorkutlag sent a reply that there was no record of V. M. Petrovs. New appeals to the Ministry of Internal Affairs and various administrative and labor camps turned out to be completely useless.

At the end of 1948, Galina Mikhailovna was summoned to the Ministry of Internal Affairs and informed that Petrovs had died while serving his sentence. However, no document was provided and no details could be obtained from the officials either. All she could do was make exhausting efforts to obtain a review of Petrovs' case and his posthumous rehabilitation. During the following four decades, the various court levels only sent standardized responses with refusals. His daughter Marina Vladimirovna had to bear the offensive stigma of a family member of an enemy of the people all her life (she died in 1985).

The situation changed dramatically with the beginning of Gorbachev's perestroika – in 1989, Galina Mikhailovna Petrova-Matisa received a certificate attesting to her husband's death, allegedly caused by pellagra and pneumonia, on August 26, 1943. Finally, in July 1989, Petrovs' widow received a letter from the KGB, which we cite in full.

"State Security Committee of the USSR Department for the City of Moscow and the Moscow region

13.07.89, Moscow No. b/m-792

Dear Galina Mikhailovna!

While examining your application, we have established that Vladimirs Mikhailovich

Petrovs, born in 1908, a native of Riga, Russian, a literary employee of the letters department of the Radio Committee under the Council of People's Commissars of the USSR, living at the following address: Moscow, B. Golovin Lane 3, apartment 3., was arrested by the NKVD on August 31, 1942. Accusations against your husband were based on the facts of his expressing dissatisfaction with living conditions in the Baltic Republics after they were jointed with the USSR; on February 3, 1943, Petrovs V. M. was sentenced by a Special Council of the NKVD of the USSR (a non-judicial body) to 10 years of imprisonment in a correctional labor camp. During the investigation, he was held in the Butyrskaya prison in Moscow; on February 14, 1943, he was sent to Vorkutlag to further serve his sentence. We regret to inform you that there is no information about the subsequent fate of your husband in the archives of the Ministry of Internal Affairs of the USSR or the KGB of the USSR (including the Komi ASSR).

In view of the destruction of prisoner's cases by the statute of limitations, there are no prisoners' files available.

We are also sending you a note on the place of work of V. M. Petrovs at the time of his arrest in 1942. In accordance with the Resolution of the Council of Ministers of the USSR No. 1655 of 08.09.1955, you have the right to receive your husband's salary for two months, for which you need to send an application to Gosteleradio, attaching to it our note and a copy of the certificate of rehabilitation of your spouse (notarized).

No property of Petrovs V. M. was confiscated following his arrest and conviction.

Yours sincerely,

Deputy head of the department

N. V. Grashoven".

So, Petrovs was finally rehabilitated, and his widow obtained the right to get his salary for two months (for the loss of her husband and decades of suffering – her own and her daughter's). But there are still many more questions than answers. What exactly was the "anti-Soviet agitation and propaganda" that Petrovs was accused of? (In a letter to the author of the book, G. M. Petrova-Matisa suggests that chess players also had a hand in her husband's tragedy.)

Why does the death certificate not indicate the place of death? By the way, his death was registered only a year later (in August 1944) in the registry office of the Dzerzhinsk district of Moscow.

As stated earlier, since this book was published in Russian two important works have been published that shed much more light on Petrovs' life (his widow's memoir, whose translation is being published together with the book you are reading) and on his final months (the second volume of Sergey Voronkov's *Masterpieces and Dramas of the Soviet Championships*, whose English translation is available already).

Petr Izmailov – The First Champion of Soviet Russia

The All-Russian Chess Olympiad held in 1920 and won by Alexander Alekhine was once considered to be the first championship of the RSFSR (Soviet Russia). However, that championship, as well as the next one, which took place three years later and ended with victory by Peter Romanovsky, only formally had All-Russian status. In reality, these were the first two championships of the Soviet Union as a whole. Therefore, when the All-Union Championship was first organized in 1924, it was assigned serial number three.

The first championship of the actual Soviet Russia, which was the largest part of the USSR, was held in 1928. That tournament in Moscow, which brought together the winners of regional and district competitions, gave the title of champion of the RSFSR to a resident of the Siberian city of Tomsk, Petr Izmailov.

It seems that we have somewhat forgotten the chess master Petr Izmailov. The magazine pages on which his games were printed have long turned yellow, personal memories about him disappeared from the memoirs of veterans. And no wonder why.

For more than half a century, his name was not mentioned in the press, and therefore there was barely a glimmer of hope to find his trace, which suddenly disappeared in 1936.

But where to look for this trace? It was known that Petr Nikolaevich Izmailov once lived in Tomsk, and I (it was in 1989) decided to write a letter to the Tomsk regional newspaper *Krasnoe Znamya ("Red Banner")*, in which I appealed for that city's veterans to tell everything that they knew about the fate of their local colleague – the former chess champion of Russia.

The newspaper with my article caught the eye of Izmailov's relatives. They sent it to his son, Nikolai Petrovich Izmailov, who now lives in

Irkutsk. Nikolai does not remember his father. He was not even two years old when, on September 10, 1936, Petr Nikolaevich was arrested and disappeared forever. His mother often talked about him, conquering her mental anguish, and it was from her words we can "complete the unfinished portrait" of the chess master Petr Izmailov. Note that since this book was published in Russian, Nikolai's own book on his father *Petr Izmailov: From Chess Champion of Russia to Enemy of the People: The Truth About My Father* was published in English in 2021 by Elk and Ruby, with analysis by Grandmaster Mihail Marin of all of Izmailov's surviving games. It provides a comprehensive description of Izmailov's life and career and was updated by Nikolai especially for the English edition.

He was born on June 13, 1906, in Kazan in the family of a priest. He studied at the local grammar school. He discovered chess at the age of 15 at his school club. Nowadays, the question at what age one should start studying chess is debated by psychologists, doctors, and teachers. While opinions differ on that question, there is broad agreement that if you want to reach heights in chess, then you should study the basics no later than at the age of 8-10. Petr's initial results were all the more striking as, just a year or two later, he was already the strongest chess player of Kazan.

He took second place in the city championship in January 1924, behind the then leader of Kazan chess players Nikolai Kosolapov. Four months later, the First Volga Tournament was held in Kazan with the participation of the strongest chess players from Astrakhan, Vyatka, Izhevsk, Kostroma, Nizhny Novgorod, and Samara. The young player from Kazan started with confident victories over strong chess players Kondybin (Samara) and Sergeev (Nizhny Novgorod) and immediately took the lead. Izmailov indeed won first prize, and was the only undefeated participant. By contrast, his recent competitor in the Kazan championship, Kosolapov, finished only fifth in the Volga tournament.

Experts noted Izmailov's strictly positional and careful style. He was faithful to this style to the end, but for the sake of objectivity, it needs to be said that, because of excessive caution, Petr drew too many times, and rarely achieved crushing victories.

In 1924, Izmailov played in the Tournament of Cities of the Third All-Union Chess and Checkers Congress. He scored 8 points out of 15 and was placed in the middle of the table. Yet he also drew his game with the winner, the Moscow master Nikolai Zubarev, and won his game against a participant of the pre-revolutionary All-Russian tournaments and the winner of the Baltic tournaments, Karl Rosenkranz. Thanks to his performance in the Tournament of Cities, Izmailov was awarded the first category title.

After graduating from Kazan grammar school in 1924, Peter moved to Omsk. Nevertheless, he managed to play in the Second Volga Tournament (Kazan, 1925), where he ended second. But the Third Siberian Championship (Novosibirsk, 1926) with its wider representation brought the newly-baked Siberian a clear victory.

Petr Izmailov delivered simultaneous exhibitions in Omsk, and in 1926 he became champion of the city, but soon moved to Tomsk to study at the faculty of physics and mathematics of the local university. This first-year student took second place in the Tomsk Championship of 1927, behind Mikhail Tronov – a well-known author of chess problems since pre-revolutionary times and an even more famous scientist: a future professor of glaciology at Tomsk University.

The All-Siberian Championship of 1927 was won by the Moscow master Boris Verlinsky, playing *hors concours*. Second place and the title of champion of Siberia went to Tronov, while Izmailov was the third.

The following year brought Petr Izmailov further success, placing him among the leading chess players of Russia. At the beginning of 1928, he confidently won the Tomsk championship, losing only one point in 13 games and finishing two points ahead of the second prize-winner. The quality of his play also improved.

Game No. 32

P. Izmailov – L. Staroverov

Tomsk Championship, 1928

Queen's Gambit D64

Commentary by M. Marin (comments to this game and the subsequent games by Izmailov cited in this chapter were originally published in Nikolai Izmailov and Mihail Marin's book mentioned earlier. Comments in italics in the below game are taken from Krasnoe Znamya *and* Shakhmatny listok*).*

1.d4 ♘f6 2.♘f3 e6 3.c4 d5 4.♘c3 ♘bd7 5.♗g5 ♗e7 6.e3 c6 7.♖c1 0-0

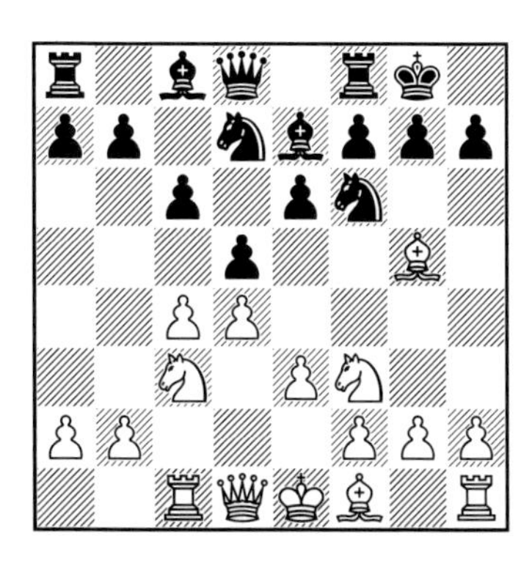

A classical tabiya on the board.

8.♕c2

Izmailov avoids the Capablanca variation 8.♗d3 dxc4 9.♗xc4 ♘d5. In order to understand why the setup chosen by black in this game is not the best, we should compare it with what could happen if white follows Izmailov's plan in this line: 10.♗xe7 ♕xe7 11.0-0 ♘xc3 12.♖xc3 e5

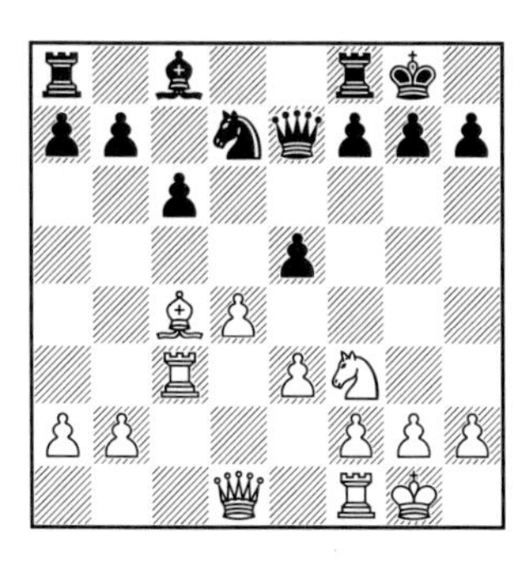

13.e4 (the traditional main line goes 13.dxe5 ♘xe5 14.♘xe5 ♕xe5 15.f4 ♕e4 with fairly sharp play) 13... exd4 14.♕xd4 (unlike Izmailov, white does not get much after taking with the knight: after 14.♘xd4 taking on e4 at once might be a bit dangerous due to black's lag in development, but 14...♘b6 looks safe and in the event of the principled move 15.♗b3, black can now play 15...♕xe4; other moves do not leave black facing any particular problem) 14...♘b6 15.♗b3 ♗e6. The white kingside pawn majority is far from advancing yet and black has a comfortable position.

8...♖e8 9.a3 dxc4

It would have been possible to postpone this exchange, carrying it out only after ♗d3 with a gain of a tempo.

Staroverov decides to play a hybrid form of the Capablanca system.

10.♗xc4 ♘d5 11.♗xe7 ♕xe7 12.0-0 ♘xc3

This second exchange only worsens black's position. 12...b6 would have been preferable.

In principle, ...b7–b6 is a better plan than ...e6–e5 (see the comment below), but in this position it runs into a concrete refutation: 13.♘xd5! cxd5 (13...exd5? loses a pawn to 14.♗d3 with a double attack on c6 and h7) 14.♗b5! (white threatens ♕c7, more or less forcing black to weaken his queenside) 14...a6 15.♗d3 ♘f6 16.♕c7! (this is the point: white attacks b6) 16...b5 17.♘e5 with a big advantage to white.

13.♕xc3

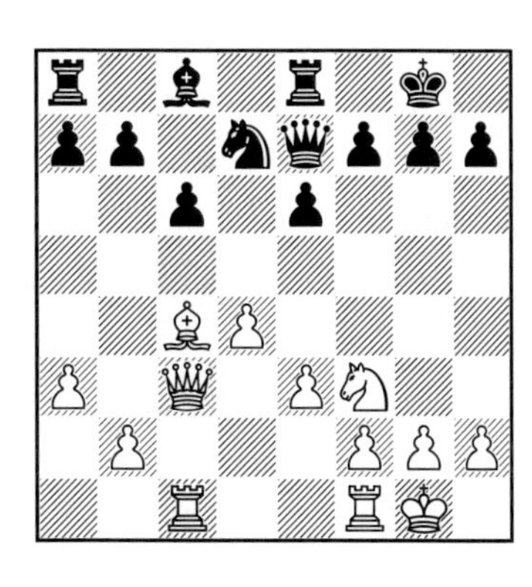

13...e5

At that time, a novelty.

Five years earlier, black played the strange 13...♕f6?! 14.♖fd1 g5 15.e4 ♘f8 16.e5 ♕g7 17.♕e3 h6 18.♘d2 followed by ♘e4, with a rapid win in Gibson – Steele, Portsmouth (Southsea) 1923.

Eleven years later, black tried the relatively better 13...b6 14.♕d3 ♗b7 and eventually equalized in Trepat de Navarro – Andersson, Buenos Aires (women's Olympiad) 1939.

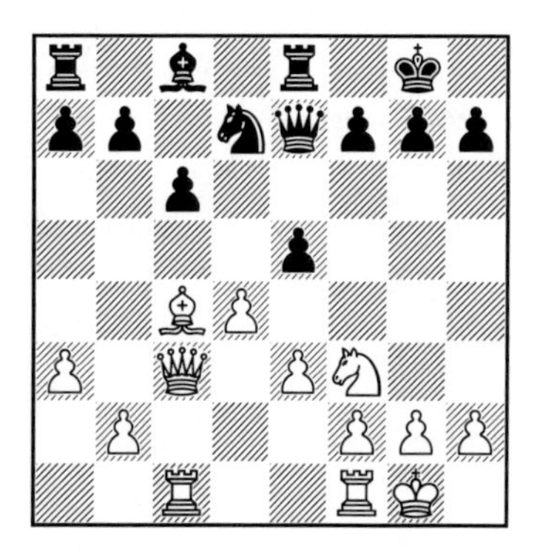

14.e4!

Under the circumstances, the most convincing way to meet black's plan. Strangely enough, nobody has tried this move since.

Izmailov must have been inspired by the following game, featuring a different opening, but leading to a similar early middlegame position:

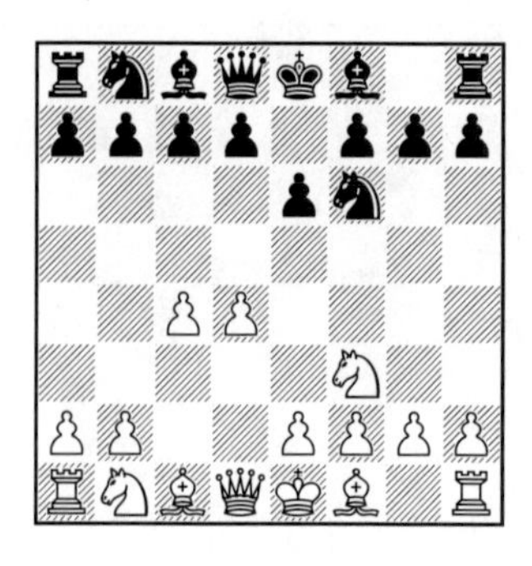

3...♗b4+ 4.♗d2 ♗xd2+ 5.♕xd2 d5. This used to be Bogoljubov's favorite way of treating "his" opening. In modern times, Ulf Andersson played it a lot, too. 6.e3 0-0 7.♘c3 ♘bd7 8.♗d3

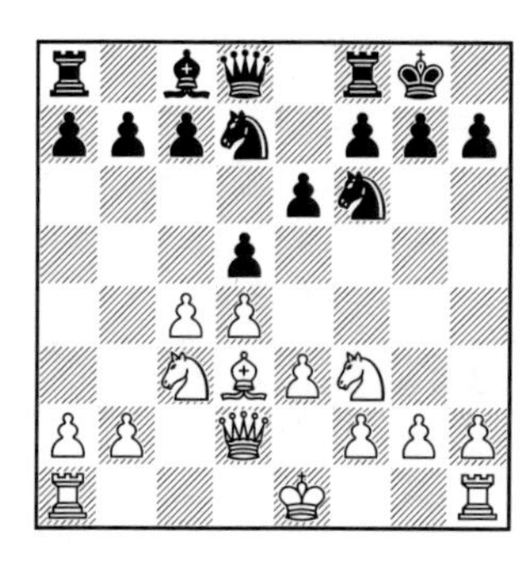

8...c6?! (this unnecessary loss of time is the main cause of black's later problems. Even though he had similar positions several times, Efim Dmitrievich never seemed to be aware of this slight inaccuracy. In such situations, Andersson used to play 8...♕e7 followed by ...dxc4 and either ...e6–e5 or ...c7–c5. Sometimes, he would insert ...♖d8 somewhere in between. Black does not need his pawn on c6 in any of these lines) 9.0-0 dxc4 10.♗xc4 e5 11.♗b3 ♕e7

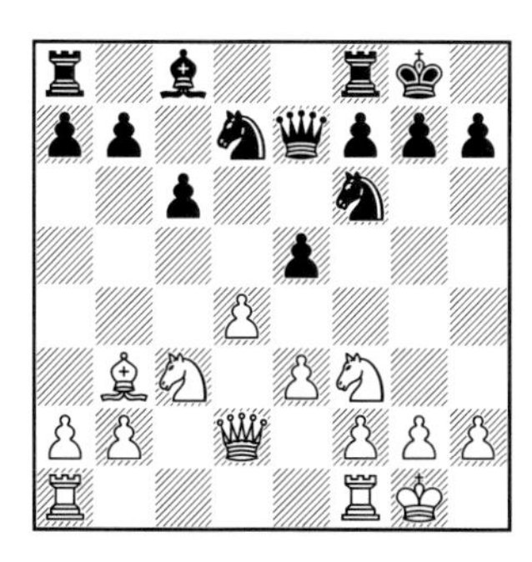

12.e4!

The similarity with our main game becomes clear now. After 12...exd4 13.♘xd4 ♘c5 14.♗c2 ♖d8 15.♖ad1 ♗g4 16.f3 ♘e6 17.♕f2 ♘xd4 18.♖xd4 ♗e6 19.♖fd1 black cannot challenge white's control over the open file and the white pawn majority will become threatening soon: 19...b6 20.h3 c5 21.♖4d2 ♖xd2 22.♕xd2 c4 23.f4 with a clear advantage for white, who won seven moves later in Alekhine – Bogoljubov, Budapest 1921.

Staroverov's idea must have been that, unlike in the genuine Capablanca system, widescale exchanges on e5 do not promise white anything: 14.dxe5 ♘xe5 15.♘xe5 ♕xe5 16.♕xe5 ♖xe5 with a comfortable ending for black.

14.d5!? is an interesting alternative, tried a few times in practice.

14...exd4 15.♘xd4

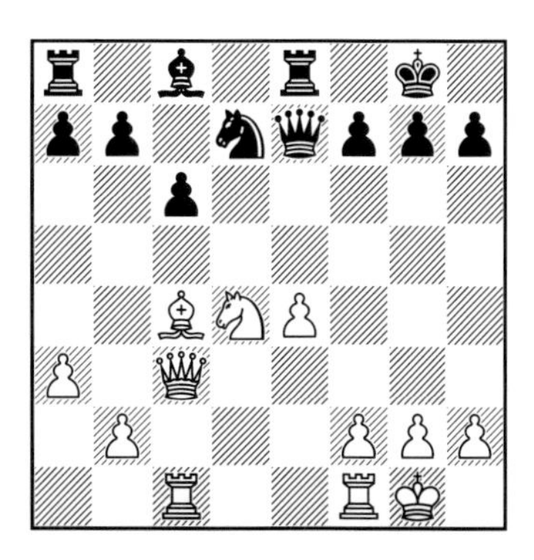

Now the rook proves misplaced on e8. Black cannot take the pawn on e4 due to ♖f(c)e1. For once, a2–a3 is just a generally useful move, sustaining a later b2–b4, but it does not influence the evaluation of the current position.

15...♘e5

A mistake, since black allows f4 with an attack against the knight. By continuing 15...♘c5, black would have obtained a satisfactory position.

I took this as a challenging comment. My first idea was that black is intended to simplify with either ...♘e6 or ...♗e6 in the proposed line. However, this would allow the white knight to jump to f5 and maybe later to d6 (after the preliminary ♗xe6 ♘xe6 in the latter case).

As I continued to examine the proposed position, I came to realize that white's main aim was to find a way of advancing his center, which is submitted to certain pressure now.

My first candidate was 16.♖ce1!? (I felt that 16.f3 was too passive, while it also weakened the dark squares, but the engines think that it ensures white a stable advantage;

16.♖fe1 is less accurate, for reasons revealed below):

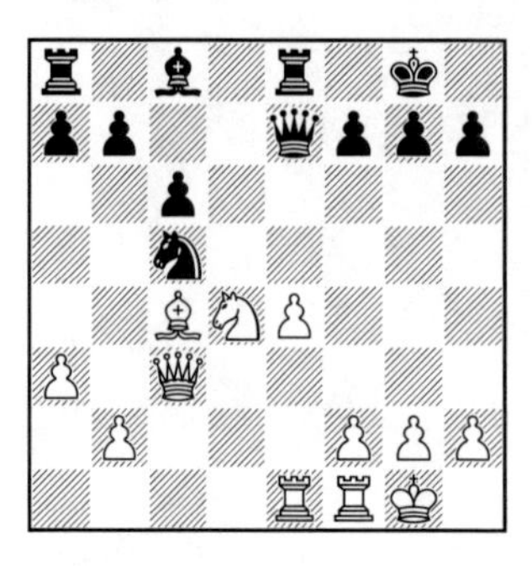

16...♘xe4 (the critical move; white was threatening to start his pawn attack with e4–e5 and f2–f4; 16...♘e6 runs into 17.♘f5 ♕g5 18.f4! (now is when white needs a rook on f1! and 18...♘xf4? is impossible because of 19.♖xf4!)):

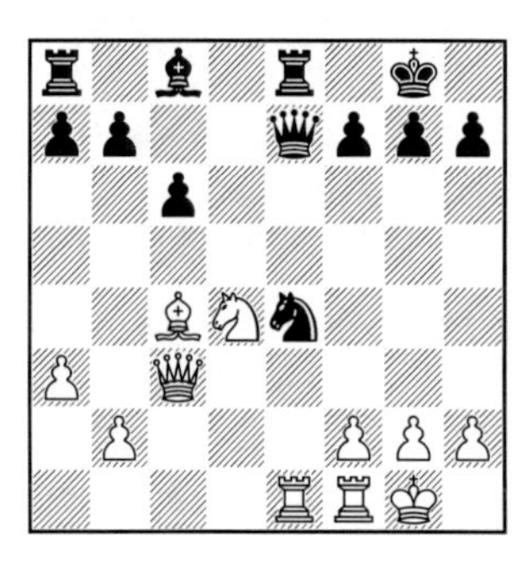

It took me some time to discover that 17.♕c2 offers black additional possibilities, for instance 17...♕e5 18.♕d3 ♗d7 19.f3 b5 when white does not have anything better than taking on f7 and e4, since 20.♗a2 leaves the queen undefended, allowing 20...♘c5!

17.♕d3 is much stronger, leaving black without any defense against f2–f3, winning a piece.

While this looked entirely satisfactory for white, I later decided that 16.e5! was even more promising.

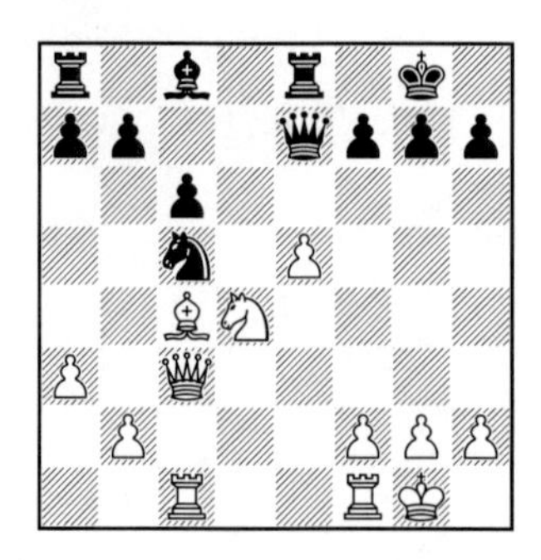

White intends to continue with f2–f4, reaching a similar attacking position as in the game. Black cannot free himself by means of exchanges: 16...♘e6 (16...♗e6 is simply met with 17.f4) 17.♘f5 ♕g5 18.♘d6 ♘f4. The only chance to generate some counterplay; the passive 18...♖f8 yields white an overwhelming initiative after 19.♗xe6 ♗xe6 20.f4 followed by f4–f5.

19.♕f3! It is better to maintain the threat of taking on f7 in his back pocket; the hurried 19.♗xf7+ leads to unclear consequences: 19...♔f8 20.♕f3 ♗g4! (after the bishop's departure from c4, the threat ...♘e2+ is an issue and white has to find only moves to maintain chances for equality) 21.h4 ♗xf3 22.hxg5 ♖xe5 23.gxf3 ♘e2+ 24.♔g2 ♘xc1 25.♖xc1 ♖d8 26.♘xb7. If now 26...♖d7 27.f4 white gets adequate compensation for the exchange; in the event of 26...♖xg5+ 27.♔f1 ♖d7 white saves the game with 28.♘c5! retrieving the exchange with a probable draw. Now is a good moment to say that the engine greatly helped during the final part of the analysis on black's last move.

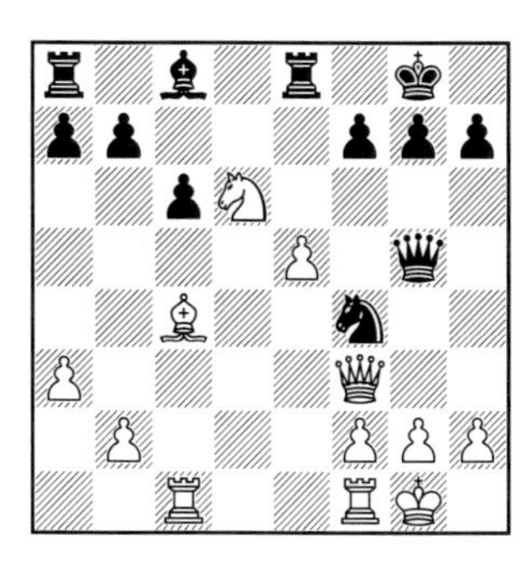

19...♖e7 (19...♗g4 is ineffective now: 20.♕g3, adding the threat f2–f3 to the existing ones and after 20...b5 the simplest is 21.h4! bxc4 22.hxg5 ♘e2+ 23.♔h2 ♘xg3 24.♔xg3 winning an exchange) 20.♘xf7 ♖xf7 21.♗xf7+ ♔xf7 22.g3 with a decisive material advantage.

16.♗b3 ♗d7 17.f4 ♘g6 18.e5

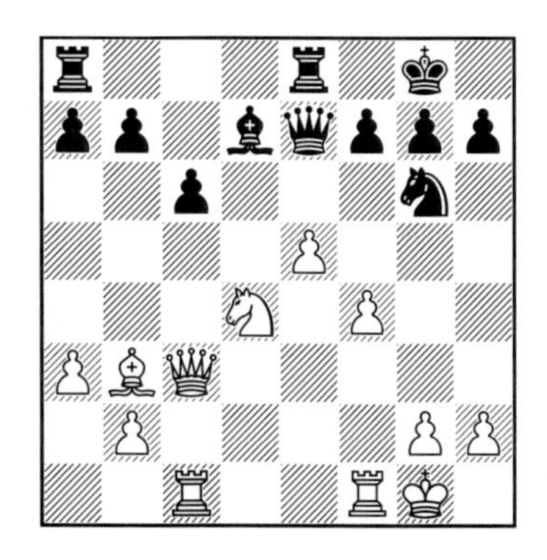

18...♖ac8

Black is unaware of the looming danger. The best move would have been 18...♔h8 evacuating the king from the bishop's diagonal.

The commentator is absolutely right, but after the recommended move white maintains a large advantage anyway. For instance: 19.♗a2 ♖ac8 20.♗b1 (preparing to create some threats on h7) 20... c5 (the only way of displaying some activity) 21.♘f5 ♗xf5 22.♗xf5 ♖c7 23.♖cd1. Just as in the game Alekhine – Bogoljubov, white has unchallenged control over the d-file, but Izmailov's pawns are even more threatening than Alekhine's.

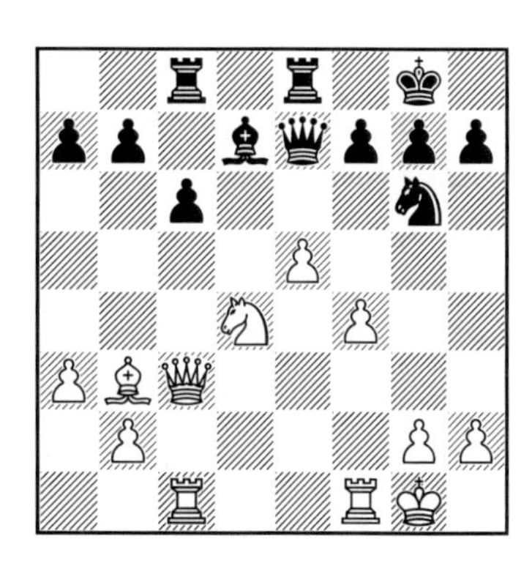

19.e6!

The decisive breakthrough!

19...♗xe6 20.♘xe6 fxe6 21.f5 ♘f8 22.fxe6 ♔h8

22...♘xe6 is impossible because of 23.♖ce1 ♕d6 24.♕e5 winning.

23.♖f7 ♕g5 24.♖cf1

and black resigned, since there is no satisfactory defense against the threat e6–e7.

Krasnoe Znamya added that Izmailov conducted the whole game in an exemplary manner and vigorously.

Petr thus regained the title of the strongest chess player of Siberia in addition to claiming the title of the champion of the city, thereby getting rid of the prefix "ex" acquired a year earlier. This time, he completed the tournament without any losses, and drew only twice. He shared 1st-2nd place with Novosibirsk player Komarov in the tournament, but won the playoff match 2:0.

In November 1928, the champion of Siberia, Petr Izmailov, took part in the first championship of the RSFSR, in which the winners of regional and district championships competed. Among them were the later famous masters Panov and Kan (both from Moscow), and Vygodchikov (Smolensk).

Unexpectedly, the young champion of Siberia immediately stormed into the lead and won with a score of 10 points out of 13. His game with a strong first-category opponent from Leningrad, Shebarshin, turned out to be key to his overall placement.

Game No. 33

P. Izmailov – M. Shebarshin

Championship of the RSFSR, Moscow, 1928

Semi-Slav Defense D46

Commentary by M. Marin (Comments in italics by P. Romanovsky)

1.d4 ♘f6 2.♘f3 e6 3.c4 d5 4.♘c3 c6 5.e3 ♘bd7 6.♗d3

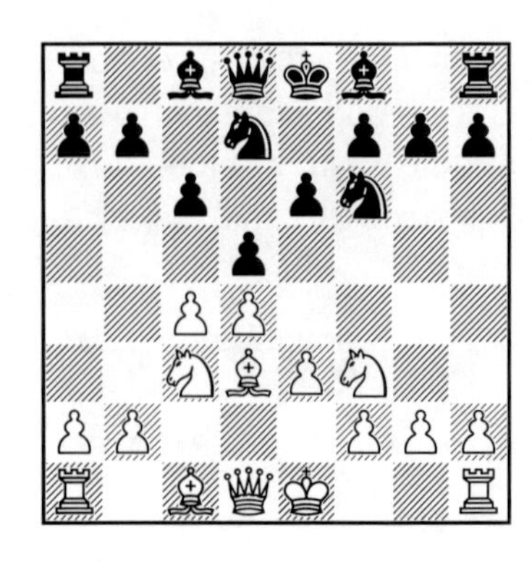

Known since the last decade of the 19th century, the Meran system came into the limelight after Rubinstein and Grunfeld played it at the Merano 1924 tournament.

6...♗e7

This move has enjoyed a burst of popularity in modern times. The main idea is to maintain the tension in the center and develop slowly with ...b7–b6 and ♗b7.

The absolute main line is 6...dxc4 7.♗xc4 b5.

7.0-0 dxc4

I have played the Meran system many times with white, but never with black, which does not make me a proper expert. I was tempted to consider the last move inaccurate, since black has already committed his bishop to e7. This judgement is correct in certain Catalan variations, where after ...dxc4 and an early ...c7–c5, the bishop should be ready to take back on c5 without wasting a tempo. However, in the Meran system, this job is usually fulfilled by the knight on d7. This explains why several very strong players from modern times have played the same variation as in the game.

8.♗xc4 b5 9.♗d3 b4 10.♘e4

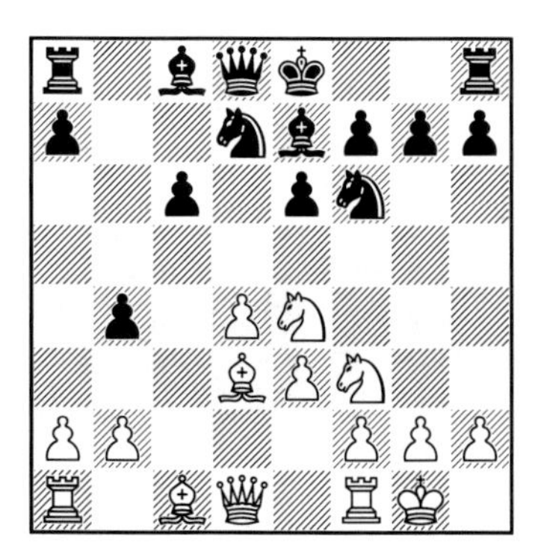

We notice that the bishop stands better on e7 than it would have on d6, because it means that black can ignore the central knight for now.

10...c5?!

This early pawn break is not consistent with black's philosophy in this line. Before advancing his c-pawn, he should have completed his development.

10...0-0 has been played by many strong grandmasters, including Anand and Mikhail Gurevich. One of the main lines goes 11.♘xf6+ ♘xf6 12.e4 ♗b7 13.e5 ♘d7, still preparing ...c6–c5.

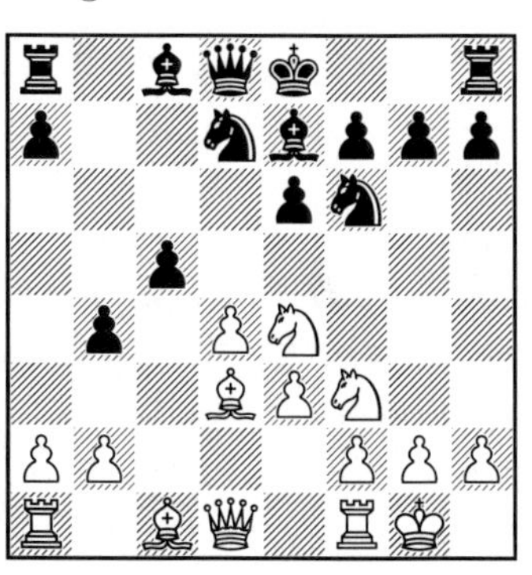

11.dxc5

This exchange allows black to unravel his forces, at a time when his opening pawn attack compromised his queenside to a certain extent.

11.♕e2 was more vigorous, and if 11...0-0 then 12.dxc5 ♘xc5 13.♘xf6+ and black has to take with the pawn because of 13...♗xf6 14.♗xh7+.

Romanovsky is wrong in more than one way. Firstly, the mini-combination mentioned by him is flawed.

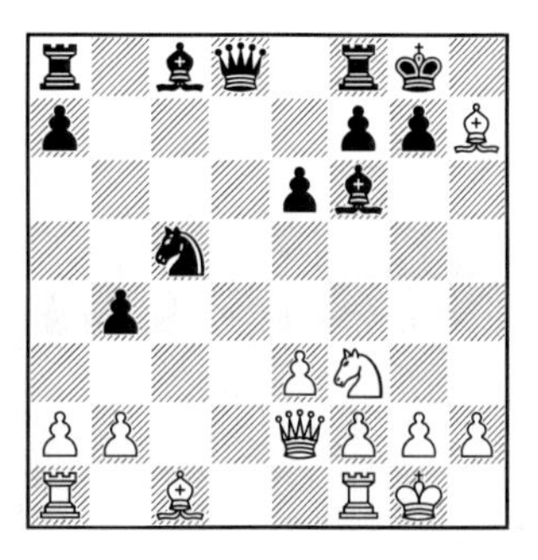

14...♔xh7 15.♕c2+ ♘d3 16.♖d1 ♗a6, maintaining the extra piece.

Instead of exchanging on f6, white should take the other knight: 13.♘xc5 ♗xc5

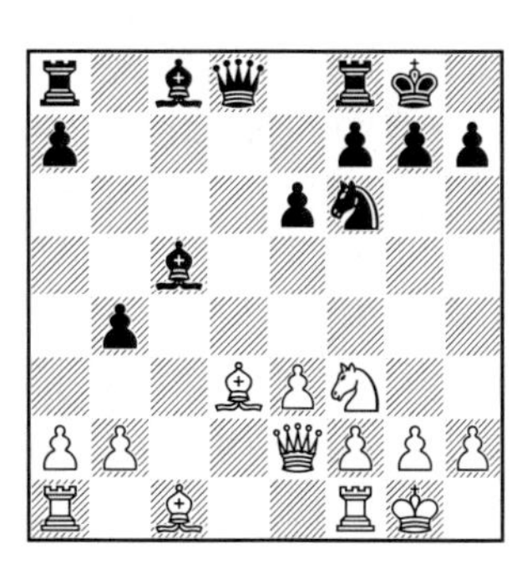

14.e4!

As we see, it is white who unravels his pieces quicker. There are several modern games with this line, confirming that white has the initiative. I will mention only the oldest example, played a few years after Izmailov's game: 14...♗b7 15.e5 ♗xf3 16.♕xf3 ♘d7 17.♕e4 g6 18.♗h6 ♖e8, Vidmar – Steiner, Ujpest 1934, and now 19.♗b5 would have put black in a decisive pin.

One year later, it was discovered that black is not forced to take on c5 at once, though. He could do better with 12...♗b7!

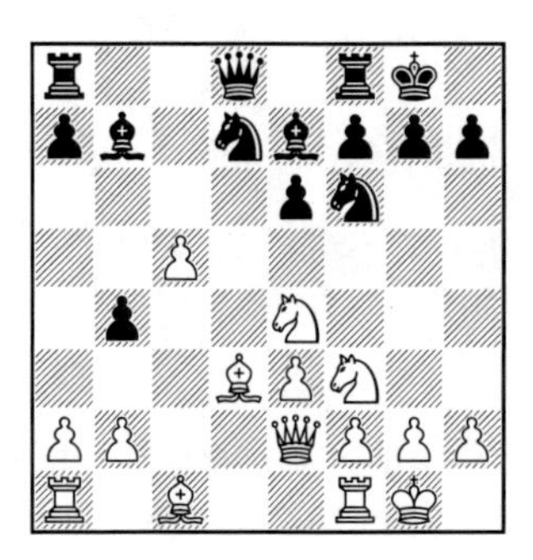

13.♘xf6+ ♘xf6 14.e4 ♘d7. Over the past decades, many games between strong players have reached this position, but as before I will only mention a classical example, Havasi – Lundin, Warsaw 1935.

One of the best reactions to black's early pawn break is 11.♘xf6+ ♘xf6 12.e4 cxd4 13.e5 ♘d5 14.♘xd4 as played in Gelfand – Korchnoi, Tilburg 1992. White has more space and some attacking chances, while black's queenside has many weak light squares.

However, Izmailov's move is at least as strong, despite Romanovsky's criticism.

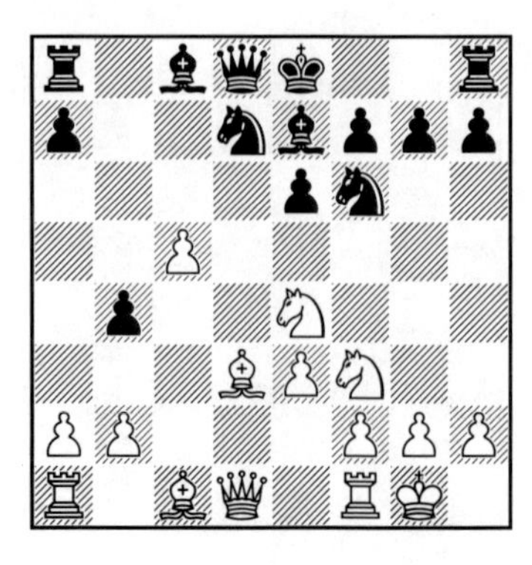

11...♘xc5

11...0-0 allows 12.♘xf6+ ♘xf6 13.c6 and although black might retrieve the pawn, the process will not be trivial, allowing white to make strategic progress in the meantime.

12.♘xc5 ♗xc5

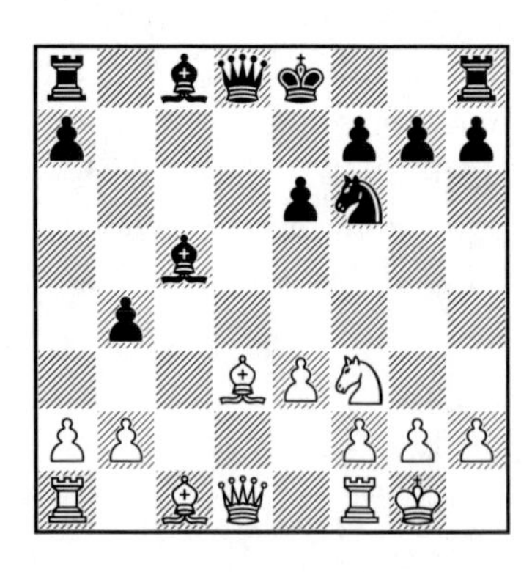

13.b3

In the event of 13.♗b5+ there follows simply 13...♗d7. White needs to focus on developing. The position is equal.

This time, Romanovsky's comment is more to the point, but white could have maintained the initiative with 13.e4! as in Giri – Tazbir, Warsaw 2013.

13...♕b6?!

Why not simply 13...0-0 in order to create real plans only after completing development, all the more so as the game move does not threaten anything and does not prevent anything, either?

14.♗b2

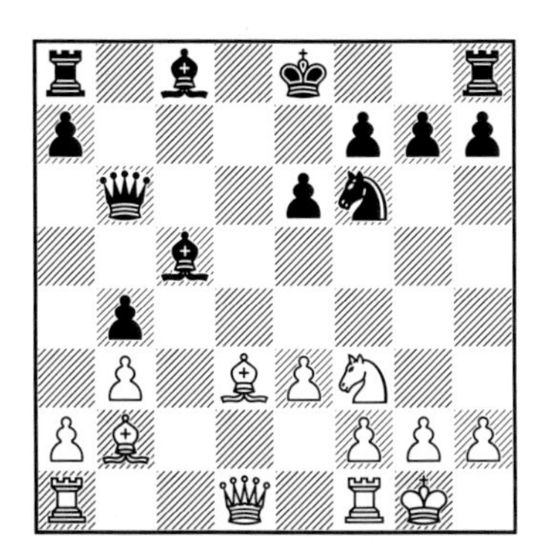

14...♗b7

14...0-0 would already be unpleasant in view of 15.♖c1, threatening ♗xf6, ♗xh7+ and ♕c2+.

After 14...0-0 white can actually win quickly with 15.♘g5: for instance 15...h6 16.♗xf6 gxf6 17.♘h7.

15.♖c1 ♖d8 16.♕e2

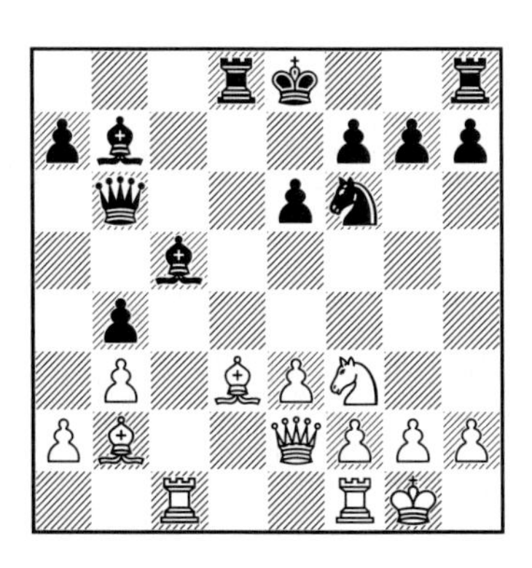

16...♗xf3

Black could not play 16...0-0 because he loses a pawn after 17.♗xf6. On the other hand, he faces the threat ♗b5+. The difficulties of the position induced him to dive into complications. Maybe he should have restricted himself to the prophylactic 16...a6.

While the general evaluation of the situation is correct, this comment is inaccurate when analyzing concretely. Winning a pawn does not promise white much after 17...gxf6 18.♗xh7+ ♔xh7 19.♕c2+ f5 20.♕xc5 ♕xc5 21.♖xc5

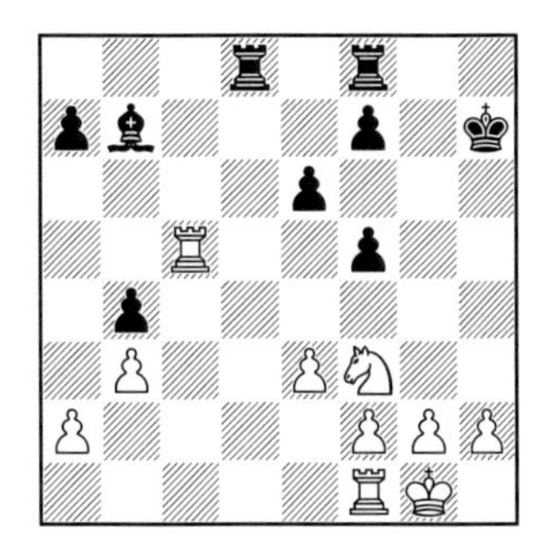

21...♖g8 22.♖c4 a5 (22...♗xf3 runs into 23.♖h4+) 23.♔h1 ♖c8 24.♖fc1 ♖xc4 25.♖xc4 ♖d8 with excellent compensation for the pawn.

After 16...0-0 white can simply prepare a massive attack with 17.♖c4, when it is hard to imagine that black's kingside can survive.

16...a6 does not improve black's position. White can complete his development with 17.♖fd1 followed by either ♖c4 or ♘e5, with an overwhelming advantage.

17.gxf3

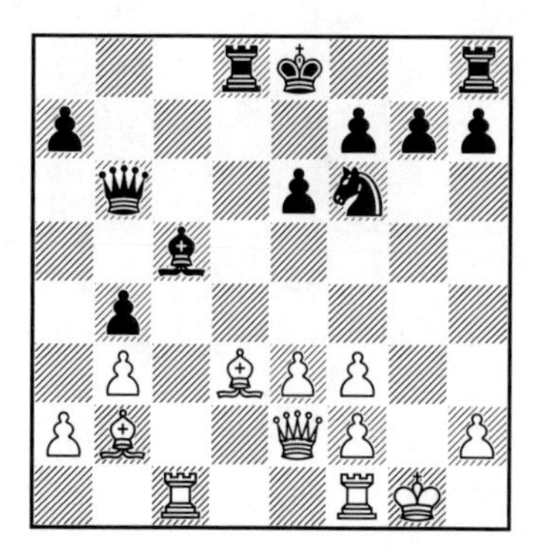

17...♖d5?!

Black misses his last chance to castle. True, after 17...0-0 18.♖c4 white can combine the pressure on light squares with concrete kingside threats, yielding him a clear advantage.

18.f4 ♔e7

18...0-0 would lead to disaster: 19.♗xf6 gxf6 20.♗e4 ♖dd8 21.♕h5 f5 22.♕g5+. Stockfish declares mate in 8 at this point.

19.♗c4 ♖d7

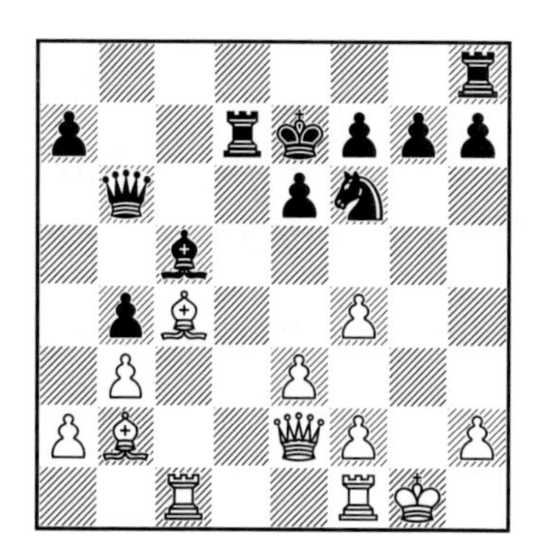

20.♕c2

Izmailov not only adds indirect pressure on the bishop on c5, but also prepares f4–f5. His last and next moves do however offer black two tempi to initiate simplifications.

The immediate 20.f5! was very strong, for instance 20...exf5 21.♕f3 g6 22.♕f4 with decisive threats. The bishops are murderous!

20...♖c8 21.♖fd1

21.f5! was better here as well.

21...♖xd1+ 22.♖xd1

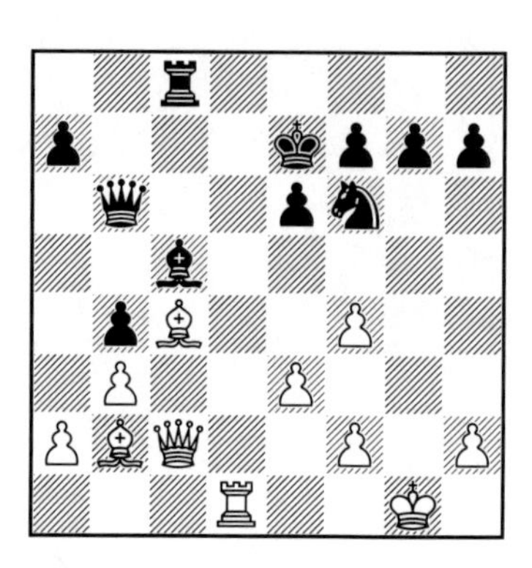

22...h6?

Black barely withstood the first assault. Now he should have played ...♖d8 with chances for a draw. After the game move, he again falls into difficulties.

Indeed, after 22...♖d8 white only retains a more pleasant position in the endgame. I entertained myself analyzing 23.♖xd8 ♕xd8 (23...♔xd8 simply loses a pawn to 24.♗xf6+ gxf6 25.♕xh7, when 25...♗xe3 does not offer black chances for a perpetual due to 26.fxe3 ♕xe3+ 27.♔g2 ♕xf4 28.♕d3+, with reasonable winning chances for white).

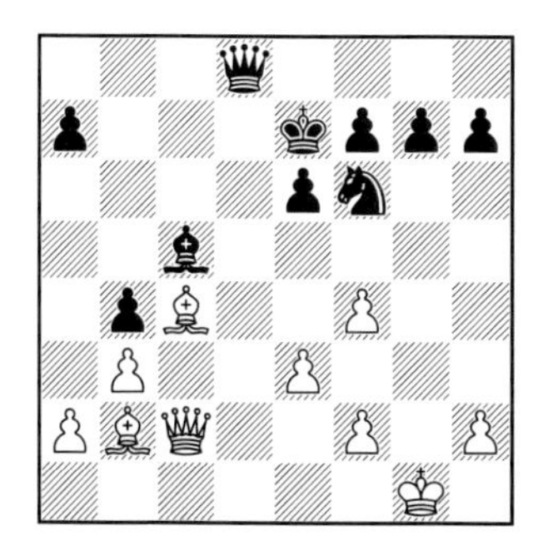

Grabbing the pawn on h7 would allow black to deliver perpetual, but white can try 24.♗xe6!? ♗xe3? (I had already found the improvement mentioned below, but this line was fun to analyze) 25.♗xf6+ gxf6 (25...♔xf6 loses to 26.♕f5+ ♔e7 27.♕xf7+ ♔d6 28.fxe3) 26.fxe3 ♔xe6 (26...fxe6 27.♕xh7+ wins a pawn and forces the exchange of queens) 27.♕e4+ ♔d7 28.♕xb4, with a promising endgame.

Black should of course play 24...♔xe6! 25.♕xc5 (25.f5+ runs into 25...♔d6, defending the bishop) 25...♕d1+ with perpetual.

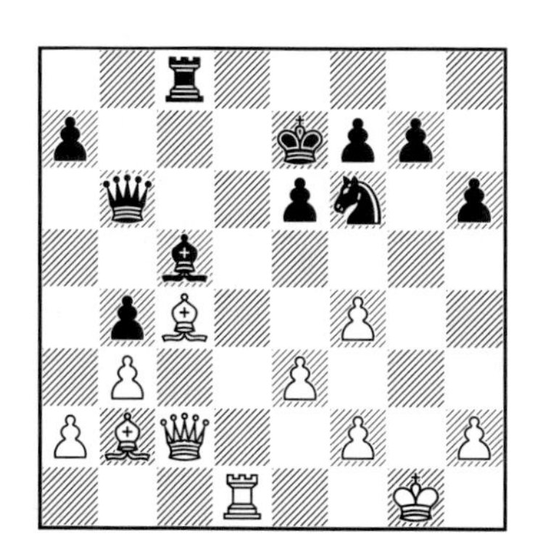

23.f5! exf5

Romanovsky attaches a question mark to this move, but black's position was bad anyway. For instance, after 23...♖d8 (recommended by him in the next comment) 24.♖xd8 ♕xd8 25.fxe6 fxe6 26.♕g6 ♕f8 (sadly, the only way to avoid losing a pawn) 27.♔f1!? White can slowly improve his position and should in all probability win, due to black's numerous weaknesses.

24.♕xf5

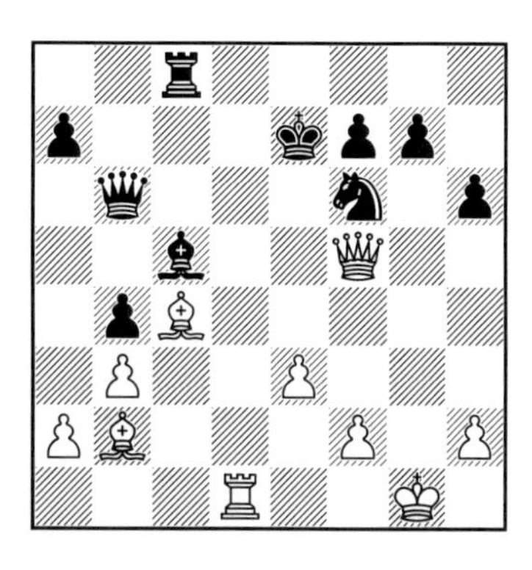

24...♕c6

Now, even after 24...♖d8 black cannot avoid losses in view of 25.♕e5+. On the previous move, it was still possible to choose the lesser evil with ...♖d8.

I would add that the rook does not have good squares at all. It has to defend d7 in view of the threat ♗xf6+ followed by ♖d7+, but 24...♖c7 loses to the same check: 25.♕e5+ followed by ♖d8+, mating next.

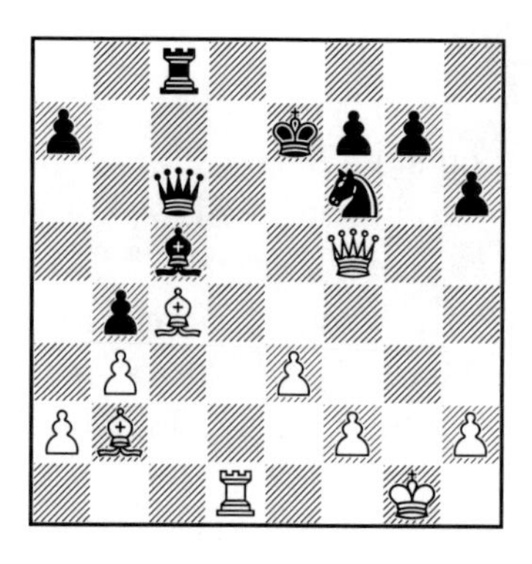

25.♗b5!

Izmailov plays this phase of the game very powerfully. Black's lack of coordination is decisive.

25...♕e6 26.♗xf6+ gxf6 27.♖d7+ ♔f8

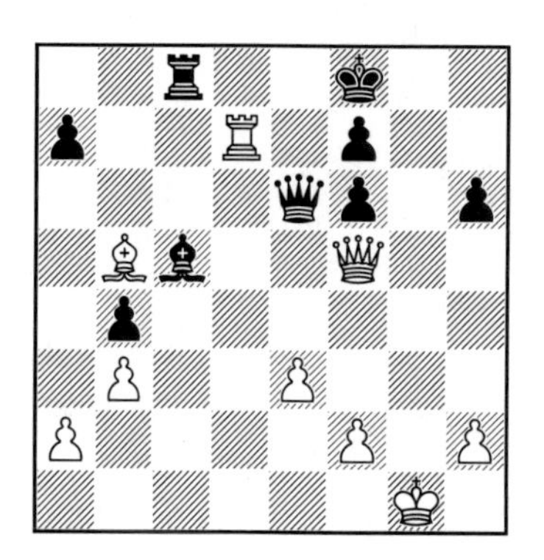

28.♖xf7+!

Not complicated, but original and beautiful.

28...♔xf7

28...♕xf7 29.♕xc8+ ♔g7 30.♕xc5 is completely hopeless, of course.

29.♗c4 ♖g8+ 30.♔f1 ♕xc4+ 31.bxc4 ♖g5 32.♕d7+ ♔g6 33.f4 ♖f5 34.♕e8+ ♔g7 35.♕e6. Black resigned.

Izmailov suffered his only defeat in the RSFSR championship at the hands of the Moscow player Ilia Kan. But even in this game, he held up well.

Game No. 34
P. Izmailov – I. Kan
Championship of the RSFSR, Moscow, 1928
Bogo-Indian Defense E11
Commentary by M. Marin

1.d4 ♘f6 2.♘f3 e6 3.c4 ♗b4+

This game allows us to continue the discussion about the Bogo-Indian Defense, initiated in the comments to the game with Staroverov, played earlier that same year. Since the moment when Efim Bogoljubov played "his" opening for the first time, in 1920, theory had advanced quite a bit.

The next move sequence shows that both opponents were aware of the most recent discoveries.

4.♗d2 ♕e7

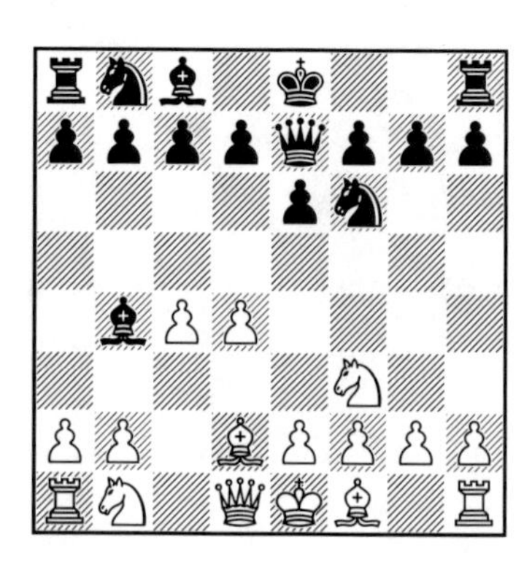

This move was introduced in the game Grunfeld – Johner, Berlin

1926. One year later, Alekhine and Nimzowitsch started using it, too. Earlier, black simply took on d2.

5.g3

In the early years of this opening, it was not obvious that white's best plan was to develop his bishop in a fianchetto. True, Bogoljubov himself had chosen this plan in 1920 against Selezniev in Gothenburg, but black had played a different variation: 4...♗xd2+ 5.♘bxd2 c5 6.dxc5 ♕a5 and now white replied with 7.g3.

Capablanca – Marshall, New York 1927, went 4...♗xd2+ 5.♘bxd2 d5 6.g3 and white eventually won. However, the game introducing g2–g3 in this position was Vidmar – Alekhine, played in the same tournament and quoted below.

5...0-0 6.♗g2 ♗xd2+

The modern plan, introduced by 6...♘c6, became popular only a few decades later.

7.♘bxd2

In those years, this was regarded as the most natural developing move.

Players discovered that 7.♕xd2 followed by ♘c3 was more active only in 1931.

Capturing with the knight is typical for positions where black plays 5...♘c6 instead of castling. Our game will transpose to this type of position after black's ninth move.

7...d6

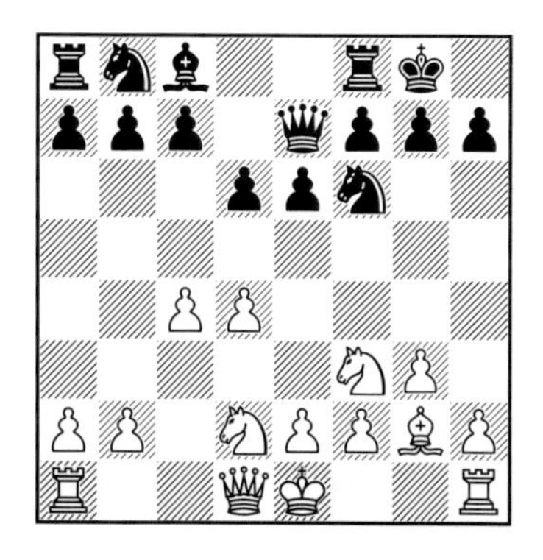

The most typical plan for the Bogo-Indian Defense, but not one used by Efim Dmitrievich himself.

8.♕c2!?

At this stage, developing the queen is not necessary and this move never became popular.

Two important games were played the year before: 8.0-0 e5 9.♕c2 (as we see, at grandmaster level the queen's early development looked natural, too) 9...♘c6 10.e3 (during the 1920s, players with white seemed to be slightly inhibited when having the chance to advance their d-pawn) 10...♗d7 11.a3 ♖ae8 12.d5 (finally!) 12...♘d8 in Vidmar – Alekhine, New York 1927.

With all the other pieces well developed, the knight can retreat to this square. After a later advance of the f-pawn, it could move closer to the attacking area with ...♘f7.

In this line, 9.e4 is more natural: 9...♗g4 10.d5 ♕d7?! (wasting developing time; 10...a5 or 10...♘bd7 would have been better) 11.♕b3 b6 12.c5! After a further c5–c6, white obtained a crushing space advantage in Grunfeld – Euwe, London Olympiad 1927. The point is that 12...bxc5 runs into 13.♕b7.

I find it reasonable to believe that both players knew these games. When playing his novelty, Izmailov planned to combine the two different plans.

8...e5 9.e4 ♘c6 10.d5

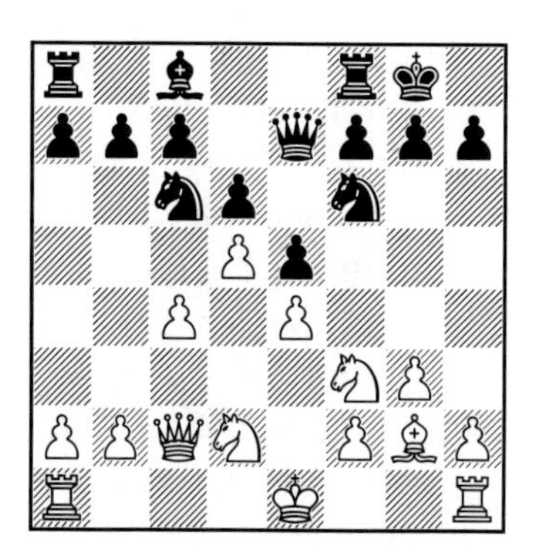

10...♘b4?!

If Izmailov had intended his novelty as a small psychological trap, his experiment was successful. This apparently active move dooms the knight to passivity for the rest of the game.

10...♘b8 was better, when 11.0-0 a5 12.♘e1 ♘a6 13.♘d3 transposes to a known opening position. True, instead of ♕c2 white has played a2–a3 many times, but developing the queen (albeit, at a later stage than Izmailov did) is also popular.

11.♕c3

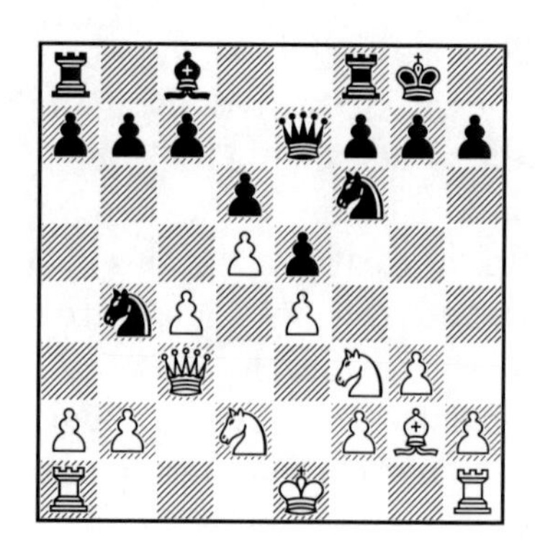

11...♘a6

A sad necessity.

The generally desirable 11...a5 loses a pawn to 12.a3 ♘a6 13.♕xa5. With his knight pinned, black does not have 13...♘c5.

12.b4 c5

A radical attempt to solve black's problems.

12...♘b8 would imply losing two tempi with respect to the normal variations. White has used them to transfer his queen to c3, where it stands much better than on d1.

12...c6 looks more flexible, but it does not solve black's space problems.

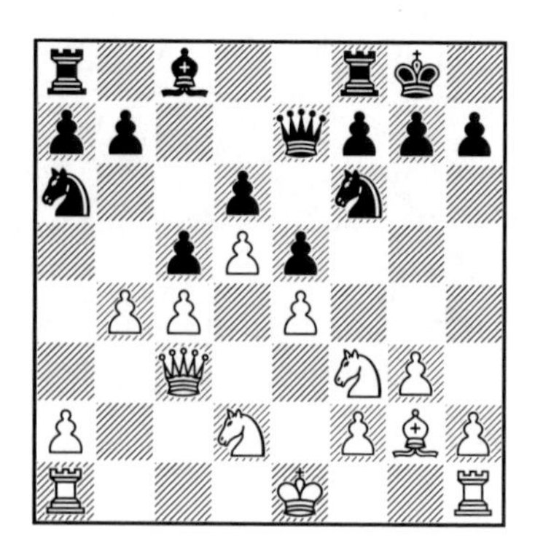

13.a3

Izmailov plays the middlegame consistently. His last move maintains the tension, allowing him to prepare the opening of the b-file after proper preparation.

13.dxc6 bxc6 clears the knight's path to e6 and, possibly, d4.

13.b5 is worth mentioning, too. True, white deprives himself of any queenside plan, but he can try to get the upper hand on the other wing. 13...♘c7 14.0-0 ♘h5 15.♘e1 f5 16.exf5 ♗xf5 17.♘c2 followed by ♘e3 and, depending on the circumstances, ♘e4 or f2–f4.

However, playing on just one wing restricts white's practical chances of success. Therefore, I find the game move the best.

13...b6 14.0-0 ♘h5

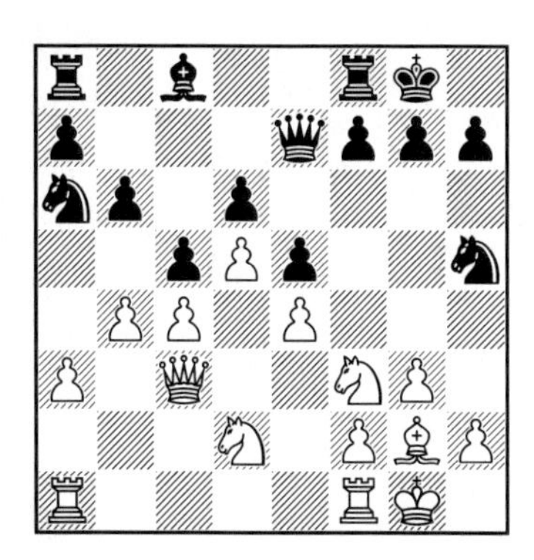

15.♘b3

The start of a fluent regrouping. White turns the threat bxc5 into a real one and clears the path for the other knight.

15...f5 16.exf5 ♗xf5 17.♘fd2

Consistent, but maybe not the best.

17.♖ae1, adapting the main plan to the changed circumstances, might have been stronger. 17... h6 (preparing ...♘f6 without allowing ♘g5) 18.♘bd2 and now white threatens ♘e4 with a stable advantage, since the knight on a6 remains passive. In the event of 18...♘f6? white gets an overwhelming initiative with 19.♘h4 ♗h7 20.f4.

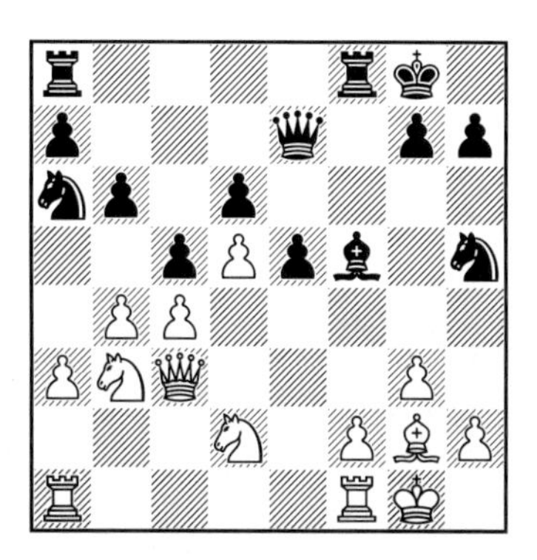

17...♕d7?!

Missing the chance to fight for the e4 square with 17...♘f6! that would have ensured good chances of equalizing.

18.♘e4

Everything returns to the normal path now.

18...h6 19.♘bd2

White has completed his regrouping, maintaining control of the center and chances to continue his queenside attack.

19...♖ad8 20.♖ab1 ♖f7

This rook lift will offer white a tactical chance after black's next move.

The immediate 20...♗h3 would not have solved his problems, though. After 21.♗xh3 ♕xh3 22.♕c2!? (threatening ♕a4) 22...♕d7 23.♖b3 white has consolidated his control of the light squares, without offering black any attacking chances. Next, he may play f2–f3 and choose a good moment for bxc5.

21.♖b2

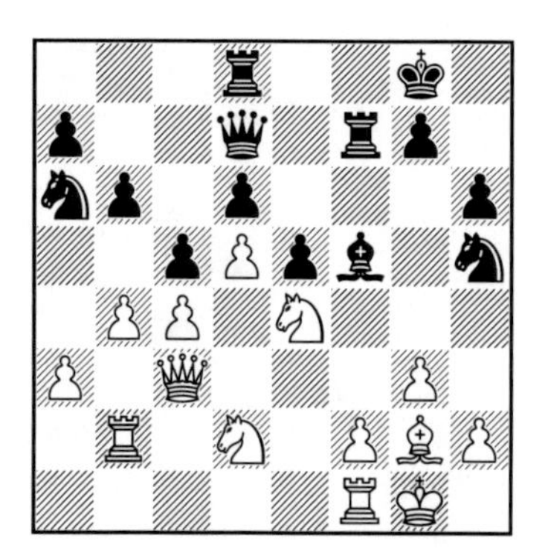

An elegant move, preparing the opening of the b-file, but also providing the kingside with some sort of indirect defense in any emergency. Unfortunately, Izmailov will not make use of the latter opportunity later in the game.

21...♗h3?

Probably intended as a tactical trap, this should have lost by force.

22.♘xd6!

The plan mentioned above would be good, but this is much stronger.

22...♗xg2 23.♘xf7 ♕h3

I can understand how confusing this position must have been for the players. When analyzing it, I had problems keeping record of the material balance, since both sides' pieces are spread all over the board. White is an exchange and a pawn up, but pieces are hanging...

It is also difficult to distinguish between the real threats and illusory ones.

24.♘xd8?!

This greedy move allows black to stay in the game.

Everything became clear when I discovered the calm move 24.♖e1! parrying all the threats and leaving black with poor coordination. After 24...♔xf7 (24...♘f4 is adequately met with 25.f3; the engine adds the variation 24...♖f8 25.♖xe5 ♖xf7 26.♖xh5 ♕xh5 27.♔xg2 winning) 25.♕xe5 white is not worse from the material point of view while the black king is exposed not only to ♕e7+, but also to ♕e6+, since the bishop is hanging. In the event of 25...♔g8, the least white can do is 26.f3 followed by ♕e2, trapping the bishop.

The engines consider 24.♘xh6+ gxh6 25.♖e1 equally good, but I find "my" move more natural.

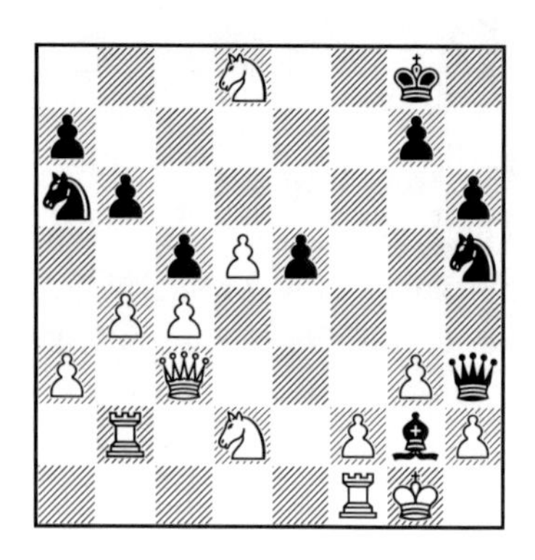

24...♘f4!

Throwing new forces into the attack. The knight is taboo due to the pin along the third rank, while the immediate threat is ...♘e2 mate.

25.♕xe5?

This way of defending e2 runs into an elegant refutation.

25.♖e1? loses to any bishop move, with the exception of ...♗f3, of course.

Now was the time to reveal the merits of white's 21st move with 25.♘f3! (clearing the second rank and preparing to defend g2 with the knight; in other words, white would bring two pieces to the defense with just one move) 25...♗xf1 26.♘h4! (white needs to leave the back rank clear, since 26.♘e1? ♗e2! wins) 26...♗d3 27.♕e1 (27.♕c1 allows black to bring the passive knight into play via 27...cxb4 28.axb4 ♘xb4! with reasonable compensation for the exchange) 27...♗xc4 28.♖d2. When reaching this position, I concluded that black was not without chances. The engines think differently: white has a large, maybe decisive advantage. The main point is that the errant knight on d8 can return home starting with ♘c6, while the knight on a6 remains passive.

From the practical point of view, black's chances are better than after 24.♖e1! mentioned above.

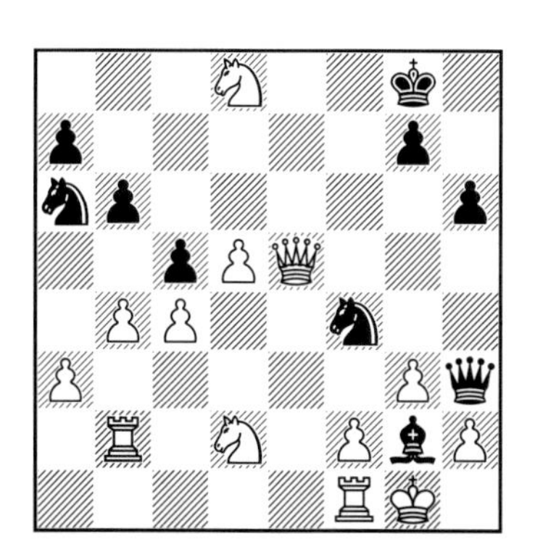

25...♗f3!

After this elegant move, threatening mate on g2, Izmailov resigned. No matter which piece white decides to take, black will still play ...♕g2 mate.

Apart from sustaining the attack, black's minor pieces also do a great job preventing white's counterplay based on checks on e6 or e4. At least this was what I thought... but the engines think that Izmailov should have played on: 26.♕xg7+!! (26.♕e6+ is a less effective way of speculating with the same ideas: 26...♔h8 27.♘f7+ ♔h7 28.♕f5+ ♕xf5 29.♘xf3 ♘g6 winning one of the knights) 26...♔xg7

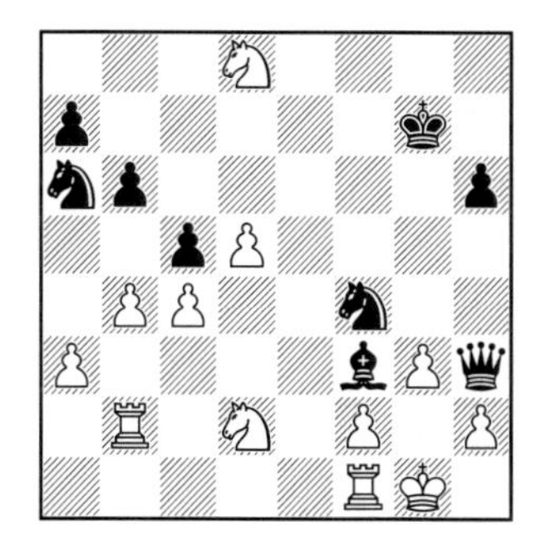

27.♘e6+! (the only way of dismantling the attacking

mechanism) 27...♘xe6 (27...♕xe6 28.♘xf3 ♕h3 transposes) 28.♘xf3 ♘f4 29.♘h4 (the material balance is unusual: a queen and a knight versus two rooks and three pawns; the d5–pawn is strong and the black king is exposed; however, the main events take place in the white king's neighborhood) 29... cxb4 30.axb4 ♘xb4! The knight is taboo, due to ...♘e2+ followed by mate. The game is very much still on.

Commenting on the outcome of the RSFSR championship, the magazine *Shakhmatny listok* noted: "Peter Nikolaevich Izmailov (born in 1906), the champion of Siberia, has already established himself with a number of successful games in regional tournaments, but has not yet had the opportunity to show his strength in a really high-level competition. We believe that after this new, well-deserved victory, this opportunity will be given to him, and he will manage to pass the test for the title of master."

And indeed, he got such an opportunity very soon – the Higher Qualification Commission decided to admit the champion of the RSFSR to the next Soviet Championship. Preparing for the All-Union Championship, Izmailov participated *hors concours* in the Leningrad regional tournament. His result, second place with 7 points out of 9, including victories over Ragozin and Ravinsky, who took first and third places, allowed for optimistic forecasts. And they came true.

In 1929, 36 chess players, of which one-third were masters, gathered in Odessa for the Sixth Soviet Championship. The competition was held under a three-stage system. Four preliminary groups were formed, and the masters were also included in them. Under the draw, Izmailov found himself in the fourth group and in the first round he played against the master Vladimir Makogonov.

The result was a victory for Izmailov, who played enthusiastically. Later, he beat the master Seleznev and the first-category player Kirillov (who later also became a master). As a result, he shared 3rd-4th place with the latter (behind the masters Grigoriev and Makogonov, both of whom scored half a point more), and, thanks to his better Berger score, he reached the next stage (as three players from each group reached the semifinal).

The twelve semi-finalists were divided into two groups of six, each of which competed for two places in the final in a round-robin system. At the end of the semifinal battles, the magazine *Shakhmatny listok* published the following: "Izmailov is a strong player; it's true that he doesn't show comprehensive mastery in his games, but his opponents may be partially at fault here, obligingly relieving him of the necessity of searching for complicated wins..." The game Izmailov – Botvinnik was illustrative of this description.

Game No. 35
P. Izmailov – M. Botvinnik
6th Soviet Championship,
Odessa, 1929
Queen's Gambit D52
Commentary by M. Marin (Comments in italics taken from Shakhmatny listok*)*

1.d4 ♘f6 2.♘f3 e6 3.c4 d5 4.♗g5

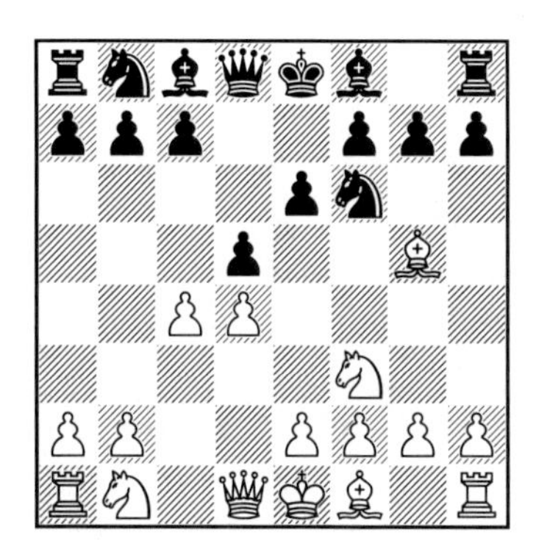

4...♘bd7

Heading for the Cambridge Springs variation.

Botvinnik started playing the system wearing his name only 12 years later. Despite the unusual move order chosen by Izmailov, black could have tried to reach the Botvinnik system with 4...dxc4 5.♘c3 (5.e4 b5 is an improved version of the system. 5.♕a4+ is known to be relatively inoffensive after 5...c6 6.♕xc4 b5) 5...c6 6.e4 b5.

5.♘c3 c6 6.e3 ♕a5

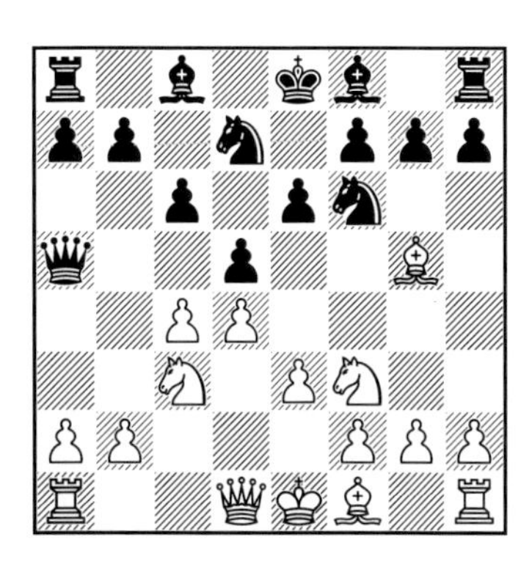

7.♕c2!?

A relatively rare move.

The main continuations are 7.♘d2 dxc4 8.♗xf6 ♘xf6 9.♘xc4 and 7.cxd5 ♘xd5. True, Bogoljubov successfully experimented with 7...exd5, which remains playable now.

7...♗b4

7...♘e4 is simpler.

8.♘d2 0-0 9.♗e2

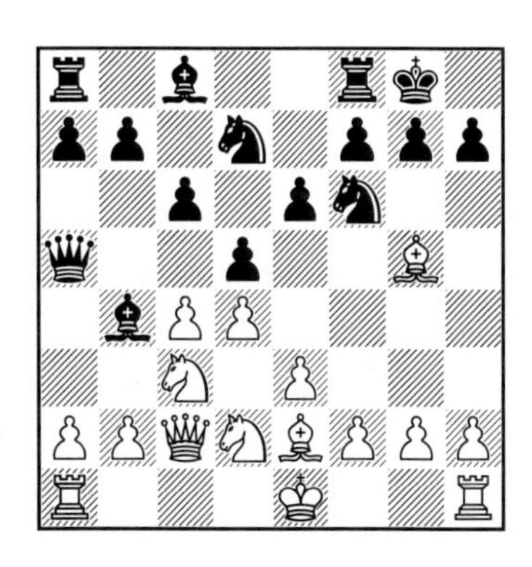

9...b6

A very ambitious move, aiming to fight for the light squares, in the spirit of the Nimzo-Indian.

In the event of 9...dxc4 10.♗xf6 ♘xf6 11.♘xc4 ♕c7 the bishop on b4 is likely to cause the loss of a tempo.

9...c5 and 9...e5 are more direct ways of fighting for the center after the knight's retreat to d2.

10.0-0 ♗xc3 11.bxc3 ♗a6 12.♗f4

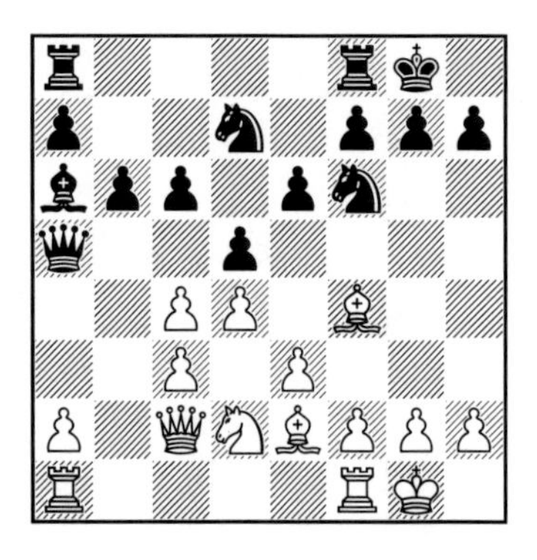

12...♖ac8

A mistake, immediately leading to material losses. 12...♖fc8 was correct.

In fact, the recommended move does not spare black problems: 13.a4! (threatening to trap the queen with ♘b3) 13...dxc4 14.♗xc4 (renewing the threat, since the bishop is hanging) 14...♗xc4 15.♘xc4 ♕a6 (15...♕d5 does not change the evaluation: 16.♘d6 ♖d8 17.c4 ♕h5 18.a5 with strong positional pressure) 16.♘d6 ♖d8 17.c4 with an obvious advantage.

In order to get some counterplay, black should have released the tension at once with 12...dxc4! 13.♗xc4 ♗xc4 14.♘xc4 ♕d5 15.♘d6

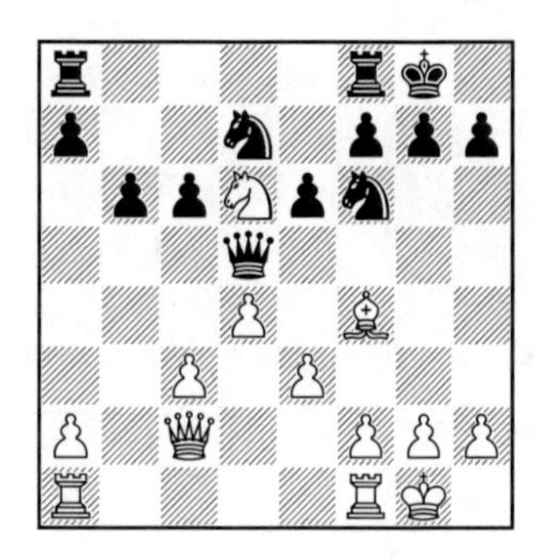

The difference with respect to the lines above is that black has a free tempo to organize his counterplay in the center. 15...e5 (15...c5 16.c4 ♕c6 is also playable) 16.dxe5 ♘xe5 17.♖fd1 ♕e6 and, in both cases, white maintains only light pressure.

13.♗d6

With the threat of ♗b4, trapping the queen, due to which black loses the exchange on f8.

13...c5 14.♗xf8 ♘xf8+–

And here, *Shakhmatny listok* concludes that the fate of the game is practically decided and states that white won. It is unknown what further moves were played in the game.

Izmailov played cautiously as always, with a "margin of safety". Having defeated Botvinnik and Makogonov, he drew his games against the rest of the semi-finalists – Kan, Vygodchikov and Silich. His score of 3.5 points out of 5 allowed him to share 1st-2nd place with Kan and reach the final.

The decisive battles for the championship title were to be waged by four players, however, there were only three of them left – Izmailov failed to participate in the final. The motive for his withdrawal mentioned in the magazine was characteristic of him: his educational leave had come to an end and he needed to take exams at his university. So, did the student of Tomsk University choose to give up the fight for the title of champion of the USSR but not to miss classes?!

What was the real reason for his "refusal" to participate in the final, even admitting Izmailov's sincere student zeal for studying? *Pravda* and *Izvestia* cited illness as the reason for Izmailov's refusal, while *Komsomolskaya Pravda* was of the opinion that the reason was overwork. As Nikolai Izmailov recalls, his mother, when recounting this episode, said that in the mid-1930s Petr Nikolaevich claimed that he was healthy and quite ready to continue fighting for the title of champion of the USSR; but that he was forced to leave the tournament...

Anyway, he was only 23 years old, and it seemed that he had his whole life ahead of him, in which there would be many opportunities to achieve top results in chess. In the meantime, Izmailov was satisfied with the fact that, thanks to his performance in the preliminary and semi-final groups of the national championship, he was awarded the title of master. He became the first chess player of the vast region of Siberia, stretching from the Urals to the Far East, to be awarded this title.

Izmailov took part in the championship of the year 1931. In the preliminary group, he scored 5 points out of 9, sharing 3rd-5th place with Konstantinopolsky and Grigorenko (behind Kasparyan and Botvinnik, who became the national champion for the first time that year). Nevertheless, that year Izmailov beat Botvinnik again.

Game No. 36
P. Izmailov – M. Botvinnik
7th Soviet Championship,
Moscow, 1931
Queen's Indian Defense E12
Commentary by M. Marin (Comments in italics by Yuri Averbakh)

1.d4 ♘f6 2.♘f3 b6 3.c4 ♗b7 4.♘c3 e6 5.♗g5

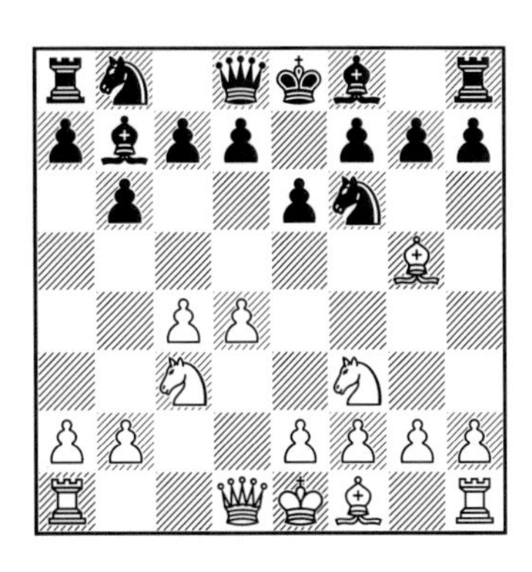

5...♗e7

5...♗b4 is more active.

Even though white's system has lost most of its initial popularity, it seems that it was not Botvinnik's lucky variation. More than three decades later he lost an important game continuing: 5...h6 6.♗h4 g5 7.♗g3 ♘h5 8.e3 ♘xg3 9.hxg3 ♗g7 10.♕c2 ♘c6 Uhlmann – Botvinnik, Varna 1962. In this game, too, Botvinnik refrained from early pawn confrontation in the center, playing more in a hyper-modern style.

6.♕c2 h6 7.♗xf6 ♗xf6 8.e4 d6

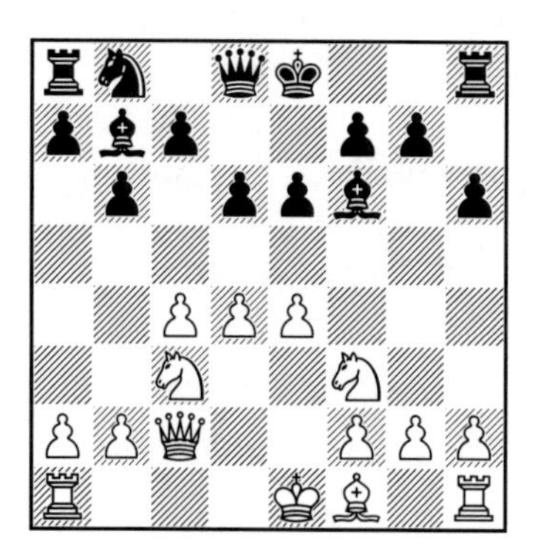

Black plays in the spirit of the Modern Defense, refraining from reaching the fifth rank with his pawns.

9.e5

A questionable plan. Opening the game plays into black's hands, since he has the bishop pair.

Indeed, white should have chosen a plan like 9.♖d1 ♘d7 10.♗e2 focusing on preparing d4–d5.

9...♗e7 10.♖d1 ♘d7 11.♗d3

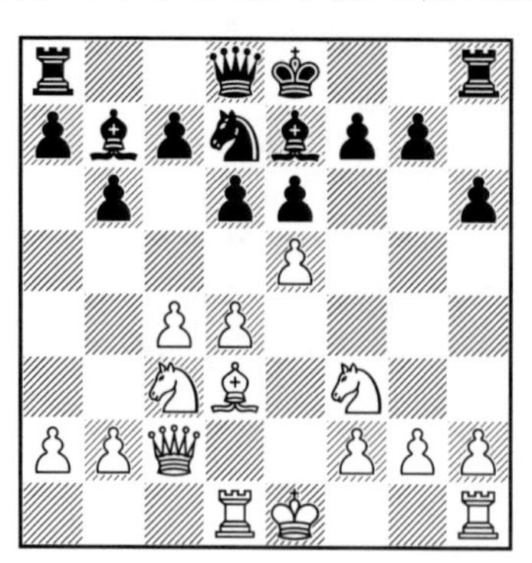

11...♕c8

But not 11...dxe5 12.dxe5 ♗xf3 13.gxf3 ♘xe5 14.♗e4±

The final position in Averbakh's line is anything but clear, though. After 14...♗d6 black gets great compensation for the exchange.

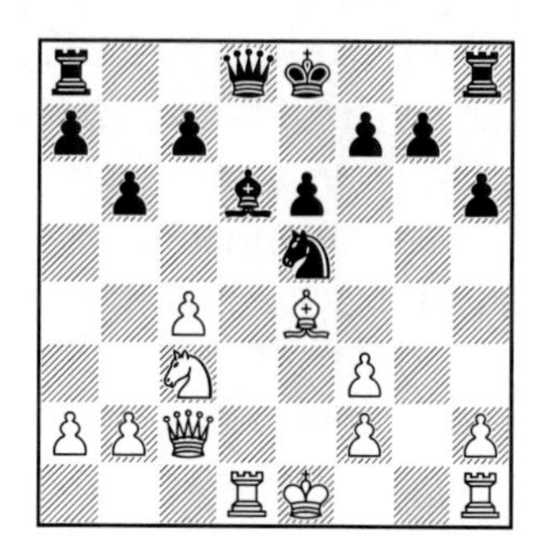

15.f4 (15.♗xa8 ♕xa8 leaves the pawns on f3 and c4 hanging, then 16.♕e4 ♕xe4+ 17.fxe4 ♘xc4 with a decent game for black; a neutral move such as 15.b4 can be met with 15...f5, forcing matters, then 16.f4 ♘d7 with unclear play) 15...♘d7 16.♗xa8 ♕xa8 17.♖g1 ♕f3 with excellent compensation.

12.♗e4

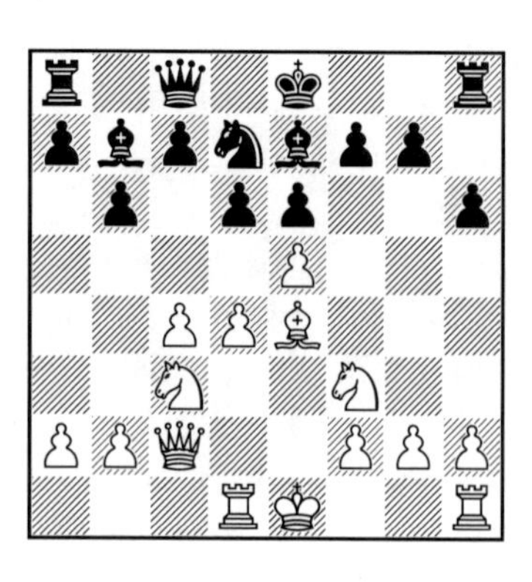

12...c6?

Botvinnik was heading for the structure arising later in the game. He must have thought that his move order was the most restricting, but in doing so, he underestimated the dynamic factors.

He probably discarded the safer 12...dxe5 because of the intermediate 13.♗xb7 (13.dxe5 c6 is likely to transpose to the game) 13...♕xb7 14.dxe5 with approximate equality.

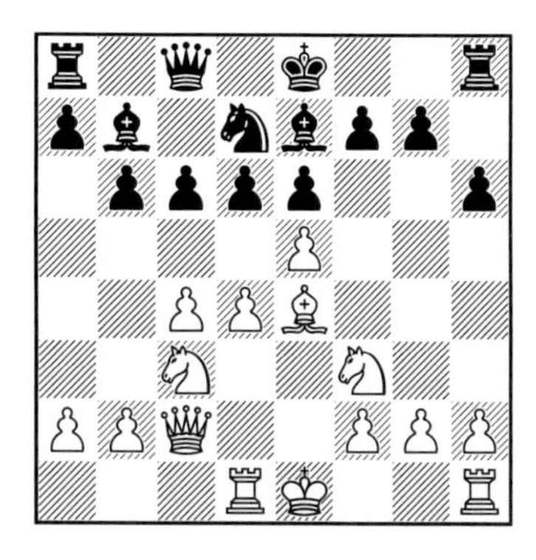

13.♕e2?!

Izmailov could have used his more natural development to break in the center with 13.d5! and black would have been in serious trouble: 13...cxd5 14.cxd5 exd5 15.♗f5 ♕c7 16.e6 with a strong initiative.

13...♕c7

Planning ...0-0-0 with a counterattack on the kingside.

For known reasons, 13...dxe5! was better.

14.0-0

Once again missing 14.d5!

14...dxe5

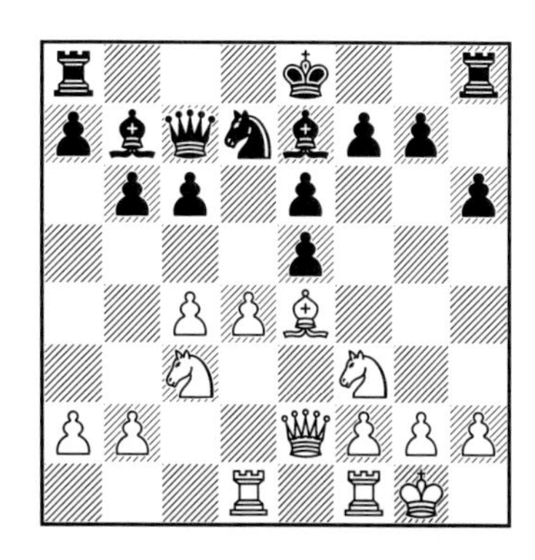

15.dxe5?!

Izmailov, too, shows his ambitions by avoiding early simplifications. However, keeping the knights on board will offer black additional ideas for developing his kingside initiative.

15.♘xe5 ♘xe5 16.dxe5 would have led to approximate equality.

15.d5!? would only offer reasonable compensation for the pawn: 15...cxd5 16.cxd5 exd5 17.♘xd5 ♗xd5 18.♗xd5 ♖d8 19.♖fe1 and if black intends to avoid any hint of trouble, he could return the pawn with 19...0-0, leading to complete equality.

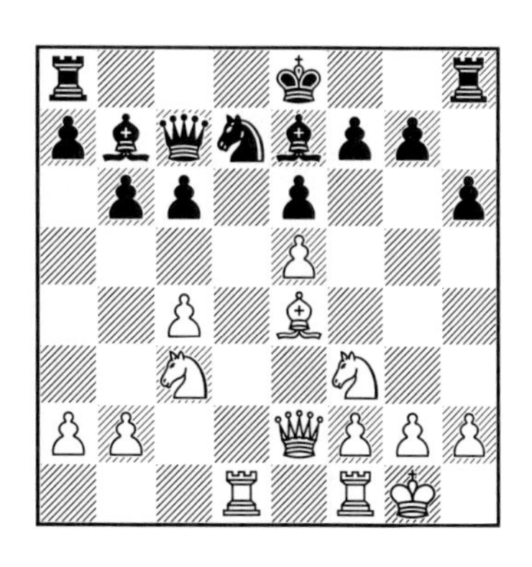

15...0-0-0

15...g5 was tempting, for instance 16.♖fe1 g4 17.♘d4 ♘xe5 18.♘db5 ♕b8!, but a stronger line is 16.♗c2 g4 17.♘d4 ♘xe5 18.♖fe1 ♗f6 (18...♘d7 19.♘xe6!) 19.♘e4 ♗g7 (19...♗e7 20.♘g3) 20.♘d6+! and black has to play 20...♔f8 (20...♕xd6 21.♘f5 ♕f8 22.♕d2 threatening ♖xe5 and ♕d7 mate)

16.♗c2

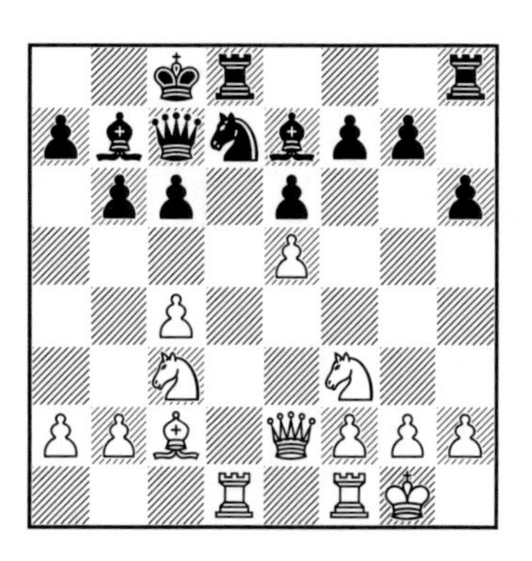

The position is not easy to evaluate. The pawn on e5 ensures white a space advantage, but can also become a target. Black's position also features a small dilemma. He would like to play ...a7–a6 and ...c6–c5, in order to clear the bishop's path, but this would leave the knight passive.

16...g5!

This resolute move combines a kingside attack with the idea of undermining the pawn on e5.

17.♖fe1 g4 18.♘d4 ♖hg8 19.f4!

White consolidates the pawn on e5, without fearing the opening of the g-file.

The unexpected 19.♗f5!? deserves consideration, too.

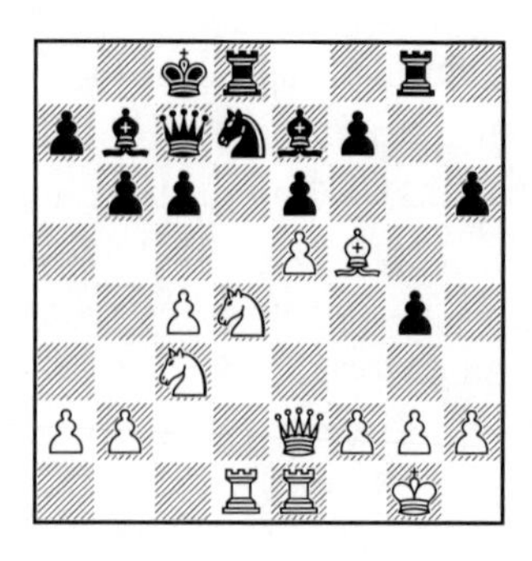

White attacks g4 and the bishop is not edible: 19...exf5? 20.e6 ♘e5 (20...fxe6 is even worse: 21.♘xe6 ♕b8 22.♘xd8 ♗xd8 23.♖xd7 ♔xd7 24.♕e6+ winning the rook and maintaining a decisive attack) 21.exf7 ♖g7 22.♕xe5 ♕xe5 23.♖xe5 ♖xf7 24.♘xf5 when white has an extra pawn and a dominant position. If black tries to activate his bishop with ...c6–c5, the knights will get the d5–square.

However, black can react better to the piece sacrifice: 19...♗c5 20.♗xg4 ♕xe5. After the simplifications, black's control of dark squares will yield him the better game.

19...gxf3 20.♘xf3

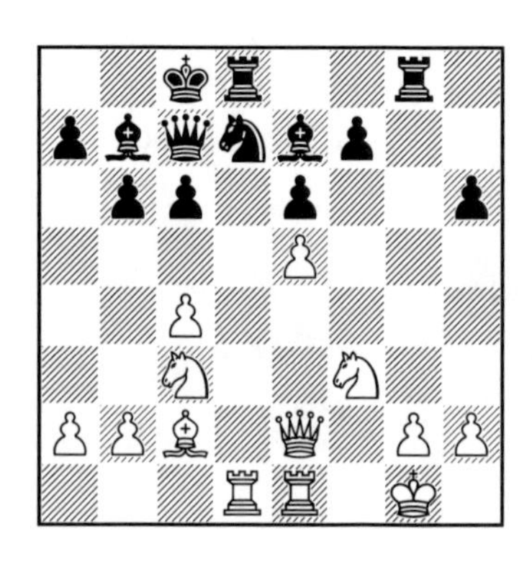

20...♗b4?!

Losing control over the dark squares; 20...♗a6!?

Averbakh is right when criticizing the last move, but his comment does not touch the core of the matter. The final evaluation of the position depends on timing. If white manages to consolidate, he will have chances to maintain an advantage. Therefore, black should develop his counterplay as quickly as he can and this is likely to yield him a superior position. 20...♖g4!

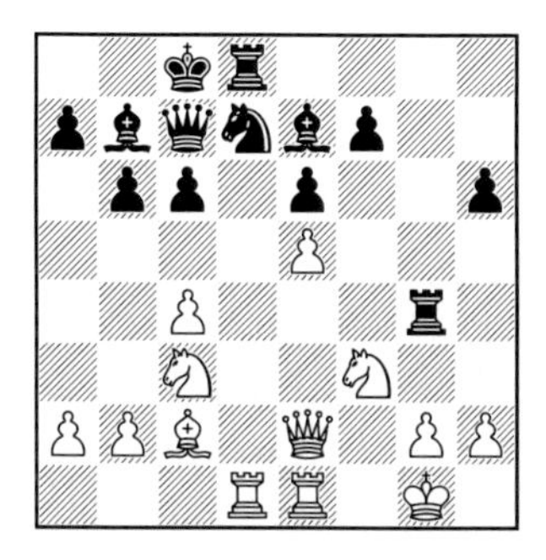

21.h3 (white cannot defend g2 with 21.♔h1 ♖dg8 22.♖g1 because of 22...♗c5; after 21.♖d2 ♖dg8, the white queen does not have the optimal e3–square available as in the game: 22.♕d3 ♗a6 23.b3 ♗b4 followed by ...b6–b5 with a strong initiative) 21...♖g7 22.♖d2 ♖dg8 (once again, the queen needs to stay away from e3) 23.♕d1 ♗b4 with excellent play for black.

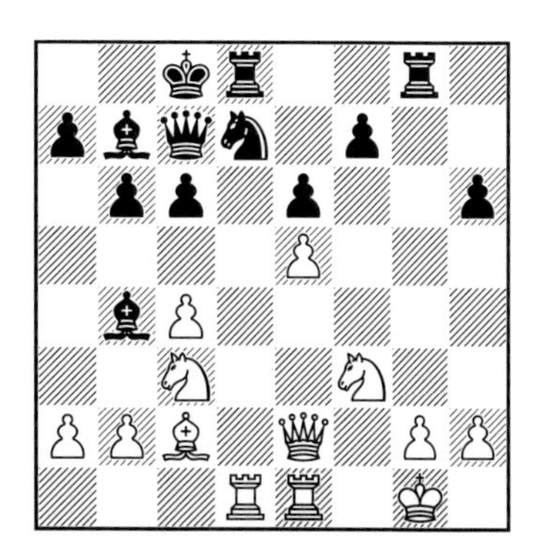

21.♔h1!

Izmailov makes use of the gifted tempo in the best way possible. His last move removes the danger of a pin along the dark-squared diagonal.

21...♖g4 22.h3 ♖g3 23.♖d2 ♗xc3

This exchange was meant to solve the aforementioned dilemma involving black's minor pieces. At some point, the knight will go to c5 and the bishop to a6.

23...♖dg8 24.♕e3 does not change much.

24.bxc3 ♖dg8 25.♕e3

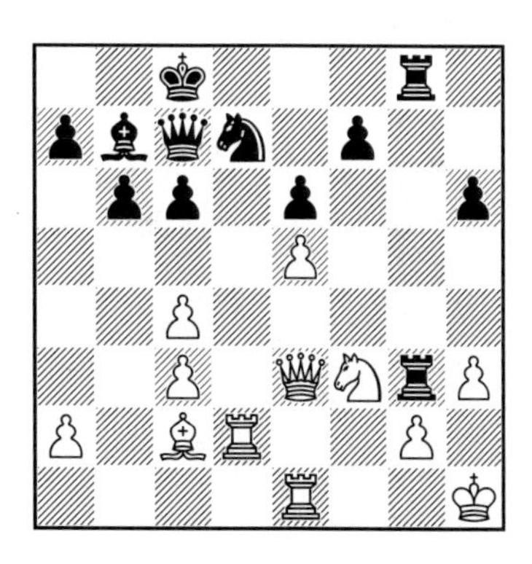

White has solved all his problems and it is now black's turn to look for a way of maintaining equality.

25...h5?

Botvinnik treats the position too statically, as though he had all the time in the world to strengthen his position.

True, 25...c5? is premature due to 26.♗e4 stabilizing white's advantage.

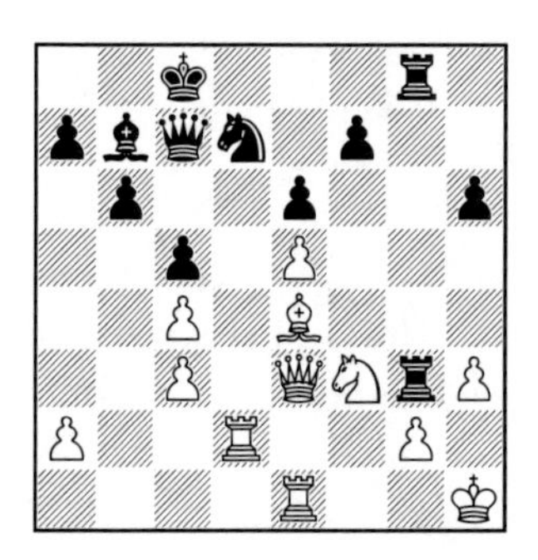

Tactics do not work for black here: 26...♘xe5? 27.♗xb7+ ♕xb7 28.♕xe5 ♖xf3 29.gxf3 ♕xf3+ 30.♔h2 when all the important squares are defended and black is simply a rook down.

The only correct continuation was 25...♔b8!, which was to a certain extent similar to Izmailov's earlier ♔h1.

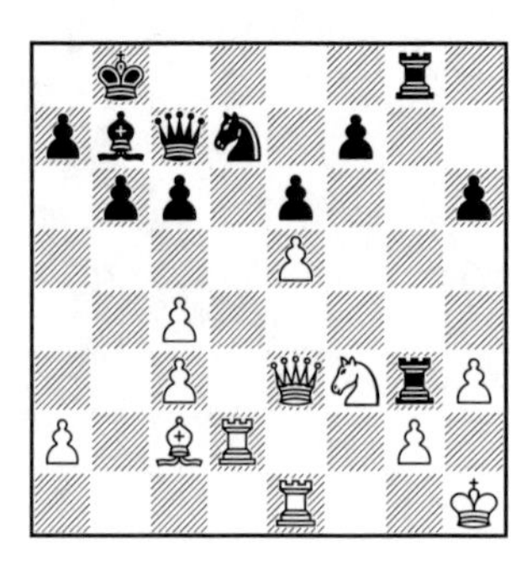

This move has two main ideas. In the lines with ...c6–c5, ♗xb7 will come without a check. Secondly, the king also clears the c8–square for the bishop, in order to overprotect the knight if necessary. Now 26.♕xh6 (26. a4? allows 26...c5 27.♗e4 ♘xe5! 28.♗xb7 ♘xc4! winning material; 26.♖ed1 is easily parried with 26...♗c8) 26...c5

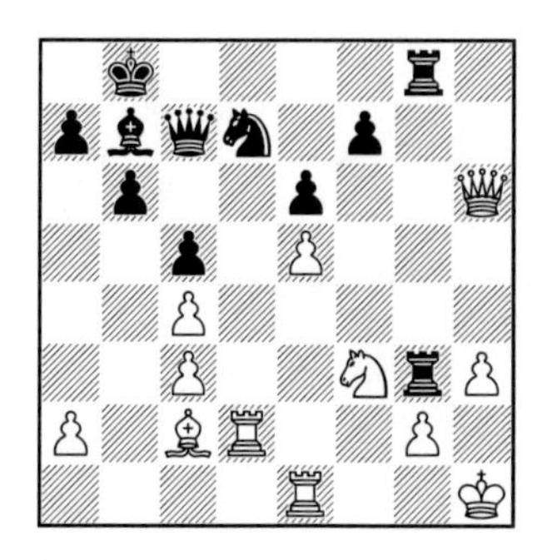

27.♗h7! (white has to be careful already; his last move induces black to weaken his back rank defense, whereas 27.♗e4? runs into 27...♘xe5! 28.♗xb7 ♕xb7! 29.♖xe5 ♖xf3! with a clear advantage: the rook is taboo now, since the square on g3 is not defended by the queen as in the above variation) 27...♖8g7 28.♗e4! ♗c8 (28...♘xe5 is impossible due to 29.♕h8+ ♗c8 30.♘xe5 ♕xe5 31.♖d8 or 29...♖g8 30.♕xe5, winning in both cases) 29.♗c2 (defending the pawn on e5) 29...♗b7 with a probable draw by repetition.

26.a4

26.♕h6 ♗a6! 27.♕xh5 ♗xc4 28.♕xf7 ♗xa2.

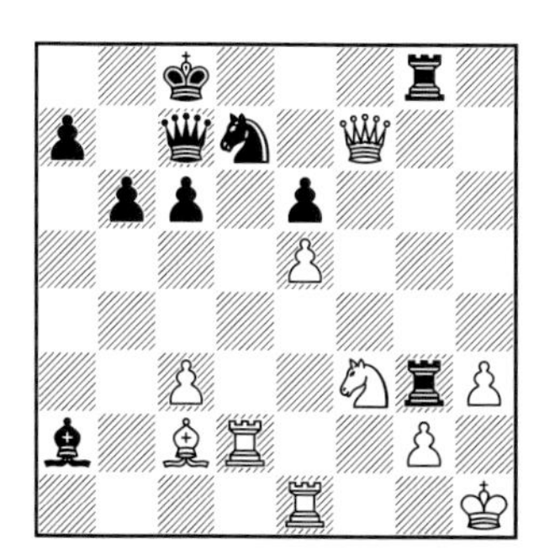

In the final position of Averbakh's variation, white has the elegant 29.♗g6! ensuring him an advantage after 29...♖3xg6 30.♖xa2, as black's king is a bit unsafe and, in the endgame, white's connected passed pawns would be more dangerous than black's queenside pawn majority.

After 26.♕h6 black once again has the prophylactic move 26...♔b8! available, for instance 27.♕xh5 f5 28.exf6 ♘xf6 29.♕e5! (otherwise, ...c6–c5 would win) 29...♕xe5 30.♖xe5 c5 and black will retrieve the pawn with approximate equality.

White's strongest continuation would have been 26.♖ed1! ♘c5 27.♖f2!? preparing to increase the pressure with, say, ♖d4 and ♕f4.

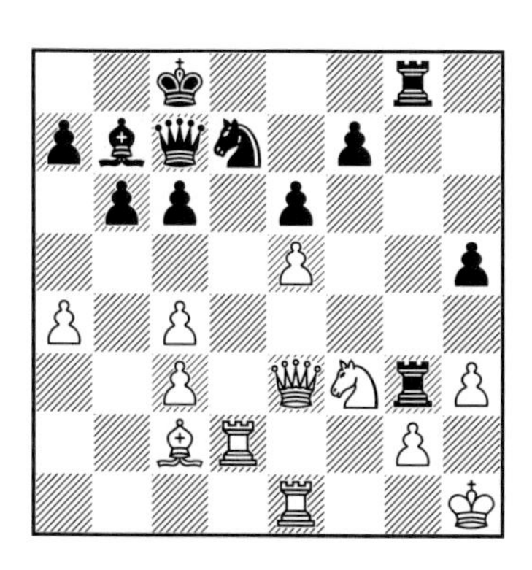

26...♔b8?

Botvinnik chooses an unfortunate moment for this move. Under the circumstances, it simply wastes a tempo.

26...a5! would have stabilized the queenside and maintained the status quo. For instance: 27.♖ed1

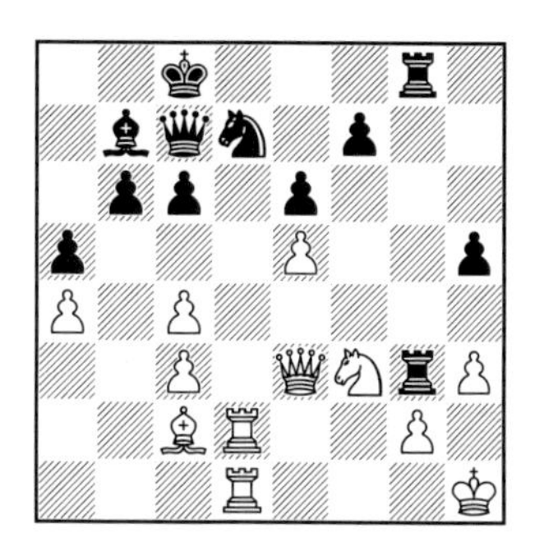

27...♘xe5!! 28.♕xe5 ♕xe5 29.♘xe5 c5 30.♔g1 (of course, not 30.♖g1 ♖xh3 mate) 30...♖xg2+ 31.♔f1 ♖g1+ 32.♔f2 ♖1g2+ and white should agree to a draw by perpetual, since 33.♔e3 ♖2g3+ 34.♔f4?! ♖xh3 would be dangerous for him. Black threatens ...f7–f6 with ideas of mate on f3 or g4.

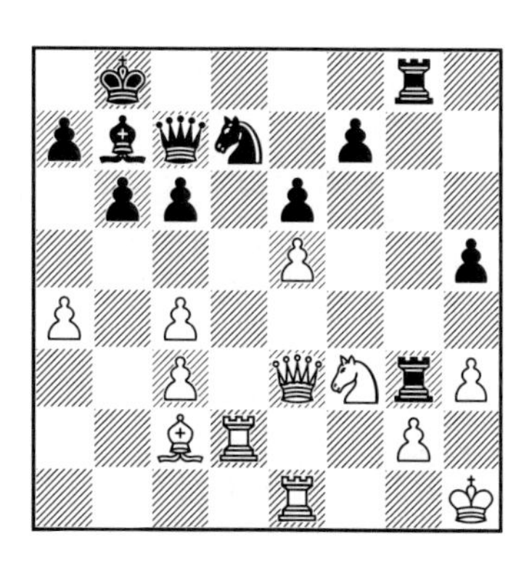

27.♖ed1!!

Against 27.♕h6 Botvinnik had prepared a combination: 27...c5 28.♗e4 ♘xe5 29.♗xb7 ♕xb7!

27...♘c5

27...♘xe5 does not work now, since after 28.♕xe5 ♕xe5 29.♘xe5 c5 white has 30.♖d8+! (a direct consequence of ...♔b8) 30...♖xd8 31.♖xd8+ ♔c7 32.♖d3 ♖xg2 33.♖d7+ ♔c8 34.♖xb7! winning.

27...♗c8 would have been fine if white could not have played 28.a5! weakening the enemy queenside, with chances to start an attack.

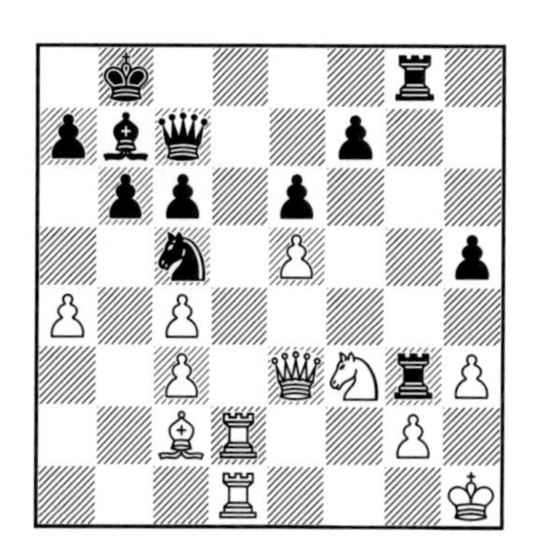

28.a5!

Ridding himself of the weak pawn.

28...♕e7 29.axb6 axb6 30.♕f4 ♔c7 31.♔h2

Creating the threat ♗h7.

31...♗a6

31...h4! was essential, defending the rook on g3 in advance.

In fact, this allows white to start a decisive attack after 32.♘xh4 ♖xc3 33.♘f5! exf5 (otherwise, black's position would be simply bad) 34.e6+ ♔c8 35.exf7 ♕xf7 36.♗xf5+ winning.

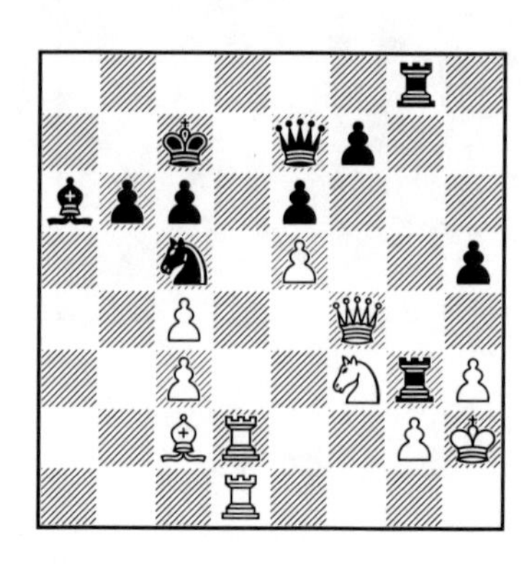

32.♗h7

A tempting continuation, which will work out well in the game.

32.♕f6 ♕xf6 33.exf6 h4 does not promise white much.

Objectively, the most constructive move would have been 32.♖f2! still preparing ♕f6 (maybe with ♖d4 in between).

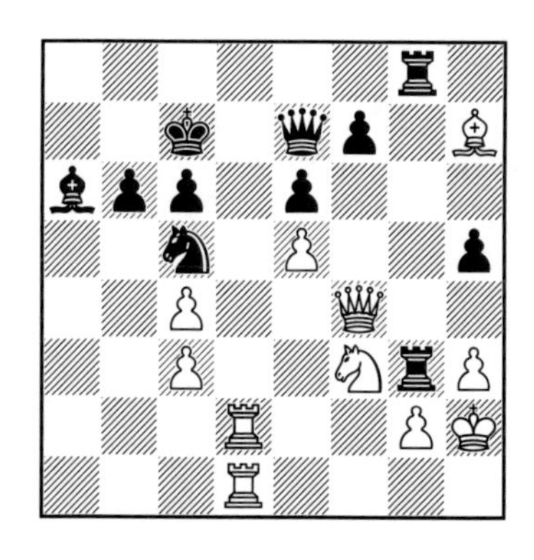

32...♖3g7?

This loses the exchange without any compensation.

32...♖8g7 33.♕f6! would be very unpleasant:

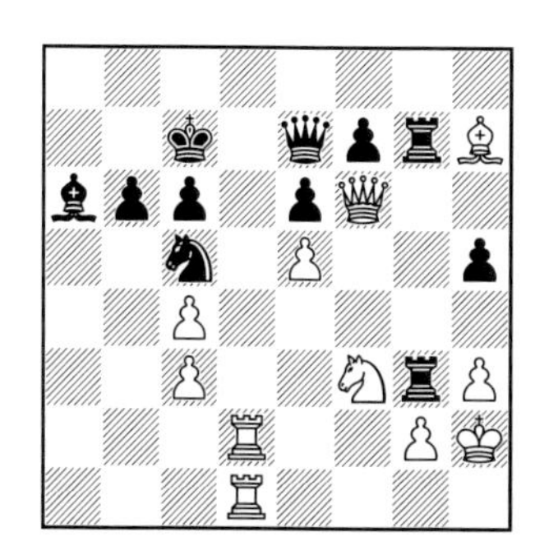

33...♕xf6 (33...♕f8 34.♖d8 ♖xg2+ 35.♔h1+−) 34.exf6 ♖xh7 35.♔xg3 ♘e4+ 36.♔h4! (36.♔f4? ♘xd2 37.♖xd2 ♖h6 38.♔e5 h4 39.♘g5 ♖h5=) 36...♘xd2 37.♖xd2 ♖h6 38.♘e5 ♖xf6 39.♖d7+ ♔b8 40.♖xf7±

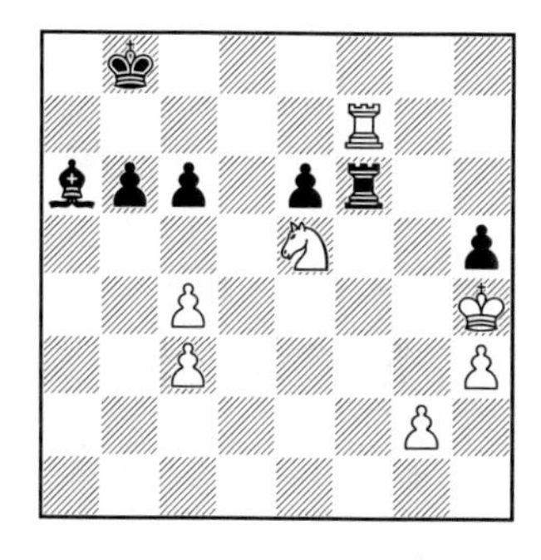

This is what both players must have calculated, too. However, the evaluation of the final position requires a considerable adjustment.

40...♖xf7 41.♘xf7 ♗xc4. The bishop will arrive on f1 just in time to avoid losing a pawn.

42.♘e5 (42.♔xh5 ♗f1 may transpose).

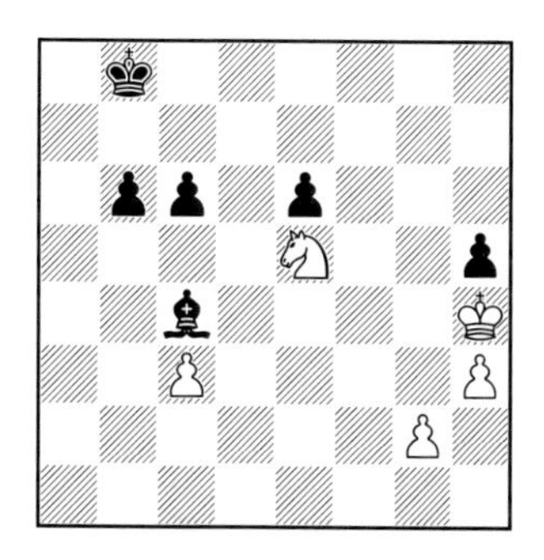

Black's position remains dangerous, but he can reach a draw with a few very precise moves.

42...♗f1! 43.♔xh5 (43.♘xc6+ ♔c7 helps black to activate his king. He will give up the bishop for the h-pawn when needed and proceed with queenside counterplay) 43... ♗xg2 44.h4

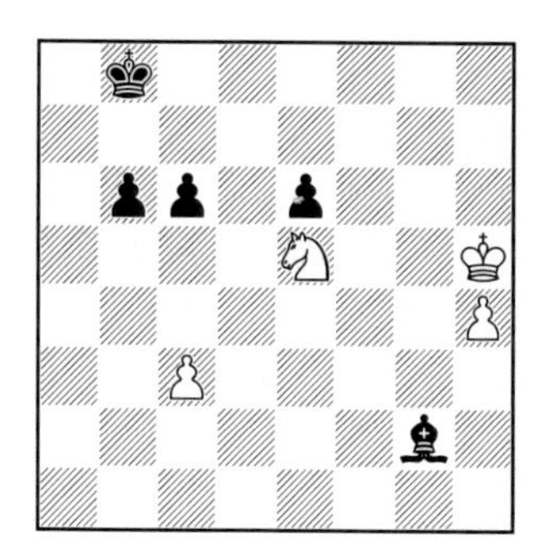

44...♗f1! (the bishop needs to start fighting against the advance of the pawn at once. In the event of say 44...♔c7? 45.♔g5 ♔d6 46.♔f6 white gains time for the race: 46...♗e4 47.h5 ♔c5 48.h6 ♗h7 49.♔g7 ♗e4 50.♘g6 winning. In the main variation, white will have to lose additional time on making the h5–square available for the pawn):

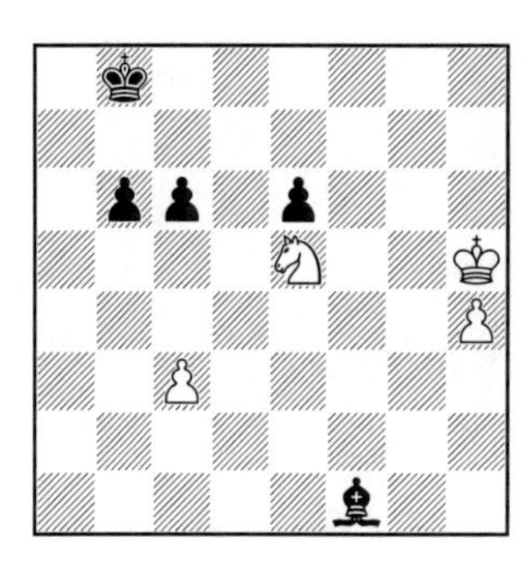

45.♔g5 ♗e2 46.♘g4 b5 47.h5 c5 48.h6 ♗d3 49.♘e5 ♗h7 50.♘d7+ ♔c7 51.♘f8 (white has almost succeeded, but only "almost") 51... b4! 52.cxb4 cxb4 53.♘xh7 b3 54.♘f6 b2 55.h7 b1=♕ 56.h8=♕ with a draw.

33.♗xg8 ♖xg8 34.♖d4

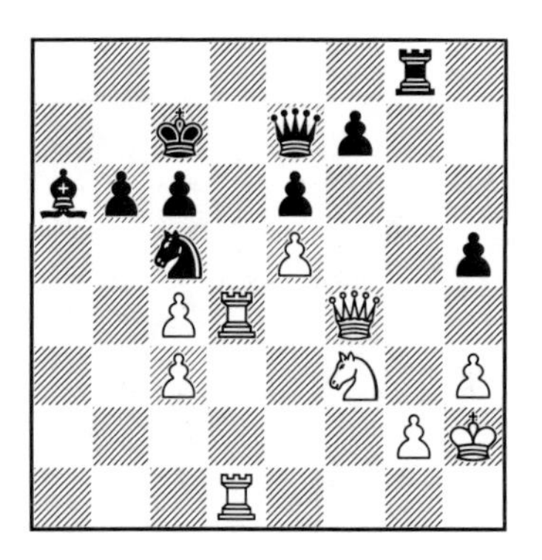

The rest is a formality.

34...♗c8 35.♕h6 ♘d7 36.♖f4 c5 37.♕xh5 ♖g7 38.♖g4 f5 39.♖xg7 ♕xg7 40.♖e1 ♗b7 41.♕g5 ♕h8 42.♕e7 ♕h6 43.♕d6+ ♔c8 44.♖d1 ♕f4+ 45.g3. Black resigned.

Averbakh gives the following line: *45...♕xf3 46.♕xd7+ ♔b8 47.♕d8+ ♔a7 48.♖a1+ ♗a6 49.♕c7+.*

Izmailov's overall performance in the 1931 national championship after his sensational success in 1929 seemed modest. "...Master Izmailov is isolated from chess life (he works in the taiga), and the lack of tournament practice affected his performance," reported the magazine *64 – Shakhmaty v Rabochem Klube* (*"64. Chess and Checkers in the Workers' Club"*).

Between 1931 and 1936, Izmailov rarely participated in tournaments. A geophysics engineer by profession, he worked as the head of a geological exploration party in the taiga. He spent every summer on geological expeditions, and when he returned home to Tomsk, he was engaged in processing materials. Nevertheless, in 1934 Izmailov easily won the

Tomsk championship (10.5 out of 12). But then the ex-champion of the RSFSR played too cautiously in the semifinal of the championship of the republic, finishing many games in a draw, which only allowed him to share 6th-7th place with a 50% result, while only the top five proceeded to the final.

Izmailov's last tournament was held in April 1936 in Leningrad. Among those who took part in this competition, which was called the All-Union Tournament of the first category, we find the names of future famous masters, as well as grandmasters Bondarevsky and Kotov. Izmailov scored 7.5 points out of 14 (6th place). "Izmailov is arguably a special case. In faraway Siberia, separated from our everyday chess life and big events, he couldn't, of course, have counted on a better result. His play, nevertheless, was highly diligent," – commented Peter Romanovsky for the magazine *64* when analyzing the tournament.

On September 10, 1936, Petr Nikolaevich called his wife in the afternoon from work and told her not to worry: he said he would come later than usual, since he had been invited for a discussion at the local NKVD office. This was their last conversation – he would never see freedom again.

At the end of the 1990s, Nikolai Izmailov got the opportunity to study his father's case, from which he learned that his father was alleged

Форма № 30

Военная Коллегия
Верховного Суда
Союза ССР

2 июля 1957 г.

№4н-025107/56

Москва, ул. Воровского, д. 13.

СПРАВКА

Дело по обвинению ИЗМАЙЛОВА Петра Николаевича, работавшего до ареста – 10 сентября 1936 года – начальником Омской электроразведочной партии Западно-Сибирского геологического треста, пересмотрено Военной коллегией Верховного Суда СССР 8 июня 1957 года.

Приговор Военной коллегии от 28 апреля 1937 года в отношении ИЗМАЙЛОВА П.Н. по вновь открывшимся обстоятельствам отменен и дело прекращено за отсутствием состава преступления.

ИЗМАЙЛОВ П.Н. реабилитирован посмертно.

ПОМ. ПРЕДСЕДАТЕЛЯ ВОЕННОЙ КОЛЛЕГИИ
ВЕРХОВНОГО СУДА СССР
ПОЛКОВНИК ЮСТИЦИИ

/М. РУСАКОВ/

33

to have been a member of a "counter-revolutionary Trotskyist-fascist terrorist organization" headed by Professor of the Industrial Institute Galakhov, which aimed to bring down the existing system and establish a fascist dictatorship. Moreover, it was supposed to install Alfred Rosenberg, an associate of Hitler, as head of state!

Further, they claimed that Izmailov's appearance at the chess tournament in Leningrad was just an excuse. The actual purpose of his trip was to attend a secret meeting at which the participants worked on a plan to kill Zhdanov.

The case of Petr Nikolaevich Izmailov was heard at a closed session of the field court of the USSR Supreme Court Military Board on April 28, 1937. The minutes of the meeting recorded the following information: "The presiding official explained the essence of the accusations to the defendant and asked the defendant if he pleaded guilty, and the defendant pleaded not guilty." And then: "In his last words, the defendant stated that he was never a member of any counter-revolutionary organization."

The entire "hearing" lasted 20 minutes, which was enough for the notorious "troika" (the three officials who would act as judge and jury, hearing the cases) to pass a sentence of execution with confiscation of property. The sentence was carried out immediately.

Petr Nikolaevich's wife Galina Efimovna Kozmina suffered the fate of a "family member of a national traitor". In 1937, she was sentenced to 8 years of correctional labor camps, which she spent at Kolyma. In January 1957, she was rehabilitated. And in June of the same year, Izmailov was posthumously rehabilitated "because of newly-found circumstances, and the case has been closed for lack of evidence."

Galina Efimovna died in February 1987. She did not live long enough to see her husband's name returned to the pages of the chess press.

The Tomsk newspaper *Krasnoye Znamya*, which published my article "A Champion Who Lived in Tomsk", reported on the organization of an All-Russian Izmailov memorial chess tournament. In the 1990s, a chess club was opened in Tomsk, which was named after Izmailov, the first champion of the RSFSR and the first chess master of Siberia.

Georgy Schneideman – The Surname That Cost His Life

You could be arrested for many "crimes" under Article 58. For a "political joke" (not just for telling one, but even for hearing one), or for an ambiguous joke, for a gesture that seemed suspicious to someone. And one famous chess player was sentenced on the basis of this article because of his surname! Moreover, for a surname that he had himself chosen in adulthood...

In the Russian-language book *People and Chess* by Vladimir Zak and Yakov Dlugolensky (Leningrad, 1988) which covers the chess history of St. Petersburg/Petrograd/ Leningrad, G. G. Schneideman-Stepanov (1907-1941) is included in the list of Leningrad masters. However, in fact there was never any chess player with this double-barreled surname. Until the middle of 1937, we find the name of Leningrad citizen G. Stepanov in the tournament tables, and after that – the name of fellow Leningrad citizen G. Schneideman.

Everything can be explained easily. He first carried his mother's surname, but at the age of 30 he suddenly changed it to his father's last name, from whom, by the way, his mother was divorced since Georgy's childhood.

When I think about his fate, I get a lump in my throat. I address this question to the man who was murdered more than half a century ago: who told you to change your surname? You could have lived happily as a Stepanov. Some of your friends even outlived Perestroika! Yet, you decided to call yourself Schneideman. And it was 1937! Perhaps you trusted Stalin's constitution? "I don't know another country like this, where a person breathes so freely". How accurate those lyrics are! Anyway, in the society of militant atheists, those who had an Orthodox surname written in their passport breathed more freely. And you just changed it to a foreign one... Those who were smarter did the opposite...

According to Georgy Schneideman's friends, he was a completely different young man to the one with sad eyes that looks from the photo. They recall a red-cheeked fun fellow, a people person. He was friends with Tolush and many other Leningrad masters, including the study composer Vitaly Chekhov, too. When, in 1936, Chekhov was preparing for an important match with Kasparyan, it was Schneideman (still Stepanov) whom he chose as his second.

By that time, the reputation of Georgy Schneideman (we will call him by the name with which he passed away) was strong. We don't yet know anything about his childhood or his first chess steps. For the first time we meet his name in 1929 – in the table of the Sovtorgs-Luzhashchy championship. The young chess player, although ending up at the bottom of the top ten, achieved impressive victories over experienced players Alatortsev and Ravinsky. The following year, Georgy was included in the city's team for the match with Moscow. Here he played against E. Baum, from whom the Leningrader managed to take only half a point in two meetings.

Just a year later, Schneideman was considered one of the strongest chess players of Leningrad. In the 1931 city championship, he scored 8.5 points out of 17, sharing 6th-8th place. This was enough to get a place in the semifinal of the Soviet Championship. The first round of the semi-final brought a sensation – the Leningrad first-category player defeated a famous Moscow master with excellent play.

Game No. 37
I. Kan – G. Schneideman
Leningrad Championship, 1931
French Defense C11
Commentary by S. Grodzensky

1.e4 e6 2.d4 d5 3.♘c3 ♘f6 4.♗g5 dxe4 5.♘xe4 ♗e7 6.♗xf6 ♗xf6 7.♘f3 ♘d7. In Spassky-Petrosian (23rd game of the 1966 World Championship match), 7...♗d7 was met by 8.♕d2 ♗c6 9.♘xf6+ ♕xf6 10.♘e5 0-0 11.0-0-0 ♘d7 12.♘xc6 bxc6 13.h4! with an advantage for white.

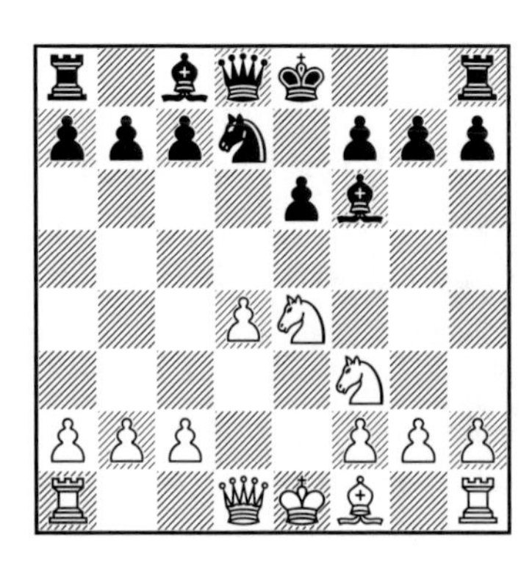

8.c3. If white's plans included long castling, then he should not have made this weakening move.

Objectively, 8.♕d2 0-0 9.0-0-0 ♕e7 10.g4 or 8...b6 9.♗b5 ♗b7 10.♘xf6+ gxf6 11.♕c3, with an active position for white, was stronger.

8...0-0 9.♕c2 e5 10.0-0-0. The move 10.♗d3 could have been followed by 10...exd4 11.cxd4 (11.♘xf6+ ♕xf6 12.♗xh7+ ♔h8 was better for black) 11...g6 12.h4 ♗g7 13.h5 ♘f6 14.hxg6 hxg6 with an equal game (game 21 of the same Spassky-Petrosian match).

10...exd4 11.♘xf6+ ♕xf6 12.♖xd4 ♘e5! The exchanges in the center help black to complete the appropriate placement of his pieces.

13.♗d3 (it was necessary to exchange on e5) **13...♘xd3+ 14.♕xd3 ♗e6! 15.b3.** White is forced to switch to defense, but it was somewhat better to continue 15.a3.

15...c5 16.♖d6. After 16.♖h4 ♗f5 the white rook is mostly locked out of the game.

16...a5 (the beginning of black's pawn offensive) **17.♖d1 a4 18.♔b2.**

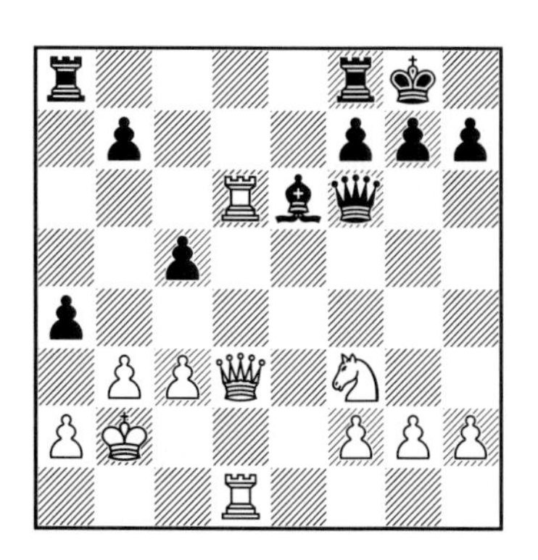

18...b5! 19.♕e3 (in the case of 19.♕xb5, 19...a3+ would have won) **19...b4 20.♘e5.** In case of 20.♕e5, it was possible to play 20...axb3 21.axb3 ♕g6, threatening 22...♖a2+.

20...bxc3+ 21.♔xc3 axb3 22.axb3 c4! Commenting on his loss here, Kan wrote: "Black literally crushed his opponent with simple moves. The following play is agony."

23.♕d4 cxb3 24.♘c6 ♕g5. A picturesque position! What is left of the white king's castling position?

25.g3 ♖fc8 26.f4. The attempt to get mass exchanges does not save white either: 26.♖d8+ ♖xd8 27.♕xd8+ ♖xd8 28.♖xd8+ ♕xd8 29.♘xd8 ♗d5! and the white knight perishes anyway.

26...♕a5+ 27.♔d3 ♖xc6 28.♖xc6 ♕b5+ 29.♖c4 ♗xc4+ 30.♕xc4 ♖d8+ 31.♔e3 ♕e8+. White resigned.

In his group, Schneideman scored 5.5 points out of 9, which brought him 4th place. It is interesting that in games with future finalists of the Soviet Championship Goglidze, Kan and Zamikhovsky, who shared 1st-3rd place, he scored 2.5 points out of 3, while against participants who remained behind him he scored only 3 out of 6 (without drawing a single game).

In the following years, Schneideman, working at the Kirov plant, defended the colors of the Leningrad Avangard team. He was not always lucky, but in every game he fought uncompromisingly.

Game No. 38
Dmitrievsky – G. Schneideman
Tournament of the first category, Leningrad, 1937
King's Indian Defense E83
Commentary by S. Belavenets

1.d4 ♘f6 2.c4 g6 3.♘c3 ♗g7 4.e4 d6 5.f3 0-0 6.♗e3 ♘c6 7.♕d2 e5 8.♘ge2 ♘d7 9.d5

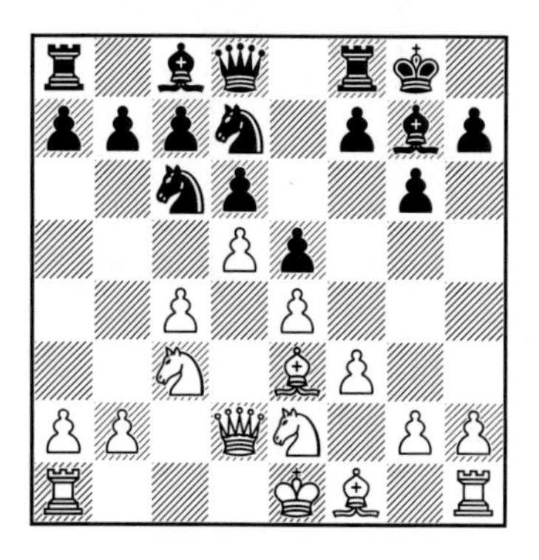

9...♘b4?! Prior to this move, the game had developed according to the latest theory, which recommends here 9...♘e7 and then f5. In that case, however, the knight on e7 occupies quite a poor position, so black is now trying to find a better position for it, on c5. This idea would undoubtedly be very good were it not for the fact that white can fairly easily prevent its implementation.

10.♘a4. The easiest way was to play 10.a3 ♘a6 11.b4, and white immediately gets play on the queenside, while the black knight on a6 looks far from ideal, having only one move available, to b8.

10...a5! Evidently, white did not expect this bold sacrifice, counting only on 10...♘a6, after which, b4 would have given him a great game.

11.a3 ♘a6 12.♕xa5 f5. Black gets some tempi for his pawn, since white will have to retreat his queen and knight. This allows black to seize the initiative on the kingside. It was undoubtedly more cautious for white to refrain from taking the pawn, but in this case he would have had to admit that the knight's diversion to a4 was an error.

13.exf5. Black would have kept the initiative even after 13.♕d2 fxe4 14.fxe4 ♘f6 15.♘ac3 ♘g4, and if now 16.♗g5, then 16...♕e8 with very unpleasant threats via 17...♘f2 and 18...♘c5.

13...gxf5

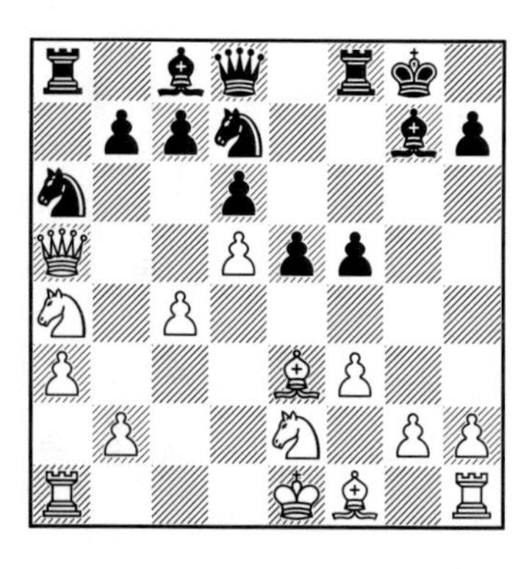

14.g3? Now black quickly gains a decisive advantage. To protect himself against the threats 14... ♕h4+ and 15...♕xc4, it was better to play 14.♕c3 (14.♕c3? f4–+, – S.G.) or even 14.♗f2, conceding the h6-c1 diagonal but preventing the opening of the game. Obviously, it is extremely dangerous for white to castle long.

14...f4! 15.gxf4 (after 15.♗f2 black wins back a pawn at least) **15...exf4 16.♗d4** (it is clear that capturing on f4 is impossible) **16...♘e5 17.♗xe5.** Forced, since 17.♕c3 is met by 17...♗d7, and the position of the a4 knight looks unenviable.

17...♕h4+! An important zwischenschach that deprives white of the right to castle.

18.♔d1 ♗xe5 19.♕e1 ♕h5 20.♕f2 ♗d7 21.♘ac3 ♘c5. Black's position strengthens with each move.

22.♖g1+ ♔h8 23.♘d4 ♗a4+ 24.♘xa4. Now there follows a small combination that gives black a material advantage. However, even after 24.♔d2 ♖f6, threatening 25...♗xd4, black's superiority is obvious.

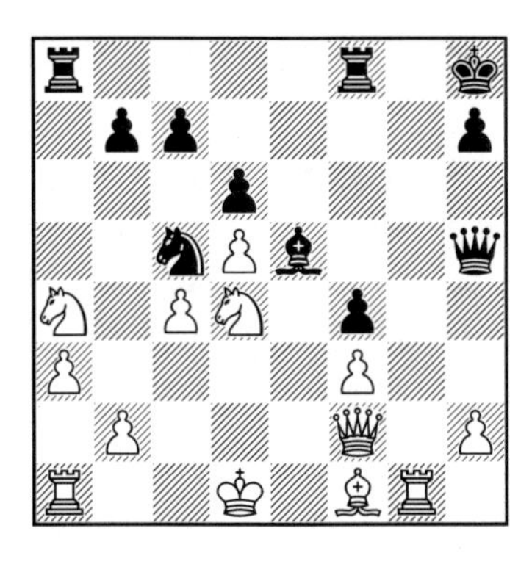

24...♘e4! 25.♕e2 ♗xd4 26.♕xe4 ♗xg1 27.♘c3 ♖ae8 28.♕d3 ♕xh2, and white resigned after a few moves.

In the final of the trade unions championship (Moscow, 1936), Schneideman scored 50% – 9 out of 18 – but played several interesting games.

Game No. 39
G. Schneideman – V. Makogonov
Trade unions championship,
Moscow, 1936
Commentary by S. Grodzensky

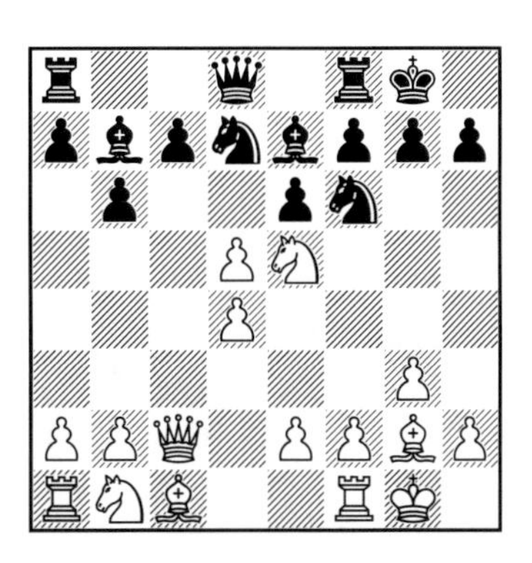

It's black to move, and he really faces a difficult choice between 9...♗xd5 and 9...♘xd5. However, he preferred the most "natural" move **9...♘xe5?,** wishing to prevent the invasion of the white knight on c6, but this was followed by **10.d6!!,** and after: **10...♗xg2 11.dxe7 ♕xe7 12.dxe5 ♗xf1 13.exf6 ♕xf6 14.♔xf1** white got great prospects.

Two of Schneideman's games from the final part of the trade union championship were of theoretical significance.

Game No. 40
E. Zagoryansky – G. Schneideman
Trade unions championship,
Moscow, 1936
Queen's Gambit D59
Commentary by S. Grodzensky

1.d4 d5 2.c4 e6 3.♘c3 ♘f6 4.♗g5 ♗e7 5.e3 0-0 6.♘f3 h6 7.♗h4. In the Belavenets-Schneideman game from the same tournament, after 7.♗f4 c5 (in the case of 7...b6, it was possible to play 8.cxd5 ♘xd5 9.♘xd5, and black must play 9...exd5, since after 9...♕xd5 10.♗xc7 ♗b4+ 11.♘d2 ♗b7 black's decent development hardly compensates for the loss of an important pawn) 8.dxc5 ♗xc5 9.♕c2 ♘c6! black got a promising position.

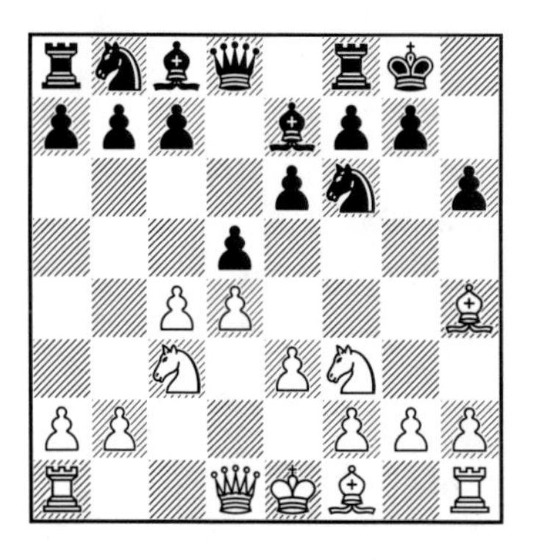

7...b6! 8.cxd5 ♘xd5! 9.♗g3 c5 10.♘xd5 ♕xd5! 11.dxc5. The move 11.♗e2 would have been met by 11...cxd4, threatening 12...♗b4+.

11...♕xc5 12.a3 ♖d8, and black gained the initiative.

Game No. 41
G. Schneideman – M. Gergenreder
Trade unions championship,
Moscow, 1936
Queen's Gambit D37
Commentary by S. Grodzensky

1.♘f3 ♘f6 2.c4 e6 3.♘c3 d5 4.d4 dxc4 5.e4 c5 6.♗xc4 cxd4 7.♘xd4. Exactly the same position occurred in Capablanca – Bogoljubov (Moscow, 1925). Bogoljubov played 7...♗c5 and later expressed the opinion that black has no satisfactory defense.

7...♘bd7 8.0-0 a6. Black decides not to bring his king's bishop into the game, leaving the g7 square protected and thus preventing the bishop's sacrifice for three pawns and an attack on e6. As will soon become clear, this risky play will anyway end with a sacrifice, regardless of the safety of the g7 square.

9.♖e1 b5. The continuation 9...♘b6 10.♗b3 ♗e7 could have prolonged the resistance.

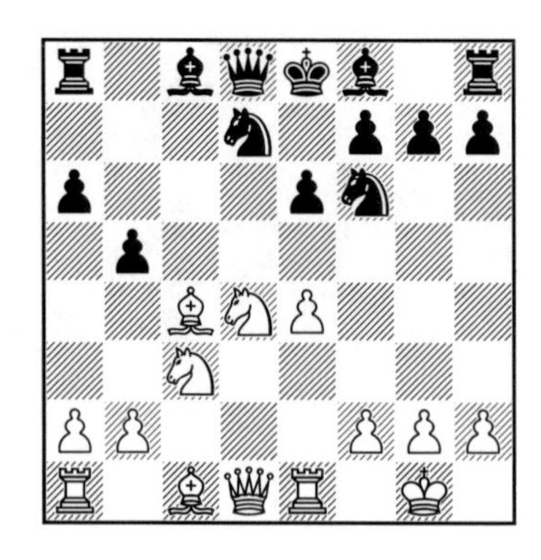

10.♗xe6! (this sacrifice quickly decides the outcome of the duel) **10...fxe6 11.♘xe6 ♕b6 12.e5 ♘xe5**

13.♖xe5 ♗xe6 14.♘d5, and black had to return the extra piece, which, however, did not save him from defeat.

Schneideman's score in his mini-match against A. Poliak – 1.5:0.5 during the traditional Leningrad-Moscow match (1937) also deserves mentioning. Further, the year 1938 brought Schneideman victory in the All-Union first-category tournament, which allowed him to be one of the first players to receive the newly established title of Candidate Master of Sport. By the way, the vast majority of the participants of that tournament later got the master title.

Game No. 42
V. Baturinsky – G. Schneideman
All-Union first-category
tournament, Gorky, 1938
Spanish Opening C79
Commentary by S. Grodzensky

1.e4 e5 2.♘f3 ♘c6 3.♗b5 a6 4.♗a4 ♘f6 5.0-0 d6 6.♗xc6+ bxc6 7.d4 ♘xe4 (7...exd4 leads to a variation of the Steinitz Defense that is advantageous for white).

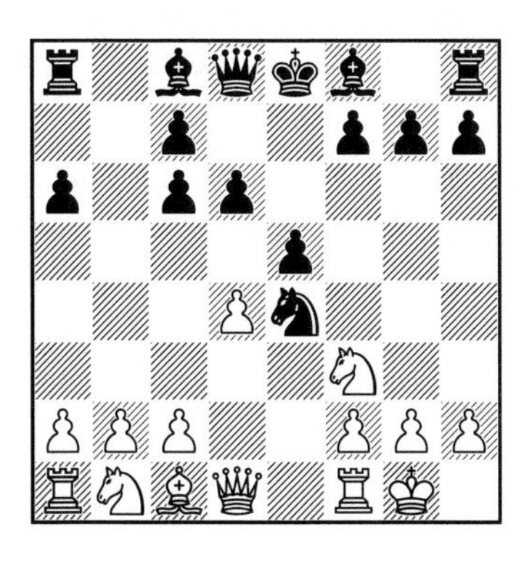

8.♕e2. The continuation 8.♖e1 f5 9.dxe5 d5 10.♘d4 ♗c5 11.c3 0-0 12.f3 ♘g5 13.♔h1 gives better chances of an opening advantage.

8...f5 9.dxe5 d5 10.♘bd2. Today, the Yugoslav *Encyclopedia of Openings* recommends 10.c4 ♗c5 11.♗e3 0-0 12.♗xc5 ♘xc5 13.♖d1 ♗b7 14.♘c3 ♘e4 15.♖ac1 and evaluates this position as somewhat better for white.

10...a5!? This move contains a threat of 11...♗a6; Reshevsky in a game with Dake from the US championship (1938) continued by playing 10...♗c5, which led to an unclear position.

11.♘xe4 fxe4. Black rejects winning the exchange via 11...♗a6, since the complications that occur after 12.♘f6+! seemed advantageous for white.

12.♘g5 ♗e7 (here, 12...♗a6 would have been met by 13.♕g4!) **13.♖d1 ♗f5!** Forcing the knight to retreat. Both 13...♗xg5? 14.♕h5+ g6 15.♕xg5 and 13...0-0? 14.♘xe4! look bad.

14.♘h3 0-0 15.♘f4 ♕d7 16.h3 ♔h8! (preparing for a pawn attack) **17.♕e3 g5 18.♘e2 c5 19.♘g3 ♕e6 20.♕b3 c6 21.♕a4 h5 22.♘xh5.**

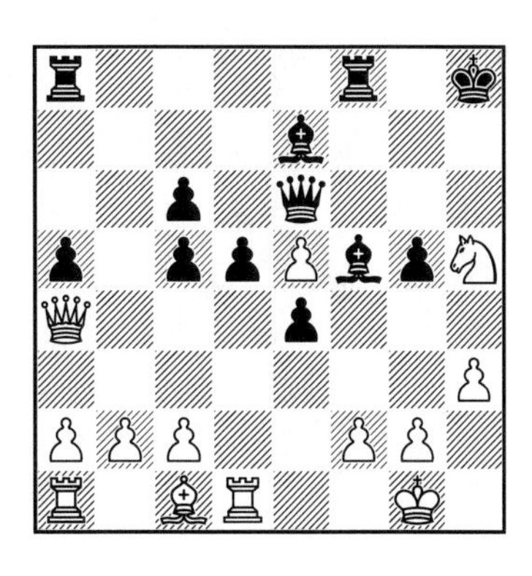

22...♗xh3! Everything has been precisely calculated. If now 23.gxh3 ♕xh3 24.♘g3, then 24...♖xf2!! 25.♔xf2 ♖f8+, with a win.

23.♘g3 ♗g4 24.♖f1 ♖f7! 25.♕b3 ♖af8 (there was an easier way of winning – 25...♕xe5) **26.c4 ♖h7 27.f3 ♕h6 28.♔f2 ♗xf3 29.♖h1 ♗d1+ 30.♔g1 ♕xh1+ 31.♘xh1 ♗xb3 32.axb3 d4,** white soon resigned.

Game No. 43

A. Konstantinov – G. Schneideman

All-Union first-category tournament, Gorky, 1938

Catalan Opening E00

Commentary by G. Schneideman

1.d4 ♘f6 2.c4 e6 3.g3 d5 4.♘f3 dxc4. This variation seems a much better way to fight for the initiative than strengthening the d5 square via 4...c6, since white easily manages to prepare a strong attack e2-e4, after which black is still unable to hold his position in the center.

5.♕a4+ ♘bd7 6.♗g2 a6 7.♘c3 ♖b8 8.♕xc4 b5 9.♕d3 ♗b7 10.0-0 c5

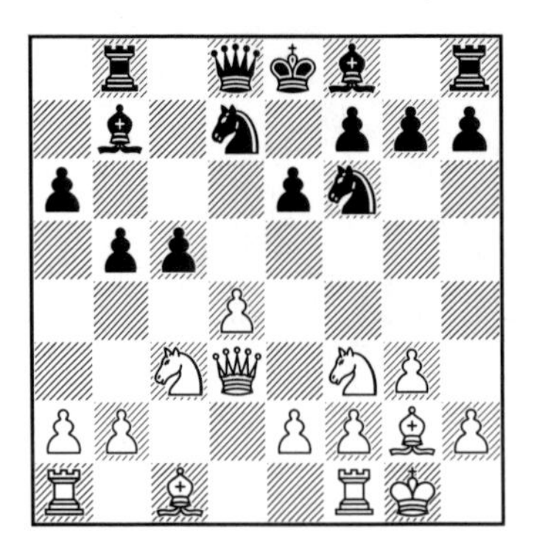

11.♗f4. Black has developed comfortably, and now after 11.dxc5 ♘xc5 12.♕xd8+ ♖xd8 he would have got a good game because of the control over the e4 square and his active pieces.

11...♖c8 12.dxc5 ♗xc5. Here, 12...♘xc5 would have been followed by 13.♕xd8+ ♖xd8 14.♖fd1 with an equal game.

13.♖ad1 (if 13.♗d6, then 13... ♗xd6 14.♕xd6 ♕e7) **13...0-0 14.♘e5 ♗xg2 15.♔xg2 ♘xe5 16.♗xe5.** It would be easier to fight for full equality after 16.♕xd8 ♖fxd8 17.♗xe5.

16...♕e7 17.♕f3 ♘d7! This is an important maneuver. The move 17...♖fd8 would have been met by 18.♖xd8+ ♖xd8 19.♕c6, however, now the poor position of the bishop on e5 tells.

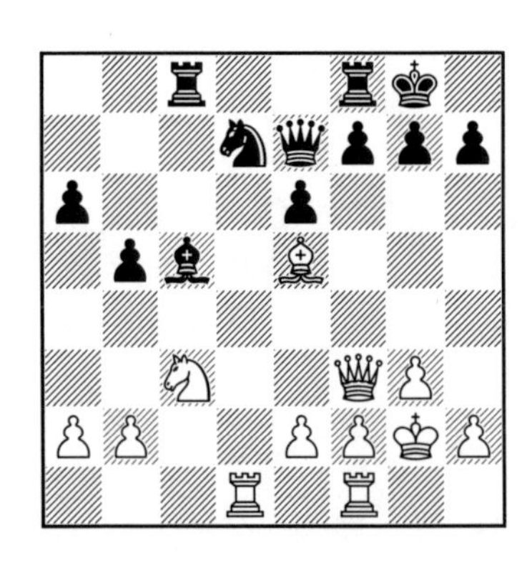

18.♗d4. After this natural move, black grabs a decisive initiative. It was necessary to play 18.♗f4 ♘b6 19.♘e4 with equal chances.

18...♗xd4 19.♖xd4 ♘e5 20.♕e4 ♘c4 21.b3 ♘b6 22.♕d3? It was better to continue 22.♘d5 ♘xd5

23.♖xd5 ♕b7 24.♖d4 ♕xe4+ 25.♖xe4 ♖c2, which is the best practical chance to save the game, since it would have been very difficult for black to convert his positional advantage in the rook endgame.

22...e5! (white cannot now continue 23.♖d6 in view of 23...♖xc3) **23.♖h4 h6 24.f4.** A desperate attempt, but white's situation already looks very bad, as black threatens ♖fd8, and the h4 rook gets locked out of the game.

24...♖fd8 25.♕f3. After 25.♕e3, it was even possible to play 25...b4, for example, 26.♕xb6 bxc3, and the c-pawn should decide the outcome of the fight; or 26.♘e4 ♘d5 27.♕f3 f5 and so on.

25...e4! The strongest choice, since it cuts off the awkward h4 rook for a long time.

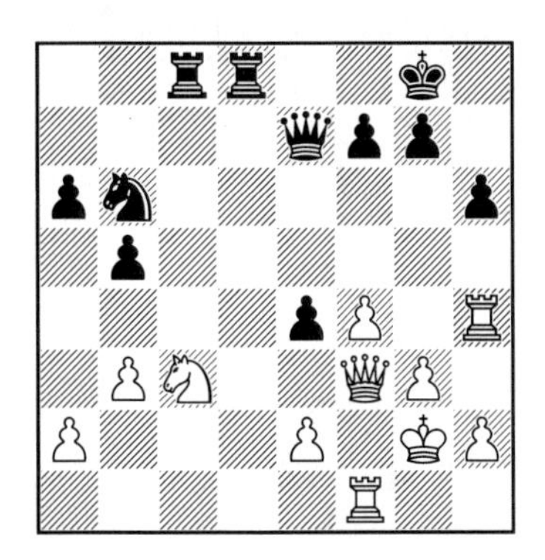

26.♘xe4 (or 26.♕xe4 ♕xe4+ 27.♘xe4 f5, and then the black rooks invades the second rank) **26...f5 27.♘f2 ♖d2 28.♖h3 ♕xe2 29.♕b7 ♕e4+ 30.♕xe4 fxe4 31.g4.** Finally! But there are still no squares for the h3 rook.

31...♘d5 32.♔g1 (if 32.♔g3, then 32...♖c3+ with an easy win) **32...♘xf4 33.♖e3 ♖cc2.** White resigned. There's no defense against 34...♘d3, and if 34.♖xe4, then 34...♘h3+ spectacularly solves the problem.

In the Leningrad championship of 1939, candidate master Schneideman scored 8 points out of 15, and as a result shared 8th-9th place with the future grandmaster Tolush, whom he defeated in their head-to-head meeting.

Game No. 44
A. Tolush – G. Schneideman
Leningrad Championship, 1939
Caro-Kann Defense B14
Commentary by G. Schneideman

1.e4 c6 2.d4 d5 3.exd5 cxd5 4.c4 ♘f6 5.♘c3 e6 6.♘f3 ♗e7 7.cxd5 ♘xd5. (The position on the board is characteristic of one of the variations of the Queen's Gambit – S.G.). The move 7...exd5 would have been also met by 8.♗b5+.

8.♗b5+

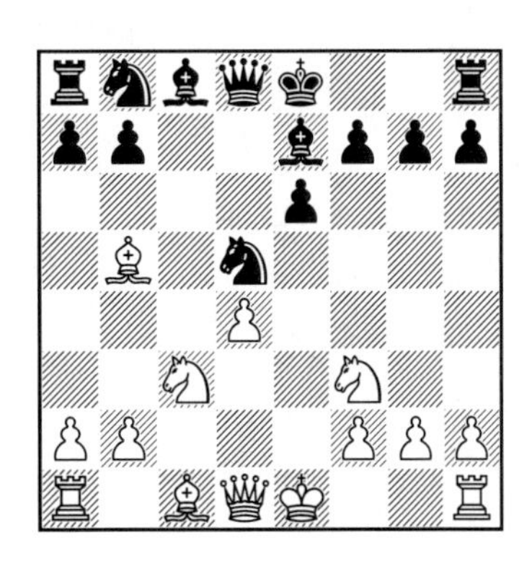

8...♘d7. In the game Alekhine – Eliskases (Tournament of Nations, 1939) black responded 8...♗d7, and got a difficult game after 9.♗xd7+ ♘xd7 10.♘xd5 exd5 11.♕b3 ♘b6 despite the simplifications – white has strong pressure along the open e- and c-files, and against the b7 and d5 pawns.

In this game, black tries to reinforce his defense with the sacrifice of a pawn, but white, wisely refusing the "Greek gift", still gets an advantage. Alekhine's novelty 7.cxd5 is still waiting for a refutation (the move 7.cxd5 is still considered one of the strongest in the Panov Attack – S.G.).

9.♘xd5 exd5 10.♕b3 0-0 11.0-0. 11.♕xd5 ♗b4+ is weak, as black gets a dangerous attack aimed at the white king stuck in the center.

11...♘f6 12.♖e1 h6. Black needs to prepare the development of his bishop to e6 and prevent the unpleasant ♗g5.

13.♗f4 ♗d6 14.♗e5 ♗e6 15.♗d3 ♕e7

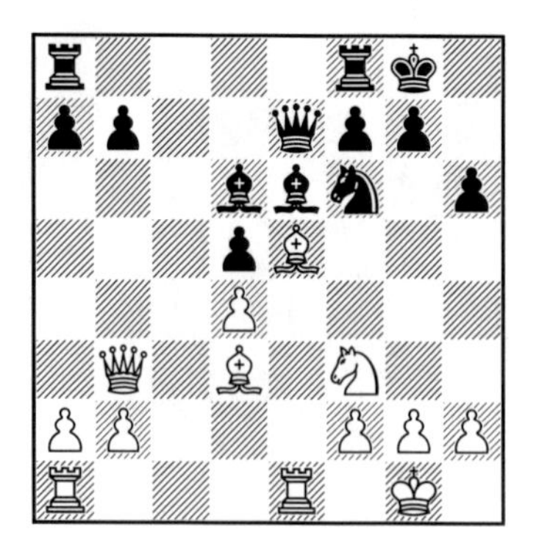

16.♖ac1. This move is stronger than 16.♗xf6 ♕xf6 17.♕xb7 ♖ab8 with a good game for black.

16...b6. Now white firmly captures the c-file.

17.♗a6 ♘e4 18.♖c6 ♗xe5 19.♘xe5 ♖fe8 20.♖ec1 ♕f6 21.f3?

So far, white has played excellently, and after 21.♕e3 he would have got a significant advantage. The move in the text is weak and meets an unexpected tactical refutation.

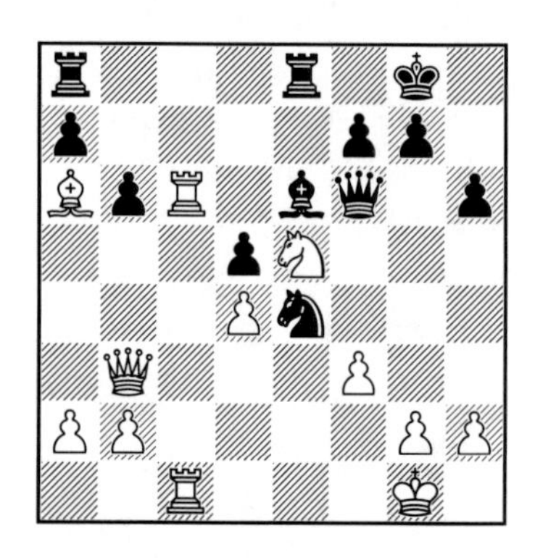

21...♘c5 22.dxc5. Forced. The continuation 22.♕a3 ♕f4 was bad (22...♕g5! –S.G.) 23.♖d1 ♘xa6 24.♕xa6 f6 (24...f6? 25.♕b7!= – S.G.).

22...♕xe5 23.cxb6 axb6 24.♖xb6 d4 25.♕d3 ♗f5. The strongest move. Now the passed d-pawn cannot be stopped.

26.♕d2 d3 27.♖d1 ♕c5+ 28.♕f2 ♕a5 29.♖b5. If 29.♗c4, then 29...♖e2 solves the problem, while in the case of 29.b4 the move 29...♕a4 wins.

29...♕xa6 30.♖xf5 ♖e2 31.♕d4 ♕e6 32.♕xd3 ♕b6+ 33.♕d4.

Or 33.♔h1 ♕f2 34.♖g1 ♖e1 with inevitable checkmate.

33...♖d8. White resigned.

Schneideman claimed victory in a sharp fight against the tournament winner Lisitsyn.

Game No. 45
G. Lisitsyn – G. Schneideman
Leningrad Championship, 1939
Reti Opening A05
Commentary by G. Schneideman

1.♘f3 ♘f6 2.g3 ♘c6. An original and, apparently, decent continuation.

3.d4 d5 4.♗g2 ♗f5 5.c4 e6 6.♕a4. Now the queen stands poorly. It was better to play 6.0-0.

6...♕d7 7.0-0 ♗e7 8.♘c3 0-0 9.♗f4 ♘e4 10.♖ac1 ♖ad8. Defending the queen and threatening to take the d4 pawn after the exchange of knights on c3.

11.cxd5 exd5 12.♕b5? Failing to notice black's main threat. It was necessary to play 12.♖fd1, defending the d4 pawn.

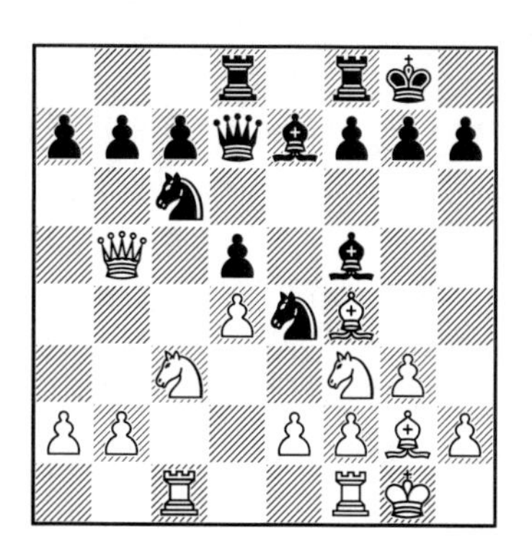

12...g5! 13.♘xe4 (13.♗e3 would have been met by 13...g4 14.♘d2 ♘xc3 15.♖xc3 ♘xd4 16.♕xd7 ♘xe2+) **13...dxe4 14.♘xg5 ♘xd4**

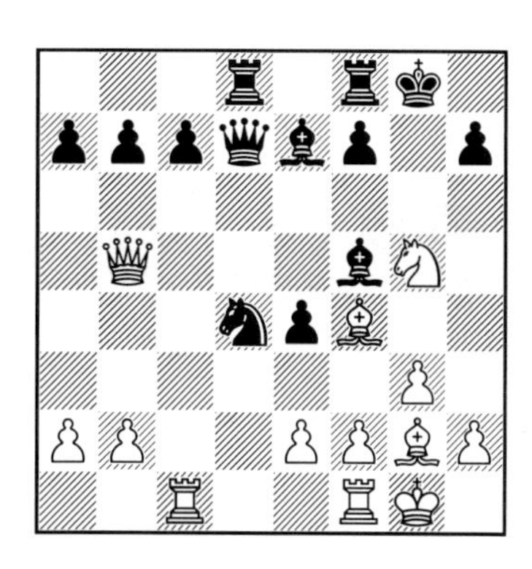

15.♕xb7. The move 15.♕c4 b5 looks no better. After 15.♕xd7 ♘xe2+ 16.♔h1 ♖xd7 17.♖ce1 ♘xf4 18.gxf4 ♗xg5 19.fxg5 ♖e8 black still has a winning position. Sacrificing the exchange, white is still trying to complicate the game, but unexpectedly meets a quick end.

15...♘xe2+ 16.♔h1 ♘xc1 17.♖xc1 ♗xg5! 18.♗xg5 ♕d1+ 19.♗f1 (not 19.♖xd1 ♖xd1+ 20.♗f1 ♗h3 and game over) **19...♕f3+ 20.♔g1 ♖d1 21.♕b5.** The "last" trap. If black thoughtlessly plays 21...♗h3, threatening to checkmate on g2, then it will be followed by 22.♖xd1 ♕xd1 23.♗h6 ♕xf1+ 24.♕xf1 ♗xf1 25.♗xf8 with a drawn ending.

21...e3 (immediately decides the outcome) **22.♗xe3 ♗e4 23.♕g5+ ♔h8 24.♕e5+ f6 25.♕xe4 ♖xf1+.** White resigned.

At the end of the 1930s, Schneideman got close to master's level. This was confirmed by the All-Union candidate masters tournament in 1939, in which he shared 5th-7th place, ahead of a whole group of future masters. In 1940's edition of that tournament, Schneideman scored 7.5 out of 11, took second place after master Belavenets, and finally fulfilled the master's norm.

Georgy was the only seeker of the master's title to manage to avoid defeat throughout the tournament. His performance would have been even better had it not been for the sporting goal that weighed him down – fulfilling the master's norm, due to which he played in an unusually cautious style and agreed to draws in better positions.

And yet, in some duels in this important tournament, too, Schneideman showed sharp, combinational play.

Game No. 46
G. Schneideman – Geyer
All-Union candidate masters tournament, 1940
Queen's Gambit D68
Commentary by G. Schneideman

1.c4 ♘f6 2.♘f3 e6 3.♘c3 d5 4.d4 ♘bd7 5.♗g5 ♗e7 6.e3 0-0 7.♖c1 c6 8.♗d3 dxc4 9.♗xc4 ♘d5 10.♗xe7 ♕xe7 11.0-0 ♘xc3 12.♖xc3 e5 13.♕c2. This continuation became popular after the well-known game Levenfish – Riumin (Moscow, 1938).

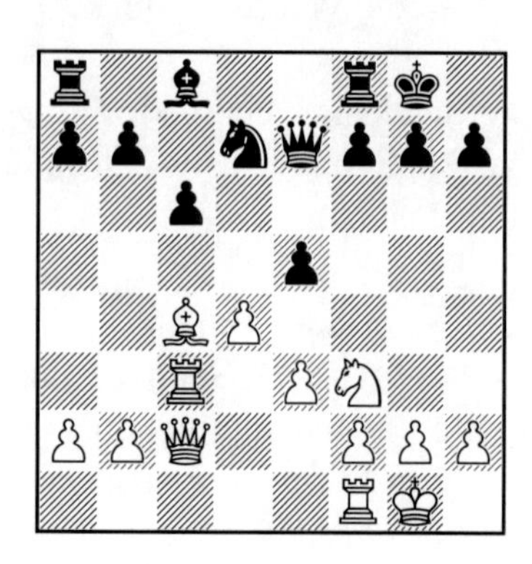

13...e4. It was also possible to play 13...exd4 here, although, as practice has shown, this variation requires very precise defense, since white is much better developed.

14.♘d2 ♘f6 15.♗b3. Threatening, if necessary, to move the rook to e5 and preparing operations along the c-file.

15...♔h8. Black intends to play 16...♗e6 to capture the d5 square in the future; if now 15...♗e6, then 16.♘xe4 ♗xb3 17.♘xf6+.

16.♖c1 ♗e6 17.♗xe6 ♕xe6 18.♖b3 ♕e7. This continuation is weak, since it ties the queen to the protection of the b7 pawn. It was better to play 18...♖ab8.

19.♕c5 ♖fe8. (19...♕xc5 led to the loss of a pawn after 20.♖xc5 ♖ab8 21.♖e5 – S.G.) **20.♘c4 ♘d5 21.♘d6.** With the move in the text, white begins a long combination.

21...♖eb8.

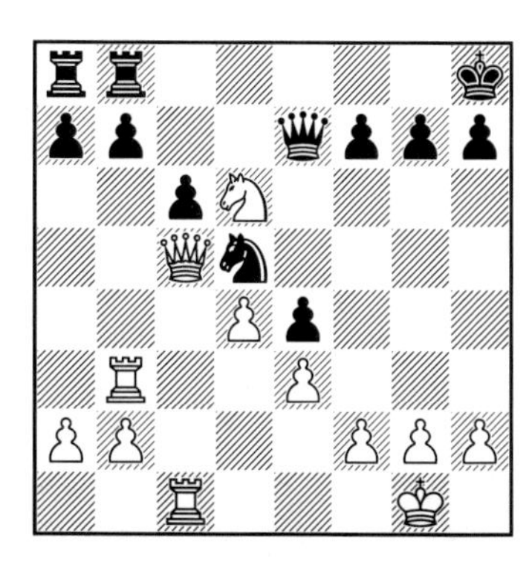

22.♘xb7! ♖xb7 23.♕xc6 ♘b6 (not 23...♘b4 due to 24.♕c8+; the weakness of the move 15...♔h8 is making itself felt – S.G.) **24.♖xb6 axb6 25.♕c8+ ♕d8 26.♕xb7 ♖xa2 27.♕xb6.** It is interesting that the tempting move 27.♕d5 could be parried via 27...♕c7! (this move does not, of course, help the situation, and only allows resistance to be prolonged for a short time – S.G.).

The game continued **27...♕a8 28.h3 h6 29.♕b3 f5 30.♕e6 ♖a1 31.♖xa1 ♕xa1+ 32.♔h2 ♕a5 33.d5.** Black resigned.

Schneideman shared 6th-8th place with Ilyin-Zhenevsky and Chekhover in the 1940 Leningrad championship, scoring 2 points out of 3 in the games against the prize winners.

Game No. 47
A. Tolush – G. Schneideman
Leningrad Championship, 1940
Spanish Opening C91
Commentary by I. Rabinovich

1.e4 e5 2.♘f3 ♘c6 3.♗b5 a6 4.♗a4 ♘f6 5.0-0 ♗e7 6.♖e1 b5 7.♗b3 d6 8.c3 0-0 9.d4 ♗g4

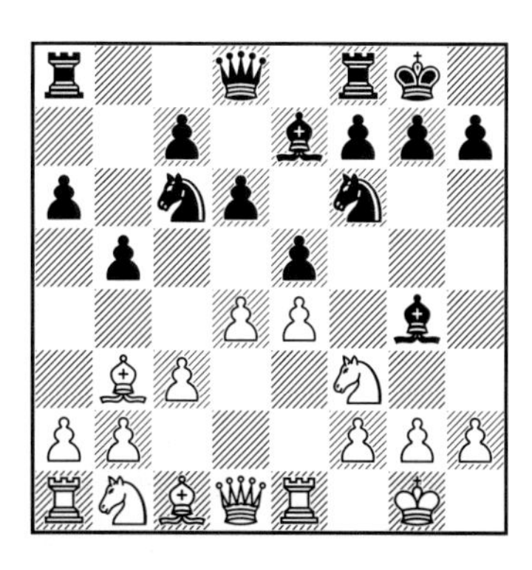

10.d5 (10.♗e3 is more common here) **10...♘a5 11.♗c2 c6 12.dxc6 ♘xc6 13.♗g5.** If 13.♘bd2, then 13...♖c8, with the idea of playing b5-b4 and d6-d5.

13...h6 14.♗h4. In the case of 14.♗xf6 black would have responded 14...♗xf6, 15...♗e6 and 16...d5.

14...♖c8. Preparing 15...b4; if white prevents this move via 15.♗d3, then it is possible to play 15...g5 with double-edged play on the kingside.

15.♘bd2 b4 16.♘f1 (if 16.c4, then 16...♘d4 17.♗d3 ♘h5) **16...bxc3 17.bxc3 ♕a5 18.h3 ♗xf3 19.♕xf3**

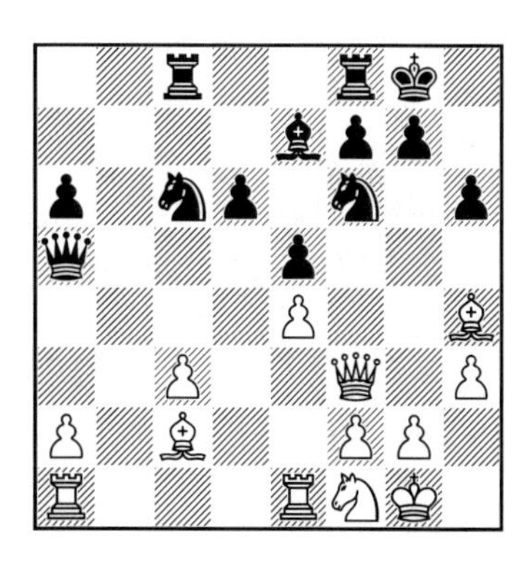

19...♘d4. Here black could have won a pawn via 19...♘a7 20.♖e3

♘b5. However, white, by playing 21.♘g3, would have received sufficient compensation for the pawn: if, for example, 21...♖xc3 22.♘f5 ♘d4, then 23.♘xe7+ ♔h7 24.♖xc3 ♘xf3+ 25.♖xf3, and white is winning.

20.cxd4 ♖xc2 21.♘e3! The beginning of major complications. A preliminary exchange on e5 led to a less sharp game, for example, 21.dxe5 dxe5 22.♘e3 ♖xa2 23.♖xa2 ♕xa2 24.♘f5 ♕e6 25.♕g3 g6 26.♘xh6+ ♔h7.

21...♖xa2 22.♖xa2 ♕xe1+. Here, this continuation looks better than 22...♕xa2, which would have been followed by 23.♘f5 ♕e6 24.d5! (the black queen is chased from protecting the f6 square) 24... ♕d7 25.♘xh6+ gxh6 26.♗xf6 ♗xf6 27.♕xf6 ♔h7 28.♖a1! ♖a8 29.♖a3 with a strong threat ♖a3-f3-f5-h5.

23.♔h2 exd4 24.♘f5 ♗d8 25.♘xd6 ♗c7 26.♗g3

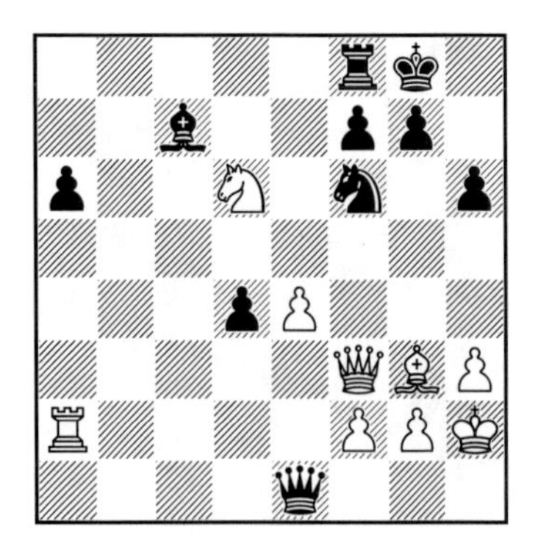

26...♖b8? In an effort to strengthen the attack aimed at the king, black rejects the correct continuation 26...♖d8 27.e5 ♗xd6 28.exd6 ♕e4 29.♖xa6 ♕xf3 30.gxf3 ♘h5 31.♔g2 ♘xg3 32.fxg3 ♔f8 33.♔f2 ♔e8 34.♔e2 ♔d7 35.♔d3 ♔e6 with a draw.

27.♖e2? White fails to exploit his opponent's mistake. At the end of the game, Tolush and Schneideman found the following forced variation here, leading to white's victory: 27.♖xa6! ♖b1 (28.e5 was threatened; the move 27...♕c3 was unfavorable for black, too, in view of 28.♕xc3 dxc3 29.♖c6! ♗xd6 30.♗xd6 and then 31.f3!, threatening ♗e5) 28.♖a8+ ♔h7 (if 28...♖b8, then 29.♖a7) 29.♗e5! ♗xd6 30.♕f5+ g6 31.♖h8+!!

27...♕c3 28.♕f5 d3. The far advanced passed pawn ensures black's victory.

29.♖e3 ♕d4

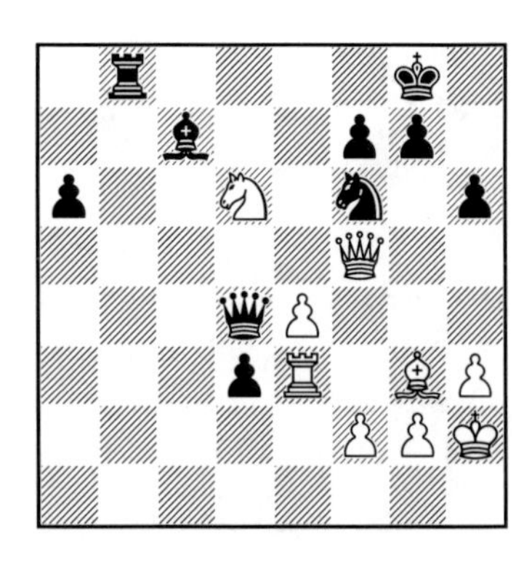

30.♘xf7! A nice trick. If black now responds with 30...♗xg3+ 31.♖xg3 ♔xf7 32.e5! d2 (but not 32...♕e4 or 32...♕d5 33.♖xg7+) 33.exf6 d1=♕? (the correct continuation was 33... ♕xf6 34.♕d5+ and 35.♕xd2 with an approximately equal game), then 33.♖xg7+ ♔f8 34.♕h7!! ♕f4+ 35.♖g3, and white wins, despite his opponent's two queens.

30...♔xf7 31.♗xc7 d2! (31...♖b5 was weaker, in view of 32.♕f3! d2 33.♖d3) **32.e5!** (32.♗xb8 d1=♕ 33.e5 would have been met by 33...♕h5) **32...d1=♕!** The move 32...♖b5 looks tempting here, however, it would not win due to the spectacular response 33.♖g3 d1=♕ 34.♖xg7+! ♔xg7 35.♕xf6+ with perpetual check.

33.exf6 ♕xf6 34.♕xf6+ gxf6! (preventing the bishop from moving to the e5 square) **35.♗xb8.** Now the situation has become clearer. Despite all white's tricks, his position is lost.

35...a5 36.♗f4 a4 (if now 37.♗xh6, then 37...♕d6+ and 38...a3) **37.♖g3 h5** (taking the pawn out of the bishop's aim and threatening h5-h4 if the opportunity arises) **38.♖f3.** If 38.h4 (preventing h5-h4), then 38...♕d4 39.♗e3 ♕b4 40.♗c1 ♕e1.

38...♔e6!

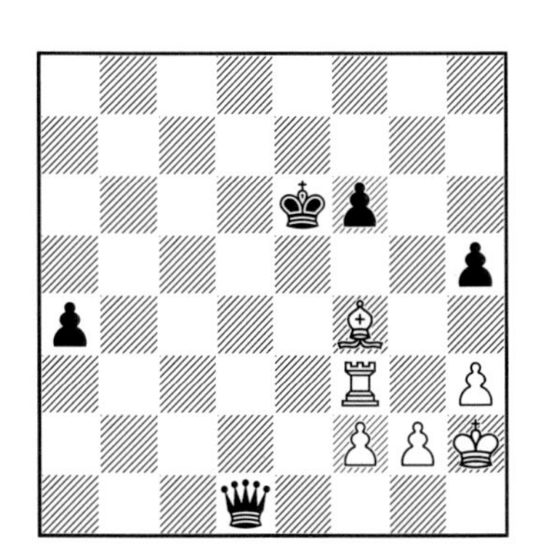

39.h4. White is caught in zugzwang. For example, 39.♖a3 looks bad due to 39...♕c2! If 39.♗g3 (39.♗h6? a3 40.♖xa3 ♕d6+ 41.♖g3 h4), then 39...♕xf3.

39...♕a1? This move negates all black's previous subtle play. (Actually, black's position remains won after the move in the text – S.G..) Now white, moving the bishop to a3, achieves a drawn position. Instead of playing 39...♕a1? it was necessary to respond with 39...♕c2!, preventing the bishop from reaching the d2 and c1 squares while threatening 40...♕b2 followed by a4-a3. If white responds with 40.♖a3, then 40...♕xf2 41.♗g3 ♕c2 (threatening 42...♕b3!) 42.♗f4 ♔f5. 40.♗h6 doesn't help either in view of 40...♕b2 41.♗g7 (or 41.♗f8 ♕b8+) 41...♔f7 42.♗h8 ♕b8+. While if 40.♗e3, then 40...♕b2 41.♗c5 ♕e5+.

40.♗d2! Threatening: 1) 41.♗c3 winning the f6 pawn and then sacrificing the bishop for the passed pawn; 2) 41.♗b4 and then ♗a3. The loss of the h4 pawn makes no difference.

40...♕d4 41.♗c1! ♕xh4+ 42.♔g1 ♕d4 43.♗a3 f5. Black has already lost his chance to win. Now he has only one trap combination left to test.

44.♔h2 ♕d1 45.♗f8 ♕f1 46.♗a3 h4 47.♖e3+ ♔f7 48.♖f3 ♔f6 49.♗b2+ ♔g5 50.♗a3 ♔g4 51.♗d6 ♕d1 52.♗a3 ♕d4 53.♔g1 ♕e5 54.♖e3 ♕a1+ 55.♔h2 f4 56.♖f3 ♕e5 57.♔g1 ♕d4.

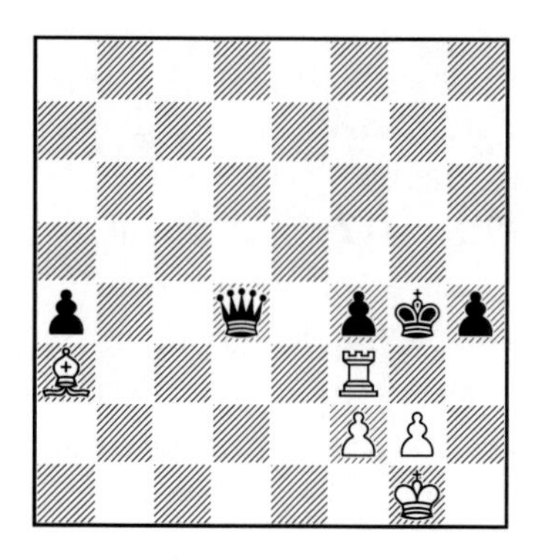

Now, in order to achieve a draw, white had to adhere to the following defensive setup: move the bishop diagonally a3-f8, and keep the king on g1, leaving this square only in case of a check and returning to it at the first opportunity. In this case, the eventual ♕e1+ ♔h2 h3 is not dangerous for white in view of ♖xh3 ♕xf2, and now it is necessary to at least play ♖f3, since after ♕xf3 and ♔xf3 white responds by playing ♗d6!, preventing the black king from penetrating on e2.

58.♖h3 ♕d5 59.♔h2?? A terrible mistake. The simplest continuation was 59.♖f3, without leaving the g1 square unnecessarily.

59...♕e5! 60.♖f3. Now even the move 60.♔g1 would not help due to 60...♕e1+. The move 60.♗b4 also loses due to 60...♕b2! 61.♗c5 ♕c2 62.f3+ ♔h5 63.♗e7 ♕f2, then ...♕e1 with the following transfer of the black king to the queenside or to the f1 square. If, finally, 60.♗f8, then 60... f3+ 61.♔g1 (or 61.g3 ♕e2! 62.♖xh4+ ♔g5 63.♗c5 ♕f1) 61...fxg2 62.♔xg2 ♕d5+ 63.f3+ ♔h5 64.♗e7 ♕c4 (threatening 65...a3 66.♗xa3 ♕a2+) 65.♔g1 a3! 66.♗xa3 ♕d4+ 67.♔g2 ♕d2 68.♔f1 ♕d1+ 69.♔f2 ♕c2+ and black wins.

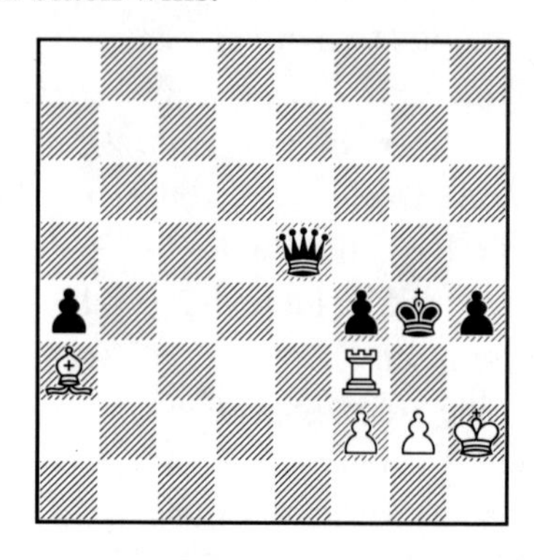

60...h3!! (threatening 61...hxg2 62.♔xg2 ♕e4) **61.♖xh3 f3+.** White resigned, since 62.♖g3+ would be followed by 62...♕xg3+ 63.fxg3 f2, while 62.♔g1 would lose in view of 62...♕a1+ and 63...♕xa3.

"A sharp and intense game, in which, perhaps, one should be surprised not by the mistakes made, but by the relatively small number of them!" – this is how master Ilya Rabinovich finished his notes.

In June 1941, Georgy Schneideman participated in the semi-final of the Soviet Championship in Rostov-on-Don.

Game No. 48

I. Tyurn – G. Schneideman

Semi-final of the Soviet Championship, Rostov-on-Don, 1941

Queen's Gambit D61

Commentary by S. Grodzensky

1.d4 ♘f6 2.c4 e6 3.♘c3 d5 4.♗g5 ♗e7 5.e3 ♘bd7 6.♘f3 0-0

7.♕c2 c6 8.cxd5 exd5 9.♗d3 ♖e8 10.0-0 ♘f8

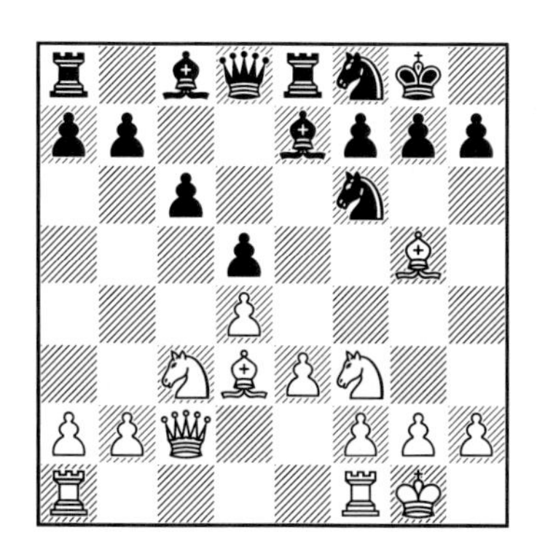

11.♗f4. Nowadays preference is given to the variation 11.♖ab1 a5 12.a3 ♘e4 13.♗xe7 ♕xe7 14.b4, which, in fact, does not give white a tangible advantage in the opening.

11...♘h5 12.♗e5 f6 13.♗g3 ♗g4 14.♘h4 g6 (14...♘xg3 15.hxg3 ♗d6 led to equality) **15.♘xg6 hxg6 16.♗xg6 ♘xg3 17.fxg3 ♕d7 18.h3.** It was possible to capture the exchange right away: 18.♗xe8 ♖xe8 19.♖ae1, retaining some advantage.

18...♗e6 19.♗xe8 ♖xe8 20.g4 ♗f7 21.♘e2 ♗d8 22.♕d2 ♘h7 23.♘g3 ♘g5 24.♘f5 ♗g6

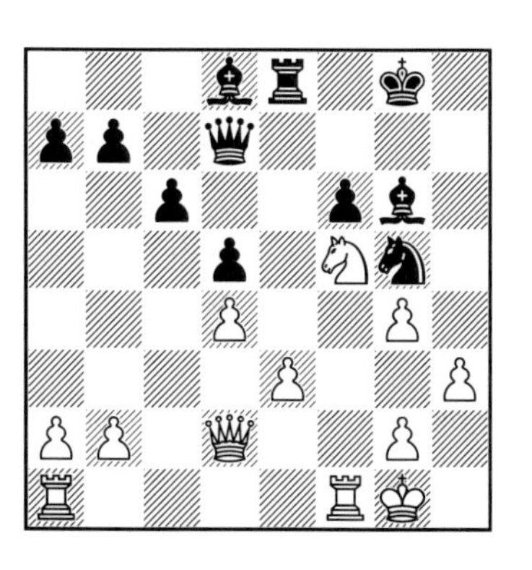

25.h4. Why does white chase the black knight to a great square?! The move 25.♕d3!? deserves consideration.

25...♘e4 26.♕e1 ♗c7 27.♖f3 ♔h8. Black has already taken the initiative, which could be emphasized by 27...♗xf5! 28.gxf5 ♕g7.

28.♕b4 a5 29.♕a3 ♘d2 30.♖f2 ♘c4 31.♕a4 ♗xf5 32.♖xf5 ♕d6 (32...♘xe3 would have won immediately) **33.♖f4 ♖xe3 34.♖af1 ♘d2 35.♖1f2 ♖e1+ 36.♔h2 ♘f1+ 37.♖xf1.** White resigned.

After the sixth round of the Soviet Championship semi-final, master Schneideman had achieved a 50% result. The seventh round did not take place. By that time, the war had started!

The life of chess master Georgy Schneideman was tragically cut short at the beginning of the war. People with German-sounding surnames suddenly felt uncomfortable, and, moreover, someone else said that there was a general in the German army by the name of Schneideman. Following a denunciation, Georgy was arrested and shot as a German spy. According to his friend, Master of Sport Mikhail Borisovich Noakh, he managed to convey that he was being sent to Askold Island, far away in the Sea of Japan – one of the places where "enemies of the people" were shot. The name of this island could

not be found on a geographical map at the time, and it sounded ominous for Leningraders.

Shortly before his death, international arbiter M. N. Volkovysky said that someone who saw G. Schneideman after his arrest heard him say, "Tell the Leningrad chess players that I am innocent. The denunciation was written by...", and he mentioned a name well-known in the city's chess circles.

P. A. Romanovsky was one of those called to the 'Big House' on Liteiny Avenue after Schneideman's disappearance. Failing to obtain any compromising evidence from him, the investigator rather irately said that there was a very important 'signal', shaking a sheet of paper in his fist. Romanovsky could only see the lines of text, but it was enough for him to recognize the handwriting with characteristic narrow and tall slanting letters. Peter Arsenyevich also saw the signature – the same one he saw many times on game sheets.

It belonged to a player who lived by the principle that it was worth doing a small vile thing to enjoy a great career. He made a great career indeed – an endgame study composer, chess writer, and piano player. And vile things are actually not that horrible when nobody, except for a few accomplices, knows about it. In our days, all the secrets are revealed, albeit slowly. When the names of the informers are named publicly, we'll know the bitter truth – even talented people could sink very low.

Back in 2004, when I wrote the Russian version of the book you are now reading, it was difficult to name the snitch. However, in advance of the publication by Elk and Ruby in 2021 of the book *Selected Games* by Peter Romanovsky with a new biography of Romanovsky contributed by Sergei Tkachenko, I agreed to clarify this information. Here I repeat the information given in that book: the denunciation was written by Romanovsky's pupil Vitaly Chekhover. My source of information was Vladimir Zak, another of Romanovsky's pupils.

While preparing material on the case I consulted Vladimir, who told me that Peter Arsenyevich had told him this story, and that the signature was indeed Chekhover's.

I can only dream of a time when our fellow citizens will no longer care what a person's surname is: Stepanov, Schneideman or any double-barreled name.

Mikhail Shebarshin – From Trade Union Champion to BelBalt Gulag Champion

Leningrad master Andrey Batuev, recalling his youth, described a grand chess evening at the Yusupov Palace: "In the blue drawing room, the highlight of the meeting was a blindfold consultation exhibition by two famous Leningrad chess players, Shebarshin and Perfiliev. At the time, they were like the popular Danish comedians Ole & Axel: a small, young student – Perfiliev, and a tall, prim mathematician with a walrus mustache and glasses – Shebarshin. The consultants played on ten boards. The blue drawing room was jam-packed. Everyone wanted to watch the blindfold games. Their opponents were seated comfortably at tables, drinking tea with lemon, snacking on sandwiches and quietly conferring about the next move. One player unexpectedly offered a draw in a cheerful voice, to which Shebarshin, smiling, replied: 'Oh, no! We will quickly organize checkmate for you now.' And they really did 'organize' it, against a background of friendly applause from the audience. The final result – the two men giving the exhibition won 8 games and drew the other two. They were carried out by their opponents' hands to the foyer and were given the bumps to the extent that poor Shebarshin had to hold the frame of his glasses with both hands."

The episode that the future master remembered is recorded in *Shakhmatny listok*, and it took place on March 17, 1926. By that time, first-year mathematics teacher Mikhail Nikolaevich Shebarshin was already well known in Leningrad. In particular, in 1925 he simultaneously worked as a chess club instructor at the factories Krasny Putilovets, Krasny Vyborzhets, Imeni Ilyich, and Krasny Gvozdilshchik, and even at the club of the Union of

Metalworkers and the Priboy publishing house.

Moreover, Mikhail Nikolaevich was a member of the section under the regional committee of the Union of Education Workers and, together with master Ilya Rabinovich and Rokhlin, led the chess section of the Leningrad Department of Public Education. He was fond of playing without looking at the board. In January 1928, he conducted a blindfold exhibition on five boards (+3–1=1).

Shebarshin came to Leningrad from Staraya Russa. He was born on September 3 (old style), 1892 in that city in Novgorod Gubernia, in the family of a retired junior captain. Like his four brothers, Mikhail graduated from the 2nd Moscow Cadet Corps. From the certificate he received after graduating from the corps in 1911, it follows that he was an excellent student, receiving the top score of 12 in almost all subjects.

In 1914, Shebarshin graduated from the engineering college. He prepared for a military career, but he did not have the chance to follow in his father's footsteps – Mikhail Nikolaevich was declared unfit for military service for health reasons.

Mikhail Shebarshin was already a strong chess player in his youth. In the *Chess Bulletin* published by the elder brother of the future world champion Alexei Alekhine for 1915, we find a game with his own annotations.

Game No. 49

M. Shebarshin – N. Katalymov

Staraya Russa, September 20, 1915

Spanish Opening C62

Commentary by M. Shebarshin

1.e4 e5 2.♘f3 ♘c6 3.♗b5 d6 4.d4 ♗d7 5.0-0 exd4

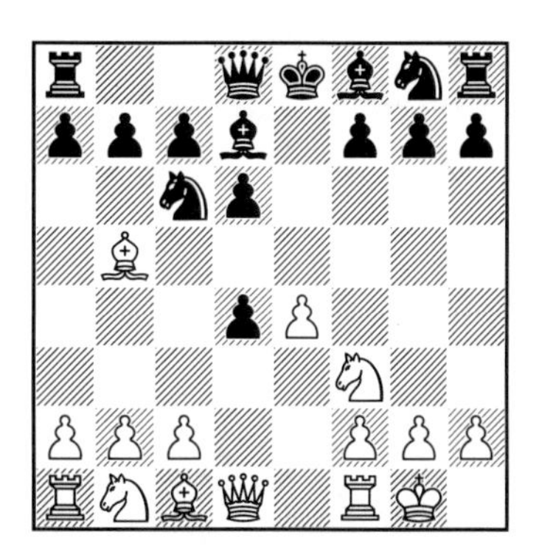

6.♗xc6 (at the end of the 20th century, the most common continuation for white was 6.♘xd4, after which black chose to fianchetto his dark-squared bishop: 6...g6 7.♘c3 ♗g7 8.♗xc6 bxc6, followed by 9.f4 or 9.♖e1 – S.G.) **6...♗xc6 7.♘xd4 ♘f6 8.♘c3 ♗e7 9.♕d3 0-0.** I think it was better to retain the bishop pair by playing 9...♗d7.

10.♘xc6 bxc6 11.b3 ♖e8 12.♗b2 ♗f8 13.♖ad1 ♕c8 14.♕c4 c5 15.f3. In view of 15...♕e6 it is necessary to protect the e4 pawn. In addition, 15.f3 frees the c3 knight and, as the continuation shows, prevents the immediate g7–g6.

15...g6 16.♘b5 ♗g7. It would have been wrong to continue by playing 16...♘d7 17.♕c3 f6 18.♕a5

♘b6 19.♗xf6, but the move 16...♖e6, after which white creates a weakness on d6 for black, seems the best.

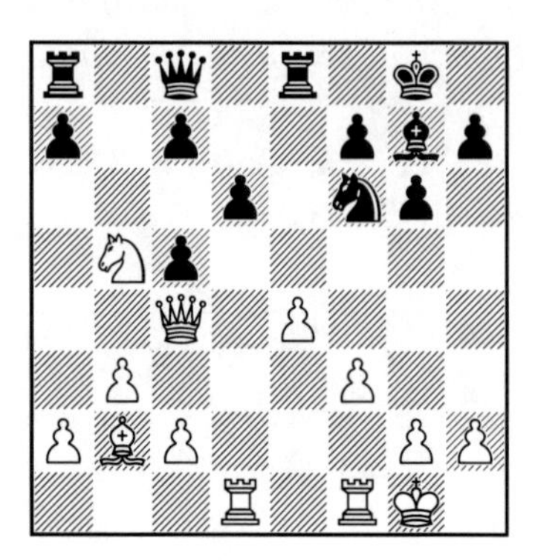

17.e5! Unexpectedly for black, this onslaught is not only possible, but should even lead to a victory for white. Black arguably chooses the best continuation from here, since, for example, 17...♘d7 18.exd6! ♗xb2 19.c3! did not promise any benefits, and it is difficult to find a completely satisfactory defense for black.

17...dxe5 18.♕xc5 c6 19.♘d6 ♗f8 20.♕c3. Perhaps 20.♗xe5 was stronger: white has an extra pawn with a good position. Starting from the 17th move, the game becomes rich in complex and interesting combinations.

20...♗xd6 21.♖xd6 ♘d5 22.♕xc6 ♘e3! This looks stronger than 22...♘b4, since after the exchange of queens and c2-c4, the c-pawn becomes unpleasant.

23.♖e1 (according to Katalymov, this move was better than 23.♖f2) **23...♘xc2 24.♕xc8 ♖exc8 25.♖xe5 ♖c7.** Otherwise, white will occupy the seventh rank. Katalymov admits that the game is lost for black, but by persistent defense he gradually increases the chances of salvation that were infinitely small.

26.♖d2 f5 27.a3.

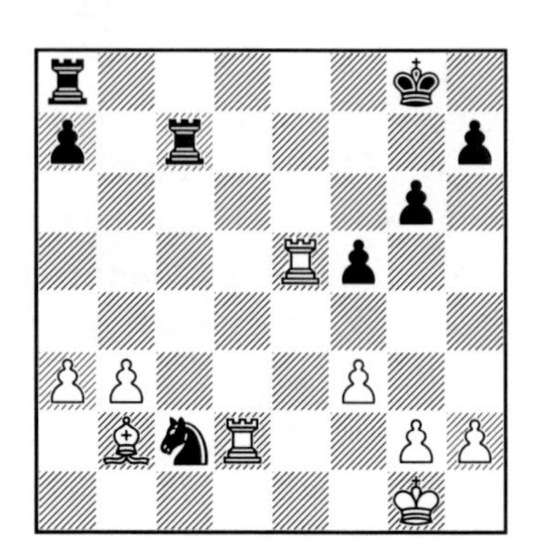

From this moment, white begins to hunt the c2 knight, whose position looks bad. Black's next move is forced, since after b3-b4 the knight risks forever sitting on the c2 or b3 squares, from which it will not have an opportunity to move.

27...a5 28.♔f2 f4 (black seeks to exchange pawns in order to sac a piece for 2-3 pawns in the future) **29.g3 fxg3+ 30.hxg3 ♔f7 31.♔e2.** The knight attracts the white king like a magnet. Maybe here white could have played better by exchanging one of the rooks, after which the knight would have been stuck on c2.

31...♖b8! 32.♔d1! If 32.♖d3, then 32...♖cb7 33.♔d1 ♖xb3 34.♖xb3 ♖xb3 35.♔xc2 ♖xf3 36.♖xa5 ♖xg3 37.♖a7+ ♔e6 38.♖xh7, and even if black did not have a g-pawn, it would hardly be possible for white to win (white has a won position according to the seven-piece tablebase – S.G.). Black could have also brought the game to the same position after the move in the text.

32...♘xa3 33.♗xa3 ♖xb3 34.♖xa5 ♖xf3. According to Katalymov, "black has managed to carry out his plan, and as a result he has gained chances for a drawn ending."

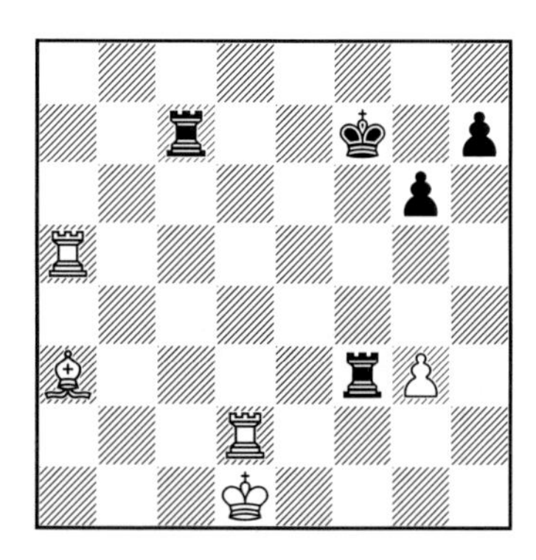

35.♗d6 ♖d7 36.♖a8! ♖f5 37.g4 ♖f1+ 38.♔e2 ♖g1 39.♔f3 h5 40.♔e4!

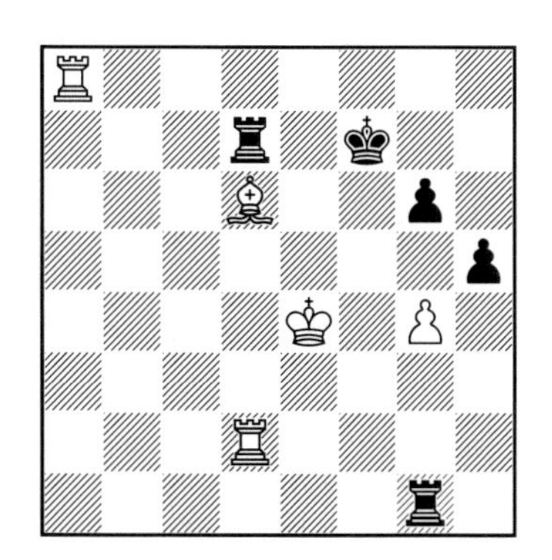

40...♔e6! After 40...♖xg4+ black has a lot of chances to lose, such as 41.♔d5 ♖g5+ 42.♔c6, with a win. If 41...♔f6, then 42.♖f2+ ♔g5 43.♔e6 ♖h7 (43...♖b7 44.♗e7+ ♔h6 45.♖h8+ ♔g7 46.♗f6#) 44.♖a5+ ♔h6 (44...♔h4 45.♖h2#) 45.♗f8+ ♖g7 46.♖f7, with a win; if 42...♔g7, then 43.♔e6 ♖b7 44.♗e5+ ♔h6 45.♖h8+ ♖h7 46.♖ff8 g5 47.♖f6+ ♔g7 48.♖f7+ ♔g6 49.♖g8+ ♔h6 50.♖f6#.

41.♖e8+ ♔f6! After 41...♔f7, it would have been difficult for white to win, but, as these interesting variations show, it seems to be possible, namely: 42.♖f2+ ♔g7 43.♗e5+ ♔h6 44.♗f4+! g5 45.♗e5 ♖xg4+ 46.♔e3, and if, for example, 46...♔g6, then 47.♖g8+ ♔h6 48.♖h8+ ♖h7 49.♖f6+ ♔g7 50.♖a6+; if47...♔h7, then 48.♖h8+ ♔g6 49.♖f6+ ♔g7 50.♖fh6+ ♔f7 51.♖8h7+ ♔e8 52.♖e6+ ♔d8 53.♖h8#. If on the 46th turn black moves his d7 rook, then it becomes clear that the rook is lost. If 45...♖e1+, then 46.♔f5! ♖f7+ 47.♔e6! ♖xf2 48.♖h8+ ♔g6 49.gxh5#. Or 44...♔h7 45.g5! and the black king gets checkmated, for example, 45...♖f7 46.♗e5! ♖e1+ 47.♔d4! ♖d1+ (47...♖d7+ prolongs the resistance – S.G.) 48.♔c5 ♖c1+ 49.♔d6 ♖d1+ 50.♔e6, with a win, or 45...♖e1+ 46.♗e3 ♖b7 47.♔d5! ♖d1+ (47...♖b5+ 48.♔c6 ♖xg5 49.♖f7+ and 50.♖h8#) 48.♔c6 ♖g7 49.♖ff8 – and black not only has no hope of salvation, but there is no good move either.

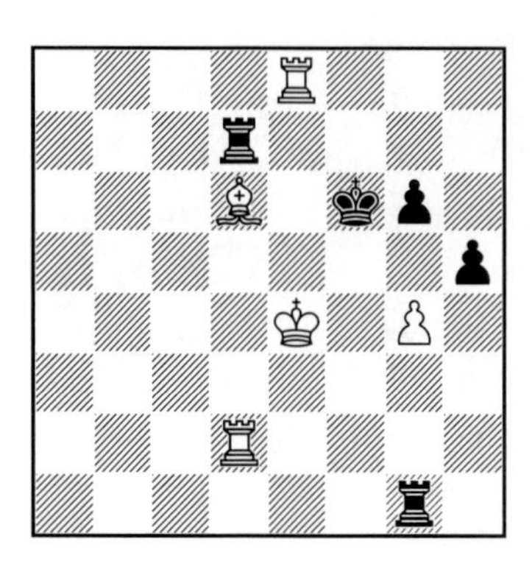

42.♖f2+ (42.♗e5+ ♔f7 43.♖xd7+ ♔xe8 44.♖a7 ♖xg4+ 45.♔d5 ♔d8! gives white nothing) **42...♔g5! 43.♖e5+ ♔xg4 44.♗c5 ♖g3 45.♗e3 ♖b7!** In the case of 45...♖c7 black would have lost: 46.♖h2 ♖c4+ 47.♔d3 ♖b4 48.♖g5+ ♔f3 49.♖f2# or 46...♖h3 47.♖g2+ ♖g3 48.♖g5+ ♔h4 49.♖5xg3, with a win; if 47...♔h4, then 48.♗g5#.

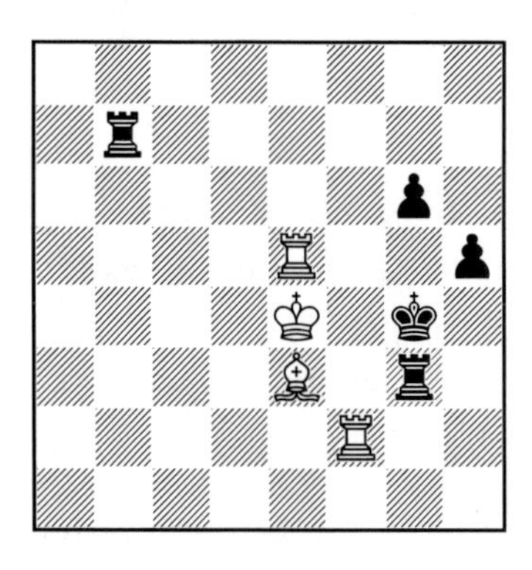

46.♖f6. Now white had to try 46.♖h2 ♖b4+ 47.♔d3 ♖b3+ 48.♔e2 ♖b2+ 49.♗d2 again, with a win. (49...♖h3 50.♖g2+ ♔h4 51.♖e4#). However, black has a way to defend himself: 47...♔f3! 48.♗f2 ♖gg4 49.♗c5 ♖b3+! 50.♔c2 ♖b7 51.♖e3+ ♔f4 52.♖f2+ ♔g5 53.♗e7+ ♔h6 54.♖f7 ♖c4+! – a draw. Not the fascinating 54...♖c7+ 55.♔d3 ♖gc4 (55...♖cc4 56.♖e5 ♖gd4+ 57.♔e3!, with a win) 56.♖e5! ♖c3+ 57.♔d4 ♖7c4+ 58.♔d5 (threatening 59.♗g5# and 59.♗f8#) 58...g5 59.♖e6#.

46...♔h3 47.♗b6 g5 48.♖ee6 ♖d7 49.♖f1 h4 50.♗f2 ♖f7 51.♖h1+ ♔g2 52.♗xg3 ♔xh1 53.♖h6 ♔g2 54.♗e5 ♔h3 55.♗f6 ♔g2 56.♗xg5 h3. Draw agreed.

We also find Shebarshin among the participants of a strong tournament organized during the Christmas holidays of 1923 by the Novgorod branch of the All-Russian Chess Union. "The strong Shebarshin's play was affected by a long lack of practice," commented *Shakhmatny listok* on the fourth place (behind I. Rabinovich, P. Romanovsky and V. Sozin) gained by the first-year student from Staraya Russa.

Those defeated by Shebarshin included professor of mathematics Boris Mikhailovich Koyalovich – an experienced St. Petersburg first-category player whose chess career began before the revolution.

Game No. 50

B. Koyalovich – M. Shebarshin

Novgorod, December 22, 1923

Bird's Opening A03

Commentary by M. Shebarshin

1.f4 d5 2.♘f3 c5 3.b3 ♘c6 4.♗b2 ♘f6 5.e3 ♗f5 6.♘h4 e6 7.♘xf5

exf5 8.♗d3. Not a good place for the bishop, which later causes white's collapse.

8...g6 9.0-0 ♗g7 10.♕f3 0-0 11.♘c3 ♖e8!

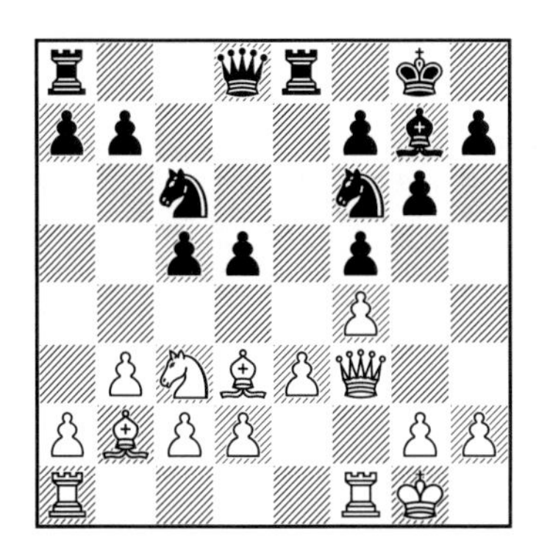

White failed to understand the significance of this seemingly harmless move. It is clear that black is preparing a pile-up on d2 via c5-c4, for which he had to first increase the pressure on the e3 pawn.

12.♘a4? c4! 13.bxc4 (if 13.♗e2, then 13...♘e4 14.♗xg7 ♘xd2, winning the exchange) **13...dxc4 14.♗xc4 ♕xd2 15.♖fe1 ♕xc2 16.♗b3** (I was expecting 16.♗b5) **16...♕e4 17.♘c5 ♕xf3 18.gxf3 ♘d7! 19.♘d3.**

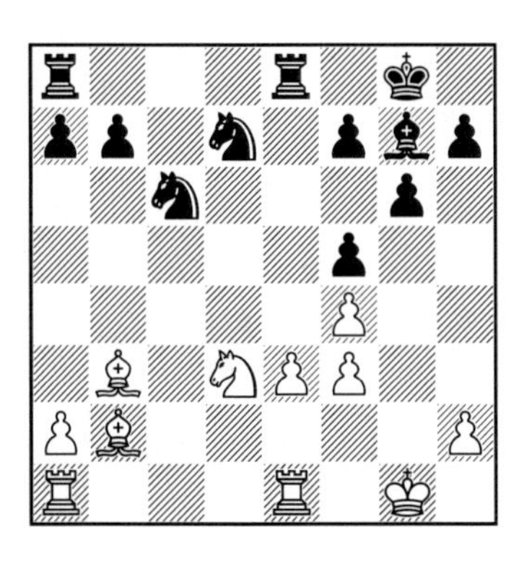

19...♘c5! An original way to pursue the knight.

20.♘xc5 ♗xb2 21.♖ad1 ♗c3 22.♖f1. If 22.♖e2, then 22...♗d4 or 22...♘d4.

22...♖xe3 23.♘xb7 ♘d4 24.♗d5 ♖ae8

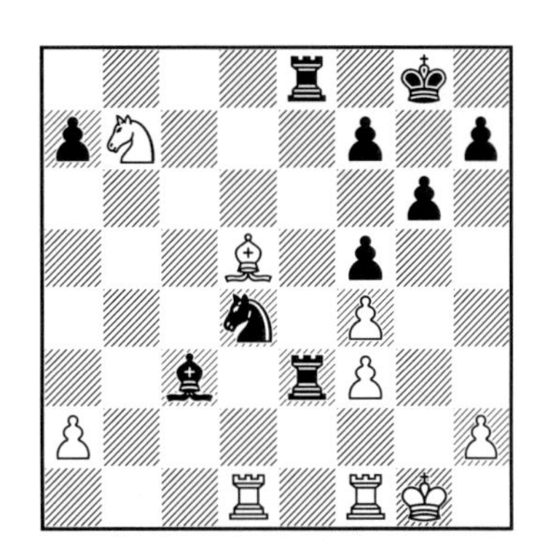

25.♔f2? A mistake in a hopeless situation. The move 25.♘d6 could have been followed by 25...♖d8 26.♘c4 ♖e2, etc.

25...♖e2+ 26.♔g3 ♖b2 27.♗xf7+ ♔xf7 28.♘d6+ ♔f8 29.♘xe8 ♔xe8 30.♖d3 ♘e2+. White resigned, since the ♖d3 was also about to get lost. The variation 31.♔f2 ♘xf4+ 32.♔e3 ♘g2# was pretty.

Soon, Mikhail Nikolaevich moved to Petrograd, by then already called Leningrad. Two years later, by decision of the Provincial Qualification Commission headed by Romanovsky, Shebarshin was confirmed as a first category player (only the thirty-odd strongest St. Petersburg chess players had this title at the time).

One of his first competitions in Leningrad was a match with Koyalovich, drawn with a 4.5:4.5 score. In 1926, Shebarshin was included in the Leningrad team for the match with Moscow. Both of his games on 11th board with Poliak ended in a draw. But in the first of them, the Leningrad player was close to victory.

Game No. 51
M. Shebarshin – A. Poliak
Moscow, May 22, 1926
Grunfeld Defense D90
Commentary by S. Grodzensky

1.d4 ♘f6 2.♘f3 g6 3.c4 ♗g7 4.♘c3 d5 5.cxd5 ♘xd5 6.e4 ♘xc3 7.bxc3 c5 8.♗b5+ ♗d7 9.♗xd7+ ♕xd7 10.0-0 cxd4 11.cxd4

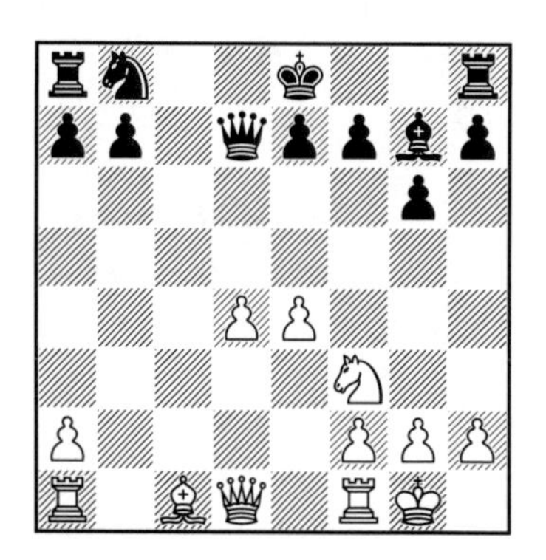

11...0-0. The continuation 11...♘c6 12.♗e3 0-0 13.♖b1 ♘a5 14.d5 ♖fc8! was more accurate – and black would have successfully solved his opening problems.

12.♖b1 ♘c6 13.d5 ♘a5 14.♕e1 b6 15.♗d2! (the impact of black's inaccuracy on his 11th move is felt) **15...♘b7 16.♗c3 ♗xc3 17.♕xc3 ♖ac8 18.♕a3 ♘a5 19.♖bc1 ♖xc1 20.♖xc1 ♖c8 21.♘e5 ♖xc1+ 22.♕xc1 ♕a4.**

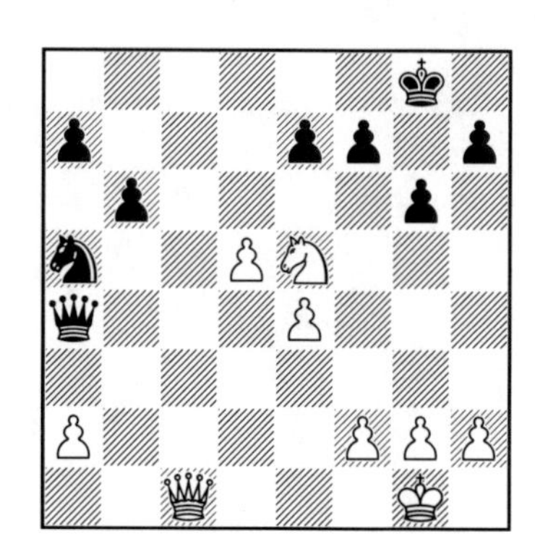

It seems that white had to play 23.♕b1 to protect the a2 and e4 pawns. However...

23.h3! ♕xe4 24.♕c8+ ♔g7 25.♘d7! (threatening checkmate) **25...g5 26.♕f8+ ♔g6 27.♕g8+ ♔h6 28.♕xf7 ♘c4 29.g4!** (winning a pawn) **29...♕e1+ 30.♔h2 ♕e4 31.♕h5+ ♔g7 32.♕xg5+ ♔f7 33.♔g3 ♕d3+ 34.f3 ♕e2 35.♕f5+ ♔e8**

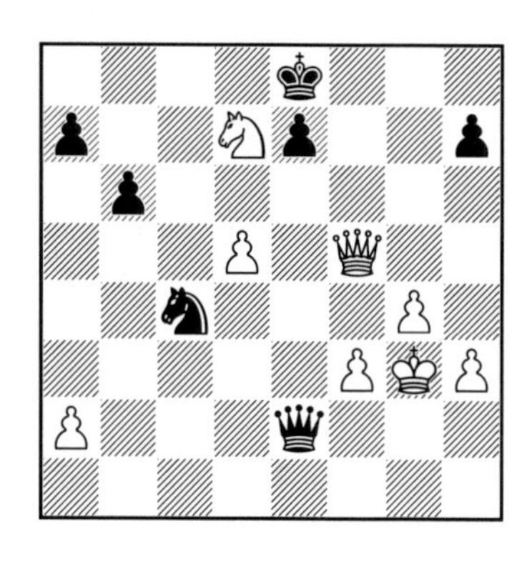

36.♕e6! ♕b2 (forced, since 37.♘f6+ was threatened) **37.♕c6!**

♔d8. If 37...♘a5, then 38.♘f6+ ♔f7 39.♕e8+ ♔g7 40.♕g8+ ♔xf6 41.♕h8+, with a win.

38.♘f8 ♕e5+ 39.♔h4 ♕f6+ 40.♕xf6 exf6 41.♘xh7 (white has a won position) **41...♔e7 42.g5 fxg5+ 43.♔xg5 b5 44.♘f6 ♘e5 45.f4 ♘f3+ 46.♔g4 ♘d2 47.♔f5 b4 48.♘e4 ♘f3 49.♔g6 a5 50.f5 ♘e5+ 51.♔g7 a4 52.d6+ ♔e8 53.h4 b3 54.axb3 axb3 55.h5 b2 56.♘c3 ♘c4.**

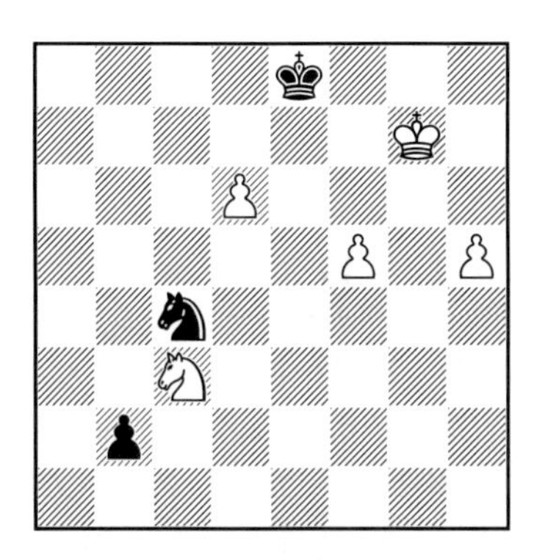

57.h6?? A blunder, ruining a well-deserved victory. After the obvious continuation 57.d7+, black would have had to give up immediately. Now, it's a positional draw.

57...♘xd6 58.h7 ♘f7 59.f6 ♘h8. Draw agreed.

Shebarshin scored 11 points out of 12 in the semi-final of the 1926 Leningrad championship! But even this result brought only second place – Mikhail Botvinnik got half a point more. The key game between the two Mikhails was very tense and brought the future world champion victory on the 97th move!

In the 1926 Petrograd Side championship, M. Shebarshin finished second after the master Romanovsky, and a year later he won the title of champion. In the same 1927 in the teachers trade union championship, Shebarshin finished fourth, but then, playing for his union team, he showed the best result on second board in the team tournament.

Perhaps the biggest competition in Mikhail Shebarshin's short career was the first championship of the RSFSR (Moscow, 1928). He took second place after Izmailov, ahead of the future masters Panov, Vygodchikov, Kan, and Sokolsky, as well as chess composition master Dmitry Petrov. "Shebarshin played well, but despite his sharp combinational style he did not have enough stamina to overtake his dangerous competitor," *Shakhmatny listok* reported.

Moreover, a jury consisting of Botvinnik and Romanovsky awarded Shebarshin a beauty prize for his victory over Sokolsky. "The jury chose the Shebarshin – Sokolsky game, the most complex in its struggle and the most original in the sudden attack carried out by white. When awarding this game the beauty prize, the jury nevertheless considers it necessary to note that it has some defects. For example, instead of the overelaborate move a2-

a3, white easily and beautifully wins with the move g4-g5. In addition, black missed the opportunity to play the move g7-g6 three times, which would have deprived white of many attacking chances." (From the conclusion by Romanovsky and Botvinnik.)

Game No. 52
M. Shebarshin – A. Sokolsky
Championship of the RSFSR,
Moscow, 1928
Queen's Gambit D67
Commentary by S. Grodzensky

1.c4 ♘f6 2.♘c3 e6 3.d4 d5 4.♗g5 ♘bd7 5.e3 ♗e7 6.♖c1 c6 (the main continuation here is 6...a6 or 6...0-0 followed by 7...c5) **7.♘f3 0-0 8.♗d3! dxc4 9.♗xc4 ♘d5 10.♗xe7 ♕xe7 11.0-0 ♘5b6** (11... ♘xc3 12.♖xc3 e5 is more common) **12.♗b3 e5**

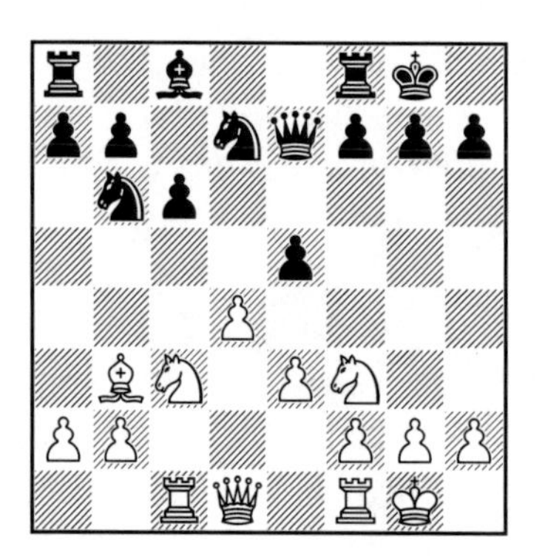

13.♘e4! The variation 13.d5 cxd5 14.♘xd5 ♘xd5 15.♕xd5 e4 16.♘d4 ♘f6 only leads to equal play.

The Yugoslav Encyclopedia attributes the authorship of the move 13.♘e4! to Capablanca, who played it against Kan at the Moscow International Tournament in 1935. However, Shebarshin played this move seven years earlier!

13...h6. 14.♘fg5 was threatened. Another possible continuation, 13... exd4 14.♕xd4, only further cramped black's position.

14.♘g3 ♔h8 15.♕d3 exd4 16.exd4. In that Capablanca-Kan game, Capa played 16.♗c2, and after 16...♘f6 17.e4 g6 18.♕xd4 got a big advantage.

16...♘f6 17.♖fe1 ♕d6 18.♘e5 ♘bd5 19.♕f3 (the move 19.f3!?, threatening 20.♘e4, deserved consideration) **19...♗e6 20.♘f5 ♗xf5 21.♕xf5 ♖ad8 22.♖cd1 ♕b4?** Black had to defend painstakingly via 22...g6 and 23...♔g7.

23.g4

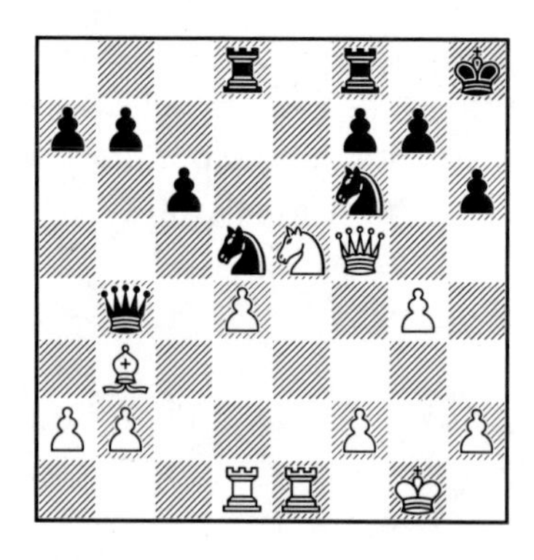

23...a5. And now it was better to play 23...g6, without fear of the white knight's sacrifice on g6 or f7. For example, 24.♘xg6+ fxg6 25.♕xg6

♘xg4 26.♗c2 ♘df6, or 24.♘xf7+ ♖xf7 25.♕xg6 ♕f8.

24.h4 a4 25.♗c2 ♘e7 26.♕d3 c5 27.a3! As Romanovsky pointed out, the continuation 27.g5 ♖xd4 28.gxf6 ♖xd3 (28...♘g6 29.♘xf7+ ♖xf7 30.♖e8+ ♖f8 31.fxg7+ or 29... ♔g8 30.♘xh6+ ♔h8 31.fxg7+, with a win) 29.fxe7 ♖e8 30.♗xd3 ♕xh4 31.♗g6! ♕g5+ 32.♔f1, was also winning.

27...♕xb2. Or 27...♕a5 28.g5 and so on. If 27...♕xd4, then 28.♕e2 followed by 29.♖xd8 and 30.♘xf7+; 27...♕b6 28.dxc5 ♕c7 29.♕xd8 ♖xd8 30.♖xd8+ ♘eg8 31.♖d7 ♘xd7 32.♘xf7#.

28.♘c4 ♕b5 29.g5 ♖xd4 30.gxf6 ♘g6.

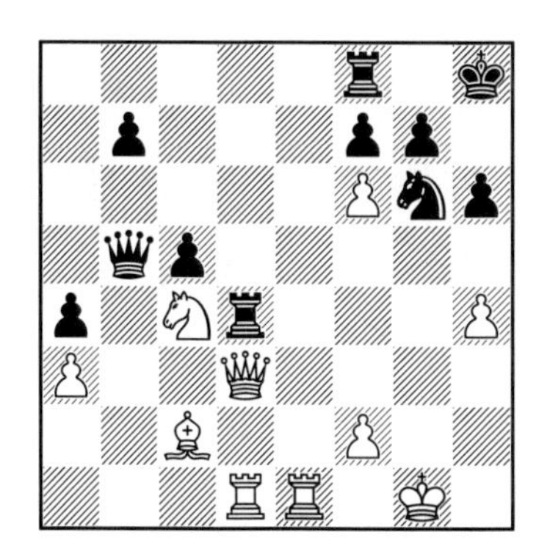

31.♘d6! The culmination of the combination conceived by white on the 27th move.

31...♕d7 32.fxg7+ ♔xg7 33.♘f5+. Black resigned.

There is also a certain theoretical significance in the game between Shebarshin and Kosolapov.

Game No. 53
M. Shebarshin – S. Kosolapov
Championship of the RSFSR,
Moscow, 1928
Nimzo-Indian Defense E24
Commentary by S. Grodzensky

1.d4 ♘f6 2.c4 e6 3.♘c3 ♗b4 4.a3 ♗xc3+ 5.bxc3 b6 (the most common continuation here is 5...c5) **6.f3**

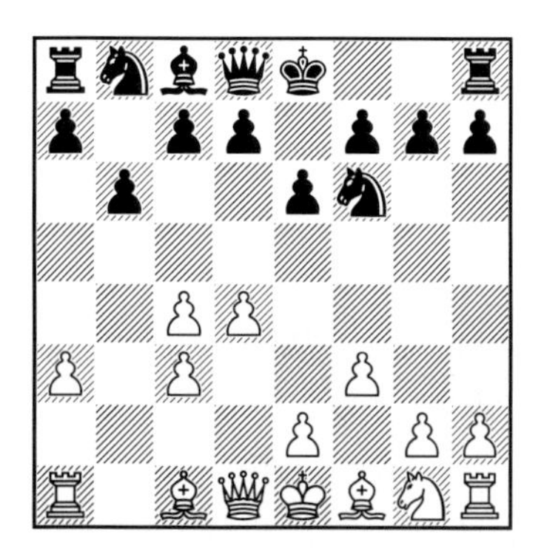

6...0-0. In the game Shebarshin – Kan from the same championship black chose 6...d5 7.e3 0-0 8.♗d3 ♘bd7 9.♘e2 ♗b7 10.0-0 c5, which led to an approximately equal game.

7.e4 d6 8.♗d3 e5 9.♘e2 ♗b7 10.0-0 ♘fd7 11.♘g3 ♖e8 12.♕c2 ♘f8 13.f4 (the outcome of the opening is that white has a minimal advantage) **13...♘bd7.** Black chooses a path that does not promise any opportunity for counterplay, but condemns him to passive defense.

14.♗e3 exf4 15.♖xf4 ♘g6 16.♖f2 ♘df8 17.♖af1 ♘h8.

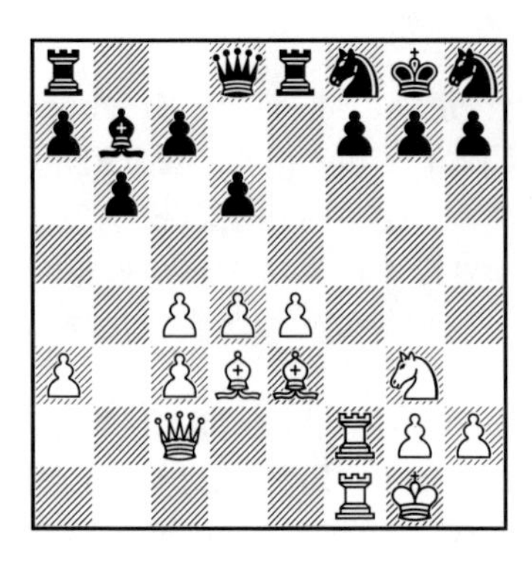

18.♕e2 ♘fg6 19.♖f5 ♗c8 20.♖h5 f6 21.♕f3 (with the unpleasant threat 22.e5) **21...♗e6 22.♘f5 ♘f8 23.g4.** Now the final pawn assault begins.

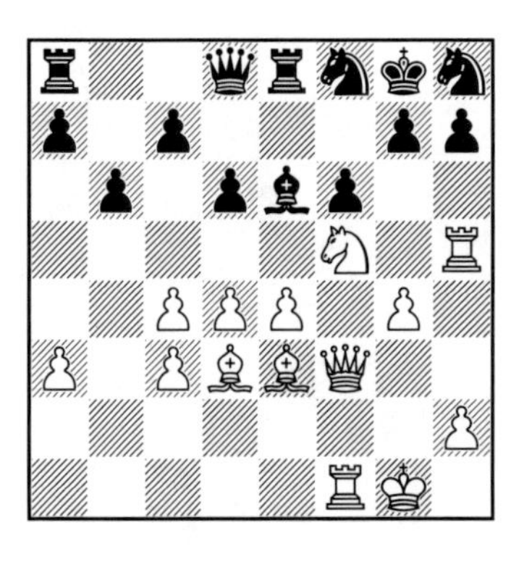

23...♗f7 24.♖h3 ♘e6 25.♖g3 ♘g5 26.♕g2 ♕d7 27.h4 ♘e6 28.♕f3 ♕a4 29.g5 fxg5 30.d5 ♘c5 31.♖xg5 ♗g6 (the move 31...♘xd3 would have been met by 32.♘h6+ ♔f8 33.♕xf7+ ♘xf7 34.♖xf7#) **32.♗d4 ♘xd3 33.♕xd3.** Black lost on time.

Mathematics teacher Shebarshin regularly participated in university competitions. For example, in the match between the educators of Leningrad and Kharkov (December 27-28, 1928), he took one-and-a half points out of two from Alexei Alekhine. He consistently showed strong results in the individual teachers trade union championships, despite the impressive opposition.

Shebarshin won second prize in the 1928 championship, half a point behind the winner Ilya Rabinovich, but ahead of Ilyin-Zhenevsky, Batuev, and Koyalovich. The next educators championship brought Mikhail Nikolaevich fourth place behind Botvinnik, Batuev and Romanovsky, but ahead of Ragozin, whom Shebarshin beat in their game.

Mikhail Shebarshin's swansong was the All-Union Championship of the teachers trade union, which took place in early 1930 in Minsk. Mikhail Nikolaevich performed confidently and consistently in this tournament. In fifteen games, he dropped only one-and-a half points, and he did not have a worse position in any of his games. He took first place.

Game No. 54
M. Shebarshin (Leningrad) – M. Shalaev (Polotsk)
Teachers trade union championship, Minsk, 1930
Queen's Gambit D43
Commentary by M. Shebarshin

1.d4 d5 2.c4 c6 3.♘f3 ♘f6 4.♘c3 e6 5.♗g5 ♘bd7 6.e4 dxe4 7.♘xe4 ♕a5+. Black has set up his pieces in a way similar to the Rubinstein Variation of the Cambridge Springs Defense. We believe that although black's bishop will move to d6 instead of e7, such a construction is erroneous. In particular, the ♗d6 gives white an opportunity to play c4-c5 with tempo.

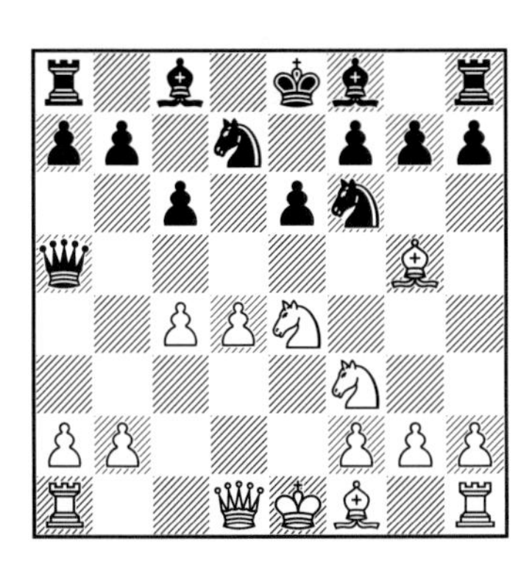

8.♗d2 ♗b4 9.♘c3 ♕c7 10.♗d3 0-0 11.a3 ♗d6 12.0-0 ♖e8 13.♕c2 ♘f8. Black should have gone for the continuation 13...♗f4, not heading straight into defense.

14.g3! h6 15.♖fe1 b6 16.b4 ♗b7 17.c5. After this move, white gets a backward d4 pawn, but wins two tempi, once and for all prevents both c5 and e5, and locks in the b7 bishop. Black takes control of the d5 square, but white, in turn, has good chances to occupy the d6 square.

17...♗e7 18.♗f4 ♕c8. If 18...♕d7, then 19.♘e5, and taking the pawn by means of 19...♕xd4 will cost black dearly after 20.♖ad1.

19.♗e5 ♗a6? We consider this move to be erroneous. Although the position of the b7 bishop is poor and, at first glance, is even worse than its opponent the d3 bishop, the b7 bishop still protects the c6 square, while the d3 bishop has nothing to do yet, since there is no attack on the black castling position in sight.

20.♘d2 ♗xd3 21.♕xd3 ♘g6.

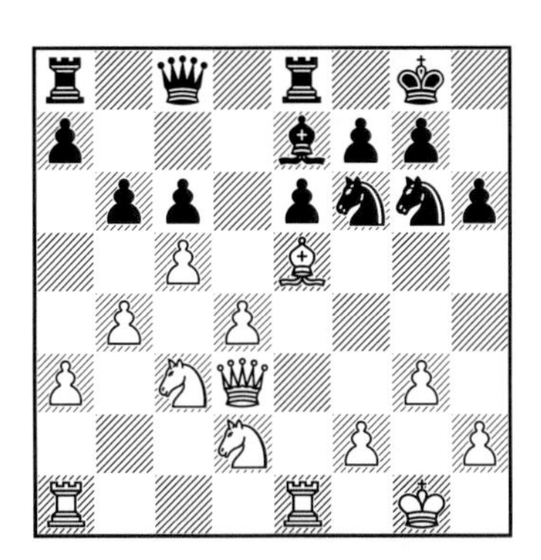

22.♘c4 ♘xe5 23.dxe5 ♕d7 24.♘d6 ♘h7. Unfortunately, black has missed his chance to get his knight to d5, since now white responds with 25.♘xe8. Not 24...♗xd6 due to 25.exf6, winning a piece.

25.♖ed1 ♖ed8 26.♕c2 ♗f8 (27.♘xf7 was threatened) **27.♖d4 ♗xd6 28.♖xd6 ♕c7 29.♖ad1.** White, carrying out his plan, failed to notice the possibility of deviating from it, but which he nevertheless found on the next move.

29...♘f8 30.cxb6 axb6. It was better to play 30...♕xb6 despite dropping a pawn after 31.♘a4 ♕c7 32.b5.

31.♘b5, and white went on to win.

After the 1930 teachers trade union championship, the name Mikhail Shebarshin, who was close to the title of master, disappeared from the chess periodicals. What happened to him?

After mentioning Shebarshin in an article about Izmailov published in the magazine *64-Chess Review*, I asked readers who had heard anything about Mikhail Nikolaevich to contact me.

The responses were not long in coming.

Professor Naum Yakovlevich Vilenkin wrote to me that he played games in 1932-1933 with Shebarshin, a prisoner of the BelBaltlag. In the early 1930s, Naum Yakovlevich studied at school in Medvezhya Gora (today called Medvezhyegorsk) – a kind of capital of the White Sea Canal. Vilenkin was fond of chess, and among his opponents Shebarshin, who was in prison at that time, made the greatest impression. The regime in BelBaltlag in the early 1930s was relatively mild, and so several qualified chess players among the prisoners were allowed to enter the city championship.

According to Vilenkin, Shebarshin enjoyed great success with the King's Gambit, and in a tournament that gathered about 20 participants (among whom several were second-category players), he easily took first place.

A fragment of Shebarshin's life was also recalled by Candidate Master from the Moscow region Vladimir Zavyalov. Vladimir spent his school years in the village of Yaya in the Kemerovo region.

The majority of the population of Yaya in the mid-1950s was made up of internal exiles – prisoners who had served time under Article 58. The latter included Shebarshin, who worked as a mathematics teacher at a local school.

Student Zavyalov had the third rank (*"razriad" – third rank was a rather weak club player's level)* in chess. This attracted him to an elderly teacher who played very strongly, but had no appropriate opponents in his village. In addition to chess, Shebarshin was interested in math teaching methodology. His articles were published in the magazine *Mathematics for School.*

Zavyalov remembered the teacher Shebarshin for his noble appearance and flowing gray hair. Just like in Batuev's recollections, Zavyalov's portrait of Shebarshin included his luxurious mustache, except that by the 1950s it had turned completely gray.

From Shebarshin's personal file, stored in the Yaya archives, we learned more about his biography, including that his freedom was interrupted on November 5, 1930. On the eve of the thirteenth anniversary of the October revolution, Mikhail Shebarshin was arrested, convicted by the "troika" under Article 58 and sentenced to 10 years. At first, he served time constructing the White Sea Canal. For his excellent work, convict Shebarshin was awarded a "shock-worker's badge", and in October 1935 he was granted the status of an exiled ("free") person.

The village of Yaya became Mikhail Nikolaevich's place of internal exile in October 1941. He taught mathematics and physics at local school No. 2 for over 15 years, until retiring.

What about his chess career? It was not forgotten. Master Vasily Grigoryevich Skotorenko wrote to the author about one of his encounters with Mikhail Shebarshin. In November 1952, Skotorenko, at that time a young engineer, played on first board for the Shakhter team in the Third Championship of the Kemerovo Regional Council Professionals. The future master easily outplayed competitors from all teams, and only the duel with the leader of the Iskra team M. N. Shebarshin, who went through the entire competition undefeated, ended in a draw.

Game No. 55
V. Skotorenko – M. Shebarshin
Kemerovo, 1952
English Opening A11
Commentary by S. Grodzensky

1.♘f3 d5 2.c4 c6 3.g3 ♘f6 4.♗g2 e6 5.b3 ♘bd7 6.♗b2 ♗d6 7.d4 b6 8.0-0 ♗b7 9.cxd5 cxd5 10.♘bd2 ♕e7.

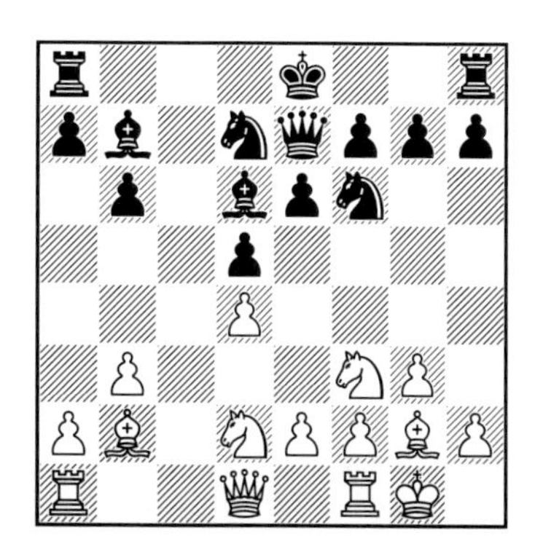

Having skillfully transposed from the Reti Opening to the English, black has not only equalized, but has also gained somewhat better prospects.

11.♘e5 ♖c8 12.♘df3 ♗a3 13.♗xa3 ♕xa3 14.♘xd7 ♘xd7 15.♕d2 0-0 16.♖fc1 a5 17.h4 ♖fd8 18.h5 ♘f6 (18...h6!? deserved consideration) **19.h6 ♘e4 20.♕f4**

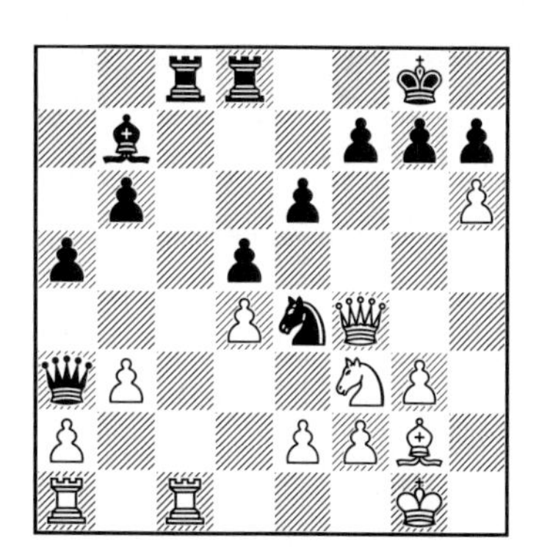

20...♕d6. Another defensive plan would be: 20...♘c3 21.♖c2 ♗a6 22.♕g5 ♕f8.

21.♘e5 f6 22.♗xe4 dxe4 23.♕g4 ♕e7. The more reliable continuation was 23...♖xc1+ 24.♖xc1 g5 with equality.

24.♖xc8 ♖xc8 25.♘c4 f5 26.♕xg7+ ♕xg7 27.hxg7 ♖c6 28.♘e3 ♔xg7.

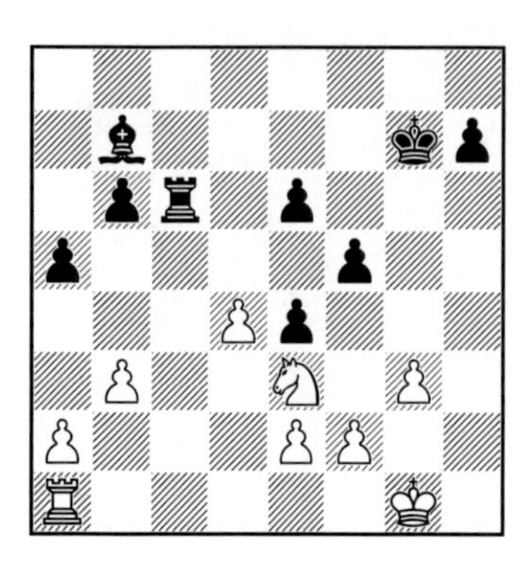

29.d5 ♖c5 30.dxe6 ♔f6 31.e7 (a tempo loss) **31...♔xe7 32.♔g2 ♗a6 33.♖e1 ♔f6 34.f4 ♖c6 35.♔f2 ♖d6 36.♖d1 ♖xd1 37.♘xd1 ♔e6 38.♘e3 b5 39.a3 ♗c8 40.♔e1 ♔d6 41.b4 a4 42.♔d2 ♗d7 43.♔c3 ♗c8 44.♔d4 ♗e6 45.♘d1 ♗d7 46.♘f2 ♗c8 47.♘h3 h6 48.♘f2 ♗e6 49.♘d1 h5 50.♘c3 ♗c4 51.♘xa4 ♗xe2 52.♘c3 ♗f1 53.♘d1 ♗c4.** Draw agreed.

During the tournament, Skotorenko lived with Shebarshin in the same room. Vasily Grigoryevich recalls that Mikhail Nikolaevich loved to play five-minute games, continuously commenting on what was happening on the board. And Skotorenko, who had a reputation as one of the strongest players in Siberia, was sincerely surprised that his opponent, being almost three times older than him, often won against him.

Local organizers invited the veteran to the regional championship without any qualification process, but he kept refusing, citing health problems. In the last years of his life (he died on July 13, 1963), Shebarshin hardly ever left Yaya. The reputation of the strongest among the local chess players was so solid that, sometimes, the old teacher was chosen to play on first board in the Yaya team, even though he did not participate in the qualifying tournaments.

Nikolai Yefimovich Babushkin, who won Yaya championships in the early 1960s, recalls that once in 1962 Mikhail Nikolaevich invited him to his home. They played two games, and Shebarshin won both of them. Perhaps these were some of the last duels of a chess player who competed with Botvinnik in the Leningrad championship in the 1920s.

To this day, Yaya veterans tell young people about an amazing man who received neither high awards nor sonorous titles, but drew others towards him with the wideness of his talent and enjoyed their unwavering respect.

Thus was the life and career of the chess player Mikhail Nikolaevich Shebarshin, who in his youth was one of the strongest players in Leningrad, who in his more mature years became a prisoner, won chess tournaments on the Gulag islands and in his old age was an internal exile who gave chess lessons to occasional students in the remote village of Yaya.

Nikolai Salmin – A Life Cut Short at Thirty

The Stockholm-Leningrad match was held on 12 boards in the Swedish capital in the first days of November 1926. It witnessed an intense struggle, which was reflected in the score – 12.5:11.5 in favor of the chess players from the banks of the Neva River.

The Leningrad team was headed by the already famous Alexander Ilyin-Zhenevsky, and the team consisted of players who do not need to be introduced to today's readers. Let us mention at least Botvinnik, Model, brothers Arvid and Leonid Kubbel, Rokhlin, Perfiliev, and Samuil Vainstein.

The team also included 19-year-old Salmin – one of the strongest first-category players of the city, who, despite his young age, had a reputation as an excellent teacher to the extent that one article at the time placed his name on a par with such luminaries as Romanovsky and Ilya Rabinovich. That was in the 1920s, yet by the end of the 20th century there were few veterans who recalled him...

Nikolai Konstantinovich Salmin was born in 1907, studied at the Leningrad Academy of Arts, and then taught at the Leningrad Institute of Precision Mechanics and Optics. He also had a part-time job taking orders to illustrate books, and therefore often played in chess competitions for the Printers Union team.

On May 17, 1936, he was arrested, and, probably in 1938, was shot by the Special Council. In 1963, his widow, Zinaida Karlovna Salmina, received a certificate of her husband's posthumous rehabilitation. Information on Salmin in this short chapter was provided by her.

Nikolai Konstantinovich's chess performances lasted only a few years, but they were notable. At the beginning of 1925, Nikolai Salmin won a second category tournament, ahead of the famous study composer Sergei Kaminer, among others. In the so-called "small" championship of Leningrad in 1926, Salmin, who had by then been awarded the first category title, shared third place with the future grandmaster Alatortsev, ahead of another future grandmaster (and world correspondence champion) Ragozin.

Salmin played a lot in 1927. In March, he led the team of the Leningrad Printers Union in a match with colleagues from Moscow, scoring one-and-a half points in two games against the leader of the Moscow printers Merolver. During the May Day holidays, Nikolai Konstantinovich played in the traditional Moscow versus Leningrad match, where he got the experienced Vasily Panov, a future international master and well-known theorist, as his opponent. Salmin lost one game but drew the other one.

In the summer of the same year, he won second prize in a first-category city tournament, while in the autumn, together with Pavel Ostrovsky and Georgy Lisitsyn, he shared 2nd-4th place in the semifinals of the city Olympiad, half a point behind Uspensky.

According to *Shakhmatny listok*, there were 5 masters and 32 first-category players in the city at the time. Nikolai Salmin was, undoubtedly, one of the strongest first-category players in Leningrad and among the top ten chess players of the city as a whole.

1928 brought him third place in the All-Union Tournament of Printers. The following year, in the next small championship of the city, he managed to score fifty percent, but in the championship of Leningrad printers he shared 1st-2nd place with Vainstein.

At the end of 1929, Salmin finished fifth in the annual championship of the Petrograd Side. The finale of one of his games was printed in periodicals.

Game No. 56
A. Sokolsky – N. Salmin
Leningrad, 1929
Commentary by S. Grodzensky

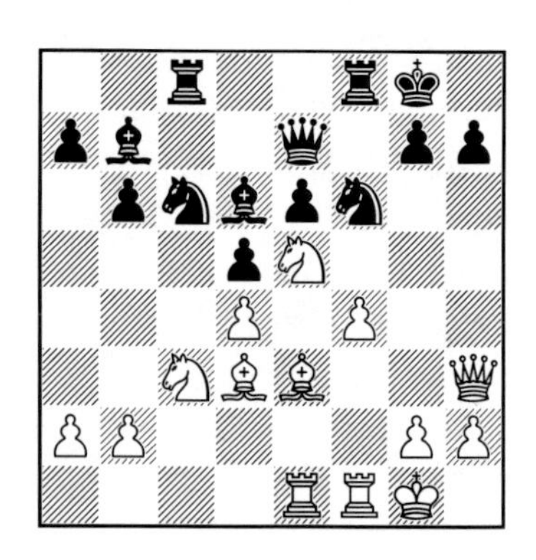

There followed by **17.♗f2! ♘b4 18.♗b1 ♗a6 19.♗h4,** threatening 20.♗xh7+ ♔h8 21.♗xf6 ♕xf6 22.♗g6+.

19...g6 20.♖f3 ♕e8 21.♘xg6 hxg6 22.♖xe6 ♕d7 23.♗xf6. Black resigned.

In the early 1930s, Nikolai Konstantinovich Salmin continued to perform in competitions, and frequently coached, as his widow recalled. But his name was no longer mentioned in the press. And again there are questions that are, alas, now traditional for our book: what was he charged with, and when did he die?

"Hoisted by their Own Petard"

Nikolai Krylenko – The Rise and Fall of the Supreme Commander

Nikolai Vasilyevich Krylenko is one of the most controversial figures in our history. Following his posthumous rehabilitation, books were published everywhere about him, from Moscow to Vladivostok. They were permeated with respect and tenderness, as can be seen from the titles: *Living for the Revolution*, *Devotion*, *Revolution Was His Profession*, *The First Soviet Commander-in-Chief*, and *The Man of Many Summits*.

The blurb for the book written about Krylenko by Arkady Vaksberg *Prosecutor of the Republic* (1974) says: "A man with a fascinating, unusual life, the holder of two university degrees, a highly educated fount of knowledge... In the first Soviet government, he headed the People's Commissariat of Military and Naval Affairs, and then all the Armed Forces of Soviet Russia. An outstanding lawyer, a prosecutor of the republic, an inspirational speaker, the People's Commissar of Justice of the USSR – these are only some of the milestones in the life of this amazing, versatile person."

In 1990, however, the same Vaksberg published an essay on the life of Vyshinsky, where he compared him with Krylenko. Here is how the essayist describes the behavior of the state prosecutor Krylenko during the "Shakhty trial": "Krylenko publicly mocked the victims, while Vyshinsky, on the contrary, beat them with logic clothed in the form of exquisite correctness. The memories of eyewitnesses present us the most interesting psychological portraits of the two pillars of the Soviet judicial system of that time. While Krylenko appears under the pen of memoirists in the guise of an insensitive brute, almost a boor, Vyshinsky is remembered, if not with warmth, then, at least, with respect, recognizing such qualities as politeness and responsiveness for him. Using his right as the owner of the process, Vyshinsky repeatedly cut off the too independent Krylenko, extinguished his ardor, rebuked him and made sarcastic comments about him... He was particularly irritated by the prosecutor's political rigor, lack of flexibility, the dull straightforwardness with which he approached the prosecution of the defendants, his primitive generalizations.

"...Several years later they change places: Krylenko will be remembered as a weak-willed and helpless person, as if waiting every minute to be attacked from around the corner, while Vyshinsky will appear in all his strength and invincibility."

(A. Vaksberg, *Pages of One Life*, Znamya No. 6, 1990)

The name of Nikolai Krylenko is repeatedly mentioned on the pages of *The Gulag Archipelago* by Alexander Solzhenitsyn. "Some well-wishers gave us a surviving copy of the book of accusatory speeches of a violent revolutionary, the first workers' and peasants' people's commissar, the Commander-in-Chief, then the initiator of the Department of Exceptional Courts of the People's Commissariat of Justice (he was preparing for the personal post of Tribune, but Lenin canceled this term), a glorious prosecutor of the grandest trials, and the then exposed fierce enemy of the people N. V. Krylenko." (Alexander Solzhenitsyn *The Gulag Archipelago, Vol. 1*)

Moreover, Solzhenitsyn used Krylenko's ominous-sounding words, which he said at the trial of the "Industrial Party", as an epigraph to the first volume of *The Gulag Archipelago*: "In the era of dictatorship, surrounded by enemies, we sometimes showed unnecessary softness, unnecessary soft-heartedness".

His praises sung in the 1920s, repressed in 1938, posthumously rehabilitated in the late 1950s, and now again subjected to criticism so harsh that you may be wondering why such a man deserves a place in this book. Is he the executioner or the victim? Does his execution in 1938 mean that the revenge of history itself got him?

It is not easy to answer these questions, but it is indisputable that he was illegally repressed in 1938 (after all, he was not arrested for creating his hellish machine of lawlessness, and the charges of sabotage against him were, of course, falsified).

Nikolai Vasilyevich Krylenko was born on May 2, 1885 in the village of Bekhteevo, in what is now the Smolensk region, in the family of a political internal exile. Krylenko's hometown now features a park and a street named after him. Memorial evenings are held annually on the birthday of the famous local.

The future leader of Soviet chess players graduated from two universities: the Faculty of History and Philology in St. Petersburg (in 1909) and the Faculty of Law in Kharkov (in 1914). At the age of nineteen, he joined the Bolshevik Party, was an active participant in the revolution of 1905-1907 and the October Revolution, and joined the first Council of People's Commissars (he was a member of the Commissariat for Military and Naval Affairs). On November 9, 1917, by Lenin's decision, Ensign Krylenko was appointed Supreme Commander-in-Chief (in place of General Nikolai Dukhonin, who was removed from office) and People's Commissar for Military Affairs.

Krylenko worked in Soviet legal institutions from March 1918, and organized the Soviet court and prosecutor's office. Solzhenitsyn cites an interesting fact about the very beginning of the Supreme Commander's legal career: "At the beginning of 1918, the newly-baked Admiral Alexei Schastny was sentenced to death for refusing to sink the Baltic Fleet. A commotion arose in the courtroom, as the death penalty had been abolished on October 28, 1917. Prosecutor Krylenko explained: 'What are you worried about? The death penalty has been abolished. And we aren't going to execute Schastny – we are going to shoot him'. And he was shot."

Krylenko, being the prosecutor in the case of F. M. Skosyrev (1918), commented on denunciations, which were just beginning to sprout: "We do not see anything shameful in this, we consider it our duty... once a person recognizes that this work is required in the interests of the revolution, he must go and do it." Commander-in-chief Krylenko gave the British chief diplomat in Moscow Bruce Lockhart the impression of a "degenerate epileptic". (R. H. Bruce Lockhart, *Memoirs of a British Agent*. London, 1932, p. 257.)

Anyway, fairness demands that we tell you about Krylenko's act of bravery. In 1924, Felix Dzerzhinsky wrote a note to the Politburo where he proposed that, in order to combat banditry, the police and the criminal investigation department should be promptly subordinated to the OGPU (the name of the secret police at the time), and that this organ be allowed to consider cases of all participants in bandit raids extrajudicially.

This proposal was strongly opposed by People's Commissar of Justice Krylenko, who wrote the following letter to the Politburo: "I consider it necessary to categorically speak out against... the suggestions by Comrade Dzerzhinsky... Recently, the OGPU has adopted the practice of expanding its jurisdiction by applying to the CEC [Central Executive Committee] Presidium for permission to consider particular cases extrajudicially. Moreover, it first considers the case and passes sentence, and then asks the CEC to approve such a sentence."

In the note that Krylenko sent to the Politburo, he drew attention to the fact that the OGPU had the right to extrajudicial consideration of cases of counter-revolutionary crimes, espionage, gangs of bandits, on-duty crimes of OGPU employees, counterfeiters, and, in any other case as an exception if it received special permission from the Presidium of the CEC.

In practice, as Krylenko noted, "exceptions have become the rule... there is literally not a single article of the Criminal Code under which the OGPU would not consider itself entitled to take cases to its proceedings". In addition, a lot of cases were considered at each meeting of the "judicial troika". And the "troika" passed harsh sentences. According to Krylenko's own data, in 1924 they sentenced 650 people to the firing squad.

Concluding his note to the Politburo, Krylenko wrote that "it has turned out that every more or less significant case passing through the OGPU ends, as a rule, with an extrajudicial verdict and does not reach the court", and proposed strictly limiting those categories of crimes that could be considered out of court, mitigating penalties, and also strengthening the prosecutor's supervision of the OGPU's activities.

But all Krylenko's comments and suggestions were rejected by the OGPU. In its response to his note, it accused the Prosecutor's Office of lacking "understanding of the political situation" and claimed that Krylenko, its chief, was only concerned about articles of laws, and ignored "the fight against counter-revolution and prevention of the growth of political parties, terrorist groups, etc". Moreover, the OGPU replied that it did not consider its sentences to be too harsh.

Krylenko combined work on creating the Soviet court system with support for sports. Nikolai Vasilyevich was one of the leaders of the Pamir expeditions in 1928-1934, and headed the All-Union Society of Proletarian Tourism and the mountaineering section.

From 1924 until his arrest in 1938, Krylenko headed the All-Union Chess and Checkers Section. Mikhail Botvinnik called Nikolai Krylenko the "Supreme Commander-in-Chief of the Soviet Chess School".

Krylenko was fond of chess since childhood. He played chess as a student and during his period of underground Bolshevik activity, too. In 1924, Krylenko established the popular magazine *64*, and in 1935 the magazine was reorganized as a newspaper at his suggestion. And, most importantly, Nikolai Krylenko was the chairman while remaining an active player. He participated in competitions, both over-the-board and correspondence.

To the question: what is chess – a sport or an art? – Krylenko responded: "Above all, chess is art! The richness of ideas and the beauty of combinations put this kind of mental creativity on a par with other manifestations of art: poetry, painting, and music. The element of struggle also gives chess a sporty character".

Game No. 57
N. Krylenko – V. Likum
Championship of the Krasnopresnensky district of Moscow, 1925
Evans Gambit C52
Commentary by S. Grodzensky

1.e4 e5 2.♘f3 ♘c6 3.♗c4 ♗c5 4.b4 ♗xb4 5.c3 ♗a5 6.0-0 (theory prefers the immediate 6.d4) **6...d6 7.d4 ♗d7.** The main variation here is 7...♘f6 8.♕a4 exd4 9.e5 ♘e4 10.cxd4 0-0 11.d5 ♘c5 12.♕a3.

8.♕b3 ♕e7 9.dxe5

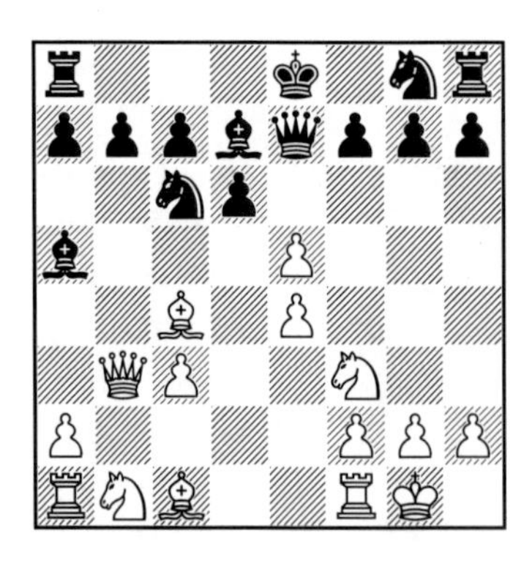

9...♗b6? By returning the gambit pawn too late, black gets a worse position. He should have continued 9...dxe5 10.♖d1 ♖d8 (or 10...0-0-0) 11.♖d5 ♗b6 12.♗b5 with chances of launching an attack.

10.exd6 cxd6 11.♕d1 (white wants to keep the two bishops) **11...0-0-0?!** A hasty decision. Perhaps it was better to play 11...♘f6 12.♗g5 0-0.

12.♘a3 (the moves 12.♗a3 or 12.♘bd2 look better) **12...♗g4! 13.♕d3 ♘f6?** The variation 13...♘e5! 14.♘xe5 dxe5 15.♕g3 ♘f6 16.♗g5 h5 left more chances for a successful defense. Now white captures the initiative and launches his strongest attack.

14.♗d5 ♖he8.

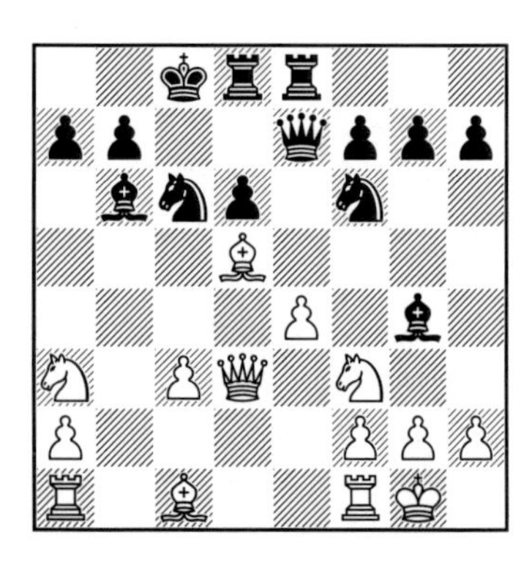

15.♕c4! This move gives white great practical chances of starting an attack, even if it's mostly off the radar screens of computers.

15...♕d7 16.♘d4 ♗c5. The continuation 16...♗xd4 17.cxd4 ♘xd5 18.exd5 ♗e2 19.dxc6 bxc6 20.♕c3 ♗xf1 21.♔xf1 f6 22.♖b1 with an advantage for white, was no better.

17.♘xc6 bxc6 18.♖b1 ♔c7 19.♗f4 ♗xa3. The move 19...cxd5 would have been met by 20.♕xc5+ ♕c6 21.♕xa7+ and checkmate coming; in the case of 19...♘xd5, the move 20.exd5 ♗b6 21.♘b5+ solves the problem, and white wins.

20.♕a6 ♖b8 21.♕xa7+ ♔d8 22.♖xb8+ ♔e7 23.♖b7. Black resigned.

Game No. 58
A. Rassadnev – N. Krylenko
Correspondence game, 1927-1928
Reti Opening A05
Commentary by N. Grigoriev

1.♘f3 ♘f6 2.c4 g6 3.d4 ♗g7 4.g3 d5 5.♘c3 0-0

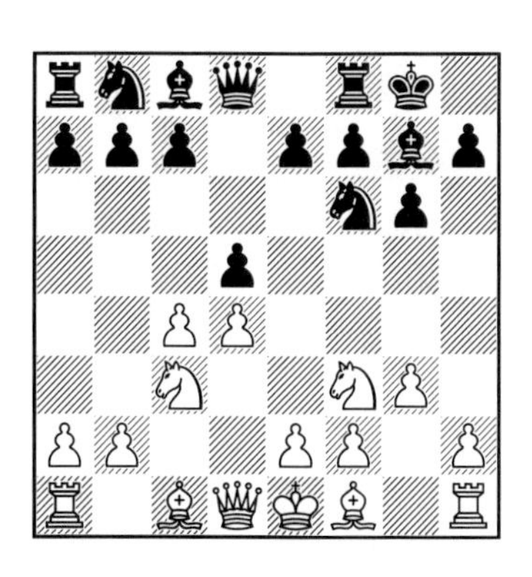

6.cxd5. The beginning of a dubious plan aimed at creating a pawn center. White actually did get a center, but one that should bring him not joy, only trouble. That is why it was better not to build broad plans yet, but to continue to develop quietly (6.♗g2).

6...♘xd5 7.e4 ♘xc3 8.bxc3. Isn't this a center? It will soon turn out that white's play is not as good as it seems now.

8...♗g4 9.h3. Continuing 9.♗a3 would have led to a clear advantage for black after 9...c5.

9...♗xf3 10.♕xf3 c5 11.d5 f5 12.♗d2 fxe4? Disappointing haste that could have destroyed all the previous successful work. He should have just played 12...♘d7.

13.♕xe4 ♖f5. With a double attack: aiming at both d5 and e5. However, the first threat turns out to be imaginary, while the second one can be easily repelled.

14.f4! ♔f8 15.♗g2 ♘d7

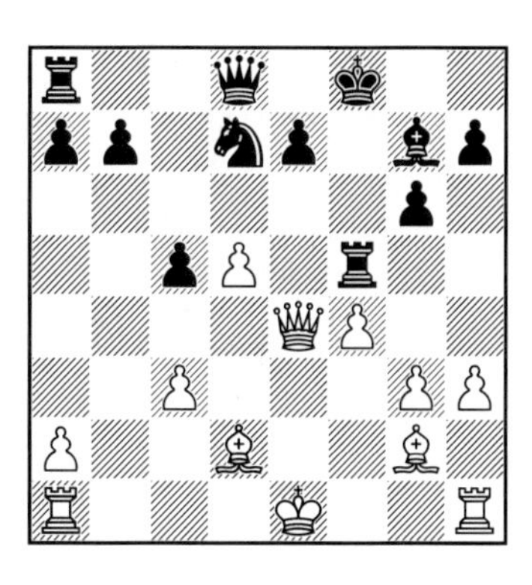

16.d6? White has failed to take advantage of the blessing that fell into his arms because of black's mistake on the 12th move. With 16.g4! he would have posed his opponent a difficult problem: either to retreat with the rook, risking falling under white's attack on the f-file, or making an exchange sacrifice via 16...♘f6 17.♕e6 ♖xd5. In the latter case, black would have achieved a good game, but at the cost of some material deficit. After the move in the text, the crisis is successfully resolved in black's favor and the game continues as though nothing had happened.

16...exd6 17.♕xb7 ♕e8+ 18.♔f2 ♖b8 19.♕e4. If 19.♖he1, then 19...♕d8! 20.♕c6 (indirectly parrying the threat of 20...♖b2) 20...♘e5!, and the black rook gets to the feeding rank anyway.

19...♖b2 20.♕xe8+ ♔xe8 21.♖he1+ ♔d8 22.♖e2 ♘e5! (22...♖xd2! 23.♖xd2 ♗xc3–+ – S.G.) **23.♗e4.** White has a weak c3 pawn, while black's pawn advantage in the center plays an important role.

23...♖f7. The subsequent events show that it was possible to retreat with the rook to f8 immediately without losing any time.

24.♖d1 ♔c7 25.♗d5 ♖f8 26.♔e3 ♘d7 27.♔d3 ♗f6 28.♗e1 ♖xe2 29.♔xe2 ♘b6 30.♗b3. 30.c4 was not a good continuation, since after 30...♘d5 it becomes impossible to capture with a rook due to 31...♖e8+ and 32...♖e4. It was somewhat better to move the bishop away immediately along the other diagonal (a8-h1).

30...c4! 31.♗c2 ♔c6 32.♗e4+ d5 33.♗h1 ♖e8+! Taking the opportunity to chase the white king to the side. And indeed, 34.♔d2 will be followed by 34...♘a4 35.♔c2 ♖e2+ 36.♔b1 ♗xc3! 37.♗xd5+ ♔c5, and black wins.

34.♔f2 ♔c5.

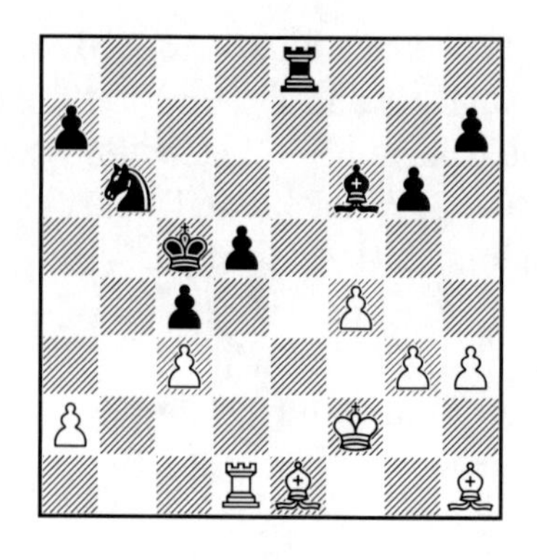

An important role now belongs to the black king.

35.♗d2. In contrast to black, the white pieces, including both bishops, are doomed to eke out a miserable existence. The advance of the white pawns on the kingside is pointless.

35...♖d8 36.♔e2 ♘a4 37.♖c1 d4 38.cxd4+ ♗xd4 39.♗e4 c3 40.♗e1 ♖e8 41.♔f3 ♔c4 42.♗c6. Or 42.g4 ♘c5 43.♗c2 ♖e3+ 44.♔g2 ♘d3 45.♗xd3+ ♔xd3, and black wins at the very least because he has the sacrifice on e1 available.

42...♖e3+ 43.♔g2 (the variation 43.♔g4 ♘c5, threatening 44...♘d3 would lose). **43...♖e2+ 44.♔f3 ♖xa2 45.♗e4 ♘c5 46.♗b1 ♖b2 47.♗c2 a5.** Black intends to create another passed pawn. The continuation 47...♘d3 48.♗xd3+ ♔xd3 was also winning.

48.f5 a4 49.fxg6 hxg6 50.♗xg6 a3 51.h4 ♘b3. White resigned.

From the mid-1920s, Nikolai Krylenko was often referred to as the "leader of Soviet chess players". And on the first page of the magazine *64*.

Chess and checkers in the workers club (1927, No. 13), the following appeal was printed: "The editorial board of the magazine *Chess and checkers in the workers club* ("64") is opening a collection of contributions for the construction of an airplane called the 'N. V. Krylenko Chess-Player Plane' with an appeal to all chess and checkers players of the USSR to support this initiative."

We do not know whether anybody managed to actually build this "chess-player plane", but we get a sense of Krylenko's autocratic mania. Increasingly often, the supreme commander promoted a class approach to chess, and this also manifested itself in inherent rigor – a strict, unyielding observance of principles.

In the late 1920s and early 1930s, Krylenko was a particularly zealous defender of extrajudicial repressions. In 1930, he wrote: "For bourgeois Europe and for the broad circles of the liberal intelligentsia, it may seem monstrous that the Soviet government does not always deal with pests in a judicial process. But every conscious worker and peasant will agree that the Soviet government is doing the right thing."

Further, Krylenko did not object to the Law of December 1, 1934 introduced following Kirov's assassination allowing for 'terrorism" cases to be heard and sentences implemented in just 10 days, all of which contradicted the Constitution, or to the repressions of 1935, 1936 and 1937. Well, back in 1931, Krylenko became the People's Commissar for Justice of the RSFSR, thereby giving up his duties as a prosecutor of the republic (the case of the "Union Bureau of the Mensheviks" proved to be his swansong in this role), and then in 1936 he was appointed People's Commissar for Justice of the whole of the USSR.

In 1934, Krylenko was awarded the degree of Doctor of State and Social Sciences. The People's Commissar and Doctor of Sciences enthusiastically backed Vyshinsky when the latter declared: "No evidence is required to find a defendant guilty of treason, espionage or sabotage, in any counter-revolutionary crime.

Москва, 27.VII.35.
В/письмо получил 25.VII.35. Положение нашей партии показал мастерам - Зубареву и Панову а также, сегодня, гроссмейстеру Флору. Все они одного мнения, что партия должна закончиться в ничью. Поэтому вторично предлагаю Вам ничью.
НКрыл

Admission of guilt by the accused is enough."

Krylenko not only supported this "doctrine", but developed it further, leading the drafting of the criminal code according to which a person could be charged with criminal responsibility even if they had not committed a specific crime but simply for being in a "dangerous state of personality". However, his bill was not destined to be legislated, since its author was himself soon declared an enemy of the people and a traitor to the Motherland, and subsequently shot.

"The task of the judicial authorities is to anticipate all possible attacks of the class enemy, to skillfully recognize them, and to direct against the enemy the powerful instrument of repression that is placed in their hands," Krylenko wrote in 1935. "Let the bourgeoisie of the whole world and all its henchmen inside and outside our country know: we will not be afraid to mercilessly crush the writhing reptile of the counter-revolution, to wipe anyone who dares to stand on the road of our planned socialist construction out of existence!" – this was in an article by Doctor of Sciences Krylenko in 1936. It is painful to admit, but the "leader of the Soviet chess players" was one of the theorists of Stalinism. Besides, in his works he wrote of his admiration for both the "father of peoples" and his Constitution!

Meanwhile, Krylenko put his heart into organizing the Moscow international tournaments and continued to participate in competitions himself. All that happened.

In the next game, the leader of the chess players played against a famous study composer.

Game No. 59
A. Gerbstman – N. Krylenko
64 correspondence tournament, 1927
Reti Opening A13
Commentary by S. Grodzensky

1.♘f3 e6 2.c4 f5 3.b3. Usually white chooses between 3.d4 ♘f6 4.e3 d5 5.♗d3 ♗d6 6.0-0 and 3.g3 ♘f6 4.d4 d5 5.♗g2 c6 6.0-0.

3...♘f6 4.♗b2 ♗e7 5.g3 0-0 6.♗g2 d6 7.d3 (7.d4 looks more natural) **7...e5 8.♘bd2**

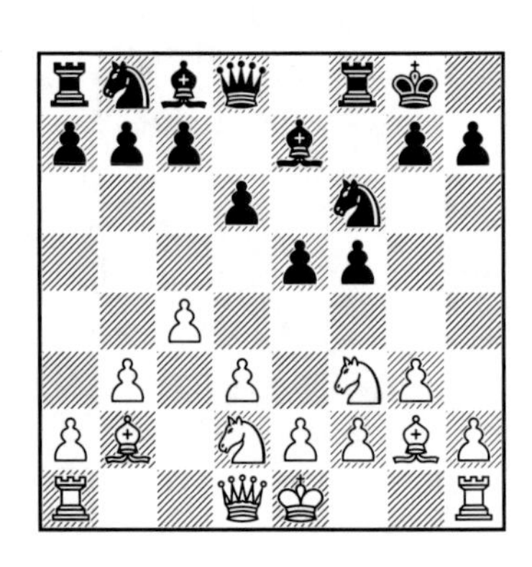

8...e4? Black makes a rash thrust with his e-pawn. It was necessary to simply develop the queenside pieces via 8...♗d7 and 9...♘c6.

9.♘d4. What was white afraid of? After 9.dxe4 fxe4 10.♘xe4 he would have got a healthy extra pawn with better development. Now black finally manages to carry out his plan.

9...e3! 10.fxe3 ♘g4 11.♘f1 ♗g5 12.h3. White voluntarily returns the e3 pawn. After 12.♘c2 ♕e7 13.♕d2 ♖e8 14.h3 black would have had to exchange his active pieces to win back the pawn.

12...♘xe3 13.♘xe3 ♗xe3 14.♘f3 (preventing 14...♕g5) **14... c5 15.♗c1 f4 16.gxf4 ♗xf4 17.♗xf4 ♖xf4.** As a result, the white king occupies a precarious position.

18.e3 ♕e7 19.♕e2 ♖f6 20.♔d2 (20.0-0-0 was probably better) **20... ♘c6**

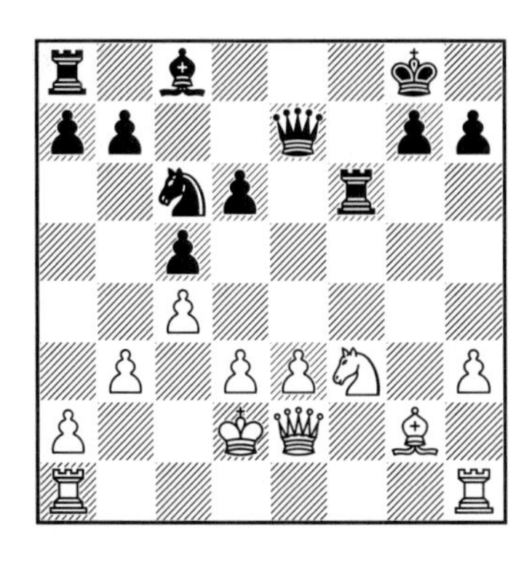

21.♘g5? Black's position looks better, and therefore white should have thought about defense, for example, 21.♘h2 with the following 22.♘g4. Black now refutes white's risky move.

21...♕e5! 22.♗d5+ ♗e6 (it was enough to continue 22...♔h8) **23.♗xe6+** (23.♘xe6 will be met by 23...♕b2+ and 24...♕xa1) **23... ♖xe6 24.♖ag1.** Not 24.♘xe6 ♕b2+ 25.♔e1 ♕xa1+ 26.♕d1 ♕e5!.

24...♕b2+ 25.♔e1 ♕c1+ (25... ♕c3+ was even more energetic) **26.♔f2 ♖f8+ 27.♘f3 ♕c3** (threatening 28...♘d4!) **28.♔g2 ♖g6+ 29.♔h2 ♘e5**

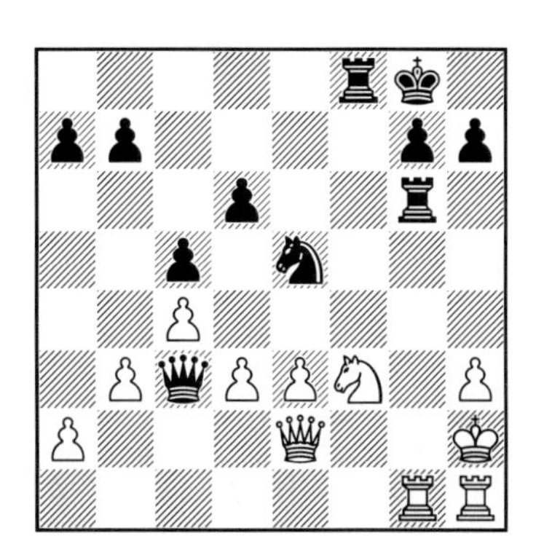

30.♘g5? This continuation loses immediately. The variation 30.♘e1 ♖gf6 could have prolonged the resistance (the line 30...♕xe1? 31.♖xe1 ♘f3+ 32.♕xf3 ♖xf3 33.♖hf1 gave nothing, and the position is close to drawn) 31.♖g2! (but not 31.♖f1?? due to 31...♖xf1 32.♖xf1 ♖xf1 33.♕xf1 ♕xe1! and 34...♘f3+), and black will have to make greater efforts to achieve victory.

30...h6 31.♘e4 ♘f3+ 32.♕xf3 ♕e5+. This does not miss the win, but a more natural finish could have been obtained with 32...♖xf3! 33.♖xg6 (capturing the queen via 33.♘xc3 is impossible due to checkmate in two moves) 33...♕xd3.

In any case, white now resigned because of 33.♕g3 ♖xg3 34.♖xg3 ♖f3.

Game No. 60
V. Likum – N. Krylenko
Match game, 1928
Alekhine's Defense B02
Commentary by F. Duz-Khotimirsky

1.e4 ♘f6 2.d4 (this sacrifice is incorrect) **2...♘xe4 3.♗d3 d5 4.♗f4 ♘f6 5.c3 ♗g4! 6.♘f3 ♘bd7** (it would be better to develop the bishop beforehand with 6...e6 and then 7...♗d6) **7.♘bd2**

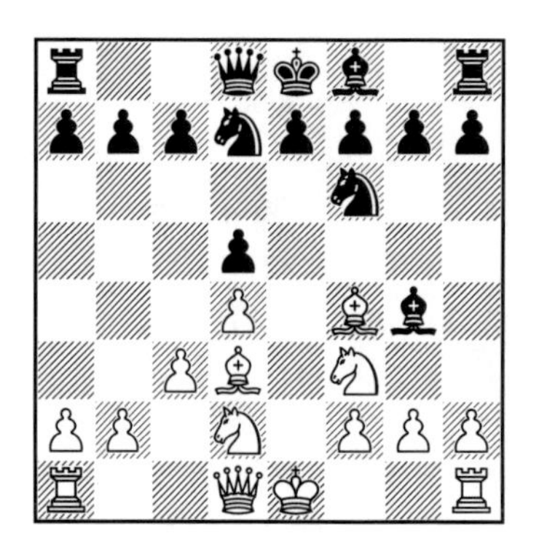

7...♘h5! An interesting plan aimed at destroying the annoying f4 bishop, which, unfortunately, black failed to implement.

8.♗e3 (it was better to accept the exchange) **8...c5?** A poor move. By playing 8...e5!, black could have obtained a clear advantage.

9.dxc5 e5 10.♗e2! (prevents all of black's threats) **10...e4 11.♘d4 ♗xe2 12.♕xe2 ♘hf6.** Black's attack has been repelled with material equality restored.

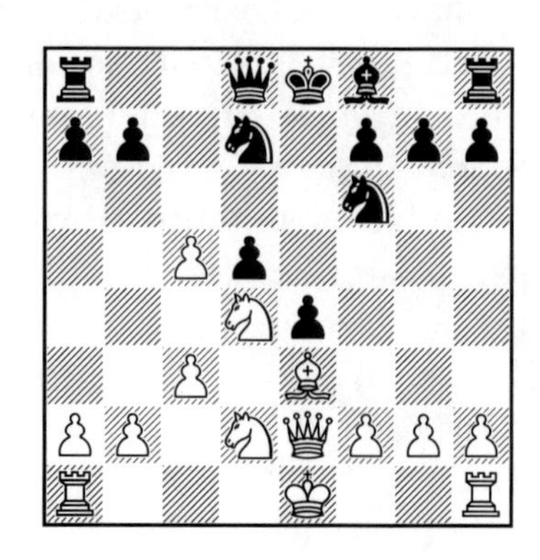

13.c6. At first glance, this continuation is very strong, but in fact it gives black new attacking opportunities.

13...bxc6 14.♘xc6 ♕c7 15.♘d4 ♘c5! (launching a formidable attack) **16.0-0 ♘d3 17.♘2b3** (17. f3+– – S.G.) **17...♗d6!** (forces a weakening of the king's position) **18.g3 ♕d7! 19.♖ad1 0-0 20.f3 ♕h3! 21.fxe4 dxe4 22.♖d2 ♘h5 23.♘c1**

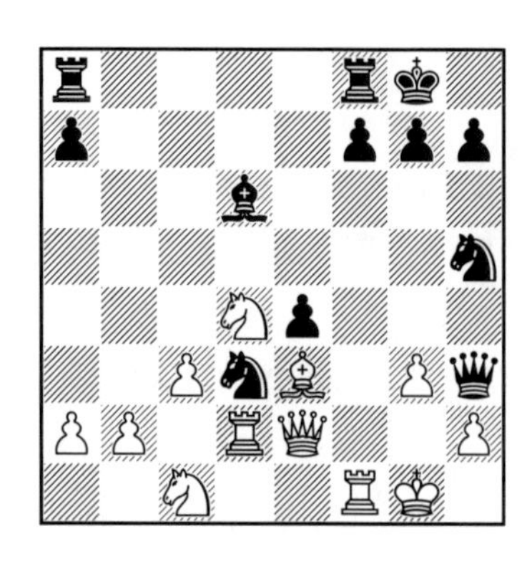

23...♗xg3 (23...♘xg3!–+ – S.G.). This sacrifice should be recognized as correct, logically flowing from the conceived plan. If black avoids a sacrifice, white will immediately strengthen his weak kingside and, with an open f-file, a strong d4 knight and formidable pawns on the queenside, can easily get an advantage.

24.hxg3 ♕xg3+ 25.♔h1 ♕h3+ 26.♔g1 ♕g3+ 27.♔h1 ♕h4+. Rejecting perpetual check, black had reason to play for a win. In the worst case, he could count on a drawn ending.

28.♔g1 ♘g3 29.♕g2? It was necessary to play 29.♕h2 and after 29...♕xh2+ 30.♖xh2 ♘xf1 31.♔xf1, the players would have reached a complex endgame, but with great winning chances for black. (Actually this was the best move – S.G.)

29...♘xf1 30.♕xf1 (A blunder turning a clear advantage into a loss. 30.♘f5! – S.G.) **30...♕g3+ 31.♔h1 ♕xe3 32.♖g2? ♕xc1.** White resigned.

Game No. 61
V. Zbandutto – N. Krylenko
Correspondence Tournament,
1935-1936
Vienna Game C29
Commentary by S. Grodzensky

1.e4 e5 2.♘c3 ♘f6 3.f4 d6 4.♘f3 ♘c6 5.♗c4. The main continuation in this variation of the Vienna Game is 5.♗b5.

5...♗e7 6.d3 0-0 7.0-0 exf4 (after 7...♗g4 8.h3 black is forced to perform an exchange on f3) **8.♗xf4 ♗e6**

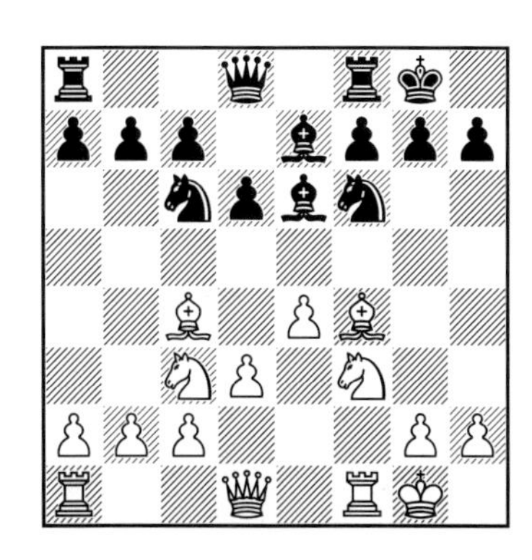

9.♘d5? White loses his opening advantage. The correct continuation was 9.♗b3.

9...♗xd5 10.exd5 (10.♗xd5 ♘xd5 11.exd5 ♘b4 12.c4 is easier for white to handle, even if the computer is indifferent) **10...♘b4 11.♘g5 h6.** If now 11...♘bxd5 then 12.♗xd5 ♘xd5 13.♘xh7 ♘xf4 (13...♔xh7? 14.♕h5+ and 15.♕xd5) 14.♘xf8 ♘d5 15.♘h7! with an advantage.

12.♘e4 ♘bxd5 13.♘xf6+ (the continuation 13.♗xd5 ♘xd5 14.♗xh6 gxh6 15.♕g4+ ♔h8 16.♕h5 ♗g5! 17.h4 ♗e3+ and 18... f5! would not have brought victory) **13...♘xf6 14.d4 d5! 15.♗d3 ♘e4 16.♕h5 ♗g5 17.♖ae1.**

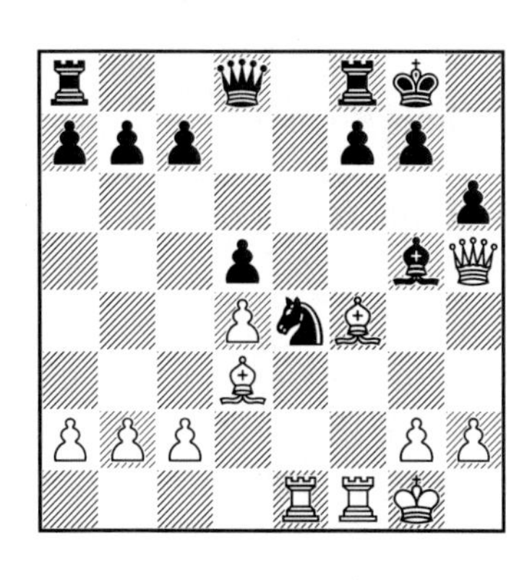

17...♕f6!?, threatening both 18...♕xd4+, and 18...♗xf4. However, it was possible to play 17...♗xf4 18.♖xf4 ♕d6 19.♖ef1 ♕e6 20.♗xe4 right away, with better chances for black.

18.♗e5 ♕b6 19.♖xe4? 19.♗xe4 was best but still tough for white.

19...g6 (19...dxe4 would have won immediately) **20.♕g4?.** White could have tried to pose black some problems via for example 20.♕f3 dxe4 21.♕xe4 and now hoping for 21...♕xb2?? 22.h4.

20...dxe4 21.♕xe4 ♖ae8 22.♗c4 ♖e7 23.♔h1 ♔h7 24.♕d3 f6 25.♗b3 ♖d8 26.♗g3 ♖xd4 27.♕f3 ♖e3 28.♕f2 ♕a6 (28...♖ee4 could have shortened the path to victory) **29.♖e1 ♖xe1+ 30.♕xe1 ♖e4 31.♕d1 ♕e2 32.♕xe2 ♖xe2.** White resigned.

The next game took place in a mixed tournament for first and second category players.

Game No. 62
N. Krylenko – A. Serebryakov
Moscow, 1935
Queen's Gambit D00
Commentary by S. Grodzensky

1.d4 d5 2.♘d2. It seems that white has refused to fight for an opening advantage.

2...♘f6 3.c4 c6 4.♘gf3 e6 5.e3 ♗e7 (it's time to attack the center through 5...c5) **6.♗d3 ♘bd7 7.b3 0-0 8.0-0 ♕c7 9.♗b2 ♗d6?** (black loses time and gives white the opportunity to seize the initiative) **10.c5 ♗e7 11.♖c1 e5?** (and this miscalculation puts black in a critical position) **12.dxe5** (perhaps 12.♘xe5 ♘xe5 13.dxe5 was stronger) **12...♘g4.**

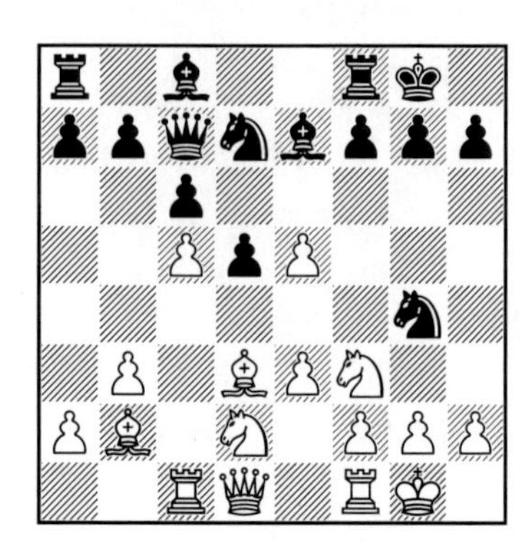

13.e6 fxe6 (it was necessary to play 13...♘xc5) **14.h3 ♘gf6 15.♘g5 ♘xc5 16.♗xf6 ♖xf6 17.♗xh7+ ♔f8 18.♕h5 ♗d6 19.♗g6 ♔e7 20.♕h7.** It was possible to win by playing 20.♘h7, for example, 20...♖xg6 21.♕xg6 ♔d8 22.♘g5.

20...♖xg6 (it was possible to continue fighting only via 20...♔d8) **21.♕xg6 ♔f8 22.♘h7+ ♔e7 23.♕xg7+.** Black resigned.

Game No. 63
Y. Karakhan – N. Krylenko
Moscow, 1937
Sicilian Defense B62
Commentary by S. Grodzensky

1.e4 c5 2.♘f3 ♘c6 3.d4 cxd4 4.♘xd4 ♘f6 5.♘c3 d6 6.♗g5 e6 7.♘db5?! The main theoretical continuation here is 7.♕d2.

7...♗e7 (7...a6 8.♗xf6 gxf6 was preferable) **8.♕d2 0-0 9.0-0-0 ♕a5 10.f4 ♖d8 11.♗c4 a6 12.♗xf6** (it was probably better to play 12.♘d4) **12...♗xf6.** By sacrificing a pawn, black gets rich tactical opportunities.

13.♘xd6 ♗e7 14.e5.

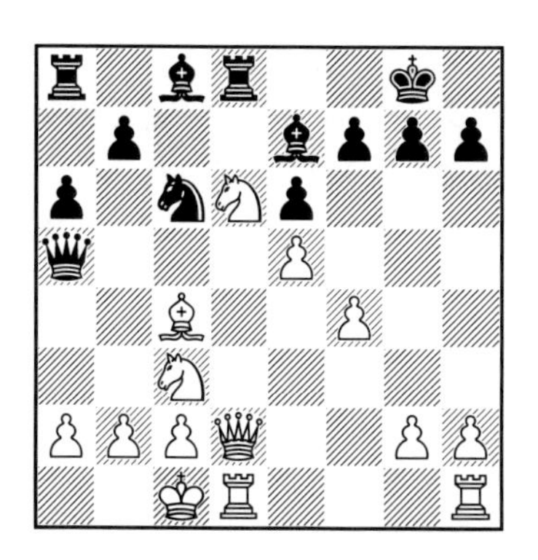

14...♘xe5! 15.fxe5 ♕xe5? The correct continuation was 15...♖xd6!, and if 16.exd6, then 16...♗g5 or 16.♕e3 ♖c6 with a good game for black.

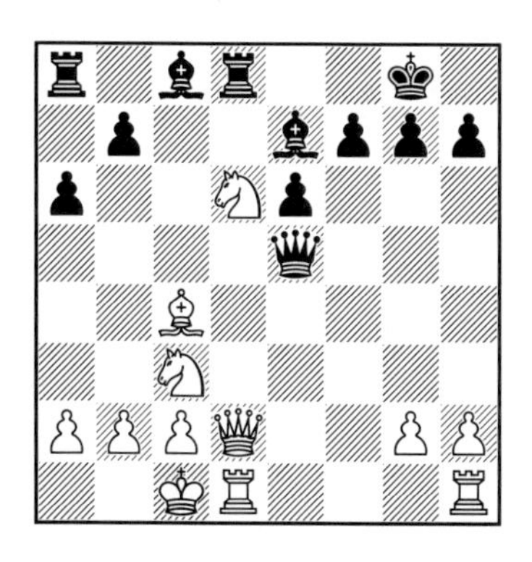

16.♘xf7! ♔xf7 17.♕f2+ ♕f6 18.♕e2 ♕f4+ 19.♔b1 ♖xd1+ 20.♘xd1 ♗f6 21.♖e1 ♕xh2 22.♗xe6+ ♗xe6 23.♕xe6+ ♔f8 24.♕d5 ♕c7 25.g4 ♖d8 26.♕f5 h6 27.♘f2 ♔g8 28.♘d3 (28.♘e4 was more active) **28...♕b6 29.♕g6 ♕d4 30.a3.** Draw agreed.

In 1938, at the first session of the Supreme Soviet of the USSR of the 1st convocation, Krylenko was criticized, formally – for spending too much time on mountaineering, "when others were doing their job". He was arrested on January 31, 1938, and was charged with having relations with the anti-Soviet organization of the right, which was allegedly headed by Bukharin. He was further accused of establishing a "wrecking organization" and carrying out subversive activities in the judicial authorities. The "trial" lasted 20 minutes. On July 29, 1938, Krylenko was shot in accordance with the verdict of the Military Board of the Supreme Court of the USSR (VKVS), as part of the case of the "counterrevolutionary fascist-terrorist organization of mountaineers and tourists". He was buried at the Kommunarka execution site. The Military Board of the Supreme Court of the USSR rehabilitated Krylenko on July 29, 1955, and the Party Control Commission restored him to the party on October 7, 1955. (Russian State Archive of Modern History, f. 6, op. 3, d. 834, pp. 25-29). In the Russian-language memoirs of R. V. Ivanov-Razumnik (*Prisons and Deportations*, Chekhov Publishing

House, New York, 1953) the author mentions that he was sitting with Krylenko in the same cell in Butyrka prison, and the sleeping place of the former commander-in-chief was under the bunks.

The author of *The Gulag Archipelago* has the following opinion on this: "I can imagine it very vividly (I had such an experience myself): there are such bunks that you reach only by crawling on your stomach across the dirty asphalt floor, but the beginner who has not got used to it crawls on all fours. He will stick his head in, but the protruding backside will remain outside. I think it was especially difficult for the supreme prosecutor to get used to it, and his not yet emaciated backside stuck out for a long time celebrating the glory of Soviet justice. Being a sinful person, I imagine this stuck out backside with malice, and during all the long description of these cases, it somehow calms me down." (Alexander Solzhenitsyn *The Gulag Archipelago, Vol. 1.*)

Why did Krylenko suffer? In the novel written by Anatoly Rybakov *The Thirty-fifth and Other Years*, we find Stalin's thoughts about Krylenko:

However, the People's Commissar of Justice, Comrade Krylenko, opposed the publication of such a decree (on the establishment of the death penalty for minors – S.G.). He even asked for an appointment with HIM. HE, of course, did not accept it. HE possesses accurate reports: Krylenko claims that such a law is unprecedented, has no analogies in world judicial practice, that supposedly no twelve-year-old children are executed in any country in the world, that children can become victims of false accusations, or even just a misunderstanding, that the acceptation of such a decree in the eighteenth year of Soviet power will make a terrible impression abroad, will undermine the prestige of the Soviet state.

Why did Comrade Krylenko suddenly become so humane, why did he suddenly take bourgeois public opinion into account?... Previously, when acting as an investigator at the trials of the Industrial Party, the Mensheviks and others, he ignored it. Just recently, Comrade Krylenko argued: "To demand absolute objectivity from a judge is the purest utopia" – he insisted on narrowing the rights to a defense, since, as he correctly said at the time, the Soviet court itself protects the accused; he virtually proposed abolishing the procedural code, called it "a fragment of bourgeois law". And suddenly he completely changed his mind. Besides the fact that he publicly renounced his views, he published a book last year called Lenin's Opinion on the Court and Criminal Policy, *in which he advocated revolutionary legality, absolute thoroughness, and strict compliance with all procedural norms...*

Right after the Mensheviks trial, Krylenko applied to join the People's Commissariat of Justice. It suddenly became clear that Krylenko does not want to appear in court anymore: he saw where everything is heading... At the 17th Congress, Krylenko was not elected either to the Party Central Committee or to the Party Control Commission. This was a warning to him. He took offense but didn't draw any conclusions. Today is his 50th birthday. Let him read a greeting from his mountain climbers in Pravda. The Central Committee is not going to welcome him. It is a warning, too. The last one. Let's see whether he draws any conclusions from that or again throws a spanner in Vyshinsky's works. (Rybakov A. *The Thirty-fifth and Other Years,* Friendship of Nations, 1986, No. 9).

Did Krylenko have an epiphany, did he really throw a spanner in the works of the infernal machine?! Was he repressed because of the fact that he opposed the decree on the establishment of the death penalty for minors?!

I would like to think that all this was not the fiction of a novelist, but the truth...

Vladimir Fridberg – The Fate of the Prosecutor

In the autumn of 1930, the First Plenum of the chess and checkers section of the All-Union Council of Physical Education elected a new leadership of Soviet chess players. Vladimir Fridberg, who headed the Moscow section in the late 1920s, joined the ruling body – the executive bureau. Issue No. 22-23 of the magazine *64* that same year published an editorial by Fridberg, called "Lessons of the Big Moscow Chess Championship", written in an acutely critical tone. Everyone gets criticized by the author – both the organizers and the participants.

After firing a hail of criticisms, Fridberg continues: "The reader undoubtedly has the question: what positive experience did the participants get after the championship? In all conscience, I would find it difficult to give a positive answer to this question." After bestowing restrained praise on the young chess players who achieved success, he also reproaches them for failing to value public work sufficiently. This ideological article ends with the following words: "The success of the upcoming competitions exclusively depends on the extent to which they will be tied to the public work of chess and checkers organizations. A strong connection will ensure the best outcome."

Fridberg was known in the capital's chess circles in the 1920s and early 1930s, until he suddenly disappeared from the pages of the chess press. That suddenness, and the fact that it happened in the year 1937, aroused your author's suspicion: and I discovered that Fridberg was ground under the millstones of the machine of arbitrariness.

Your author expressed his assumption in a note to an article about Krylenko published in *64. Chess Review* (1990, No. 21, pp. 24-26), and appealed to readers to share what they knew about the fate of Vladimir Isaakovich Fridberg.

Literally the day after the publication of the magazine, one of the regular readers, a first-rank chess player with more than half a century of experience, Kirill Vladimirovich Zlotkovsky, called me. He was none other than Fridberg's son.

Kirill Vladimirovich bears his mother's surname, but he remembers his father, who died in Stalin's jail in 1938, very well. Based on Zlotkovsky's story, we have reconstituted his father's biography.

He was born in 1884 in a Belarusian village in the family of a doctor. Vladimir managed to get a higher legal education, which was not at all easy for a boy from a village in pre-revolutionary Russia. Sworn attorney Fridberg enthusiastically met the October Revolution, and in 1919 he joined the Bolshevik Party and moved to the Prosecutor's Office of the RSFSR, where he worked as an assistant to Krylenko until 1931.

At the same time (perhaps under the influence of his superior), he seriously started studying chess. Playing in departmental competitions, he gained the first category.

One of Fridberg's games was published in the magazine *64* in 1931.

Game No. 64
N. Krylenko – V. Fridberg
1931
Queen's Gambit D35
Commentary by S. Grodzensky

1.d4 ♘f6 2.c4 e6 3.♘c3 d5 4.e3 c6 5.♕c2 ♘bd7 6.b3 ♗b4 7.a3 ♗xc3+ 8.♕xc3 0-0

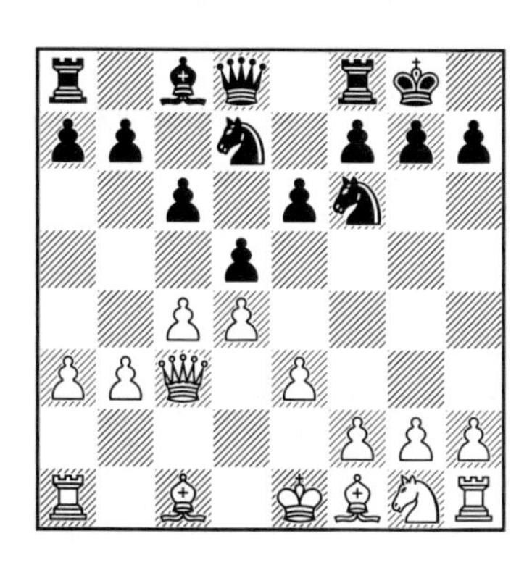

9.c5. (9.♘f3 looks more solid) **9...a5.** The variation 9...e5 10.dxe5 ♘e4 11.♕c2 ♘xe5 12.♗b2 ♘g4 deserved consideration.

10.b4 ♖e8 11.♘f3 ♕c7. The

continuation 11...♘e4! 12.♕b2 b6 13.♗d3 axb4 14.axb4 ♖xa1 15.♕xa1 bxc5 and 16...e5 was more energetic.

12.♗d3 b6 13.♗b2 b5? Locking the c8 bishop out of the game. The move 13...♗a6 seemed most natural.

14.0-0 a4 15.♖ae1 h6 16.♕c2 ♘f8 17.♘e5 ♗b7 18.f3 ♘6d7 19.e4 ♘xe5 20.dxe5 ♖ad8 21.exd5 exd5. It would have been worse to continue 21...♖xd5 22.♗e4 ♖d7 23.f4 ♖ed8 24.♗c3! with an advantage for white.

22.f4 ♗c8 23.f5

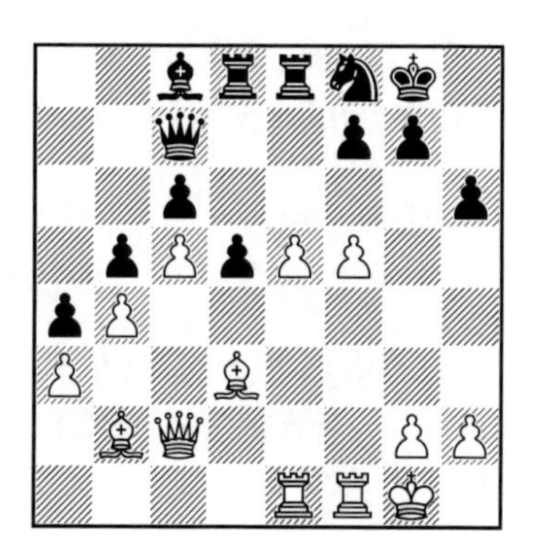

23...d4! A successful attempt to seize the initiative even if, objectively, black is completely lost here.

24.♕e2 ♖d5 25.♕g4 ♕d8 26.♕f4 ♘d7 27.e6 ♘f6.

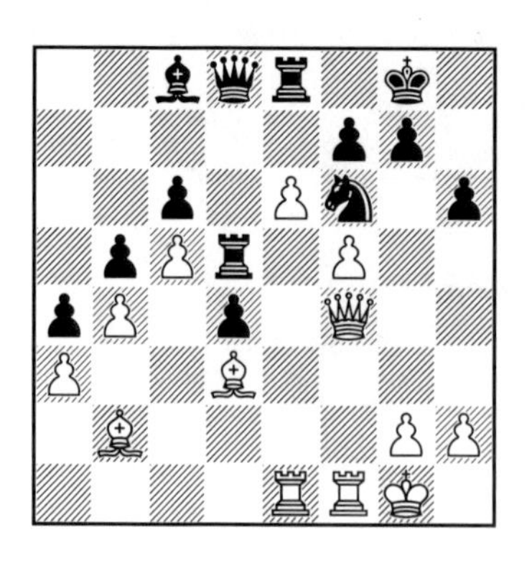

28.exf7+ ♔xf7 29.♖xe8 ♔xe8 30.♖e1+ ♔f7 31.♖e5 ♖xe5 32.♕xe5 ♘g4 33.♕f4. After 33.♕xd4 and the exchange of queens, it seemed that the game could finish in a draw, and this outcome apparently did not suit the "commander-in-chief" who was playing white. The computer has a different opinion though.

33...♘e3 34.♗xd4 ♘d5 35.♕e5 ♘f6 36.♗b1 ♕d5 37.♕f4 ♗d7 38.♕f2 ♔f8 39.h3 ♕b3 40.♕b2 ♕xb2 41.♗xb2 h5 (black should have waited and played 41...♔f7) **42.♗xf6 gxf6 43.♔f2 ♔g7 44.♔g3 ♔h6**

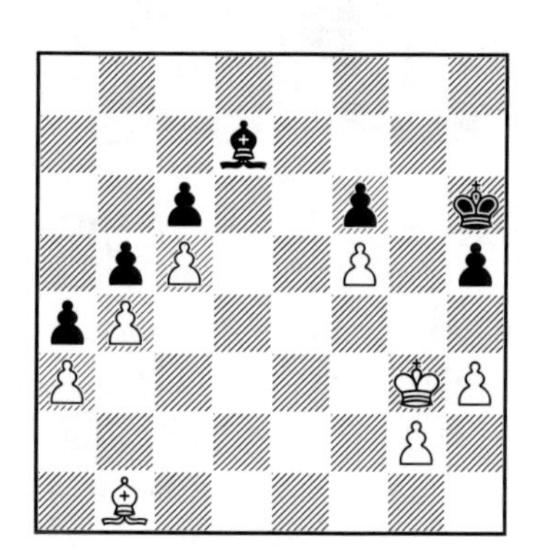

45.h4? White throws away an easy win. Grigoriev, who commented on this game in the magazine *64*, gives the exact plan: 45.♔h4! ♗e8 46.♗e4 ♗d7 47.♗f3 ♗e8 48.g3 ♗d7 49.♗xh5 ♗xf5 50.♗f3 ♗d7 51.g4, with a win.

45...♗e8 46.♗e4 ♗d7 47.♔f4 ♗e8 48.♗f3 ♗d7 49.♔e4 ♗e8 50.♔d4

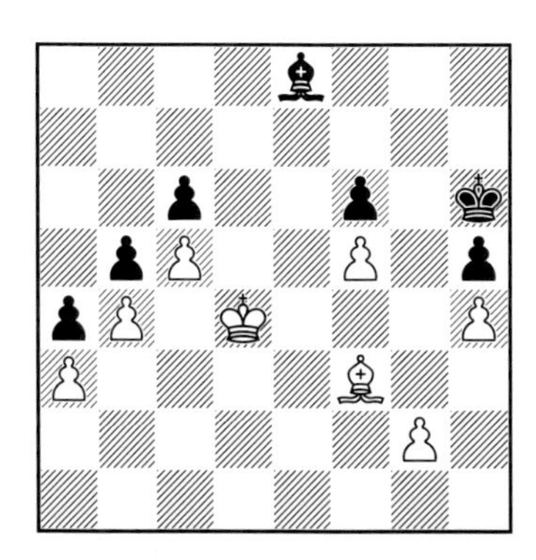

50...♗d7? Returning the favor – black misses a draw, which he should have got with the correct continuation 50...♔g7! 51.♗e2 ♔f8, and so on.

51.g3 ♗e8 52.♗e2 ♗d7 53.♗xb5 cxb5 54.♔d5 ♗xf5 55.c6 ♔g6 56.♔c5 ♗c8 57.♔xb5 ♔f5 58.♔b6 ♔g4 59.♔c7. Black resigned.

Grigoriev's detailed comments on the game end with the following words: "An eventful, interesting endgame. The whole game is also interesting, although not perfect. However, how many perfect games can we observe even in international tournaments?" We have not found any other examples of Fridberg's chess career.

According to his son, Vladimir Isaakovich was transferred to Rostov as a prosecutor of the North Caucasus Region in 1931. A trace of his work as a prosecutor remained in the press. (Fridberg V. I., *Thieves and Robbers – Enemies of the People*. Rostov-on-Don: Party publishing house, 1933).

In 1934, Fridberg received a new assignment – he moved to Irkutsk as a prosecutor of the East Siberian Territory. Here he was elected chairman of the Regional Committee for Physical Education and Sports. He carried out a lot of voluntary work to develop the physical education movement in Eastern Siberia and also played in local chess competitions.

The last sharp turn in his life occurred in the spring of 1937. Vladimir Isaakovich was summoned to Moscow. It seemed that a new promotion was on the cards: there was talk about appointing him Deputy Prosecutor of the USSR, working under Vyshinsky. But things turned out differently.

When on July 2 an unsuspecting Kirill called his father's office phone, he heard an unfamiliar voice, stating twice firmly: "There is no such person here!"

On that same summer's day, July 2, 1937, Fridberg was arrested. About a year later, his son Zlotkovsky was told in the OGPU that his father was an enemy of the people and, according to the verdict of June 5, 1938, he was sentenced to 10 years in prison without the right of correspondence.

Kirill Vladimirovich once met his father's former driver from the days when his father was a prosecutor in Irkutsk. This driver had heard that Vladimir Isaakovich was sent to Irkutsk after his arrest, where he was convicted. Despite the pressure exerted on him, Fridberg refused to sign the charges and, in the end, unable to withstand the beatings, he lost his mind.

Later, though, his indictment came to light. It says that Fridberg, "exploiting his position as a regional prosecutor, on the instructions of a counter-revolutionary organization, was engaged in sabotage in the prosecutor's office of the region, that is, in order to save counter-revolutionary rightist Trotskyists... He stood for individual terror against the leaders of the CPSU(b) and the Soviet government. For this purpose, he created a terrorist organization of young people." On June 5, 1938, V. I. Fridberg was hence in actuality sentenced to death by shooting.

In 1956, Fridberg's widow was issued a certificate of her husband's posthumous rehabilitation, which stated that the sentence of June 5, 1938 "was annulled due to newly discovered circumstances and the case was terminated due to the absence of any crime".

According to Kirill, some people suggested that Fridberg suffered because, as an assistant to Krylenko, he supervised the OGPU courts. And when the time came, they dealt with him, too. Who knows whether or not this is the truth...

Rodion Shukevich-Tretyakov – Devoted to the Revolution

A 1915 issue of *Shakhmatny vestnik* published in Moscow by Alexei Alekhine contained an interesting article: "We have received a letter from organizer of correspondence tournaments R. K. Shukevich-Tretyak (in pre-revolutionary chess magazines, his surname was written Shukevich-Tretyak rather than Shukevich-Tretyakov – S.G.) from the Lechfeld camp (Bavaria), informing interested parties that any unfinished business in relation to correspondence chess tournaments will be completed by him immediately upon his return from captivity."

Although captivity in Germany during the First World War does not bear any comparison with Hitler's camps or the Gulag, a chess organizer who did not forget his social duties while in captivity deserves respect.

The name of the chess player from Minsk R. K. Shukevich-Tretyakov was well known at the beginning of the 20th century. I found more information on him from his niece Zinaida Ivanovna Yanushkevich. Rodion Konstantinovich was born in 1893 in the village of Novina, Rakovskaya parish of Minsk county. Since his youth, he had aspired to knowledge and, although he was left without a father early on and was forced to earn his daily bread from a young age, he managed to get a higher education, and studied several foreign languages on his own.

Shukevich-Tretyakov accepted the October Revolution with all his heart, and in 1919 he joined the Bolshevik Party. He even gave his children "Bolshevik-like" names: his daughter was named Revolutsia ("Revolution") and his son was named Artem (in honor of the famous Bolshevik Fyodor Sergeev, who made history under the pseudonym "Artem"). In the post-October period, his organizational abilities in the chess field were fully on display.

In 1924, as a representative of Belarus at the Third All-Union Congress of Chess Players in Moscow, Shukevich-Tretyakov was elected to the Plenum of the All-Union Chess Section. In the following years, he headed the chess organization of Belarus, edited the chess column in the Bulletin of the Supreme Council of Physical Education published in Minsk, and regularly participated in republican championships.

In the Belarus championship of 1924, Rodion Konstantinovich inflicted the only defeat on the winner of the tournament, Solomon Rozental. Shukevich-Tretyakov also played in an interesting consultation game in Minsk on November 3, 1924.

Game No. 65
E. Bogoljubov and D. Gaukhberg – R. Shukevich-Tretyakov and A. Kaspersky
Consultation game, Minsk, 1924
French Defense C13
Commentary by S. Grodzensky

1.e4 e6 2.d4 d5 3.♘c3 ♘f6 4.♗g5 ♗e7 5.e5 ♘fd7 6.h4

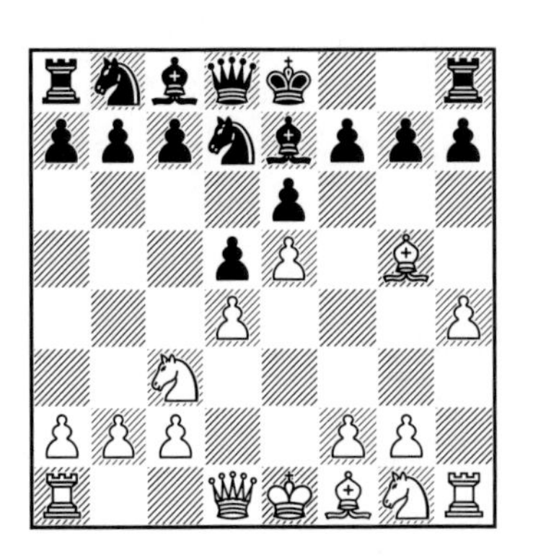

6...a6. Accepting the pawn sacrifice in this variation, called the Alekhine-Chatard Attack, is quite dangerous. Black follows Maroczy's recommendations, preparing to blow open the center with c7-c5.

7.♕g4! ♔f8. Modern theory recommends 7...♗xg5, since other continuations allow white to get an advantage.

8.♘f3. Eleven years later, Czerniak continued 8.♕f4 against Trifunovic at the Tournament of Nations in Warsaw (1935). After 8...c5 9.dxc5 ♘c6 10.♘f3 ♕c7 11.b4 ♘dxe5 12.♗xe7+ ♔xe7 13.♘xe5 ♕xe5+ 14.♕xe5 ♘xe5 15.♘a4 white achieved some advantage.

8...c5 9.0-0-0 ♘c6 10.dxc5 ♘dxe5. The exchanges in the center highlight white's advantage in development. The move 10...♘xc5 deserved consideration.

11.♘xe5 ♘xe5 12.♕g3 ♘d7. In case of 12...♘c6 white would have had the move 13.♗c4!? at his disposal.

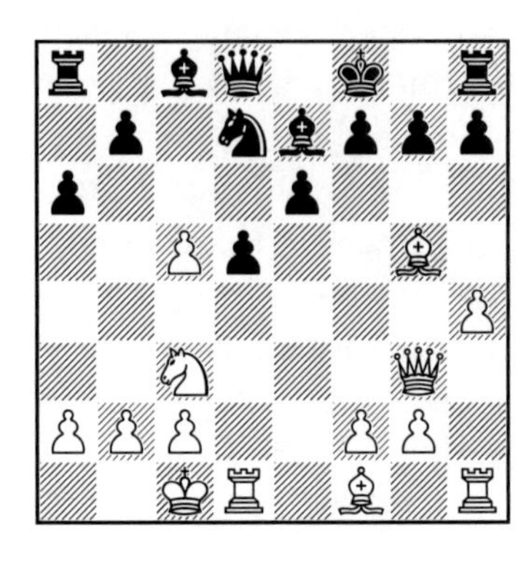

13.♘xd5! White attempts a combinational solution to the position.

13...exd5. In case of 13...♗xg5+ 14.hxg5 exd5 15.♖xd5 ♕a5 (15...♕e8 16.♗d3 with a clear advantage) 16.♕d6+ ♔g8 (or 16...♔e8 17.c6) 17.c6 with a win.

14.♖xd5 f6 15.♗f4 ♗xc5 16.♗c4! This continuation is more concrete than the obvious 16.♖xc5 ♘xc5 17.♗d6+ ♔f7 18.♗xc5 ♗e6.

16...♗e7. The move 16...♗b4 deserved consideration.

17.♖e1 g6 18.♗d6 ♗xd6 19.♕xd6+ ♔g7 20.♖e7+ ♕xe7 21.♕xe7+ ♔h6 22.g4. Black resigned.

As in his younger days, Rodion Konstantinovich was interested in correspondence chess. He regularly played in the tournaments for first-category players organized by the magazines *Shakhmatny listok* and *64*, where among his many rivals we find such famous names as Ragozin and Krylenko. First-category player Rodion Shukevich-Tretyakov demonstrated strong abilities in the next game.

Game No. 66
R. Shukevich-Tretyakov – A. Alexeev
28th *64* correspondence tournament, 1930-1931
Sicilian Defense B83
Commentary by S. Grodzensky

1.e4 c5 2.♘f3 e6 3.d4 cxd4 4.♘xd4 ♘f6 5.♘c3 d6 6.♗e2 ♗e7 7.0-0 0-0 8.♗e3 ♘bd7 9.f4 ♘c5?! The move 9...a6 would be in the spirit of this opening.

10.e5 dxe5?! Opening the file was in white's favor. It was better to play 10...♘e8.

11.fxe5 ♘d5 12.♘xd5 ♕xd5? The move 12...exd5 was stronger.

13.♘f3. White could have easily won via 13.♘f5 ♕d8 14.♕xd8 ♗xd8 15.♗xc5.

13...♕e4? The exchange of queens was clearly to white's advantage. However, after the move made by black, white gets the opportunity to attack.

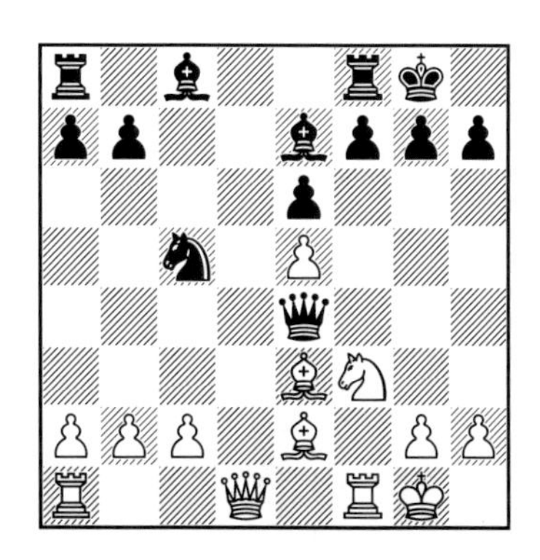

14.♗xc5 ♗xc5+ 15.♔h1 h6 16.♗d3 ♕g4 17.♕e1 ♗d7 18.h3 ♕h5?! The queen retreat looks poor. It was better to continue 18...♕f4.

19.♕e4 f5? Leads to a quick defeat. It was possible to tighten the resistance via 19...g6.

20.exf6 ♖xf6 21.♘e5 ♗e8 22.♖xf6 gxf6 23.♘g4 ♕h4 24.♕xe6+ ♔g7 25.♖f1 ♗c6 26.♘e5 ♗xg2+ 27.♔xg2 ♖g8 28.♕f7+. Black resigned.

In 1932, Shukevich-Tretyakov participated in the Kharkov–Minsk telegraph match, where his opponent was the well-known Kharkov chess player Romashkevich.

Zinaida Ivanovna recalled hearing in the mid-1930s that her uncle worked as a chess club methodologist in the Committee for Arts Affairs under the Council of People's Commissars of Belarus, but then his name irrevocably disappeared from the pages of periodicals.

The answer to the author's request to the Prosecutor's Office of Belarus was that Rodion Konstantinovich

Shukevich-Tretyakov "was arrested by the NKVD of the BSSR on August 15, 1938 for committing crimes under Article 72 of the BSSR Criminal Code (anti-Soviet agitation) and under Article 76 of the BSSR Criminal Code (organizational activities aimed at preparing counter-revolutionary speeches).

By resolution of a Special Meeting under the People's Commissar of Internal Affairs of the USSR dated February 9, 1940, Shukevich-Tretyakov was imprisoned in a correctional labor camp for a period of 5 years. He died on January 10, 1942 in the city of Sevastopol. By decision of the judicial board for criminal cases of the Supreme Court of the BSSR of February 2, 1956, Shukevich-Tretyakov R. K. was rehabilitated."

We can add to the official response from the Prosecutor's Office that he was rehabilitated posthumously. And we note that it was much more difficult to survive in the Gulag system than in German captivity during the First World War.

Chess in the "Destructive-Labor Camps"

Introduction

Stalin's camps had poetic names: Ozerlag, Steplag, Kamyshlag, Rechlag, Dubrovlag... This is what Solzhenitsyn wrote: "You might think that an unrecognized poet is sitting in the Ministry of Internal Affairs. He has not written a poem or any rhyme yet, so he gives poetic names to the camps." (Alexander Solzhenitsyn *In the First Circle*, Moscow, Khudozh.- lit., 1990.)

Now that much is known about Stalin's correctional labor camps, which Solzhenitsyn dubbed "destructive-labor", their locations – Vorkuta, Kolyma, Norilsk and Dzhezkazgan – sound as ominous as Hitler's mass extermination camps. Bringing together the facts that are becoming known about the Gulag Archipelago (one of the symbols of the 20th century), I constantly recall the ironic couplet of Stanislaw Jerzy Lec:

Don't admire Dante.
He was an amateur when it comes to hell.

Looked at from the 20th century, the Omsk prison described by Dostoevsky seems patriarchal. "The danger of dying from exhaustion never hung over Dostoevsky's convicts. What would you expect, if geese were walking in their prison and yet the prisoners did not break their necks." (Alexander Solzhenitsyn *The Gulag Archipelago, Vol. 2*). Along the way, the author of *The Gulag Archipelago* cites a characteristic critical point expressed by Varlam Shalamov in respect of *One Day in the Life of Ivan Denisovich*:

"Given the standards of many hard camps, Shalamov rightly reproached me, writing: 'and what kind of hospital cat is walking there with you? Why hasn't he been stabbed and eaten yet?.. And why does Ivan Denisovich carry a spoon with him, when it is known that everything cooked in the camp was eaten in liquid form by drinking straight from the dishes?'

"And with respect to *Notes of Maria Volkonskaya*, Shalamov points out that the Decembrists in Nerchinsk were given a lesson on how to extract and load three *poods* of ore per person per day (forty-eight kilograms! – you can lift it all at once!), Meanwhile, Shalamov in Kolyma was taught to load eight hundred *poods*. Shalamov also writes that sometimes their working day in summer lasted up to 16 hours!" (Alexander Solzhenitsyn *The Gulag Archipelago, Vol. 1*).

The Chateau d'If described by Alexandre Dumas causes Alexander Isayevich to respond with irony: "I also reread *The Count of Monte Cristo* in prison, though not to the end. I noticed that, although Dumas tries to create a sense of horror, he paints a completely patriarchal prison in the Chateau d'If. Not to mention the distortion of such small details as the daily removal of a slops pail from the cell, which Dumas, by his own folly, is silent about – do you understand why Dantes was able to escape? Because there hadn't been any searches of their cells for years, when it was supposed to be done every week, and this is the result: the tunnel was not detected. Then, they did not change the assigned screws – they should, as we know from the experience of Lubyanka, be changed every two hours, so that each watchman would look for anything missed by the previous one. And in the Chateau d'If they do not enter the cell for days and do not look in. They didn't even have spy holes in their cell doors – so If was not a prison, but just a seaside resort! It was considered plausible for a metal pot to be left in Dantes' cell – and he hammered the floor with it. Finally, the deceased was trustfully sewn up in a bag, without his body being incinerated in the morgue with a hot iron and without it being punctured with a bayonet during watch. Dumas should have mixed in not gloominess, but elementary procedure." (Alexander Solzhenitsyn *In the First Circle*).

At one of the first exhibitions organized by the Memorial Society, there were posters that made it possible to compare the conditions of detention in the camps of pre-revolutionary Russia and during the era of Stalinism. This comparison shows in all respects that conditions were much harsher in the Gulag.

I remember how, when visiting the Peter and Paul Fortress, my father, listening to the excited voice of the guide who told of the horrors of imprisonment in Petropavlovsk, sighed that he could not even have dreamed of such tolerable conditions while locked in Butyrka.

In the middle of the 20th century, the civilized world was shocked at the horrors committed in Hitler's camps. When attempts were made to objectively compare Stalin's camps with Hitler's, it turned out that the latter featured much better sanitary conditions of detention.

History shows that prisoners played chess in order to preserve their mental health. The newspaper *Shakhmatny listok* bitterly ironized that the first correspondence games in Russia were played by Decembrists imprisoned in the Peter and Paul and Shlisselburg fortresses. They passed the moves from cell to cell, tapping on the walls.

My father, who was imprisoned in Butyrskaya prison in 1935, recalled that even prisoners who were indifferent to chess on the outside got into it in prison. Craft artists made a board and simple pieces, and battles took place right in the cells. They were interrupted when the warden suddenly burst in and scattered and broke the pieces while swearing. It was forbidden to play chess in the cell. You were supposed to "sit and think about your case".

Ivanov-Razumnik recalled that, when in 1933 he found himself in a solitary cell in the Pre-Trial Detention House at the Shpalernaya prison in Leningrad, he fought insomnia by solving chess problems and studies (obviously without a chess set), and even managed, without looking at the board, to reconstruct the first game of the Alekhine – Capablanca world championship match (1927). When he managed to get to "freedom" (he was sent into exile to Saratov), he was able to confirm that the duel was reproduced in his mind without a single mistake.

In 1938, in his Butyrskaya prison cell, Ivanov-Razumnik spent many hours playing blindfold with a member of the collegiate of defense council lawyers called Malyantovich, who was imprisoned for being the nephew of a minister of the Provisional Government.

Here are some essays on the subject of chess in the Gulag.

The Gulag Prisoners – "Vorkuta, Vorkuta, a Wonderful Planet..."

The plane to Vorkuta took off from Moscow's Sheremetyevo Airport on a warm May morning – I set off on a work trip to a city completely unfamiliar to me, but whose name has haunted me my entire life: Vorkuta is indicated in my passport as my place of birth. It so happened that soon after my birth, in the place of my father's exile, I was taken by my mother to her homeland – to Ryazan.

I must admit that I often find it difficult to choose a title for an article. But there I was, leaving for my work trip, and various options for the future title came to mind: "To Vorkuta On My Own", "Chess in the Arctic", "Checkmate on the 67th Parallel". I could see green meadows through the porthole, but I could not get rid of the familiar motif of a simple and always for some reason fun-sounding song: "Vorkuta, Vorkuta, a wonderful planet! Twelve months of winter, and the rest is summer".

However, the words of the song got a real meaning when endless white fields began to float under the wing of the plane, which appeared so unexpectedly that I did not immediately realize that it was not a cloud, but a snowy plain. After landing, I got to appreciate that the weather in Vorkuta on Victory Day, May 9, is somewhat cooler than in Moscow on International Women's Day, on March 8. It is perfectly possible to take a cross-country skiing trip around the city.

The history of Vorkuta starts in the early 1930s. There was bare, deserted tundra here, when in June 1930 a group of six people led by 24-year-old Moscow geologist Georgy Chernovoi discovered deposits of coking coal in the middle reaches of the wild, unexplored Vorkuta River.

Now at this place, near the first ever mine in the Arctic, there is a granite complex entangled with barbed wire – Vorkutlag, alas, outweighed the names of courageous explorers in the public's memory.

For many years, there was an opinion that Vorkuta was tamed and then built up by young people who arrived in this harsh region on trips organized by Komsomol or thanks to the dictates of their hearts. Democratization and publicity have, however, made significant adjustments to this judgment that was so convenient during those years, and now it is known for certain that the main productive force during the creation of this polar boiler room consisted of thousands of prisoners, and, you know, most of them were innocent.

On the streets of Vorkuta, there were often stands with the city's emblem – a deer standing near a pithead that was topped with a five-pointed star. But perhaps the most respected society in the city was the local Memorial branch, which chose three rows of barbed wire and a small circle of the sun on a black background as its emblem, as on the picture.

In the early 1960s, during the Khruschev "thaw", the Vorkuta Museum of Local Lore asked my father to share his memories. The reply from Yakov Davidovich Grodzensky dated March 20, 1965 is kept in the museum archive:

"...The city of Vorkuta is young even from the point of view of just one human life, let alone on a historical scale – it is not even forty. The city is young, but its history is unique, full of tragic events and bitter fates generated by the years of the Stalinist cult, which has left a sad memory. I lived in Vorkuta from 1935 to 1950. I served a three-year prison sentence, then, without trial or investigation, without a case or a crime, it was prolonged – another 5 years and, having worked as a convict for more than 8 years, instead of three, I was released for good work on April 17, 1943 – on the first day of arrival of the new head of the Vorkutstroi, M. M. Maltsev.

"Free people of our type were considered 'directive workers', i.e., they were assigned to construction in accordance with a directive from above. We considered ourselves lucky not to be serving in the prison surrounded by barbed wire, but on the other side, even with some restrictions, without the right to leave and without many other actual rights. But even such 'freedom' seemed to some people too much for the 'enemies of the people' who diligently mined coal and built the city: on December 13, 1949, I, among many others, was arrested. And only in the summer of 1950 after interrogation and ordeals in prison, were we gradually moved out of Vorkuta, a city created mainly by the work of people indicted under Article 58.

"I hope you will not see in my words an immodest desire to speak about myself: my fate is the fate of thousands of others, just like me, many of whom 'gave their soul to God' and were forgotten. With their sufferings, sweat, and blood, they inhabited the dead tundra, erecting a polar boiler room. It was them, and not those who stood on their bones, those who were awarded Stalin's laureateships, orders, medals, monetary awards and all sorts of bonuses for long service. Vorkuta is rich in minerals. But its history is immeasurably richer, the history of those who, deprived of human rights, heroically strengthened the force and power of their country during the Great Patriotic War and long before it. That's why the history section should be the most important in the local museum..."

And how did the history of chess in Vorkuta begin? Afanasy Mikhailovich Sfinaris, a veteran of the Vorkutlag, told the author that chess battles were often arranged in the dormitories. The games were sometimes played over-emotionally. They also led to physical altercations. In any case, trash talking your opponent, rejoicing at his bad moves, was fraught with the danger of an acute conflict arising.

Chess was the only entertainment in the camp, and that's why all the prisoners became amateur players, learning the basics of the game on the job.

Candidate Master Leonard Melkonyan, a multiple champion of Vorkuta and the Komi Republic, recalled that, when he arrived in the polar city in the early 1960s, fascinated by the romance of the North, he found many people who had gone through Vorkutlag. One of them, Sergey Vladimirovich Sukhorsky, gave him a present, a homemade chess set that had been used to play in prison.

Vorkutlag prisoners played using these chess pieces

Although many prisoners at Vorkutlag played chess, there were no official tournaments in the pre-war years. Prisoners were periodically reallocated to different dormitories, so the chess players were unable to form close groups.

Among the prisoners, Dmitry Lozhenitsyn had a reputation as a strong chess player. Dmitry Borisovich had a good memory and was famous for his ability to play well blindfold. In fact, Lozhenitsyn had suffered because of chess. When a student in the early 1920s, he became friends with the son of the Belgian consul on the basis of a common interest in chess. When it was time for the consul to return to his homeland, Lozhenitsyn decided to maintain relations with his friend by playing correspondence chess. Many years passed after the completion of these correspondence duels, but it was 1937, and Lozhenitsyn, who had become a surgeon by that time, was convicted on the basis of this correspondence from his school years "for his links with the global bourgeoisie".

The camp was divided in 1947, and the convicts under Article 58 were allocated to a special camp – Rechlag. There were no chess competitions for the camp as a whole, but there were tournaments held in each separate camp point (SCP). The strongest players there were N. Korovin, V. Pankratov, G. Arakelyan (Arakelov), A. Kriger, V. Kushnir, A. Savenko, and A. Samutin.

Right after Stalin's death, the regime in Rechlag was eased, and the prisoners were allowed to hold team competitions between the camp departments. In September 1953, the operative officer N. Lyutov (who was distinguished by a humane attitude to prisoners according to the memoirs of veterans of the Rechlag), even allowed a fragment of the SCP championship for mine No. 40 to be captured on film.

Only one print was made, and even that one came out blurry. And yet we reproduce this technically weak photo, because it is the only visible recording of the prisoners playing in the Rechlag.

The decisive game in the SCP championship in September 1953 was V. Kushnir – A. Kriger, in which the following position appeared after white's 23rd move:

Game No. 67
V. Kushnir – A. Kriger
Vorkuta, SCP for mine No. 40, 1953
Commentary by S. Grodzensky

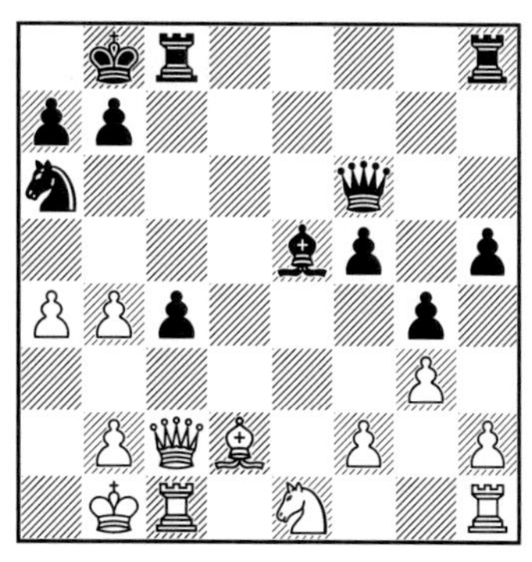

Black continued **23...♗d6 24.♕c3.** White offers to exchange queens in the hope of strengthening his b4 pawn. Black probably should have done this, preserving somewhat better chances in the endgame. Instead, he made a superficial move **24...♗e5?** and after white's response **25.♗f4!**, which he had failed to anticipate, he found himself in a difficult situation.

There followed **25...♖he8 26.♘f3 gxf3 27.♖he1 ♔a8 28.♖xe5** and black resigned.

Black should have drawn from here, but it seems that he suffered a psychological shock due to the sharp deterioration of his position, which only five moves earlier had looked quite attractive.

Having won this meeting, Vladimir Kushnir became champion of his SCP. It actually took him a long time to reach this semi-official title. He took up chess seriously when, in 1947, after graduating from school, he got a place at the History Department of Leningrad University. There he met the master L. Zhukhovitsky and the future masters E. Stolyar and V. Byvshev. But as soon as he started his studies, Kushnir was arrested following a denunciation by a provocateur on January 1, 1948, and half a year later he was convicted on several counts under Article 58 and sentenced to 25 years of correctional labor camps as well as five years of deprivation of rights.

Kushnir (right) versus Shved, Vorkuta championship, 1956

He served his time in special purpose camps: Dubrovlag (Mordovia), Peschanglag (Karaganda region), Luglag (Kemerovo region), and on the day of Stalin's death on March 5, 1953, he was moved to Rechlag. In 1956 he was released, and in 1964 he was rehabilitated "due to the absence of any crime".

For several years after his release, Kushnir played in local competitions, but then retired from playing chess seriously. He graduated from the Leningrad Mining Institute as a part-time student. On the threshold of his 50th birthday, he gained his candidate's degree in economics.

Vladimir Petrovich, who had once gained the first rank in chess in Vorkuta, regularly confirmed his level in competition after competition over several decades.

While the prisoners in the dormitories had to make do with one-on-one games with homemade chess sets, the exiles were allowed to take part in the official championships of the city. Those were first held immediately after the end of the war. And so we note an important detail: illegally repressed players are on the list of champions of Vorkuta from 1945 to 1960.

In the late 1950s, freed prisoners participated in competitions together with their former guards, and consistently outperformed them.

In 1945, Nikolai Korovkin, who at that time worked as an engineer at a thermal power plant, and who before that had spent many years in camps, won the first city championship. The second Vorkuta championship, in 1947, was won by another veteran of Vorkutlag – Valentin Pankratov. He also won the city championship in 1959 and 1960, after rehabilitation.

The third citywide championship was held in 1950, won by Georgy Yanchuk, a teacher at the mining college. He ended up in Vorkuta because he had suffered the misfortune of living in territory temporarily occupied by the Nazis (he had not been a collaborator with the Germans: six years of internal exile was punishment for the mere fact of residing on territory occupied by them). Yanchuk reaffirmed his title of the best chess player in the city twice more – in 1952 and 1954, while in 1951 the competition was won by Georgy Morozov, who was exiled to the Arctic in 1948.

In the 1960s, the population of Vorkuta began to grow, mainly thanks to those who came here voluntarily, while many former prisoners convicted under Article 58 got certificates of rehabilitation and preferred to move to other lands. New names appeared in the table of Vorkuta champions, but this is not the place for their story.

***

...I wandered around Vorkuta's outskirts and saw swollen mounds, from which rotten stakes with numbers stick out in some places. The prisoners of the early fifties are laid to rest here. The graves of those whom the tundra accepted earlier had long since been leveled to the ground. This reminds me of the lines of Varlam Shalamov:

I carve letters on abandoned tombs,
I will write down dates and names for the birds to remember.

...The plane has reached its cruising altitude, leaving Vorkuta airport and the snowy plain below, and a couple of hours later I am already inhaling the May Moscow air. And again, I hear: "Vorkuta, Vorkuta, a wonderful planet!..." But now the song sounds so sad.

Varlam Shalamov – Chess in the Life and Work of the Author of *Kolyma Tales*

Two great writers, A. I. Solzhenitsyn and V. T. Shalamov, played a significant role in my life. Alexander Solzhenitsyn was my school teacher, and Varlam Shalamov was a close friend of my father. Personal communication with these writers allows me to conclude that their differences were manifested not only in their works and in their worldviews, but even in hobbies. Solzhenitsyn, a former Komsomol member, did not hide that he believed in God, whereas the priest's son Shalamov was a convinced atheist. He often repeated: "I'm not religious. This is not for me. It's like a musical ear: you either have it or you don't." Alexander Isayevich Solzhenitsyn considered himself a "broad internationalist", but from his work "Two Hundred Years Together" on Russian-Jewish relations, it is clear that he was concerned about the question of "good" and "not so good" ethnicities. For Varlam Shalamov, a person's ethnicity did not matter, and he considered anti-Semitism a crime.

Unlike Solzhenitsyn, Shalamov loved chess. Even as a child he attended the Vologda Chess Club, and in his work you won't find a single bad word about the game.

My first memory of Varlam Shalamov comes from TV and goes all the way back to May 1962, when I watched a program presented by Boris Slutsky dedicated to a person who at that time was a completely unknown poet. My father found out about it in advance and looked forward to it with joy and excitement. Then we watched it carefully together, with my father commenting on it.

At the end of the program, I asked my father: who is this poet? He told me that it was his old friend – they studied at the same university. "He is not well known among the public for now, but in the future his work will be studied in schools." When I asked when this would happen, my father suggested that he and Shalamov would not get to see it, but that it would certainly happen during my lifetime.

After the program, my father sent a greeting card to Shalamov and, as Varlam Tikhonovich Shalamov recalled much later, he was the only person who reacted to it. Soon, Shalamov sent him a gift: it was a miniature book in a spacious envelope. It was *Ognivo ("Flintstone")* – the first collection of poems written by the author of *Kolyma Tales*, on the

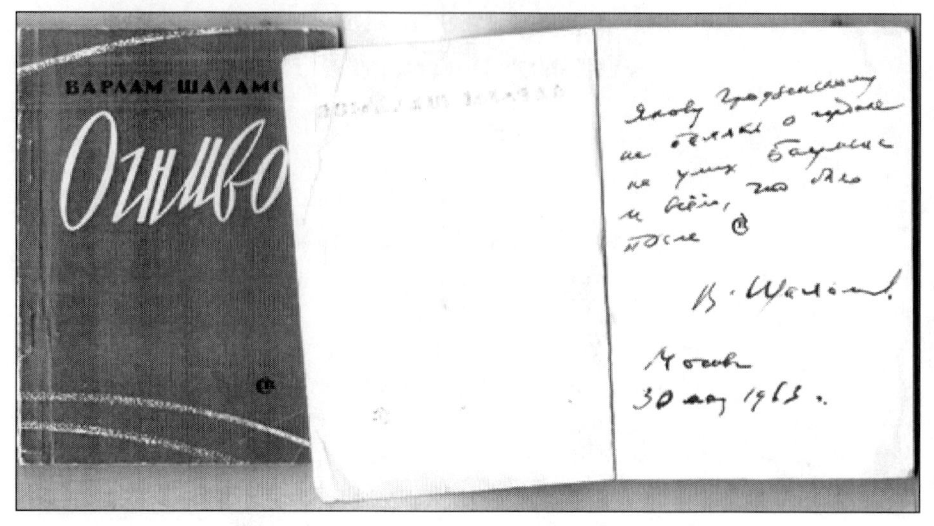

Flintstone – the first collection of Varlam Shalamov's poems

title page of which he had especially inscribed: "To Yakov Grodzensky, in memory of the attic on Bauman Street and everything that happened after. V. Shalamov".

Shalamov had been a friend of my father since they were young. They once studied at the Moscow University law faculty together (then it was called the "Faculty of

Varlam Tikhonovich Shalamov. 1968

Photos of my father – as a student at Moscow State University on September 30, 1931, and then in 1957

Soviet Law"). The said attic was a student dormitory in a building on Staro-Basmannaya Street, next to Bauman Garden.

The writer considered my father his close friend, from his youth until his final days. He referred to him as "a righteous man of a special kind". Y. Grodzensky and V. Shalamov's paths in life diverged, or, more precisely, were forcibly separated during their student years. Varlam Shalamov was a victim of the first series of mass arrests.

The first time Shalamov was arrested was on February 19, 1929, in an ambush on 26 Sretenka Street, which housed an underground printing house and where Lenin's Testament and other opposition materials were printed. The warrant for his arrest was signed by the head of the OGPU, Genrikh Yagoda. Yakov Grodzensky first entered the prison gates much later, in March 1935. He, like Shalamov, was accused of counterrevolutionary Trotskyist activity.

My father returned in the mid-1950s, after 20 years of prisons, a "destructive-labor" camp (Vorkutlag), and "eternal" exile (Kengir-Rudnik). At first after returning to Moscow, he liked to walk along the central streets and once told me that if he walked all the way along Tverskaya Street (he refused to use the Soviet-era name "Gorky Street", just like Shalamov, by the way – Tverskaya was its pre-revolutionary name, and is also its post-Soviet name today), he would definitely encounter an old acquaintance.

One day, walking along Tverskaya Street, my father saw a man with a sharp, piercing look, walking and slightly swaying. There was something of an outlaw in the face of the strange pedestrian, which made some passers-by look around fearfully. It was not easy for my father to recognize him as his old friend Varlam Shalamov.

Shalamov returned to Moscow, having survived Kolyma, which symbolizes the limit of human suffering for any veteran prisoner. In response to my father's enthusiastic evaluation of the novel *One Day in the Life of Ivan Denisovich* that had just been published, Shalamov took a restrained view of Solzhenitsyn, describing him as "another whitewasher".

Yakov Davidovich, while barely acquainted with the first set of *Kolyma Tales*, appreciated the talent of "my friend Varlam" and predicted his place in literature. My father made efforts – and considerable ones – to get Shalamov a significant increase in his pension.

"I owe Grodzensky for dealing with my pension troubles – this is an extremely important issue for me. <...> The state has just left all of us in a hopeless situation – for example, I received a disability pension of the 3rd group – 26 rubles a month, and for the second disability group – 46 rubles. A disabled person of group 2 is not allowed to do any work," Shalamov writes in his memoirs.

And I remember suddenly hearing my father's joyful exclamations while walking near our single-story house in Ryazan – Shalamov had sent a letter reporting that he had won his case. "Yakov. I received the entire 'settlement' today and thank you from the bottom of my heart for your help in this very important matter for me. This is not just help, but something that must be called much more expressively. Thank you so much." (From a letter dated September 10, 1964.)

When Varlam Tikhonovich worked, his black cat Mukha was by his side. He loved her more than the "chess king" Alexander Alekhine loved his cat Chess. Some nasty person killed Mukha. "People do not care about cats," Shalamov said, and sent my father a photo of him holding the dead body of his favorite pet with the following inscription: "To Yakov from me and Mukha. Mukha – the day after her death, and what about me? March 29, 1965, Moscow. V. Shalamov". And the postscript: "Mukha knew you for many years and loved you very much. V. S.," which was a big compliment.

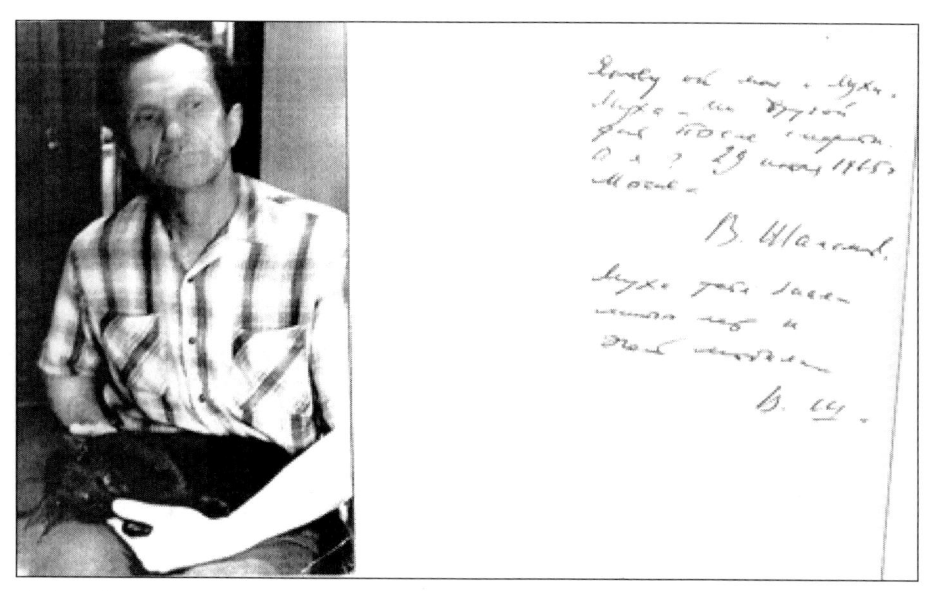

Varlam Shalamov and Mukha

The "Chronicler of Kolyma" was a passionate football fan, which brought him closer to my father, who in his youth was known throughout the district as the goalkeeper of the local boys team. Shalamov often watched games at Dynamo, but supported Spartak. I think that his sympathy for this club reflected the dislike for the departments that were represented by Spartak's rivals – Dynamo and CDSA Moscow (the precursor to CSKA).

Having heard that a football match was going to be broadcast on TV, Varlam Tikhonovich would become excited and rub his hands with glee: "We are going to see some footie now!" This did not cause enthusiasm among the household, because the following hour and a half would be accompanied by loud shouts and jumping up and down at great risk to the furniture, a common situation when watching "footie". After the defeat of his favorite team, Varlam Tikhonovich would sometimes enthusiastically discuss the failure as a fan, but overemotionally. Once, in a conversation on the same subject, he mentioned a famous coach whom he considered the main culprit of a loss by the USSR national team and unleashed a tirade of Kolyma swear-words for selecting "this shameful whore" as the goalkeeper.

Sometimes, my father's recollections of Shalamov would turn to Varlam Tikhonovich's interest in chess. By the way, Shalamov's first place of residence after returning to Moscow from exile in October 1956 was Gogol Boulevard, 25, opposite the newly opened Central Chess Club of the USSR.

In Shalamov's notebooks we find the following musings on chess: "Tal is not Alekhine. Tal's success is more of a psychological than a chess nature." In a chapter of memoirs called "The Twenties", we read about a well-known fragment of chess history as portrayed by Shalamov: "Once, there was the following case in the chess world. Morphy, having defeated all his contemporaries and challenged all chess players with the offer of a pawn handicap and an extra move, suddenly gave up chess, refused to play chess anymore. Chess life continued; the young Wilhelm Steinitz became world champion. One day, Steinitz was in Paris and found out that Morphy was visiting Paris from America. Steinitz went to the hotel where Morphy was staying, and sent him a note asking to meet. Morphy sent a spoken reply: if Mr. Steinitz agrees not to talk about chess, he, Morphy, is ready to accept the invitation. Steinitz left."

The chess motif sometimes pops up in his stories, about which he said, "all my stories have been lived, in agony," each one "is totally authentic. It has the authenticity of a document." Another time, we read the following comment: "My stories are full documentaries, but it seems to me that they contain so many dramatic and tragic events that no one document could bear them."

In *Butyrskaya Prison* (1929) he notes: "The food in Butyrka was excellent. 'Simple, but convincing', in the terminology of chess commentators".

In the 1960s, he wrote a story about events in the Vishera camp in 1929 – *Chess and Poetry*. The plot was as follows: the wife of the big camp chief was a chess fan. In order not to spoil relations with the authorities, the two best players among the prisoners regularly lost their games against her. And then the author, who was considered the third strongest chess player, decided to take her on. It turned out that the boss's wife, who had previously "played almost like Vera Menchik," was a weak player, and Shalamov won several games in a row. The prisoners were scared – you mustn't beat the authorities! The author's moral was characteristic of his style: "You see, I play chess. Chess players don't like sycophants."

The plot of the story *Chess of Dr. Kuzmenko*, from the sixth and final book in *Kolyma Tales*, called by Shalamov "new prose", is quite dramatic. The surgeon Kuzmenko and the narrator, both former prisoners, are going to play using a unique chess set, sculpted in prison by the artist Kulagin from chewed bread and depicting characters of the Time of Troubles. Two pieces are missing – the black queen and the white rook. The fact is that, having reached hunger-driven dementia, the sculptor began to eat his work, but died, having managed only to swallow a rook and bite off the head of the queen.

At the end of the story, the surgeon Kuzmenko admits:

"I did not ask to take the rook out of his stomach, though it could have been done during the autopsy. And the queen's head as well... Therefore, we will play without two pieces. It's your turn, Maestro.

'No,' I said. 'I don't feel like playing anymore...'"

Although the narrator knows many similar stories from the camp, he loses the desire to play chess with Dr. Kuzmenko, who did not commit sacrilege by extracting the chess pieces out of Kulagin's body, pieces which up until then had survived "everything in the camps – both disinfection and the greed of thieves." But the mere fact that Dr. Kuzmenko thought about asking for them prevents the narrator from playing a game with him – at least, with this chess set.

Shalamov's interest in chess was genuine. Varlam Tikhonovich played in chess tournaments in the camp. Kolyma resident Ivan Ivanovich Pavlov in his memoirs noted the following episode: "I once met Varlam Tikhonovich at the chess board, when a chess tournament was organized in the camp."

Shalamov told me about a time when he won a chess tournament in the camp, but the prize was awarded not to him, but to another, more "trustworthy" prisoner. Meanwhile, after winning the tournament, he was appointed a member of the arts council of the camps, since chess was treated in the zone as an art. Later, a fragment in the story *Rusalka* talked about this episode: "I won a chess tournament – I took first place and received a prize, a chess set, which I still have, only the sticker *(stating that it was a prize – S.G.)* got burned off, although for me this chess set without a sticker is both a prize and not a prize. It was my wife's acumen which erased this proof from the chess set."

My personal memories of Shalamov are rather bare. And I only saw him a few times. Usually, my father visited Shalamov on his own. Varlam Tikhonovich appeared here occasionally. Chess was not discussed much at my home, because my father did not approve of my passion for it.

One day, on my way home, I ran into my father and Shalamov coming out of the door. Varlam Tikhonovich greeted me, and my father asked:

"Varlam says that he saw some article of yours about chess. What kind of graphomania is this?"

My parent's face expressed both amazement and irony, since he did not know anything about my chess journalism and, apparently, believed that his son was not capable of writing anything more meaningful than a statement to the trade union committee. I looked at Shalamov with feigned surprise, and he said in a hollow voice:

"The one in the newspaper *Shakhmatnaya Moskva*. I liked the column 'Chess Andersens'. I also saw your article on the subject of composition in the magazine *64*."

"Do you read these newspapers?" I asked.

"I regularly read *Football* and *64*."

At that time, I was more interested in correspondence play than in chess composition. Varlam Tikhonovich asked me about postal chess. I started explaining its key features. Shalamov listened with interest, and in response to my father's ironic remarks he took my side ("Yashka, you don't understand anything about this. Seryozha, tell me, I'm interested"). Many years later, in his published diaries, I read the following lines: "I can only perform in a correspondence tournament. I have kept my mind, but my capacity to use it is less than that of any other person." Maybe Varlam Tikhonovich wrote this, remembering the following story that I told him.

One day he asked me:

"Have you heard of the chess master Blumenfeld?"

I responded affirmatively, and Varlam Tikhonovich said that he knew his nephew Mark Abramovich Blumenfeld, with whom he served time in the Vishera camp. Everyone called Mark Blumenfeld "Max".

Just then, in the late 1960s, Shalamov was working on a series of autobiographical stories and essays, called *Vishera. An Anti-Novel.* In the *Vishera* cycle there is a story called *M. A. Blumenfeld*, whose plot boils down to the fact that in April 1931, Shalamov, together with Blumenfeld – one of the newly arrived prisoners from Moscow from the opposition case – tried to send a letter to the Gulag administration and to the Central Committee of the CPSU(b) protesting against the disenfranchised status of women in the camp.

And so, believing that I was saying something pleasing to Varlam Tikhonovich, I said:

"In 1938, the Chairman of the Chess Federation Nikolai Vasilyevich Krylenko fell victim to the repressions and perished. He was a fantastic organizer. Thanks to his enthusiasm, the famous Moscow international tournaments were held in the 1930s."

Shalamov's face turned to stone.

"Krylenko!.. Chairman of the Chess Federation!.. A fantastic organizer!.." he uttered dully, separating one word from another with a heavy, long pause. "Do you know who this Krylenko was? Have you heard of the 'Krylenko eraser'?!" And he began to explain to me the essence of Krylenko eraser. I do not remember all his words, so I therefore give two quotes from Shalamov's story *There are No Guilty People in the Camp*, which I read later:

"In the twenties, there was the famous 'Krylenko eraser', the essence of which was as follows. Every sentence was theoretical and approximate: depending on behavior, on diligence at work, on mending their ways, on honest work for the benefit of the state. The sentence could be reduced to a spectacular minimum – a year or two instead of ten years, or endless extensions: people were put in prison for a year, but were kept there for their whole life anyway, extending the official term, not allowing 'unofficial years' to accumulate. I myself am a student who has listened to Krylenko's lectures. They had little relation to the law and were inspired by non-legal ideas".

"The starkest expression of the 'Krylenko eraser', of mending their ways, was self-guarding, when prisoners were given rifles – to order, guard, beat their yesterday's neighbors from the same camp and dormitory. Self-service, self-guarding, the investigative corps consisting of prisoners was probably cheap, but it completely erased the concept of guilt."

The last time I saw Varlam Tikhonovich Shalamov was in the Lenin Library. I recognized him immediately by the way he walked. And when I caught him up, I felt that I had the right to smile at a friend. Varlam Tikhonovich stopped and looked at me carefully. (People said that Shalamov saw a snitch in everyone he met.) I, continuing to smile, identified myself. Varlam Tikhonovich misheard me, and when I repeated my long surname again loudly, he smiled in response:

"You are Yakov's son." And, meeting my nod, he continued: "Sorry, Seryozha, I know that it is difficult to communicate with me."

And he started talking about chess, because he had nothing else to talk about with me:

"Are you in the Lenin Library on chess matters?! Yashka complains about you: 'My idiot', he says, 'he spends tons of time on chess.' But I told him: 'Do not prevent your son from doing what he loves.' So, if your father bothers you for your interest in chess, say to him: Shalamov advised me not to give up chess."

He spoke, as always, slowly, with a stutter, but in a friendly manner. It was difficult to hold a dialogue with him as he could not hear too well. Our conversation took place shortly after the "match of the century" (1970). Varlam Tikhonovich knew the results of this historic match. He was shocked at the blunder by the reigning world champion Boris Spassky in a game with Bent Larsen. At parting, Shalamov said that he would like to see me again and talk about chess.

However, I never saw him again. At the end of 1970, my father had a heart attack. We received a letter from Shalamov dated January 7, 1971: "Yakov, you should be rewarded with immortality for your good deeds, but immortality does not exclude short-term ailments, all

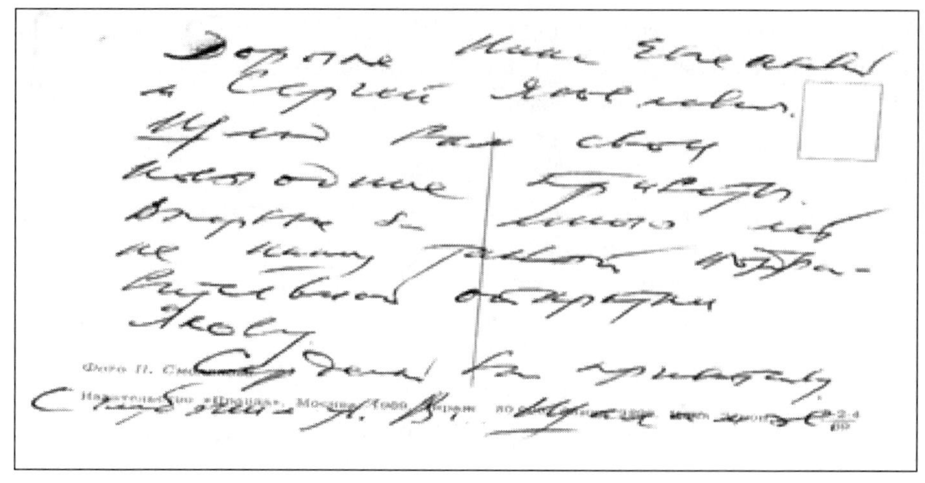

Greetings from V. T. Shalamov on the New Year 1972

sorts of crises! If you can hold a pen in your hand, answer in two words. Yours V. Shalamov".

On January 23, 1971, my father died. Varlam Tikhonovich took it very badly. "One day I came home and found V. T. in deep silent sadness (V. T. was never silent, his thirst for speaking out was always boiling inside of him). 'Yashka is gone,' – said V. T." (Sirotinskaya I. *About Varlam Shalamov, Literary Review*. 1990. No. 10).

Before New Year's Eve, 1972, a greetings card came from him:

"Dear Nina Evgenyevna and Sergey Yakovlevich.

I send you my New Year greetings. For the first time in many years, I am not writing such a greetings card to Yakov. I send you a warm hello.

With deep respect, V. Shalamov".

After that, we exchanged holiday greetings cards for some time. Then, Shalamov's infamous renunciation of the *Kolyma Tales* appeared in the *Literary Newspaper* with reproaches against those who contributed to the appearance of the book in a foreign publishing house.

I remember the angry reaction of Gulag veterans known to me to Shalamov's act. I heard that someone, not limited to breaking off relations with him, destroyed books and photos that Shalamov had once given him. I think that had my father been alive, he, a liberal man who had experienced grief himself, might not have approved of this renunciation, but he would not have turned away from his old friend either. Realizing that I was no replacement of my father for him, I stopped calling Varlam Tikhonovich...

From archival materials, Shalamov's published diaries and memoirs written about him, we learn about his interest in chess in the last years of his life. In his own memoir written in the 1970s, we read: "Fifty years ago, I attended the Moscow International Chess Tournament. The first Lasker-Capablanca game was played in the then Metropol restaurant. The crowd gathered at the entrance guarded by mounted police. The policemen were shouting: "Draw agreed! But the crowd was also fairly small – about three hundred people – no more. All the other tournament games were played in a different section of the building and there were no crowds of fans outside it. That was the Sovnarkom club, in the next entrance, where the Aeroflot ticket offices are now located. About a hundred people went to see those games..."

The Shalamov file at the Russian State Archive of Literature and Art contains a clipping from the *Soviet Sport* newspaper dated September 19, 1974 with an article by P. Dembo "Crash on the opening rails" about the second game of the Karpov – Korchnoi candidates final and a comment on this by Shalamov: "It's more like a crash on the chess rails, because Karpov does not let you get away with such carelessness, such sloppiness, such mistakes. Korchnoi will lose the match." Shalamov also made the following point in his diary: Karpov is wearing a suit and tie with a neat haircut, while Korchnoi is badly dressed with tousled hair.

Shalamov's ticket to the Column Hall of the House of Unions (where the editorial offices of the magazines in which he worked were located in the 1930s) with the stamp "September 18, 1974" has been preserved. "Column Hall of the House of Unions, parterre, row 3, place 12. The price is 2 rubles". As was perfectly understandable, Shalamov attended the Karpov – Korchnoi match rooting for Karpov.

The last time Shalamov wrote about chess was shortly before he moved to a nursing home. "I gave up chess the very day I became convinced that it takes more than it gives – both in terms of time and mental energy. No matter how insignificant the role of poetry in life is, it is still more than that of chess."

In 2005, I managed to find Shalamov's early publications. Previously, it was believed that the first work written by Shalamov was the story *The Three Deaths of Dr. Austino* (October Publishing House, 1936) – an episode of the Spanish Civil War between the international brigades and the forces of General Franco. But it is known that after serving his first camp term in Vishera, he returned to Moscow in 1932, began working in magazines, and later began publishing his works. In a letter dated December 2, 1973 to L. N. Chertkov (the author of an article about Shalamov in the *Short Literary Encyclopedia*) he mentions three articles published in the newspaper *Vechernaya Moskva* in 1935, which, evidently, should be considered his first works in print.

After discovering these materials, I realized that all three were about chess! They covered the Second Moscow International Tournament, which started on February 15 that year, and on February 19 the first article by the still unknown Shalamov appeared in *Vechernaya Moskva* under the title "64 Squares". A week later, an entire half page article "Grandmaster in time pressure" was published on the lower half of the third page. Reading these materials, we see that their author was not only passionate about chess, but also knew its history well, reflected on the topic "What is chess?" which became fashionable decades later, and understood many nuances of the game.

Of course, it was impossible to live without ideological cliches at that time. They permeate all publications, especially the last one – in the issue dated March 8. Among the materials dedicated to International Women's Day, there was a column with the title "Woman and Chess" on the third page. Shalamov explains the poor performance of the women's world champion Vera Menchik at the Second Moscow International Tournament by the fact that "nothing is being done in the West for women's chess... In modern England – the 'advanced' country of 'democratic freedoms' – you need to be fairly wealthy to be a member of the club. The women of the proletariat have more important things to worry about than chess."

Of course, everything was different in the "country of victorious socialism": "All sixty-four squares of the chessboard are available to a Soviet woman. Work with women is included in the plan of any chess organization, in the chess circle of any club." And the future author of *Kolyma Tales* ends his article with the following appeal: "The game of chess should become the favorite game of female workers of the Soviet Union."

That was the last publication of the young journalist on the subject of chess, and soon a new arrest followed. He was now to experience almost 20 years of appalling hardship in Kolyma, followed by a return to the capital and poverty after rehabilitation, the publication of his first collections of poems, and a lonely death in a nursing home.

All over the world, Shalamov is recognized as a great Russian writer, in a certain sense as the direct successor of the Dostoevsky tradition, with whom he seemed to conduct a spiritual dialogue. Dostoevsky's *Notes from the Dead House* and Shalamov's *Kolyma Tales* reflect the polemics between these writers. My father's prediction came true: the works of Varlam – his fellow student, and a close friend in my father's late years – are now included in the school literature curriculum. The importance of his work continues to grow.

***

I attended a function dedicated to the life and work of the author of *Kolyma Tales* in the Central House of Writers at the end of the 1980s. The highlight came when the organizer turned on a recording of Shalamov's voice, and everyone listened in the silence. He was reading *Chess of Dr. Kuzmenko*. It is symbolic that this particular story was recorded on tape. Listening to it performed by the author, I remembered the same voice speaking to me: "It's good that you have a favorite thing. Keep studying chess and keep writing on chess matters."

May future literary historians not forget that the author of *Kolyma Tales* began his career with publications on chess – a game he enthusiastically loved his entire life.

Alexander Solzhenitsyn – As I Remember Him

I graduated from secondary school No. 2 in Ryazan in 1961. During my childhood, the school was known for the future academician, the first Russian Nobel Prize winner, physiologist Ivan Petrovich Pavlov, who studied at the theological seminary located within its walls in the 1860s, and for the multiple Stalin laureate, the writer Konstantin Mikhailovich Simonov, who studied in the primary school here in the 1920s.

In my school years, a physics and astronomy teacher called Alexander Isayevich Solzhenitsyn, whom we called "Isaich" behind his back, was quite popular among the pupils. And I consider it my duty to write about the little-known side of his activities in the late 1950s, when Alexander Isayevich's name was known only to a narrow circle of acquaintances, a few colleagues and several dozen pupils.

A. I. Solzhenitsyn. On his 50th birthday, December 11, 1968.

A. I. Solzhenitsyn, a mathematician by education (he graduated from the mathematical department of the Physics and Mathematics Faculty of Rostov University), taught physics and astronomy at our school. He had an undoubted teacher's talent, and the creative principle living in him led to fascinating lessons. He gradually instilled in us a love for physics, one of the most difficult school subjects. Methodical, demanding, and sometimes strict, he happily combined that with sensitivity and kindness.

Knowing about my passion for chess, Alexander Isayevich sometimes spoke about the game. Recalling his youth, he told me there was a time when he himself was fond of it. He played in tournaments and gained third category. Later, he became disillusioned with the "royal game", believing that it pointlessly forces a person to waste a lot of energy. Evidence that Sanya Solzhenitsyn was fond of chess as a child can be found in his early story in verse *The Road*. The following lines are addressed to a childhood friend called Sergei:

I remember your child's velvet jacket,

Stubborn disagreement with German verbs

Our chess passions, between two football games.

In my presence, Isaich repeatedly claimed that our chess successes were publicized in order to cover up the gap in other, more important areas. I remember the following dialogue between us:

"After all, Seryozha, chess is wrongly attributed to sports."

"Why?!"

"Simply because sport involves a person's physical development. And if chess is a sport, then why not count dominoes, card games and God knows what else as sports?"

"Alexander Isayevich, let's agree on the terminology. In my opinion, a sports competition is a competition whose participants are on equal terms, and success does not depend on chance. That's why chess is a sport, but dominoes and cards are not."

"Anyway, sport necessarily involves physical competition."

"What, then, in your opinion, is chess? Is it a game, or a means to kill time?"

"Probably, chess is closer to science. There are also textbooks on chess, and success in it largely depends on how conscientiously the materials and manuals are studied."

I wish I remembered how our argument ended. I could not imagine then that there would come a time when the opinion of my school teacher on various issues would be of public interest.

It was noticeable that among the famous chess players, Alexander Isayevich's sympathies were aroused by those who combined the game with achievements in other intellectual fields. So, he spoke with respect about the longstanding world champion Emanuel Lasker, a doctor of philosophy and mathematics. At the same time, he did not hide that he did not like Doctor of Sciences Mikhail Botvinnik for his, as it seemed to him, overly rational style, lack of romanticism in games, the desire to win not by direct attack, but to wait for the opponent to make a mistake.

Solzhenitsyn spent his whole life "rooting against" the chess player Botvinnik, and as I later learned, Botvinnik could not stand the writer Solzhenitsyn, either. In an article recalling the patriarch of Soviet chess, Grandmaster Genna Sosonko writes that when asked if he had read Solzhenitsyn, Botvinnik replied: "I read *One Day in the Life of Ivan Denisovich* and *Matrenin Yard* and began to view him negatively. So, I consider Ivan Denisovich plagiarism. He took everything from Tolstoy, from *War and Peace*. This is just Platon Karataev, transferred to the present. It is written cleverly of course, but he needed to add content, and *Matrenin Yard* is an appeal to Russia's reactionary peasant past. No, I haven't read anything else written by him – that was enough."

During the matches for the world championship between the chess scientist Botvinnik and the professional chess player Tal, Solzhenitsyn supported the young Rigan. Tal's first defeats in the rematch left Alexander Isayevich feeling upset. "What a shame!" he exclaimed with a mournful expression on his face. When the rematch ended, he concluded that the result was unnatural and caused by Tal's illness.

One day, order was brought to the school – at the beginning of the first lesson, the teacher was required to spend a few minutes on "political information". Our form tutor asked me to tell Alexander Isayevich about this before the lesson. He frowned and launched a hail of questions: "What other political information? What's the point of this? And why exactly should I do this?" When I explained that it was not his "political reliability" that was being checked, he reacted with a deep sigh, and reduced the discussion to a couple of sentences about the most important foreign policy events. Then he suggested that on future occasions when the school day starts with physics, the pupil on duty, having previously prepared, should deliver a two-minute message.

Once, after political information had ended, and Alexander Isayevich had rushed to the blackboard, I allowed myself a remark from my seat:

"What about sports news?!"

Isaich only muttered: "That's enough. They even want to hear sports news!"

And after having started to write a physics formula on the blackboard, he glanced at my side and continued: "I heard that the school chess championship is being held, in which Grodzensky, secretly of course, hopes to gain first place. When the tournament ends, I will announce its results during the political information lesson."

I felt my face turn red, the class was amused, but Isaich knew how to curb the mood, directing the energy of his pupils in the right direction. And we really were holding the school championship at that time. In the absence of a dedicated room, the games were held in a spare classroom. Sometimes, chess players even occupied the physics room. I remember Alexander Isayevich lingering near one of the boards. Watching the first moves, he said:

"The Sicilian Defense."

"Do you know that, too?" I asked.

"Once I knew a little about opening theory. Now I only remember the names of a few of them," Solzhenitsyn replied.

He named the openings that he preferred at the time of his passion for chess, but, honestly, I wasn't paying attention: I was not particularly interested in the chess tastes of a former third-grader. Suddenly, one of the tournament players rose abruptly from the table and, without looking at anyone, left.

"Have you lost, Valery?" asked a voice sitting in the far corner. It was Solzhenitsyn's, who had seemed absorbed in his own business. Reacting to my nodding, he commented:

"Yeah, I realized that. He's too impatient for chess."

When he heard that some Swiss tournament was being held, he wondered what that meant, since up to then he only knew of round-robins and knock-outs. When I explained the essence of a Swiss tourney, he called it "the method of successive approximations in determining the relative strength of a chess player".

The mathematician Solzhenitsyn treated games that contribute to the development of cognitive combinational analysis with disdain. Examples of this can be found in his works. In *Cancer Ward* we find a former camp guard who hates prisoners, a stupid soldier called Akhmadzhan, characterized by Solzhenitsyn as a person "no more developed than dominoes". Two of the guards in *One Day in the Life of Ivan Denisovich* turn out to be checkers fans.

And although he compared himself to a chess player who was fighting an extremely strong and dangerous opponent (the communist regime) on the "great chessboard", which, as Zbigniew Brzezinski said, embodied global international politics, he disliked chess and, during the years that he knew me, criticized me for playing it.

When asked to play a game of chess, Solzhenitsyn once replied: "I only played it in prison, when there were no interesting people." Of course, he did not approve of chess training. During a lesson, after I had given a rather poor answer, he sadly noted: "The effect of chess failures." On that day, a local newspaper reported the results of the Ryazan youth championship, in which I played quite poorly. And at the end of my last academic year, when he saw my name in the newspaper among the participants of the region's youth championship, Alexander Isayevich remarked reproachfully: "You will probably play chess all summer, and then you will disgrace the school at the institute entrance exams."

Nevertheless, I and almost all of Solzhenitsyn's students of our year received A's for physics in the entrance exams. Meeting me, Alexander Isayevich asked in detail about how the exam went, rejoicing at the success of his students.

Did we know that he was a writer? No, I can definitely say that. This was partly explained by his behavior during his time in Ryazan. As he wrote, "I worked with my colleagues while never revealing my breadth of interests, always demonstrating disinterest in literature." Alexander Isayevich could not stop "showing his breadth of interest" with his students, but he tried not to touch the field of literature.

In general, Solzhenitsyn's life beyond the school entrance was unknown to us. We knew less about him than about other teachers, whose joys and sorrows were vividly discussed by the students. But for some reason, the opinion of this physicist interested me most of all when it came to literature, and Isaich was the person whom I sought out to discuss those subjects that were very far from the academic disciplines taught by him.

What can we say about his hobbies at that time? Recalling the years of his youth, he would say that there was a time when he could not imagine life without football. He loved tennis and complained: "Ryazan is an uncultured city. There is not a single decent court." I remember that Isaich helped in the construction of a tennis court on the sports ground near the Radio Engineering Institute. Having already become a student at this educational institution, I once watched him play. "Come on, Isaich!" reverberated from the stands. Many of his students gained a place at this institute.

He was also interested in hiking, especially cycling. When one of his students pointed out that, traveling by car, you could see much more, Isaich replied: "You are the son of the twentieth century, and I am more of the nineteenth. It is important for me to go all the way myself. You ride a bike, look around and see that everything is yours. And what about travelling by car?! You shoot past something at 80 kilometers per hour and it doesn't get noticed." He said that he did not like boat trips for only one reason – he had to listen to the loudspeaker all day long. I remember the aphorism of the Polish poet Julian Tuwim: "The radio is a remarkable invention: one turn of the handle – and you can't hear anything."

I found out that my school teacher was a writer on November 19, 1962. As I remember now, I – a second-year student of the Ryazan Radio Engineering Institute – came home, my head focused on the upcoming examination session. As soon as I crossed the threshold, my father asked:

"Didn't you have a teacher at school named Solzhenitsyn?"

"I did, the physics teacher," I answered in surprise, since my father had never shown much interest in my school affairs, and I had finished school over a year before.

"Look, it turns out that he is a great writer," my father said, handing me the latest issue of *Izvestia*, in which the bottom of the fifth page contained an article by K. Simonov entitled "About the past in the name of the future", beginning with the words: "Many articles will probably be written about a small story by Solzhenitsyn *One Day in the Life of Ivan Denisovich* recently published in the 11th book of *New World*. In the meantime, having just turned the last page of it, I want to express a few thoughts out loud."

Having "expressed his thoughts out loud", Simonov concludes the article: "The story *One Day in the Life of Ivan Denisovich* was written by the confident hand of a mature, original master. A strong talent has arrived in our literature. I personally have no doubts about this."

On the eve of 1963, I send a letter to Solzhenitsyn, in which, in addition to New Year wishes, I provide information that may interest him. "Much of what is written in the story is known to me from my father, who was also repressed and served a sentence in Vorkutlag, where I was born in August 1944," I wrote, and continued: "Speaking in the language of cinema, *One Day in the Life of Ivan Denisovich* is a still shot, brilliantly shown in close-up. We are waiting for the full-length film from you.

"I'll tell you my childhood secret. You know, of course, that students always reward their teachers with various nicknames. We, your students, always called you with respect and affection – Isaich. We called you that even when we had to admit bitterly: 'Isaich gave me bottom marks today.' I, like all of us, have always known that you are a great and versatile teacher. I liked the fact that the mathematician, physicist and astronomer Isaich easily replaced the literature teacher. But how surprised I was when I found out that you are also a talented writer."

I added that my father has two small comments on the text of the story. Firstly, it follows from the story of Brigadier Tyurin that in 1930 the regiment commander wore four stripes, which could not be true, and secondly, when trying to reason with a person, it was usually said: "You understand a lot about yourself", rather than "You think a lot about yourself", as Ivan Denisovich Shukhov states.

A few days later, the answer came.

"Dear Seryozha!

I am touched by your letter and your unwavering affection. I was interested to read your news. I wouldn't mind talking to you sometime in the evening, but I'm having a hard time naming a date in advance. I am leaving the school now until September, but I promised the headmaster to be at the meeting

9.1.63.

Милый Сережа!

Я тронут твоим письмом и твоей неизменной привязанностью. С интересом прочел новые о тебе сведения.

Я не возражал бы как-нибудь с тобой побеседовать вечерком, но затрудняюсь заранее назвать дату.

Школу я сейчас покидаю до сентября, однако обещал директору быть на вечере встречи с быв. выпускниками (он же — „вечер за честь школы"). М.б. ты заглянешь туда после сессии? (это будет, наверно, 26 января).

Относительно шпал ты мне напомнил что-то смутное, что я забыл. Ромбов четырех, во всяком случае, долго не было, верно.

А „о себе понимает" — несколько затрепано и к тому же уже по объёму понятия, — неприемлемо.

Мой поклон твоим маме и папе.

А.И.

Letter from Solzhenitsyn dated January 9, 1963

with former graduates (also called the 'evening for the school's honor'). Maybe you would like to go there after your exams? (It will probably be on January 26.) Regarding the stripes, you reminded me of something foggy that I forgot. He didn't have four diamond-shaped rank badges for a long time, that's correct. And "to understand a lot about oneself" is somewhat cliched and, moreover doesn't fit the concept.

Give my regards to your mom and dad. A. I.".

Solzhenitsyn was interested in news of my father, a veteran of Vorkutlag and Karlag. My father spent several years in exile in

Novorudny near Dzhezkazgan, which Solzhenitsyn in the unfinished tale *Love the Revolution* would call "one of the most terrible places on Earth," and in *The Gulag Archipelago* he would write the following about its nature: "There is desert all around, salt marshes and dunes, sometimes laced with swarth or camel thorn. In some places, Kazakhs with herds roam this steppe, but in others there is no one."

I told him everything I knew, though it was not much, recalling my father's sad but humorous comment: "I received three terms from three enemies of the people: one each from Yagoda, Yezhov and Beria." Saying goodbye to Isaich after spending an evening with him, I repeated what I had written to him in the letter: "*One Day in the Life of Ivan Denisovich* is a still shot... We are waiting for the full-length film."

"There will be a full-length film," Solzhenitsyn promised.

I didn't know then that the "film" was being written and already had a name – *The Gulag Archipelago*.

That book begins with the following words: "It would have been impossible for one person to create this book. In addition to everything that I took away from the Archipelago – my skin, memory, ears and eyes, 227 witnesses gave me the material for this book, in stories, recollections and letters. I am not expressing my personal gratitude to them here: this is our common collective monument to all those who were tortured and killed. ...But the time when I dare to name them has not yet come." In later editions, the "witnesses of the Archipelago" are listed by name and among them is my father – Yakov Davidovich Grodzensky. The book's index of names contains the entry: "Yakov Davidovich Grodzensky (1906-1971) – a comrade of V. T. Shalamov, imprisoned (Vorkuta, 1935-1950), a resident of Ryazan".

Shortly after the decision not to award the Lenin Prize to the author of *One Day...* was made, I saw Solzhenitsyn in the Ryazan Regional Library. Alexander Isayevich said that he had been nominated for a prestigious foreign award, but that he was defeated in the last round. "Prizes are a lucrative business," Isaich concluded. We talked about another liberal magazine – *Youth*. After making a negative comment about the editor-in-chief Boris Polevoi, Solzhenitsyn added: "It is clear that those young people on the editorial board confused the chief editor."

When I asked about his own affairs, he frowned: "It's unclear. My novel *In the First Circle* is still in GB." That's exactly what he said – "in the GB", meaning the State Security Committee (KGB). There was a pause. We talked about a chess matter that was close to me. At that time, I was fond of chess composition, and a problem which I composed had been published in *Priokskaya Pravda* with flattering praise. Alexander Isayevich, having inquired about my affairs, suddenly asked:

"What does zugzwang mean in a chess problem?" and he continued in his usual rapid delivery: "I understand what zugzwang in a game means, but how can zugzwang arise in a problem, all the more so in a two-mover?"

I enthusiastically began to explain the difference between problems involving threats and zugzwang. He listened as if interested. But when I began to give definitions of model and pure mates and was about to explain how a heterodox composition differed from an orthodox one, Alexander Isayevich put on his typical ironic smile, which in this case meant that he was not interested in learning the basics of chess composition.

The last time I saw Solzhenitsyn was on a May evening in 1970. After leaving the building of the Central Telegraph Office and walking a block up Gorky Street (Tverskaya Street), I noticed two men talking. The face of one would have seemed very familiar to me, were it not for the beard. I involuntarily slowed down my pace. The bearded man glanced at me and called out: "Seryozha?!"

We hugged. Isaich introduced me to his companion: "This is my student from Ryazan, Seryozha Grodzensky," and added, addressing me, "Seryozha. Meet my colleague. This is the writer Boris Mozhaev." He answered my routine question about how he was doing with hopeless sadness. Everything was bad: constant headaches, and personal issues. I didn't ask for details.

Suddenly his voice trembled, and I saw tears rolling down his cheeks. At the end, Alexander Isayevich hugged me with the words: "Be happy, dearest." I trudged up Tverskaya Street. After a dozen steps, he looked back. Isaich looked towards me. He smiled and waved a friendly hand...

These days, acquaintance with Solzhenitsyn is no longer a dark spot on one's biography. I get asked to share my memories. I pick up my pen, something appears in print. I once sent a clipping to Alexander Isayevich in the USA, accompanied by a note in which I expressed the hope that he remembered one of his students. The answer from Vermont came quickly:

"Dear Seryozha!

How could I 'not remember' you? You were no ordinary student. And after all, you introduced me to your father, I once was in your house. Thank you for the memory. It is not the first time I'm reading your recollections. In your article in the magazine *Shakhmaty* you fantasized a bit in my opinion, but the rest is probably true.

I wish you all the best and bow to your mother.

A. Solzhenitsyn.
30.9.90"

30.9.90.

Дорогой Серёжа!

Как же я мог бы тебя "не помнить"? - ты был не рядовой ученик. И ведь с отцом твоим ты меня познакомил, я был у вас. Спасибо за память. Воспоминания твои читаю уже не первые. В "Шахматах", по-моему, ты прифантазировал, остальное - наверно, так.

Всего тебе доброго

и кланяюсь твоей маме.

А.Солженицын

Letter from Solzhenitsyn dated September 30, 1990

After Solzhenitsyn's triumphant return to his homeland, I carefully followed his speeches, trying not to miss a single publication about him. Finally, I decided to send him one of my books.

One day, it was in February 2001, the phone rang at my house.

"Is it Sergey Yakovlevich?"

"It is, how can I help you?"

"Seryozhenka, this is Alexander Isayevich."

Isaich asked about various matters – both professional and family. I felt that he was pleased to hear about my progress in science. I told him that one of the areas that I was engaged in was the application of the theory of Markov processes to the study of reliability of systems. So the name of the outstanding mathematician of the 19th century, academician Andrey Andreevich Markov, came up in our dialogue.

Alexander Isayevich got excited, remembering that he studied probability theory at the physics department at university using Markov's textbook *Calculus of Probabilities*, and I immediately mentioned that Markov was one of the strongest Russian chess players of his time, a friend of Mikhail Chigorin.

And getting carried away, I began to talk about my book *Chess in the Life of Scientists*. Isaich sighed: "Chess again". But I didn't want to interrupt the story, because at that time I was collecting material for a book about repressed chess players (the one you are reading) and hoped that it would interest him. After all, one of the chapters was going to be called "Muses in the Gulag", and I really wanted *The Lubyanka Gambit* to be published with a foreword by Solzhenitsyn himself.

After listening to the request, Alexander Isayevich expressed sympathy for the chess players who suffered during the years of timelessness, but refused to write a foreword: "You see, Seryozha, I don't write forewords at all. And were I to do so, I would first need to read the manuscript. But I have neither the energy nor the time to read a chess book." There was slight irritation in his voice, and Isaich turned the conversation to another topic.

When the Russian version of *The Lubyanka Gambit* was published *(without the chapter you are reading, which was especially added to the English version)*, Solzhenitsyn was already seriously ill, and I sent him the book with an inscription. After a while, I got a call from his representative, who thanked me for the book on behalf of Alexander Isayevich.

Concluding my recollections of Alexander Solzhenitsyn, I can say that I will consider my mission not completely useless if the image of a Teacher rather than of a writer whose place in the history of literature will be determined by time appears in the reader's mind, even if to a small extent.

***

At the school graduation party, Isaich, hinting at me, said with a smile that many years later there would be a memorial plaque in honor of one of the 1961 graduates in our school. The grade book of class 10A would be exhibited in the school's history museum, but after grades unworthy of a genius were cleaned up... "You will have a lot to clean up, Alexander Isayevich!" I responded in the same tone.

The pediment of my old grammar school building, now named after the famous Russian scientist, academician Ivan Pavlov, sports a memorial plaque testifying that a great writer and citizen once worked there. But my memory contains an image not of the prophet who wrote *Rebuilding Russia*, and, it seems, of a person who knew how to rebuild the whole world, but of a 40-year-old mentor who had a huge teaching talent, learning from whom was a real joy, and one of whose lucky students many, many years ago was me.

Vladimir Levitsky – Champion of the Step Gulag

Vladimir Ivanovich Levitsky (1923-2001) believed that chess helped him overcome all the "circles" of Stalin's hell and at the same time saved his mental health.

Levitsky spent his childhood and adolescence in the mining town of Kadiyevka, the birthplace of the "Stakhanovite movement". Here he learned to play chess, and after he won a simultaneous game against Master Seleznev, he became a local celebrity. After completing school, Vladimir went to study at the Chelyabinsk Pedagogical Institute. As a student, he gained success in the city and regional championships. And he was also fond of poetry, having penned a lot of poems by the age of twenty.

But he was not destined to complete his institute studies at the time. His chess tournament appearances were also interrupted, and the NKVD investigators issued an assessment of his poetic output.

Everything happened as described in his poem "Arrest":

My life on Earth's circle came to the end,
A black raven flew down for me,
It hid in the yard. They took me away at dawn.
They took me away from my family,
From friends and good books.
From Voltaire and from Zola,
They didn't allow me to take anything.
From Tolstoy and from Rousseau
The wheel of fortune turned
From the Earthly, from the usual goods,
They took me away to the Gulag country.
A star rolled down from the sky,
And trains sobbed far away.

Vladimir Levitsky, a third-year student of the Chelyabinsk Pedagogical Institute, a Komsomol activist, was arrested in 1946. A number of young poets and prose writers were arrested with him. All of them were charged with participating in the publication of the handwritten magazine *Snow Wine* and preparing the magazine *Drummer* for publication, with the latter's epigraph intended to consist of what at the time were seditious lines by Heinrich Heine, translated by Levitsky:

Wake people from sleep with a drum,
Drum, raising the people,
Beat while the heart is beating in your chest,
Go forward boldly with a drum beat!

When at the first interrogation the investigator asked from what age Vladimir composed poems, he heard in response: "Since I was seven years old".

This was absolutely true, and an entry appeared in the interrogation minutes that the defendant was engaged in counter-revolutionary activities... from the age of seven (!). It is clear that such a dangerous state criminal could not count on leniency (however, who could count on mercy during Stalinism?) and, therefore, having received eight years of camp at once under two points of Article 58 (anti-Soviet agitation – point 10 and anti-Soviet organization – point 11), he believed, not without reason, that he was lucky.

Levitsky was convicted, as we would say now, for an attempt at self-publishing. He served his sentence without a crime at first in a camp near Chelyabinsk, where he worked at a stone quarry – using a shovel, a crowbar, a pickaxe, and even a sledgehammer, he crushed the stone, loaded it on a trolley and took it to the railway line. Thus, he was used for "general work", where even the most healthy prisoners already accustomed to physical work died from hard labor, malnutrition and constant bullying by the authorities.

Fortunately, the former student of philology was recognized as a participant in the regional chess championship by a quarry foreman, who worked there as a regular employee. The foreman managed to release Vladimir from general work and assign him a position of accountant, or in the camp slang – "an idiot".

For a while, his service became easier. But after being transferred to a taiga camp near Verkhny Ufaley, Levitsky was sent to work in logging. Here, the conditions were such that it took little time to waste a man. When Vladimir's physical condition turned critical even by camp standards, he was sent to the infirmary. And here the assistant to the head of the medical unit – a second category chess player – proved to be his guardian angel.

And Vladimir's life continued under a particular regimen: he slept during the day and played chess with the doctor on duty at night. The doctor wanted to gain more chess lessons and therefore kept his qualified opponent on bed rest longer than the procedures at the destructive-labor camps provided for. It proved to be an important chance of survival. No wonder that they used to say in the camp: "a day of rest is a month of life".

The next stage of Vladimir Levitsky's "steep journey" was at the infamous Steplag in Dzhezkazgan. Dzhezkazgan means "copper field" in Kazakh. Here, in the arid semi-desert, where there was no housing for hundreds of kilometers, special camp No. 4 Osoblag Steplag was located behind a stone camp fence.

The Gulag Archipelago gives a brief description of those places: "At the Novorudnoye station, they (the prisoners – S.G.) jumped out of red railcars right onto the reddish ground. It was Dzhezkazgan copper, the extraction of which no one's lungs could withstand for more than four months."

I remember well the village of Novorudnoye, which became the new place of exile (after Vorkuta) of my father. Steplag was a convict colony which included the copper field and stone quarry, and where mines and a railway were under construction.

After hard work, Vladimir wanted to lose himself in chess. He recalls:

We used to erect a six-cube stack of sleepers with our shift partner, lie down on it, draw a board, choose stones that resembled chess pieces, and play... Once, before the changing of the guard, I was called to the "Cunning House" for interrogation by the "Godfather" – this is how prisoners called the operative, whom everyone was afraid of: he could prolong one's term. When I entered, the Godfather closed the door and began to try and "recruit" me:

"Well," he began, "how's everyone doing, what are they talking about in the dormitory?"

I replied that I didn't talk to anyone about anything except work.

Suddenly, the operative took out a new chess set and suggested we play.

He thought about each move for a long time, played at about third-category strength, but did not let me go until I deliberately lost one of the games. Such challenges were repeated, and I was plunged into despair. They might suspect that I'm a snitch. Informers got killed in the camp. Perhaps the challenges themselves were aimed at getting me eliminated at the hands of my own comrades. As it turned out later, the operative's duty prisoner was, so to speak, a representative of the "prison counterintelligence": he followed our conversations and was in a position to assert my innocence to our comrades. And near the end of my term, the operative allowed me to receive a chess set sent to me from home.

From that day, we began real chess battles. My opponents included the well-known geneticist, Professor Vladimir Pavlovich Efroimson.

Vladimir Pavlovich played impulsively, he got nervous. My friendship with Efroimson, which was born at some point in the camp, eventually lasted for decades, until his death in 1988. He was a real man, a staunch fighter against Stalinism and the Lysenkoism pseudo-science. He played at second category level.

The prisoners in the Steplag included titled chess players. The match for the title of champion of the Dzhezkazgan branch of the Steplag between Nikolai Miroshnichenko and Vladimir Levitsky was won by the latter. Whenever he went for a game with Miroshnichenko, Levitsky was granted a special pass to walk from the second camp point to the first, where his opponent was serving time. The warden graciously let the chess player through the passage in the stone wall, and on his return he invariably inquired about the result, because he was rooting for Levitsky – he was a patriot of his camp point.

I spent a lot of time with Vladimir Ivanovich Levitsky and later corresponding with him. His archive preserved the scoresheets of two games from that match, sealed with the signatures of both players and the match arbiter – I. Rotar. We give these games with comments, sometimes forgetting that at that time these chess players were deprived even of their own name. For example, Levitsky bore the name "SM-846".

Game No. 68
N. Miroshnichenko – V. Levitsky
Steplag, 1951
King's Gambit C35
Commentary by S. Grodzensky

1.e4 e5 2.f4 exf4 3.♘f3 ♗e7 4.♗c4 ♗h4+ 5.g3. In this line, which now belongs to the archives, it is almost mandatory for white to continue 5.♔f1.

5...fxg3 6.0-0 d5. There is another good variation for black: 6... gxh2+ 7.♔h1 d5 etc.

7.♗xd5 ♗h3? (and now the most effective continuation was

7...gxh2+! with a clear advantage) **8.♘xh4?** White could have seized the initiative via 8.♗xb7! and for example 8...g2 9.♖f2 ♗xf2+ 10.♔xf2 ♘d7 11.♗xa8 ♕xa8 12.♘g5 ♗e6 13.♘xe6 fxe6 14.♘c3.

8...♕xh4 9.♕f3 ♗xf1. The winning continuation was 9...gxh2+ 10.♔h1 (10.♔xh2?? ♗g4+ with a win) 10...♘h6 11.♕f2 ♕xf2 12.♖xf2 c6, and black retains both a material and positional advantage.

10.hxg3 ♕h3.

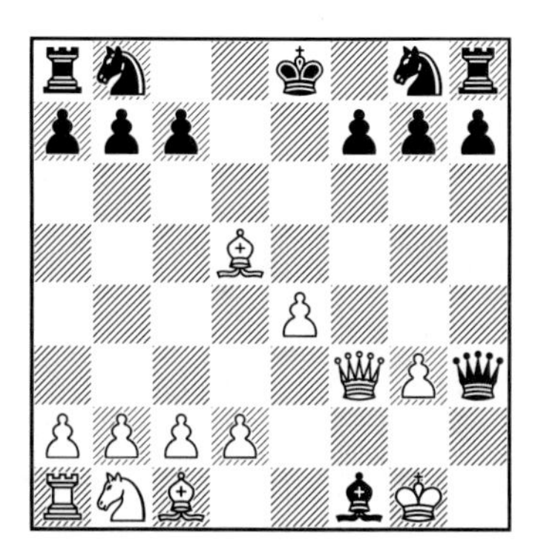

11.e5?? The variation 11.♕xf7+ ♔d8 12.♕xf1 ♕xg3+ 13.♕g2 ♕xg2+ 14.♔xg2 c6 doesn't achieve anything useful, and black is a full exchange ahead. However, the simple continuation 11.♗xb7! would have forced black to deal with problems.

11...♘d7 12.♕xf7+ ♔d8 13.♕xg7 c6 14.♕xh8 cxd5! Black seems to have gained confidence.

15.♕xg8+ ♔c7 16.♕xd5 ♕xg3+ 17.♔h1 ♖g8 18.♕a5+. A pre-death check.

18...♔b8. White resigned.

Game No. 69

V. Levitsky – N. Miroshnichenko

Steplag, 1951

Spanish Opening C70

Commentary by S. Grodzensky

1.e4 e5 2.♘f3 ♘c6 3.♗b5 a6 4.♗a4 b5 5.♗b3 ♗c5 6.♘xe5 ♗xf2+ 7.♔xf2 ♘xe5 8.d4 ♕f6+ 9.♔g1 ♘g6 10.e5 ♕b6. Not a good retreat. It was necessary to choose between 10...♕h4 and 10...♕c6.

11.♕f3! ♕xd4+ 12.♗e3?! This natural move gives away the opening advantage. It was necessary to play 12.♔f1!

12...♕xe5. The move 12...♕xb2!? with the approximate continuation 13.♗xf7+ ♔d8 14.♗g5+ ♘8e7! 15.♕c3 ♕xc3 16.♘xc3 h6! deserved consideration, and black has every chance of repelling the attack while maintaining a material advantage.

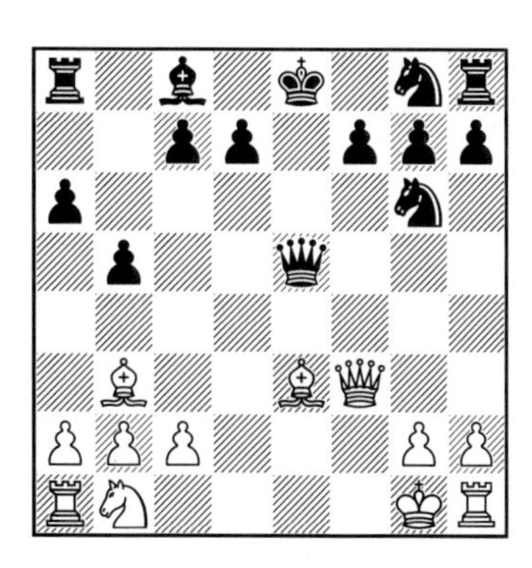

13.♗xf7+! ♔e7 14.♗xg6 hxg6 15.♔f2 ♕f5 16.♗g5+ ♘f6 (16...♕xg5?? 17.♖e1+ with a win.) **17.♖e1+ ♔f7 18.♗f4?** It was better to exchange queens, although black's position would still have been preferable.

18...d5? Black misses a probable chance to win after 18...♗b7!! 19.♕xb7 ♕xf4+ 20.♕f3 ♕d4+ 21.♔f1 ♖xh2!.

19.♘c3 c6 (19...b4! maintained the advantage) **20.♔g1 ♗e6 21.♘e2 ♘h5.** Completely losing the advantage that could have been retained by continuing 21...c5, 21...g5 or even 21...♕xc2.

22.♕c3 ♘f6 23.♕xc6 ♖ac8? Having lost chances of winning, black also complicates the path to a drawn ending, which seemed realistic after 23...♘d7. However, we should make allowances for the fact that this game was not played in an ordinary tournament and the players did not have an opportunity to train at home or rest...

24.♕xa6 ♖c4 25.♗g3 g5 26.♘d4! Black resigned, as he loses the exchange while retaining weaknesses.

Among Levitsky's opponents in the Steplag were the marine writer Alexander Ilyich Zonin and David Alexandrovich Budyonny, the latter mentioned in Anatoly Zhigulin's novel *Black Stones.*

After the expiration of his eight-year term, Levitsky was sentenced to permanent exile in Temir-Tau. Fortunately, the "permanence" lasted little more than a year. In 1955, he was rehabilitated. Two years later, he graduated with top marks from his institute. Then he settled in the mining town of Skopin (Ryazan region). He worked as a literature teacher at a technical college and a school, collaborated with magazines and was even accepted into the Union of Journalists of the USSR.

And, of course, he got fully involved in chess. He achieved several victories in a row in the championships of Skopin, as well as successes in regional championships.

In his declining years, he became interested in correspondence play, became the correspondence champion of the Ryazan Region, and among international competitions even managed to reach the final of the ICCF World Cup. He died on October 2, 2001 aged 75.

Solovki Special Purpose Camp – The Original Gulag

The first camp of the Gulag system was established in Solovki in 1923 and it was called the Solovki Special Purpose Camp (SSPC). At the end of the 1930s, the SSPC was transformed into the SSPP (Solovki Special Purpose Prison).

In those years, the future professor Yuri Ivanovich Chirkov (1919-1988) served a term in Solovki. In his recollections, he talks about chess competitions in SSPC (Chirkov Y. *Big Solovki Tournament – Shakhmaty v SSSR*, 1988, No. 9).

Yuri Ivanovich recalls that the Solovetsky Islands had always been a place of interest: amazing nature, a famous monastery with a top secret prison, and for some time by then, a camp with an extremely diverse community of prisoners – from "fragments of the empire" and prominent figures of science and culture to famous revolutionaries (including communists). The great scientist and philosopher P. A. Florensky, who was here in 1935-1937, called this strange cluster "a tragic panopticon."

In 1936, while working in the camp library, Chirkov discovered the broad nature of the Solovetsky intelligentsia. The library turned out to contain chess literature, and since 1934 it kept the magazine *Shakhmaty v SSSR*, which was in high demand.

One day in the winter of 1936, a tall, gray-haired old man in a burnt astrakhan hat and a tattered pea jacket came in to the library. After looking around and taking off his cap, he smiled, bowed and requested in a somewhat singsong voice: "Will you deign to sign me up as a reader".

It turned out that the old man was the famous lawyer Bobrishchev-Pushkin. He was known as one of the defenders of Menahem Beilis, but his name could also be found in pre-revolutionary chess publications. Bobrishchev-Pushkin also demonstrated his chess abilities at Solovki. He composed several problems and, with the permission of the head of the library, G. P. Kotlyarovsky (a former deputy head of the political department of the Black Sea Fleet, who was serving a ten-year term in Solovki), placed them on the bulletin board for new books. The problems aroused interest because they were distinguished by the originality of the form and the difficulty in solving them.

At the beginning of the summer, the Solovki chess players decided to organize a tournament for their section of the camp (their so-called *'lagpunkt'*). The organizing committee, in addition to Bobrishchev-Pushkin, included Yasenev-Krukovsky and Bestuzhev, well-known first-category players in the 1920s. The cultural and educational department of the camp administration allowed this event to be organized and even gave some assistance: it provided what for the winner was a great prize in those conditions, a men's satin kaftan and cotton trousers.

So many people wanted to participate that they had to organize qualifying tournaments, in which more than fifty chess amateurs played. Two winners from each qualifying group advanced to the final, called by the organizers the "Big Solovki Tournament".

The Big Solovki Tournament started in early June 1936 with 16 participants. Among them were the favorites: Bobrishchev-Pushkin, Yasenev-Krukovsky, and Bestuzhev, professors Yavorsky and Grushevsky, student of the Plekhanov Institute Khablenko, secretary of the Comintern executive committee Rudnyansky, and Stalin's colleague in the People's Commissariat for Nationalities and Panturkism ideologist Izmail Firdevs.

Play was held in the open air, and numerous spectators, unable to keep their emotions at bay, discussed the course of the battles in whispers. The white night approached imperceptibly and the prisoners were called back inside – it was time to return to their cells. But even on the bunks, the discussion of the tournament continued.

The winner of the tournament was Yasenev-Krukovsky. Bobrishchev-Pushkin absentmindedly lost two games in the endgame, which noticeably upset him. The winner of the tournament shared the prize with the old man, gifting him the kaftan. The gift was very useful: the old lawyer's own shirt had almost disintegrated.

In addition, he received a prize from the fans for his subtle play – his own portrait drawn in ink by the Leningrad artist Klinge. The old man was depicted at the chessboard, wearing the same astrakhan hat, stroking his beard with his left hand, and holding out his right hand to the board – he was going to make a move! In addition, he was handed a bag of dried bread snacks.

In the middle of 1937, after the transformation of the camp into the Solovki Special Purpose Prison, the prisoners were partially liquidated and partially taken to the mainland. Their places were taken by new ones from the "harvest" of that year. Bobrishchev-Pushkin – a descendant of an ancient family, a lawyer, and a chess player – was executed on October 27, 1937 at Sandormokh, Karelia. This information can be found on the bessmertnybarak.ru website, which adds that he was rehabilitated in 1963.

Georgy Brenev – A Career Split in Two

In 1993, a candidate masters tournament was held in the Central Chess Club. This overtly ordinary competition seemed interesting, because the clear favorite was an intelligent-looking gentleman who clearly surpassed his opponents in age. With the great score of 11 points out of 13 and no defeats, 75-year-old candidate master Georgy Evgenyevich Brenev, better known as a chess composer who had authored around 200 chess problems and 30 studies, won the tournament.

Georgy Brenev was well-known among Moscow composers in the 1930s. He began his composition career together with the authors of problems and studies who became masters and even grandmasters years later, whereas Georgy quietly disappeared.

Many chess players disappeared without trace, whereas only a few were "resurrected". Georgy Evgenyevich returned to composition in the mid-1950s and proved that he had not lost his technique. What happened to him in his youth? It is now time to tell his biography, keeping no secrets.

Brenev was born in Moscow in 1916 in a family that could be proud of its pedigree. Georgy's great-great-grandfather was the famous Russian traveler and naturalist Grigory Silych Karelin (1801-1872), while the poet Alexander Blok was his second cousin on his mother's side. His father, Evgeny Konstantinovich Brenev, taught mathematics at a university, played chess well and even achieved second category before the revolution. He once lost a game to Alexander Alekhine.

And it is no wonder that Georgy was introduced to chess before he learned to read and write. When he was very young, he liked to watch his father play with his friends, and he especially liked the final positions. The boy started a notebook, in which he carefully sketched various mating pictures, analyzed the endings of the games and looked for beautiful combinations. And at the age of nine, he composed his first study!

The work of the young author was published in the magazine *64*. Soon, Brenev reached the level of a mature composer and gained success in competitions.

Composition No. 139
64, 1931
3rd honorable mention of the competition of the first semester

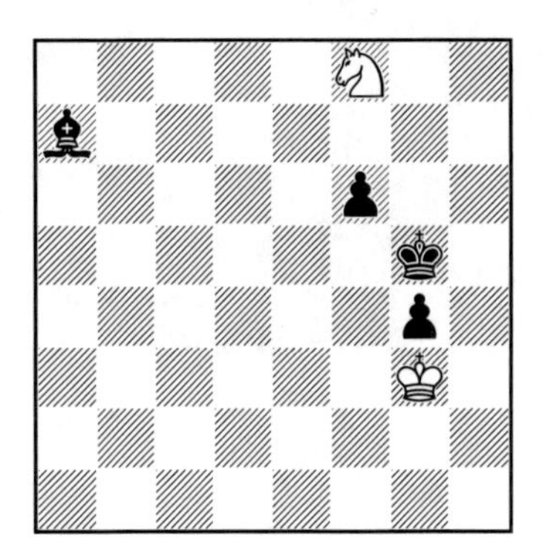

White to move and draw

1.♘h7+! ♔f5 2.♘xf6 ♗b8+ 3.♔h4 g3 4.♘h5 g2 5.♘g3+! ♗xg3+. It was necessary to take the knight, otherwise it would have held the pawn after 6.♘e2.

6.♔h3! g1=♕(♖). Stalemate.

Georgy used to show his studies to his friends, unwittingly infecting them with his love of composition. One of them, a classmate of his older brother, Boris Sakharov, was "infected" for his whole life, and this "infection" got so serious that he became a master of composition.

Meanwhile, Georgy began to compose problems as well. He submitted an excellent two-mover at the All-Union competition held in honor of the 17th Party Congress.

Composition No. 140
All-Union competition
1934, 7th prize

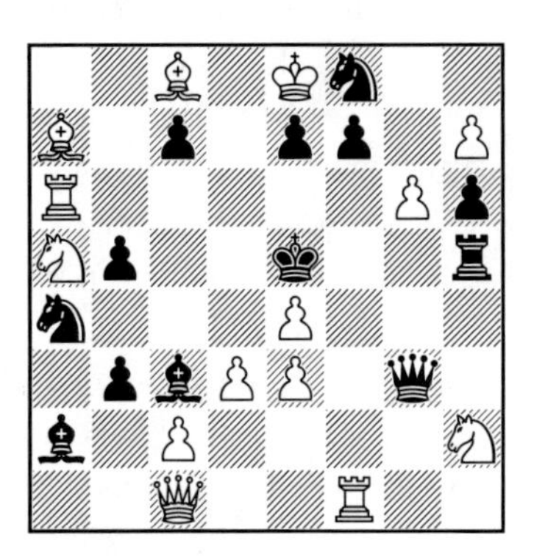

White to mate in 2 moves

1.♕a3! Threatening 2.♘c6#. In this threat variation, the a6 rook gets locked out of the game. Black defends himself by blocking one of the white pieces ♕a3, ♗c8 or ♖f1, from the d6, e6 or f6 squares, respectively, which causes a weakening in his position, leading to checkmate. There are ten (!) variations in the problem with such a complex blocking (Barulin's Defense). This is a record that no one has even managed to repeat as yet!

However, that competition, in which works of various genres competed with each other: studies, problems with direct and reverse mates, and even fairy problems with additional pieces – "grasshoppers" and "riders" among others – was strange. And therefore it is not clear what the jury was guided by when awarding only the seventh prize to this record problem.

To top it all off, it turned out that a bust of Stalin was due to be presented as a prize for the tournament winner... Georgy, already annoyed at the competition result, preferred not to appear for it...

By that time, Brenev had already graduated from high school and got a place at the Bauman Moscow State Technical University, from where he qualified as a mechanical engineer. He composed new problems and studies, continuing to receive distinctions at competitions.

Composition No. 141
Shakhmaty v SSSR
1940, Honorable mention

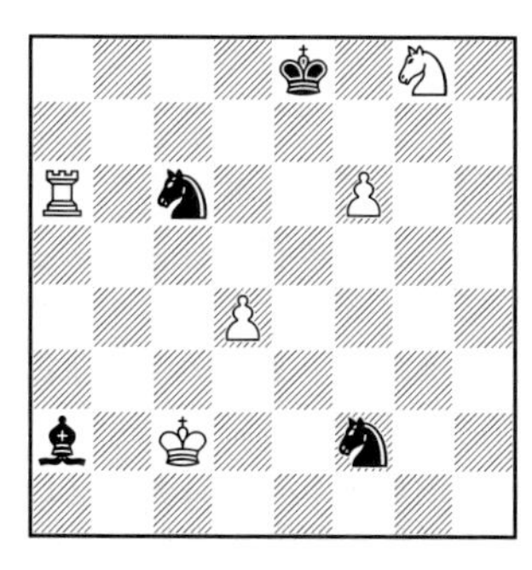

White to move and win

1.f7+ **♔xf7** 1...♗xf7 2.♘f6+ ♔e7 3.♖xc6 **2.♘h6**+ **♔e6 3.♖xc6**+ **♔d5 4.♖f6 ♘e4,** otherwise, white will protect the pawn with his knight.

5.♖a6 ♗c4 6.♖a5+ **♔xd4 7.♘f5#.**

This study turned out to be one of the last, compiled, as Georgy Evgenyevich put it, "before the arrest". In December 1942, he was arrested, and from that day on, his life and work were divided in two, and every event began to be mentally marked by whether it happened before or after the arrest.

Before his arrest, engineer Brenev worked in a design bureau that carried out defense projects, and therefore had some protection – he was exempt from being sent to the front. But there was no institution in the country that could protect against Beria's satraps, and in just a few days in December 1942 almost half of the design bureau's employees were arrested. They were all charged with participating in an anti-Soviet group. And the specific cases of "anti-Sovietism" should have only caused a smile, had it not been that their consequences were the broken lives of so many people.

So, Georgy Evgenyevich was accused, among other crimes, of saying the following about the awarding of the Stalin Prize for 1941 to Ivan Kozlovsky: "Rather than giving a hundred thousand rubles to a singer, it would be better to divide this money among the workers who are grafting day and night." Such a judgment was considered a criticism of Party and government activities.

By decision of a Special Council, Brenev was sentenced to eight years in prison. He composed a two-mover while waiting for the verdict in the NKVD cell on Lubyanskaya Square in Moscow.

Composition No. 142
Zvyazda (Minsk)
1954

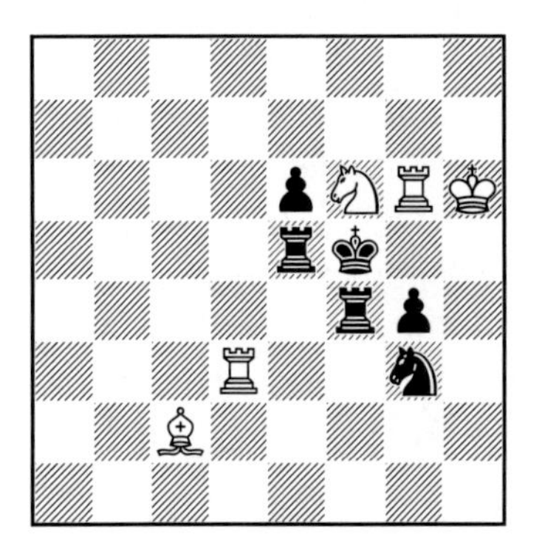

White to mate in 2 moves

1.♘e8!, threatening 2.♘d6#.

There was no paper or pencil in the pre-trial detention cell (and chess sets were obviously out of the question). Therefore, this small problem was composed by Brenev on January 13, 1943 blindfold, though it was only published many years later, in 1954. There were long years of camps and deportations between the dates of its creation and publication.

The camp regime did not bring any creative insights, but chess was played as a means of survival. "In the camp, in order not to turn into a goner doing the main work, we had to take on any, as we are now say, menial jobs," Georgy Evgenyevich told the author. "I was really happy when I got the opportunity to work as a clerk. Another time I wrote poems for a bulletin. I wasn't a great poet, but you learn to rhyme when circumstances force you to. Chess was also useful. I remember that the deputy head of the planning and production section of the camp found out that I was a chess player, called for me and suggested we play. By that time I was already swollen from hunger, I had no strength to play and, no matter how hard I tried, every game finished in a draw. But then, when I managed to eat a little, I began to play confidently, and the amateurs there could not make a single draw with me".

And forty years after these events, Georgy Evgenyevich's brightest memory of the chess battles in the Norilsk camp, Norillag, was how well he got fed after the game with the deputy head of the planning and production section.

Famous scientists, arts figures, and athletes served their sentences in Norillag. The strongest chess player of Eastern Siberia, Konstantin Gaiduk, served about two years in the Norilsk prison "for espionage". Experienced candidate masters Andrey Gabovich and Zinovy Berkovich lived there in exile. According to the chess veteran

E. V. Pavlovsky, chess players exiled to Norilsk in the first post-war years were favorites for the city's championships. And in the early 1950s, Norilsk residents played matches over the radio with Vorkuta and Krasnoyarsk.

The camp was usually followed by exile to the Krasnoyarsk region. In exile, Brenev continued to play chess and published more than twenty-odd compositions in the local press.

Composition No. 143
Krasnoyarskiy Rabochiy
1955

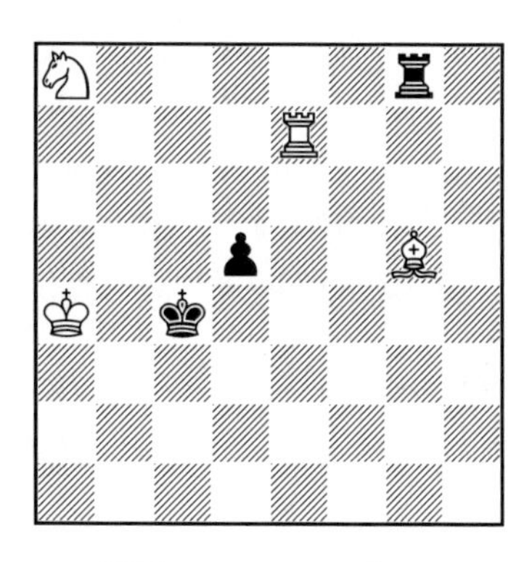

White to move and win

1.♘b6+! ♔c5 2.♘d7+ ♔d6 3.♗f6 ♖a8+ 4.♔b5! ♖a7 5.♖e8! ♖xd7 6.♗e5#.

In 1956, he was rehabilitated and got the opportunity to return to Moscow. The former convict quickly gained a reputation as a highly qualified specialist, began to contribute to a contemporary topic in science, and defended his candidate's degree thesis in his fifties.

The chess composer Brenev was already over fifty when he played his first official over-the-board tournament. After quickly gaining the first qualifications, he became a candidate master and regularly confirmed his level. Georgy Brenev returned to composing, too.

Composition No. 144
First team championship of the USSR
1956-1957, 1st place

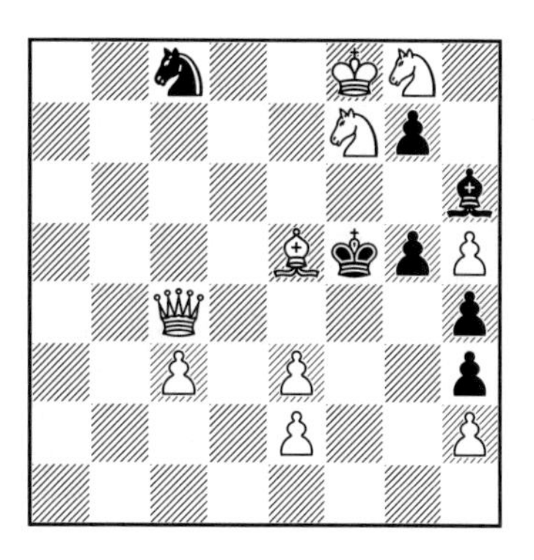

White to mate in 2 moves

A block problem. In the initial position, white has answers to all of black's moves: 1...♘~ 2.♘e7#, 1...g4 2.e4#, 1...g6 2.♘gxh6#. However, white has no waiting moves. After **1.♗f6!** all of black's moves are met by new checkmates: 1...♘~ 2.♘d6#, 1...g4 2.♕d5#, 1...g6 2.♘fxh6.

Composition No. 145
Shakhmatnaya Moskva, 1965
Honorable mention

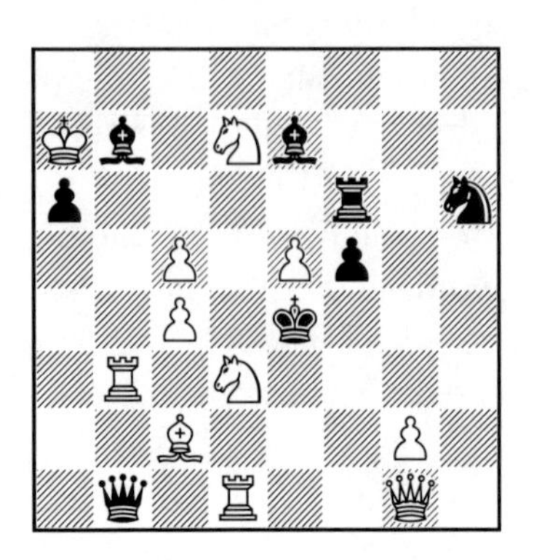

White to mate in 2 moves

In the initial position, the move 1...♗xc5 is met by 2.♘3xc5#. 1.♕f1!, threatening 2.♕f4#, 1...♔e3 2.♘b2#, 1...♔d4 2.♘c1#, 1...f4 2.♘f2#.

Although his composing career was interrupted forcibly, unfairly and for a long time, Georgy Evgenyevich Brenev achieved genuine mastery in his best works.

***

Mikhail Alekseevich Shishkin from the Novosibirsk region told me about the dramatic fate of another prisoner of Norillag. This was Ivan Dmitrievich Chetyrkin (1891-1978). Chetyrkin, a student of the Faculty of History and Philology at Warsaw University, had embarked upon what until his arrest was a successful chess career. Having arrived from

the Smolensk region to study, he played in university tournaments, and in the Warsaw championships he fought with none other than Akiba Rubinstein, who was recognized at that time as a contender for the world championship.

After graduating from university in 1914, Chetyrkin was sent to work in Ekaterinoslav (now Dnepropetrovsk). Here he taught Russian language and literature at the local grammar school, and, of course, introduced children to chess. In September 1915, the young philologist was called up for military service. Chetyrkin hence worked for only a short time in the city on the Dnieper, but left pleasant memories of himself that lasted for many years.

Information about his work as an organizer of tournaments was posted on a special stand at the city chess club.

After demobilization in 1923, Ivan Dmitrievich was sent to Moscow, where, in addition to teaching, he devoted a lot of efforts to improving teaching methods. This capable teacher got noticed, and he became a senior researcher at a research institute. Despite the heavy workload at his main job, Chetyrkin still managed to run a school chess club, and occasionally participated in competitions, where he gained first category.

Ivan Dmitrievich played an active role in designing school textbooks, sometimes expressing beliefs that were becoming more dangerous to hold... He was arrested in February 1938. The sentence was ten years with confiscation of property (he was fully rehabilitated in 1957).

As soon as he left the camp in 1947, Ivan Dmitrievich got involved in correspondence chess. He had enjoyed this type of chess creativity back in his youth.

Playing in tournaments of the Central Chess Club of the USSR, the veteran beat chess players who were old enough to be his grandchildren. In 1968 (at the age of 77), Ivan Dmitrievich Chetyrkin got a candidate's norm, and until the age of 85 he invariably proved his first rank level! One can only wonder what he would have achieved had he not spent his best years in prison...

Natan Sharansky – The French Defense, Lefortovo Variation

In the 1970s, the name of Anatoly Borisovich Shcharansky (now Natan Sharansky), breaking through the intense jamming, was often heard in the USSR on short waves. A simple staff member of the Institute of Oil and Gas, he became world-famous due to his human rights campaigning. Once the youngest member of the Public Group to Promote Fulfillment of the Helsinki Accords in the USSR (the "Moscow Helsinki Group") since its foundation, he was an activist trying to implement in the USSR the agreements of heads of European states, and, in particular, the right of citizens to emigrate. Sharansky challenged the authorities, and they responded with repression.

He was arrested on March 15, 1977. Sharansky was not the first member of the group to be arrested, but the authorities decide that he played a leading role. Natan spent fifteen months in a solitary cell in Lefortovo prison. On June 10, 1978, the "traitor" appeared in court. It quickly, and wrongly, handed down a sentence of 13 years of confinement, of which 3 years in prison and 10 years in high-security camps.

In his book *Fear No Evil*, which was published in many countries, and, in 1991, was released in the dissident's homeland, Sharansky writes in detail about the nine years spent in prisons and camps. He used lines from Psalm 23 as an epigraph: "...Though I walk through the valley of the shadow of death, I will fear no evil, For thou art with me".

What helped him to withstand it?! Belief in the rightness of his cause, the help of his mother, wife, relatives, a powerful support movement that has swept through the entire civilized world, and... chess!

Sharansky was born in 1948 in Donetsk. In his youth, he sometimes won the adult championship of the city and played for the local Spartak club. During his studies at the Moscow Institute of Physics and Technology, candidate master Sharansky played on first board for the university team.

Game No. 70
N. Sharansky – N.N.
Universities team championship,
Moscow, 1971
Queen's Pawn Game D00
Commentary by S. Grodzensky

1.d4 d5 2.♘c3 ♗f5 3.♗g5. White tries to avoid theoretical variations from the first moves.

3...♕d7 4.♘f3 e6 (4...f6 looks more natural, and if 5.♗f4 then 5...

e6) **5.e3 c5 6.dxc5.** The continuation 6.♗b5!? ♘c6 7.♘e5 ♕c7 8.♗f4 with an advantage deserved consideration.

6...♗xc5 7.♗d3 ♗g6 8.h4 ♗xd3 9.♕xd3 ♘c6 10.e4 f6 11.exd5! White sacrifices a piece for an attack.

11...♘b4 12.♕e2 fxg5 13.dxe6 ♕c6.

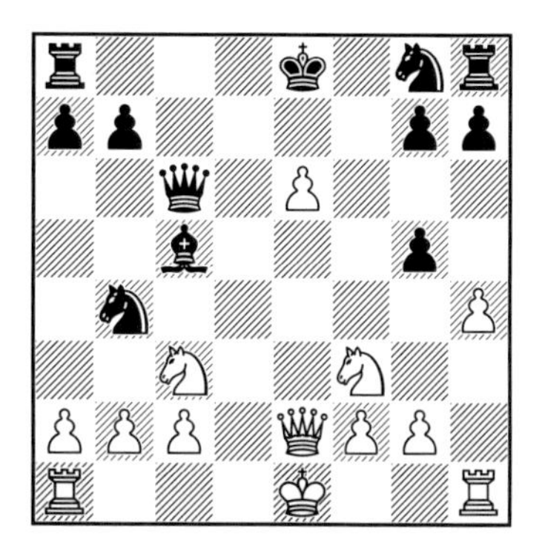

14.0-0-0! ♘e7 15.♘e5. Perhaps it was better to chase the knight away first with 15.a3 ♘a6 and then 16.♘e5.

15...♕xe6 16.♕b5+ ♘bc6 17.♖he1! (with the idea of playing 18.♘d7!) **17...♗xf2 18.♘xc6 ♕xc6 19.♖xe7+! ♔xe7 20.♕e2+ ♔f7 21.♕xf2+ ♔g8** (if 21...♕f6, then 22.♖d7+) **22.♘d5 ♖e8 23.♕f3 ♕e6** (or 23...h6 24.♘e7+ ♖xe7 25.♖d8+ ♔h7 26.♕f5+ g6 27.♖xh8+ ♔xh8 28.♕f8+ ♔h7 29.♕xe7+ ♔g8 30.hxg5 with a big advantage in the endgame) **24.♖f1?** The move 24.♘c7 would have easily won. After this blunder, black should win easily with 24...gxh4 or 24...g4.

24...h6?! (ceding much of his new-found advantage but black is still close to winning) **25.h5! ♔h7?!** (25...♖d8 or 25...b5 was called for, now white should hold with accurate play) **26.♕d3+ ♕e4** (not 26...♔g8 27.♘f6+ gxf6 28.♕g6+ ♔f8 29.♖xf6+, with a win) **27.♖f7! ♕xd3??** Blundering a mate in one. After 27...♔g8 black is still better. **28.♘f6#.**

Sharansky's book reminded me of *The Royal Game* by Stefan Zweig. When he was asked about the similarity of his story with that described by Stefan Zweig, he replied:

"Indeed, the fate of Dr. B., Zweig's hero and mine are very similar. Thanks to chess, both of us kept our minds intact, we did not lose self-control. Playing chess – unfortunately, like the Doctor, I mostly had to play blindfold against myself – and just thinking about chess helped us find the right move in our behaviour, to select the keys to our investigators, who never managed to break us. However, there is a small difference. My literary predecessor (Dr. B. – S.G.) spent about a year "training" as a guest of the Gestapo, while the KGB essentially forced me to study chess in the camps for a total of nine years..."

In real life, everything turned out to be more dramatic than in the novel. *Fear No Evil* begins with a description of the arrest. Natan finds himself in solitary confinement in Lefortovo. On the first day, he is visited by the deputy head of the political section of the prison. He asks whether the prisoner has requests for his cell.

And what does the prisoner ask for? Among other request, chess! The jailer and political commissar is somewhat puzzled:

"...but you're alone in here. What do you want with a chess set?"

"The rules stipulate that the prison must provide a chess set for every cell, without specifying how many people there must be."

Sharansky had managed to study the rules hanging on the wall and remembered the part about chess. As soon as he received the chess set, he began to analyze:

...I arranged the pieces on the board. I immediately began to feel better, for I have always used chess to escape from pressure and anxiety...

...I began to analyze a variation of the French Defense, my favorite chess opening. Its distinctive feature is that black opens with his king's pawn, but advances only one square instead of the customary two, thereby yielding the center and inviting his opponent to mount an early attack. But while black is exposed to strong pressure during the opening moves, he eventually has the resources to mount a successful counterattack...

Unable to rein in my thoughts, which threatened to gallop off again in various wayward directions, I start whipping the pieces around as if I were playing both sides in a blitz match. When I reached the endgame I caught myself and returned to the opening position that had intrigued me in the first place...

Ten minutes passed, then twenty, then thirty. Finally, I began to calm down. I moved the pieces much more deliberately and took time to consider each move. I formed some ideas and reached some conclusions and counterconclusions. Gradually, my feverish state of mind gave way to a sustained analysis.

While getting into the weeds of the French Defense, Natan knew that he was charged under article 64-a: "Treason against the Motherland in the form of espionage, transfer of state or military secrets to a foreign state", which provided for punishment right up to the death penalty. The investigators constantly reminded him of the coming punishment. The threat of execution followed the hero until trial. Waiting for the case, he prepared for it while playing chess with a cellmate.

Sharansky writes about duels with a cellmate who turned out to be an avid chess player: "...after a few test games, we came to the following agreement: I would cede him a rook, and we would play three games. If I won the match, he would do the next cleanup. If he won or if our game ended in a draw, I would clean up.

As a result of this arrangement our cell was always in model shape, for Leonid Yosifovich washed the floors with great diligence."

If the crews of spaceships are selected based on the psychological compatibility of the expedition members, then when placing people in cells, the KGB proceeded from the opposite considerations, skillfully provoking conflicts between prisoners. Chess was a lightning rod in this situation. Candidate Master Sharansky would cede his opponents material up front, so that chances were equalized and the game became interesting for both players. Sometimes it was possible to play blindfold, passing the move to the opponent through a window or tapping on the wall (a method known since the time of the Decembrists, imprisoned in the Peter and Paul Fortress).

But what do you do while sitting in the punishment cell? When in complete isolation, having been tortured by starvation for many days. "...my sleepy mind was increasingly occupied with chess," Sharansky writes, and he continues: "Once, in a student chess competition, I lost a game to a professional, a chess master who represented Moscow University. Playing black, I had used a rare and risky variation of the Spanish Opening... My opponent responded with a completely new line of play, and when the game was over he told me he had found it in a Swedish chess magazine..." Eventually, after the game, Sharansky recounts how he spent much time in his cell analyzing the moves, and eventually found a refutation of the novelty.

Later in the book, the author recounts how he used chess as a means of simulating his "game" with the KGB. Moreover, a team of twenty investigators worked day and night on his case. So Sharansky started to treat his "game" with them as a simultaneous exhibition. Chess motifs in fact permeate his memoir.

Having gained his freedom, Sharansky told the *Jerusalem Report* in 1991 that if you expected to go to prison, you should learn to play blindfold chess, as well as the Morse code. Playing hundreds of games sitting in a punishment cell, unable to read or write is a great advantage: you control your time, while your opponents think that you live by their rules. Meanwhile, you are training your brain for other activities; for example, for conversations with the investigator.

***

Sharansky won his game:

On February 11, 1986, he was stripped of his Soviet citizenship, like Solzhenitsyn before him. He was put on a plane and sent to the West. Sharansky spent a total of 3,255 days in a Gulag in the era of Brezhnev and his followers, 430 of which were spent in solitary confinement.

In Israel, where he moved to, Sharansky became a politician and, eventually, a government minister. One of his Party's election slogans in 1995 came from chess: "Stop being a pawn in someone else's game!"

In the 1970s, Sharansky fought for the right of Soviet Jews to emigrate to Israel, including for himself. Now, this problem no longer exists. But did all the Jews who found themselves in the "promised land" also manage to find happiness there? The response of the Minister of the Israeli Government was as follows:

"I fought not so much for emigration, but for freedom of choice: every person, regardless of nationality, should have the right to decide for himself where to live. And as for happiness... Let's think of chess again... The game has been around for a thousand years, maybe more. But is there anyone who will assert definitively which move is better, 1.e2-e4 or l.d2–d4, which of them will bring success?..."

Natan Sharansky plays both open and closed openings very well. In October 1994, when Garry Kasparov came to visit Israel, Natan decided to relive the good old days and took part in a 15-board simul that the world champion gave at the Tel Aviv Hilton Hotel. After the game, which finished in a draw, Sharansky shared his impressions:

"We played the Queen's Gambit. At some point, Kasparov sacrificed a piece, probably considering that he would crush me during his attack or in the endgame. However, his plan did not work out. Journalists, of course, immediately called this game a 'Russian conspiracy', but that is nonsense..."

A few days later, speaking at an event in front of repatriates from the former USSR, Garry answered a question about this draw in this way: "I believe that this game has no relevance to politeness. Sharansky plays well." (V. Teplitsky. "Russian Conspiracy?" *Shakhmaty v Rossii*, 1996, No. 10-11).

Game No. 71
G. Kasparov – N. Sharansky
Simultaneous exhibition,
Tel Aviv, 1994
Queen's Gambit D53
Commentary by S. Grodzensky

1.d4 d5 2.c4 c6 3.♘f3 ♘f6 4.♘c3 e6 5.♗g5 ♗e7 6.e3 ♘bd7 7.♕c2 My computer doesn't approve of this move and insists on developing the king's bishop to either available square. Black has equality now.

7...h6 8.♗f4 ♕a5?! Castling or chasing the bishop with the knight would have preserved equality for black.

9.♗d3?! The world champion returns the compliment.

9...dxc4 10.♗xc4 b5 11.♗b3?! c5!

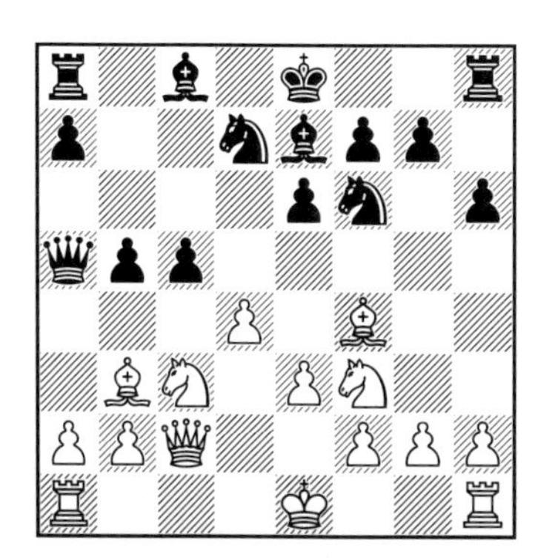

12.♗xe6 Sharansky assigned a "?!" sign to this sac, but white didn't have any good options. The computer recommends capturing on c5 but black is already better.

12...fxe6 13.♕g6+ ♔d8? (13...♔f8 kept a close to winning advantage) **14.0-0 ♗b7 15.dxc5 ♘f8 16.♕c2 ♘6d7 17.a3 ♕a6 18.♖fd1 ♗xf3 19.gxf3 ♖c8 20.b4 e5 21.♗xe5 ♕g6+ 22.♕xg6 ♘xg6 23.♗g3 ♗f6 24.♖ac1 ♗xc3 25.♖xc3 ♔e7 26.a4 a6 27.♖d6 ♘de5 28.♖xa6 bxa4 29.f4 ♘f3+ 30.♔g2**

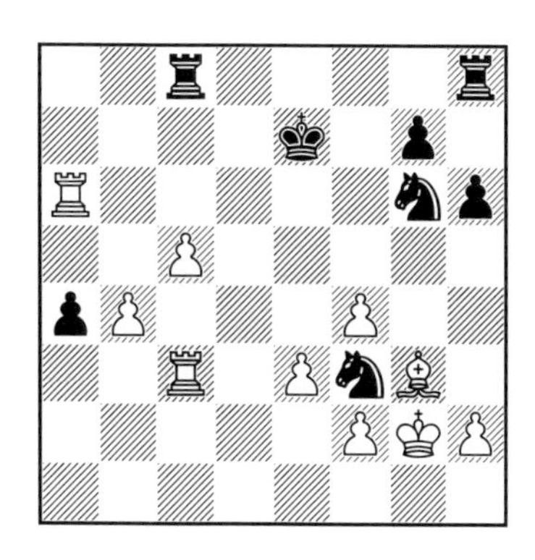

30...♘gh4+! 31.♗xh4+.

Or 31.♔h3 g5!, threatening 32...♘g1+ 33.♔g4 h5+ 34.♔xg5 ♘gf3!#.

31...♘xh4+ 32.♔h3 ♘f5 33.♖xa4 ♖a8 34.♖xa8 ♖xa8 35.b5 ♔d7 36.♔g4 ♘e7 37.♖d3+

Photo by Gideon Markowiz, courtesy of The Pritzker Family National Photography Collection, The National Library of Israel

♔c7 38.c6 ♔b6 39.♖d7 ♖a7 40.f5 ♖xd7 41.cxd7 ♔c7 42.f6 gxf6 43.♔h5 ♔xd7 44.♔xh6 ♔e6 45.♔g7 ♘f5+ 46.♔f8 ♘d6 47.b6 f5 48.f3 ♔f6

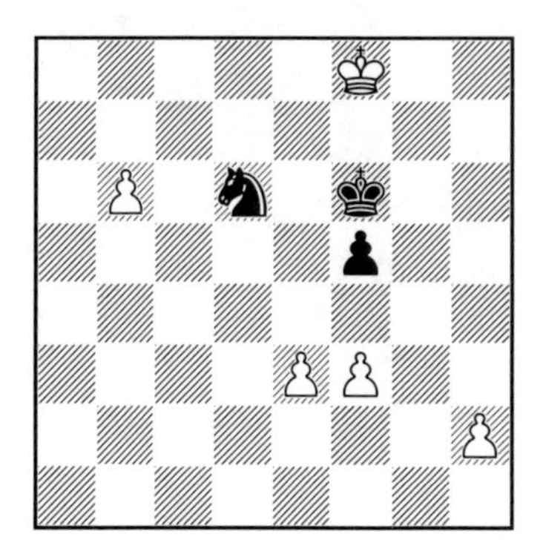

49.♔g8. "Kasparov was going to play 49.e4, but at the last moment he noticed that I was going to respond with 49...fxe4 50.fxe4 ♘xe4 51.b7 ♘c5 and 52...♘d7+" – Sharansky.

49...♔g6 50.e4 fxe4. Draw agreed, proposed by Kasparov. After 51.fxe4 ♘xe4 52.b7 ♘f6+ the b7 pawn cannot make progress.

"Our life is full of emotional and other pleasures but is very poor in intellectual pleasure," Natan complained after the game. "I would say that this game reminded me of the pleasure I experienced playing blindfold with myself in a prison cell about 15 years ago..."

In 1996, in another simultaneous game, he won a brilliant game against that same Garry Kasparov.

Game No. 72
G. Kasparov – N. Sharansky
Simultaneous exhibition,
Jerusalem, 1996
French Defense C01
Commentary by S. Grodzensky

1.e4 e6 2.d4 d5 3.exd5. In Lefortovo prison, Sharansky analyzed the French Defense main line, which begins with 3.♘c3.

3...exd5 4.♘f3 ♘f6 5.♗d3 ♗e7. 6.h3 ♘c6 7.a3 ♘e4 8.c4 ♗f5. We have now reached a Petroff Defense-type position which is very safe for black.

9.0-0 dxc4 10.♗xc4 0-0 11.d5 ♘a5 12.♗a2 c5?! The move 12... ♗f6 retains a positional advantage for black.

13.♖e1 c4 14.♘bd2. Now, after 14...♕xd5 15.♘xc4 ♕xd1 16.♖xd1 ♘xc4 17.♗xc4 the game would end in a draw. However, Sharansky found a spectacular combination to take down the reigning world champion.

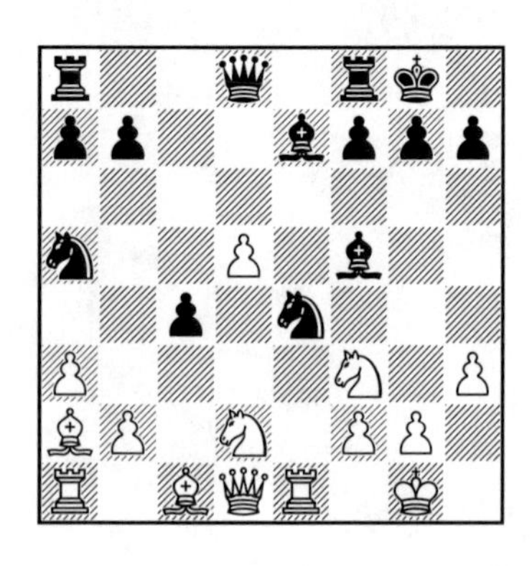

14...♘xf2!! 15.♔xf2 ♗c5+ 16.♖e3. White's position is hopeless. After 16.♔g3 (or 16.♔f1

♗d3+, with a win) 16...♕d6+ 17.♘e5 and then for example 17...f6 (or 17...♖ae8, which the computer prefers) 18.♘dxc4 ♘xc4 19.♗xc4 fxe5 he has no prospects of salvation.

16...♗xe3+ 17.♔xe3 ♕xd5 18.♔f2 ♖ad8 19.♔g1 ♖fe8 20.♔h1 b5 21.♕f1 ♗d3 22.♕g1 ♘c6 23.♘b1 ♘d4 24.♘xd4 ♕xd4 25.♘c3 ♕xg1+ 26.♔xg1 ♖e1+ 27.♔f2 ♖de8. White resigned.

Unlike the hero of *The Royal Game*, Natan Sharansky gained the upper hand over the chess king.

Afterword

In this book, we were unable to write about many chess figures who fell victim to political repression. In some cases, it wasn't possible to collect the necessary materials, while in others we didn't have complete confidence that the fate of the person belonged to the book's subject. The words from Anna Akhmatova's *Requiem*, the epigraph at the beginning of this book, are so appropriate here: *I would like to name everyone by name, but they took away the list and there is no way to find them out.*

In his monograph *Notes of a Non-Conspirator*, first published in Russian in 2001, the outstanding philologist Efim Etkind noted: "our Talleyrands ran the university departments of the international workers movement... Our Napoleons were chess grandmasters." He also proposed the law of "conservation of intellectual energy": "in culture, it happens that if you once shut someone up, a thought, a talent, a word will eventually escape another time." Etkind claims that the outstanding French generals Hoche, Moreau and even Bonaparte could have become chess players. Perhaps Lenin himself, had he lived in Stalin's era, would have built a career not in politics, but in chess.

Taking such a point of view, the incredible flourishing of chess culture in the USSR is explained by the fact that the party and government leadership encouraged the spread of the ancient game as a safe way of preserving intellectual creativity. And chess players effectively contributed to the propagation of the Soviet agenda: "And even in the field of ballet, we are ahead of the whole planet!" One can argue about ballet, but the fact that we were "ahead of the whole planet" in chess never caused doubt even among the most ardent anti-Soviet observers.

There was an opinion among some political emigrants that in the USSR society was divided into executioners and victims; there could be no "middle class": the intelligentsia either sold its soul to the communists or perished in the Gulag.

However, there was another point of view, which the author adheres to: the true Russian intelligentsia continued to fulfill its duty, only using legal means and without entering into a political confrontation with the regime. And the regime was forced to tolerate it. This stratum of the intelligentsia created cultural assets, including in chess.

The twentieth century came to an end, and here is what Osip Mandelstam said about the last century: "The century of wolfhounds grabs me from behind..." The following lines by Nikolai Glazkov also come to mind:

I look at the world from under the table.
The twentieth century is an extraordinary one,
The more interesting it is for the historian,
The more tragic it is for the contemporary.

Finishing this book about the tragic events of the last century, I would like to hope that all the variations of the Lubyanka Gambit will stay in the past.

Epilogue – Bullet Chess

To be honest, I have never been either a sports fan or a chess fan; but nevertheless I knew that chess was a part of Russian culture, like fine art, literature, and music. Naturally I, like most Soviet citizens, admired the talent of Botvinnik and Tal and obviously, when I read the press, I felt for all Soviet chess players. And I wore the blinkers of Soviet mythology which recounted that chess was one of the many branches of knowledge supported by the authorities.

And yet, the Soviet government viciously invaded all spheres of culture that it patronized. In particular, it destroyed many outstanding chess players. At best, it drove them out of the country (for that we might say "thank you"!); at worst, there was another outcome – CHECKMATE.

I agreed to write these lines only so that people opening this book would never forget about the system that Stalinism gave birth to. After all, the young people of the 1920s-1930s, high on Bolshevik ideology, adopted this system with great pleasure. That includes young chess players under the leadership of the People's Commissar of Justice Nikolai Krylenko, who, as it happens, died in this same vicious circle of lawlessness. And I also agreed because both my late husband Ernest Ametistov and I were to a certain extent victims of this same era.

Professor Olga Nikolaevna Zimenkova,
President of the Ametistov Foundation

Made in United States
North Haven, CT
02 September 2023